AI and Game-Based Literacy Learning:

Innovative Pathways for Diverse Learners

Leslie Haas
https://orcid.org/0000-0002-8941-5696
Texas A&M University-Texarkana, USA

Jill T. Tussey
https://orcid.org/0000-0003-0870-0637
Buena Vista University, USA

IGI Global
Scientific Publishing
Publishing Tomorrow's Research Today

Vice President of Editorial Melissa Wagner
Director of Acquisitions Mikaela Felty
Director of Book Development Jocelynn Hessler
Production Manager Mike Brehm
Cover Design Jose Rosado

Published in the United States of America by
IGI Global Scientific Publishing
701 East Chocolate Avenue
Hershey, PA, 17033, USA
Tel: 717-533-8845 | Fax: 717-533-7115
Website: https://www.igi-global.com E-mail: cust@igi-global.com

Library of Congress Cataloging-in-Publication Data

Names: Haas, Leslie, 1969- editor | Tussey, Jill, 1982- editor
Title: AI and game-based literacy learning : innovative pathways for diverse learners / Edited by Leslie Haas, Jill T. Tussey.
Description: Hershey, PA : IGI Global Scientific Publishing, [2026] | Includes bibliographical references and index. | Summary: "This book explores how artificial intelligence and game-based learning transform literacy education. Bridging theory and practice, it presents research, frameworks, and classroom applications that promote equitable, inclusive, and culturally responsive literacy instruction across global contexts and diverse learner populations"-- Provided by publisher.
Identifiers: LCCN 2026002100 (print) | LCCN 2026002101 (ebook) | ISBN 9798337374727 hardcover | ISBN 9798337374734 paperback | ISBN 9798337374741 ebook
Subjects: LCSH: Artificial intelligence--Educational applications | Educational games--Technological innovations | Literacy--Study and teaching | Culturally relevant pedagogy
Classification: LCC LB1028.43 .A374 2026 (print) | LCC LB1028.43 (ebook)
LC record available at https://lccn.loc.gov/2026002100
LC ebook record available at https://lccn.loc.gov/2026002101

British Cataloguing in Publication Data
A Cataloguing in Publication record for this book is available from the British Library.

Table of Contents

Detailed Table of Contents

accessible resources under pedagogical supervision. Prototype quality was assessed with an analytic rubric aligned with inclusive design and Universal Design for Learning, and instructors' perspectives were collected through semi-structured interviews. Findings indicate that adopting a designer role strengthened situated professional learning, inclusive decision-making, and digital pedagogical competence, while also highlighting the need for ethical guidance and critical AI literacy. Overall, the intervention increased readiness for inclusive practice in diverse contexts.

This chapter develops a cognitive load framework for designing AI-supported game-based literacy environments for diverse learners. Responding to the growing use of large language models, adaptive feedback, and automated scaffolds in reading and writing platforms, the chapter argues that AI features should be evaluated as cognitive-load interventions rather than as neutral enhancements. The chapter links three themes: AI, game-based literacy learning, and diverse learner participation. It synthesizes cognitive load theory, reading-comprehension research, writing-process research, game-based learning, formative feedback, self-regulated learning, Universal Design for Learning, culturally sustaining pedagogy, and automation trust. The central contribution is an Adaptive Scaffolding Matrix that maps AI support families to phases of literacy activity: orientation, comprehension and encoding, composition and revision, and reflection and consolidation. The chapter then develops design propositions, four illustrative scenarios, and a multi-method evaluation agenda.

This chapter theorises AI-infused, game-based literacy environments as equity-centered multiliteracies ecosystems rather than technocentric novelties. It synthesises autonomous, sociocultural, multiliteracies, critical literacy, Universal Design for Learning, translanguaging, neurodiversity, and design justice constructs to re-specify how multilingual and neurodiverse learners are positioned within algorithmically orchestrated games. AI functionalities are reframed as sociotechnical infrastructures whose affordances, risks, and safeguards co-determine epistemic inclusion. The chapter articulates literacy-first, pedagogy-first design blueprints, neurodiversity-sensitive interfaces, and culturally responsive narrative architectures that preserve teacher agency and learner dignity. A polycentric governance matrix distributes responsibilities across students, families, educators, developers, researchers, and regulators. Collectively, these architectures delineate how AI-GBL systems can be re-engineered as infrastructures for critical, culturally grounded, plurilingual literacies.

Differentiation in secondary English Language Arts classrooms is essential for equitable literacy outcomes, especially in inclusive settings where students with and without disabilities learn together. Integrating artificial intelligence (AI) and game-based learning (GBL) offers teachers tools to individualize instruction, boost engagement, and align learning with students' diverse needs. Using Universal Design for Learning (UDL) and T-TESS Dimension 2.4: Differentiation, this chapter examines how AI and GBL support differentiation through adaptive feedback, multimodal learning, and interactive storytelling. Additionally, by drawing on research and utilizing a classroom case study, it explores how these technologies enhance literacy, inclusion, and equity in secondary ELA. The findings suggest that combining AI's adaptive features with GBL's motivational elements creates accessible, responsive learning aligned with T-TESS 2.4. The chapter concludes with implications for instruction, co-teaching, and policy in diverse classrooms.

This chapter presents the design and development of AI-generated classroom scenarios and video simulations created to advance intercultural and global literacies in teacher education. Grounded in culturally responsive pedagogy, intercultural and global competence frameworks, and experiential learning theory, the project treats competence as a reflective, action-oriented literacy. AI was used to draft scenarios and videos, while all pedagogical and ethical decisions were guided through a human-centered, iterative process. Fifty scenarios aligned with six intercultural and four global competencies were created, extensively reviewed and edited, and transformed into video simulations with accompanying instructional guides. The simulations were then integrated into teacher preparation courses and professional development settings. The chapter demonstrates how AI can support experiential, scenario-based learning while human expertise ensures ethical representation and instructional quality, offering a scalable model for preparing educators to teach in diverse classrooms.

This chapter examines how Game-Based Learning (GBL) can be used as an equity-oriented instructional approach for supporting multilingual learners (MLs) in secondary science classrooms. Drawing on Second Language Acquisition theory (SLA) and Self-Determination Theory (SDT), it argues that review activities can function as powerful, literacy-rich, and motivational learning spaces when intentionally designed. The chapter demonstrates how GBL supports language development, scientific literacy, and student motivation. Review game design guidelines are outlined following SLA and SDT principles.

The chapter presents classroom-based examples of both non-digital and digital review games, detailing materials, setup, gameplay, and reflections on their alignment with SLA and SDT principles. It also explores the role of AI, future directions, and instructional implications.

In this chapter, the AI-driven storytelling and adaptive game-based learning are explored as the methods to make literacy education an inclusive, critical, and culturally responsive practice. It theorizes AI-generated narratives and adaptive literacy games as dynamic scaffolds and personalize learning, maintains interest, and promotes vocabulary, fluency, writing, and critical literacy among diverse learner groups, based on the multiliteracies theory, socio-constructivism, and digital game-based learning. The chapter presents the findings of recent empirical studies and systematic reviews, discusses ethical and accessibility issues (authorship, bias, surveillance, and equity), and suggests principles of pedagogical design and an equitable AI literacy practice model based on the idea of cultural responsiveness, explainability, and learner agency.

This chapter examines the role of serious games in supporting the development of multidimensional literacies across safety, energy, STEM, and health domains. Literacy is understood as a situated practice that involves interpreting information, making decisions, and reflecting on outcomes within specific contexts. The chapter presents a design-based synthesis of four case studies, including simulations of emergency evacuation, energy systems, chemical reasoning, and health decision-making. These cases illustrate how structured game environments can support the application of disciplinary knowledge through interaction and feedback. While artificial intelligence is not fully implemented, the designs are prepared for future adaptive extensions. The chapter discusses implications for instructional design, inclusive educational practice, and the use of simulation-based environments to support applied learning.

Ensuring sustained student engagement in the biological sciences is an increasing educational challenge, particularly with regard to 'plant blindness' and limited engagement with climate change. This study presents PLANT-A-QUESTION, an analogue board game designed to promote botanical and environmental literacy, and to support SDGs 13 (Climate Action) and 15 (Life on Land). Based on active and GB learning, the game involves players in collaborative problem-solving and covers topics such as biodiversity, climate resilience, and botany.The tool was evaluated with 86 secondary school pupils and validated by 11 subject experts and educators. The results showed that the game was well received. Expert feedback confirmed its value as a motivational and educational resource. Overall, PLANT-A-QUESTION demonstrates the potential of analogue, game-based learning to encourage engagement and promote environmental literacy and ecological understanding, while emphasising the importance of low-tech, interactive strategies in an AI-driven context.

This chapter examines the integration of game-based learning (GBL) and artificial intelligenceto advance literacy development in hospitality education. Using the CESIM simulation platform over multiple years in undergraduate and graduate hospitality programs, it reframes literacy as a broad construct encompassing reading, writing, and interpreting complex data. The pedagogical design combines adaptive teaching, flipped classroom, inquiry-based learning, Montessori principles, and technology-enhanced strategies to create an immersive, literacy-centered environment. Findings indicate that this approach increased student engagement and improved literacy outcomes. Implications include enhanced student readiness for industry, a shift in instructor roles toward facilitation, the need for faculty training, and the need for institutional support to implement such innovative approaches. The chapter also acknowledges limitations such as the simulation's scope and context-specific factors, and calls for further research including longitudinal studies on career impacts and deeper AI integration.

Preface

Literacy learning continues to evolve alongside the technologies, communication practices, and digital spaces that shape how individuals interact with the world around them. As classrooms become increasingly diverse and technology becomes more embedded within educational environments, educators are being challenged to rethink traditional approaches to literacy instruction and explore innovative pathways that promote engagement, accessibility, and meaningful learning experiences for a wide range of learners. *AI and Game-Based Literacy Learning: Innovative Pathways for Diverse Learners* was developed in response to these changing educational realities and the growing need for instructional practices that are both academically rigorous and responsive to contemporary learners.

This volume explores the intersection of artificial intelligence (AI), game-based learning (GBL), and literacy education across a variety of educational contexts and age groups. Spanning early childhood through higher education, the chapters within this collection examine how emerging technologies, interactive learning environments, and GBL pedagogies can support literacy development in engaging, adaptive, and culturally responsive ways. Contributing authors from countries including Indonesia, India, the United States, Spain, Portugal, the United Arab Emirates, and Mexico provide diverse international perspectives on the opportunities and challenges associated with AI and GBL across educational settings. Collectively, the contributors explore how AI and GBL may create opportunities for learners to participate more actively in literacy experiences while also supporting educators as they navigate increasingly complex and technology-rich learning environments.

The contributors to this volume explore literacy as more than a set of isolated academic skills. Throughout the book, readers will encounter discussions related to engagement and motivation, disciplinary literacy, instructional supports, vocabulary development, comprehension, fluency, and the integration of AI-driven tools within literacy instruction. Several chapters examine how GBL environments can foster collaboration, persistence, problem solving, and learner participation across content areas, while others investigate how AI may support differentiated instruction, feedback, scaffolding, and personalized learning experiences for diverse learners.

SUMMARY OF CHAPTERS

An important focus throughout this collection is the recognition that literacy practices extend beyond traditional language arts instruction. Literacy is embedded within STEM disciplines, social sciences, professional and industry-based learning environments, digital spaces, and creative contexts where learners must navigate multiple forms of communication, interpretation, collaboration, and meaning-making. As a result, several contributors explore disciplinary literacy practices and the ways AI and

GBL may support learners as they engage with the unique language, problem-solving processes, and communication expectations associated with different academic fields.

The volume also includes selected discussions related to storytelling and narrative-centered learning experiences. These chapters explore how storytelling, digital narratives, and interactive experiences may support literacy concepts such as vocabulary, comprehension, fluency, creativity, and learner engagement across diverse educational settings. In doing so, the contributors highlight the continued importance of narrative as both a literacy practice and a meaningful way for learners to connect with content, culture, and personal experience.

Importantly, this volume does not position AI or GBL as replacements for effective teaching or meaningful human interaction. Rather, the contributors emphasize thoughtful implementation, learner-centered instructional design, and educational practices that recognize the diverse experiences, strengths, and needs students bring into learning environments. Across the chapters, there is a shared recognition that literacy learning is closely connected to engagement, belonging, identity, collaboration, and authentic participation.

This collection arrives at a time when conversations surrounding AI in education continue to expand rapidly across educational settings. While emerging technologies offer exciting possibilities for instruction, assessment, and learner support, they also raise important questions related to ethics, equity, access, and the evolving role of educators. Several contributors within this volume encourage readers to critically examine both the opportunities and challenges associated with integrating AI and GBL into literacy instruction while remaining attentive to the human dimensions of teaching and learning.

It is our hope that this book serves as both a practical and reflective resource for educators, researchers, instructional designers, graduate students, and educational leaders interested in innovative approaches to literacy learning. As conversations surrounding AI, educational technology, and GBL continue to evolve, we hope this collection contributes to ongoing discussions about inclusive, engaging, and future-oriented literacy practices for diverse learners across educational contexts.

Chapter 1
AI-Driven Game-Based Literacy Learning Innovative Pathways for Diverse Learners

Dandi Akbar
http://orcid.org/0009-0004-9421-7928
Universitas Esa Unggul, Indonesia

Binastya Anggara Sekti
http://orcid.org/0000-0001-5489-4888
Universitas Esa Unggul, Indonesia

Vinsens Aji Pamungkas
http://orcid.org/0009-0003-3036-0699
Universitas Esa Unggul, Indonesia

Didin Wahidin
Universitas Esa Unggul, Indonesia

Gerry Firmansyah
http://orcid.org/0000-0002-5047-3880
Universitas Esa Unggul, Indonesia

Gusti Muhamad Sardana
http://orcid.org/0009-0001-4281-2432
Universitas Esa Unggul, Indonesia

ABSTRACT

Literacy in the digital era requires skills beyond traditional reading and writing, including critical thinking, digital awareness, and multimodal communication. This chapter explores the integration of artificial intelligence and game-based learning as an innovative approach to literacy education. AI enables adaptive and personalized learning through data-driven feedback, while game-based learning enhances engagement and motivation through interactive experiences. The proposed framework combines these strengths to create inclusive, responsive, and learner-centered environments. This integration supports diverse learners by addressing varying abilities, promoting active participation, and improving literacy outcomes in dynamic digital contexts.

1. INTRODUCTION

Literacy in the digital era extends well beyond the traditional ability to read and write printed text. It now involves the ability to interpret, evaluate, and produce information across a wide range of digital platforms. As technology continues to develop, particularly through the growth of the internet and intelligent systems, the ways people access knowledge and communicate have changed significantly.

DOI: 10.4018/979-8-3373-7472-7.ch001

Information is created and shared on a massive scale, requiring learners to navigate sources that differ in quality, reliability, and intention. In this environment, digital literacy has become not only an essential academic skill but also an important competency for meaningful participation in contemporary society (Kasapidis, Petrou, Konstantinidi, Kostalias, & Kakogianni, 2025). Learners are expected to navigate complex information environments, assess credibility, synthesize knowledge from multiple sources, and engage with interactive content that continuously evolves in form and structure.

Beyond functional skills, literacy in the digital age also requires critical awareness and ethical responsibility. Individuals are expected to recognize misinformation, understand the implications of digital footprints, and engage responsibly in online environments. These demands involve higher-order thinking skills that extend beyond simply decoding text. Consequently, literacy education must broaden its focus to include analytical, evaluative, and creative dimensions that reflect contemporary communication practices. This transformation creates both opportunities and challenges for educators as they adapt their teaching approaches to meet evolving learning needs.

Despite these developments, conventional approaches to literacy learning continue to dominate many educational environments. Traditional methods often place strong emphasis on passive reading, memorization, and standardized instruction that may not fully reflect the needs of contemporary learners. These approaches are generally teacher-centered and depend heavily on fixed curricula and uniform forms of assessment. Although they provide structure and consistency, they may struggle to engage learners who are familiar with interactive and fast-changing digital environments. As a result, learner motivation can decline, limiting opportunities to develop deeper and more meaningful literacy skills.

Moreover, traditional literacy instruction often pays limited attention to the diversity of learning preferences and abilities found in contemporary classrooms. Learners who respond better to visual, auditory, or experiential approaches may find it difficult to engage with instruction that relies mainly on text-based methods. Standardized teaching practices may also provide insufficient support for learners from different linguistic backgrounds or those with varying levels of prior knowledge. As a result, a disconnect can emerge between the ways literacy is taught in schools and the ways it is used in everyday digital environments (Muawanah, Marini, & Sarifah, 2024). Consequently, there is a growing need to rethink how literacy education is designed and delivered.

The integration of artificial intelligence and game-based learning offers a promising way to address these challenges. Artificial intelligence can support adaptive learning experiences by analyzing learner behavior and providing personalized feedback in real time. Through data-driven insights, AI systems are able to identify individual strengths, weaknesses, and learning patterns, allowing instruction to be adjusted according to the needs of each learner (Aguado-García, Alonso-Muñoz, & De-Pablos-Heredero, 2025). This level of personalization helps ensure that learners receive appropriate support and challenge, which is essential for effective skill development. In addition, AI can automate routine tasks such as assessment and feedback, enabling educators to focus more on facilitating meaningful learning experiences.

At the same time, game-based learning introduces elements that enhance engagement and motivation. Features such as challenges, rewards, progression systems, and storytelling create an interactive environment where learners are actively involved in the learning process (Horvat, Jagušt, Veseli, Malnar, & Čižmar, 2022). These elements support intrinsic motivation by making learning more engaging and purpose-driven. Game-based environments also encourage exploration and experimentation, giving learners opportunities to learn through both success and failure. When literacy activities are presented within meaningful contexts, learners are more likely to develop a deeper understanding of the material and apply their skills in practical situations.

The combination of AI and game-based learning reshapes literacy education into a more dynamic and learner-centered process. AI helps personalize learning experiences, while game-based approaches maintain engagement and encourage active participation in learning. Together, these approaches support the diverse needs of modern learners by offering flexible and inclusive experiences that adapt content, provide multimodal forms of representation, and encourage collaboration. They also create opportunities for learning beyond traditional classroom settings, although their effective implementation still depends on adequate infrastructure, digital access, and user readiness. To better understand how these innovations influence literacy practices, it is important to examine the theoretical foundations that support the use of AI and game-based learning in education.

2. THEORETICAL FOUNDATIONS OF AI AND GAME-BASED LITERACY LEARNING

2.1 Multiliteracies and Digital Literacy

The concept of literacy has changed significantly with the growth of digital technologies and global communication networks. Literacy today extends beyond reading and writing static texts to include the ability to interpret visual, auditory, interactive, and multimodal information across digital environments. As a result, learners are expected to develop broader competencies that support critical thinking and digital engagement. In this context, medieval-themed video games have gained attention as educational tools that can support historical understanding, digital literacy, and critical thinking in different learning settings (Villatoro Moral, Serra Vives, & Capellà Galmés, 2026).

The theory of multiliteracies provides a strong foundation for understanding this transformation. It emphasizes the importance of cultural and linguistic diversity as well as the integration of various modes of communication such as visual, audio, and digital media (Si, Hodges, & Coleman, 2022). From this perspective, meaning making is not fixed but shaped by context, culture, and the tools used to communicate. Learners must be able to navigate different forms of expression and adapt their understanding depending on the situation. This approach recognizes that literacy is inherently social and dynamic, reflecting the complexities of communication in a globalized world.

Closely related to multiliteracies is the concept of digital literacy, which focuses on the skills required to function effectively in digital environments. Digital literacy includes the ability to locate, evaluate, and create information using digital technologies. It also involves critical thinking, ethical awareness, and the capacity to manage information overload. In an era where misinformation can spread rapidly, the ability to assess credibility and verify sources becomes a crucial component of literacy. Therefore, digital literacy is not only a technical skill set but also a cognitive and ethical framework that supports responsible participation in digital spaces.

2.2 Constructivism in Literacy Learning

In parallel with the evolution of literacy concepts, learning theories have also expanded to accommodate new forms of knowledge acquisition. Constructivism posits that learners actively construct their own understanding through interaction with their environment. Knowledge is not simply transmitted from teacher to student but is built through experience, reflection, and problem solving (Zajda, 2021).

This perspective highlights the importance of active engagement and meaningful interaction in the learning process. Learners are encouraged to explore, question, and experiment, which leads to deeper understanding and long-term retention.

Constructivist principles align closely with modern digital learning environments, where learners can interact with content in dynamic and flexible ways. For example, interactive platforms allow learners to manipulate information, receive immediate feedback, and adjust their learning strategies. This creates opportunities for personalized learning experiences that are responsive to individual needs. In literacy education, constructivism supports activities such as interpreting texts, creating content, and engaging in discussions that promote critical thinking and reflection.

2.3 Connectivism and Networked Learning

Another important theoretical perspective is connectivism, which reflects the realities of learning in a networked world. Connectivism suggests that knowledge exists within systems of connections and that learning involves the ability to access and navigate these networks (Dziubaniuk, Ivanova-Gongne, & Nyholm, 2023). In this framework, the capacity to find and connect information is more important than the possession of static knowledge. Technology plays a central role by linking learners to a vast array of resources, communities, and information sources. Learning becomes a continuous process of connecting, updating, and applying knowledge in different contexts.

Connectivism is particularly relevant in the digital era, where learners are constantly exposed to new information through online platforms. It encourages collaboration, sharing, and participation in knowledge networks. In literacy learning, this may involve engaging with online texts, participating in discussions, and creating content that contributes to a broader community. This approach supports the development of communication and collaboration skills that are essential in modern society.

2.4 Artificial Intelligence in Education

Artificial Intelligence introduces a new dimension to these theoretical perspectives by enabling systems that can simulate aspects of human intelligence in educational contexts. AI in education is grounded in the ability of machines to process large amounts of data, recognize patterns, and make decisions based on learner behavior (Wang et al., 2024). This capability supports the development of adaptive learning systems that personalize content and feedback according to individual needs. By analyzing learner performance, AI can identify strengths and weaknesses, adjust difficulty levels, and provide more targeted support (Putri & Sekti, 2026).

The use of AI aligns with constructivist principles by providing interactive environments where learners can explore concepts and receive immediate feedback. It also reflects connectivist ideas by linking learners to relevant resources and networks based on their needs and interests. In literacy education, AI can support reading comprehension, writing feedback, and personalized content delivery, making learning experiences more responsive and efficient.

2.5 Game-Based Learning Theory

Game based learning further complements these theoretical foundations by incorporating elements that enhance motivation and engagement. Games are designed to create meaningful experiences through challenges, goals, feedback, and rewards. These elements encourage active participation and sustain learner interest over time (Wang et al., 2023). Motivation in game-based learning is often driven by intrinsic factors such as curiosity, achievement, and a sense of progression. Extrinsic elements such as points, badges, and recognition also play a role in reinforcing engagement.

Engagement in game-based learning is achieved through immersive environments and interactive tasks that require learners to think critically and make decisions. This approach aligns closely with constructivist learning, as it emphasizes learning through experience and action. Learners are not passive recipients of information but active participants who shape their own learning journey. In addition, game-based learning supports connectivist principles by enabling collaboration and interaction within digital spaces, where learners can share knowledge and work together to solve problems.

2.6 Integrated Theoretical Framework

The integration of these theories within the context of literacy learning creates a comprehensive framework for understanding how learners develop skills in the digital age. Multiliteracies and digital literacy define the competencies that learners need, while constructivism and connectivism explain how learning occurs. Artificial Intelligence and game-based learning act as enablers that bring these theories into practice. Together, they form an ecosystem where learners engage with content in dynamic, interactive, and meaningful ways.

This integrated framework also supports diverse learning needs by providing flexible pathways and multiple forms of representation. Learners can access information in ways that suit their preferences, receive personalized support, and engage with content that is relevant to their experiences. This not only enhances learning outcomes but also promotes equity and inclusion in education. By combining theoretical insights with technological innovation, educators can design literacy learning environments that are better suited to the demands of the digital era.

Building upon these theoretical perspectives, the next section explores how AI technologies concretely support literacy development.

3. AI IN LITERACY EDUCATION: PERSONALIZATION AND INTELLIGENT SUPPORT

The integration of artificial intelligence into literacy education has created new opportunities for developing personalized and responsive learning environments. Unlike traditional instructional approaches that often use the same methods for all learners, AI allows systems to adapt dynamically to individual needs. This capability is especially important in literacy development, where learners differ in reading levels, writing abilities, and comprehension skills. These differences are shaped by factors such as prior knowledge, language background, and learning pace. Through data-driven analysis, AI can support more effective and inclusive literacy instruction that responds to learner diversity in meaningful ways.

3.1 AI for Reading and Writing Development

One of the most widely used applications of AI in education is adaptive learning. These systems monitor learner interactions, performance, and progress over time to adjust the level and type of content provided. In literacy education, this allows reading materials to be matched more closely to a learner's abilities, helping ensure that activities are not overly simple or excessively difficult. Maintaining this balance is important for keeping learners engaged and supporting continuous skill development. When learners face challenges that fit their current level, they are generally more motivated and more likely to make consistent progress. As learners improve, the system can gradually adjust learning pathways, creating a more personalized and responsive learning experience.

Beyond personalization, adaptive systems can also make learning more efficient. Rather than following a fixed sequence of instruction, learners are able to focus on the areas where they need the most support. For instance, a learner who struggles with vocabulary may receive activities that strengthen word recognition and meaning, while another learner may work more on comprehension strategies. This flexibility helps ensure that instructional time is used more effectively and that learners receive support that matches their individual needs. Over time, adaptive systems can develop detailed learner profiles that help improve instructional decisions and learning outcomes.

In the context of reading comprehension, AI plays a critical role in supporting deeper understanding of texts. Intelligent systems can assess how learners interact with reading materials, including the time spent on passages, responses to comprehension questions, and patterns of errors (Hsiao & Chang, 2024). Based on this data, AI can provide targeted support such as simplifying complex sentences, offering vocabulary explanations, or generating guiding questions that prompt critical thinking. These features help learners engage more actively with texts rather than passively reading them. In addition, AI can simulate interactive reading experiences where learners receive immediate feedback, enabling them to identify misunderstandings and correct them in real time.

Such interactive support is particularly valuable in developing higher order literacy skills. Learners are encouraged to analyze, interpret, and evaluate texts rather than simply recall information. AI systems can also introduce scaffolding strategies, gradually reducing support as learners become more proficient. This approach helps build independence and confidence, which are essential for long term literacy development. By transforming reading into an active and reflective process, AI enhances both comprehension and engagement.

3.2 AI-Generated Content and Feedback Systems

AI also contributes significantly to the development of writing skills through automated feedback systems. Writing is a complex process that involves grammar, structure, coherence, and creativity. AI powered tools can analyze written text and provide instant feedback on various aspects of writing (Yildiz Durak & Onan, 2025). This includes identifying grammatical errors, suggesting improvements in sentence structure, and offering recommendations for enhancing clarity and coherence. Immediate feedback allows learners to revise their work iteratively, which is crucial for improving writing skills. Instead of waiting for delayed feedback, learners can make adjustments in real time and observe the impact of their revisions.

More advanced AI systems extend beyond surface level corrections to evaluate deeper aspects of writing. They can assess the organization of ideas, the strength of arguments, and the logical flow of a text. Some systems even provide suggestions for improving tone and style, helping learners develop more effective communication skills. This continuous feedback loop supports the development of writing as a process rather than a one-time task. It encourages reflection, revision, and refinement, all of which are essential components of effective writing practice.

Another emerging application of AI in literacy education is the generation of content. AI generated texts can be used to create reading materials that are customized to specific themes, difficulty levels, or learner interests. This personalization enhances engagement by aligning content with topics that are meaningful to learners. For example, a learner interested in science may receive reading passages related to scientific topics, while another learner may explore narratives based on storytelling themes. AI can also generate writing prompts, discussion questions, and practice exercises, providing a diverse range of resources that support literacy development.

However, the use of AI generated content requires careful consideration. While it offers flexibility and variety, it is important to ensure that content remains accurate, relevant, and aligned with educational objectives. Educators play a critical role in curating and guiding the use of such materials to maintain quality and pedagogical value. When used effectively, AI generated content can enrich the learning experience and provide opportunities for personalized exploration.

3.3 Learning Analytics and Personalization

Learning analytics further enhances the role of AI in literacy education by providing insights into learner behavior and progress. Through the collection and analysis of data, educators can gain a comprehensive understanding of how students interact with learning materials (Alfredo et al., 2024). This includes identifying patterns of engagement, areas of difficulty, and overall progress. Learning analytics enables data informed decision making, allowing educators to adjust instructional strategies and provide targeted interventions. It also supports early identification of learning challenges, enabling timely support that can prevent long term difficulties.

In addition, learning analytics can support learners by giving them access to information about their own progress. When learners are able to see their achievements and identify areas that still need improvement, they are often more motivated to take an active role in their learning process. This encourages self-reflection and independent learning, both of which are important skills in the digital era. By combining analytics with adaptive systems, AI helps create a feedback-rich environment that supports continuous development. The different applications of AI in literacy learning can be categorized according to their instructional functions, as summarized in Table 1.

Table 1. Applications of AI in Literacy Learning

AI Application Area	Function in Literacy Learning	Example of Implementation
Adaptive Learning	Personalizes reading levels and learning pathways	Dynamic text difficulty adjustment
Reading Comprehension	Enhances understanding through guided support	Automated question generation and hints
Writing Feedback	Provides real time corrections and suggestions	Grammar and coherence analysis tools
AI Generated Content	Produces customized learning materials	Personalized reading passages and prompts
Learning Analytics	Tracks and analyzes learner performance	Dashboards for progress monitoring

As shown in Table 1, AI technologies not only support personalization but also provide continuous feedback that is important for literacy development. These applications illustrate how AI can assist multiple aspects of literacy learning in a more integrated way.

Overall, the integration of AI into literacy education represents an important shift in how learning experiences are designed and delivered. By combining adaptive learning, intelligent feedback, content generation, and learning analytics, AI can create a more responsive support system for learners with different needs. This approach makes literacy learning more interactive, personalized, and data-informed, helping learners develop essential skills more effectively. At the same time, educators continue to play a central role in guiding the use of these technologies so that they remain meaningful and pedagogically appropriate. While AI strengthens personalization, game-based learning contributes engagement and motivation, both of which are equally important in literacy education..

4. GAME-BASED LEARNING FOR LITERACY DEVELOPMENT

Game-based learning has become an important approach in modern education, particularly in supporting literacy development in the digital era. In general, game-based learning involves the use of game elements and design principles to create meaningful learning experiences. Unlike traditional instructional methods that often depend on passive content delivery, game-based learning encourages interaction, exploration, and active participation. Learners engage with content through challenges, tasks, and feedback systems that are designed to strengthen understanding and skill development. In literacy education, this approach allows learners to practice reading, writing, and comprehension skills in ways that are more engaging and contextually meaningful (Glas, van Vught, Fluitsma, De La Hera, & Gómez-García, 2023).

4.1 Principles of Game-Based Learning

Game-based learning is based on the idea that learners understand concepts more effectively when they are actively involved in the learning process. Instead of only receiving information passively, learners interact with challenges, make decisions, and experience the outcomes of their actions within structured environments. This approach aligns well with literacy learning because reading and writing are often used in real-life situations that require interpretation, problem-solving, and communication. When literacy activities are placed within meaningful game scenarios, learners are encouraged to use language with a clear purpose rather than treating it as a set of isolated exercises. This contextual learning experience can strengthen understanding and improve retention over time.

Narratives are also an important element of many game-based learning environments. In narrative-driven activities, learners become part of a story that changes according to their choices and actions. Reading and writing are no longer separate classroom tasks but become tools for progressing through the experience. Learners may need to interpret clues, understand conversations between characters, or produce written responses that influence how the story develops. These activities encourage learners to think critically and engage more deeply with texts. Narrative elements can also strengthen emotional engagement because learners often become attached to characters or invested in the storyline, which helps maintain motivation and attention during learning activities.

Game-based learning is often associated with both gamification and serious games, although the two approaches are not identical. Gamification involves adding game elements such as points, badges, or leaderboards to existing learning activities in order to increase participation and motivation. For example, learners may receive rewards for completing reading tasks or reaching certain milestones. Serious games, in contrast, are designed specifically for educational purposes and integrate learning objectives directly into gameplay. While gamification can encourage participation, serious games tend to create more immersive learning experiences where literacy skills are practiced naturally through interaction and problem solvin (Pando Cerra, Fernández Álvarez, Busto Parra, & Iglesias Cordera, 2022).

In contrast, serious games are developed specifically for educational purposes, with learning objectives integrated directly into the gameplay. In literacy education, these games may include interactive storytelling, problem-solving activities, or collaborative tasks that require learners to use reading and writing skills as part of the experience. This distinction between gamification and serious games highlights the importance of intentional design in game-based learning. Effective implementation involves more than simply adding rewards or points; it requires creating learning experiences where educational goals and gameplay are closely connected.

The motivational impact of game-based learning has been widely recognized because games often include clear goals, immediate feedback, and a visible sense of progression. These elements encourage learners to remain engaged and continue practicing over time. In literacy education, where consistent practice is essential for improvement, making activities enjoyable can significantly increase learner participation. Engagement in game-based learning also goes beyond surface-level interaction, as learners are often encouraged to think critically, make decisions, and reflect on their actions throughout the learning proces (Lin, Wang, & Hsieh, 2024). This active engagement promotes deeper learning and helps develop skills that are transferable beyond the game environment. In addition, the interactive nature of games allows for immediate feedback, enabling learners to identify and correct errors in real time. This continuous feedback loop supports skill development and reinforces learning.

4.2 Applications in Literacy Learning

A simple example can illustrate how game-based learning supports literacy development. Imagine a digital storytelling game in which learners play as characters exploring a fictional world. To move through the story, they need to read dialogues, understand instructions, and make decisions that influence what happens next. At different stages of the game, learners may also complete writing activities, solve language-related puzzles, or interact with other players. The system can adapt to their performance by offering hints, additional support, or more challenging tasks when appropriate. Through these activities, learners practice reading comprehension, vocabulary, and writing skills in a connected and engaging way.

Examples like this show how game-based learning can make literacy instruction more interactive and meaningful. By combining storytelling, challenges, and feedback, games encourage learners to engage more deeply with content. At the same time, the success of this approach depends heavily on thoughtful design. If game elements are not connected clearly to learning objectives, they may distract learners instead of supporting literacy development. For this reason, gameplay mechanics need to be carefully aligned with educational outcomes so that engagement contributes directly to learning.

Overall, game-based learning offers an innovative approach to literacy development that reflects the needs of learners in the digital era. Instead of relying mainly on passive instruction, it creates interactive environments where learners actively build knowledge and apply their skills in meaningful contexts. Narrative-driven experiences, continuous feedback, and adaptive challenges can strengthen both motivation and engagement while also supporting diverse learning needs. The potential of this approach becomes even greater when game-based learning is combined with artificial intelligence within a unified literacy framework.

5. INTEGRATING AI AND GAME-BASED LEARNING: A CONCEPTUAL FRAMEWORK

5.1 Concept of AI-Game-Based Integration

The convergence of Artificial Intelligence (AI) and game-based learning (GBL) represents a transformative approach in literacy education, offering a powerful synthesis of personalization and engagement. While AI focuses on delivering intelligent, data-driven support tailored to individual learners, game-based learning emphasizes motivation, immersion, and active participation. When these two paradigms are thoughtfully integrated, they create a learning ecosystem that is not only adaptive but also deeply (Hsu & Lin, 2025). This integration goes beyond the mere use of digital tools; it reflects a deliberate alignment of pedagogical strategies, technological capabilities, and learner-centered design principles. The result is a holistic framework that supports literacy development in a way that is interactive, responsive, and meaningful.

At the core of this integration lies the concept of synergy between adaptive intelligence and interactive experience. AI systems continuously analyze learner data such as performance, behavior, and engagement patterns to build dynamic learner profiles. Meanwhile, game-based environments provide structured yet flexible spaces where learners can actively engage with content through exploration, challenges, and feedback. When combined, these elements enable real-time adjustments within a game context. For instance, the difficulty level of reading tasks, the complexity of narratives, or the type of feedback provided can evolve based on the learner's progress. This creates an experiential learning process where literacy is not passively consumed but actively constructed through interaction, decision-making, and problem-solving.

From this synergy emerges a hybrid learning model that blends traditional instructional approaches with intelligent and interactive technologies. In this model, foundational literacy skills such as decoding, vocabulary building, and sentence construction can still be introduced through structured guidance by educators. However, these skills are reinforced and expanded through adaptive game environments that provide contextualized practice. This hybrid approach allows educators to retain control over learning objectives and curricular alignment while leveraging AI to personalize instruction and GBL to enhance engagement. It also supports multiple modes of learning, including individual progression and collaborative interaction, enabling learners to work independently or in groups within shared digital environments.

5.2 Framework Design and Components

A key component of this framework is the development of adaptive game environments. These environments are designed to dynamically adjust gameplay elements based on learner input and performance (Chiotaki, Poulopoulos, & Karpouzis, 2023). For example, a learner who struggles with reading comprehension may be presented with simplified texts, additional visual aids, or scaffolded hints to support understanding. Conversely, learners who demonstrate higher proficiency may encounter more complex narratives, inferential questions, or time-based challenges that require advanced critical thinking. This adaptability ensures that learners remain within their optimal learning zone, where tasks are sufficiently challenging to promote growth without causing frustration. By embedding literacy tasks within meaningful game scenarios, learners are encouraged to apply their skills in context, thereby enhancing retention and transfer of knowledge.

Another critical dimension of this integration is the incorporation of AI-driven narrative systems. Narratives are central to game-based learning because they provide context, purpose, and emotional engagement. When enhanced by AI, narratives become dynamic and responsive, adapting to the learner's choices and actions. This creates personalized storylines where characters, plot developments, and outcomes evolve in real time. In literacy education, such narrative systems can be used to develop both reading and writing skills. Learners may be required to interpret story elements, predict outcomes, or create their own narrative responses, thereby engaging in higher-order cognitive processes. AI-driven narratives not only sustain engagement but also foster creativity, critical thinking, and deeper comprehension.

To better understand how these components interact, a conceptual framework is illustrated in Figure 1.

Figure 1. Conceptual Framework of AI-Driven Game-Based Literacy Learning

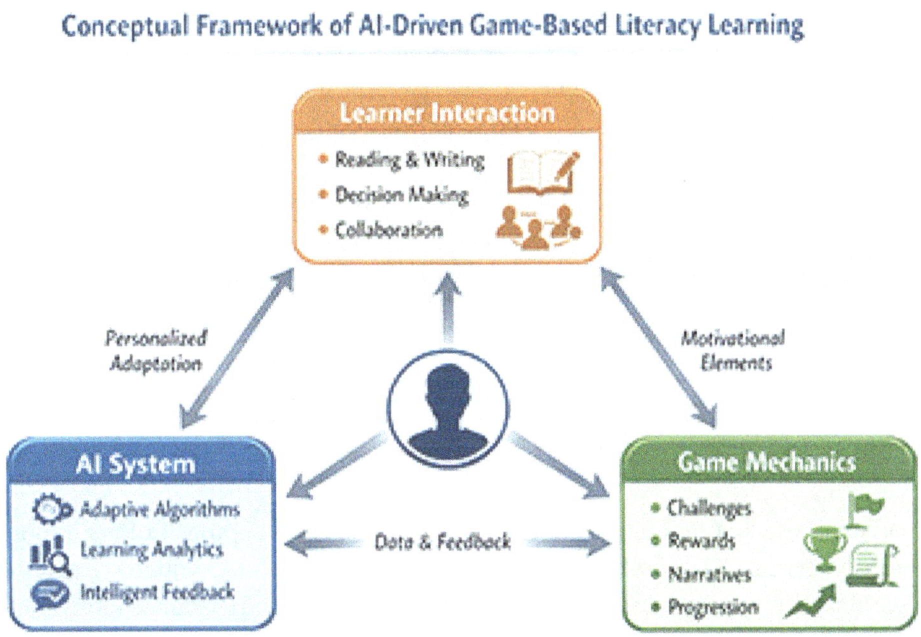

The framework consists of three interconnected components. The first is the AI system, which includes adaptive algorithms, learning analytics, and intelligent feedback mechanisms. This component is responsible for analyzing learner data and generating personalized responses. The second component is learner interaction, encompassing activities such as reading, writing, decision-making, and collaboration. This represents the active engagement of learners within the system. The third component is game mechanics, which include elements such as challenges, rewards, narratives, and progression systems that structure the learning experience.

Figure 1 demonstrates how these components form a continuous feedback loop. Learner interactions generate data that is processed by the AI system, which then adapts the game mechanics to better suit the learner's needs. In turn, these adjusted game elements influence subsequent learner interactions, creating an ongoing cycle of personalization and engagement. This dynamic interplay ensures that learning experiences remain relevant, responsive, and aligned with individual progress.

5.3 Comparative Analysis of Learning Approaches

In addition to understanding how these approaches are integrated, it is also important to compare them with traditional and standalone methods of literacy instruction. Conventional literacy teaching often depends on static materials, fixed pacing, and teacher-centered delivery, which may not fully address differences in learner abilities and learning preferences. AI-based approaches provide stronger personalization through adaptive feedback and data-driven analysis, although they may not always maintain learner motivation over long periods. In contrast, game-based approaches are highly effective in creating engaging and immersive learning experiences but may offer limited personalization or instructional accuracy when used independently. A comparison of these approaches is presented in Table 2.

Table 2. Comparison Between Traditional, AI-Based, and Game-Based Approach

Aspect	Traditional Approach	AI-Based Approach	Game-Based Approach	Integrated Approach
Personalization	Low	High	Moderate	Very High
Engagement	Low to Moderate	Moderate	High	Very High
Feedback	Delayed	Real-time	Immediate	Continuous and adaptive
Learning Experience	Passive	Interactive	Immersive	Interactive and immersive
Adaptability	Limited	High	Moderate	Very High
Skill Application	Theoretical	Contextual	Experiential	Contextual and experiential

The comparison presented in Table 2 suggests that an integrated approach offers a more balanced solution for literacy learning. By combining the adaptive capabilities of AI with the engaging nature of game-based learning, this approach can provide both personalization and sustained motivation. Learners receive feedback that is immediate and continuously adjusted to their progress, while learning activities become more interactive and immersive. This combination supports not only skill development but also contextual understanding and practical application of literacy skills.

Another important advantage of this integrated framework is its flexibility. AI-driven game-based platforms can be accessed through different devices and learning environments, making literacy education more accessible to a wider range of learners. In addition, the data generated through these systems can help educators and researchers better understand learner behavior, identify challenges, and improve instructional strategies. As a result, the learning environment becomes more responsive and capable of continuous improvement over time.

At the same time, successful implementation requires careful attention to inclusivity and accessibility. Learners come from different backgrounds and may have varying levels of digital literacy, access to technology, and learning needs. For this reason, AI-driven game-based systems should be designed with clear interfaces, culturally relevant materials, and appropriate support for learners with special needs. Without these considerations, technological innovation may unintentionally increase existing educational inequalities rather than reduce them.

Overall, the integration of AI and game-based learning provides a promising framework for literacy education in the digital era. By combining adaptive intelligence with interactive experiences, this approach addresses both the cognitive and motivational aspects of learning. It creates opportunities for literacy instruction that are more engaging, flexible, and meaningful for diverse learners. However, the long-term success of these approaches will depend on how thoughtfully they are designed and implemented in real educational contexts.

6. INCLUSIVE AND EQUITABLE LITERACY LEARNING FOR DIVERSE LEARNERS

The rapid advancement of Artificial Intelligence (AI) and game-based learning (GBL) in literacy education offers transformative potential, but it also raises critical questions about inclusivity and equity. As education becomes increasingly technology-driven, it is essential to ensure that these innovations benefit all learners, regardless of their linguistic background, abilities, or socio-economic conditions. Inclusive literacy education requires more than access to technology; it demands intentional design that recognizes diversity and ensures equitable opportunities for participation, engagement, and achievement (Song et al., 2024).

6.1 Addressing Diverse Learners

One of the most important groups to consider in this context is multilingual learners. These learners navigate multiple languages in their daily lives, which can serve as both an asset and a challenge in literacy development. Traditional literacy instruction often prioritizes a dominant language, potentially overlooking the linguistic richness that multilingual learners bring. AI-driven systems, however, offer new possibilities for addressing this gap. Through features such as real-time translation, contextual vocabulary support, and adaptive multilingual content, AI can create more inclusive learning pathways. Game-based learning further enhances this experience by embedding language use within interactive and meaningful contexts. For instance, learners may engage in narrative-driven scenarios where understanding and using multiple languages becomes part of gameplay. This approach not only supports language acquisition but also strengthens cognitive connections between prior knowledge and new learning.

Learners with disabilities represent another critical dimension of inclusivity. Disabilities may include visual, auditory, cognitive, or motor impairments, each of which affects how learners interact with literacy materials. Inclusive design principles emphasize accessibility as a foundational requirement rather than an optional feature. AI technologies can significantly enhance accessibility by personalizing content delivery. Features such as text-to-speech, speech-to-text, customizable font sizes, and adaptive interfaces allow learners to interact with content in ways that suit their needs. Game-based environments can complement these features by offering multiple modes of interaction, such as visual storytelling, audio narratives, or simplified task structures. For example, a learner with visual impairment may benefit from immersive audio-based storytelling, while a learner with cognitive challenges may require step-by-step guidance and scaffolded instructions. Ensuring accessibility is not only a technical necessity but also a moral imperative in building equitable education systems.

Socio-economic disparities present another major challenge in achieving inclusive literacy learning. Not all learners have equal access to digital devices, stable internet connectivity, or supportive learning environments. This digital divide can significantly limit the reach and effectiveness of AI and GBL innovations, particularly in underserved communities (Khalid, Chuanmin, Shahid Rasheed, & Kamdar, 2025). Addressing this issue requires a multi-layered approach. Technological solutions such as offline-capable platforms, low-bandwidth applications, and affordable hardware can help reduce access barriers. At the same time, institutional and governmental support is crucial in providing infrastructure, subsidies, and community-based learning spaces. Without such coordinated efforts, technological advancements risk reinforcing existing inequalities rather than alleviating them.

Cultural relevance is another essential component of inclusive literacy education. Learners come from diverse cultural backgrounds that shape how they interpret, engage with, and respond to content. Literacy instruction that fails to reflect this diversity may feel disconnected or even alienating. AI systems can be designed to incorporate culturally responsive content by adapting examples, narratives, and contexts to align with learners' lived experiences. Game-based learning is particularly well-suited for this purpose, as it can integrate diverse storylines, characters, and settings that reflect a wide range of cultural perspectives. When learners see their identities and experiences represented in learning materials, they are more likely to feel engaged and motivated. This not only enhances comprehension but also fosters a sense of belonging and validation.

6.2 Accessibility and Equity Challenges

Access to technology remains a central issue that intersects with all aspects of inclusivity. While digital tools are becoming more widespread, access is still uneven across regions and communities. Factors such as cost, infrastructure, and digital literacy significantly influence how effectively learners can engage with AI-driven and game-based systems. Providing devices alone is not sufficient; learners and educators must also be equipped with the skills needed to use these technologies effectively. Digital literacy training plays a crucial role in ensuring that users can navigate platforms, interpret feedback, and engage meaningfully with interactive content. Educators, in particular, need professional development opportunities to integrate these tools into their teaching practices in pedagogically sound ways.

Beyond access, the design of technological systems must prioritize usability and inclusivity. Interfaces should be intuitive, flexible, and adaptable to users with varying levels of digital experience. AI systems should offer transparency in how they generate recommendations or feedback, helping learners understand and trust the system. Game-based environments should provide multiple pathways to success, allowing learners to approach tasks in ways that align with their strengths and preferences. For example, some learners may prefer exploratory gameplay, while others may benefit from structured guidance. By accommodating different learning styles, these systems can create more inclusive and supportive learning experiences.

Another important consideration is the role of educators in fostering inclusive environments. While technology can provide powerful tools, it cannot replace the human element of teaching. Educators play a critical role in interpreting data, providing emotional support, and ensuring that learning experiences remain meaningful and contextually appropriate. They also serve as mediators who can identify potential gaps in technology and adapt instruction accordingly. In inclusive literacy education, the collaboration between educators and technology becomes essential in addressing the diverse needs of learners.

Ultimately, achieving inclusive and equitable literacy learning requires a holistic and systemic approach. It involves not only the development of advanced technologies but also thoughtful design, policy support, and continuous evaluation. AI and game-based learning have the potential to democratize education by making it more personalized, engaging, and accessible. However, this potential can only be realized if inclusivity is embedded at every stage of development and implementation.

By addressing linguistic diversity, accessibility needs, socio-economic barriers, cultural relevance, and technological access, stakeholders can create literacy learning environments that truly serve all learners. Such environments not only improve individual outcomes but also contribute to broader educational equity and social inclusion. In this way, the integration of AI and game-based learning becomes not just a technological advancement, but a meaningful step toward a more just and inclusive education system.

Beyond inclusivity, ethical considerations must also be addressed to ensure responsible use of AI in literacy education.

7. ETHICAL CONSIDERATIONS AND CHALLENGES IN AI-ENHANCED LITERACY LEARNING

The integration of Artificial Intelligence (AI) into literacy education offers substantial benefits, yet it also introduces a range of ethical challenges that must be addressed with careful consideration. As AI systems become increasingly embedded in educational environments, concerns related to fairness, privacy, authorship, dependency, and implementation emerge as critical issues. These challenges are not only technical in nature but also deeply connected to pedagogical values and social responsibility. Therefore, the responsible use of AI in literacy learning requires a balanced approach that combines innovation with ethical awareness, transparent design, and continuous evaluation (Usher & Barak, 2024).

One of the most pressing ethical concerns in AI-enhanced literacy learning is algorithmic bias. AI systems rely heavily on training data, and when such data contains historical or cultural biases, these biases can be replicated or even amplified in system outputs. In literacy education, bias may appear in various forms, such as the prioritization of certain linguistic styles, cultural narratives, or forms of expression over others. For instance, automated writing evaluation tools may favor standardized grammar conventions while undervaluing diverse linguistic identities, including those of multilingual learners. Similarly, reading recommendations generated by AI may reflect dominant cultural perspectives, limiting exposure to diverse viewpoints. Addressing this issue requires deliberate efforts in curating inclusive datasets, conducting regular audits of AI outputs, and involving diverse stakeholders in system development. Without these safeguards, AI risks perpetuating inequities rather than fostering inclusive learning environments (Sekti, 2025b).

Data privacy is one of the most important ethical concerns in AI-driven literacy education. Adaptive systems often collect large amounts of learner data, including reading behavior, writing patterns, engagement levels, and interaction histories. Although this information helps systems provide more personalized learning experiences, it also raises questions about how data is collected, stored, and protected. Risks such as unauthorized access, data misuse, or security breaches can have serious consequences, particularly for younger learners. For this reason, ethical implementation requires strong security measures, transparent data policies, and clear communication about how learner information is being used.

Learners and educators should also have greater awareness and control over the data generated through these systems (Sckti, 2026).

Another challenge involves authorship and originality in the use of AI-generated content. Modern AI systems are capable of producing essays, summaries, and other written materials that closely resemble human writing. While these tools can support learning through feedback and examples, they may also encourage learners to depend too heavily on automated content generation. This creates concerns about academic integrity and may weaken the development of independent thinking and writing skills. To address this issue, educators need to establish clear guidelines regarding the appropriate use of AI tools in literacy activities. AI should function as a support tool rather than a replacement for genuine learning and critical reflection.

Over-reliance on AI can also affect the quality of learning experiences. When learners depend excessively on automated systems to interpret texts, summarize information, or generate responses, they may engage less deeply with the material. This can limit the development of critical thinking and communication skills, which are central goals of literacy education. Educators may face similar challenges if they rely too heavily on automated assessment and feedback systems without considering the value of human judgment. A balanced approach is therefore necessary, where AI enhances learning while still maintaining meaningful interaction between teachers and learners.

In addition to ethical concerns, practical barriers can also affect implementation. Integrating AI into literacy education requires reliable infrastructure, technical expertise, and continuous system maintenance. Educational institutions do not always have equal access to these resources, which can create disparities in the availability and quality of AI-supported learning tools. Teachers may also encounter difficulties adapting to new technologies, particularly when training and institutional support are limited. Addressing these challenges requires long-term commitment through infrastructure development, professional training, and supportive educational policies. Key ethical challenges and their corresponding mitigation strategies are summarized in Table 3.

Table 3. Ethical Challenges and Mitigation Strategies

Ethical Challenge	Description	Mitigation Strategy
Algorithmic Bias	AI systems reflect biased training data	Use diverse datasets and conduct regular audits
Data Privacy	Risks in data collection and storage	Implement strong security and transparent policies
Authorship Issues	Unclear ownership of AI-generated content	Establish guidelines and promote academic integrity
Over Reliance on AI	Reduced critical thinking and interaction	Balance AI use with active learning strategies
Implementation Barriers	Limited resources and technical expertise	Provide training and institutional support

Table 3 highlights the importance of proactive governance and ethical design in ensuring that AI-driven literacy tools remain fair, transparent, and accountable. These strategies show that ethical challenges can be reduced through careful planning, continuous evaluation, and collaboration among different stakeholders. Ethical considerations should be treated as an essential part of educational innovation rather than as barriers to technological development.

Ultimately, the responsible integration of AI into literacy education depends on shared commitment from educators, developers, policymakers, and learners. Each group contributes to shaping how technology is designed, implemented, and used in educational settings. By addressing concerns related to bias, privacy, authorship, dependency, and implementation barriers, it becomes possible to develop literacy learning environments that are both innovative and ethically responsible. Having explored the opportunities and challenges of AI-driven literacy learning, the next section discusses future directions and practical implications for education.

8. FUTURE DIRECTIONS AND PRACTICAL IMPLICATIONS

The rapid evolution of Artificial Intelligence and game-based learning continues to shape the future of literacy education in profound ways. As technological capabilities expand, new opportunities emerge to create more adaptive, immersive, and inclusive learning environments. These developments are not only transforming how literacy is taught but also redefining the roles of educators, learners, and institutions (Lim, Gunasekara, Pallant, Pallant, & Pechenkina, 2023). Literacy is no longer a static skill but a dynamic competence that evolves alongside technological change. Understanding future trends is therefore essential for ensuring that the integration of AI and game-based learning remains aligned with educational goals and broader societal needs.

8.1 Future Implications for Practice

One of the most noticeable developments in this field is the emergence of more intelligent and context-aware learning systems. Future AI technologies are expected to become better at understanding learner behavior, emotional responses, and cognitive patterns during learning activities (Sekti, 2025a). This means that AI systems may eventually move beyond simple performance tracking and develop a more complete understanding of how learners interact with content. In literacy education, such systems could recognize when learners are confused by difficult texts, disengaged because tasks are too repetitive, or highly motivated during interactive activities. Based on these observations, the system could adjust reading materials, provide additional guidance, or introduce new challenges to maintain engagement. At the same time, game-based learning is likely to become more immersive through the use of virtual reality and augmented reality, allowing learners to participate directly in interactive story worlds and literacy-based experiences.

Another important direction involves the growth of collaborative and social learning within AI-driven game environments. Future literacy platforms may support real-time interaction among learners from different regions and cultural backgrounds. In these environments, learners could work together to create stories, solve narrative-based problems, and participate in discussions that strengthen reading and writing skills. AI systems may also help facilitate these interactions by recommending peer groups, moderating communication, and providing feedback on collaborative work. This development reflects the growing importance of communication, collaboration, and digital citizenship in modern education. It also reinforces the idea that literacy is not only an individual ability but a social practice shaped through interaction and shared understanding.

These technological developments also have important implications for teachers and educational institutions. Educators are increasingly expected to move beyond the traditional role of content delivery and become facilitators, mentors, and designers of learning experiences. This shift requires teachers to guide learners in interpreting AI-generated feedback, using digital tools critically, and engaging responsibly with technology-supported learning environments. As a result, educators need broader competencies that include digital literacy, data interpretation, and a basic understanding of how AI systems function. Institutions also need to adapt by investing in technological infrastructure, professional development, and policies that support innovation while maintaining ethical standards. Without adequate institutional preparation, even advanced educational technologies may have limited impact on learning outcomes.

Practical implementation of AI and game-based literacy learning also requires careful planning. One effective strategy is to adopt a gradual implementation process rather than introducing complex systems all at once. Pilot programs allow institutions to test technologies, identify technical or instructional challenges, and refine systems before wider adoption. Continuous evaluation is equally important to ensure that technology supports literacy development rather than becoming a distraction from educational goals. Involving different stakeholders throughout the implementation process is also essential. Teachers, learners, parents, and administrators each provide perspectives that can help improve usability, relevance, and effectiveness. Their participation increases the likelihood that these systems will reflect actual educational needs rather than purely technological priorities.

Inclusivity and accessibility must remain central considerations in both the design and implementation of these systems. Learners come from diverse linguistic, cultural, and socio-economic backgrounds, and educational technologies need to accommodate these differences. AI-driven game-based systems should therefore include multilingual support, accessible interfaces, and flexible learning pathways that respond to varying abilities and needs. Training and technical support are also necessary to ensure that both educators and learners can use these tools effectively. Without sufficient digital literacy skills, users may struggle to benefit from advanced features, reducing the overall impact of the system. Partnerships between educational institutions, technology providers, and policymakers can help create solutions that are sustainable and adaptable across different contexts.

Future research will continue to play an important role in shaping AI-enhanced literacy learning. More long-term studies are needed to understand whether improvements in engagement and short-term performance lead to lasting literacy development. Researchers should also examine how different groups of learners interact with AI and game-based systems, particularly in relation to motivation, accessibility, and educational equity. Another important area of research involves developing ethical and pedagogical frameworks that guide the responsible use of AI in education. As technologies continue to evolve, these frameworks will need to be updated regularly to address new challenges while remaining aligned with educational values and learner well-being.

Interdisciplinary collaboration can further strengthen innovation in this area. Combining perspectives from education, computer science, psychology, and sociology can lead to more balanced and effective learning systems. Psychological research, for example, can help explain how motivation and engagement develop within game environments, while educational theory can guide the alignment between AI systems and literacy objectives. Sociological perspectives are equally important because they help address issues related to equity, inclusion, and access. Collaboration among universities, technology companies, and government institutions can also support the development of standards and policies that encourage quality, accountability, and responsible innovation in AI-supported education.

Overall, the integration of artificial intelligence and game-based learning represents an important step forward in literacy education. These technologies create opportunities for more personalized, engaging, and inclusive learning experiences that reflect the realities of the digital era. At the same time, their effectiveness depends on thoughtful implementation, continuous evaluation, and a strong commitment to ethical and equitable practices. Educators and institutions need to remain adaptable by embracing innovation while continuing to prioritize meaningful learning and pedagogical goals. When implemented carefully, AI and game-based learning can help literacy education evolve in ways that better prepare learners to participate in an increasingly connected and information-rich world..

9. CONCLUSION

The integration of artificial intelligence and game-based learning offers a promising approach for transforming literacy education within increasingly diverse and complex learning environments. Throughout this discussion, literacy has been treated not simply as a learning outcome but as the primary focus of educational innovation, where technology functions as a support tool rather than a replacement for meaningful learning experiences. Maintaining this perspective is important to ensure that developments in digital education continue to prioritize pedagogical value and the real needs of learners.

The discussion also demonstrates that combining artificial intelligence with game-based learning can create learning environments that are both adaptive and engaging. Artificial intelligence supports personalization through data-driven analysis, enabling systems to respond to individual learner progress, preferences, and challenges. At the same time, game-based learning introduces motivation, interaction, and immersive experiences that help sustain learner engagement. When these approaches are integrated, they can support literacy development in ways that are both effective and enjoyable, particularly in reading and writing activities that require continuous practice and reinforcement.

From a theoretical perspective, this integration reflects principles associated with constructivism and connectivism. Learners are encouraged to become active participants who build knowledge through interaction, exploration, and collaboration rather than passive recipients of information. Game environments provide meaningful contexts for these interactions, while artificial intelligence enhances the learning process through adaptive pathways and timely feedback. Together, these elements support deeper comprehension and stronger critical engagement with texts, both of which are essential aspects of literacy in the digital era.

In practical terms, the use of artificial intelligence in literacy education has shown considerable potential in areas such as automated feedback, reading comprehension support, and writing development. These functions become even more effective when integrated into game-based systems that encourage learners to engage with content through stories, challenges, and reward structures. Such environments can transform traditional literacy activities into more meaningful and engaging experiences that encourage curiosity and persistence. As learners remain actively involved in these activities, they are more likely to strengthen their literacy skills over time.

The importance of inclusivity and equity has also emerged as a central issue in the design and implementation of these technologies. Learners from different linguistic, cultural, and socio-economic backgrounds may benefit significantly from adaptive and accessible learning systems. Artificial intelligence can support differentiated instruction by adjusting content and feedback according to individual needs, while game-based learning can provide culturally relevant and engaging contexts for participation. However, ensuring equal access to these technologies remains a significant challenge. Without thoughtful planning and institutional support, technological developments may unintentionally reinforce existing educational inequalities instead of reducing them.

Ethical considerations are equally important in shaping the future use of artificial intelligence in literacy education. Concerns related to data privacy, algorithmic bias, and transparency must be addressed to ensure responsible implementation and maintain trust among users. Educators and developers need to work collaboratively to create systems that are fair, accountable, and aligned with educational values. It is also essential to preserve the role of educators as facilitators and mentors so that technology enhances, rather than replaces, meaningful human interaction in the learning process. A balanced approach is necessary to maximize the benefits of innovation while minimizing potential risks.

Looking ahead, literacy education will likely continue to evolve alongside advancements in artificial intelligence and interactive technologies. Emerging developments such as immersive storytelling, augmented environments, and more advanced language-processing systems may further enrich literacy learning experiences. Future research should therefore focus on evaluating the long-term effects of these approaches, examining their effectiveness across different educational contexts, and identifying scalable solutions that can be implemented more broadly. Interdisciplinary collaboration will remain important for encouraging innovation while ensuring that educational quality and equity continue to be prioritized.

Overall, the integration of artificial intelligence and game-based learning represents an important step in the ongoing development of literacy education. By combining adaptive technologies with engaging learning environments, these approaches can create experiences that are both meaningful and inclusive for diverse learners. Although challenges remain, the opportunities offered by this integration highlight the value of continued exploration, careful implementation, and ethical consideration. These developments provide a strong foundation for supporting more effective literacy education in an increasingly digital and interconnected world.

REFERENCES

Aguado-García, J.-M., Alonso-Muñoz, S., & De-Pablos-Heredero, C. (2025). Using Artificial Intelligence for Higher Education: An Overview and Future Research Avenues. *SAGE Open, 15*(2), 21582440251340350. DOI: 10.1177/21582440251340352

Alfredo, R., Echeverria, V., Jin, Y., Yan, L., Swiecki, Z., Gašević, D., & Martinez-Maldonado, R. (2024). Human-centred learning analytics and AI in education: A systematic literature review. *Computers and Education: Artificial Intelligence, 6*, 100215. https://doi.org/https://doi.org/10.1016/j.caeai.2024.100215

Cerra, P., Pablo, F. Á., & Humberto, B. P. (2022). Effects of Using Game-Based Learning to Improve the Academic Performance and Motivation in Engineering Studies. *Journal of Educational Computing Research, 60*(7), 1663–1687. DOI: 10.1177/07356331221074022

Chiotaki, D., Poulopoulos, V., & Karpouzis, K. (2023). Adaptive game-based learning in education: a systematic review. *Frontiers in Computer Science, Volume 5-2023.*

Dziubaniuk, O., Ivanova-Gongne, M., & Nyholm, M. (2023). Learning and teaching sustainable business in the digital era: A connectivism theory approach. *International Journal of Educational Technology in Higher Education, 20*(1), 20. DOI: 10.1186/s41239-023-00390-w PMID: 37096023

Glas, R., van Vught, J., Fluitsma, T., De La Hera, T., & Gómez-García, S. (2023). Literacy at play: an analysis of media literacy games used to foster media literacy competencies. *Frontiers in Communication, Volume 8-2023.*

Horvat, M., Jagušt, T., Veseli, Z. P., Malnar, K., & Čižmar, Ž. (2022). An overview of digital game-based learning development and evaluation models. In *2022 45th Jubilee International Convention on Information, Communication and Electronic Technology (MIPRO)* (pp. 717–722). DOI: 10.23919/MIPRO55190.2022.9803333

Hsiao, J.-C., & Chang, J. S. (2024). Enhancing EFL reading and writing through AI-powered tools: Design, implementation, and evaluation of an online course. *Interactive Learning Environments, 32*(9), 4934–4949. DOI: 10.1080/10494820.2023.2207187

Hsu, T.-C., & Lin, Y.-T. (2025). Effects of integrating AI image recognition and robot game-based learning on computational thinking. *Journal of Educational Technology & Society, 28*(4), 225–240.

Kasapidis, V., Petrou, A., Konstantinidi, N., Kostalias, K., & Kakogianni, E. (2025). AI and Data Literacy: Challenges and Opportunities for Teachers and Students. *European Journal of Education and Pedagogy, 6*(3), 7–11. DOI: 10.24018/ejedu.2025.6.3.957

Khalid, J., Chuanmin, M., Shahid Rasheed, M., & Kamdar, I. (2025). Towards an inclusive and equitable future: Transformation of digital learning design in the digital era. *Information Technology & People*, •••, 1–24. DOI: 10.1108/ITP-09-2024-1144

Lim, W. M., Gunasekara, A., Pallant, J. L., Pallant, J. I., & Pechenkina, E. (2023). Generative AI and the future of education: Ragnarök or reformation? A paradoxical perspective from management educators. *International Journal of Management Education, 21*(2), 100790. https://doi.org/https://doi.org/10.1016/j.ijme.2023.100790. DOI: 10.1016/j.ijme.2023.100790

Lin, Y.-L., Wang, W.-T., & Hsieh, M.-J. (2024). The effects of students' self-efficacy, self-regulated learning strategy, perceived and actual learning effectiveness: A digital game-based learning system. *Education and Information Technologies*, *29*(16), 22213–22245. DOI: 10.1007/s10639-024-12700-4

Muawanah, U., Marini, A., & Sarifah, I. (2024). The interconnection between digital literacy, artificial intelligence, and the use of E-learning applications in enhancing the sustainability of Regional Languages: Evidence from Indonesia. *Social Sciences & Humanities Open*, *10*, 101169. https://doi.org/https://doi.org/10.1016/j.ssaho.2024.101169. DOI: 10.1016/j.ssaho.2024.101169

Putri, A. A., & Sekti, B. A. (2026). Human–AI Collaboration in Creativity, Design, and Innovation. In *Redefining Global Creative Sectors Through AI and Human Augmentation* (pp. 273–303). DOI: 10.4018/979-8-3373-7153-5.ch009

Sekti, B. A. (2025a). AI Technology Management Concepts and Strategies. In *AI Technology Management and Value Creation* (pp. 1–32). DOI: 10.4018/979-8-3373-2497-5.ch001

Sekti, B. A. (2025b). Foundations of Artificial Intelligence Ethics. In *Navigating Social Trust in the AI Era* (pp. 23–47). DOI: 10.4018/979-8-3373-7011-8.ch002

Sekti, B. A. (2026). Data Privacy and Cybersecurity in Wind Power Systems. In *AI-Powered Analysis* (pp. 335–366). Modeling, and Monitoring of Wind Energy Systems., DOI: 10.4018/979-8-3373-4159-0.ch009

Si, Q., Hodges, T. S., & Coleman, J. M. (2022). Multimodal literacies classroom instruction for K-12 students: A review of research. *Literacy Research and Instruction*, *61*(3), 276–297. DOI: 10.1080/19388071.2021.2008555

Song, Y., Weisberg, L. R., Zhang, S., Tian, X., Boyer, K. E., & Israel, M. (2024). A framework for inclusive AI learning design for diverse learners. *Computers and Education: Artificial Intelligence, 6*, 100212. https://doi.org/https://doi.org/10.1016/j.caeai.2024.100212

Usher, M., & Barak, M. (2024). Unpacking the role of AI ethics online education for science and engineering students. *International Journal of STEM Education*, *11*(1), 35. DOI: 10.1186/s40594-024-00493-4

Villatoro Moral, S., Serra Vives, N., & Capellà Galmés, M. À. (2026). Medieval-Themed Video Games For History Teaching: A Systematic Review. *Electronic Journal of e-Learning*, *24*(1), 45–60. DOI: 10.34190/ejel.24.1.4431

Wang, S., Wang, F., Zhu, Z., Wang, J., Tran, T., & Du, Z. (2024). Artificial intelligence in education: A systematic literature review. *Expert Systems with Applications*, *252*, 124167. https://doi.org/https://doi.org/10.1016/j.eswa.2024.124167. DOI: 10.1016/j.eswa.2024.124167

Yildiz Durak, H., & Onan, A. (2025). A systematic review of AI-based feedback in educational settings. *Journal of Computational Social Science*, *8*(4), 96. DOI: 10.1007/s42001-025-00428-1

Zajda, J. (2021). Constructivist Learning Theory and Creating Effective Learning Environments BT - Globalisation and Education Reforms: Creating Effective Learning Environments. In Zajda, J. (Ed.), (pp. 35–50). Springer International Publishing., DOI: 10.1007/978-3-030-71575-5_3

KEY TERMS AND DEFINITIONS

Adaptive Learning Systems: Technologies that adjust content and instruction based on individual learner performance and needs.

AI-Generated Content: Text or media created by artificial intelligence to support learning activities and instruction.

Artificial Intelligence in Education: The use of intelligent systems to support, personalize, and automate learning processes.

Digital Literacy: The ability to effectively access, evaluate, and create information using digital technologies.

Game-Based Learning: An instructional approach that uses game elements to enhance engagement and learning outcomes.

Gamification: The application of game elements such as points, badges, and rewards in non-game learning contexts.

Inclusive Education: An approach that ensures all learners, regardless of background or ability, have equal access to education.

Learning Analytics: The measurement and analysis of learner data to improve learning experiences and outcomes.

Literacy Learning: The development of reading, writing, and comprehension skills across various contexts and media.

Multiliteracies: A framework that recognizes multiple forms of literacy, including visual, digital, and cultural literacies.

Chapter 2
Case Studies of AI and Game-Based Approaches to Literacy Learning:
Insights Across Diverse Educational Contexts

Shruti George
http://orcid.org/0009-0006-6955-4628
Christ University, India

S. Chanti
http://orcid.org/0000-0003-4055-0333
Christ University, India

Jossy P. George
http://orcid.org/0000-0003-3285-5081
Christ University, India

ABSTRACT

Literacy has been found to be one of the greatest determinants to success in education, economic empowerment as well as civic action in life. In the world we live in today, which is increasingly digital, technological innovation is transforming traditional forms of teaching literacy. The use of artificial intelligence and game-based learning systems especially demonstrates this change. These newer methods are to address the problems that have been present in the literacy education since then, including student engagement, personalized learning, and the equitable access of various groups of learners to programs. Game based learning has demonstrated tremendous potential in enhancing literacy performance through intrinsic motivation, instant feedback and able relevant feedback. These systems, together with AI, can provide previously unattainable rates of personalization because they can analyse an individual learning pattern and modify the delivery of content in real time.

DOI: 10.4018/979-8-3373-7472-7.ch002

INTRODUCTION

Contextual Background

Educational achievement, social interaction and lifelong learning still require literacy. It is important to be able to read, write, and be entertained to communicate in a meaningful way to contribute to society. It assists people in going through academic, professional and civic worlds (UNESCO, 2004; Vlieghe, 2015). Even with its significance, there are still issues of learning literacy which include; how to capture the attention of the learners, how to overcome language barriers, and how to provide equal access to above par educational resources. The continuous and sustained growth of digital technologies and worldwide interconnections complicate these issues.

However, with recent technological advancements, the shift in circumstances has seen teachers and schools consider new methods of teaching literacy. Game-Based Learning (GBL) and Artificial Intelligence (AI) have become promising tools for the present and future of education (Zhan et al., 2022). AI algorithms are developed to adapt to individual pupil's strength, allowing customisable learning paths that promote user engagement and growth. GBL uses game mechanics and graphics to incorporate educational curricula into the students learning. They provide new strategies which can serve the needs of different learners in a refined manner. The techniques can establish an inclusive, flexible, and learner-focused approach to teaching literacy in different learning institutions.

Digital Transformation in Literacy Learning

The use of digital technology has transformed the design and the method of teaching literacy. This is because different applications of AI and gaming environments offer interactive and adaptive capabilities that are unlike the traditional approach. GBL promotes active learning through the integration of literacy activities with activities of interest; this stimulates long-term follow-up. Such environments accommodate reading/writing and multimodal communication practices that are appealing to learners born into the digital era (Wilson et al., 2017).

With AI, games focused on education and academic performance are able to react to individual interactions with the learner and modify instructional resources accordingly. The systems have the potential to facilitate individualized learning by providing feedback, pace, and task complexity based on the performance of the individual learners (Hartt et al., 2020). These can be examples such as adaptive reading platforms, vocabulary-turned games, and writing assistance which help the learners to get through the writing process. The combination of AI and GBL preconditions more adaptable and interactive approaches to teaching literacy.

The importance of technology in literacy practices became prominent due to the rise in the application of digital learning spaces in remote and hybrid learning. Although these innovations increased the application of AI and game-based tools in the classroom, they also put an emphasis on the necessity to investigate the functioning of these tools in various learning situations and among students of different groups. GBL is also seen to have an inclusive view on education by motivating learners and helping them engage with different learner materials. As seen in the years before, compared to traditional, text-heavy instructional approaches, digital and game-based pedagogies focus primarily on active learner participation, feedback and student autonomy (Yasir et al., 2021).

Purpose of the Chapter

The case studies of AI and GBL strategies of acquiring literacy in various educational environments are presented and discussed in this chapter. It intends to demonstrate the integration of these technologies into literacy teaching and their impact on the interactions of learners with reading, writing, and literacy processes as a whole through the review of practical uses. Students have been demonstrated to be able to enhance their literacy using AI-based teaching methods, which provide them with personal feedback, flexible content delivery, and guided practice (Chen and Lin, 2020). In other research, game-based learning was associated with increased engagement and motivation, which can promote more in-depth multimodal literacy engagement (Hartt, Hosseini, and Mostafapour, 2020; Wilson et al., 2017). The existing studies on blended or tech-heavy classrooms indicate that these solutions may offer the different types of formats that can satisfy the needs of different learners (Gligorea et al., 2023; Nadeem, Oroszlanyova, and Farag, 2023). Also, the studies of inclusive teaching observe that instructional technologies can open numerous opportunities to learn and communicate, which can be beneficial to students with various needs when the technologies are developed. Simultaneously, research reviews admit that the results of interventions on the level of literacy skills are different in various settings. It may depend on the quality of the implementation, support provided to learners, and the learning context (Boeker et al., 2013; Yasir, Shaheen, and Hafeez, 2021). This body of evidence portrays a complicated scenario of how AI and game-based approaches can be applied in enhancing literacy experiences and where future studies are required in order to comprehend the interactions of these technologies with aspects of education.

The chapter examines the benefits of instruction and context-specific considerations of AI and game-based literacy programs with the help of case studies. It elucidates more about the application of such practices in various setups and how they encourage equitable and inclusive literacy acquisition. The chapter also adds to the current debates regarding the role of new technologies in changing literacy education by providing knowledge about the educational environments.

LITERATURE REVIEW

Theoretical Underpinnings of Literacy Learning

Literacy development in a digital learning environment (DLE) depends on the constructivist and the socio-cognitive theory. The process of learning is social and individual (Zhang et al., 2004). These theories can give some insights into the interaction of students with digital text, technology, and their peers. Within a digital environment, literacy development may emerge as an opportunity for collaboration and shared problem-solving facilitated through digital tools. Consequently, interactions with digital texts may support the quest for knowledge and the gradual development for high-order literacy skills.

Substantivism Foundations of Digital Literacy

Constructivism theory deeply emphasises that learning is active as it entails the development of knowledge through the connection of the new knowledge with prior experiences and the background of the learner (Piaget, 1952). The theory in an online setting takes the form of self-regulated learning that is student-focused, rather than the learner passively absorbing information. When it comes to digital literacy, students proactively get to know their learning requirements and strategies as these approaches are associated with increased learner engagement (Zhang et al., 2004).

- **Active Meaning Construction**: Reading is not just about how different words and letters appear on a page. It is an interactive and multilayered cognition process during which the readers interact with text. They produce, as well as construct meaning for interpretability.
- **Adaptive and Personalized Learning**: AI-based algorithms allow adaptive learning, which delivers customisation of learner experiences. They go in line with constructivism by assisting the students to build knowledge based on meaningful experiences at their own pace and level of skill, implying that programs adjust based on the performance and needs demonstrated by the learner (Piaget, 1952).
- **Self-Regulation and Metacognition**: In order to be successful in digital literacy education, learners should primarily take part in defining their learning objectives. In the absence of strict supervision, it is important for them to learn how to hold themselves accountable. They are also supposed to adopt the metacognitive practices of keeping track of their progress and evaluating the worth of the acquired knowledge (M et al., 2024).

Social-Cultural and Socio-Cognitive Perspectives

The socio-cognitive theory emphasises the fact that learning takes place in particular communities. The view is important in the analysis of the role of digital space in supporting literacy, such as through private Facebook groups, Reddit sub groups and Discord communities. Such digital platforms offer support to learner's that share similar interests, becoming a means of communication to help connect students to their fellow peers (M et al., 2024).

- **Social Interaction and Vygotskian Concepts**: Vygotsky (1978) did not just think, but researched about the necessity of social interaction when developing an environment in which language and knowledge are created in a community of learners.
- **Collaborative Learning Theory (CLT)**: CLT advocates the utilization of e-learning as a method of collaboration. This partnership can be seen through the application of online tools to exchange knowledge, provide feedback, and discuss potential solutions to different problems in collaboration with other students.
- **Social Presence**: Social-emotional literacy is a determinant of the quality of outcomes in online learning. It entails social skills such as the capability to introduce oneself and share feelings and considerate the opinion of others in a debate (Porat et al., 2018).

Multidimensional Interactivity Integration and New Literacies

The New Literacy theory further explains literacy acquisition. It introduces literacy as an interactive, non-linear, and dynamic way of approach to digital text, beyond traditional print (Alneyadi et al., 2023). Also, according to the Technology Acceptance Model (TAM), digital natives are more likely to reach a literacy level when they consider digital tools to be useful and convenient (Alneyadi et al., 2023).

The interrelationship between these theories makes sure that the relationship between learners, content and technology in the creation of digital literacy is achieved (Alotaibi, 2025). This relationship is amplified by the use of digital platforms which allow learners to interact and grow. This will lessen mental processing and enable students to concentrate on advanced processes, including information organization and the critical analysis (Alsowat, 2022). Within this context, learners are not only consumers of knowledge, they also turn into investigators and discoverers of their learning process (Alneyadi et al., 2023).

AI in Literacy Instruction

Introducing the concept of AI in the field of literacy and language teaching is the transition towards the old-fashioned one-fit-all model and a more adaptable system. The new system will serve the cognitive differences and learning pace of individual students (Sari et al., 2024; Jiao, 2024). The recent applications are based on three primary technologies, including adaptive learning models, Natural Language Processing (NLP) and systems of data-driven feedback. The purpose of such technologies is to ease the cognitive load and improve knowledge retention and student engagement (Sajja et al., 2023; Gligorea et al., 2023).

Individual Processes and Personal Learning

Adaptive learning models are the foundation of the current education platforms that apply machine learning to the learning process to make it unique. Knowledge spaces are used by such systems as Smart Sparrow, Knewton, and DreamBox Learning that monitor the existing knowledge of a student and modify the level of content (Dutta et al., 2024; Sari et al., 2024). Adaptive learning also uses the Teaching at the Right Level (TaRL) model, which means that tasks do not become either overly challenging or too simple to be completed by learners in literacy education (Ezzaim et al., 2023; Naseer et al., 2025). As an illustration, the Smart Sparrow system has seen a 20% higher course completion rate through designing student-specific learning paths through student performance data (Sari et al., 2024). Also, more sophisticated systems, such as the AI-Based Intelligent Assistant (AIIA), combine text embeddings and cosine similarity to identify the most relevant course materials on the request of the users, which makes personalized assistance work more accurate (Sajja et al., 2023).

Language Acquisition and Natural Language Processing (NLP)

NLP has altered the way of teaching literacy, as machines can think, and talk like people. Advanced Large Language Models (LLM) like GPT-3.5 can also be used in generating study plans tailored to the user, automating time-consuming tasks, such as grading tests within fractions of a second, and providing 24-hour virtual assistance (Sajja et al., 2023; Eltahir & Babiker, 2024). NLP systems, such as EAP TALK and the Arabic Language and Speech Tutor, are also used in language literacy and offer feedback on pronunciation, fluency, and grammar in real-time (Stasolla et al., 2025). These systems are based on speech recognition and Deep Learning (DL) models, such as BiLSTM models, capable of detecting linguistic errors with high precision, up to 99% in proficiency classification in the case of some of them (Stasolla et al., 2025). Moreover, NLP summarization devices can assist students to comprehend complicated writings or technical records by delivering a simplified version that brings out the core theme of the indented text (Sajja et al., 2023; Qurbunova & Yusupova, 2024).

Feedback Systems and Automated Assessment

Data-driven feedback systems serve as a diagnostic tool that provides immediate feedback, which nurtures continuous improvement in the client. Auto-graded assessment systems such as OpenEssayist and the Auto-Evaluator offered by the AIIA help instructors by grading their assignments and justifying the rationale behind every mark (Sari et al., 2024; Sajja et al., 2023). Such systems are used to process patterns of interaction including time taken on tasks, number of quiz attempts left, or to detect at-risk students who may be prone to disengagement from the program in their early stages. The dropout prediction models have proven to have accuracy rates of up to 99.1% (Stasolla et al., 2025). These feedback loops can be adapted in a way that supports long-term engagement through the use of adaptive gamification: the rewards, such as points, digital badges, and levels, are dynamically awarded according to trends in performance (Naseer et al., 2025). It has been shown that not only do such integrated systems contribute to the improvement of average assessment scores, the increase seen from 68.4 to 82.7 but also increase intrinsic motivation through the visualization of progress (Sari et al., 2024; Naseer et al., 2025).

Future Projections and Ethical implications

While perspectives may vary, AI can prove to be beneficial in literacy education, issues such as algorithmic bias, data privacy, and the digital divide have to be solved (Oubagine et al., 2025; Alotaibi, 2025). LLM institutions and model providers should make sure that AI must only enhance and not override human expertise. They need to pay attention to a co-creation model, in which teachers apply AI-related data to more personalized mentorship (Joshi, 2023; Dutta et al., 2024). Future research has picked up a focus in the direction of affective computing, a technology that will identify the state of the learner, including frustration or anxiety, to provide them with a more adaptive learning environment (Oubagine et al., 2025; Naseer et al., 2025).

Gamification and Engagement in Literacy Learning

GBL and gamification are recent trends in the field of education. It is a shift in the approach from the teacher-centered model towards the learner-centered, one that addresses the demands of digital natives (Yasir et al., 2021; Kenwright, 2018). While certain people may consider gamification and GBL as interchangeable terms, that notion is incorrect and the two concepts are quite distinct. Gamification is the integration of game-based features (points, rewards, negative markings etc.) in non-game situations with the aim of encouraging the learner along the intended behavioral trajectory to encourage dedication and user engagement (Gillis & Barney, 2025). On the contrary, GBL is a real-time game in which learners grasp material concepts and theory through practical experience by playing (Kenwright, 2018; Bawa, 2020). They are particularly effective in the field of literacy and language learning since they provide a contextual and interactive learning environment that decreases anxiety associated with learning a foreign language (Poole & Clarke-Midura, 2020).

Gamification Principles and their Impacts

Effective learning has strategies which are heavily dependent on engagement and involvement of the students. This strategy involves certain game designing elements, which are given below (Nadeem et al., 2023).

- **Currencies and Scoring Systems**: Points are one of the major currencies and are used to monitor the progress. They can be used to self-assess by giving immediate feedback (Jose and Vinay, 2017; Nadeem et al., 2023). Students can obtain points on activities such as vocabulary retention and speed in literacy-oriented GBL, which encourages them to have a growth mentality and increase their score by doing more tasks (Nadeem et al., 2023).
- **Badges and Achievements**: Badges are a symbol of mastery and they are meant to encourage students to do more (Tavares, 2022). This motivation can however diminish over time. A study of nursing students found that interest in earning digital badges decreased drastically during one module at the 15% mark at the end of the module, compared to 66% at the beginning (Tavares, 2022).
- **Social Comparison and Leaderboard**: Leaderboard promotes competition and social acknowledgment and makes students aim to achieve a higher position (Nadeem et al., 2023). According to research, male students tend to use leaderboards to measure their capabilities more frequently than female students (Nadeem et al., 2023). On the other hand, the use of leaderboards may demoralize students with worse performance, who will believe that they will never appear in the top positions, which can prompt them to lose interest in studying (Nadeem et al., 2023).

Influence on Student Motivation

These principles behind gamification are effective and based on the Self-Determination Theory (SDT) developed by Deci and Ryan, and the ARCS model developed by Keller, which is an acronym of Attention, Relevance, Confidence, and Satisfaction (Nadeem et al., 2023; Hartt et al., 2020). SDT emphasises intrinsic motivation in learning. According to it, learners must experience relatedness, competence, and autonomy. These psychological needs are satisfied thereby increasing motivation (Deci & Ryan, 2000). On the same note, the ARCS model focuses on ensuring that the learners are motivated and achieve their objectives by engaging their attention, relating with their objectives, developing confidence in their ability to complete the tasks, and offering rewarding feedback (Keller, 1987). When used in the context of gamified learning, the frameworks can be used to explain the way in which structured game elements can enhance engagement, persistence, and positive learning experiences.

- **Intrinsic vs. Extrinsic Motivation**: GBL encourages intrinsic motivation through addressing the needs of autonomy, competence, and relatedness (Hartt et al., 2020). Although the elements of gamification, such as points, offer external incentives, the best designs associate such incentives with pleasant and valuable learning activities (Hartt et al., 2020).
- **Affective Outcomes**: It has been reported by students that games as a way of teaching will be more entertaining and enjoyable than traditional lectures (Nadeem et al., 2023; Wang et al., 2016). This pleasure satisfies a basic need of a human and improves socialization, which results in improved information memory (Yasir et al., 2021).

Persistence in tasks and Development of skills

A characteristic of GBL that deserves discussion is that it fosters persistent work because it builds a simulated world in which a student is free to learn from their mistakes without the fear of judgement, supporting continued engagement and educational gain (Mariappan, 2024).

- **Trial-and-Error Mastery**: It can be referred to as the most expedient method of learning in the game. It enables the players to resume fast after making mistakes and this creates curiosity and persistence.
- **Repetition and Engagement**: Games can be used to present new ideas and instill them during repetitive engagement (Kenwright, 2018). These activities include exploration, analysis, and higher-order thinking and improve memory, short-term, in comparison with passive listening or reading (Mariappan, 2024; Rondon et al., 2013).

Gamified tools must be supported by explicit training on the self-regulated learning (SRL) strategies in order to maximize the effectiveness of literacy learning. It means that students will not perceive the game as a resource limited to just a specific course, but they will also be able to learn more about the process of self-regulated learning.

Research Gaps and Limitations

AI in education, learning literacy and GBL is a quickly developing concept, yet it suffers a lot of challenges in sustaining the benefits, ethical applications and the provision of robustness in the evaluation techniques. Motivational design frameworks, such as those relying on gamification and adaptive systems, have been used to explain how learner engagement and persistence may be supported across digitally mediated environments. However, the effectiveness of such frameworks often depends on contextual factors, including learner characteristics, instructional design choices, and the mode of delivery. The latest research indicates that developing comparative frameworks is important in establishing which strategies are most effective when applied to various groups of learners in a virtual, hybrid, or traditional classroom (Alsowat, 2022).

Methodological and Ethical Problems of AI in Education

- **Long-term Effects**: One of the key weaknesses of research, which is now being conducted, is its emphasis on immediate academic gains. It also does not provide consideration to the long-term effects of AI on the learning process, memory, and self-control of students (Sari et al., 2024; Alotaibi, 2025; Eltahir and Babiker, 2024).
- **Scalability and Resource Requirement**: A number of advanced AI and deep learning models have large computational requirements. This poses scalability and technical preparedness challenges on institutions (Sari et al., 2024; Stasolla et al., 2025).
- **Ethical and Transparency Issues**: Black-box AI models are not transparent. To construct the trust in the existence of these models and mitigate algorithmic bias, Explainable AI (XAI) needs to be developed (Alotaibi, 2025; Stasolla et al., 2025).

- **Small Sample Sizes**: Numerous empirical studies are based on the outcomes of one or two particular institutions or academic settings and make such studies less applicable to larger, more heterogeneous groups of students (Sari et al., 2024; Stasolla et al., 2025; Naseer et al., 2025).

Literacy Learning: Environmental and Underlying Gaps

- **The Digital Literacy Paradox**: Despite the high rates of daily interaction with digital tools, students usually lack the necessary skills to evaluate the information critically to find their way in the multi-layered information. This is also referred to as the digital literacy paradox (Porat et al., 2018).
- **Skill Foundations Interaction**: The knowledge gap on the low-tech nature of poor foundational reading competence to constrain the efficacy of high-tech literacy interventions is great. It means that digital technology cannot substitute the traditional literacy basis (Odvina et al., 2024).
- **Digital Distraction**: The inclusion of too much online gaming and social media should be discussed on, as they curb the reading abilities and concentration of students on their studies (Odvina et al., 2024).
- **Comparative Effectiveness**: The effectiveness of virtual learning versus the hybrid learning has not been completely determined, especially in its capacity to impart certain literacy skills such as writing of essays of high school level (Alsowat, 2022).

GBL: Gap in Synergy and Design

- **Striking a balance between Adaptivity and Motivation**: The main deficiency in the research literature is that the majority of adaptive systems are not designed with intentional motivation. They fail to bridge the gap between AI-assisted personalization and the gameplay (Naseer et al., 2025; Alotaibi, 2025).
- **Superficiality**: The existing constraints tend to be concerned with superficial aspects of games, like points and badges. These properties do not always facilitate deep learning when not incorporated into the fundamental adaptive processing of the learning system (Naseer et al., 2025).
- **Multi-group Comparisons**: Future researchers should involve intensive studies that will compare gamification-only, AI-only, and a combination of the two interventions. This would assist in explaining the individual and interactive impacts of each on the student outcomes (Naseer et al., 2025).

The Requirement of Inclusion and Evaluation Models.

- **Solving the Digital Divide**: The research has to focus on the improvement of the digital divide because the lack of access to technology is the factor, which diminishes the possible advantages of AI tools to educational fairness (Alotaibi, 2025).
- **Strong Evaluation Models**: There are no standardized, data-driven evaluation models in the field that are not based on self-reported data. The reliability of the research could be improved with the help of objective measures or observations (Eltahir and Babiker, 2024).
- **Addressing Diverse Needs**: Future research efforts should focus on inclusiveness through the research of the way these technologies can be applied to diverse students, such as stu-

dents with disabilities and students with different socio-economic backgrounds (Alotaibi, 2025; Stasolla et al., 2025).

METHODOLOGY

Research Design

The chapter represents what the authors have researched into AI-based and game-based platforms of learning literacy. The study adopts a literature review and comparative study of different platforms. This method enables one to take a glance at the application of AI and gamification as applied in literacy teaching in various educational technologies. The qualitative component of the current work allows delving into the educational basis, design of the chosen platforms, and terms of their usage. The analysis section aids in the comparison and synthesis of the results in a logical way.

The descriptive section dwells upon specific characteristics of every platform such as inner AI processes, the game design, instruction techniques, and accessibility. The analytical dimension is the evaluation of these qualities in comparison with the conventional educational models and theories of learning. This chapter is not merely descriptive, but it offers excellent information, based on credible background research, on the pros and cons of various platforms and establishes suitable application in various learning institutions through systematic synthesis.

The approach is especially applicable to rapidly evolving fields where a comparative framework is not present at all. Instead of the primary empirical research, which could have offered little information on a particular situation, in this study, the available evidence and experts are synthesized to offer general insights that can be applied in different educational settings. The research design acknowledges that the systematic review of diverse information sources and perspectives is necessary to gain an insight into AI-driven game-based literacy tools. The method assists educators, administrators, and policymakers to make evidence-based decisions.

Data Sources and Selection Criteria

In order to establish the basis of this chapter, the aim is to collect information to do such a comparative review, a wide range of sources were incorporated to address the technical characteristics, aspects and educational application of the selected platforms. Primary sources of data will include peer-reviewed scholarly articles on educational technology and literacy journals, technical documents and white papers provided by platform developers, case studies of educational establishments, research reports of other credible organizations, and publicly available analytics and user experience metrics about these platforms under examination.

The choice of scholarly materials was systematic on relevancy and quality. Articles were required to be published in the past ten years to consider up-to-date technology and instruction methods, be specific to the AI integration or GBL in literacy education, include empirical information or theoretical models, and have to be published in a peer-reviewed journal or academic conference. Favors were given to the studies that studied actual results, user interactions, or comparisons of education technologies. Articles were included on a theoretical basis because they provided information on the background on AI or gamification in education.

The sources of technical documentation and white papers were selected at official platforms and known educational technology organizations. The sources were subsequently essential to gather important data on the AI algorithms employed, mechanics of the games in the platforms, concepts that the contents were based upon, and privacy and security policies. This documentation proved to be particularly helpful in the context of technical complexity of AI integration and deliberate design choices relying on learning outcomes.

The choice of the implementations case studies and educational reports was determined by the degree of credibility, detailing and applicability to different educational contexts. The literature contained real-life applications of the grade levels, and had documented quantifiable results in literacy or engagement, and the variables that contributed to or impeded implementation. It also reflected various geographic and socioeconomic settings. This prevented the analysis of theoretical applications of education, as opposed to hypothetical scenarios that prevail in marketing.

Even selection of platforms was influenced by certain criteria in order to provide the stakeholders with a significant comparative outcome. The six platforms discussed in this chapter were chosen based on their great market penetration and common use in the education sector. They are deeply embedded in AI technologies, including GBL or gamification as one of the main characteristics and have a range of possible ways of integrating AI into the game design. These selection criteria will help to make sure that the platforms are not only applicable to contemporary choices of education and inform theories at the cross of AI, gamification, and literacy teaching.

Comparative Framework

It was found that there were five major dimensions of comparison of the platforms that would allow concluding about their essential features in terms of their educational efficiency and application. This model enables one to give a closer examination on features that exceed surface comparisons. It also examines the efficiency of teaching practices and the suitability of each platform to various circumstances.

The first dimension is the AI integration. It looks at the sophistication and the inner mechanics of the AI applications in every platform. This discussion takes into consideration the illustrations of AI technologies in application, including natural language processing, machine learning algorithms and predictive analytics. It examines the extent to which AI can be utilized in personalization as opposed to simple application of branching logic. It as well evaluates the quality and responsiveness of AI feedback, how the platform will respond to individual learning patterns as time progresses and the transparency of the AI decisions. Detailed attention is given to how AI functionality directly supports objectives targeting literacy learning rather than just serving its purpose as an engagement tool.

The second dimension takes into account game design mechanisms. This dimension examines the aspects of gamification and elements of GBL in every platform and how it corresponds to the learning objectives of literacy. It also judges motivational mechanics such as points, badges, leaderboards, and visualization of progress, the existence and the quality of narrative features or thematic context. The extrinsic rewards and intrinsic motivation, the challenge progression and difficulty level design, and possibilities to work collaboratively, compete and learn socially are also analyzed. The review determines whether the elements of the games indeed help in learning or they are just activities of the students which do not meet the learning outcomes.

The third dimension is pedagogical coherence. It evaluates the suitability of the design of each platform in terms of effective principles of literacy teaching. This dimension examines the theoretical learning frameworks that inform platform design, the quality and authenticity of literacy curriculum and tasks, the support provided to skills development, chances of valuable practice, and incorporation of the formative evaluation and feedback connections. This dimension is essential in establishing whether platforms are effective teaching tools or mere products of entertainment that are labeled to be educative.

The fourth dimension measures inclusivity and accessibility. It evaluates the ability of every platform to suit various learners. The factors that are taken into consideration in the analysis include multilingual support, culturally relevant materials, compliance with universal design principles, and the differentiation of skills and needs of learning to differentiate. It also looks at the cultural responsiveness of materials and examples and taking into account the learners with disabilities or special educational needs. Since there is still the problem of equity in educational technology, this aspect is essential to comprehend what tools can deliver equitable literacy results.

The fifth dimension dwells on evidence of implementation and reported outcomes. This section is a mixture of research and case studies on the effectiveness of each of the platforms in actual school environments. The review evaluates the reported improvements in literacy or skills growth, student involvement and persistence and teacher and student satisfaction, and scalability and sustainability of implementation. It does not accept marketing claims on a face value basis and insists on conducting independent research and reports of credible implementation that gives realistic expectations of the stakeholders on the result that could be expected.

The evaluation criteria of each dimension are the same, and the platforms can be meaningfully compared under the condition that the platforms might be best in different aspects depending on their design priorities and target audience. The framework recognizes that the platform cannot be ideal in all cases, but that each platform has its various strengths that apply to particular educational objectives, student population, and factors of implementation.

Limitations

The findings and recommendations have some critical limitations that should be considered during their analysis. First, the study is based solely on secondary sources as opposed to using empirical research. Although the approach enables one to synthesize the existing knowledge and perform a general comparative analysis, the findings also rely on the availability and quality of literature and records, as well as possible biases. This analysis will not be able to answer questions that were not sufficiently addressed by earlier studies and has the same methodological weaknesses as the underlying studies.

It does not contain any novel primary empirical testing in classrooms. Consequently, the analysis is unable to deliver first-hand observation regarding the ways platforms are practiced, how the students and teachers make use of these tools in the real-life educational settings, and how the implementation considerations can impact the results. Due to the lack of experimental comparative analysis, any remarks concerning relative effectiveness are to be regarded as an integration of different available pieces of evidence, rather than an experiment. Different methods, measures, and settings used in the studies may have been applied and it would be difficult to compare them directly.

The other major weakness is that learning technology is rapidly changing. The characteristics of AI platforms are constantly improved. Thus, the analyses which are conducted on the basis of the available documentation and research may get outdated soon. After the analysis, it is possible to introduce new features, optimize AI algorithms, and change teaching strategies. Thus, outcomes must be considered as a moment in time of these platforms, but not permanent descriptions.

Research evidence can be of various quality and availability depending on the platform. Certain platforms especially those that have existed longer or have been in the market have been researched more stringently. Some might not have primary research and they might depend mainly on records and assertions of the company. Such an asymmetry of evidence creates discrepancies in the rigor and confidence of analysis between platforms, i.e., results on less-studied platforms would be regarded as less confident.

Also, the argument in this discussion is limited to the application of AI and game-based aspects of literacy instruction. Other relevant factors regarding platform selection and implementation are, therefore, given less attention. Such practical issues as price, technical infrastructure requirements, compatibility with existing curricula and systems, professional development needs, and support maintenance are mentioned but not described in detail. These concerns should also be taken into account by stakeholders together with pedagogical and technical analysis introduced in this chapter.

Lastly, the chapter is restrictive to six platforms of choice. Even though they capture major strategies in the area, they are not the full picture of AI-based game-based literacy devices. There are a lot of other platforms and new tools are coming up. The platforms analysed were selected by the virtue of visibility, usage, and documentation that necessarily excludes other potentially useful tools. These six platforms might not be applicable to the rest of the teaching and learning technologies in this category because of the results and models that were developed.

Despite these constraints, this systematic comparative review, addresses a major gap in the literature by offering a systematic evaluation of the predominant platforms on the basis of similar evaluation measures. By recognizing these limitations, this facilitates an acceptable interpretation and application of findings and also indicates areas that need further investigation to enhance the evidence base on which to make decisions about educational technology.

CASE STUDIES OF LEADING PLATFORMS

Duolingo

Platform Overview

Duolingo is a language learning application, which applies AI and adaptive learning. The system integrates reinforcement learning algorithms and games in order to produce personalized experiences to learners. The platform uses data-driven personalization systems, such as reinforcement-learning-influenced algorithms, to adapt the difficulty of the lesson, the sequence of content, and the amount of practice by the performance and engagement trends of learners. To facilitate lasting engagement and motivation the gamified aspects like points, streaks, levels and instant feedback are incorporated. Duolingo can offer multimodal exposure of language input through the short and interactive exercises comprising a mix of reading, writing, listening, and translating texts, which can facilitate incremental development of literacy in a digital learning setting. Nevertheless, it has also been studied to be contingent upon variables like goals of the learners, regularity of application, and degree to which the learning done through apps receive support through a wider-based instruction (Ramanathan & Tara, 2026; OpenAI, 2024).

AI Architecture and Learning Models

Reinforcement Learning Framework. Duolingo relies on algorithms to improve learning activities and select material. It sees all learning processes as decision points whereby the AI has to decide between exploring some new content and re-enforcing what the learner has already begun to comprehend. The platform is based on spaced repetition algorithms that determine the likelihood of a learner recalling a word or concept at a specific time. These models take into account such aspects as the time of the practice and the number of times a word was observed, the error trends of the learners, and the complexity of the content. Subsequent deep learning models determine interaction among learners to discover the most efficient lesson content. These systems consider response times, types of errors, skip rates and indicators of engagement to change the difficulty level when necessary (Loewen et al., 2019).

Adaptive Instructional Processes. The machine behind the platform is adaptive and it works on varying periods of time. In-session adaptation varies exercise intensity in relation to short-term performance, whereas between-session adaptation varies the order of lesson sequences in relation to long-term learning courses. The system will record the level of mastery of a vocabulary, grammar and pronunciation of every learner.

Gamification and Motivational Mechanics

Progression Systems. Duolingo uses experience points as a system of recognition based on frequent use as opposed to intensive study of the language that can be timely. Goals will motivate people to be committed, and streak systems will make the user feel engaged in their continued presence. The study of the most appropriate levels of challenge has revealed that moderate levels of difficulty, where learners succeed more frequently than fail yet not very easily, can be more effective at retaining information in the long term than both high levels of difficulty and low levels of difficulty.

Social and Competitive Factors. Leaderboard systems provide competitions between learners that are in divisions based on the same level of activities, and there are no instances of futile competition. Social accountability is applied in friend quests and shared challenges, whereas milestones are given through achievement badges. Research indicates that badges could increase intrinsic motivation associated with mastery and not participation.

Narrative Integration. Recent releases features new character-based storylines that unlock consecutively with learner progression. These narratives help attain a solid background of vocabulary and grammar, as they create an emotional investment in the learning process.

Educational Effectiveness and Outcomes

Studies show that language learning applications such as Duolingo have actual advantages, however, the advantages are different depending on the language proficiency of the learners. These mediums are specifically good with the development of reading and writing skills whilst speaking and listening comprehension might progress more slowly without further conversation practice. The retention rates on the platform seem to be greater than the retention rates of the conventional mobile learning platforms, indicating that gamification and adaptive learning can be effective in ensuring that the user is retained (Loewen et al., 2019).

Limitations and Pedagogical Problems

Despite its strengths, this platform faces numerous disadvantages too. Concentration on the practice of translating and on specific words can become an obstacle to acquire the skills of spontaneous speaking. This focus on gamification occasionally rewards behaviors that focus on gaining points instead of real learning, and some players are pressurized to keep streaks to gain points instead of pushing themselves. The disjointed nature of the grammar instructional process can also be such that it does not allow the students to develop a coherent view of the structures of the target language. Isolated exercises may be effective in training particular skills but may not be training the integrated needs of communication in the real life.

Grammarly

Platform Overview

Grammarly has transformed itself into a multi-purpose AI writing assistant, which is more than a grammar checker. The site uses the methods of natural language processing to give context sensitive feedback on the clarity, tone, coherence, and genre-specific conventions of a diverse range of writing scenarios. Grammarly can potentially help learners build metalinguistic awareness and the reflective writing habits by providing real-time suggestions and explanations. Their adaptive feedback features also demonstrate the ability of AI-driven tools to scaffold the writing process in accordance with the needs of individual users, though their teaching efficacy can be lower in case of learners with different levels of proficiency, writing goal, and use of automated assistance (Chesson, 2026; Slater-Robins, 2025.

NLP Architecture and Mechanisms of Correction

Multi-Layer Analysis System. Grammarly uses a pyramid structure of certain NLP models, which focus on various aspects of a given language. This system has a number of key levels of processing. The rule-based systems of surface-level processing identify simple errors such as spelling errors, punctuation errors, and simple subject-verb agreement errors. These are the quick systems and very dependable. Syntactic analysis is used to study the structure of the sentence and detect complex grammatical mistakes, some of which include syntax and structure, which are misplaced modifiers and sentence fragments. The system constructs the parsing trees in order to comprehend relationships between the elements of sentences. Semantic understanding and establishment of meaning and coherence is done using transformer-based models. Such models are able to recognize ambiguous pronouns, logical errors, and vocabulary error in the form of contextual word embeddings and sentence relations.

Context-Sensitive Correction. The most advanced feature of the platform is context adaptability. Grammarly is differentiated into multiple models based on the writing style such as, academic, business, casual, technical, with different purposes like to inform, describe, persuade or tell a story. The system examines document characteristics in order to identify the context and consequently modifies its recommendations. As an example, sentence fragments that would be marked as such in an academic writing style can be okay in a creative or marketing context because of its stylistic worth.

Adaptive Feedback Systems

Progressive Disclosure Architecture. Rather than overwhelming users with constant corrections simultaneously, the platform concentrates on the severity of the suggestions and learning potential. Serious mistakes are highlighted and addressed immediately, whereas the stylistic recommendations are made subsequently when the users resolve fundamental problems as they progress on. Such an organized approach helps prevent cognitive overload and focuses on impactful changes effectively.

Customized Learning Models. The platform monitors the patterns of errors made by the user per writing session in order to create user profiles. There are weaknesses that machine learning algorithms detect and adjust the feedback techniques. Users that often have trouble with certain errors are promptly given explanations, and forewarned of the possible problem spots, whereas those who have understood the concept well are barely bothered.

Explanatory Frameworks. Every correction contains stratified explanations, ranging between brief reasons consisting of one sentence each, to intricate grammatical explanations with examples. The natural language generation models generate idiomatic explanations allowing the users to get a grasp of abstract grammatical concepts by referring them to their text. The evidence in studies of writing feedback indicates that the encouragement to use explanations, as opposed to accepting corrections, results in the measurable advancement of subsequent writing of the user.

Tone and Clarity Analysis

Beyond correction, Grammarly also has advanced features that evaluate the effectiveness of communication. Sentiment analysis models assess such dimensions of tone as formality, confidence, and approachability. The system is able to identify the inconsistencies on tone and propose revisions according to the intentions of the user. Various methods are used to evaluate complexity in the readability algorithms, such as variability in sentence length, challenge in vocabulary and density of concepts.

Educational and Professional Applications

Teachers are saying that automated writing assistants can supplement formative feedback by performing mechanical corrections so that teachers can concentrate on more advanced problems such as argumentation and organization. However, this may lead to dependency issue and makes it difficult to transfer the skills of editing to non-assistive situations. When used in professional writing, the tools assist in maintaining consistency in long documents and adherence to the style guide because they generate individual rule sets.

Limitations and Pedagogical Debates

It has been criticized that too much use of automated corrections may make the development of independent editing skills more difficult. Although the recommendations provided on the platform are usually quite reasonable, they may at times be based on the biases expressed in the training data or may fail to consider some purposeful stylistic decisions. It is understandable why the writers with high skills get frustrated when the suggestions do not take into account the complex rhetorical techniques. The effectiveness of the platform is highly contingent upon the way the users engage with the explanations as opposed to the situation when they will be actively offered corrections, though the vast majority of users are inclined to choose the latter.

NoRedInk

Platform Overview

NoRedInk is a specialized program of teaching grammar and writing with an emphasis on more adaptive systems of practice. The platform takes the data of the learner performance to customize the exercises, increase or decrease the difficulty level, and focus on specific learner-hard to grasp grammatical concepts. NoRedInk aims to enhance relevance and commitment in the writing activities by positioning grammar teaching in the context of the interest chosen by the student and the important sentence structures. This method exemplifies how individualisation algorithms can reinforce sustained practice of the so-called difficult areas, as well as the significance of the adaptive feedback to strengthen grammar and writing skills in a digital learning setting (Edwards, 2024; Snowe & Snowe, 2017).

Adaptive Exercise Generation

Interest-Based Personalization. The peculiarity of NoRedInk is the creation of practice sentences which include the interests declared by students, for example, favorite athletes, musicians, hobbies, video games. This individual approach handles the motivation issue in grammar practice, which the students find boring. Personalization studies have demonstrated higher engagement measures and time-on-task with exercises with personally relevant material, but there is concern that this may not be reflective of a more profound grammatical comprehension but may more probably be associated with surface-level compliance.

Diagnostic Evaluation and Competency Charting. The site uses preliminary diagnostic test to chart student knowledge in a wide-ranging taxonomy of grammar skills. In this taxonomy, the grammar competency is broken down into fine-grained elements, for example, not just all errors to do with sentence boundary but to make a distinction between comma splice errors, run-on errors, and fragment errors. Models of item response theory are used to determine the performance patterns of students to determine the level of proficiency in each of the elements of skills.

Scaffolding Architecture

Mastery-Based Progression. NoRedInk has a high mastery before moving students to dependent skills. In its skill taxonomy, the system creates prerequisite relationships and does not allow advancement until the base competencies have attained threshold levels. As an example, before students are allowed to access exercises about the construction of complex sentences, they need to prove the level of skills in determining independent clauses.

Dynamic Difficulty Adjustment. The platform is adaptive in terms of challenge level in each area of skills by applying the following mechanisms:

- **Hint availability**: The first introduction to concepts consists of gradual hints; with student demonstration of the material scaffolding is gradually removed.

- **Distractor sophistication**: Multiple-choice tests use distractors that are matched to the difficulty of the student, where beginners would be shown prototypical errors, whereas higher-level students would be shown less apparent differences.
- **Complexity of sentences**: The grammatical context under target constructions will span the simple, clear examples to complex passages that will need more complicated parsing.

Integration of Spaced Repetition. The platform uses spaced repetition algorithms to remind the learner to revise at a later date concept that have already been practiced. These algorithms hit a balance between the necessity of consolidation and the necessity of moving through curriculum. There are periodic spiral review exercises, during which students go through previously acquired skills in an ever-increasing time frame, and the schedule is changed according to the trends in performance of students.

Mechanisms of Feedback and Metacognitive Development

Instant Remedial Feedback. Upon delivering incorrect responses, the students get specific explanations about the given type of error, as well as grammatical reasoning. The feedback generation system of the platform uses the templates that are tailored to specific categories of errors, providing uniform explanatory patterns that allow students to develop mental paradigms of grammar rules. This structured and consistent feedback approach supports metacognitive awareness by helping learners reflect on their mistakes and gradually internalize grammatical rules through repeated, guided practice.

Progress Visualization. The platform offers progress dashboards with detailed progress that can be seen in relation to skill dimensions. The learners are able to see the mastery levels, the recent progress trends, and the areas the focus will be made in future. This openness facilitates self-reflection and self-ambitions. By visualizing learning trajectories over time, the dashboards enable learners to monitor their development and make informed decisions about their study strategies. Such transparency also supports goal setting and sustained motivation, as learners can clearly associate effort with measurable improvement.

Classroom Part and Teacher Tools.

NoRedInk helps to offer granular data on student performance to teachers in order to target intervention. The system identifies students who are having difficulties with a particular concept and recommends the use of differentiated instruction. The teachers may give practice collections in accordance with classroom teaching or leave the adaptive engine of the platform to guide the student work. The assignment system in place in the platform can be used to facilitate both independent practice and formative assessment whereby the teachers can go to and review the work of the students and provide personalized feedback which is overlayed on top of the automated corrections.

Educational Findings and Research Data

Research into adaptive grammar systems demonstrates that they lead to better performance in grammar knowledge and use in the writing of students, although the effect sizes differ significantly across implementations. The most apparent benefits are seen in situations where educators are actively incorporating the platform with the direct instruction as opposed to it being independent practice. The student engagement measures of personalized grammar practice always go beyond the expectations of the baseline, which indicates the effectiveness of the personalization strategies in overcoming the motivational barriers. Nevertheless, some questions regarding whether the increase of engagement can be seen as a way of showing interest in the grammar concepts or just a more enjoyable means of wrapping traditionally unpopular contents are present.

Limitations

The transfer to real life writing settings is questionable given the fact that the platform focuses on the discrete skills practice. In actual composition, grammar requires the coordination of a range of competencies at once and focus on purpose of communication, neither of which is replicated in disconnected practice. Moreover, the mastery-based progression model, despite its theoretical soundness, can cause frustration to students who cannot get to the next level in specific skills and may behave as disengaged with the platform in spite of its efforts to personalize it.

Kahoot

Platform Overview

One example of applying the GBL to promote active engagement and knowledge retention with a competitive and collaborative quiz is Kahoot. Through the platform, instructors can create game-based assessments with points, leaderboard, and real-time feedback, thus motivating and encouraging attention to learners. Focusing on social interaction, peer competition, and instant response, Kahoot makes assessment an interactive learning tool, which promotes formative assessment and engagement in a variety of educational environments (Alsswey & Malak, 2024; Licorish, Owen, Daniel, & George, 2018; Özdemir, 2024; Wang, Zhu, & Sætre, 2016).

Game Mechanics and Motivational Design

Competitive Structure. The theme of Kahoot is the competition of groups against each other with the help of multiple choices and the time limit. Competitive aspect is observed at other levels:

- **Speed-accuracy trade-off:** The score decreases with time, and tension arises between the need to consider the answers and to take time. This arrangement would ensure quick recall and accuracy was not compromised.
- **Live leaderboards:** These leaderboards spark social comparison. It has been found that competitive motivation can be achieved by observing the performance of the peers, yet the effect of observation differs depending on individual objectives and self-confidence.
- **Podium recognition:** The best performers are given a high-profile credit, which provides social rewards as opposed to just points. This may enhance intrinsic motivation among a group of learners and augment anxiety or disengagement among others.

Streak Advanced Question Distribution Mechanics. The site shows the group response after every question. This understanding helps to dispel the usual misunderstandings and forms learning experiences whereby a majority of people make incorrect solutions. This transparency could reduce the stigma around errors and creates a positive towards growth.

Team and Collaborative Modes

In addition to personal competition, Kahoot has team-based ones that redirect competitive aspects to collaborative problem-solving. In team mode, answers are to be discussed in the groups, this involves verbal reasoning and group decision making. Such design encourages peer explanations, which is a useful learning approach, as students are able to understand better, when they have to explain something to others. Studies of cooperative learning demonstrate that such discussions have the capacity to build cognitive conflict and comprehension.

Balanced Challenge Design. To be effective, Kahoot should be implemented in a way that calibrates question difficulty objectively. When the questions are mostly answered wrong or right by most people, they will reduce the participation since competition thrives on conspicuous differences. The most effective questions produce diverse answers and definite learning experiences in case the correct answers are provided.

Reinforcement of Learning and Instant Feedback

Knowledge of Results. Kahoot automatically shows the correct answers on each question, whether with or without the involvement of the instructor. This is consistent with the timing research which identified feedback to be most effective when provided right after a respondent has responded to an inquiry when the query is still in their mind. This immediacy helps reduce misconceptions by reinforcing accurate understanding before incorrect assumptions are consolidated. Additionally, the visibility of correct responses can stimulate peer discussion and collective reflection, further strengthening conceptual clarity and engagement (Özdemir, 2024).

Chances of rectifying mistakes. The competitive type enables students to get a first-hand response on their answers which gives them an opportunity to reflect on their thought. When students realize that they have made a mistake, the shock and the visibility of the mistakes can make students think more in-depth and be reminded of the correct information, assuming that the classroom atmosphere allows admitting the mistakes. Over time, repeated exposure to immediate correction in a low-stakes, game-based environment can enhance confidence and promote deeper cognitive processing.

Contribution and Interaction

Universal Response Systems. Kahoot also involves every learner in real-time as opposed to classic classroom questioning where a student is addressed one at a time. This general type of response discourages observation and establishes an information flow on student understanding. Teachers also get the knowledge of the general misconceptions not only by depending on volunteers.

Flow State Cultivation. The difficulties and the speed associated with the platform can trigger flow states, which are defined by engagement and pleasure. A balance between the difficulty of the questions and the ability of the students will ensure that they are not bored through their inability or anxiety to answer. When this balance is achieved, learners are more likely to remain fully immersed in the activity, sustaining attention and motivation throughout the learning process.

Instructional integration and Pedagogical applications

Kahoot can be used in different teaching ways:

- **Formative assessment**: It is fast evaluation of what has been learnt prior to instruction. The immediate feedback allows the teacher to improve the teaching process according to the misconceptions that arise.
- **Review process**: It gives the practice in form of intervals, which strengthens retention. Interactive style enables reviews to remain more interactive and not monotonous which encourages active retrieval.
- **Energizer**: It can be used in case of long classes, as it helps to shift the concentration and get away with lecturing. The format of the game is stimulating and opposes mental exhaustion.

Outliers and Pedagogical Problems

Depth vs. Engagement Trade-off. The multiple-choice format restricts depth and complexity of questions. Although Kahoot is useful in assisting students to remember facts and recognize concepts, it lacks in challenging the students to perform tasks such as application, analysis, or synthesis. This restriction is compounded by the time factor of focusing on expeditious retrieval, rather than critical thinking. As a result, the platform is better suited for formative assessment or revision activities than for evaluating higher-order cognitive skills. Educators may need to supplement it with open-ended or project-based tasks to ensure deeper learning.

Competitive Anxiety. Social comparisons and leaderboards involving the general public may stress struggling students, which may negatively affect their academic self-esteem. It has been found that competitive formats are more advantageous to the high-performing students than the low-performing ones, which pose a risk of even greater achievement gap. In some cases, anxiety induced by time pressure and ranking can reduce participation rather than enhance motivation. This highlights the importance of using optional anonymity or team-based modes to mitigate negative emotional effects.

Personality Bias. The game-based system can encourage shallow learning with the goal of winning instead of grasping the concepts. Students may come up with test taking strategies that can be effective in the game but not in actual understanding. Over time, this can lead to a preference for recognition over reasoning. Without guided reflection or follow-up discussion, learning may remain superficial.

Equity Considerations. The race towards speed is not in favor of the student with slower information processing abilities such as students with learning disabilities and English language learners that need more time to process the information. This makes one ask the question of whether performance is an expression of real knowledge, or merely fastness of processing. Unequal access to devices or stable internet connections can further intensify these disparities. Consequently, careful instructional design is required to ensure fair and inclusive use of such platforms.

Newsela

Platform Overview

Newsela solves an important issue in the sphere of education the need to offer reading tools that will be accessible to students with different levels of learning abilities. The site provides entertaining and up to date information that belongs to credible sources, such as newspapers, magazines, and primary documents. This content is rewritten with the help of AI and checked by human editors to fit various levels of reading (Newsela, n.d.; Nushi & Fadaei, 2020).

AI-Driven Content Curation and Adaptation

Choosing Sources of Information and Algorithms. Information provided by Newsela is filtered by machine learning algorithms that analyse potential articles that include the most important information that is educational, the right topic, and the possibility to be modified. The selection algorithms are used to measure:

- **Curriculum Alignment**: Natural language processing models find the connections to the standards and teaching topics in many subjects, allowing a teacher to find reading materials that may support their lesson.
- **Potential Interest and Engagement**: Models that are trained on student interaction data give information on the topic and presentation style that is likely to result in interest of particular age groups.
- **Adaptation Feasibility**: Algorithms consider both structural and linguistic variations to find out how articles can be restated to suit a lower level of reading without losing the original meaning of the article.

Leveled Text Generation. The outstanding feature of Newsela is that every article can be read at various levels, which are usually elementary level to high school level. It is an adaptation process that incorporates AI support and human edits.

The AI methods of adaptation involve:

- **Syntactic Simplification**: These algorithms recognize syntactically complex sentences and generate simpler equivalents by decomposing the complex-compound syntactic structures to simpler syntactic structures.
- **Lexical Substitution**: Word embedding systems identify problematic vocabulary and replace it with synonyms that accommodate the reading level without changing the meaning which balances both accessibility and vocabulary exposure.
- **Discourse Simplification**: Machine learning models restructure paragraph order, implicitly linking links to the language, and decreasing inferential workload at the lower reading level.

Human Quality Control. AI drafts are revised and edited by professional editors. They make sure that simplification does not create misinterpretations, bring prejudices, and deprive the cultures of their value. This human intervention deals with AI weaknesses in understanding nuances, culture and learning in the right word choice. It is a hybrid strategy that guarantees accuracy and pedagogical correctness, especially when dealing with sensitive or complicated informational materials. Through AI effectiveness and professional control, the platform will ensure the quality of content and will fit a variety of literacy and learning requirements.

Differentiation and Instructional Support

Individualized Reading Assignments. A single article can be distributed to a whole class with the students being provided with versions of the same that are reading level appropriate to them. This approach can be used to discuss content together and access it in a differentiated manner. The students are also allowed to select their level of reading, and this promotes their self-reliance and understanding of how they understand.

Characteristics of Progressive Challenges. The website assures students to solve more difficult versions of already read articles. The scaffolding method can ensure that the students are well exposed to the material and how it is organized as the language complexity is steadily raised to support their attainment of grade sophistication. Such progression supports confidence building and reduces brain overload as students advance toward grade-level proficiency. It also allows teachers to differentiate instruction without changing core content.

Note-Taking and Vocabulary Support. The site contains an explanation of hard words, the background concerning new ideas and marking important parts. The support available is adjusted dynamically depending on the level of the text and reading ability by the student. As a result, students are encouraged to actively interact with the text rather than passively read it. This functionality also promotes independent reading strategies that can transfer to non-digital contexts.

Knowledge of Evaluation and Tracking

AI-Generated Quiz Questions. The articles have automatically generated comprehension questions that evaluate literal recall, inferential reasoning and vocabulary comprehension. The model of natural language processing works to generate the questions covering:

- **Important Objectives and Indicators**: Determining whether students can understand the primary arguments, as well as differentiate between major and minor details.
- **Inferential Comprehension**: Calling on students to make conclusions which were not made.
- **Contextual Vocabulary**: Evaluating the skills of students in words sense deducing.

Writing Prompts and Response Analysis. Constructed-response prompts are also available on the platform and students need to synthesize information, construct arguments, or make connections. Although it is still up to the teachers to do the grading, new technologies based on AI give preliminary ratings on the quality of the responses, paying attention to whether the student answers the prompt, uses the material, and demonstrates knowledge.

Progress Tracking Systems. Such websites as Newsela keep precise data about the reading habits of students and their level of understanding. The dashboards available to teachers show:

- Volume and consistency of reading.

- Tendencies of comprehension accuracy in references to text difficulty.
- Growth in doing more complicated written text.
- Patterns of interaction, e.g. reading durations and completion.

Cross-Curricular Applications

Literacy Instruction in Content Areas. The wide range of topics covered by Newsela has a large library that covers science, social studies, arts, and current events. This diversity will aid in the development of literacy in the framework of a particular subject teaching. It is related to the necessity of students to work with discipline-specific forms of text, vocabulary, and structure of argument.

Primary Source Access. The site provides the altered editions of historical documents, which allows students with different reading skills to study the primary sources. This makes sure that high level of literacy historical texts do not go to waste among historical studies. By adapting primary sources to multiple reading levels, the platform enables broader access to authentic historical materials without excluding struggling readers. This approach supports inclusive history instruction by allowing all learners to engage with original documents while still preserving their educational value.

Effectiveness and Research Evidence of Education. Studies carried out on the effects of leveled text platforms on the reading comprehension have yielded mixed findings. Certain research reports accelerated reading, especially with the struggling readers who gain advantage of well-leveled reading materials, which are interesting to read. Other reviews indicate that not even the traditionally distinct reading methods can have growth rates significantly higher when well applied. The most distinctive benefit is the volume of reading that is enhanced since such platforms enable the student to read more due to the interest and updated content offered at the right level of difficulty. The interconnection between the amount of reading and literacy development is well developed.

Limitations

Simplification Concerns of Quality. By applying human editing, simplified texts sometimes lose the gravity of the original script, challenging the complexity and cultural authenticity of the intended text. There are some of the linguistic characteristics available in original texts that are useful in the process of literacy development and can be eliminated inadvertently in the simplification process.

Scaffolding Dependency. Concerns surrounding text modifications are valid as learners may become overly reliant on simplified materials and consequently struggle to develop the skills necessary to engage independently with complex, age-appropriate texts. The existence of simplified versions may reduce the challenge of solving challenging material.

Assessment Validity. Automatically generated comprehension questions might only provide a superficial assessment of the knowledge. The multiple-choice format constrains the capturing of more complex processes of comprehension, including critical evaluation, source synthesis or subtle interpretation.

AI Bias and Representation. Simplification algorithmic methods may produce systematic biases depending on their training cards. It has been demonstrated that such simplification in certain instances has resulted in omission of mentioning of marginalized communities or skewed presentation of cultural significant information.

Quizlet

Platform Overview

Quizlet represents the digital evolution of flashcard-based study, serving users across educational contexts from elementary vocabulary learning to professional certification preparation. The platform demonstrates how AI algorithms can optimize one of education's oldest learning tools through adaptive scheduling and personalized practice. With the incorporation of gamified study features like quizzes, matching exercises, and collaborative learning tasks, the platform allows students to engage with the material repeatedly in a way meaningful and entertaining. These characteristics facilitate active recall and retention with data spacing and this type of practice is usually associated with better retention and comprehension. Consequently, Quizlet emphasizes the opportunities offered by game-based features and adaptive technologies to improve independent learning and keep it in line with the official learning objectives (Setiawan & Wiedarti, 2020; Tool in School: Quizlet, 2018).

Cognitive Science Foundations

Retrieval Practice Principles. Quizlet's core functionality rests on decades of cognitive science research demonstrating that active retrieval strengthens memory more effectively than passive review. The testing effect research shows that attempting to recall information, even unsuccessfully, enhances long-term retention more than repeated study. Quizlet's various modes all emphasize this active generation of responses rather than passive recognition.

Spacing Effect Implementation. The platform incorporates spacing algorithms designed to present information at increasing intervals, leveraging the robust finding that distributed practice produces superior retention compared to massed practice. Effective spacing requires precisely timed reviews: too soon and the practice is inefficient; too late and the memory trace has degraded, requiring relearning. By adjusting review intervals based on learner performance, the system aims to reinforce memory just before forgetting occurs, thereby strengthening long-term retention. This adaptive implementation demonstrates how cognitive psychology principles can be operationalized within digital study tools to support efficient and personalized learning.

AI-Driven Adaptive Learning Systems

Personalized Scheduling Algorithms. Quizlet's adaptive modes employ machine learning models that predict individual forgetting curves for each term-definition pair. These models incorporate multiple factors:

- **Performance history**: The system tracks whether students answered correctly or incorrectly for each item, how many times they have seen it, and how long since last exposure
- **Response latency**: Faster responses indicate stronger memory traces while hesitant responses suggest weaker encoding even when ultimately correct
- **Item difficulty**: Some concepts prove universally challenging while others are quickly mastered, with aggregate user data helping to estimate item-specific difficulty

- **Learning context**: Performance varies across study modes like, flashcards vs. written response vs. multiple choice, and algorithms adjust predictions accordingly

Optimized Spaced Review Systems. The platform implements sophisticated versions of spaced repetition, where items move through increasingly spaced review schedules based on mastery. Correctly recalled items graduate to longer intervals, while errors return items to more frequent practice. Machine learning enhancements optimize the specific interval lengths and graduation criteria based on population-wide performance patterns.

Diverse Study Modes and Cognitive Variability

The platform offers multiple study modes to support varied cognitive demands:

- **Flashcard mode**: Presents term-definition pairs for student-paced review. Research suggests that self-directed pacing allows students to allocate more time to difficult items, though it also permits non-optimal behaviors like rushing through challenging material.
- **Learn mode**: Combines multiple question formats such as written response, multiple choice, true/false answers and adjusts difficulty based on ongoing performance. The system introduces new terms gradually while cycling in review of partially mastered content. The mixed format approach potentially enhances transfer by requiring flexible retrieval under varied conditions.
- **Write mode**: Requires students to type complete definitions or terms, demanding generative rather than recognition-based retrieval. This format demands deeper processing and more complete memory traces, though it's more time-intensive than recognition tasks.
- **Test mode**: Provides simulated assessments that combine multiple question types, helping students develop test-taking strategies and providing practice in time-pressured retrieval conditions that mirror actual examination contexts.
- **Match and game modes**: Transform retrieval practice into timed challenges, pairing terms with definitions against a clock. The competitive element and immediate feedback can enhance engagement, though the speed emphasis may encourage surface processing for some learners.

Collaborative and Social Learning Features

Shared Study Sets. The platform's open ecosystem allows students to search for and use study sets created by others, dramatically reducing set-up time. However, this raises quality control concerns, as student-generated content varies in accuracy and pedagogical quality.

Classroom Integration. Teachers can create curated study sets for classes, assign specific study modes, and monitor student progress. The platform provides data on which terms students find most challenging, enabling targeted instructional response.

Collaborative Games. Team-based classroom games divide students into groups who must correctly match terms and definitions. These formats require communication and knowledge sharing, transforming individual memorization into social learning activity.

Memory Optimization Techniques

Desirable Difficulties Integration. The platform incorporates several evidence-based *desirable difficulties* that enhance long-term learning despite temporarily slowing acquisition:

- **Interleaving practice**: Mixes different terms and categories rather than blocking practice by concept, preventing context-dependent learning and promoting discrimination between similar concepts
- **Varied retrieval contexts**: Requires accessing the same knowledge in different ways through different study modes, strengthening flexible retrieval abilities
- **Generative practice**: Write mode requires students to produce answers rather than selecting from options, engaging more effortful and effective processing

Metacognitive Calibration

The platform provides progress indicators and mastery percentages, helping students develop accurate assessments of their own knowledge. Research suggests many students have poor metacognitive awareness, continuing to study material they have mastered while neglecting content they do not know (Porat et al., 2018). Feedback systems in adaptive learning platforms can improve this calibration.

Educational Applications Across Domains

Vocabulary Acquisition. Foreign language learning represents a primary use case, with flashcard platforms particularly suited to the memorization-intensive demands of vocabulary building. The spaced repetition approach aligns well with research on optimal vocabulary learning conditions.

Professional Education. Professional programs with substantial memorization requirements such as anatomy, pharmacology, legal concepts, frequently employ digital flashcard systems for foundational knowledge acquisition, allowing class time to focus on application and clinical reasoning.

Standardized Test Preparation. Students preparing for standardized assessments use flashcard platforms for memorizing vocabulary, formulas, and factual knowledge, though questions remain about how well decontextualized memorization transfers to complex test questions.

Research Evidence on Effectiveness

Studies examining digital flashcard platforms' impact on learning outcomes generally show positive effects, though with important nuances. Research comparing adaptive digital study to traditional methods finds advantages for retention, particularly when students use adaptive modes rather than simple flashcard review (Dutta et al., 2024). The spacing algorithm's effectiveness depends on student compliance with recommended study schedules, which proves variable. Other findings also suggest students overuse recognition-based modes relative to more challenging generative modes, potentially because recognition tasks feel easier and produce inflated confidence (Porat et al., 2018; Setiawan & Wiedarti, 2020). This highlights ongoing challenges in motivating students to engage in optimally effortful study strategies.

Limitations and Pedagogical Considerations

Atomistic Knowledge Representation. The flashcard format inherently fragments knowledge into discrete units, potentially impeding development of integrated conceptual understanding and relational knowledge structures. Complex concepts that require understanding relationships and contexts fit poorly into term-definition formats.

Depth of Processing Concerns. While retrieval practice is demonstrably effective, the rapid cycling through flashcards may encourage surface-level, rote memorization rather than elaborative processing that connects new information to existing knowledge structures. Students may develop strong cued recall, for example, given term, produce definition etc., without flexible understanding that supports application.

Self-Regulation Demands. Platform effectiveness depends on student engagement with adaptive modes and compliance with spaced practice schedules. Many students lack the self-regulation skills to use platforms optimally, gravitating toward easier but less effective study approaches.

Quality Control Challenges. The open nature of shared study sets means students may encounter inaccurate information or poorly constructed materials. While platforms include reporting mechanisms, quality assurance remains imperfect.

Overemphasis on Memorization. Particularly in contexts where flashcard platforms become primary study tools, there's risk of over-prioritizing factual recall relative to higher-order thinking skills. These platforms effectively support memory development but cannot replace conceptual instruction, problem-solving practice, or authentic application opportunities.

RESULTS AND COMPARATIVE ANALYSIS

This section will comprise a comparison of the chosen AI-based and game-based literacy platforms according to their design patterns, teaching frameworks, and aspects of implementation. To assess the effectiveness in quantitative terms, the approach is to assess how individual platforms contribute to adaptation, engagement, teaching strategies, and inclusivity in literacy learning. In addition, this review will examine similarities and contrasts across platforms in terms of feedback mechanisms, personalization depth, and learner agency. Attention will also be given to contextual factors such as learner age, instructional setting, and access constraints, which may influence how these platforms perform in practice. This comparative perspective aims to identify strengths, limitations, and conditions under which specific approaches are most effective for literacy development.

AI Integration Patterns

The main areas of AI usage in the platforms examined are adaptive learning paths, responsive feedback and different degrees of personalization. Although both platforms react to learners, the complexity and presence of these variants vary. There are platforms where a difficulty or pacing of the content is adjusted in real time according to the interaction of learners, and there are platforms that follow a constant sequence that is altered at predefined points.

Platforms also differ regarding the quality and richness of feedback. Some provide real-time feedback that is context sensitive to enhance learning and correct errors. Other ones are based on cumulative feedback which shows overall performance trends. Personalization can be enabled by personalized content recommendation, adaptive practice activities, or personalized learning paths, but the extent of visibility of these personalization features and the extent to which learners can affect them can differ. Overall, AI in the learning environment is an invisible facilitator.

Game Design Mechanisms

The aspects of game design contribute greatly to the ability to keep the learners engaged. The common features are the use of points, achievement badges, progress tracking and tasks which are challenging. Leaderboards may also be employed to encourage improvement in an individual without incurring direct competition particularly in literacy settings so that learners are not disheartened.

Narrative structures in learning activities are used differently in the form of either stories or mission-centered learning. Online sites that include some narrative tendencies tend to be more engaging because they provide meaning and the learners some continuity. The problems and incentives are usually in line with the achievement of the task and mastery of the skills which encourages perseverance and frequent participation. The intrinsic motivation and extrinsic reward balance may be more or less, with some websites focusing on play and exploration and others having a more structured form of gamification.

Pedagogical Coherence

The level of pedagogical adherence is represented by the degree of correspondence of each platform with the principles of the literacy development and learning goals. Platforms that have greater coherence have evident progression of simple to complex skills, and the elements of gamification facilitate the learning objectives. Certain platforms bring the learning content and the interaction very close together, enabling learners to exercise the relevant skills. Other platforms provide a weaker linking, whereby the mechanics of the games proceed alongside instructional materials without much conceptual integration. The best designs are those which consistently apply to the learning goals, assessments, and feedback to support the development of literacy in an interesting manner.

Inclusivity and Accessibility

The inclusiveness and accessibility of different platforms vary greatly. One of the powerful distinguishing factors is multilingual support, especially in the case of a tool targeting various or international students. Certain websites are flexible in their interfaces, adjustable speeds, and content displays, which is a universal designing concept (Nushi & Fadaei, 2020; Gameil & Al-Abdullatif, 2023). Cultural flexibility can be handled by means of localized content, contextually relevant tales, or customized learning paths that consider the background of the learner. There are however platforms of different degrees of cultural responsiveness where some of them are more superficially customizable and some of them put more emphasis on cultural relevance in learning. The crucial issues to use in choosing a platform that can be embraced by different learners are readability, visual comprehension, and the flexibility of devices.

Implementation Evidence

Cross-platform implementation reports present favourable tendencies of engagement among learners and their long-term participation especially where the aspects of AI-driven adaptation and gamification are very similar to the goals of teaching. It has been observed that in many cases, there are positive changes in motivation among learners, patterns of their use, and confidence to learners in literacy activities. Although directly tracing the results to particular aspects of design is not possible, adaptive feedback combined with a systematic progress and captivating mechanics seem to influence positive learning experiences. Practices in various learning settings have indicated that learning platforms that combine pedagogical facilitation and interactive design have higher probabilities to realize significant literacy increase in the long run.

DISCUSSION

Pedagogical Implications

With AI and the game-based learning in the context of learning literacy, there are great changes in the relationship between the learners and contents used, processes involved, and the outputs. These methods can facilitate active learning as long as they are structured in a proper manner and ensure that the learners are made to assume an active role throughout the learning process as opposed to being the passive receivers or listeners (Piaget, 1952; Zhang et al., 2004). Game-based designs are likely to promote exploration, choice and progress that could make the learners independent and increase their interest in the literacy practices.

The participation of AI-driven systems in these changes in the educational field should also be noted as an important issue since it renders the process more receptive. These tools will enable them to customize the learning experience into a personal level and a personal learning pace through adaptive pathways and feedback systems. It is a form of learning that enables the practice and reflections of the development of literacy to take place through practice other than through instructions. The integration of AI and game-based strategies have the potential to build the learning environments which focus on engagement, self-management, and significant interaction with texts, leading to deeper and lasting literacy.

Challenges and Ethical Considerations

However, these are not the only challenges and ethical issues associated with AI and game-based literacy devices to consider. One of the main ones is data privacy since AI systems are traditionally based on the information given in the interactions between learners. This information requires a correct governance and responsible administration to ensure that the rights and autonomy of the learners are not compromised when gathering, storing and making use of this information.

The algorithmic transparency can also be regarded as a problem, especially when it comes to automated systems, specifically when making instructions. The weakness regarding knowledge in the manner the recommendations are presented may present a challenge in understanding or questioning the projections of the system by the educators. In addition, the application of gamification in the teaching of literacy should be done with a cautious approach. Although play is useful in some aspects to enhance the degree of engagement, undue focus on any of the rewarding or the competition can hamper achievement of meaningful teachings or the necessary literacy (Hartt et al., 2020; Manesis, 2020). The solution to such problems includes serious instructional design and continuous emphasis on the ethical character of the technology-enhanced learning.

Contextual Suitability

The educational environment of the application of AI and game-based tools of literacy is where they greatly rely to achieve their success. These resources can be implemented in the primary and lower-level education as a foundation of literacy, through the interactive and visual interaction. In secondary level (ages 11-18 years), they can be used assisting in more complicated literacy practices, such as reading activities analytically and systematic writing activities. However, conversely, the adult literacy programs might have to adopt non-rigid and context-specific methods, which take into account the life experience of the learners and the diverse goals of these learners.

The resources that are available, readiness of the educator and access to technology by the learners is also the situational fit (Zhang et al., 2004; Gameil & Al-Abdullatif, 2023). The effective tools in one particular environment may be needed to be adjusted to other curriculum needs or cultural or aspects of the students. Therefore, AI and game-based literacy strategies could not be effective because they have to be universal but might be employed considering various degrees of education and the environments under which they are to be applied.

CONCLUSION

The comparison of AI-based and game-oriented literacy platforms demonstrates evident dissimilarity in the design and the method of learning literacy. Language and writing assistants that are powered by AI are called adaptive learning platforms, and they place importance on personal feedback as well as user input (Chen et al., 2020; Dutta et al., 2024). Such systems facilitate the progressive learning of new skills such as vocabulary, grammar and clarity in writing by interactive feedback programmes. Conversely, game-based platforms promote interaction, involvement, and socialisation as the key points of literacy practice. These tools provide dynamic learning by way of competition, collaboration and prompt responses. Although there are platforms that combine adaptive intelligence with gamification, each one of them has priorities in education. They both possess advantages and disadvantages. In general, the reviewed tools demonstrate that AI-based game platforms are most effectively implemented as flexible and evolving ecosystems that complement literacy instruction, supporting diverse teaching objectives and addressing the varied needs of learners rather than serving as a single, fixed solution.

Recommendations for Stakeholders

Most AI and game-based literacy applications are not a stand-alone solution but should be used in addition to teaching. The choice of adaptive features might be used to bolster differentiated instruction by supporting teacher-directed discussions and reflections as well as activities not provided by the platforms.

Administrators might desire to take investment decisions basing on the curricular objectives, student demographics, and the needs of the institution than just taking decisions based on the technological advancements. Other areas that should be taken into account are transparency, data management, and teacher support during the implementation of systems that are based on learner data and automation.

To the developers, the tools reviewed underline the ethical design. This involves ensuring that system behavior is comprehensible, learner autonomy is respected, and that system behavior is diminished to the extent of necessitating external reward. The main issue with the AI-enhanced literacy environment is how to develop systems which promote reflection, independence, and active involvement rather than compliance.

Future Research Directions

The variety of platforms and instructions that were mentioned in this chapter suggests that AI-enhanced literacy learning requires further and more in-depth research. Longitudinal research would be more beneficial in understanding how there is a long-term impact of the long-term use of adaptive and game-based systems on the literacy practices with time passing by, especially following the initial interactions.

Cross-cultural research is also required in order to observe how these tools operate in various language, cultural and institutional settings, where platform design assumptions might not correspond with local literacy practices. Also, the influence of multimodal literacy including text, visuals, audio, and interactive media needs further investigations in the future to comprehend the influence of AI and GBL environments on literacy in digital contexts.

These research fields could help to better comprehend how AI and game-based technologies could be used in promoting literacy learning without violating many contexts, ethical guidelines, and pedagogical principles.

REFERENCES

Alneyadi, S., Abulibdeh, E., & Wardat, Y. (2023). The Impact of Digital Environment vs. Traditional Method on Literacy Skills; Reading and Writing of Emirati Fourth Graders. *Sustainability (Basel)*, *15*(4), 3418. DOI: 10.3390/su15043418

Alotaibi, J. (2025). Digital communication in Middle East cultural institutions: Developing a theoretical framework for the use of digital platforms. *Humanities & Social Sciences Communications*, *13*(1), 51. Advance online publication. DOI: 10.1057/s41599-025-06345-y

Alsowat, H. H. (2022). Hybrid learning or virtual Learning? Effects on students' essay writing and digital literacy. *Journal of Language Teaching and Research*, *13*(4), 872–883. DOI: 10.17507/jltr.1304.20

Alsswey, A., & Malak, M. (2024). Effect of using gamification of "Kahoot!" as a learning method on stress symptoms, anxiety symptoms, self-efficacy, and academic achievement among university students. *Learning and Motivation*, *87*, 101993. DOI: 10.1016/j.lmot.2024.101993

Bawa, P. (2020). Game on! *International Journal of Game-Based Learning*, *10*(3), 16–46. DOI: 10.4018/IJGBL.2020070102

Boeker, M., Andel, P., Vach, W., & Frankenschmidt, A. (2013). Game-Based E-Learning Is More Effective than a Conventional Instructional Method: A Randomized Controlled Trial with Third-Year Medical Students. *PLoS One*, *8*(12), e82328. DOI: 10.1371/journal.pone.0082328 PMID: 24349257

Chen, L., Chen, P., & Lin, Z. (2020). *Artificial Intelligence in Education: a review*. IEEE Journals & Magazine | IEEE Xplore. DOI: 10.1109/ACCESS.2020.2988510

Chesson, D. (2026, January 13). *Grammarly review: Is Grammarly still worth it in 2026?* Kindlepreneur. https://kindlepreneur.com/grammarly-review-is-grammarly-good/

Dutta, S., Ranjan, S., Mishra, S., Sharma, V., Hewage, P., & Iwendi, C. (2024). Enhancing Educational Adaptability: A Review and Analysis of AI-Driven Adaptive Learning Platforms. In *IEEE* (pp. 1–5). DOI: 10.1109/ICIPTM59628.2024.10563448

Edwards, L. (2024, May 22). *NoRedInk: How to use it to Teach writing*. Tech & Learning. https://www.techlearning.com/how-to/noredink-how-to-use-it-to-teach

Eltahir, M. E., & Babiker, F. M. E. (2024). The Influence of Artificial intelligence Tools on Student Performance in e-Learning Environments: Case study. *Electronic Journal of e-Learning*, *22*(9), 91–110. DOI: 10.34190/ejel.22.9.3639

Ezzaim, A., Dahbi, A., Haidine, A., & Aqqal, A. (2023). Enhancing Academic Outcomes through an Adaptive Learning Framework Utilizing a Novel Machine Learning-Based Performance Prediction Method. *Data & Metadata*, *2*, 164. DOI: 10.56294/dm2023164

Gameil, A. A., & Al-Abdullatif, A. M. (2023). Using digital learning platforms to enhance the instructional design competencies and learning engagement of preservice teachers. *Education Sciences*, *13*(4), 334. DOI: 10.3390/educsci13040334

Gillis, A. S., & Barney, N. (2025, February 24). What is gamification? how it works and how to use it: Definition from TechTarget. Search HR Software. https://www.techtarget.com/searchhrsoftware/definition/gamification

Gligorea, I., Cioca, M., Oancea, R., Gorski, A., Gorski, H., & Tudorache, P. (2023). Adaptive Learning Using Artificial Intelligence in e-Learning: A Literature review. *Education Sciences*, *13*(12), 1216. DOI: 10.3390/educsci13121216

Hartt, M., Hosseini, H., & Mostafapour, M. (2020). Game On: Exploring the Effectiveness of Game-based learning. *Planning Practice and Research*, *35*(5), 589–604. DOI: 10.1080/02697459.2020.1778859

Jiao, D. (2024). AI-Driven Personalization in Higher Education: Enhancing Learning Outcomes through Adaptive Technologies. *Adult and Higher Education*, *6*(6). Advance online publication. DOI: 10.23977/aduhe.2024.060607

Jose, J., & Vinay, M. (2017). Performance Analysis of gamification over the traditional classroom in Education. *Indian Journal of Science and Technology*, *10*(13), 1–5. DOI: 10.17485/ijst/2017/v10i13/109065

Joshi, M. (2023). Adaptive Learning through Artificial Intelligence. SSRN *Electronic Journal*. DOI: 10.2139/ssrn.4514887

Keller, J. M. (1987). Development and use of the ARCS model of instructional design. *Journal of Instructional Development : JID*, *10*(3), 2–10. DOI: 10.1007/BF02905780

Kenwright, B. (2018). *Game-Based Learning in Higher Education The good, the bad and the ugly*. https://www.semanticscholar.org/paper/Game-Based-Learning-in-Higher-Education-The-Good,-Kenwright/b478c377bcbecfedec1f4ee671490f17e958d4e5

Licorish, S. A., Owen, H. E., Daniel, B., & George, J. L. (2018). Students' perception of Kahoot!'s influence on teaching and learning. *Research and Practice in Technology Enhanced Learning*, *13*(1), 9. Advance online publication. DOI: 10.1186/s41039-018-0078-8

Loewen, S., Crowther, D., Isbell, D. R., Kim, K. M., Maloney, J., Miller, Z. F., & Rawal, H. (2019). Mobile-assisted language learning: A Duolingo case study. *ReCALL*, *31*(3), 293–311. DOI: 10.1017/S0958344019000065

M, A., Asdam, M., & Asdar, A. (2024). Investigating students' reading strategies and reading comprehension through digital literacy environment. *AL-ISHLAH Jurnal Pendidikan*, *16*(3), 3370–3379. https://doi.org/DOI: 10.35445/alishlah.v16i3.5510

Manesis, D. (2020). Barriers to the use of Games-Based learning in Pre-School settings. *International Journal of Game-Based Learning*, *10*(3), 47–61. DOI: 10.4018/IJGBL.2020070103

Mariappan, L. (2024). From Boredom to Excitement: Transforming Classroom Activities with Realia-Based Games. *Journal of Electrical Systems*, *20*(5s), 1600–1606. DOI: 10.52783/jes.2493

Nadeem, M., Oroszlanyova, M., & Farag, W. (2023). Effect of Digital Game-Based Learning on student engagement and motivation. *Computers*, *12*(9), 177. DOI: 10.3390/computers12090177

Naseer, F., Khan, M. N., Addas, A., Awais, Q., & Ayub, N. (2025). Game Mechanics and Artificial Intelligence Personalization: A framework for Adaptive learning systems. *Education Sciences*, *15*(3), 301. DOI: 10.3390/educsci15030301

Newsela. (n.d.). LINCS | Adult Education and Literacy | U.S. Department of Education. https://lincs.ed.gov/professional-development/resource-collections/profile-916

Nushi, M., & Fadaei, M. H. (2020). Newsela: A Level-Adaptive App to improve reading ability. *Reading in a Foreign Language*, *32*(2), 239–247. DOI: 10.64152/10125/67381

Odvina, R. A., Baylon, L. A., Ayop, R. M. M., & Evardo, O. J.Jr. (2024). Use of Cybergogy in Improving Reading Comprehension among High School Students: A Systematic Literature Review. *Journal of Digital Learning and Education*, *4*(3), 210–222. DOI: 10.52562/jdle.v4i3.1330

Oubagine, R., Laaouina, L., Jehgal, A., & Tairi, H. (2025). Smart Adaptive Learning Systems in Education: Current state and future Perspectives. In *International Conference on Circuit, Systems and Communication (ICCSC)*. IEEE. https://doi.org/DOI: 10.1109/ICCSC66714.2025.11135254

Özdemir, O. (2024). Kahoot! Game-based digital learning platform: A comprehensive meta-analysis. *Journal of Computer Assisted Learning*, *41*(1), e13084. Advance online publication. DOI: 10.1111/jcal.13084

Piaget, J. (1952). The origins of intelligence in children. In *W W Norton & Co eBooks*. DOI: 10.1037/11494-000

Poole, F. J., & Clarke-Midura, J. (2020). A Systematic review of Digital games in second language learning studies. *International Journal of Game-Based Learning*, *10*(3), 1–15. DOI: 10.4018/IJGBL.2020070101

Porat, E., Blau, I., & Barak, A. (2018). Measuring digital literacies: Junior high-school students' perceived competencies versus actual performance. *Computers & Education*, *126*, 23–36. DOI: 10.1016/j.compedu.2018.06.030

Qurbunova, B., & Yusupova, A. (2024). The Deep investigation of the part of AI integ in the field of Education: A Technical review. In *4th International Conference on Advance Computing and Innovative Technologies in Engineering (ICACITE), Greater Noida, India*. IEEE. https://doi.org/DOI: 10.1109/ICACITE60783.2024.10617224

Ramanathan, & Tara. (2026, February 12). *Duolingo | App, Languages, Background, & Virality*. Encyclopedia Britannica. https://www.britannica.com/topic/Duolingo

Rondon, S., Sassi, F. C., & De Andrade, C. R. F. (2013). Computer game-based and traditional learning method: A comparison regarding students' knowledge retention. *BMC Medical Education*, *13*(1), 30. DOI: 10.1186/1472-6920-13-30 PMID: 23442203

Ryan, R. M., & Deci, E. L. (2000). Intrinsic and Extrinsic Motivations: Classic definitions and new directions. *Contemporary Educational Psychology*, *25*(1), 54–67. DOI: 10.1006/ceps.1999.1020 PMID: 10620381

Sajja, R., Sermet, Y., Cikmaz, M., Cwiertny, D., & Demir, I. (2023, September 19). *Artificial Intelligence-Enabled Intelligent Assistant for Personalized and Adaptive Learning in Higher Education*. arXiv.org. https://arxiv.org/abs/2309.10892

Sari, H. E., Tumanggor, B., & Efron, D. (2024). Improving Educational Outcomes Through Adaptive Learning Systems using AI. [ITALIC]. *International Transactions on Artificial Intelligence*, *3*(1), 21–31. DOI: 10.33050/italic.v3i1.647

Setiawan, M. R., & Wiedarti, P. (2020). The effectiveness of Quizlet application towards students' motivation in learning vocabulary. *Studies in English Language and Education*, *7*(1), 83–95. DOI: 10.24815/siele.v7i1.15359

Slater-Robins, M. (2025, February 11). *What is Grammarly? Everything we know about the best AI writing assistant*. TechRadar. https://www.techradar.com/pro/what-is-grammarly-everything-we-know-about-the-best-ai-writing-assistant

Snowe, A., & Snowe, A. (2017). *Exploring the use of NoRedInk as a tool for composition instruction*. DOI: 10.23860/diss-snowe-alyson-2017

Stasolla, F., Zullo, A., Maniglio, R., Passaro, A., Di Gioia, M., Curcio, E., & Martini, E. (2025). Deep Learning and Reinforcement Learning for Assessing and Enhancing Academic Performance in university Students: A scoping review. *AI*, *6*(2), 40. DOI: 10.3390/ai6020040

T, S. T., & B, I. A. S. (2024). Artificial intelligence effects on student learning outcomes in higher education. In *Ninth International Conference on Science Technology Engineering and Mathematics (ICONSTEM), Chennai, India*. DOI: 10.1109/ICONSTEM60960.2024.10568868

Tavares, N. (2022). The use and impact of game-based learning on the learning experience and knowledge retention of nursing undergraduate students: A systematic literature review. *Nurse Education Today*, *117*, 105484. DOI: 10.1016/j.nedt.2022.105484 PMID: 35917707

UNESCO. (2017). Literacy rates continue to rise from one generation to the next global literacy trends today. Retrieved from https://on.unesco.org/literacy-map

Vlieghe, J. (2015). Traditional and digital literacy. The literacy hypothesis, technologies of reading and writing, and the 'grammatized' body. *Ethics and Education*, *10*(2), 209–226. DOI: 10.1080/17449642.2015.1039288

Vygotsky, L. S. (1978). Mind in Society: the development of higher psychological processes. In *Medical Entomology and Zoology*. https://ci.nii.ac.jp/ncid/BA03570814

Wang, A. I., Zhu, M., & Sætre, R. (2016). The effect of digitizing and gamifying quizzing in classrooms. *ResearchGate*. https://www.researchgate.net/publication/309292274_The_Effect_of_Digitizing_and_Gamifying_Quizzing_in_Classrooms

Wilson, S. N., Engler, C. E., Black, J. E., Yager-Elorriaga, D. K., Thompson, W. M., McConnell, A., Cecena, J. E., Ralston, R., & Terry, R. A. (2017). Game-Based learning and information literacy. *International Journal of Game-Based Learning*, *7*(4), 1–21. DOI: 10.4018/IJGBL.2017100101

Yasir, G. M., Shaheen, A., & Hafeez, M. (2021). A Systematic Review on Digital Game-Based Versus Traditional Learning Approaches. *Global Social Sciences Review*, *VI*(IV), 124–135. DOI: 10.31703/gssr.2021(VI-IV).12

Zhan, Z., Tong, Y., Lan, X., & Zhong, B. (2022). A systematic literature review of game-based learning in Artificial Intelligence education. *Interactive Learning Environments*, *32*(3), 1137–1158. DOI: 10.1080/10494820.2022.2115077

Zhang, D., Zhao, J. L., Zhou, L., & Nunamaker, J. F.Jr. (2004). Can e-learning replace classroom learning? *Communications of the ACM*, *47*(5), 75–79. DOI: 10.1145/986213.986216

Zulkarnain, I., Sitepu, Y. S., Sutatminingsih, R., & Rajagukguk, M. (2024). Student's digital literacy competence and its implications for the learning process. [IJERE]. *International Journal of Evaluation and Research in Education*, *13*(2), 997. DOI: 10.11591/ijere.v13i2.25767

Chapter 3
Designing ELA Chatbots With a Simulation-Informed Process:
A Practical Framework and Use Cases for Inclusive Literacy Instruction

Alicia M. Drelick
http://orcid.org/0000-0002-4485-5858
Rowan University, USA

Casey Woodfield
Rowan University, USA

Justin E. Freedman
Rowan University, USA

ABSTRACT

Generative artificial intelligence (GenAI) chatbots offer new possibilities for dialogue-rich learning in English language arts, yet educators lack practical guidance for designing tools that are instructionally purposeful, inclusive, and classroom-safe. This chapter presents a simulation-informed framework for designing custom ELA chatbots that center teacher decision-making, student agency, and ethical implementation. Drawing on principles from clinical simulation research, the framework outlines a four-step, tool-agnostic design process, conceptualization, protocol design, technical design, and iterative revision. This process is paired with an instructional routine that emphasizes preparation, real-time debriefing, and structured reflection. Three classroom-based case studies illustrate how educator-designed chatbots can provide low-risk, scaffolded practice that complements teacher expertise while mitigating risks related to bias, accuracy, and student overreliance.

INTRODUCTION

English language arts (ELA) educators are known for their creative and experiential pedagogical approaches that allow students to construct knowledge through discussion, writing, inquiry, and interaction. Generative artificial intelligence (GenAI)-based chatbots offer ELA teachers new ways to support students

DOI: 10.4018/979-8-3373-7472-7.ch003

by engaging in iterative structured conversations with them. Students can receive feedback, rehearse academic language, revise their work, or build or refine an idea. A chatbot is an AI-based conversation platform that can simulate interaction through text and/or voice (Adamopoulou & Moussiades, 2020). Educational chatbots can serve as personalized tutors, writing companions, or motivational supports (Labadze et al., 2023). Well-designed chatbots can complement teacher feedback while supporting students in building writing and discussion skills (Yao et al., 2025).

However, the value of these learning experiences depends on purposeful design, clear guidelines and guardrails, and active teacher engagement and oversight (U.S. Department of Education, Office of Educational Technology, 2023; McMahon, 2025). Memarian and Doleck (2024) note that the benefits of using educational chatbots rely heavily on keeping humans in the loop of the learning process. Involving humans in the loop while engaging with GenAI involves applying human knowledge and skills to improve and ensure the quality of machine-automated processes (Holzinger et al., 2019). This can reduce miscommunication, exposure to misinformation, and the development of problematic relationships with GenAI (Memarian & Doleck, 2024).

GenAI tools can introduce new instructional and ethical challenges if they are adopted without clear learning purposes, boundaries, and routines for use (Mishra et al., 2023; U.S. Department of Education, Office of Educational Technology, 2023). With new guidelines from the U.S. Department of Education, educators in the United States are encouraged to use federal funds to adopt GenAI tools for instruction, tutoring, and advising, with the caveat that these experiences should be teacher-led and have a responsible use plan in place to ensure safe and ethical adoption (McMahon, 2025).

Custom chatbots represent a promising application of GenAI for ELA instruction. While creating a chatbot can be done quickly, a pedagogically sound custom chatbot is more complicated than entering a basic prompt into a generative tool. In education, chatbots have been used to support both teaching and learning through personalized tutoring, concept understanding, planning and preparation, and collaboration (Labadze et al, 2023). ELA teachers can leverage chatbots in various ways to support their students, including using them as a writing tool for workshopping drafts, a peer-like partner for rehearsing academic talk, a fictional character for role-playing, or a motivational agent (Kuhail et al., 2023). Each of these roles would produce a different type of learning conversation, requiring both a knowledge base and a structure for interacting with students to create a meaningful learning experience. According to Kuhail et al. (2023), there are four different types of conversational agents:

- Teaching agents can scaffold close reading and text-based reasoning.
- Peer agents can collaborate during writing revision or vocabulary practice.
- Teachable agents can prompt students to explain and justify ideas.
- Motivational agents can encourage persistence and reduce anxiety during literacy tasks.

Despite the rapid growth of chatbot-building tools, practical guidance for educators on creating educationally sound chatbots remains limited. Educators should apply guidelines and guardrails to create purposeful, classroom-safe, and inclusive learning experiences using chatbots. This ease of creation can interfere with the pedagogical rigor needed for meaningful educational impact. Without careful design, chatbots can drift off target, provide overwhelming or inconsistent responses, amplify bias, or mishandle student input (Drelick et al., 2025; Pérez et al., 2020). Ganguly and colleagues (2026) remind educators that GenAI can influence academic outcomes in different ways across content which reinforces the need for educator design, intentional implementation, and ongoing evaluation, rather than the set-it-and-forget-it model. With mindful planning, custom chatbots can create low-risk opportunities for authentic practice and scaffolded support that complements teacher expertise and peer learning (Drelick et al., 2025). In support of efforts to create meaningful and responsible opportunities for authentic practice, this chapter seeks to answer the following question: *How can educators design custom ELA chatbots to maximize meaningful literacy learning while minimizing risks related to accuracy, bias, privacy, and overwhelming students?*

This chapter provides a feasible, educator-led process for designing chatbots for inclusive literacy instruction. This process is tool-agnostic, meaning it is designed to be applied across evolving platforms rather than tied to one platform or interface. Further, this process is presented through a design framework and coupled with an implementation routine that keeps humans in the loop of conversations by centering teacher decision-making, student experience, and reflection on instruction and learning (U.S. Department of Education, Office of Educational Technology, 2023; Drelick et al., 2025; McMahon, 2025). This is especially important at the high school level, where students have described chatbots in various ways, including as a "teacher, tutor or friend," highlighting the need for educator oversight, intentional framing, and collective reflection (Gupta et al., 2025, p. 3686).

The approach presented in this chapter is a design framework informed by clinical simulation, which draws on decades of research in medical education and teacher education (Barrows 1987; Dotger, 2015). Clinical simulations were developed to provide authentic, low-risk opportunities to practice professional skills by using standardized roles and protocols to ensure consistency and meaningful assessment (Barrows, 1987). This approach has been proposed as a signature pedagogy in teacher education to allow novices to rehearse complex interpersonal and instructional situations, followed by a structured debriefing and reflection (Dotger, 2015; Dotger & Chandler-Olcott, 2022). Features of clinical simulations translate well to the creation of custom chatbots, where the quality of the learning experience depends on the clarity of the chatbot's role and the responses it provides to users. These features include the use of a purpose-driven, clear persona with consistent cues and iterative revisions based on observation (Drelick et al., 2025).

This simulation-informed approach to chatbot design also aligns closely with principles found in game-based learning. Well-designed educational games place learners in structured scenarios where they assume roles, make decisions, receive feedback, and learn through iterative practice in low-risk environments, features that closely mirror the purposes of clinical simulation (Barrows, 1987; Dotger, 2015). Similarly, custom educational chatbots function as interactive simulation spaces in which students rehearse academic behaviors within clearly bounded roles and rule-based interactions. When AI-based chatbots are embedded in learning environments, they can adaptively support student metacognition, engagement, and problem solving, reinforcing structural parallels between conversational agents and game-like learning contexts (Liang et al., 2024). Like simulations and pedagogically grounded chatbots, game-based environments emphasize active participation, problem-solving, and feedback loops rather than passive content consumption (Kuhail et al., 2023). From this perspective, chatbots can be understood as dialogic learning spaces that share features with both simulations and educational games, underscoring the importance of intentional design that aligns conversational structure with instructional purpose.

Additionally, game-based learning principles can strengthen the educational chatbot engagement experience by structuring the simulation using game design techniques. Setting goals, assuming roles, facing challenges, receiving and responding to immediate feedback, and iterating towards mastering are gaming principles that can improve the design of educational chatbots (Liang et al., 2024). Embedding gaming mechanics such as clear goals, levels, checkpoints, or rewards can increase motivation and support the generalization of skills while preserving the pedagogical intent of the design (Kuhail et al., 2023). Integrating these elements into simulation-informed educational chatbots provides a real space that can increase engagement while delivering intentional outcomes. Deepening learning experiences with rich storylines delivered through educational chatbots can improve the cognitive and affective learning experience for students (Xiao et al., 2025).

BACKGROUND

ELA instruction is inherently interactive, built on dialogue, interpretation, perspective-taking, and iterative composing. Conversational technologies are not new to ELA. What is new is the scale and flexibility with which GenAI can simulate dialogue, offer feedback, and adapt responses in real time. The widespread accessibility of chatbot creation tools has shifted the central question for educators. The question is no longer *whether* chatbots belong in ELA classrooms, but rather *how* to design and implement them with clear instructional purpose, appropriate boundaries, and inclusive practices (Drelick et al., 2025). Recent literature comparing chatbot-supported learning with traditional learning approaches reveals a key consideration: the importance of aligning chatbot use with specific instructional goals and intended forms of student interaction (Pinter et al., 2025; Labadze et al., 2023). In this section, authors will discuss clinical simulations as a foundation for chatbot design, review the role of custom chatbots in ELA, and present a chatbot design framework and an implementation guide.

Clinical Simulations as a Foundation for Chatbot Design

Because chatbots can approximate real-world conversations, grounding their development in authentic learning simulations can significantly boost their pedagogical fidelity. The foundation of education based simulations is rooted in medical education. In the 1900s, neurologist Howard Barrows began developing problem-based learning experiences where medical students were asked to interact with an actor portraying a patient displaying a standard set of symptoms and needs, or what later became known as a "standardized patient." A standardized patient is an individual who is trained to portray the symptoms and communication patterns associated with a particular medical condition (Barrows, 1987). The portrayal is standardized in that each individual actor is trained to portray the patient in the same manner, consistently, across all medical students with whom they interact. The standardized patient model has become widely used in medical school as a method of immersing future healthcare providers in meaningful learning experiences. Clinical simulations are problem-based scenarios that provide novice learners with low-risk opportunities to practice performance-based skills in a low-risk environment and serve as a core method for assessing professional competencies in medical education (Williams et al., 2001).

Dotger (2015) later adapted this approach for teacher education to create structured, authentic practice opportunities for pre-service teachers. In these simulations, a trained actor, known as a standardized individual, engages candidates in interactions that reflect core competencies of teaching, such as collaborating with colleagues, communicating with families, or explaining content to students. The simulation is followed by structured debriefing, opportunities to review a recording, and guided reflection, both individually and with peers (Dotger, 2015). In adapting clinical simulations for teacher education, Dotger (2015) has drawn on Barrows' (1987) considerations for making design decisions about the problem-based context of simulations. These include four tenets for developing diverse and authentic clinical simulations. Simulations focused on *prevalence* address common professional situations. *Instructional importance* suggests a focus on rare but high-stakes problems. Simulations focused on *clinical impact* target specific competencies. Simulations that address *social impact* attempt to respond to issues that disproportionately affect particular groups.

Freedman and colleagues (2024) extended the use of clinical simulation methods to provide an opportunity for university students with disabilities in practice and reflect on their use of self-advocacy. In this study, students participated in one-on-one meetings with professors portrayed by trained actors, focused on discussing accommodations. Participants then processed the experience through small-group reflection and later revisited key moments by watching video recordings of their meetings. Students reported that the simulation and reflection process helped them examine their current self-advocacy strategies and identify intentional adjustments for future accommodation conversations.

Simulation design offers a useful framework for developing chatbot personas and guardrails. Drelick and colleagues (2025) proposed that educational chatbots can be designed using the same logic that guides clinical simulation development. In simulation design, developers create a protocol that clarifies the standardized individual's persona and includes specific prompts or verbal cues the actor will use. For instance, in the simulated meetings between student and professor to discuss accommodations, the standardized professor role was informed by interviews with staff from the university's disability service office and a focus group with students with disabilities to surface common professor dispositions and recurring questions or statements. That information was then translated into a protocol used to train actors, including clear parameters for how they should respond to anticipated interactions. Similarly, educators can draw on practitioners' expertise and local context to define a chatbot's persona and establish guardrails that support similar conversations with students.

Educational Chatbots as ELA Learning Tools

Chatbots are conversational systems that simulate dialogue with users through text and/or voice in ways that support learning activities (Adamopoulou & Moussiades, 2020). When paired with GenAI, chatbots can produce more flexible responses, expanding the range of educational tools teachers can develop as conversational partners for their students. Current research on chatbots in education shows this practice can be promising, but the results are uneven (Labadze et al., 2023). In an analysis of 67 studies, Labadze and colleagues (2023) found researchers report benefits to students engaging with chatbots, including scaffolded learning experience, study help, or the development of metacognition skills. However, there are concerns around the reliability of interactions and the overall effectiveness of chatbots due to a lack of tools to evaluate their impact on learning (Labadze et al., 2023). Memarian and Doleck (2024) assert the importance of teachers serving as the humans in the loop to provide supervision, prompting support, and monitoring for biases, privacy, and accessibility concerns. These findings stress the importance of teacher-centered, simulation-informed design to creating chatbots in order to generate more meaningful learning experiences.

In the ELA context, Yao and colleagues (2025) studied the effectiveness of AI-guided chatbots, trained by specific rubrics, used by students during the writing and revision process. The researchers found that the custom chatbot offered complementary feedback to their teacher and was effective in supporting students. However, they noted that the role of teachers and their capacity to implement AI tools in conjunction with traditional or personal feedback was key (Yao et al, 2025). Character-anchored conversational agents have also been used to structure literary interactions and promote dialogue during reading by offering a character-based chatbot experience in ELA settings (He et al., 2025). Rather than constituting a single instructional strategy, chatbots serve multiple pedagogical functions. Different purposes shape different types of student interaction, which can result in varied learning outcomes.

Understanding whether a chatbot scaffolds the delivery of content or provides motivational support can help educators develop chatbot-based learning experiences that layer intentionality into their design (Drelick et al., 2025; Kuhail et al., 2023). A chatbot designed for social dialog, rehearsed to practice academic talk, will look and interact differently than a chatbot designed to scaffold revisions aligned with a set rubric for a writing assignment. The instructional value lies not in the novelty of GenAI, but in the pedagogy underlying the design of chatbot conversations (Kuhail et al., 2023).

Emerging research shows that pairing chatbots with gaming-based and storytelling narrative designs can increase engagement and positive impact on learning outcomes in ELA (Liang et al., 2024; Xiao, et al., 2025; Han & Han, 2024). Increased motivation and improvements in higher-order thinking were observed when quest-like storyline elements were embedded into educational chatbots designed for high school students learning English as a second language (Xiao, et al., 2025). Han & Han (2024) note that story-oriented chatbots can be successful in scaffolding the writing process for young writers when engagement is increased and targeted feedback is provided to boost confidence. These early findings can be applied alongside a sound pedagogical framework to designing and implementing chatbots in order to boost the instructional credibility of an educational chatbot.

Design Process

Drelick and colleagues (2025) introduced the following design framework to provide guidance for the creation of custom chatbots for education. In this section, the authors will briefly review the four steps: conceptualization, protocol design, technician design, and trials and revisions.

Figure 1. 4-Step Chatbot Design Process Informed by Clinical Simulations. Image Source: Drelick et al., (2025)

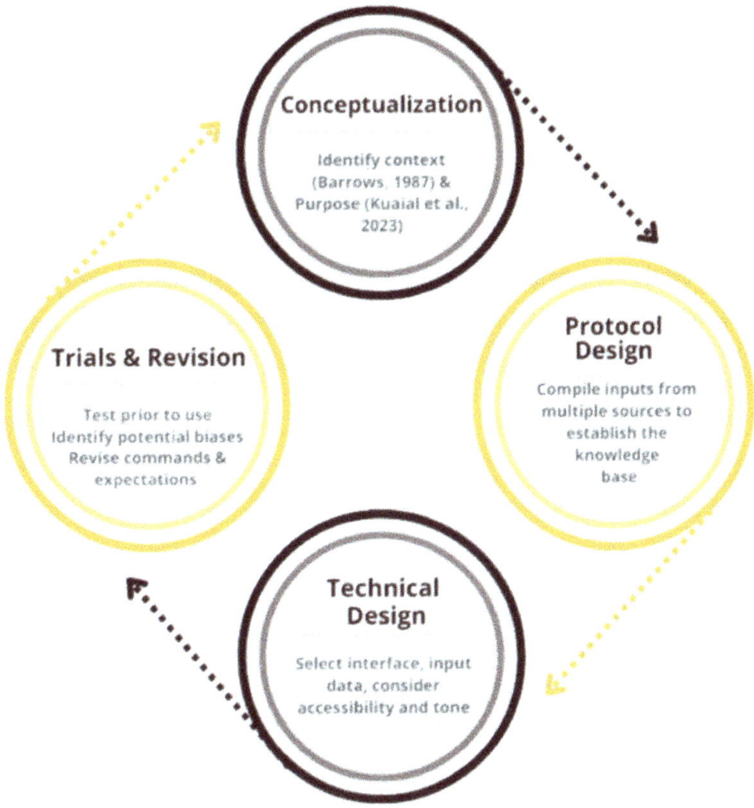

Guiding frameworks used for developing chatbots:

- tenets of clinical simulation design (Barrows, 1987),
- principles of designing educational chatbots (Kuhail et al., 2023),
- components of clinical simulations in educator education (Dotger & Chandler-Olcott, 2022).

Conceptualization

During the planning phase, chatbot designers should start by clarifying the learning outcomes they want the interaction to support. One way to identify a conversation worth simulating with a chatbot is to apply Barrows' (1987) tenets of clinical simulation design. Educators might prioritize a situation that happens frequently and benefits from repeated practice (prevalence); an event that occurs less often but carries significant consequences (clinical impact); an experience that supports key skill development over time (instructional importance); or a concern that is especially relevant for a particular student or group (social impact) (Drelick et al., 2025). Naming and prioritizing these tenets helps educators intentionally design learning experiences that are both meaningful and instructionally useful. Beyond selecting the event or conversational scenario, designers should also consider what that real-world interaction feels like for students, including the social-emotional, academic, and cognitive demands involved (Drelick et al., 2025). This understanding can guide decisions about how the chatbot will communicate, respond, and scaffold student participation.

Designers can integrate basic game-design principles during the conceptualization phase to shape student motivation and increase engagement. For example, learning outcomes can be framed as play goals or challenges, then mapped into levels or checkpoints, noting levels of mastery (Liang et al., 2024). Additionally, brainstorming thematic elements can add storytelling to the design, creating a more immersive learning experience.

It is also essential to determine the knowledge base the chatbot will draw from during interactions to set boundaries for where information is gathered to generate responses. Educational chatbots can be trained on datasets that include previously collected or constructed sources, such as instructional materials, student work samples, interviews, or open-source sites, e.g., Wikipedia (Ramandanis & Xinogalos, 2023). Some chatbots can also generate responses by searching the web. However, the authors recommend using closed datasets to create safer *walled gardens* (Klein, 2023), where students can engage more securely within carefully designed parameters.

Protocol Design

Once the training data has been identified, the next step is to develop a protocol that uses those sources to build and organize the chatbot's knowledge base. In clinical simulations, protocols are grounded in existing research and often strengthened through new data, frequently gathered through interviews. These protocols are then used to train actors to portray standardized individuals, e.g., parents, students and colleagues, in simulated interactions with participating students (Dotger, 2015). The chatbot design process described in this chapter draws on this approach: the protocol helps structure the knowledge base and includes sample prompts and likely responses. Because a chatbot cannot ask follow-up questions in the same flexible way an actor can, the protocol also needs to anticipate common student directions and include *predictive* responses to help bridge that gap (Drelick et al., 2025).

Here, designers can lean into game design principles as they map learning goals to levels or quests. If a particular persona is being developed, a storyline can be created in addition to the script to have the chatbot function as a character with whom students interact (Xiao et al., 2025).

Technical Design

Building a chatbot also requires an intentional choice of platform. Educators should examine key features of accessibility, such as speech-to-text, text-to-speech, cost, and how easy the interface is to use (Drelick et al., 2026). It is also essential to consider student privacy and data security (USDOE, 2023). In many cases, school or district IT (Information Technology) teams can help vet options and recommend tools that are secure and already licensed for organizational use.

Once a platform is selected, designers can begin building the chatbot using prompts or commands. At this stage, it is important to clearly specify the bot's role, the standardized individual that they are portraying, the type of chatbot being created (peer agent, teaching agent, motivation agent or teachable agent), and the learning objectives identified in the conceptual phase. The protocol developed then becomes the foundation for the chatbot's knowledge base. Depending on the platform, developers may choose whether the chatbot generates responses only from the provided data or is allowed to search the web and expand its knowledge through machine learning. Designers can also add additional details to strengthen the chatbot's persona or character during this step (Drelick et al., 2025).

Finally, within the technical design phase, selecting an intentional pedagogical approach can strengthen the interaction and better support the targeted learning outcomes (Drelick et al., 2025). Kuhail and colleagues (2023) describe seven design principles for educational chatbots that can help shape purposeful conversational exchanges. Kuhail et al. (2023) have established principles that align with familiar instructional approaches and can help make chatbot interactions more meaningful and directed:

- Personalized Learning: tailors output to individual users' needs
- Experiential Learning: encourages users to construct knowledge through active engagement
- Social Dialog: emphasizes conversational exchange over content delivery
- Collaborative Learning: co-constructs knowledge by working together to complete a task
- Affective Learning: provides encouraging or empathetic feedback based on user interaction
- Learning by Teaching: builds mastery as users explain concepts and demonstrate understanding
- Scaffolding: supports learning through gradual, structured engagement

Trials and Revisions

U.S. Department of Education, Office of Educational Technology (2023), recommends that teachers play an active role in the design and evaluation of AI tools, including piloting, reviewing, and revising them over time. When developing a custom chatbot, this evaluation phase can be directly led by the creator. During trials, it is especially important to talk with students and learn from their experiences using the bot. Teachers can also monitor whether the chatbot produces biased responses during interactions, including biases associated with characteristics the system may infer, such as gender (Pérez et al., 2020). In addition, educators can use this phase to fine-tune the bot's overall tone and adjust the length and usefulness of its responses.

Ongoing accessibility review is also essential during testing. Teachers should consider individual student needs and select platforms, or enable features, that provide access to supports such as text-to-speech, translation, or picture-based scaffolds. Many education-focused chatbots include built-in accessibility options, while more individualized support may require additional extensions or device-based accessibility tools. Ultimately, accessibility should be treated as an iterative process that requires continued reevaluation and revision (Drelick et al., 2026).

Introducing Chatbots in the Classroom as an Instructional Tool

Even with an intentional, thorough, and research-based process like this one, chatbot activities still need to be thoughtfully framed and facilitated by educators to be effective and keep humans in the loop. It is recommended that educators use the simulation-informed chatbot design process to treat pre-activity preparation and post-activity discussion as essential parts of the learning experience (Drelick et al., 2025). Drawing on research on clinical simulations in higher education (Freedman et al., 2020; Dotger, 2015), the authors recommend integrating three phases when using chatbots:

- preparation before students interact with the chatbot
- real-time debriefing directly after the simulation experience

- structured reflection after completion.

Activity Set-Up

The authors recommend intentionally introducing chatbot activities as simulated practice, an opportunity for students to rehearse skills and build experience in a new, low-stakes way. Consistent with a clinical simulation-informed approach, this setup should include clear reminders that the activity is non-evaluative, low-risk, and supportive (Drelick et al., 2025).

Real-Time Small Group Debrief

Shortly after students engage with the chatbot, it is recommended to facilitate a short small-group debrief to capture their initial reactions and begin making meaning of the experience. This creates space for joint analysis and deeper learning by encouraging students to reflect, compare perspectives, and name what stood out in the interaction (Dotger & Chandler-Olcott, 2022). These conversations can also yield practical feedback that informs chatbot revisions as needed.

In-Depth Reflection

Finally, the simulation-informed activity should close with a more structured reflection in which students revisit their interaction and engage in a guided discussion. Instructors can prompt students to identify the skills they practiced, evaluate how the conversation unfolded, and consider how they might respond differently in the future. When possible, this reflection can occur about one week after the chatbot interaction to give students time to process the experience and return with more thoughtful insights.

SOLUTIONS AND RECOMMENDATIONS

Educators need pragmatic steps for design, implementation, and evaluation in order to translate simulation-informed chatbot design into practice. This section applies the framework with three custom ELA-based chatbots. These examples show how educator-designed chatbots can support literacy instruction when they are purpose-driven, pedagogically sound, and embedded in reflective routines (Labadze et al., 2023). Below are examples to illustrate the design and implementation of ELA chatbots:

- **Writing Revision Coach (Grade 9-12, ages 14-18)**: A peer-to-peer feedback partner designed to stimulate thoughtful revisions through questions and rubric-aligned guidance.
- **Socratic Seminar Prep Partner (Grades 7-12, ages 12-18)**: A rehearsal tool that supports students in making claims, gathering evidence, predicting counterarguments, and practicing academic language.
- **Public-Domain Character Chatbot Grades 5-12, ages 10-18):** A literature-focused role-play chatbot that supports character analysis and text comprehension.

The following vignettes elaborate on the applications of these three chatbots. Each vignette addresses a common classroom need, presents clear learning goals and follows the chatbot design framework

(Drelick et al., 2025). Suggestions for implementing the chatbot within a class routine are also included. The purpose of these vignettes is to provide a guide through the design and implementation process for custom educational chatbots, from the perspective of a classroom teacher.

Writing Revision Coach (Grade 9-12)

Mr. Elder, a 10th-grade English language arts teacher, wants to provide one-on-one coaching for his students during the revision process of their argumentative essays. He knows that he does not have time to meet individually with all 104 students in his classes. Mr. Elder decides to create a chatbot to help students revise their drafts to convey clearer meaning, provide stronger evidence, and make intentional style choices. He was inspired by Yao and colleagues (2025) work with the Kami chatbot, which showed that chatbot feedback, when properly trained, can complement teacher feedback and support students' writing development. He also wants to incorporate gaming elements so students can progress through levels and meet checkpoints to unlock different features or rewards.

Conceptualization

He begins identifying an instructional goal. The goal is not to simply fix students' writing, but to structure prompts to help students notice, decide, and revise with agency. This chatbot combines elements from the following types of education chatbots (Kuhail et al., 2023): scaffolding, personalized learning, and collaborative learning. The chatbot would take on the persona of a peer-like partner (peer-to-peer agent) and occasionally offer instructional guidance (teaching agent) (Kuhail et al., 2023). To infuse elements of game design, he wants students to progress through levels and receive awards or "level up" after completing each stage of the revision process. Students will review their claim, evidence, organization, and style, which each align with rubric criteria, and pass a checkpoint. As a reward, they will "unlock" scaffolding suggestions to make improvements to their writing.

Protocol Design

Next, Mr. Elder begins to design his chatbot training protocol. He first retrieves the rubric from the assignment, along with samples of detailed feedback he has previously provided. Thinking through the structure of writing conferences with students, Mr. Elder first drafts levels for working through revisions, which will serve as the conversation progression.

- **Level 1 Claim**: Students state a one sentence claim and explain its focus.
  - Checkpoint: claim is clear and on topic
  - Unlocked revision tip suggestions: give a target example, suggestions for word choice
- **Level 2 Evidence**: Student selects one quote and explains relevance.
  - Checkpoint: evidence directly supports the claim
  - Unlocked revision tip suggestion: scaffolded support for integrating claim with evidence
- **Level 3 Organization:** Student identifies paragraph purpose and suggests one structure revision
  - Checkpoint: The paragraph has a coherent structure
  - Unlocked revision tip suggestion: model transitions
- **Level 4 Style and Revision:** Student applies two edits and reflects the impact of suggested changes

- Checkpoint: edits improve clarity or cohesion
- Unlock: full review and holistic feedback

Next, he drafts a chatbot protocol by creating a blueprint of what a conversation should look like. Protocol:

1. **Intake and goal setting**: Ask the student what part they want to revise based on the elements of the rubric.
2. **Solicit worksample**: Ask the student for an excerpt, not the entire draft
3. **Rubric-aligned prompts:** Ask 3-5 questions to structure the student's thought process about the revisions (e.g. What is your claim in one sentence? Which sentence is your best evidence and why?)
4. **Offer advice:** Provide 2-3 next steps (e.g. "add examples, " clarify")
5. **Check for understanding and reflection:** Ask what they will try first or what they will change and why.
6. **Graduate through checkpoints**: After the student passes through the checkpoint, provide positive feedback and encouragement before beginning the next round of prompts.

Because the chatbot cannot ask follow-up questions with the same flexibility as a teacher, Mr. Elder also creates a list of common sticking points students encounter so the chatbot can respond in a way that will help move revisions forward by getting students to think further.

Technical Design

Now he is ready to begin the technical design for the chatbot. Mr. Elder selects the platform Magic-School AI to create this custom chatbot. His district provides access to this tool, and parents are aware that they are using it, which makes him feel more comfortable with students interacting and uploading their narratives. Mr. Elder uploads the documents he prepared and provides boundaries for the chatbot. It will be a closed chatbot that will not search the internet, and if a student asks it to write something for them, they will be redirected. He reviews some of the accessibility options on the platform and ensures speech-to-text, text-to-speech, and transition features are activated so students can use them as needed.

Trials and Revisions

After the chatbot is up and running, it is time for trials and revisions. After observing some student interactions with the chatbot, Mr. Elder decides to break up some of the questions in his original protocol to reduce the amount of text that is produced. He breaks the rubric-aligned prompts into separate steps to ensure they are not presented together, as this can be overwhelming for students. Next, he readjusts the tone of the chatbot as it sounds overly authoritarian in its current responses. With these changes, the Writing Revision Coach is ready for his students!

Classroom Implementation

Mr. Elder introduces the Writing Revision Coach with a setup activity. He informs the students that he created a chatbot to provide support during their writing. He says he would love to provide one-on-one feedback on each section of the essays before final grading, but he cannot do that with each student in all of his classes. He guides the class through a modeled conversation session with the Writing Revision Coach, displaying the interaction on the classroom smartboard. Next, students are encouraged to use the chatbot to revise one section of their essays. After about 20 minutes, Mr. Elder has a real-time group discussion in which students provide their initial feedback and reactions. These debriefing sessions also provide insights for revisions to the chatbot as needed (Drelick et al., 2025). Now, students have the opportunity to use the Writing Revision Coach throughout the revision process. After the essays are complete, Mr. Elder engages the students who elected to use the chatbot in an in-depth reflection, during which they can review their interactions and reflect on their experiences.

Socratic Seminar Preparation Partner

In recent years, Mrs. Felice has observed that her 9th-grade students are increasingly reluctant to participate in Socratic Seminars. While many students have strong ideas in one-on-one or informal conversations, they are hesitant to speak up in whole-group discussions. Mrs. Felice also notices that students who are receiving academic or language support, including multilingual learners and students with disabilities, are more likely to opt out of the seminar, even when they have done the reading and work to prepare. She decides to create a chatbot to prepare students for a Socratic seminar. It will be designed as a rehearsal space where students can practice discussion techniques, refine their ideas, and build confidence before the live seminar. Her students enjoyed learning about ancient Greece, so she wants to work with storytelling, building a narrative centered in an Athenian agora where Socrates developed the method.

Conceptualization

Mrs. Felice begins by defining her instructional goals. Students should practice decision-ready training by making claims, citing textual evidence, engaging with counterarguments, and using academic language. The chatbot is not meant to provide students with scripted responses they can recite or the right answers. This chatbot draws from the following approaches to designing chatbots for education: scaffolding, experiential learning, affective learning, and learning by teaching (Kuhail et al., 2023). Mrs. Felice wants to create a character who will serve as the persona behind the chatbot, functioning as the mentor. The chatbot will serve as a supportive seminar tutor from the agora, Sokrates, prompting and modeling discussion moves under a student's guidance.

Protocol Design

Next, Mrs. Felice builds the chatbot training protocol. She gathers the seminar norms she uses in class and the discussion rubric. Next, she finds a student guide for Socratic seminars that lists sentence starters and stems. She finds online videos of effective Socratic seminars and notes what is strong in these examples. She maps her learning goals to levels or checkpoints that students will complete to advance. The chatbot persona, Sokrates, will ask questions and prompt students in character while keeping language plain enough to be understood by modern 9th graders. The leaving levels, which correspond to badges (delivered as emojis), are as follows:

- **Level 1 (Novice) Claim:** Students state a claim
  - Checkpoint: claim answers essential question and is on topic
  - Unlock: example of a strong claim
  - Badge: Olive leaf ( )
- **Level 2 (Questioner) Evidence:** Student provides a quote to support claims and explains why it fits
  - Checkpoint: evidence is text-based and linked to the claim
  - Unlock: sentence starters
  - Badge: Scroll ( )
- **Level 3 (Dialectician) Counterargument:** Student provides one counterclaim and rebuttal that uses evidence
  - Checkpoint: rebuttal cites evidence
  - Unlock: rebuttal stems
  - Badge: Lightening bolt ( )
- **Level 4 (Orator) Decision Moves:** Student selects two discussion prompts then will practice and draft an opening statement/conversation starters
  - Checkpoint: two distinct opening contributions drafted
  - Unlock: pep talk, motivation from Sokrates
  - Badge: Greek building ( )

Mrs. Felice is now ready to draft an outline of what a conversation might look like when a student engages with the chatbot:

1. **Text and purpose check:** Gather information. Ask what text(s) the seminar is about and the essential question.
2. **Claim building:** Ask the student to state the claim in one sentence. If they need help, unpack the essential question.
3. **Evidence rehearsal:** Prompt the student to choose a quote that supports their claim.
4. **Counterclaim practice:** Ask the student to predict a counterargument. Prompt them to respond and pull evidence from the text to support.
5. **Discussion moves:** Coach students to practice at least two discussion techniques such as asking a clarify question, building on a peer's idea, respectfully disagree, etc. Provide talking stems/sentence starters.
6. **Action Plan:** Ask the student for the first point they will share in the live discussion.

Because the chatbot is not flexible in its responses, Mrs. Felice tries to anticipate responses that might not align with the above protocol and to get students back on track. She anticipates students saying, "I don't know what to say," "I can't find evidence," or "I am nervous." She includes supportive responses that redirect students and keep them moving forward. She also puts in some guidelines that the chatbot will not generate ideas for students. Instead she directs the chatbot to provide a more direct response if a student asks the chatbot to "write my seminar answers for me". The chatbot will now refer them to the text and ask them to come when they are ready for support.

Technical Design

Mrs. Felice selects a platform that is already approved by her district so she and her students have access to the premium features for added security. She uses ChatGPT's ability to create a custom GPT, which will allow her to build out her Socratic Seminar Preparation Partner. She uploads the materials she collected and created, outlines the conversational script with guidelines and guardrails, and makes the chatbot closed, so it does not search the web and only pulls from what she has uploaded. Mrs. Felice's students are familiar with the accessibility features of ChatGPT, so they will be able to use the features like text-to-speech, voice mode, and custom fonts and displays that they commonly access. She spends time ensuring the welcome prompt is inviting to students so they will be encouraged to use this tool.

Trials and Revisions

After some trials with the chatbot, Mrs. Felice pilots it with another colleague, running through a planned lesson and asking the colleague to engage in a conversation with the tool. With her colleague's feedback, Mrs. Felice makes a few targeted revisions. She shortens the chatbot's responses to reduce cognitive load for students. Next, she adjusts the tone to be conversational and encouraging. Finally, she adds additional pathway responses for when students get stuck, e.g., "Do you want help finding a claim?", so students can overcome common barriers.

Classroom Implementation

Mrs. Felice introduces the Socratic Seminar Preparation Partner to her students as a practice space, explaining that the goal is to help build confidence and strengthen their decision-making skills. It is not to replace their thinking skills. She models an interaction with the chatbot for the class to show what a productive conversation can look like. Students then practice with the chatbot for 20 minutes the day before a planned Socratic seminar. After their rehearsal, Mrs. Felice has a short debrief with the class. She asks what was helpful, what felt frustrating, and how what they did will apply to the live discussion. One student shares that they felt confident about the interaction they had, but they would like to have a summary sheet to review right before the seminar to refresh their memory. Mrs. Felice incorporates this feedback and revises the chatbot to ask students whether they would like a summary sheet at the end of their conversation, which she provides as a model. After a few uses of the tool and seminar sessions, Mrs. Felice returns to reflection with students to identify successful discussion techniques and to determine whether and how the chatbot supported them. This helps keep teachers in the loop and provides feedback for refining instruction, student support, and the chatbot over time.

Public-Domain Character Chatbot

Ms. Gaton's 9th-grade English class is reading *The War of the Worlds* by H.G. Wells (1898). She recounts the dramatized radio reading of the novel in the 1930s and how many listeners believed Earth was under an alien invasion — the original *fake news*. Students make direct connections to today's media and the need to fact-check their sources. This conversation prompts Ms. Gaton to consider creating a chatbot based on the novel to help students enhance their media literacy by verifying claims, identifying missing information, and recognizing misleading reports. She sees an opportunity for students to engage in story-based learning using modern learning tools by creating a custom chatbot.

Conceptualization

Ms. Gaton clarifies the chatbot's overall learning objectives: guide students through the fact-finding process by identifying the claim, evaluating a source, checking evidence, seeking corroboration, and assessing the source's overall trustworthiness. This is not to be a *myth-buster* for students, but rather to provide practice as they work through the steps of finding evidence themselves. Students will use the chatbot after they find a source to evaluate. She selects the persona of a newspaper editor because it fits with the text and would provide authentic prompts about credibility. It could also provide opportunities later to incorporate writing assignments on ethical reporting. This chatbot draws on scaffolding, experiential learning, and social dialogue (Kuhail et al., 2023). It will employ a question-first approach to maintain students' engagement in reasoning.

Protocol Design

Since *The War of the Worlds* is in the public domain, Ms. Gaton uses selections from the text as part of the closed knowledge base. She also identifies a fact-checking framework aligned with the routines she uses in the classroom, based on state standards. Next, Ms. Gaton maps out the conversation sequence for the chatbot:

1. **The "report":** Ask students the title of the article so you can refer to it as needed.
2. **Identify the claim**: Prompt the student, "What is the main claim being made? Write it in one sentence."
3. **Source check:** Ask the student in two prompts who is reporting this information in the story? Who is quoted in the article, and what is their proximity to the event (witness, secondhand)?
4. **Evidence assessment:** Ask what evidence is included, followed by what is missing
5. **Corroboration:** Ask to find a source to confirm/verify this claim.
6. **Bias and tone check**: Ask if there is a sense of urgency, overly biased, or fear-mongering in the article; ask if the tone is neutral, sensationalized or persuasive.
7. **Rate and Reflect:** Ask the student to rate the source as reliable or unreliable and state why.

Ms. Gaton establishes some guardrails to ensure the chatbot is focused on literacy and safety. It should also have a neutral tone, knowing that confronting misinformation and grounded misconceptions can be difficult for students. As such, a neutral chatbot that adheres to the script and prompts students to reflect is essential.

Technical Design

Ms. Gaton's district does not have a license for a tool that creates custom chatbots. After exploring some options, she finds Botpress, a platform where you can create and share custom chatbots openly. After getting approval from the technology director, Ms. Gaton uploads her materials to create *The Editor* chatbot. She selects an image from the novel as an icon for the chatbot and provides an overview with directions about finding a source to the welcome page of the chatbot. This approach ensures students possess the necessary foundational knowledge prior to engaging with the chatbot.

After some trials, Ms. Gaton makes adjustments. First, she shortens the responses so *The Editor* asks one question at a time. Next, she adds hints for students who need support in naming biases or identifying missing evidence. Lastly, she adjusts the tone to ensure the experience is motivating and classroom-safe. The chatbot is now ready to share with the class.

Classroom Implementation

Ms. Gaton introduces *The Editor* chatbot as part of a digital literacy mini-lesson on misinformation that coincides with the novel. She frames the activity as a simulated conversation with an editor so students can practice determining the credibility of sources. Ms. Gaton models using the chatbot with two different sources she has selected from a credible source and a non-biased source. She uses a think-aloud during this activity as she identifies the claims, names evidence, states what is missing, and finds key language. Students then work in pairs to go through the process using articles from a curated list provided by Ms. Gaton. After a debrief, the class provides feedback on their interaction, sharing what was helpful and what was frustrating. Some minor tweaks are made to the chatbot based on the students' feedback, including uploading the article to the chatbot so they can get more support when needed.

Throughout the unit featuring *The War of the Worlds*, Ms. Gaton's class is invited to use *The Editor* chatbot. At the conclusion of the unit, the class reflects on using a chatbot to assess the credibility of sources. The class decides to make some decisions together and share the chatbot widely with the community, as they see a need for others to be able to identify misinformation. Using the platform Botpress, students modify the chatbot and ensure it is open-source so anyone can access the tool.

FUTURE RESEARCH DIRECTIONS

This chapter has focused on an educator-led, simulation-informed process for designing and implementing custom ELA chatbots to support students. While this framework is grounded in research in clinical simulations and emerging work in educational chatbots, there is still a clear need for systemic research examining when, how, and for whom these tools are most beneficial. Notwithstanding, the disadvantages of implementing this emerging tool should also be explored so that educators and developers can weigh its lasting impact relative to other teaching methods. Determining the effects of chatbots on learning goals is also key to understanding their value in the classroom over time.

The presented framework emphasizes preparation, real-time debrief, and reflection as attention components of implementation. Future research should explore how different implementation approaches influence student learning and experiences. For example, studies could compare the use of chatbots with and without guided debriefing routines, examine how reflection time affects learning, or investigate how students perceive the chatbot's role. This could determine how a structured routine impacts student experience, engagement, and perception of a chatbot.

Emerging evidence suggests that embedding chatbots within game-based and narrative contexts can boost engagement, higher-order thinking, and writing outcomes, making game-informed chatbot design a promising avenue for ELA research (Liang et al., 2024; Xiao et al., 2025). Future studies should move beyond effective pilots. Larger-scale use and inquiry with students can help unpack the effectiveness and quality of gamified chatbot designs, narrative framing, progression mechanics (levels/checkpoints), adaptive difficulty, and micro-rewards. Such research could also examine how game-informed chatbot design features interact with pedagogy to support transfer to classroom tasks. Researchers should also test differential effects for multilingual learners and students with disabilities, assess long-term impacts on writing processes, or general skill retention.

CONCLUSION

This chapter outlined a simulation-informed, evidence-based approach for designing and implementing custom ELA chatbots that support students in meaningful, intentional, and inclusive ways. Across the proposed framework and illustrative vignettes, the authors emphasized the value of chatbots as a structured, low-risk practice that can enhance existing instructional routines, not replace teacher expertise or student thinking. By grounding chatbot design in principles from clinical simulation, educators are better positioned to create conversational agents with clear purposes, consistent roles, and well-defined boundaries that align with authentic literacy practices.

Those seeking to adopt or build an educational chatbot in their ELA classroom should begin by setting a clear goal aligned to their curriculum outcomes. Next, it is important to ensure that these learning goals are met by designing protocols that map prompts and learning checkpoints in meaningful and interactive ways. Keeping humans in the loop, teachers can pilot and review the tools they create before mindfully implementing them in the classroom through structured debriefing with students. For classroom teachers, it is recommended to start small by piloting one chatbot-based activity, building on familiar materials or lessons. This allows teachers to expand engaging elements, including game-based options, into their activities.

After thoughtful design, intentional implementation is critical to keeping humans firmly in the loop of GenAI use in the classroom. Preparation, real-time debriefing, and post-activity reflection are presented not as optional add-ons, but as essential instructional moves that anchor chatbot use in pedagogical intent and collective meaning-making. These routines reinforce the role of teachers as designers, facilitators, and reflective practitioners, while positioning students as active agents in their own learning. As generative technologies continue to evolve, educators will increasingly be asked not only whether to use AI tools, but how to do so responsibly, equitably, and effectively. The simulation-informed design and implementation process presented here offers a practical pathway for navigating that complexity, while offering novel and engaging experiences to support students' growth.

Finally, future research should focus on the use of educational chatbots and how students actually engage with them. It is crucial for educators to understand not only whether chatbots work but also how students use them, what role they assign to them, e.g., tutor, friend, and how these perceptions shape learning and behavior. Importantly, future work should investigate how chatbot use interacts with well-being, self-efficacy, and content mastery.

REFERENCES

Adamopoulou, E., & Moussiades, L. (2020). Chatbots: History, technology, and applications. *Machine Learning with Applications*, *2*, 100006.

Barrows, H. S. (1987). *Simulated (Standardized) Patients and Other Human Simulations.* Health Sciences Consortium.

Dotger, B. H. (2015). Core pedagogy: Individual uncertainty, shared practice, formative ethos. *Journal of Teacher Education*, *66*(3), 215–226. DOI: 10.1177/0022487115570093

Dotger, B. H., & Chandler-Olcott, K. (2022). *Clinical simulations as signature pedagogy: Educator preparation across the disciplines.* Harvard Education Press.

Drelick, A. M., Woodfield, C., & Freedman, J. E. (2026). Designing and using custom chatbots to support students with disabilities: An educator's guide. *Journal of Special Education Technology*, **•••**, 01626434261420392.

Drelick, A. M., Woodfield, C., & Freedman, J. E. (2025). Educational chatbot development informed by clinical simulations. *Interactive Learning Environments*, *33*(3), 2044–2055.

Freedman, J. E., Woodfield, C. L., & Dotger, B. H. (2020). Using Simulated Meetings to Practice Advocating for Disability-Related Accommodations (Practice Brief). *Journal of Postsecondary Education and Disability*, *33*(4), 387–394.

Freedman, J. E., Drelick, A. M., & Dotger, B. H. (2024). Use of Simulated Discussions of Postsecondary Accommodations to Inform Self-Advocacy Instruction. *Learning Disabilities Research & Practice*, *39*(1), 26–36.

He, K., Cervera, K., Levine, J., Xu, Y., Collins, P., & Warschauer, M. (2025). Promoting parent-child shared reading with a bilingual conversational agent. *International Journal of Human-Computer Studies*, *199*(103489). Advance online publication. DOI: 10.1016/j.ijhcs.2025.103489

Holzinger, A., Plass, M., Kickmeier-Rust, M., Holzinger, K., Crişan, G. C., Pintea, C. M., & Palade, V. (2019). Interactive machine learning: experimental evidence for the human in the algorithmic loop: A case study on Ant Colony Optimization. *Applied Intelligence*, *49*(7), 2401–2414.

Ganguly, A., Mehjabin, N., & Malik, A.. (2026). Conversational AI agents in education: An umbrella review of current utilization, challenges, and future directions for ethical and responsible use. *AI and Ethics*, *6*(72). Advance online publication. DOI: 10.1007/s43681-025-00916-0

Gupta, S., Mehta, V., Kam, R., Ehmann, C., Orgad, A., Kuang, E., Barrantes, A. C., Posada, M., Shah, S., Prasad, N., Pai, T., Ho, E., Xi, S., Zhou, T., Li, E., Wan, S., Paranjape, S., Dearling, Z., Peng, S., & Muse, A. (2025). A Teacher, a Tutor, a Friend: ChatGPT and the High School Experience. *Qualitative Report*, *30*(5), 3686–3719. DOI: 10.46743/2160-3715/2025.7324

Klein, A. (2023). Welcome to the 'walled garden.' Is this education's solution to AI's pitfalls? *Education Week*, *43*(2).

Kuhail, M. A., Alturki, N., Alramlawi, S., & Alhejori, K. (2023). Interacting with educational chatbots: A systematic review. *Education and Information Technologies*, *28*(1), 973–1018. DOI: 10.1007/s10639-022-11177-3

Labadze, L., Grigolia, M., & Machaidze, L. (2023). Role of AI chatbots in education: Systematic literature review. *International Journal of Educational Technology in Higher Education*, *20*(1), 56. DOI: 10.1186/s41239-023-00426-1

Liang, H. Y., Hwang, G. J., Hsu, T. Y., & Yeh, J. Y. (2024). Effect of an AI-based chatbot on students' learning performance in alternate reality game-based museum learning. *British Journal of Educational Technology*, *55*(5), 2315–2338. DOI: 10.1111/bjet.13448

McMahon, L. E. (2025, July 22). Guidance on the use of federal grant funds to improve education outcomes using artificial intelligence (AI) [Dear Colleague Letter]. U.S. Department of Education. https://www.ed.gov/media/document/opepd-ai-dear-colleague-letter-7222025-110427.pdf

Memarian, B., & Doleck, T. (2024). Human-in-the-loop in artificial intelligence in education: A review and entity-relationship (ER) analysis. *Computers in Human Behavior: Artificial Humans*, *2*(1), 100053. Advance online publication. DOI: 10.1016/j.chbah.2024.100053

Mishra, P., Warr, M., & Islam, R. (2023). TPACK in the age of ChatGPT and Generative AI. *Journal of Digital Learning in Teacher Education*, *39*(4), 235–251. DOI: 10.1080/21532974.2023.2247480

Pérez, J., Daradoumis, T., & Marquès Puig, J. M. (2020). Rediscovering the use of chatbots in education: A systematic literature review. *Computer Applications in Engineering Education*, *28*(6), 1549–1565. DOI: 10.1002/cae.22326

Pinter, R., Bagosi, Z., Abari, K., & Katona, J. (2025). Traditional learning methods versus chatbots. In G. Rózsa, K. Abari, & J. Katona (Eds.), *New solutions based on generative artificial intelligence for human-computer interaction* (Lecture Notes in Networks and Systems, Vol. 1308, pp. 38–49). Springer. https://doi.org/DOI: 10.1007/978-3-031-85561-0_4

U.S. Department of Education, Office of Educational Technology. (2023). *Artificial Intelligence and Future of Teaching and Learning: Insights and Recommendations*. Washington, DC. https://www.ed.gov/sites/ed/files/documents/ai-report/ai-report.pdf

Williams, R. G., Makoul, G., Hawkins, R., Hallock, J. A., Scoles, P., & Reichgott, M. J. (2001). Standardized/simulated patients in medical education. In *Annual Meeting of the American Medical Association Section on Medical Schools*, Chicago. IL.

Xiao, Y., Li, D., & Guo, K. (2025). Using ChatGPT to bring non-player characters to life: Effects on students' storyline-driven game-based writing learning. *Computers & Education, 238*, 105414. Advance online publication. DOI: 10.1016/j.compedu.2025.105414

Yao, Y., Zhu, X., Xiao, L., & Lu, Q. (2025). Secondary school English teachers' application of artificial intelligence-guided chatbot in the provision of feedback on student writing: An activity theory perspective. *Journal of Second Language Writing, 67*, 101179. Advance online publication. DOI: 10.1016/j.jslw.2025.101179

ADDITIONAL READING

Gupta, S., Mehta, V., Kam, R., Ehmann, C., Orgad, A., Kuang, E., Barrantes, A. C., Posada, M., Shah, S., Prasad, N., Pai, T., Ho, E., Xi, S., Zhou, T., Li, E., Wan, S., Paranjape, S., Dearling, Z., Peng, S., & Muse, A. (2025). A Teacher, a Tutor, a Friend: ChatGPT and the High School Experience. *Qualitative Report, 30*(5), 3686–3719. DOI: 10.46743/2160-3715/2025.7324

He, K., Cervera, K., Levine, J., Xu, Y., Collins, P., & Warschauer, M. (2025). Promoting parent-child shared reading with a bilingual conversational agent. *International Journal of Human-Computer Studies, 199*, 103489. DOI: 10.1016/j.ijhcs.2025.103489

Liang, H. Y., Hwang, G. J., Hsu, T. Y., & Yeh, J. Y. (2024). Effect of an AI-based chatbot on students' learning performance in alternate reality game-based museum learning. *British Journal of Educational Technology, 55*(5), 2315–2338. DOI: 10.1111/bjet.13448

KEY TERMS AND DEFINITIONS

Educational Chatbot: A conversational digital tool designed to support learning by interacting with users through text and/or speech.

Guardrails: Design features and rules that shape what GenAI will do and what it will refuse. Guardrails may include restrictions on content, response format, tone, and privacy practices, as well as redirection prompts that keep learners focused on the task and safe classroom norms.

Protocol: A structured " blueprint" that specifies how the interaction should unfold during a clinical simulation or chatbot conversation.

Simulation-Informed Design: An approach to design that draws on the logic of clinical simulations: selecting purposeful scenarios, defining roles, using structured protocols, and improving the experience through debriefing and iterative revision.

Chapter 4
Innovative Approaches in Literacy Education Through AI and Game-Based Learning

K. Ganesh Kumar
http://orcid.org/0000-0002-5719-6193
Velalar College of Engineering and Technology, India

N. V. Keerthana
http://orcid.org/0000-0001-8878-2083
Velalar College of Engineering and Technology, India

K. Balamurugan
http://orcid.org/0000-0003-4560-3801
K.S.R. College of Engineering, India

M. A. Kaviya
Velalar College of Engineering and Technology, India

ABSTRACT

Literacy in the twenty-first century extends beyond basic reading and writing to include digital literacy, critical thinking, creativity, collaboration, and information evaluation across digital platforms. Rapid technological advancement requires learners to assess information critically and develop higher-order thinking skills. Diverse classrooms demand flexible, learner-centered approaches, as traditional methods often fail to address varied backgrounds and abilities. Artificial Intelligence (AI) supports personalized literacy instruction through adaptive content, real-time feedback, and learning analytics. Game-based learning enhances engagement by integrating challenges, narratives, and interactive tasks. Combining AI with game-based strategies creates adaptive, inclusive environments that personalize learning pathways, reduce disparities, and promote equitable literacy development for future academic and professional success in a digital world.

DOI: 10.4018/979-8-3373-7472-7.ch004

1.INTRODUCTION

People in the twenty-first century now understand literacy as more than basic reading and writing skills which were previously considered sufficient (Evmenova et al., 2025). Modern educational systems require students to possess multiple skills which include digital literacy and critical analysis and problem-solving and teamwork and their ability to handle and assess and combine information from different digital systems (Kassenkhan et al., 2025). All around the world, educational systems must change their teaching methods because technology now dominates communication and work and socializing, which creates new literacy requirements that diverse learners must fulfil (Leitner et al., 2023). The quick development of digital technologies brings both advantages and difficulties to the field of literacy education (Liu, 2025).Students in the present day display diverse learning needs because they come from different cultural backgrounds and have different access to educational resources and possess different language skills and cognitive capabilities and learning preferences (Xiao et al., 2025). Students who need different educational approaches require traditional instructional methods to be customized because these methods lead to disengagement from learning and they create unequal educational results and they prevent students from achieving basic reading and writing skills (Cross et al., 2025). Learning through personalized methods that keep students engaged while making education open to all has become more popular in modern times (Fiorentini et al., 2025).The combination of Artificial Intelligence and game-based learning has created two educational technologies that work together to enhance literacy instruction(Huber et al., 2024). Artificial Intelligence describes software systems that can complete tasks which normally need human cognitive functions to operate including pattern identification and decision creation and natural language understanding and personalized educational development (Holmes & Gee, 2016). AI-driven educational tools utilize machine learning algorithms to process vast amounts of student information which helps them find performance trends and identify student learning problems and create personalized teaching solutions (Lester et al., 2013). AI in literacy education creates adaptive reading material systems and automatic writing assessment tools and speech and language assessment systems and intelligent tutoring systems which provide immediate learning support based on individual student needs (Emihovich, 2024).

Game-based literacy uses the engaging and interactive elements of games to improve the educational experience (Li et al., 2024). Game-based literacy uses the engaging and interactive elements of games to improve educational experiences (Govender & Arnedo-Moreno, 2025). Interactive text and symbol and narrative and problem-solving activities create immersive environments which educational games provide to learners for active learning(Zão, 2025). Game mechanics which include challenges and rewards and feedback loops and storytelling elements create an environment which stimulates curiosity while developing determination and internal motivation (Mirmotahari et al., 2025). Students who experience anxiety and low confidence and present disengagement problems in traditional classrooms need to experience literacy instruction inside meaningful game contexts which will help them develop positive reading and writing attitudes (Pavloff-Pelkonen et al., 2025).AI technology serves as a prerequisite to altering all epochs of custom design with the advent of gamified designs (Junruang & Kanjug, 2025). AI technology enhances game-based learning environments through systems which automatically create feedback and develop personalized learning paths according to each student's unique learning characteristics (Song et al., 2024). Game-based systems create extensive interaction data streams which AI technologies use to analyze student learning activities and their patterns of engagement and academic achievement(Alam & Mohanty, 2023). The system develops adaptive learning environments which support continuous educational development while keeping students engaged and enabling all students to learn (Hsu & Lao, 2025). The integrated systems show great potential to resolve the main obstacles that have existed in literacy education for years which include teaching methods for diverse learners and maintaining student engagement and providing equal educational opportunities (Foster & Shah, 2020).

The combination of intelligent technologies with pedagogically grounded game design allows AI game-based literacy frameworks to help students who belong to different age groups and skill levels and study in different educational settings (Lin et al., 2025). The systems provide teachers with essential analytical data which helps them make decisions about developing instructional materials and selecting specific teaching methods (Jiang et al., 2025). The chapter investigates how AI and game-based literacy programs create new educational opportunities for all students (Palmquist et al., 2025). The framework establishes an educational system which combines teaching methods with artificial intelligence and gaming design components to support literacy development (Nolan & McBride, 2014). The chapter presents a literature review, a methodological framework description, a system architecture overview, case study presentation (Tsai et al., 2025).

2. RELATED WORKS

Researchers have expanded their Artificial Intelligence (AI) research in educational applications since 2003 by investigating three specific educational technologies which include intelligent tutoring systems and adaptive learning platforms and learning analytics systems (Lester et al., 2014). Educational institutions used AI-based systems during their initial development to implement rule-based educational systems which managed structured content presentation and automated feedback systems (Groff, 2018). The basic instructional methods of the systems developed from their ability to monitor student learning progress and give appropriate feedback (Lin & Tan, 2025).The development of AI educational applications became possible after machine learning and natural language processing technologies reached their current advanced computational power (Bhuvaneswari & Kumar, 2025). Recent studies show that AI-based tools effectively teach literacy skills to students (Bharathi et al., 2024). In the existing global e-learning context, AI and ML algorithms and technologies are helping foster a way in which intelligent reading systems assess the reading speed and comprehension accuracy with error patterns to customize reading materials and exercises for learners (Mohammadi, 2024).AI-powered writing tools help students enhance their writing skills because they provide automatic feedback on grammar and vocabulary and writing coherence which students need to improve their writing(Darvishinia et al., 2025). Research shows that students achieve better learning outcomes when they receive prompt feedback which corresponds with their unique learning requirement(Babu, 2025).Educational institutions adopted AI technology for classroom purposes while educators developed game-based learning methods which effectively boost student excitement and learning outcomes (Fan & Zhang, 2024). Game-based literacy interventions commonly target phonics instruction and vocabulary development (Fernando & Premadasa, 2025). Studies demonstrate that games help students develop literacy skills through their design which integrates language learning into real-world educational situations (Wu et al., 2024).Recent research investigates how artificial intelligence technology works with game-based learning systems (Chen et al., 2021). The adaptive educational games use AI technology to change their game content and challenge level according to player ability which helps students learn optimally (Neville et al., 2009). Existing studies still focus on two separate research areas which study AI-based learning systems together with game-based literacy approaches(Romero, 2025). The author of this chapter presents an integrated AI game-based literacy framework which enables personalized learning together with student engagement and inclusive education and scalable implementation of modern literacy programs (Brom et al., 2010).

3. METHODOLOGY

The method provides an extensive academic framework through its 10,000 word academic system which uses artificial intelligence to create Game Based Literacy Systems that support multiple learning needs. The system requires mathematical foundations and educational standards and allows for technological expansion. The system combines artificial intelligence models and game mechanics and learning analytics and literacy assessment into a complete educational computational system. The approach is a continuous analytical process that provides individualized learning experiences through its constant assessment of learning progress and tracking of particular educational milestones.

3.1 Conceptual Foundation of AI Based Game Literacy

Learning literacy is conceptualized as a dynamic cognitive process rather than a static skill acquisition process. The learner engages with text, image, and symbol representations within a game environment, where AI dynamically adjusts content difficulty, feedback, and pacing.

Assume literacy competence to be a multidimensional construct:

$$L = \{R, W, V, C, F\} \quad (1)$$

Where:

- R = Reading comprehension
- W = Writing proficiency
- V = Vocabulary knowledge
- C = Critical reasoning
- F = Fluency

Each component is continuously updated through gameplay interactions.

3.2 Learner Representation and Profiling Model

The system uses a feature vector system to track learner progress by collecting essential data points which measure their reading skills and study habits. The indicators which measure student performance include reading accuracy and comprehension skills and vocabulary knowledge and student engagement and error rate and time used to finish tasks. The system uses this method to represent students because it enables performance assessment between different students and throughout their academic journey. The process of min-max normalization transforms all data points into a common measurement system which results in standardized values that range from 0 to 1. The process creates a foundation which enables equal assessment of all data points while the system uses this data to develop models and make choices. The system uses neighbourhood similarity averaging to fill in missing data which it does by estimating learner details from their profile matches. The approach maintains the flow of data between points with bias at minimal levels.

Each learner i is represented as a **feature vector**:

$$Li = [ai, bi, ci, di, ei, ti] \qquad (2)$$

Where:

- ai = reading accuracy
- bi = comprehension score
- ci = vocabulary mastery
- di = engagement index
- ei = error frequency
- ta = task completion time

To facilitate comparability across learners, min max normalization is carried out:

$$Yi' = (Yi - Ymin) / (Ymax - Ymin) \qquad (3)$$

This ensures that all features are normalized between 0 and 1.Missing data for learners is handled using neighbourhood similarity averaging:

$$Yi = (1/k)\ \Sigma\ Yj,\ j \in N(i) \qquad (4)$$

Where N(i) is the set of k most similar learners.

3.3 Literacy Skill Quantification Model

Performance metrics for each literacy component measure two different aspects of student progress that include their exact performance and their progress in learning activities. Vocabulary development is measured by a growth index that measures improvement rather than the achievement of overall performance. The model helps beginners because it understands their progress. Every literacy skill is measured by performance metrics that use weight factors for evaluation. The Reading Proficiency Score (RPS) is the assessment tool for reading proficiency.

$$RPS = (\alpha 1 \times A) + (\alpha 2 \times S) + (\alpha 3 \times Q) \qquad (5)$$

Where:

- A = accuracy
- S = speed
- Q = question correctness
- $\alpha 1 + \alpha 2 + \alpha 3 = 1$

Writing Proficiency Score (WPS):

$$WPS = \beta 1G + \beta 2C + \beta 3L \quad (6)$$

Where:

- G = grammar score
- C = coherence score
- L = lexical diversity

Vocabulary Growth Index (VGI):

$$VGI = (Vpost - Vpre) / Vpre \quad (7)$$

3.4 Game-Based Interaction Modeling

Dynamic Difficulty Adjustment (DDA) makes it possible for the game-based learning environment to offer levels of difficulty that correspond to the capabilities of individual learners. The adaptive system holds the interest of students by ensuring that they do not experience both frustration and boredom. The game applies the Dynamic Difficulty Adjustment (DDA) system to adjust the level of difficulty in the game. The function D(t) represents the level of difficulty that exists at time t.

$$D(t+1) = D(t) + \lambda(Ptarget - Pactual) \quad (8)$$

Where:

- λ = learning rate
- Ptarget = optimal performance threshold
- Pactual = learner performance

This ensures learners remain in the **Zone of Proximal Development (ZPD)**.

3.5 Engagement and Motivation Index

The development of literacy skills is based on learner engagement as the core ingredient in digital learning environments. Engagement is quantified through behavioural factors that comprise time-on-task and interaction rates and responsiveness to rewards. The process of measuring learner engagement requires the use of behavioural metrics which include time-on-task and student participation and their response to rewards.

$$E = (w1T + w2I + w3R) / 3 \quad (9)$$

Where:

- T = time-on-task

- I = interaction frequency
- R = reward response rate

Higher E values indicate stronger intrinsic motivation.

3.6 Reinforcement Learning for Content Adaptation

The main reinforcement learning method of the system employs Q-learning to enhance both content sequencing and task selection processes. The AI agent treats each learner interaction as a state-action-reward process, where learning gains serve as rewards. The agent develops understanding of game-based literacy tasks which provide maximum educational value to various learner profiles through its continuous learning process. The system evolves from basic rule-based adjustment processes to an intelligent system that relies on continuous user interaction to create personalized user experiences. The AI agent applies Q Learning to determine which literacy tasks are optimal.

$$Q(s,a) \leftarrow Q(s,a) + \alpha[r + \gamma \max Q(s',a') - Q(s,a)] \tag{10}$$

Where:

- s = learner state
- a = game action
- r = reward (learning gain)

γ = discount factor

3.7 Natural Language Processing for Literacy Assessment

The critical functions of Natural Language Processing (NLP) techniques make it possible to evaluate the results of reading and writing. The evaluation of writing quality is carried out by using two approaches that involve the measurement of lexical diversity and readability, which is calculated by using the Flesch-Kincaid system. The system monitors the progress of the students because it uses NLP assessment to identify every small accomplishment and emerging issue. The system assesses writing quality by using its automated text analysis. Lexical Diversity:

$$LD = (\text{Unique Words}) / (\text{Total Words}) \tag{11}$$

Readability Score (Flesch-Kincaid):

$$FK = 0.39(W/S) + 11.8(Sy/W) - 15.59 \tag{12}$$

3.8 Adaptive Feedback Generation Model

Feedback is the critical ingredient that makes effective literacy instruction possible. The framework varies the intensity and type of feedback in accordance with the confidence levels of the students. Low confidence students require scaffolded feedback, and high confidence students require reflective prompts.

The approach to differentiated feedback allows students to develop their skills and take control of the learning process. Students with high confidence levels require intensive feedback, while those with low confidence levels require less intensive feedback.

$$Flevel = 1 - Ei \quad (13)$$

Low confidence students require scaffolded feedback, while high confidence students require reflective prompts.

3.9 Inclusive Design for Diverse Learners

The methodology comprises an inclusive approach by means of accessibility weighting mechanisms that evaluate all learner disabilities and their particular educational needs. The system employs accessibility indicators along with their corresponding weights to modify content that ensures learners with visual and auditory and cognitive and motor disabilities can access learning content.

$$Aw = \Sigma (Di \times Wi) \quad (14)$$

Di represents the disability indicators, and Wi represents the accessibility weights.

3.10 Learning Outcome Prediction Model

The learning outcomes of the students will be approximated by creating regression models that rely on literacy performance measures and engagement metrics. The system relies on engagement metrics and literacy performance outcomes to determine students who need support while offering educators information to improve their teaching practices. The system checks the performance of the model by using error metrics such as Mean Square Error since these metrics provide critical information without compromising their accuracy levels. The regression analysis process forecasts academic outcomes.

$$LG = \theta0 + \theta1RPS + \theta2WPS + \theta3VGI + \theta4E (15)$$

Mean Square Error (MSE):

$$MSE = (1/n)\ \Sigma (Yi - \hat{Y}i)^2 \quad (16)$$

3.11 System Validation Metrics

The system should be validated by using various validation metrics such as learning improvement rate and engagement retention ratio and skill transfer index. The metrics determine both direct performance improvements and sustained active participation by users and their ability to apply gained knowledge in new contexts.

- Learning Improvement Rate (LIR)
- Engagement Retention Ratio (ERR)

- Skill Transfer Index (STI)

$$ERR = Active Sessions / Total Sessions \quad (17)$$

3.12 Continuous Learning Loop

The system applies a closed-loop system that constantly provides data feedback to the analysis and adaptation functions. The loop serves as a support system for lifelong learning since it enables the system to develop alongside the academic development of learners.

The system applies a closed loop cycle that involves:

Data → Analysis → Adaptation → Interaction → Feedback → Data

Ensuring lifelong literacy development.

3.13 Scalability and Deployment Considerations

The system applies computational complexity that varies depending on the number of learners and tasks that require processing. The system enables continuous processing and ensures system availability while allowing institutions to develop their operations through cloud-based optimization.

Time Complexity:

$$O(n \times m) \quad (18)$$

Where n = learners, m = tasks

Cloud-based optimization allows for real-time scaling.

3.14 Ethical AI Constraints

The system promotes ethical standards by ensuring bias mitigation requirements that limit the use of protected attributes in the decision-making process. The system sets ethical standards to ensure responsible use of AI in literacy learning while ensuring that its operations remain open to public view.

Bias mitigation constraint:

$$\Sigma\, WiDi \leq \varepsilon \quad (19)$$

Fairness and inclusiveness.

4. SYSTEM ARCHITECTURE

System architecture for AI and game-based literacy: The system architecture for AI and game-based literacy ensures it retains its ability to extend which enables its operation to adjust to varying learning environments while maintaining its core operations and its ability to integrate with other systems. The system sets two separate paths that link data management operations with intelligent processing systems and student learning educational video games and decision support systems thus ensuring tailored literacy development that meets varying needs. The Data Layer serves as the fundamental architectural element which secures and manages all system data through its designated storage facilities. The system maintains complete learner profiles which contain demographic details and literacy skill assessments and accessibility needs and records of past learning experiences. The system maintains storage for gameplay interaction logs and assessment results and textual inputs and metadata about learning materials and game components. The system protects data through encryption and role-based access control and follows educational data protection standards. The system relies on its organized data layer system to support all its analytical and adaptive functionality. The Processing Layer exists above the data layer because it converts raw data into formats that intelligent analysis systems can understand. The system needs to perform data cleaning processes which include data normalization and feature extraction and data aggregation. The system uses learner interaction data to detect behavioural patterns and learning trends and performance indicators. The system processes feature vectors from this stage to enter learner modeling algorithms. The system's initial layer employs educational activities which occur within entertaining game-based environments for teaching purposes that require learners to complete educational tasks. The Analytics and Decision-Support Layer provides additional support to learners through its tools that help teachers and administrators and decision-makers. The system uses processed data to create dashboards and visual reports and predictive analytics through its data aggregation and intelligence output capacity. Educators use educational tools to track student development and discover students who need extra help and measure how well their teaching methods work. System-level insights provide administrators with information that helps them decide about curriculum development and resource distribution and policy implementation. The analytics layer connects intelligent automation systems with human decision-making processes. The system architecture which consists of multiple layers provides both flexible and complete support for AI-driven educational games that teach literacy skills. Educational institutions can enhance their systems through the architecture which connects different layers while they implement extensive solutions and utilize the system across various educational environments.

Figure 1. System Architecture

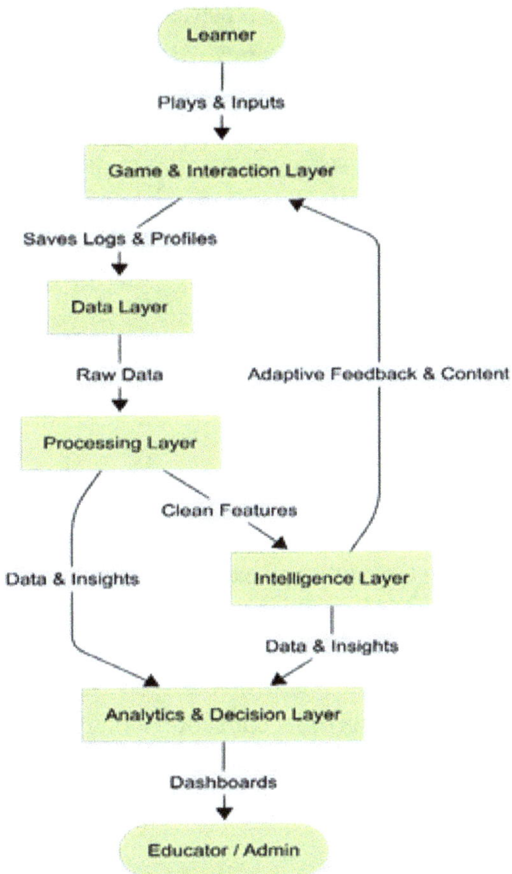

5. CASE STUDY AND EXPERIMENTAL ANALYSIS

The proposed system for teaching reading through game-based learning shows its real-world application and educational value which this research study uses to demonstrate its effectiveness through testing. The study investigates how artificial intelligence combined with three-dimensional virtual games affects reading skills development in students when compared to traditional teaching methods. The case study demonstrates the educational framework through real-world educational testing which was established in previous sections that define theoretical foundations and system design principles. The analysis examines six components which include study design and participant characteristics and data preparation and experimental workflow and observed learning outcomes and interpretive insights from quantitative and qualitative assessments. The study evaluates the framework's effects on literacy instruction through performance data and engagement metrics which provide a complete view of its effectiveness.

5.1 The Case Study's Goals and Purpose

The overall aim of case study has been to assess the effectiveness of an 'AI-enhanced game-based approach to literacy learning' through an 'in situ world' along with a 'simulated world.' Theoretical models signify that 'game-based involvement' of learning through 'AI-based personalised learning' will improve 'literacy learning outcomes.' In order to achieve 'educational progress proof' and 'student involvement assessment,' which requires 'diverse teaching strategies to cater to diverse student groups,' researchers need to perform 'experimental tests. To illustrate the effectiveness of intelligent adaptations in enhancing learning achievement, the case study also includes an evaluation of these intelligent adaptations in relation to the student's specific literacy activities and the use of the "game mechanics." This framework attempts to address issues related to learner diversity that earlier literacy learning models failed to solve.

The following are the specific objectives of this case study:

- Vocabulary Acquisition
- Writing
- Reading

By focusing on behavioural patterns, the study will explore student interaction with an AI-supported gamification method. This study discusses how language learners of different proficiency levels can utilize such a system of adapting difficulty levels and providing feedback. The current study compares traditional methods of literacy education that do not involve adaptive technology with an AI technology-assisted method of game development in terms of its educational outcomes as well as students' interest in it. The study's intention provides full guidelines that will aid in assessing the effectiveness of this framework as a teaching aid, as well as its applicability in a classroom environment.

5.2 Study Context and Learner Profile

The experimental study took place in a mixed-ability educational setting which included students from different linguistic backgrounds and different literacy levels and different learning styles. The study participants were selected from urban and semi-urban educational settings which created a diverse participant group that reflected real-world classroom environments. The assessment required this diverse group of participants because it needed to test the abilities of the AI-based game literacy system to include all users and adjust to different situations while maintaining its performance across various users. The students showed different levels of experience with digital educational tools while they also displayed different abilities in reading fluency and vocabulary knowledge and writing proficiency. The research established a perfect setting to investigate how AI-driven personalized educational methods meet individual student needs while providing equal educational access to all students.

The study participants were separated into two distinct groups.

- Control Group The Control Group consisted of students who obtained their literacy education through standard teaching methods which used textbooks and worksheets and instructor demonstrations. Students received instruction which progressed at a constant speed while instructors provided them with standard learning assessments.

- Experimental Group The Experimental Group used an AI-based game literacy system which provided them with customized learning experiences through its adaptive content and story-based activities and student assessment systems.

The two groups used the same educational framework which included specific learning goals and teaching methods and instructional time to create an equal environment that would evaluate their academic performance. The groups showed different instructional methods which created observable differences in how students performed and participated with the AI-based game learning system.

5.3 Data Collection and Experimental Design

An eight-week research study was conducted by researchers using a quasi-experimental research method. Both the experimental group and control group had pre-tests and post-tests to assess their reading skills, which made it possible to compare the results of their learning outcomes. The standardized tests measured essential reading skills that included reading comprehension and vocabulary mastery and writing skills. The experimental group generated data on continuous gameplay, which offered in-depth information on the learning behavior of the experimental group. The researchers gathered data on the following:

- The task completion rates show how long learners worked before finishing tasks.
- The data on error frequency reveals the regions that were difficult for students and the regions where improvement occurred during the period.
- The time-on-task indicator indicates the amount of time students spent on reading tasks.
- The system monitored user behavior by analyzing navigation and response to questions.
- The reward engagement measurement shows how well users respond to game-based rewards and how motivated they become during gameplay.

The sources of data allowed researchers to investigate developments among learners and the performance of the system in a more detailed analysis, which was more than the normal evaluation process. The experimental process involved four different levels of practice.

1. The first literacy test provided a foundation for evaluating learner ability.
2. For the particular study, the approaches to instruction delivery included the AI game and the normal approaches.
3. The experimental group was subjected to active tracking and system modification as provided by the AI analytics technology.
4. The researchers applied an evaluation process to monitor how learners fared and how they reacted to the curriculum at the end of the learning period.
5. The approach was of high quality, yet it also enabled the researcher to take into account particular adaptive skills of the AI.

5.4 Literacy Performance Analysis

The results of the assessment indicated that the learners in the experimental group made significant improvements in their literacy skills. The results of the reading comprehension test indicated that the learners made continuous progress throughout the duration of the study, especially those who had lower reading skills. The adaptive reading passages and the support systems helped the learners to develop skills that would help them manage difficult reading passages. The rate at which the learners acquired vocabulary was at its peak when they were exposed to the vocabulary through storytelling and gaming activities. The learners were taught vocabulary through direct experience, which helped them to understand the vocabulary as they would use it in real life. Students learned vocabulary through direct experience which enabled them to comprehend words as they would use them in real life situations. Students needed personalized learning materials together with ongoing assessments to achieve advanced literacy skills development. This Figure2 represents the Literacy Performance Analysis.

Figure 2. The Literacy Performance Analysis.

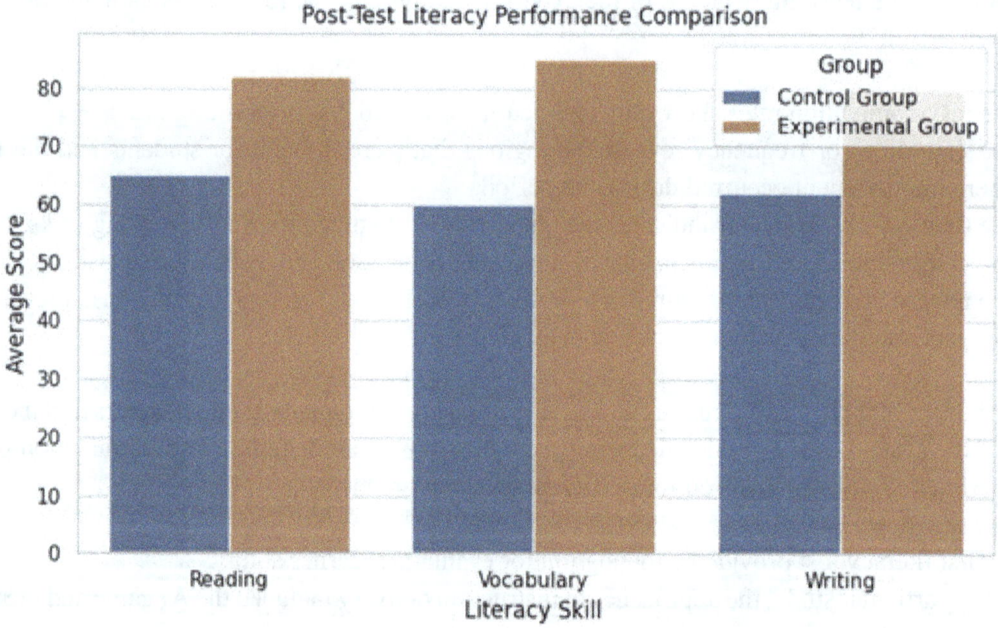

5.5 Engagement and Motivation Outcomes

The AI-based game literacy intervention produced learner engagement as its primary measurable result. The study maintained student engagement through implementation of game elements which included rewards and progress indicators and narrative progression. The experimental group maintained consistent engagement throughout all study sessions because its members showed different patterns of motivation compared to traditional learning environments which experience declining engagement throughout their duration.

Quantitative engagement metrics revealed:

- Higher session completion rates which showed that students showed better ability to complete their studies.
- Students showed more cognitive involvement because their interaction times lasted longer with the material.

Students showed less tendency to avoid learning activities especially students who had previously selected to skip learning activities. Figure 3 represents Engagement and Motivation Outcomes

Figure 3. Engagement and Motivation Outcomes

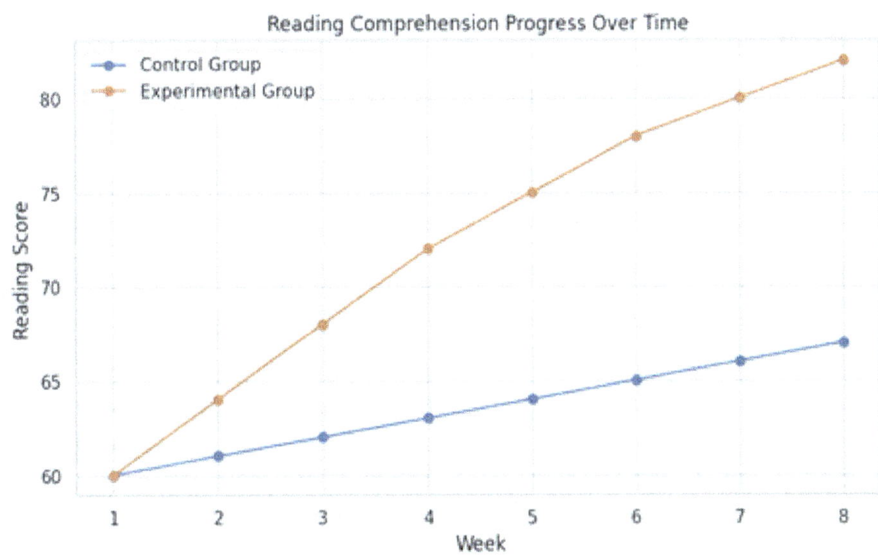

The game-based environment created a less stressful atmosphere which allowed students to complete reading and writing tasks. Students found literacy activities to be less scary and more fun when they were presented through game-based learning because this method created a positive bond between them and educational content. The change in student attitude resulted in students developing greater confidence which pushed them to tackle difficult literacy requirements.

5.6 Adaptive Learning and Personalization Effects

AI-based educational games which use literacy systems demonstrate their primary strength through their ability to change according to new information. The system uses real-time performance tracking to modify its task difficulty and content complexity while providing feedback which matches the skills of each individual learner. The system creates an optimal learning environment which challenges learners enough to enhance their skills while offering them protection against mental overload. The system offers scaffolded support to learners who need assistance through its provision of contextual hints and simplified texts and step-by-step guidance. The interventions help learners to overcome educational obstacles because they maintain the instructional process without creating negative effects on students. Figure 4 represents the Summary of Adaptive Learning and Personalization Effects.

Figure 4. Adaptive Learning and Personalization Effects.

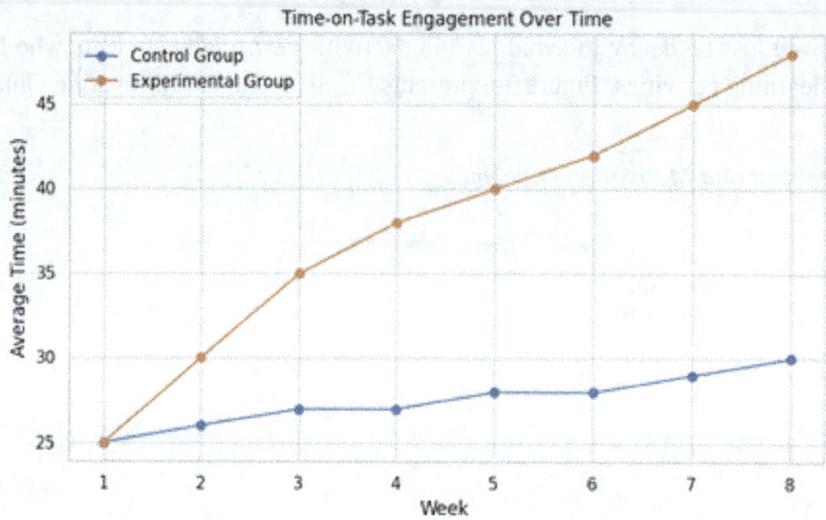

Advanced learners receive enhanced learning materials which include complex texts and advanced analytical questions and problem-solving exercises that develop their critical thinking skills and deep understanding abilities. Personalization at this level decreases two main barriers which prevent people from developing literacy skills in conventional classroom environments. AI-based systems at their best provide students with equal chances to learn because they adapt to the different learning styles and paces of students in classrooms with mixed abilities. The result makes learners show greater engagement with their studies and strengthens their motivation while increasing their confidence during literacy development.

5.7 Comparative Analysis with Traditional Instruction

The AI-enabled game-based approach shows its clear benefits when it gets compared to traditional literacy instruction. The standard teaching methods use fixed learning speeds and common teaching resources and typical assessment methods, which fail to meet the needs of different student learning styles. The assessment methods create problems because they fail to give adequate support to students who need extra help while they create unnecessary challenges for students who excel at their studies. The system made possible by the AI enables personalized learning paths, which assist students in progressing with their learning at their optimal speed. The research study revealed that the learning outcomes in AI-supported environments were equal for all students after comparing the experimental group with the control group. The study revealed that personalized learning systems assisted struggling students, which caused significant development among these students. Students demonstrated more interest in participating in class activities when they utilized the game-based learning system. The players maintained focus on the game while their motivation to learn increased because the game used interactive game mechanics which included rewards and progress tracking and instant feedback systems. The students showed increased active learning and risk-taking and perseverance through difficulties, which created a more engaging and accessible environment for learning literacy skills. Figure 5 represents Comparative Analysis with Traditional Instruction

Figure 5. Comparative Analysis with Traditional Instruction

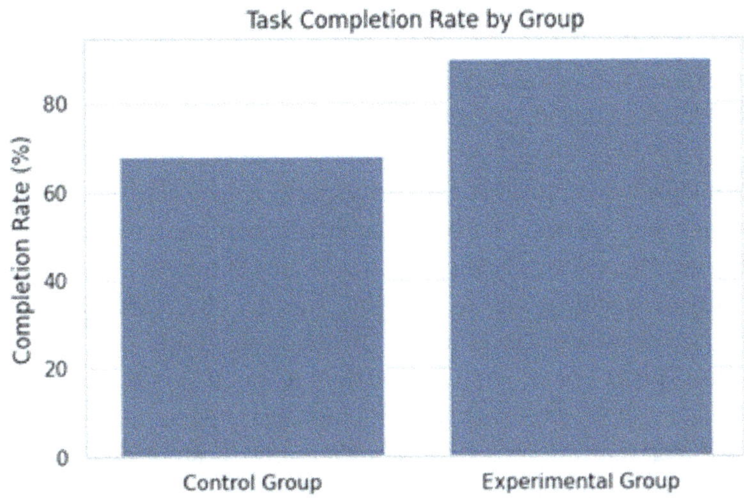

5.8 Discussion of Experimental Findings

The experimental findings show strong evidence that artificial intelligence combined with game-based literacy teaching methods results in better learning outcomes and improved student engagement. The most important finding shows that students who used the AI-based gaming system exhibited better engagement and study persistence and motivation than students who used conventional teaching methods. The results show that literacy skills development depends on both content delivery methods and students' emotional and motivational responses. The results demonstrate that literacy tasks gain learning value when students complete them in authentic educational contexts which combine genuine literacy activities with compelling game-based storytelling elements. When learners face reading and writing and vocabulary difficulties during a story-based or problem-solving task they tend to view those tasks as meaningful instead of mandatory. The system design ensured that learners would stay in their most effective learning area while the system prevented them from experiencing cognitive overload and losing interest in their studies. This helps students who face difficulties with learning the normal methods of teaching by being provided with learning paths customized to fit their learning styles and speeds. This study proves that there are good ways of teaching, as identified by the teachers through data collected from the games. By being provided with full analytics of how students behave, how they progress in the games, as well as how they learn to do various things in their games, thorough evaluations of what they need to learn are carried out. The data provides educational leaders with a foundation for making choices about teaching methods and implementing specialized programs and refining instructional methods through proven teaching methods. The experimental results demonstrate that AI-powered game-based literacy systems provide an effective solution which helps students develop reading skills while enhancing their cognitive and motivational abilities thus making it effective for teaching students from multiple backgrounds.

5.9. Practical Implications of the Case Study

The case study shows that educational institutions can implement AI-based game literacy systems in their actual educational settings. The research faces another restriction because the sample size does not provide enough representation of various contextual backgrounds. The research study tested students who had different skill levels but needed more participants from different backgrounds to achieve better research results. Future research should investigate how different socio-economic backgrounds and digital access and technology experience affect learner performance. These technical or infrastructural features produce hindrances to be cleared.AI-based game literacy systems require both digital devices and internet access to function effectively. The resource constraints of the environment establish boundaries which restrict the ability to execute the necessary requirements. The degree of learner experience with digital interfaces will determine their level of participation in activities and their ability to complete tasks which will cause different results to emerge. Future research should address these limitations by conducting large-scale, long-term studies across multiple educational contexts and cultures. The research will demonstrate how AI-driven game-based literacy frameworks can be applied at different scales and sustainable ways across diverse cultures.

5.10 The Experimental Study's Limitations

Although it is satisfactory to note the excellent outcome, various shortcomings in the experiment should not be ignored. One major flaw in the experiment is the brief period in which the intervention occurred. Since literacy learning takes a significant period of time to achieve, it requires a significant period as well to be able to gauge the outcome. Sample size and contextual diversity form two more constraints here. While learners of different proficiency levels were chosen for the study, the sample needs to be increased for more generalisable findings to be drawn. Learner outcomes need to be further explored regarding their relationship to factors such as their socioeconomic status and the availability of digital infrastructure in the country process, long-term studies are required to assess long-term effects. Sample size and contextual diversity are two more constraints. Although learners with a range of proficiency levels were included in the study, a larger and more varied participant pool would improve the findings' generalisability. Future research should look into how learner outcomes may be impacted by variations in socioeconomic background, access to digital infrastructure, and prior technology use. It is also important to consider other factors such as technical and infrastructural issues with regards to game literacy systems based on AI, and for this to be achieved, there is a need to consider access to digital devices and to the internet, which may pose challenges due to resource constraints and consider other factors such as learners and their familiarity with digital devices as factors that may introduce variability to the results to be achieved. Therefore, future investigations need to ensure that the aforementioned disadvantages of the present study are addressed by undertaking vast and wide-reaching research in various educational domains and cultures to further throw more insights into the applicability of the AI-based game-based literacy framework.

6. RESULTS AND DISCUSSION

The results from the case study and experimental analysis of AI-enabled game-based literacy functions as the main result of this section. The research aims to explain how learners develop reading skills and different student learning behaviours together with the success of adaptive learning programs and the way students from various backgrounds can access their educational materials. The analysis explains how AI and game-based learning methods improve literacy skills through their integration of learning analytics and performance metrics and experimental data .The results show performance improvements because they show the importance of understanding literacy analytics according to specific contexts. The system combines gameplay analytics with visual progress maps to provide user-friendly methods for monitoring student progress which research-based literacy gain scores and engagement indices demonstrate as evidence of student growth. The combined approach improves understanding through its ability to describe results to teachers and academic staff members who lack technical knowledge about AI systems. The research shows that the AI and game-based literacy framework creates significant learning results which help teachers make better educational choices in actual classroom environments.

6.1 Literacy Performance Results

The experimental analysis showed that learners who practiced their skills with the AI-driven game-based platform achieved better reading skills than before. Multiple learning groups demonstrated steady progress in reading comprehension and vocabulary acquisition and written expression skills. The results show that literacy development occurred at different rates because students participated in different ways and received different learning materials. The performance analytics showed that students with low literacy skills at the beginning of the program made higher progress than their peers because they used personalized learning support and adaptive difficulty systems. The results of the study revealed that students who engaged in game-based literacy activities showed better information retention and understanding of concepts than those who learned using conventional teaching methods. The findings of the research demonstrate that interactive game environments incorporating storytelling components act as effective tools for teaching literacy skills to students. Figure 6 depicts the Literacy Performance Results.

Figure 6. The Literacy Performance Results.

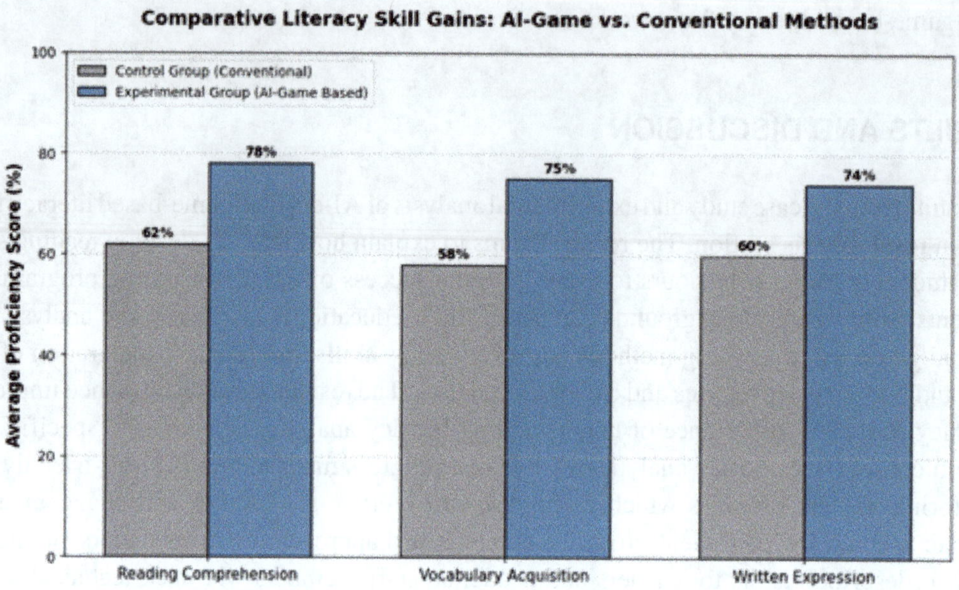

6.2 Engagement and Adaptive Learning Patterns

The experimental analysis yielded significant findings that revealed students retained their active engagement throughout the entire duration of the intervention period. The game mechanics incorporating reward and progress systems and storytelling components and challenge systems resulted in increased student motivation and prolonged engagement with their tasks. The adaptive learning patterns indicated that students progressed through different levels of difficulty since they obtained instant feedback for their performance. The results indicate that personalized learning using AI technology acts as a crucial tool that helps students stay motivated to learn in a classroom setting where students demonstrate different learning speeds and abilities.

6.3 Discussion and Educational Implications

The findings from the results reveal that the AI-based game-based literacy framework is effective in assisting users in developing skills and achieving better learning outcomes. The framework incorporates adaptive learning, immediate feedback, and contextual literacy activities to enhance cognitive engagement through its learning elements. The findings from the educational research reveal that effective learning and teaching in education require both learner-centered teaching and evidence-based teaching practices. The framework enables teachers to assess learning gaps and track learning continuously. The development of literacy skills acts as an assessment process that remains flexible for immediate improvement. The findings from the research show that game-based learning environments help students with low self-esteem, who lacks formal reading skills, to learn literacy skills without experiencing educational anxiety.

6.4 Implications for Inclusive Literacy Education and Decision Support

The findings from the research show that the AI systems and the game-based literacy systems are effective educational decision-making tools that can be employed by educational institutions to support all student groups. The proposed system provides real-time performance information as well as information on learner engagement and learning progress, which is not provided by learning materials. The system assists institutions of learning in identifying students who require extra support, which helps the institution to develop strategies for such students. Multilingual students and students with learning disabilities are greatly assisted by the adaptive feedback feature of the system, which assists such students in scaffolded learning activities. The system allows literacy education programs to cover more students while ensuring that all students have equal access to education. The system allows educational institutions to provide personalized literacy learning paths, which assist them in providing quality literacy programs in resource-constrained environments. The system is beneficial for environments that involve large groups of students and remote learning environments that lack necessary educational resources.

6.5 Experimental Dataset and Learning Analytics Overview

The experimental dataset was generated from learner interactions within the AI-enabled game-based literacy platform. The dataset captures both literacy performance indicators and engagement-related attributes, which enable a complete assessment of learning progress and adaptive behavior. The organization used anonymized aggregate data of all learner information to achieve both ethical standards and data protection requirements. The dataset is an important element that verifies the success of the proposed framework by providing measurable evidence of literacy improvement and engagement and personalized learning outcomes that various groups of students experience.

Table 1. Average Reading of Experimental Dataset and Learning Analytics Overview.

Learner Group	Average Reading Score (%)	Vocabulary Mastery (%)	Writing Coherence Score	Engagement Time (minutes/session)	Adaptive Level Progression
Group A (Beginner)	58	54	52	32	Low → Medium
Group B (Intermediate)	71	68	65	38	Medium → High
Group C (Advanced)	84	82	78	42	High → Advanced
Multilingual Learners	66	70	61	40	Medium → High
Learners with Special Needs	62	60	58	45	Adaptive Scaffolding

Table 1 summarizes the results of literacy performance and engagement metrics that measure performance for different learner groups. The AI system employed adaptive progression to dynamically alter content difficulty based on the needs of each learner.

Figure 6.1 illustrates the literacy progress of learners based on the results of experimental research. The experimental period indicated that the learner groups progressed at different rates in developing their literacy skills. The learner groups demonstrated continuous progress in reading comprehension skills and vocabulary acquisition abilities. The application of adaptive game-based learning enabled learners to attain faster and more sustained improvement, thus indicating the effectiveness of AI-supported personalized learning.

6.6 Correlational Analysis: Dynamic Difficulty Adjustment and Cognitive Load Optimization

The enhanced literacy skills achieved by the experimental group require that the researcher study the effects of variations in system algorithms on the mental processes of the learners. The strategy employed Dynamic Difficulty Adjustment (DDA) as its core component to help learners enhance their skills within the constraints of their Zone of Proximal Development (ZPD).The experimental results provide empirical validation for this theoretical construct which shows that algorithmically optimized task difficulty leads to an inverse relationship with non-productive learner anxiety.

The study found that participants spent more time interacting with the system because of cognitive load management practices which controlled their mental workload. The AI system activated "scaffolded feedback" mechanisms from the methodology after it detected a confidence level drop through response time delays and navigation pattern changes. The correlation analysis shows that the micro-interventions achieved two results because they solved particular mistakes while preserving the learner's "flow" state. The literacy gains described in Section 6.1 should not be considered a result of gamification because they emerged from an ongoing process which used mathematical methods to enhance the learning curve. The system provided educational content while it eliminated cognitive overload which normally obstructs learning for different types of students. Figure 7 represents Dynamic Difficulty Adjustment and Cognitive Load Optimization

Figure 7. Dynamic Difficulty Adjustment and Cognitive Load Optimization

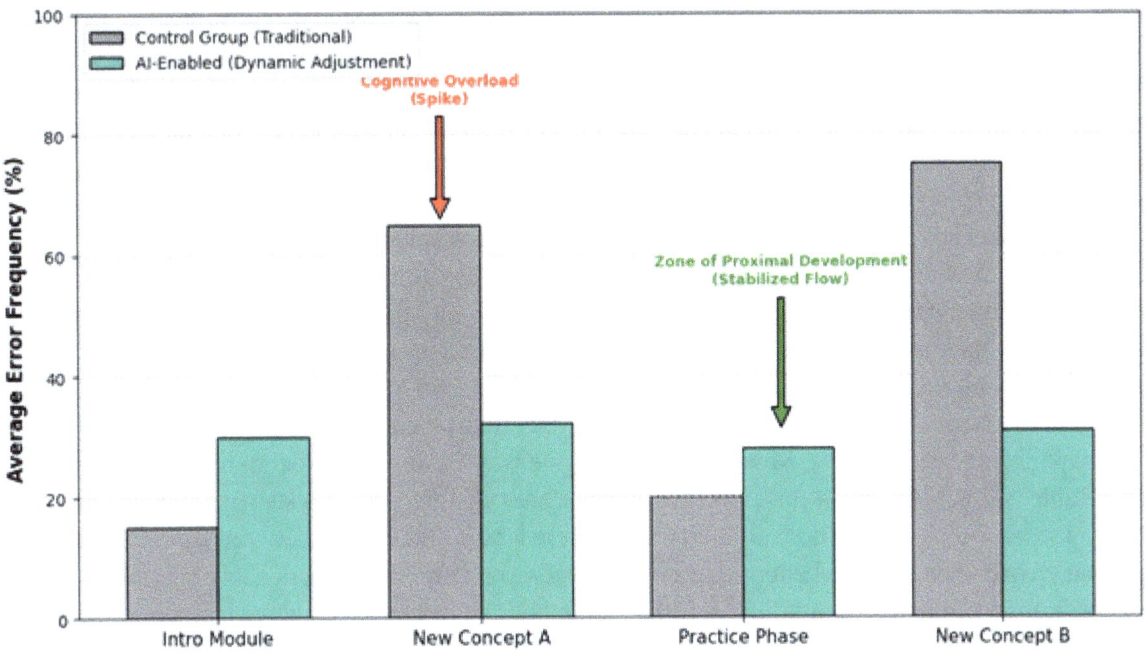

7.CHALLENGES AND LIMITATIONS

AI-based game-based literacy systems show strong potential to improve learning outcomes for diverse learners but face multiple obstacles which need to be recognized. The constraints of the system refer to four main factors which include technological limitations, pedagogical restrictions, ethical considerations, and contextual education requirements that determine how well the solution functions in actual learning environments. The primary obstacle which exists in this situation requires organizations to depend on their technological assets. AI-based game-based literacy platforms need users to have digital devices and users to have stable internet and users to have adequate computational capacity. Many areas especially rural regions and economically disadvantaged communities experience problems with their basic technological infrastructure. The digital divide prevents equal distribution of advanced learning systems while creating educational inequalities that can only be solved through inclusive deployment approaches. The second main constraint relates to the quality and accessibility of data. AI systems need large amounts of precise learner information in order to produce valuable insights which lead to adaptive system responses. The performance of personalization algorithms gets affected by incomplete data and noisy data and biased data. The initial learning period shows limitations because early-stage learners and new users generate only limited interaction data which restricts system accuracy in adapting to their learning needs. The cold-start problem causes temporary reductions in AI personalization systems because of their dependency on user data. The alignment of pedagogical methods faces multiple obstacles. Game-based environments enhance learner engagement but learners tend to concentrate more on game mechanics than on important educational content. The two main areas which need to be addressed involve teacher readiness and their willingness to accept new methods. The effective use of AI-driven game literacy systems requires educators to comprehend and apply AI-developed insights into their classroom methods. The adoption process will face challenges when educators have limited digital skills or refuse to accept new technological advancements. Teachers will not use system functions properly because they lack proper training and professional development which leads to their distrust of automatic suggestions that decrease the system's total framework effectiveness. Algorithmic bias occurs when AI systems train on datasets which do not reflect actual linguistic and cultural and socioeconomic characteristics of all student groups. The solution to these problems needs effective governance systems which include ethical protection mechanisms. The process of AI systems making decisions becomes complex due to their decision-making methods. AI systems use their intricate design to produce results which do not provide users with any understandable insights. Educators struggle to determine the reason behind the specific educational modifications and feedback which were given to students. People will trust AI recommendations less because AI systems fail to explain their operations clearly and this problem prevents users from making educated choices. Researchers investigate ways to improve system transparency through explainable AI methods which currently present a research challenge. The system performance depends on two factors which are learner variability and differences in motivation between users. Game-based learning environments create better engagement results yet different learners show varying responses to gamification elements. The traditional learning methods are preferred by some learners who become distracted by competitive elements and reward systems. The design process of engagement strategies needs to adapt to multiple motivational profiles while the design process requires ongoing development. Experimental research results cannot be applied to other situations because this generalization problem needs to be recognized. Researchers use case studies and experimental studies to examine specific research questions within controlled environments or restricted research conditions. Research results cannot be transferred to different educational contexts because of variations in curriculum requirements and student language abilities and cultural practices and institutional boundaries.

8.ETHICAL, PRIVACY, AND GOVERNANCE CONSIDERATIONS

The convergence of Artificial Intelligence (AI) technology and game-based learning systems offers substantial educational benefits for literacy education, but it also offers critical challenges that must be addressed by following ethical standards and privacy policies. The systems require responsible and fair and just implementation because they rely on two factors: learner data and their automated decision-making processes. The section discusses critical ethical considerations together with necessary privacy protection policies that must be put in place to ensure the sustainable functioning of AI-enabled game-based literacy systems.

8.1 Ethical Use of Artificial Intelligence in Literacy Education

The application of artificial intelligence in the education sector needs to have ethical standards that form the basis of the necessary framework for the application of AI. The AI literacy systems produce direct effects on the students' academic development because they influence the way students learn and receive educational feedback. The systems should define their core emphasis on the protection and fair treatment of learners. The primary ethical problem in this particular case arises from bias. The AI systems will produce disadvantages for particular learning groups because they will be trained using datasets that do not include the particular groups or have biased information. The literacy education sector applies models that are biased, which produce inappropriate results because they are unable to identify different patterns of language and dialects and writing styles.

8.2 Learner Data Privacy and Protection

Educational games that utilize AI create serious privacy concerns because they gather a lot of information about students. The systems track multiple user activities which include their reading habits and documented writing and system usage patterns and their academic results and their emotional states. The improper handling of such data creates multiple risks which include data exploitation and unauthorized access and identity theft. The solution requires the implementation of data reduction rules because they establish framework for solving these issues. The system needs to collect only the necessary data which will serve two purposes: developing customized learning experiences and enhancing system performance. The system needs to transform all sensitive data into either anonymous or pseudonymous formats which will protect student identities. The organization requires both safe data storage facilities and encryption methods which will protect its information against unauthorized access. Privacy protection needs informed consent as its fundamental requirement.

8.3 Governance Frameworks and Policy Alignment

The successful implementation of AI-based literacy systems requires effective governance systems to manage their operational processes. Governance frameworks establish the specific functions and responsibilities together with the accountability mechanisms that each stakeholder group which includes developers and educators and institutions and policymakers must follow. Educational institutions must establish clear policies regarding data usage, system monitoring, and ethical compliance. The system requires regular audits to evaluate its operational effectiveness, biases, and protection of confidential information. The framework of governance must ensure adherence to national as well as international norms of data protection, along with educational needs. The formulation of guidelines that facilitate innovation in education while ensuring the rights of students calls for collaboration between technologists, educators, and the governing authority at the policy level. The implementation of governance mechanisms needs to enable organizations to enhance their operations through ongoing progress while responding to the changing nature of AI technologies.

9.CONCLUSION

The field of digital technology has developed at an accelerated speed which led to complete educational system transformations in all parts of the world. The chapter examined how Artificial Intelligence (AI) and game-based learning technologies work together to create new methods which effectively help various learners develop their reading skills. The proposed framework combines intelligent adaptation with engaging learning environments to solve three educational challenges which include developing learner diversity and maintaining student motivation and providing all students with equal access to quality educational resources. The authors of this research demonstrate that when teachers use personalized and contextualized instructional content students achieve better literacy results. AI-driven systems enable continuous analysis of learner behavior performance and engagement which enables educational institutions to create customized learning experiences that meet the needs of each student. Students who study literacy skills require this form of adaptability because their language skills and cognitive abilities and cultural backgrounds and learning speeds show wide variations. The AI system adaptation enables students to experience appropriate challenges which they can handle while receiving instant feedback that assists their confidence building and skills development. The chapter demonstrates that game-based learning methods lead to increased student motivation and drive for academic activities which students conduct in their classroom environment. Traditional literacy instruction methods face challenges because they fail to connect with students who show anxiety and low confidence and disengagement from standard teaching methods. Game-based learning methods enable students to work with reading tasks through interactive. The implementation of stories together with the implementation of obstacles and reward mechanisms leads to better user participation which results in enhanced cognitive development and reading skill retention. The research study and experimental evaluation which the chapter presents show that AI-based game literacy programs demonstrate successful educational results. The research findings show that reading skills and vocabulary knowledge and writing skills improved through measurable advancements which benefited students with initial low proficiency levels. The framework proves its effectiveness in establishing an inclusive learning environment through its personalized learning paths that cater to both struggling and advanced learners. The results from the engagement metrics and learning analytics illustrate that motivation and adaptive feedback are key components that contribute to literacy development. The chapter illustrates that the implementation of responsibility and ethical implementation is of more importance than learning outcomes. Technological advancement demands ethical and privacy and governance norms since these norms ensure that technological development adhere to the principles of fairness and transparency. Learning environments that incorporate AI technology must establish trust through three key practices that include protecting learner data, minimizing bias in algorithms, and human control over decision-making. The successful implementation of intelligent learning technologies requires organizations to establish ethical governance as a fundamental requirement. The chapter identifies existing issues which limit progress despite presenting promising outcomes. The organization needs to develop specific deployment methods and conduct continuous assessment because existing problems with technological infrastructure and data quality and teacher readiness and contextual differences make deployment difficult. The framework extension will facilitate support for multilingual literacy and informal learning environments that will widen its scope and impact on society. The integration of AI and game-based literacy will provide a robust educational system that will revolutionize literacy education for students with diverse learning needs. The systems that develop adaptive and engaging learning environments will assist students in developing their digital literacy skills when these systems are designed and implemented in a responsible manner. This chapter contributes to the growing research community that advocates for educational approaches that prioritize learners while utilizing data and adhering to ethical norms that will establish AI-enabled game-based literacy as an effective pathway to offer equal educational opportunities to students.

REFERENCES

Alam, A., & Mohanty, A. (2023). Educational technology: Exploring the convergence of technology and pedagogy through mobility, interactivity, AI, and learning tools. *Cogent Engineering*, *10*(2), 2283282. DOI: 10.1080/23311916.2023.2283282

Brom, C., Šisler, V., & Slavík, R. (2010). Implementing digital game-based learning in schools: Augmented learning environment of 'Europe 2045'. *Multimedia Systems*, *16*(1), 23–41. DOI: 10.1007/s00530-009-0174-0

Chen, X., Zou, D., Xie, H., & Cheng, G. (2021). Twenty years of personalized language learning. *Journal of Educational Technology & Society*, *24*(1), 205–222.

Cross, B., Gollek, C., Ai, J., & Hainey, T. (2025). How parents read young learners' digital engagement: a posthumanist inquiry into the temporality of co-evolving learning practices in AI game space. *Early Years*, 1–14.

Darvishinia, N., Rios, A., & Clark, J. S. (2025). Innovative Pathways in STEM: Virtual Reality for Empowering English Language Learners. *Journal of Interactive Learning Research*, *36*(3), 269–292. DOI: 10.70725/141357ylqajb

Emihovich, B. (2024). Game-based learning and systems thinking: An innovative instructional approach for the 21st century. *TechTrends*, *68*(1), 174–185. DOI: 10.1007/s11528-023-00915-0

Evmenova, A. S., Regan, K., Mergen, R., & Hrisseh, R. (2025). Educational Games and the Potential of AI to Transform Writing Across the Curriculum. *Education Sciences*, *15*(5), 567. DOI: 10.3390/educsci15050567

Fan, J., & Zhang, Q. (2024). From literacy to learning: The sequential mediation of attitudes and enjoyment in AI-assisted EFL education. *Heliyon*, *10*(17), e37158. DOI: 10.1016/j.heliyon.2024.e37158 PMID: 39286160

Fernando, P. A., & Premadasa, H. S. (2025). Use of Game-Based Activities in Predicting the Sequential-Global Learning Dimension for Primary Schoolers. *IEEE Access : Practical Innovations, Open Solutions*, *13*, 204606–204627. DOI: 10.1109/ACCESS.2025.3637994

Fiorentini, J. P., Leif, S. A., Fasching-Varner, K. J., & McCreery, M. P. (2025). Learning to Read or Reading to Learn: A Narrative Literature Review of Literacy within Digital Game-Based Learning Environments. *Technology, Knowledge and Learning*, 1–20.

Foster, A., & Shah, M. (2020). Principles for advancing game-based learning in teacher education. *Journal of Digital Learning in Teacher Education*, *36*(2), 84–95. DOI: 10.1080/21532974.2019.1695553

Govender, T., & Arnedo-Moreno, J. (2025). Narrative alchemy: Co-creating a game-based extensive reading framework for adult language learners. *Entertainment Computing*, *52*, 100870. DOI: 10.1016/j.entcom.2024.100870

Groff, J. S. (2018). The potentials of game-based environments for integrated, immersive learning data. *European Journal of Education*, *53*(2), 188–201. DOI: 10.1111/ejed.12270

Holmes, J. B., & Gee, E. R. (2016). A framework for understanding game-based teaching and learning. *On the Horizon*, *24*(1), 1–16. DOI: 10.1108/OTH-11-2015-0069

Hsu, T.-C., & Lao, N. (2025). From Policy to Pedagogy–Building Human-Centered AI Literacy Across Educational Contexts. *Informatics in Education*, *24*(4), 645–651. DOI: 10.15388/infedu.2025.00

Huber, S. E., Kiili, K., Nebel, S., Ryan, R. M., Sailer, M., & Ninaus, M. (2024). Leveraging the potential of large language models in education through playful and game-based learning. *Educational Psychology Review*, *36*(1), 25. DOI: 10.1007/s10648-024-09868-z

Jiang, X., Wang, R., Hoang, T., Ranaweera, C., Dong, C., & Myers, T. (2025). Ai-powered gamified scaffolding: Transforming learning in virtual learning environment. *Electronics (Basel)*, *14*(13), 2732. DOI: 10.3390/electronics14132732

Junruang, C., & Kanjug, I. (2025). The Relationship between Computational and Creative Thinking in Preschool Children: An Application through Gamification and Artificial Intelligence-supported Constructivist Personalized Learning Environment. *Educational Process: International Journal*, *17*, e2025337.

Kassenkhan, A. M., Moldagulova, A. N., & Serbin, V. V. (2025). Gamification and Artificial Intelligence in Education: A Review of Innovative Approaches to Fostering Critical Thinking. *IEEE Access : Practical Innovations, Open Solutions*, *13*, 98699–98728. DOI: 10.1109/ACCESS.2025.3576147

Leitner, M., Greenwald, E., Wang, N., Montgomery, R., & Merchant, C. (2023). Designing game-based learning for high school artificial intelligence education. *International Journal of Artificial Intelligence in Education*, *33*(2), 384–398. DOI: 10.1007/s40593-022-00327-w

Lester, J. C., Ha, E. Y., Lee, S. Y., Mott, B. W., Rowe, J. P., & Sabourin, J. L. (2013). Serious games get smart: Intelligent game-based learning environments. *AI Magazine*, *34*(4), 31–45. DOI: 10.1609/aimag.v34i4.2488

Lester, J. C., Spires, H. A., Nietfeld, J. L., Minogue, J., Mott, B. W., & Lobene, E. V. (2014). Designing game-based learning environments for elementary science education: A narrative-centered learning perspective. *Information Sciences*, *264*, 4–18. DOI: 10.1016/j.ins.2013.09.005

Li, J., Bai, J., Zhu, S., & Yang, H. H. (2024). Game-based assessment of students' digital literacy using evidence-centered game design. *Electronics (Basel)*, *13*(2), 385. DOI: 10.3390/electronics13020385

Lin, X., & Tan, H. (2025). A Systematic Review of Generative AI in K–12: Mapping Goals, Activities, Roles, and Outcomes via the 3P Model. *Systems*, *13*(10), 840. DOI: 10.3390/systems13100840

Lin, Z., Dai, Y., & Ng, O.-L. (2025). Constructionism in K-12 AI Literacy Education: A Systematic Review of Pedagogical Designs, Student Outcomes, and Learning Mechanisms. *Journal of Educational Computing Research*, *63*(7-8), 1748–1781. DOI: 10.1177/07356331251360442

Liu, L. (2025). Impact of AI gamification on EFL learning outcomes and nonlinear dynamic motivation: Comparing adaptive learning paths, conversational agents, and storytelling. *Education and Information Technologies*, *30*(8), 11299–11338. DOI: 10.1007/s10639-024-13296-5

Mirmotahari, O., Grun, H. N., & Berg, Y. (2025). Gamification as a transferable pedagogical innovation for technology education: developing 21st-century skills through collaborative game-based learning. Frontiers in Education, Nolan, J., & McBride, M. (2014). Beyond gamification: reconceptualizing game-based learning in early childhood environments. *Information Communication and Society*, *17*(5), 594–608.

Mohammadi, M. (2024). Language teachers' assessment literacy in AI-aided adaptive learning environments. *Journal of Research in Applied Linguistics*, *15*(2), 73–88.

Neville, D. O., Shelton, B. E., & McInnis, B. (2009). Cybertext redux: Using digital game-based learning to teach L2 vocabulary, reading, and culture. *Computer Assisted Language Learning*, *22*(5), 409–424. DOI: 10.1080/09588220903345168

Palmquist, A., Sigurdardottir, H. D. I., & Myhre, H. (2025). Exploring interfaces and implications for integrating social-emotional competencies into AI literacy for education: A narrative review. *Journal of Computers in Education*, •••, 1–37.

Pavloff-Pelkonen, E., Hakkarainen, K., & Korhonen, T. (2025). Educational design and implementation of game literacy in a multiliteracy learning environment. *Journal of Research on Technology in Education*, •••, 1–19. DOI: 10.1080/15391523.2025.2487284

Romero, M. (2025). From Consumption to Co-Creation: A Systematic Review of Six Levels of AI-Enhanced Creative Engagement in Education. *Multimodal Technologies and Interaction*, *9*(10), 110. DOI: 10.3390/mti9100110

Song, Y., Weisberg, L. R., Zhang, S., Tian, X., Boyer, K. E., & Israel, M. (2024). A framework for inclusive AI learning design for diverse learners. *Computers and Education: Artificial Intelligence*, *6*, 100212. DOI: 10.1016/j.caeai.2024.100212

Tsai, S.-K., Chuang, T.-Y., & Lin, Z.-J. (2025). Enhancing environmental literacy through digital game-based learning: A technology-integrated attitude change approach. *Sustainability (Basel)*, *17*(16), 7416. DOI: 10.3390/su17167416

Wu, D., Chen, M., Chen, X., & Liu, X. (2024). Analyzing K-12 AI education: A large language model study of classroom instruction on learning theories, pedagogy, tools, and AI literacy. *Computers and Education: Artificial Intelligence*, *7*, 100295. DOI: 10.1016/j.caeai.2024.100295

Xiao, Y., Li, D., & Guo, K. (2025). Generative AI-powered non-player characters in digital storyline-based learning: An innovative approach to EFL writing. *Innovation in Language Learning and Teaching*, •••, 1–15. DOI: 10.1080/17501229.2025.2545397

Zão, H. (2025). AI and Marketing: Bridging the Gap Through a Game-based Tool Among Higher Education Students. *Comunicar*. Babu, M. S. (2025). AI-Driven Educational Assessments: Navigating the Intersection of Innovation, Equity, and Ethical Concerns for Future Learning. *Journal of Cultural Analysis and Social Change*, 1368–1382. Bharathi, G., Chandra, I., Sanagana, D. P. R., Tummalachervu, C. K., Rao, V. S., & Neelima, S. (2024). AI-driven adaptive learning for enhancing business intelligence simulation games. *Entertainment Computing*, *50*, 100699. Bhuvaneswari, G., & Kumar, T. P. (2025). The game of language learning and rewiring biocognitive receptors. *MethodsX*, *14*, 103143.

Chapter 5
Pre-Service Teachers as Game Designers for Children With Dyslexia:
Game-Based Learning Enhanced With Artificial Intelligence

Paula Rodríguez-Rivera
http://orcid.org/0000-0002-0415-4125
Universidad de las Illes Balears, Spain

Ana Manzano León
http://orcid.org/0000-0001-6966-0355
University of Almería, Spain

José M. Rodríguez-Ferrer
Universidad de Burgos, Spain

ABSTRACT

This chapter examines an educational intervention in initial teacher education that integrates Game-Based Learning, Service-Learning, and generative artificial intelligence to support the design of educational games for learners with dyslexia. Pre-service teachers worked in teams to develop adaptive digital game prototypes for a community partner, using AI tools to generate variants, multimodal supports, and accessible resources under pedagogical supervision. Prototype quality was assessed with an analytic rubric aligned with inclusive design and Universal Design for Learning, and instructors' perspectives were collected through semi-structured interviews. Findings indicate that adopting a designer role strengthened situated professional learning, inclusive decision-making, and digital pedagogical competence, while also highlighting the need for ethical guidance and critical AI literacy. Overall, the intervention increased readiness for inclusive practice in diverse contexts.

DOI: 10.4018/979-8-3373-7472-7.ch005

INTRODUCTION

Specific learning difficulties require innovative, personalized, and motivating didactic responses that help students achieve the proposed educational objectives (Clark et al., 2016; Qi & Zhonggen, 2022). Game-based learning (GBL) emerges as a strategy that can transform educational interventions into meaningful experiences adaptable to diverse student profiles (Clark et al., 2016; Connolly et al., 2012; Plass et al., 2015).

Their real potential, however, is maximized when future teachers assume the role of designers of playful experiences with solid curricular foundations and accessibility criteria (Maxim & Arnedo-Moreno, 2025; Othman et al., 2023; Viudes-Carbonell et al., 2021; Žilak & Car, 2025). Achieving this requires an approach that connects pedagogical foundations with current technological possibilities, without treating them as separate dimensions of teacher training. This research works across three lines that define its scope: playful strategies in higher education, service-learning (SL) as a structuring methodology, and the deliberate use of generative artificial intelligence in learning contexts oriented toward diversity (Aramburuzabala & Cerrillo, 2023; Brandl & Schrader, 2024; Moon et al., 2025; Wan et al., 2025).

In this chapter, the connection between game-based learning, service-learning, and generative AI is situated in literacy learning. Dyslexia affects children's access to written language, so the design of game-based resources for this population requires attention to reading demands, representation, feedback, and task structure. Generative AI can support this work by helping pre-service teachers produce and adapt materials at different levels of reading complexity, provided that final decisions remain pedagogically justified and reviewed by the teacher (Gooch et al., 2016). In this context, designing games becomes a way to learn to make literacy-oriented decisions under real-world conditions of inclusion and accessibility.

Game-based learning and playful strategies in teacher education

In higher education, playful strategies are didactic approaches that intentionally incorporate game elements to achieve curriculum objectives. Dynamics, rules, challenges, and narratives serve as mediators of learning (Kapp, 2012), and under this shared logic, GBL, gamification, educational simulations, and other designs that incorporate immersive scenarios are grouped. What they have in common is a capacity to promote academic engagement, motivation, and meaningful learning, one that tends to sharpen when these designs are articulated with emerging technologies and specific training needs (Alnuaim et al., 2024; Dichev & Dicheva, 2017; Lauricella & Edmunds, 2022; Plass et al., 2015). These approaches are grounded in constructivist understandings of learning as an active process shaped by interaction with the environment, with others, and with cognitive activity itself (Richardson, 1997). In well-designed playful experiences, students face real problems, make decisions with verifiable consequences, and receive immediate feedback, configuring iterative cycles of action and reflection that, when sustained over time, favor critical thinking processes and transfer to situations linked to professional practice (Baldrich et al., 2024; Jiang & Shangguan, 2022; Panadero, 2017; Sailer et al., 2017).

These perspectives do not operate in the same way, and this distinction is relevant for understanding their pedagogical scope (Qi & Zhonggen, 2022). Game-based learning uses digital or analog games with explicit educational goals, in which mechanics structure instructional design and progress is linked to expected learning outcomes (Plass et al., 2015). Gamification incorporates game elements (e.g., narrative, competition, points, badges, levels, or rankings) into non-play activities and is most effective when it is geared towards measurable objectives and avoids "*pointsification*" (Dichev & Dicheva, 2017). Educational simulations place students inside realistic or semi-realistic versions of professional practice, where the stakes are low enough to allow for error. Still, the conditions are close enough to matter (Chernikova et al., 2020). The evidence points in a relatively consistent direction: effects tend to be positive at the cognitive, motivational, and socio-formative levels, though how pronounced they are depends on the type of intervention, the quality of the design, how well it fits into the curriculum, and the disciplinary context in which it's applied (Chernikova et al., 2020; Qi & Zhonggen, 2022). The relationship between instructional alignment and the magnitude of effect is a key factor in learning: benefits increase when there is a clear correspondence among mechanics, activities, and evaluation; when this correspondence weakens, the effects diminish (Clark et al., 2016). In GBL, results tend to be more robust when games are integrated as a structural component of the curriculum and are accompanied by teacher support, including guidance, formative feedback, and transfer-oriented reflection spaces (Vlachopoulos & Makri, 2017).

In terms of design, students' decision-making margin is associated with greater cognitive involvement and persistence in the face of challenge; actively exploring, making decisions with consequences, and monitoring progress reinforce commitment to the task (Adipat et al., 2021). A PRISMA review in higher education identifies recurring benefits (critical thinking, problem-solving, applied creativity, and greater depth of knowledge), along with implementation challenges: instructional design time, specific teacher training, and the need to sustain alignment between objectives, mechanics, and expected outcomes (Khoo et al., 2025). Research on gamification offers a qualified picture of its effects. Sailer and Homner's (2020) meta-analysis found small but significant positive effects on cognitive, motivational, and behavioral learning outcomes, although these effects were not equally stable across methodological conditions. Motivational and behavioral outcomes, in particular, appeared less consistent in studies with stricter designs, which suggests treating gamification as an effective strategy is not warranted, regardless of how it is planned and implemented. Zainuddin et al. (2020) reached a similar conclusion from a systematic review of empirical studies: gamification was associated with learner engagement, motivation, academic achievement, and social connectivity, but its educational value depended on the theoretical grounding of the intervention, the methodological approach adopted, the mechanics selected, and the learning outcomes assessed. Pelizzari and Garzoni (2024) also stress this point, noting that gamified practices are more effective when playful elements are connected to clear educational objectives. In addition, evidence suggests that gamification can directly affect commitment and disciplinary knowledge. At the same time, satisfaction is indirectly influenced by these gains, limiting the value of superficial incentives when there is no substantive learning (Murillo-Zamorano et al., 2023).

Empirical studies show that playful approaches influence several dimensions of the university experience (Connolly et al., 2012). In the motivational and affective domains, increases in interest, enjoyment, and perceptions of a participatory climate are reported when the experience combines calibrated challenges, immediate feedback, and collaborative components (Rodríguez-Ferrer et al., 2023a). In serious games, improvements have been observed over traditional methodologies, with more pronounced effects when students participate in co-designing mechanics and narratives, suggesting added value in the appropriation of the didactic device (Rodriguez-Calzada et al., 2024). Convergent results have been reported in serious games, educational escape rooms, and simulations, where engagement and satisfaction are associated with meaningful tasks, difficulty adjusted to the level of competence, and narratives that contextualize the application of the content (Manzano-León et al., 2021; Sáiz-Manzanares et al., 2020; Sánchez-Ruiz et al., 2022).

At the cognitive level, the effects depend on the coherence among the pedagogical foundation, design decisions, and evaluation, since deep learning and procedural skill acquisition require more than simply adding playful elements to a task (Akour et al., 2020). Mao et al. (2022), in a meta-analysis that synthesized 21 effect sizes from 20 empirical studies involving 1,947 participants, reached a similar conclusion, finding a significant positive effect of game-based learning on students' critical thinking. The heterogeneity reported across studies relates this effect to the characteristics of the intervention, the educational context, the type of game used, and the alignment among mechanics, disciplinary content, and evaluation criteria. In software engineering, an educational escape room outperformed an expository masterclass in performance, satisfaction, and retention, supporting the usefulness of designs with explicit disciplinary integration (Gordillo & López-Fernández, 2024). Evidence from Veldkamp et al. (2020) also links sustainable outcomes to the correspondence between disciplinary objectives, game structure, and specific mechanics. In the health sciences, a systematic review reported escape-room-associated improvements in clinical decision-making, critical thinking, and problem-solving, as well as benefits in motivation, retention, and self-perception of competence (Köse et al., 2025). Socio-formative gains relevant to professional performance are also reported when the design incorporates interdependence and cooperative roles, particularly in communication, coordination, perspective negotiation, and shared decision-making (Maraza-Quispe et al., 2024). Relationships between self-regulation, technological acceptance, and performance have also been observed in play-mediated learning contexts, with academic self-efficacy acting as a key explanatory variable (Lin et al., 2024). In initial teacher training, these strategies take on particular relevance: they require designing, critically analyzing, and integrating them into broader didactic sequences (Hu & Sperling, 2022). Evidence indicates that theoretical exposure is often insufficient for sustained change; active participation in design, adaptation, or facilitation tasks is associated with a greater perception of competence for curricular integration and with more realistic conceptual frameworks on conditions of effectiveness and pedagogical limits (Kaimara et al., 2022; Rüth et al., 2022). Brief interventions can increase the willingness to use playful strategies and foster a continuous-learning attitude, especially when they incorporate guided reflection and critical review of the curricular fit (Belda-Medina & Calvo-Ferrer, 2022; Hernández & Ramírez, 2024; Hu & Sperling, 2022). This trend is accompanied by a sustained growth of publications on gamification and game-based learning in teacher education (Islam et al., 2025). An emerging line integrates ethical and inclusive objectives into the analysis and design, recognizing that pedagogical responsibility is grounded in educational justice and coexistence (Manzano-León et al., 2024). When games place students in scenarios of inequality or discrimination and are accompanied by a final discussion, they can activate perspective-taking and critical reflection, with implications for professional dilemmas and for teaching ethical dispositions.

Nevertheless, the literature still shows limitations in articulating these methodologies in relation to digital resources and AI-based support. Many studios rely on existing games or on designs without explicit AI assistance; therefore, their contribution to the design, personalized adaptation, and continuous improvement of playful strategies created by pre-service teachers has received less study (Gómez Niño et al., 2025). Recent research describes a transition scenario in which generative AI can assist with ideation, challenge variation, and narrative construction, with human verification and adherence to ethical criteria, especially in programs oriented to the design of educational games (Moon et al., 2025). The use of AI to evaluate games has revived debates over reliability, the limits of automation, and the need for AI literacy to make informed educational decisions (Tinterri et al., 2024). Teacher education, then, faces a dual demand: designing and implementing playful strategies that hold up to serious curricular scrutiny, while developing enough AI literacy to use personalization as a genuine pedagogical tool without outsourcing the judgments that matter most, those around ethics, equity, and learning intent. Both sit in conversation with broader questions about university innovation and the role AI is beginning to play in creating, assessing, and refining play-based experiences (Chergarova et al., 2024).

Service-learning and educational game design in teacher education

Service-learning (SL) is built on a demanding premise: that academic training and social engagement can happen in the same act. Students work with disciplinary content while providing a real service to a community or collaborating entity, with clear objectives, contextual relevance, and a social purpose that can be assessed alongside academic learning outcomes (Aláez et al., 2022; Dapena et al., 2022). This integration distinguishes SL from external internships or volunteering that is not connected to the curriculum. The service is not intended as an add-on at the end of the course. It functions as a pedagogical resource that incorporates real conditions, external agents, and utility requirements. This necessitates justifying didactic decisions, collecting evidence, and maintaining systematic reflection on foreseen and unforeseen effects (Aramburuzabala & Cerrillo, 2023; Schultes et al., 2025).

In initial teacher training, SL acquires strategic value when linked to the design of educational games. Design is a demanding professional practice: it involves translating learning outcomes into rules and tasks, anticipating how they'll be used in authentic contexts, calibrating the progression of challenge, and defining feedback and evaluation mechanisms that stay consistent with the formative intention (Boysen et al., 2023; Palha et al., 2024). The connection between SL and game design becomes clearer if we start from something basic, that learning deepens when community experience is accompanied by a pedagogical guide that turns it into material for analysis and reflection (Ding et al., 2025; Engin, 2023; Ribeiro et al., 2021; Screpnik et al., 2024). This type of work can promote deeper learning because it requires students to confront some of the most demanding aspects of teaching: balancing motivation with cognitive demand, combining clarity with autonomy, adjusting personalization to what is feasible, and sustaining creativity without losing formative purpose (Rosenthal & Ratan, 2022). Recent literature points in a consistent direction: education students who design games oriented toward real needs show a more grounded understanding of diversity and stronger professional self-efficacy (Rodríguez-Ferrer et al., 2025). The results are usually superior to those obtained when analyzing commercial products or participating only as players (Ding & Yu, 2024; Duarte et al., 2024; Engin, 2023). That potential, however, is not automatic. SL without sustained attention to its quality conditions tends to drift toward material production, losing the formative monitoring that gives it meaning (Rodríguez-Ferrer et al., 2023b).

Curricular intentionality comes first: learning outcomes, evidence, and evaluation criteria need to be made explicit, and their relationship to design decisions can't be left implicit. Without this, the risk is that the game becomes a product disconnected from the training process it was supposed to serve (Fiuza-Asorey et al., 2022; Santos Rego et al., 2024). Closely tied to this is reciprocity with the collaborating entity, which means agreeing on the service in response to well-formulated needs and building in verifiable feedback channels. This isn't simply a procedural requirement: unilateral solutions or demands that bypass the entity's actual context tend to undermine both the social value of the service and the authenticity of the learning experience (Martín-García et al., 2021; Martín-Sánchez et al., 2024). Running alongside both is guided reflection throughout the project, the mechanism through which experience becomes professional knowledge rather than accumulated activity. Students justify decisions, identify errors, analyze unforeseen effects, and begin constructing criteria that can actually travel with them into teaching practice, none of which happens without deliberate pedagogical structuring (Martín-García et al., 2021). Evaluation, for its part, needs to operate at several levels simultaneously, covering student learning, the quality of the game as an educational resource, and the practical usefulness of the service itself. It's this multi-level accountability that keeps academic rigor and social relevance from drifting apart over the course of the project (García-Gutiérrez et al., 2024). These conditions define the formative scope of the experience: they require future teachers to justify design decisions, work with external educational agents, and understand pedagogical innovation in terms of coherence among purposes, means, and equity criteria, rather than as the novelty of the resource itself (Salvador-García et al., 2023). The inclusive dimension becomes concrete when diversity is treated as a design criterion from the outset, shaping decisions about interface, rhythm, representation, and feedback as anticipated barriers rather than afterthoughts (Othman et al., 2023; Resch & Schrittesser, 2023; Screpnik et al., 2024). This is what shifts the professional valuation of play: it's assessed by its curricular alignment, its accessibility, and its capacity to sustain genuine learning, rather than by how engaging it feels in isolation (Pistono et al., 2024; Žilak & Car, 2025). Social responsibility, explicit evaluation, and ethical reflection aren't added to the design process here; they're built into what gives the innovation its value (Compare & Albanesi, 2023; Culcasi et al., 2023).

Generative AI can be understood as a practical extension of this pedagogical orientation. Within the constrained time of a university course, it can support ideation, content generation, prototyping, and revision from feedback gathered in authentic contexts, widening the design possibilities available to trainee teachers without demanding technical mastery they do not yet have (Baig et al., 2024; Barnes et al., 2025; Giannakos et al., 2024; Memarian & Doleck, 2024; Moon et al., 2025; Wan et al., 2025). The obligation to produce something that actually serves a real community tends to raise the bar on how AI is used: it discourages uncritical automation. It pushes toward monitoring, correction, and accountability. In that sense, the service itself becomes a check on the technology, and the technology becomes something the future teacher learns to handle with criteria (Barus et al., 2025; Maddox & Trost, 2025).

Digital and methodological innovation in teacher education

The university has never been a static institution. Since its consolidation, it has reorganized itself repeatedly in response to scientific, social, and professional change (Ashwin, 2022), and the current moment is no different. Digitalization has accelerated the pace and broadened the scope of what's being asked of it, particularly as technologies capable of intervening in planning, teaching, and assessment move from the margins to the mainstream (Hashim et al., 2022). Educational innovation, then, is better understood as a continuous process of adjustment among training purposes, methodologies, evaluation, and institutional conditions, rather than as the adoption of tools or formats in isolation. What it aims to guarantee is quality, not technological currency (Ashwin, 2022; Gkrimpizi et al., 2024; Kezar et al., 2025).

Recent research shows that change is not reduced to the integration of platforms or resources, as it depends on organizational and cultural factors that shape classroom implementation (Hashim et al., 2022; Shohel et al., 2025). Systematic reviews describe recurring barriers related to leadership, infrastructure, digital competence, organizational structure, and institutional capacity to sustain change. This explains why isolated initiatives tend to remain fragmented in the absence of professional development and teacher support strategies, as well as time, recognition, and curricular coordination (Singun, 2025). The scale of the current shift is evident in the review by Ogunleye et al. (2024), who analyzed 355 studies selected from 625 Scopus-indexed records, using PRISMA guidelines and topic modeling. Their synthesis shows the rapid expansion of GenAI research in higher education, particularly in teaching and learning practices, while also identifying unresolved issues related to effective integration, assessment, ethical use, academic integrity, privacy, and institutional guidance.

These tensions become especially relevant in teacher education. In the field of initial language teacher education, Moorhouse and Kohnke (2024) interviewed 13 English language teacher educators from the four government-funded universities in Hong Kong that offer this program. The participants anticipated substantial effects of GenAI on curriculum, instruction, and assessment: future teachers would need to understand the possibilities and limits of these tools, consider their implications for language teaching and learning, use them for lesson planning, material development, and language learning activities, and rethink assessment tasks that can be easily completed with generative systems. At the same time, most participants reported insufficient confidence and competence to address these changes, underscoring the need for professional development and explicit preparation to integrate GenAI into teacher education.

The impact of these technologies depends on their connection with subject redesign, coherent assessment, and continuous improvement, especially in contexts where bureaucracy and teaching workload restrict informed experimentation (Alsharefeen, 2025). The diversification of the student body also places pressure on university innovation, as expectations of accessibility, participation, and educational justice have expanded, now requiring decisions at the level of curriculum and assessment design (de la Fuente-González et al., 2025; Moriña et al., 2025). Veytia Bucheli et al. (2024) analysed the perceptions of 235 pedagogy and education students from the Mexican public university system using a Likert-scale questionnaire with high internal consistency (Cronbach's $\alpha = .97$). The students reported favourable perceptions of digital technologies across the three UDL principles: representation, action and expression, and engagement, particularly in relation to access to information, flexible participation, and skill development in higher education. In practice, methodologies such as game-based learning or escape rooms are not justified because they are novel. They are justified if they help achieve course objectives, offer different forms of participation, facilitate feedback, and promote in-depth learning in diverse groups, with assessment aligned with learning activities and outcomes (Makri et al., 2021).

The expansion of playful methodologies and experiential design can be read as a coherent response to several of the pressures described, provided pedagogical coherence is maintained. The literature on serious games in higher education, in the context of the so-called Education 4.0, frequently associates serious games with motivation and engagement, yet underscores the need for design concepts and implementation models that avoid artifact-centric uses and reinforce verifiable learning and congruent assessment (Brandl et al., 2024). In the specific case of digital educational escape rooms, positive results have been reported as a tool for review and motivation in university contexts, with perceived improvements in interaction and academic preparation when the design is integrated into the subject and accompanied by monitoring and evaluation instruments (Maroto Sánchez, 2023). González-Yubero et al. (2023) examined the motivational dimension of an educational escape room with 135 first-year university students from the perspective of self-determination theory. Creative thinking, activation, and dominance were associated with intrinsic motivation toward knowledge, achievement, and stimulating experiences, whereas negative affect was linked to amotivation and external regulation. Broader evidence on GBL, particularly escape rooms, reports favorable effects on learning outcomes and motivational variables, with differences across studies related to design decisions, evaluation, and implementation quality (López-Pernas et al., 2024). University educational innovation gives meaning to the integration of AI, game-based learning, and other emerging tools by linking them to the training of education professionals. Their contribution depends on the institutional capacity to sustain teaching practices that combine rigor, participation, accessibility, and coherent evaluation. These practices also model for future teachers how to teach in diverse and technologically mediated classrooms, with institutional responsibility and explicit governance and accountability criteria (Oncioiu & Bularca, 2025).

Generative AI in teacher education: inclusive design, critical use, and diversity

Designing for diversity means ensuring that students with heterogeneous needs can actually participate and progress, not just in principle but in practice. Expectations around accessibility and educational justice have gained real centrality in both university and school contexts, and that shift is reshaping what teacher training needs to address (de la Fuente-González et al., 2025; Moriña et al., 2025). AI enters this picture through what it makes possible: more granular personalization, closer monitoring of learning, and the production of adjusted supports that can reduce barriers when they're integrated with clear pedagogical criteria rather than deployed as standalone solutions (Crompton & Burke, 2017; Wang et al., 2024). That potential, though, only holds if the discussion moves beyond instrumental use toward verifiable decisions about design, evaluation, and professional responsibility, particularly in classrooms that are growing more heterogeneous, not less (Bouakaz & Khalid, 2025).

Recent systematic reviews document how AI is consolidating in education, in both research volume and the diversity of applications, and describe an expanding field that includes adaptive systems and generative tools, which are increasingly present in planning and evaluation (Garzón et al., 2025; Wang et al., 2024). In school education, these reviews highlight its potential to personalize learning and track student progress through approaches linked to intelligent systems, automated assessment, and analytics, while highlighting barriers associated with teacher preparation and ethical considerations (Akgun & Greenhow, 2022; Cheah et al., 2025; Crompton & Burke, 2017; Martin et al., 2024; Tagare et al., 2025). In parallel, frameworks and revisions on AI in K–12 emphasize principles related to justice and equity, children's rights, and AI literacy, and place inclusion as a structural criterion rather than an add-on (Adams et al., 2023; Gouseti et al., 2025).

In higher education, reviews point to a growing integration of AI into adaptive and student-profiling systems and call for more robust frameworks to guide its responsible use in university teaching (Crompton & Burke, 2017; Mustafa et al., 2024). In teacher education, AI appears both as an object of study and as a mediating artifact that can support planning, reflection and design of materials, which requires the articulation of technical competence, ethical judgment and pedagogical criteria to decide what role AI should occupy in teaching practice and which decisions should remain under human professional deliberation (Hsu et al., 2024; Kılıçkaya & Kic-Drgas, 2025; Pinargote Castro et al., 2023). This requirement becomes especially relevant when working with vulnerable students or those with specific learning difficulties, where support and assessment require traceability and substantiation (Bouakaz & Khalid, 2025).

Empirical evidence with future teachers suggests that AI literacy is multidimensional and uneven across profiles and contexts. In a study of 529 trainee teachers, a deeper understanding of AI was associated with better use, greater detection capacity, greater ethical consideration, and improved creation and problem-solving. At the same time, other dimensions did not advance at the same pace, resulting in heterogeneous competence profiles (Ayanwale et al., 2024). Across different contexts, differences have been observed that are linked to the field of specialization, the availability of technological applications, and prior exposure to digital training, whereas demographic variables such as gender and class level are not associated with significant differences (Çayak, 2024; Cetin & Celen, 2025). Among experienced professionals, differences have also been observed in the critical evaluation of AI applications, with novice teachers showing an advantage over more veteran teachers, reinforcing the need for continuous training and standardized assessment criteria (Drajati et al., 2025). AI literacy, therefore, draws on digital, media, informational, and data literacy frameworks, which often overlap in educational practice (Mills, 2024; Ng et al., 2021). Almatrafi et al. (2024), after reviewing 47 articles published between 2019 and 2023, describe AI literacy as a multidimensional construct that involves recognizing AI systems, understanding how they work, using and evaluating them, creating with them, and navigating their ethical implications. In teacher training, this overlap is manifested in the fact that students tend to handle digital tools with ease but show more difficulties in explaining the operation of AI models, critically analyzing the data with which they are trained, or anticipating social and ethical implications (Dayagbil et al., 2025; Sperling et al., 2024).

In language teacher education, these tensions become especially visible because GenAI affects areas closely linked to literacy learning, including grammar, writing, feedback, lesson planning, and assessment. Chung and Jeong (2024), in a quantitative study with 134 English pre-service teachers in China, found generally favorable perceptions of the use of generative AI, particularly ChatGPT, in English language teaching. Participants valued its potential to improve teaching efficiency and support language acquisition, especially in grammar and writing. However, they also raised concerns about over-reliance on AI, critical thinking, the authenticity of AI-mediated interaction, data privacy, and academic integrity. Kerr and Kim (2025) add a practice-based perspective from a South Korean university course in which pre-service EFL teachers used generative AI to design lesson plans for middle-school English classes. In their study, GenAI was used for lesson organization, language checking, material creation, activity ideation, and topic selection, with lesson planning and language checking appearing as the most consistent uses. Across these studies, GenAI is entering language teacher education through concrete pedagogical tasks, while also requiring future teachers to evaluate the quality, accuracy, and educational fit of the outputs they produce.

Generative AI can support inclusive design by producing variants of the same resource, adjusted to different levels of competence, pacing, and support needs, and by adapting prompts, examples, and formats. Its relevance lies partly in feasibility: differentiation has long been pedagogically desirable, although difficult to sustain under ordinary teaching workloads. The possibility of generating adjusted materials more quickly may help bring curricular coherence and differentiated support closer together, provided that the outputs are reviewed and adapted through pedagogical judgment (Chiu, 2024; Kurtz et al., 2024; Tlili et al., 2024; Viberg et al., 2024). The multimodal dimension is also important. AI-assisted generation of images and visual resources can support comprehension when learners need perceptual scaffolding or alternative access routes to information, especially in tasks where visual organization is central to understanding the content (Chiu, 2024; Wan et al., 2025). In educational design projects, AI can also facilitate prototyping and iteration within the time frame of a course, enabling the production of revised versions of materials based on feedback and making the creation process more manageable (Giannakos et al., 2024; Moon et al., 2025).

This guidance aligns with the idea that the quality of resources should be assessed on accessibility and usability as central criteria, rather than on the surface appeal of the artifact (Othman et al., 2023; Screpnik et al., 2024; Žilak & Car, 2025).

Attitudes towards AI tend to be positive, although uncertainty remains about ethical use, reliability, and evaluation expectations. In higher education, students in teacher training use generative AI for ideation, drafting, and concept clarification, while maintaining a cautious stance toward academic integrity and the limits of legitimate support (Hsu et al., 2024; Johnston et al., 2024). The acceptance of AI technologies is associated with perceived usefulness, ease of use, and availability of clear guidelines, nuanced by concerns about equity in access and about the appropriate role of technology in learning (Aksoy & Kurşun, 2024; Johnston et al., 2024; Mienye et al., 2024; Sousa & Cardoso, 2025). Barrett and Pack (2023) situate these tensions within academic writing. In a survey of 68 educators and 158 university students, the researchers compared perceptions of acceptable GenAI use across six writing-process tasks: brainstorming, outlining, writing, revising, feedback, and evaluating. Acceptability was higher in the early stages of the writing process, especially during brainstorming and outlining, whereas full-text production raised clearer concerns about authorship and academic integrity. The study also reported small differences between students and educators regarding acceptable uses of GenAI, and identified classroom and institutional preparation as areas requiring clearer guidelines and teacher professional development.

The educational value of AI depends on how it is integrated into teaching practice. In classroom contexts, one recurring risk is that textual fluency may be mistaken for validity. Generative systems can produce plausible texts, although plausibility still requires verification for accuracy, relevance, and fit with the specific teaching task (Huang et al., 2025; Kasneci et al., 2023).

When used as a substitute for reasoning, they can reduce the effort of analysis and weaken the ability to justify decisions, with a cumulative risk of loss of intellectual agency if the tool becomes a default resource without contrast or traceability (Gerlich, 2025; Lo et al., 2024; Stojanov et al., 2024; Zhai et al., 2021). Added to this is the lack of transparency in the generation processes, which makes it difficult to explain why a result is obtained, what assumptions it incorporates, and what limits it presents, reinforcing the need for critical literacy aimed at evaluating content, detecting biases, contrasting with reliable sources, and documenting the production process (Khosravi et al., 2022; Ng et al., 2021).

Data management and protection become a priority in training contexts where sensitive information is handled or decisions are made that affect evaluation and performance. The literature identifies as key issues the information entered into the tools, where it is processed, the privacy guarantees in place, and the implications of its use, especially when working with students in vulnerable situations (Barus et al., 2025; Gujjula & Sanghera, 2023; Ismail, 2025). Frameworks on AI in education increasingly organize around principles of equity, transparency, and accountability, with particular attention to justice and rights in the use of educational technologies (Adams et al., 2023; Akgun & Greenhow, 2022; Gouseti et al., 2025; Tagare et al., 2025). These principles are especially relevant in contexts that attend to diversity, where personalization requires teachers to justify which supports are appropriate, what evidence supports them, and how they affect participation and learning. In these cases, AI can inform pedagogical decision-making, provided that the selection, adaptation, and evaluation of supports remain under professional responsibility (Bender et al., 2021; Kasneci et al., 2023).

The debate over authorship and academic integrity also requires precision. Regardless of whether a text or resource has been produced with the support of AI, it matters who defines the approach, selects evidence, makes conceptual decisions, and assumes responsibility for the outcome, and this principle is critical in teacher training due to its professionalizing dimension (Bozkurt, 2024; Eke, 2023; Kofinas et al., 2025). In multimodal resources, controversies over intellectual property and rights related to model training and the use of prior works are also present, reinforcing the need for clear institutional policies on attribution, licensing, and reuse limits (Bozkurt, 2024). On this point, training proposals with contact with real contexts can act as a mechanism of responsibility, because they force us to justify decisions, review effects, and respond to needs formulated by external educational agents, sustaining an accountability that hinders uncritical automation (Aramburuzabala & Cerrillo, 2023; Oncioiu & Bularca, 2025; Schultes et al., 2025). In addition, when inclusion is designed as a criterion for specific situations, the translation of equity principles into verifiable actions that affect participation and effective access to tasks is reinforced (Moriña et al., 2025; Resch & Schrittesser, 2023).

AI contributes to teacher training and attention to diversity when it supports inclusive design and responsible personalization without displacing the professional judgment it's supposed to inform (Giannakos et al., 2024; Tsirantonaki & Vlachou, 2025). That requires explicit criteria of quality, equity, and institutional responsibility, and an honest accounting of collateral effects: on pedagogical deliberation, on transparency, on data protection. Integration without that accounting tends to be neither sustainable nor genuinely inclusive (Barus et al., 2025; Ivanov et al., 2024; Lelescu et al., 2025).

This chapter is situated within the field of AI and game-based literacy learning by examining how pre-service teachers design inclusive game-based resources for children with dyslexia. In this context, literacy learning is understood as a pedagogical process that involves access to written language, comprehension, motivation, and participation. The chapter, therefore, connects game-based learning, generative AI, and inclusive education as complementary dimensions of teacher preparation for diverse learners.

METHODOLOGY

This study employs a quasi-experimental design with a single experimental group. This design is widely used in education and is considered appropriate for exploratory studies in which randomizing the sample is not possible or not ethically desirable. As this is a teaching innovation project, we selected this method to examine the proposal in a real-world setting, preserving ecological validity and instructional coherence (Gopalan et al., 2020).

The intervention was embedded in regular university coursework and linked to a service-learning experience focused on designing educational games for children with dyslexia. Introducing a control group would have compromised both the pedagogical integrity of the instructional design and the ethical commitment to equitable learning opportunities for all students involved. Single-group quasi-experimental designs are particularly suitable for innovation-oriented studies in higher education, where the primary aim is to explore processes, feasibility, and pedagogical mechanisms rather than to establish causal relationships in a strict experimental sense (Marsden & Torgerson, 2012).

Participants

The participants in this study were two university teachers and 29 undergraduate students enrolled in courses associated with the Faculties of Education Sciences at the University of Almería (Spain). The students were enrolled in a Bachelor of Primary Education program.

A non-probabilistic intentional sampling strategy was employed. Specifically, courses were selected based on their instructors' involvement in the university-funded teaching innovation project (25_26_1_24C): "*Learning by creating with AI: development of educational content by students of Education Sciences*". This selection criterion ensured that the intervention could be integrated into the regular academic curriculum while preserving its methodological consistency and alignment with the course's instructional goals.

Instruments

Two primary instruments were employed for data collection: an ad-hoc learning rubric and a semi-structured teacher interview.

First, the learning rubric was explicitly developed for this study to assess the educational games designed by the student groups. The rubric evaluated multiple dimensions aligned with the study's theoretical framework, including the transformation of the teaching role, an applied understanding of dyslexia, the pedagogical use of artificial intelligence, accessibility based on Universal Design for Learning principles, equity of access to information, inclusive motivation, and ethical considerations related to AI use (see Table 1). Rubrics are widely recognized as practical tools for assessing complex, performance-based learning outcomes, particularly in project-based and design-oriented educational contexts. According to Brookhart (2013), analytic rubrics support formative and summative assessment by making evaluation criteria explicit and facilitating consistent, transparent judgment across evaluators.

Table 1. Learning rubric elements

Item	Evaluated Dimension	1 – Insufficient	2 – Basic	3 – Adequate	4 – High
R1	Transformation of the teaching role (from consumer to pedagogical designer)	Reproduces existing resources without adaptation or pedagogical justification.	Introduces superficial changes while continuing to rely on pre-existing models.	Designs an original resource aligned with learning objectives and justified pedagogical decisions.	Designs a coherent, contextualized, and well-grounded intervention, demonstrating professional autonomy.
R2	Applied understanding of dyslexia	The design does not consider dyslexia-related cognitive characteristics or address them in an inaccurate way.	Recognizes some dyslexia-related difficulties, but support is incomplete or poorly adjusted.	Shows clear correspondence between dyslexia-related difficulties and the support incorporated.	Accurately and consistently translates dyslexia-related processes into instructional design decisions.
R3	Pedagogical use of artificial intelligence	Uses AI uncritically or automatically, without supervision or pedagogical adaptation.	Uses AI functionally, with limited review or weak instructional justification.	Uses AI in a supervised and reviewed manner, adapting outputs to learning objectives.	Integrates AI strategically and reflectively to support pedagogical design and personalization.
R4	Accessibility by educational design (UDL)	Displays evident barriers to access, such as visual overload or reliance on written text.	Incorporates some accessibility alternatives in a limited or unsystematic way.	Offers multiple means of representation and interaction, reducing learning barriers.	Systematically anticipates barriers and provides a fully accessible learning environment.
R5	Equity and access to information	Access to information relies exclusively on written text or a single modality.	Partially reduces access barriers while maintaining relevant limitations.	Provides clear alternatives for accessing information for diverse learner profiles.	Ensures equitable, multimodal access to information while minimizing error penalties.

continued on following page

Table 1. Continued

Item	Evaluated Dimension	1 – Insufficient	2 – Basic	3 – Adequate	4 – High
R6	Inclusive motivation and ludic value	The proposal is weakly motivating or includes potentially exclusionary dynamics.	Includes ludic elements with limited or inconsistent motivational impact.	Integrates narratives and calibrated challenges that foster learner engagement.	Generates high engagement, emotional safety, and enjoyment from an inclusive perspective.
R7	Ethical consideration and critical AI literacy	No ethical reflection on AI use or authorship is evident.	Superficially acknowledges ethical risks but does not integrate them into the design.	Demonstrates responsible and supervised AI use, addressing authorship and reliability.	Explicitly integrates critical and ethical reflection on AI into design and justification.

Second, a semi-structured interview (Braun & Clarke, 2006) was conducted with the two participating teachers. The interview was selected to capture their reflections on the innovative project, perceived student learning, challenges encountered during the practice, and ethical considerations regarding the use of AI in their classes.

Procedure

The project took place over one academic semester and was designed as an educational intervention integrated into two subjects of the Primary Education Degree, both focused on special education and language, speech, and hearing disorders. The practice was structured around the design of IA-mediated educational games, framed within a service-learning methodology, and carried out in collaboration with a local association that supports children with dyslexia. In this way, the students' academic work was linked to a real educational need of their context.

A total of seven groups of students, each comprising between four and seven members, participated and developed their practical work on dyslexia. The proposal was structured into five phases that progressively guided the learning and practical application process.

In the first phase, students received a series of learning profiles that had been previously agreed upon with the collaborating association. These profiles described anonymous cases of students with dyslexia, incorporating their specific learning difficulties, their potentialities, and learning preferences, and contextual and emotional information relevant to educational design. For example, one of the profiles described David (fictitious name), a 12-year-old student who had repeated the fifth year of primary school, with a special interest in mathematics but with significant difficulties in reading and writing, which constituted the core literacy barriers the game design had to address. Despite this, he felt integrated into his class group and, with the appropriate support and adaptations, was able to achieve the expected curriculum objectives. These types of profiles served as a standard reference for the groups to identify learning barriers and adjust the mechanics, narratives, and supports of their educational games.

Before beginning the collaborative design work, one to three practical sessions (each lasting 2 hours) were devoted to analyzing and exploring different types of games and playful dynamics with educational potential. In these initial sessions, students familiarised themselves with the principles of game-based learning, reflected on its educational possibilities, and analyzed how games can be designed or used for academic and social purposes. Special emphasis was placed on identifying game mechanics, narrative structures, and forms of interaction that could be adapted to inclusive educational contexts (Manzano-León, 2025; Plass et al., 2015).

In a second phase, a two-hour training workshop was conducted by faculty from another university with experience in applying artificial intelligence to education. This workshop presented various AI tools (Genially, Canvas, Suno, ChatGPT, Gemini, and Leonardo.ai). The teacher instructed the students to create various learning resources using the tools and explicitly addressed the ethical implications of their use, including authorship, bias, the reliability of results, and the responsible integration of these technologies into educational contexts. This phase aimed to develop both technical skills and critical literacy in AI, understood as a professional skill relevant to future teaching practice (Ng et al., 2021).

In a third phase, the students had three to four face-to-face sessions (each lasting 2 hours) for independent and collaborative work in the classroom. During this period, the groups designed and developed their educational game prototypes, integrating theoretical knowledge about dyslexia, principles of Universal Design for Learning, and AI-supported resources.

In the next phase, each group presented its final project to the rest of the class, explaining the educational and game decisions made. Subsequently, they implemented the games for the dyslexia association's children during a two-hour game workshop. This phase constituted the core of the service-learning, as it allowed pre-grade students to compare their proposals with real students and observe aspects such as accessibility, motivation, and participant engagement (Lavery et al., 2018).

Finally, each group submitted a written report detailing the process. This document included a theoretical framework on dyslexia, a description of the designed educational game, and a critical reflection on the design process and implementation experience.

Examples of the educational games developed by the student groups are presented in Figure 1.

Figure 1. Sample of students projects

RESULTS

The results of the learning rubrics and the semi-structured interviews highlighted various aspects to consider, including both explicitly positive elements and limiting aspects or concerns regarding their use. The analysis was conducted using an inductive thematic approach. The following categories were identified and are presented below.

Figure 2. Diagram of relationships among qualitative categories

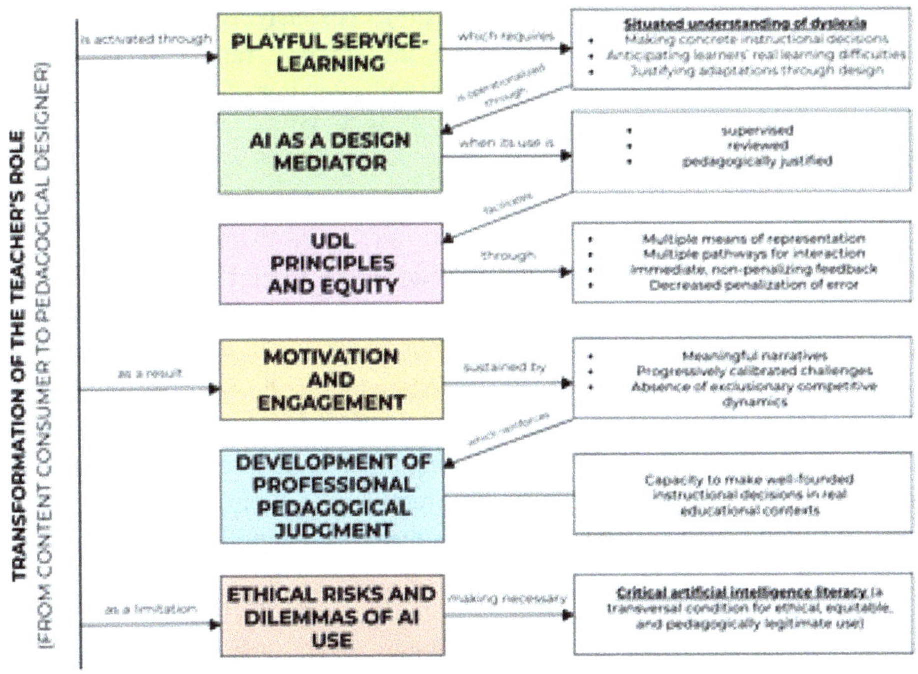

Table 2. Student scores in the learning rubric

Item	G1	G2	G3	G4	G5	G6	G7	Mean
R1	4	4	4	4	4	3	4	3.86
R2	4	4	4	3	4	3	4	3.71
R3	4	3	4	3	4	3	4	3.57
R4	4	4	4	4	4	4	4	4.00
R5	4	4	4	4	4	4	4	4.00
R6	4	4	4	4	4	4	4	4.00
R7	3	3	4	3	3	3	4	3.29

Transformation of the pre-service teacher's role through teaching innovation: from consumer to pedagogical designer

From the instructors' perspective, this process fostered a deeper understanding of what it means to design for diversity, as "when theory is taught, it seems to be just about memorizing the DSM-V, but through this practical approach, they are already working directly for the children and have to create a game that is fun while genuinely addressing their needs, adaptations, and characteristics... and that is important for them to understand the level of responsibility they will have in their future professional practice" [Interview 2]. This finding aligns directly with the Universal Design for Learning (UDL) framework, in which design is conceived as a systematic anticipation of barriers rather than a subsequent adaptation.

The rubric corroborated this perception, showing that most of the games analyzed exhibited an explicit alignment between learning objectives, game mechanics, and specific supports, reinforcing the idea that adopting the role of designer promotes a situated and professional understanding of educational practice.

Artificial intelligence as a mediating element of inclusive design and personalization

Another central category concerned the role attributed to generative artificial intelligence as a mediating tool. In the interviews, both instructors highlighted that AI accelerated ideation, enabled the generation of multiple duplicate content versions, and facilitated the exploration of narrative, visual, and auditory alternatives. This was particularly relevant for addressing the heterogeneity of learners with dyslexia. For instance, the teachers noted that "there were tools I did not know before the training [*Suno* and *Leonardo.Ai*], and I found them remarkably interesting for creating interactive content. This is highly relevant for students with disabilities, so offering these resources to our undergraduate students so that they become familiar with them and can later integrate them meaningfully into their teaching practice is valuable" [Interview 1].

Faculty members stressed that students were required to review, adapt, and justify the generated content, particularly regarding linguistic simplification, clarity of instructions, and the appropriateness of visual and auditory stimuli. "Several projects were reviewed multiple times because they were too complex or included too many distracting elements. We also need to ensure that not all resources are integrated at once, as this can be overwhelming for students with disabilities. Therefore, we worked in class on how to use digital resources coherently and in ways that are useful for the entire class" [Interview 1].

This reflective use aligns with UDL principles, particularly the provision of multiple means of representation and expression, which AI supports by generating diverse formats. According to the rubric, this category was reflected in high scores on items related to personalization and accessibility, especially in games that offer graduated levels of difficulty, complementary auditory support, and interaction options not exclusively dependent on reading.

Situated understanding of dyslexia and pedagogical translation in game design.

The thematic analysis showed that the experience contributed to a more situated and applied understanding of dyslexia, beyond purely theoretical definitions. Faculty members indicated that game design required students to explore in depth concepts such as phonological awareness, working memory, and visual processing, and to translate these into concrete design decisions, such as the use of legible fonts, control of visual load, and the incorporation of immediate, non-penalizing feedback. Instructors perceived this as an indicator of meaningful learning. In their words, "when students must decide whether an instruction is too long or whether an item stimulus helps or distracts, they begin to understand how a child with dyslexia truly learns. Just as we explain executive functions in the theoretical component, having to design something related to them allows students to understand better the differences between these functions and how to support them across different learning situations." [Interview 2].

The rubric confirmed this trend, showing that all evaluated games received adequate scores for the correspondence between dyslexia-related difficulties and the supports incorporated, thereby reinforcing the validity of this category through triangulation.

Motivation, engagement, and ludic value from an inclusive perspective

A fourth emergent category was the relationship between motivation and inclusive design. Faculty members highlighted that students valued the activity's ludic component and the service-learning thread underlying it. "For our undergraduate students, becoming familiar with different games before creating their own was very motivating. They really enjoyed those sessions. Later, the idea of gamification and having the children from the association 'visit continents' was entirely their idea. They designed it themselves and created all the materials, and I think that reinforced their belief that they can design real, motivating, and enjoyable educational interventions. The moment of implementing it with the association was beautiful; the children and the mothers enjoyed it immensely. For that reason alone, I would repeat the experience without hesitation" [Interview 2].

The analysis showed that the games tended to incorporate simple narratives, progressive challenges, and positive feedback, while avoiding exclusionary competitive dynamics. This orientation aligns with an inclusive conception of game-based learning, in which motivation is articulated through emotional safety and perceived competence, which are key elements for equitable access to information and learning.

Equity, accessibility, and the elimination of learning barriers

Equity and accessibility were identified as transversal categories in the analysis. For faculty members, ensuring that pre-service teachers learn to design accessible, coherent, and inclusive activities in these courses is central to the curriculum. For this reason, the interviews repeatedly highlighted the value of collaborating with an external association, as students worked with real children during the final phase of the project. This experience "allowed them to understand that accessibility is necessary and is achieved when motivating educational designs are created for everyone, where all learners can participate" [Interview 1]. This perspective aligns with the Universal Design for Learning (UDL) framework, shifting the focus from "adapting to the learner" to designing flexible, inclusive educational environments from the outset.

Technology, and AI tools in particular, lowered the threshold for producing multimedia materials: students could develop visual and audiovisual content without prior training in illustration or video production. This multimodal approach supported the integration of visual, auditory, and kinesthetic channels, thereby reducing reliance on written text. The evaluation rubric confirmed that the games provided genuine alternatives for accessing content through visual and auditory resources.

Ethical tensions, limitations, and the need for critical AI literacy

The qualitative results also highlighted several challenges and limitations associated with the use of artificial intelligence. Both instructors indicated that, despite the project being positive for their students' professional development, they still have concerns about the potential misuse of AI, particularly regarding inappropriate practices involving generative writing tools and the possible risks to the educational validity of the materials. These concerns translated into an explicit need to train students in critical AI literacy, understood as part of their professional competence. "One interesting aspect of this practice is that it cannot be done entirely with ChatGPT. When we assign written coursework to other courses, it is no longer possible to be 100% certain that the students completed it themselves. Anti-plagiarism tools also fail in this respect, and students are aware of this, which leads some less committed groups to use AI uncritically. However, here they had to create the game no matter what, which gives instructors some reassurance that "competencies are actually being developed" [Interview 1]. "I think all my groups did an excellent job, but we cannot ignore that AI can still be used to ask it to design everything, and that will always be a risk. That is why we need recurrent meetings and perhaps to give more weight to the resource itself and its presentation than to the final report. This is something we still need to resolve as teachers" [Interview 2].

DISCUSSION

Designing educational games for children with dyslexia within a service-learning framework placed pre-service teachers in a role centered on pedagogical decision-making and on the development of a teaching resource for a specific group of learners. The task required them to translate inclusive principles into concrete decisions about representation, interaction, rhythm, feedback, and assessment. In this experience, educational value was linked to the coherence achieved between curricular intention, accessibility, and playability (Brookhart, 2013; Moriña et al., 2025; Plass et al., 2015; Qi & Zhonggen, 2022). In initial teacher training, the movement from consumer to pedagogical designer brings students closer to the situated decisions that define professional practice: justifying didactic choices, anticipating barriers to access, responding to real educational needs, and assuming responsibility for the effects of the resource created (Maxim & Arnedo-Moreno, 2025; Resch & Schrittesser, 2023). Studies on "learning by designing" educational games show that creating games requires pre-service teachers to integrate pedagogical content, inclusion criteria, and disciplinary knowledge more deeply than when they simply implement or analyze commercial games (Ding & Yu, 2024; Engin, 2023).

The combination of game-based learning and service-learning also provides an ethical and social dimension that reconfigures the meaning of playful design in teacher training. Contact with real contexts and specific recipients shifts the focus from motivation or engagement to educational utility, accessibility, and equity, which are central elements of the inclusive approach (Aramburuzabala & Cerrillo, 2023; Compare & Albanesi, 2023). Within this logic, play ceases to be an isolated motivational resource and becomes an assessable pedagogical material, whose quality is judged by its ability to reduce barriers and sustain significant learning in diverse profiles (Othman et al., 2023; Screpnik et al., 2024).

The findings help to clarify the role that generative AI can play in teacher training. Rather than replacing pedagogical design, AI supported specific moments of the process: ideation, prototyping, revision of materials, generation of alternatives, adaptation of instructions, and creation of visual resources. Its value, therefore, depended on how the outputs were reviewed, selected, and adjusted to the learning needs of children with dyslexia. The same point appears in studies that describe AI as a tool for enhancing differentiation and personalization, provided its use remains pedagogically supervised and guided by explicit quality criteria (Giannakos et al., 2024; Moon et al., 2025). That value depended, in practice, on students' review, selection, and justification of the generated products, with professional judgment maintained as the central axis of the process (Kasneci et al., 2023; Ng et al., 2021).

The experience also shows that AI literacy cannot be reduced to knowing how to use generative tools. In this case, students had to evaluate whether the generated materials were accessible, reliable, understandable, and appropriate for children with dyslexia, which made ethical and critical AI literacy part of the design process itself. This aligns with previous studies showing that AI literacy is strengthened when students must deliberate pedagogically, assume responsibility for the materials produced, and justify decisions that affect real teaching situations (Adams et al., 2023; Ayanwale et al., 2024; Bouakaz & Khalid, 2025; Sperling et al., 2024).

The findings suggest that Universal Design for Learning principles gained pedagogical value when operationalized as explicit, assessable design criteria. In the students' work, diversity had to be translated into decisions about representation, interaction, expression, rhythm, and feedback, rather than remaining a general inclusive statement. Earlier reviews have underlined the need for specific teacher training to implement UDL effectively in higher education (Moriña et al., 2025), and this experience points in the same direction. The rubric supported this process by making accessibility, equity, inclusive motivation, and educational value visible during game design, thereby serving as a formative guide before becoming an assessment instrument (Brookhart, 2013). The collaborative nature of the task also contributed to this process, as the groups had to negotiate mechanics, supports, narratives, and accessibility criteria.

Previous studies have indicated that the collaborative design of educational games favors pedagogical reflection and the meaningful integration of theoretical frameworks, particularly when accompanied by precise assessment instruments and spaces for guided discussion (Boysen et al., 2023; Kaimara et al., 2022).

Among the main limitations of the study is the inability to establish firm causal relationships, given that it is a descriptive, mixed-methods design without a comparison group or pre-test and post-test measurements (Marsden & Torgerson, 2012). Likewise, the collection of evidence was concentrated in a limited period and focused on prototypes and the design process, without a prolonged implementation to assess the stability of the game's performance under continuous use. On the other hand, although the rubric made it possible to systematize the evaluation of dimensions linked to accessibility, playability, personalization, and pedagogical use of AI, external learning indicators of the target students were not incorporated, nor was there a longitudinal monitoring that would allow estimating the sustainability of the impact (Brookhart, 2013).

This limits a fine-grained analysis of AI's specific role in the final products and prevents a precise assessment of the extent to which technological support was accompanied by critical literacy and explicit ethical criteria throughout the process (Kasneci et al., 2023; Ng et al., 2021).

The study suggests that placing pre-service teachers in the role of game designers can support a richer understanding of inclusive educational practice when the task is linked to real needs, explicit assessment criteria, and guided reflection (Aramburuzabala & Cerrillo, 2023; Brookhart, 2013). In this experience, the combination of game-based learning and service-learning was especially valuable because it required students to test the educational usefulness of their designs beyond the university classroom, connecting playful creation with community needs and inclusive criteria (Plass et al., 2015; Qi & Zhonggen, 2022). Generative AI expanded the possibilities for prototyping and adapting materials. However, its educational value depended on supervision, review, and human pedagogical judgment, especially in contexts where equity and accessibility are central criteria (Giannakos et al., 2024; Ng et al., 2021). Future studies should document AI use more systematically, include external indicators from the recipient children, and examine whether the resources maintain their accessibility and pedagogical value in sustained implementation contexts.

REFERENCES

Adams, C., Pente, P., Lemermeyer, G., & Rockwell, G. (2023). Ethical principles for artificial intelligence in K–12 education. *Computers and Education: Artificial Intelligence*, *4*, 100131. DOI: 10.1016/j.caeai.2023.100131

Adipat, S., Laksana, K., Busayanon, K., Asawasowan, S., & Adipat, B. (2021). Engaging students in the learning process with game-based learning: The fundamental concepts. *International Journal of Technology in Education*, *4*(3), 542–552. DOI: 10.46328/ijte.169

Akgun, S., & Greenhow, C. (2022). Artificial intelligence in education: Addressing ethical challenges in K-12 settings. *AI and Ethics*, *2*(3), 431–440. DOI: 10.1007/s43681-021-00096-7 PMID: 34790956

Akour, M., Alsghaier, H., & Aldiabat, S. (2020). Game-based learning approach to improve self-motivated students' self-learning. *International Journal of Technology Enhanced Learning*, *12*(2), 146–161. DOI: 10.1504/IJTEL.2020.106283

Aksoy, N., & Kurşun, E. (2024). Behind the scenes: A critical perspective on GenAI and open educational practices. *Open Praxis*, *16*(3), 457–470. Advance online publication. DOI: 10.55982/openpraxis.16.3.674

Aláez, M., Díaz-Iso, A., Eizaguirre, A., García-Feijoo, M., & Roldán, M. (2022). Bridging generation gaps through service-learning in higher education: A systematic review. *Frontiers in Education*, *7*, 841482. DOI: 10.3389/feduc.2022.841482

Almatrafi, O., Johri, A., & Lee, H. (2024). A systematic review of AI literacy conceptualization, constructs, and implementation and assessment efforts (2019–2023). *Computers and Education Open*, *6*, 100173. DOI: 10.1016/j.caeo.2024.100173

Alnuaim, A. A., Al-Wabil, A., & Alaqeeli, A. (2024). The impact and acceptance of gamification by learners in a digital literacy course at the undergraduate level. *JMIR Serious Games*, *12*, e52017. DOI: 10.2196/52017 PMID: 39177662

Alsharefeen, R., & Al Sayari, N. (2025). Faculty as street-level bureaucrats: Discretionary decision-making in the era of generative AI. *Frontiers in Education*, *10*, 1662657. DOI: 10.3389/feduc.2025.1662657

Aramburuzabala, P., & Cerrillo, R. (2023). Service-learning as an approach to educating for sustainable development. *Sustainability (Basel)*, *15*(14), 11231. DOI: 10.3390/su151411231

Ashwin, P. (2022). The educational purposes of higher education: Changing discussions of the societal outcomes of educating students. *Higher Education*, *84*(6), 1227–1244. DOI: 10.1007/s10734-022-00930-9

Ayanwale, M. A., Adelana, O. P., Molefi, R. R., Adeeko, O., & Ishola, A. M. (2024). Examining artificial intelligence literacy among pre-service teachers for future classrooms. *Computers and Education Open*, *6*, 100179. DOI: 10.1016/j.caeo.2024.100179

Baig, M. I., Yadegaridehkordi, E., & Zamani, F. (2024). ChatGPT in the higher education: A systematic literature review and research challenges. *International Journal of Educational Research*, *127*, 102411. [REMOVED HYPERLINK FIELD] DOI: 10.1016/j.ijer.2024.102411

Baldrich, K., Pérez-García, C., Domínguez-Oller, J. C., & Amo Sánchez-Fortún, J. M. (2024). Gamified experiences in educational academic contexts: A systematic review. *Qualitative Research in Education, 13*(3), 221–242. DOI: 10.17583/qre.13552

Barnes, M., & Tour, E. (2025). Teachers' use of generative AI: A 'dirty little secret'? *Language and Education*, •••, 1–16. DOI: 10.1080/09500782.2025.2485935

Barrett, A., & Pack, A. (2023). Not quite eye to A.I.: Student and teacher perspectives on the use of generative artificial intelligence in the writing process. *International Journal of Educational Technology in Higher Education, 20*(1), 59. DOI: 10.1186/s41239-023-00427-0

Barus, O. P., Hidayanto, A. N., Handri, E. Y., Sensuse, D. I., & Yaiprasert, C. (2025). Shaping generative AI governance in higher education: A multi-stakeholder and sustainable approach. *International Journal of Educational Research Open, 8*, 100452. DOI: 10.1016/j.ijedro.2025.100452

Belda-Medina, J., & Calvo-Ferrer, J. R. (2022). Preservice teachers' knowledge and attitudes toward digital-game-based language learning. *Education Sciences, 12*(3), 182. DOI: 10.3390/educsci12030182

Bender, E. M., Gebru, T., McMillan-Major, A., & Shmitchell, S. (2021). On the dangers of stochastic parrots: Can language models be too big? FAccT '21: *Proceedings of the 2021 ACM Conference on Fairness, Accountability, and Transparency,* 610–623.https://doi.org/DOI: 10.1145/3442188.3445922

Bouakaz, L., & Khalid, S. (2025). AI in education: A sociological exploration of technology in learning environments. *Frontiers in Education, 10*, 1700876. DOI: 10.3389/feduc.2025.1700876

Boysen, M. S. W., Lund, O., Jørnø, R. L., & Skovbjerg, H. M. (2023). The role of experience in playful learning activities: A design-based self-study within teacher education aimed at the development of tabletop role-playing games. *Teaching and Teacher Education, 128*, 104128. DOI: 10.1016/j.tate.2023.104128

Bozkurt, A. (2024). GenAI et al.: Cocreation, Authorship, Ownership, Academic Ethics and Integrity in a Time of Generative AI. *Open Praxis, 16*(1), 1–10. https://doi.org/. DOI: 10.55982/openpraxis.16.1.654

Brandl, B., & Schrader, C. (2024). Serious games in higher education in the transforming process to Education 4.0—Systematized review. *Education Sciences, 14*(3), 281. DOI: 10.3390/educsci14030281

Braun, V., & Clarke, V. (2006). Using thematic analysis in psychology. *Qualitative Research in Psychology, 3*(2), 77–101. DOI: 10.1191/1478088706qp063oa

Brookhart, S. M. (2013). *How to create and use rubrics for formative assessment and grading*. Association for Supervision and Curriculum Development.

Çayak, S. (2024). Investigating the relationship between teachers' attitudes toward artificial intelligence and their artificial intelligence literacy. *Journal of Educational Technology & Online Learning, 7*(4), 367–383. DOI: 10.31681/jetol.1490307

Cetin, O., & Celen, G. (2025). Investigation of pre-service teachers' artificial intelligence literacy and views on the use of artificial intelligence in education. [JESEH]. *Journal of Education in Science, Environment and Health, 11*(4), 285–304. DOI: 10.55549/jeseh.850

Cheah, Y. H., Lu, J., & Kim, J. (2025). Integrating generative artificial intelligence in K-12 education: Examining teachers' preparedness, practices, and barriers. *Computers and Education: Artificial Intelligence, 8*, 100363. DOI: 10.1016/j.caeai.2025.100363

Chergarova, V., Tomeo, M., Morgan, H., & Andrade, S. (2024). Integrating artificial intelligence (AI) into game development to elevate diverse gameplay elements. *Issues in Information Systems, 25*(2), 408–417. DOI: 10.48009/2_iis_2024_132

Chernikova, O., Heitzmann, N., Stadler, M., Holzberger, D., Seidel, T., & Fischer, F. (2020). Simulation-based learning in higher education: A meta-analysis. *Review of Educational Research, 90*(4), 499–541. DOI: 10.3102/0034654320933544

Chiu, T. K. F. (2024). The impact of generative AI (GenAI) on practices, policies and research direction in education: A case of ChatGPT and Midjourney. *Interactive Learning Environments, 32*(10), 6187–6203. DOI: 10.1080/10494820.2023.2253861

Chung, J. Y., & Jeong, S.-H. (2024). Exploring the perceptions of Chinese pre-service teachers on the integration of generative AI in English language teaching: Benefits, challenges, and educational implications. *Online Journal of Communication and Media Technologies, 14*(4), e202457. DOI: 10.30935/ojcmt/15266

Clark, D. B., Tanner-Smith, E. E., & Killingsworth, S. S. (2016). Digital games, design, and learning: A systematic review and meta-analysis. *Review of Educational Research, 86*(1), 79–122. DOI: 10.3102/0034654315582065 PMID: 26937054

Compare, C., & Albanesi, C. (2023). Belief, attitude and critical understanding. A systematic review of social justice in Service-Learning experiences. *Journal of Community & Applied Social Psychology, 33*(6), 1234–1258. DOI: 10.1002/casp.2639

Connolly, T. M., Boyle, E. A., MacArthur, E., Hainey, T., & Boyle, J. M. (2012). A systematic literature review of empirical evidence on computer games and serious games. *Computers & Education, 59*(2), 661–686. DOI: 10.1016/j.compedu.2012.03.004

Crompton, H., Burke, D., & Gregory, K. H. (2017). The use of mobile learning in K–12 education: A systematic review. *Computers & Education, 110*, 51–63. DOI: 10.1016/j.compedu.2017.03.013

Culcasi, I., Cinque, M., Manasia, L., & Ianos, G. (2023). Learning virtual services for a higher education system in Europe that is more digital and inclusive. *RIDAS. Ibero-American Journal of Service-Learning, 16*, 159–182. DOI: 10.1344/RIDAS2023.16.10

Dapena, A., Castro, P. M., & Ares-Pernas, A. (2022). Moving to e-service learning in higher education. *Applied Sciences (Basel, Switzerland), 12*(11), 5462. DOI: 10.3390/app12115462

Dayagbil, F. T., Boholano, H. B., & Sumalinog, G. G. (2025). Are they in or out? Exploring pre-service teachers' knowledge, perceptions, and experiences regarding artificial intelligence (AI) in teaching and learning. *Frontiers in Education, 10*, 1665205. DOI: 10.3389/feduc.2025.1665205 de la Fuente-González, M. C., Armijos-Armijos, P. M., González-González, C. S., Aguilar-Parra, J. M., López-Liria, R., & Roig-Vila, R. (2025). Use of digital tools and digital competence in university students during the COVID-19 pandemic. *Alterity*, *20*(1), 85–95. DOI: 10.17163/alt.v20n1.2025.09

Dichev, C., & Dicheva, D. (2017). Gamifying education: What is known, what is believed, and what remains uncertain: A critical review. *International Journal of Educational Technology in Higher Education*, *14*(1), 9. DOI: 10.1186/s41239-017-0042-5

Ding, A.-C. E., DuBois, M. J., Asher, S., Mick, K., Fu, W., Ellison, G., & Nair, M. (2025). Let's make a game! A case of co-designing with teachers to develop game-based learning curriculum. *Journal of Research on Technology in Education*, *57*(4), 784–799. DOI: 10.1080/15391523.2024.2313619

Ding, M., & Yu, M. (2024). Serious game-based learning and learning by making games: Motivational mechanisms in EFL education. *Computers & Education*, 208, 105075. [REMOVED HYPERLINK FIELD] DOI: 10.1016/j.compedu.2024.105075

Drajati, N. A., Cahyaningrum, D., Handayani, E. I. P., & Handayani, A. (2025). Understanding the artificial intelligence literacy between novice and experienced English teachers in Indonesia. *TEFLIN Journal*, *36*(1), 44–60. DOI: 10.15639/teflinjournal.v36i1/44-60

Duarte, J., Gerritsen, N., Lourenço, M., Melo-Pfeifer, S., & Pinto, S. (2024). Service learning for linguistic and cultural diversity in higher education: Proposals for pre-service (language) teacher education. *Education Sciences*, *14*(7), 750. DOI: 10.3390/educsci14070750

Eke, D. O. (2023). ChatGPT and the rise of generative AI: Threat to academic integrity? *Journal of Responsible Technology*, *13*, 100060. DOI: 10.1016/j.jrt.2023.100060

Engin, R. A. (2023). The effect of designing educational digital games on pre-service teachers' some competencies. *Journal of Pedagogical Sociology and Psychology*, *5*(3), 195–208. DOI: 10.33902/jpsp.202323576

Fiuza-Asorey, M. J., Sotelino Losada, A., Mella Núñez, I., & Lorenzo Moledo, M. (2022). Service-Learning & Inclusive Education in Teacher Training. Evaluating student satisfaction. *Revista Fuentes*, *24*(2), 210–221. DOI: 10.12795/revistafuentes.2022.17611

García-Gutiérrez, J., Ruiz-Corbella, M., Chiva-Bartoll, O., & Paz-Lourido, B. (2024). *Service-Learning in Higher Education: Current and Future Challenges* (Working Papers Series No. 1). UNED. https://hdl.handle.net/20.500.14468/24228

Garzón, J., Patiño, E., & Marulanda, C. (2025). Systematic review of artificial intelligence in education: Trends, benefits, and challenges. *Multimodal Technologies and Interaction*, *9*(8), 84. Advance online publication. DOI: 10.3390/mti9080084

Gerlich, M. (2025). From offloading to engagement: How AI can enhance or replace our thinking. *Data*, *10*(11), 172. DOI: 10.3390/data10110172

Giannakos, M., Azevedo, R., Brusilovsky, P., Cukurova, M., Dimitriadis, Y., Hernandez-Leo, D., Järvelä, S., Mavrikis, M., & Rienties, B. (2024). The promise and challenges of generative AI in education. *Behaviour & Information Technology*, *44*(11), 2518–2544. DOI: 10.1080/0144929X.2024.2394886

Gkrimpizi, T., Peristeras, V., & Magnisalis, I. (2024). Defining the meaning and scope of digital transformation in higher education institutions. *Administrative Sciences*, *14*(3), 48. DOI: 10.3390/admsci14030048

Gómez Niño, J. R., Árias Delgado, L. P., Chiappe, A., & Ortega González, E. (2025). Gamifying learning with AI: A pathway to 21st-century skills. *Journal of Research in Childhood Education*, *39*(4), 735–750. DOI: 10.1080/02568543.2024.2421974

González-Yubero, S., Mauri, M., Cardoso, M. J., & Palomera, R. (2023). Learning through challenges and enigmas: Educational escape room as a predictive experience of motivation in university students. *Sustainability (Basel)*, *15*(17), 13001. DOI: 10.3390/su151713001

Gooch, D., Vasalou, A., Benton, L., & Khaled, R. (2016). Using gamification to motivate students with dyslexia. In *Proceedings of the 2016 CHI Conference on Human Factors in Computing Systems* (pp. 969–980). ACM. https://doi.org/DOI: 10.1145/2858036.2858231

Gopalan, M., Rosinger, K., & Ahn, J. (2020). Use of quasi-experimental research designs in education research: Growth, promise, and challenges. *Review of Research in Education*, *44*(1), 218–243. DOI: 10.3102/0091732X20903302

Gordillo, A., & López-Fernández, D. (2024). Are educational escape rooms more effective than traditional lectures for teaching software engineering? A randomized controlled trial. *IEEE Transactions on Education*, *67*(3), 245–256. DOI: 10.1109/TE.2024.3403913

Gouseti, A., James, F., Fallin, L., & Burden, K. (2025). The ethics of using AI in K-12 education: A systematic literature review. *Technology, Pedagogy and Education*, *34*(2), 161–182. DOI: 10.1080/1475939X.2024.2428601

Gujjula, R., & Sanghera, K. (2023). Ethical considerations and data privacy in AI education. *Journal of Student-Scientists' Research, 5*. https://doi.org/DOI: 10.13021/jssr2023.3958

Hashim, M., Tlemsani, I., & Matthews, R. (2022). Higher education strategy in digital transformation. *Education and Information Technologies*, *27*(3), 3171–3195. DOI: 10.1007/s10639-021-10739-1 PMID: 34539217

Hernández, J., & Ramírez, R. (2024). Introducing pre-service teachers to game-based learning. *International Journal of Educational Technology and Learning*, *17*(1), 1–8. DOI: 10.55217/101.v17i1.825

Hsu, H.-P., Mak, J., Werner, J., White-Taylor, J., Geiselhofer, M., Gorman, A., & Torrejon Capurro, C. (2024). Preliminary study on pre-service teachers' applications and perceptions of generative artificial intelligence for lesson planning. *Journal of Technology and Teacher Education*, *32*(3), 409–437. DOI: 10.70725/869859beoezu

Hu, H., & Sperling, R. A. (2022). Pre-service teachers' perceptions of adopting digital games in education: A mixed methods investigation. *Teaching and Teacher Education*, *120*, 103876. DOI: 10.1016/j.tate.2022.103876

Huang, L., Yu, W., Ma, W., Zhong, W., Feng, Z., Wang, H., Chen, Q., Peng, W., Feng, X., Qin, B., & Liu, T. (2025). A survey on hallucination in large language models: Principles, taxonomy, challenges, and open questions. *ACM Transactions on Information Systems*, *43*(2), 3155. Advance online publication. DOI: 10.1145/3703155

Islam, M., Karimi, A., Ahmad, S., Wani, J. A., Butdisuwan, S., Rahman, M. H., Habiba, U., Islam, M. E., & Rahman, M. O. (2025, December 07). N., Karimi, A., Ahmad, S., Wani, J. A., Butdisuwan, S., Rahman, Md. H., Habiba, U., Islam, Md. E., & Rahman, Md. O. (2025). Gamification and game-based learning in teacher training and education: Quantifying through bibliometric paradigms. *Journal of Education*, 00220574251406241. Advance online publication. DOI: 10.1177/00220574251406241

Ismail, I. A. (2025). Protecting privacy in AI-enhanced education: A comprehensive examination of data privacy concerns and solutions in AI-based learning. In Mutawa, A. (Ed.), *Impacts of generative AI on the future of research and education* (pp. 117–142). IGI Global., DOI: 10.4018/979-8-3693-0884-4.ch006

Ivanov, S., Soliman, M., Tuomi, A., Alhamar Alkathiri, N., & Al-Alawi, A. N. (2024). Drivers of generative AI adoption in higher education through the lens of the Theory of Planned Behaviour. *Technology in Society*, *77*, 102521. DOI: 10.1016/j.techsoc.2024.102521

Jiang, F., & Shangguan, D. (2022). Researching and designing educational games on the basis of "self-regulated learning theory". *Frontiers in Psychology*, *13*, 996403. DOI: 10.3389/fpsyg.2022.996403 PMID: 36438312

Johnston, H., Wells, R. F., Shanks, E. M., Boey, T., & Parsons, B. N. (2024). Student perspectives on the use of generative artificial intelligence technologies in higher education. *International Journal for Educational Integrity*, *20*(1), 2. DOI: 10.1007/s40979-024-00149-4

Kaimara, P., Fokides, E., Oikonomou, A., & Deliyannis, I. (2022). Pre-service teachers' views about the use of digital educational games for collaborative learning. *Education and Information Technologies*, *27*(4), 5987–6005. DOI: 10.1007/s10639-021-10820-9

Kapp, K. M. (2012). *The gamification of learning and instruction: Game-based methods and strategies for training and education*. Pfeiffer.

Kasneci, E., Seßler, K., Küchemann, S., Bannert, M., Dementieva, D., Fischer, F., Gasser, U., Groh, G., Günnemann, S., Hüllermeier, E., Krusche, S., Kutyniok, G., Michaeli, T., Nerdel, C., Pfeffer, J., Poquet, O., Sailer, M., Schmidt, A., Seidel, T., & Kasneci, G. (2023). ChatGPT for good? On opportunities and challenges of large language models for education. *Learning and Individual Differences*, *103*, 102274. DOI: 10.1016/j.lindif.2023.102274

Kerr, R. C., & Kim, H. (2025). From prompts to plans: A case study of pre-service EFL teachers' use of generative AI for lesson planning. *English Teaching*, *80*(1), 95–118. DOI: 10.15858/engtea.80.1.202503.95

Kezar, A., Hallett, R. E., Corwin, Z. B., & Hypolite, L. (2025). Moving toward institutional culture change in higher education: An exploration into cross-functional professional learning communities. *Innovative Higher Education*, *50*(2), 687–714. DOI: 10.1007/s10755-024-09753-1

Khoo, Y. Y., Ramdan, M. R., Abdullah, N. L., Abd Aziz, N. A., & Mahjom, N. (2025). The impacts of game-based learning on thinking and learning in higher education context: A scoping review. [IJEMST]. *International Journal of Education in Mathematics, Science, and Technology, 13*(3), 623–637. DOI: 10.46328/ijemst.4776

Khosravi, H., Buckingham Shum, S., Chen, G., Conati, C., Tsai, Y.-S., Kay, J., Knight, S., Martinez-Maldonado, R., Sadiq, S., & Gašević, D. (2022). Explainable Artificial Intelligence in education. *Computers and Education: Artificial Intelligence, 3*, 100074. DOI: 10.1016/j.caeai.2022.100074

Kılıçkaya, F., & Kic-Drgas, J. (2025). Pre-service language teachers' experiences and perceptions of integrating generative AI in practicum-based lesson study. *Humanities & Social Sciences Communications, 12*(1), 1478. Advance online publication. DOI: 10.1057/s41599-025-05715-w

Kofinas, A. K., Tsay, C.-H., & Pike, D. (2025). The impact of generative AI on academic integrity of authentic assessments within a higher education context. *British Journal of Educational Technology, 56*(6), 2522–2549. DOI: 10.1111/bjet.13585

Köse, A., & Özcan, S. (2025). Effectiveness of escape rooms in nursing education: A systematic review. *Nurse Education Today, 151*, 106745. DOI: 10.1016/j.nedt.2025.106745 PMID: 40250204

Kurtz, G., Amzalag, M., Shaked, N., Zaguri, Y., Kohen-Vacs, D., Gal, E., Zailer, G., & Barak-Medina, E. (2024). Strategies for integrating generative AI into higher education: Navigating challenges and leveraging opportunities. *Education Sciences, 14*(5), 503. DOI: 10.3390/educsci14050503

Lauricella, S., & Edmunds, T. K. (2022). Ludic pedagogy: Taking a serious look at fun in the COVID-19 classroom and beyond. *Educational Considerations, 48*(1), 7–24. DOI: 10.4148/0146-9282.2324

Lavery, S., Chambers, D., & Cain, G. (Eds.). (2018). *Service-learning: enhancing inclusive education.* Emerald Group Publishing.

Lelescu, A., Sava, S., Grosseck, G., & Malita, L. (2025). Exploring trust in generative AI for higher education institutions: A systematic literature review focused on educators. *Humanities & Social Sciences Communications, 12*(1), 1961. Advance online publication. DOI: 10.1057/s41599-025-06253-1

Lin, Y.-L., Wang, W.-T., & Hsieh, M.-J. (2024). The effects of students' self-efficacy, self-regulated learning strategy use, and flow experience on learning performance in digital game-based learning environments. *Education and Information Technologies, 29*(12), 15165–15192. DOI: 10.1007/s10639-024-12700-4

Lo, C. K., Hew, K. F., & Jong, M. S. (2024). The influence of ChatGPT on student engagement: A systematic review and future research agenda. *Computers & Education, 219*, 105100. DOI: 10.1016/j.compedu.2024.105100

López-Pernas, S., Gordillo, A., Barra, E., & Quemada, J. (2024). Educational escape rooms are effective learning activities across educational levels and contexts: A meta-analysis. *IEEE Transactions on Learning Technologies, 17*, 711–724. DOI: 10.1109/TLT.2023.3328913

Maddox, P. L., & Trost, J. L. (2025). Who benefits? Building a critical service-learning model. *Teaching Sociology, 53*(1), 31–45. DOI: 10.1177/0092055X241262787

Makri, A., Vlachopoulos, D., & Martina, R. A. (2021). Digital escape rooms as innovative pedagogical tools in education: A systematic literature review. *Sustainability (Basel)*, *13*(8), 4587. DOI: 10.3390/su13084587

Manzano-León, A. (2025). *Playful Service-Learning: development of games for social transformation*. University of Almeria. https://editorial.ual.es/libro/aprendizaje-servicio-ludico-elaboracion-de-juegos-para-la-transformacion-social_166197/ (20/01/2026).

Manzano-León, A., Rodríguez-Ferrer, J. M., Aguilar-Parra, J. M., Martínez, A. M., Luque de la Rosa, A., Salguero, D., & Fernández, J. M. (2021). Escape Rooms as a Learning Strategy for Special Education Master's Degree Students. *International Journal of Environmental Research and Public Health*, *18*(14), 7304. DOI: 10.3390/ijerph18147304 PMID: 34299753

Manzano-León, A., Rodríguez-Rivera, P., Raposo-Rivas, M., & Rodríguez-Ferrer, J. M. (2024). Digital game-based learning for transgender identity awareness: A qualitative study in Spanish social education degree. *Current Psychology*, *43*(20), 18065–18073. DOI: 10.1007/s12144-023-05556-3

Mao, W., Cui, Y., Chiu, M. M., & Lei, H. (2022). Effects of game-based learning on students' critical thinking: A meta-analysis. *Journal of Educational Computing Research*, *59*(8), 1682–1708. DOI: 10.1177/07356331211007098

Maraza-Quispe, B., Choquehuanca-Quispe, W., Rosas-Imán, V. H., Quispe-Flores, L. M., Alcázar-Holguín, M. A., Feliciano-Yucra, G., & Martínez-López, A. C. (2024). Impact of gamification on collaborative learning development: A quantitative experimental approach. *IEEE Revista Iberoamericana de Technologias del Aprendizaje*, *19*(1), 51–60. DOI: 10.1109/RITA.2024.3368360

Maroto Sánchez, A. (2023). Using digital educational escape rooms as a motivational strategy in higher education. *International Journal of Management Education*, *21*(3), 100852. DOI: 10.1016/j.ijme.2023.100852

Marsden, E., & Torgerson, C. J. (2012). Single group, pre- and post-test research designs: Some methodological concerns. *Oxford Review of Education*, *38*(5), 583–616. DOI: 10.1080/03054985.2012.731208

Martin, F., Zhuang, M., & Schaefer, D. (2024). Systematic review of research on artificial intelligence in K-12 education (2017–2022). *Computers and Education: Artificial Intelligence*, *6*, 100195. DOI: 10.1016/j.caeai.2023.100195

Martín-García, X., Bär-Kwast, B., Gijón-Casares, M., & Puig-Rovira, J. M. (2021). The map of the values of service-learning: An instrument for reflection & improvement. *Alterity*, *16*(1), 10–23. DOI: 10.17163/alt.v16n1.2021.01

Martín-Sánchez, M., González-Gómez, M., & Jeong, J. S. (2024). Service-learning in the education system: Evaluation of the degree of implementation as a teaching strategy for education for sustainable development. *Apex. Journal of Scientific Education*, *8*(2). Advance online publication. DOI: 10.17979/arec.2024.8.2.10682

Maxim, A., & Arnedo-Moreno, J. (2025). Learning by designing games: A scoping review. *JMIR Serious Games*, *13*, e54075. DOI: 10.2196/54075 PMID: 40053743

Memarian, B., & Doleck, T. (2024). Teaching and learning artificial intelligence: Insights from the literature. *Education and Information Technologies*, *29*(16), 21523–21546. DOI: 10.1007/s10639-024-12679-y

Mienye, I. D., Swart, A. J., & Obaido, G. (2024). Fairness metrics in AI healthcare applications: A review. In *2024, IEEE International Conference on Information, Reuse and Integration for Data Science (IRI)* (pp. 284–289). IEEE. https://doi.org/DOI: 10.1109/IRI62200.2024.00065

Mills, K. A. (2024). Critical Literacy and Digital Futures: Looking Ahead. In *Text-Critical Classroom*. Scandinavian University Press., DOI: 10.18261/9788215071114-24-17

Moon, J., Lee, U., Koh, J., Jeong, Y., Lee, Y., Byun, G., & Lim, J. (2025). Generative artificial intelligence in educational game design: Nuanced challenges, design implications, and future research. *Technology. Knowledge and Learning*, *30*(1), 447–459. DOI: 10.1007/s10758-024-09756-z

Moorhouse, B. L., & Kohnke, L. M. A. (2024). The effects of generative AI on initial language teacher education: The perceptions of teacher educators. *System*, *122*, 103290. DOI: 10.1016/j.system.2024.103290

Moriña, A., Carballo, R., & Doménech, A. (2025). Faculty training in Universal Design for Learning: A systematic review of the benefits and challenges. *Teaching in Higher Education*, *30*(7), 1722–1739. DOI: 10.1080/13562517.2025.2465994

Murillo-Zamorano, L. R., López-Sánchez, J. Á., López-Rey, M. J., & Bueno-Muñoz, C. (2023). Gamification in higher education: The ECOn+ star battles. *Computers & Education*, *181*, 104699. DOI: 10.1016/j.compedu.2022.104699

Mustafa, M. Y., Tlili, A., Lampropoulos, G., Huang, R., Jandrić, P., Zhao, J., Salha, S., Xu, L., Panda, S., Kinshuk, , López-Pernas, S., & Saqr, M. (2024). A systematic review of literature reviews on artificial intelligence in education (AIED): A roadmap to a future research agenda. *Smart Learning Environments*, *11*(1), 59. Advance online publication. DOI: 10.1186/s40561-024-00350-5

Ng, D. T. K., Leung, J. K. L., Chu, S. K. W., & Qiao, M. S. (2021). AI literacy: Definition, teaching, evaluation and ethical issues. *Proceedings of the Association for Information Science and Technology*, *58*(1), 504–509. DOI: 10.1002/pra2.487

Ogunleye, B., Zakariyyah, K. I., Ajao, O., Olayinka, O., & Sharma, H. (2024). A systematic review of generative AI for teaching and learning practice. *Education Sciences*, *14*(6), 636. DOI: 10.3390/educsci14060636

Oncioiu, I., & Bularca, A. R. (2025). Artificial intelligence governance in higher education: The role of knowledge-based strategies in fostering legal awareness and ethical artificial intelligence literacy. *Societies (Basel, Switzerland)*, *15*(6), 144. DOI: 10.3390/soc15060144

Othman, N. I., Mohamed, H., & Mat Zin, N. A. (2023). Serious games accessibility design model for low-vision children. *Advances in Human-Computer Interaction*, *13*(52), 1–13. DOI: 10.1155/2023/9528294

Palha, S., Bouwer, A., Webb, K., van Smaalen, D., & Agterberg, D. (2024). Game-based pedagogy in teacher training. *European Conference on Games Based Learning Proceedings, 18*(1), 677–684. https://doi.org/DOI: 10.34190/ecgbl.18.1.2698

Panadero, E. (2017). A review of self-regulated learning: Six models and four directions for research. *Frontiers in Psychology, 8*, 422. DOI: 10.3389/fpsyg.2017.00422 PMID: 28503157

Pelizzari, F., & Garzoni, A. (2024). Gamification in higher education: A systematic literature review. *Italian Journal of Educational Technology, 31*(3), 21–43. DOI: 10.17471/2499-4324/1335

Pinargote Castro, M. A., Solórzano Ortega, C. V., Ruilova Alvarado, N. A., & Bulgarín Sánchez, R. M. (2023). Artificial intelligence in the context of teacher training. *Scientific research journal update of the world of science. RECIAMUC, 7*(4), 153–161. https://doi.org/. (4).Oct.2023.153-161DOI: 10.26820/reciamuc/7

Pistono, C., Santos, P., Baptista, A., & São Mamede, H. (2024). Framework for adaptive serious games design. *Computer Applications in Engineering Education, 32*(4), e22731. DOI: 10.1002/cae.22731

Plass, J. L., Homer, B. D., & Kinzer, C. K. (2015). Foundations of game-based learning. *Educational Psychologist, 50*(4), 258–283. DOI: 10.1080/00461520.2015.1122533

Qi, Z., & Zhonggen, Y. (2022). Meta-analysis on investigating and comparing the effects on learning achievement and motivation for gamification and game-based learning. *Education Research International, 1519880*, 1–19. Advance online publication. DOI: 10.1155/2022/1519880

Resch, K., & Schrittesser, I. (2023). Using the service-learning approach to bridge the gap between theory and practice in teacher education. *International Journal of Inclusive Education, 27*(10), 1118–1132. DOI: 10.1080/13603116.2021.1882053

Ribeiro, Á., Aramburuzabala, P., & Paz, B. (2021). Reflections on the learning service of European higher education. *RIDAS. Ibero-American Journal of Service-Learning, 12*(12), 3–12. Advance online publication. DOI: 10.1344/RIDAS2021.12.2

Richardson, V. (1997). *Constructivist teacher education: Building a world of new understandings*. Falmer Press.

Rodríguez-Calzada, L., Paredes-Velasco, M., & Urquiza-Fuentes, J. (2024). The educational impact of a comprehensive serious game within the university setting: Improving learning and fostering motivation. *Heliyon, 10*(16), e35608. DOI: 10.1016/j.heliyon.2024.e35608 PMID: 39220894

Rodríguez-Ferrer, J. M., Manzano-León, A., & Aguilar-Parra, J. M. (2023b). Game-based learning and service-learning to teach inclusive education in higher education. *International Journal of Environmental Research and Public Health, 20*(4), 3285. [REMOVED HYPERLINK FIELD] DOI: 10.3390/ijerph20043285

Rodríguez-Ferrer, J. M., Manzano-León, A., Fernández-Jiménez, C., Luque de la Rosa, A., Fernández-Campoy, J. M., & Aguilar-Parra, J. M. (2023a). Shall we play together? Game-based learning for engagement and classroom climate in Spanish socially deprived communities. *Frontiers in Psychology, 14*, 1163441. DOI: 10.3389/fpsyg.2023.1163441 PMID: 37333587

Rodríguez-Ferrer, J. M., Rodríguez Rivera, P., & Manzano León, A. (2025). Effects of the combination of service-learning and play-based learning on the cooperative competences of university students. *Interuniversity Electronic Journal of Teacher Training, 29*(1), 155–168. DOI: 10.6018/reifop.672301

Rosenthal, J., & Ratan, R. (2022). Balancing learning and enjoyment in serious games: A Kerbal Space Program case study examining the communication mediation model. *Computers & Education, 182*, 104480. DOI: 10.1016/j.compedu.2022.104480

Rüth, M. (2022). *Learning and teaching with video games: Toward theoretical progress and educational practice* [Doctoral thesis, Universität zu Köln]. KUPS – Köln University Publication Services. https://kups.ub.uni-koeln.de/52965/

Sailer, M., Hense, J. U., Mayr, S. K., & Mandl, H. (2017). How gamification motivates: An experimental study of the effects of specific game design elements on psychological need satisfaction. *Computers in Human Behavior, 69*, 371–380. DOI: 10.1016/j.chb.2016.12.033

Sailer, M., & Homner, L. (2020). The gamification of learning: A meta-analysis. *Educational Psychology Review, 32*(1), 77–112. DOI: 10.1007/s10648-019-09498-w

Sáiz-Manzanares, M. C., Rodríguez Arribas, S., Pardo Aguilar, C., & Queiruga-Dios, M. Á. (2020). Effectiveness of self-regulation and serious games for learning STEM knowledge in primary education. *Psicothema, 32*(4), 516–524. DOI: 10.7334/psicothema2020.30 PMID: 33073757

Salvador-García, C., Chiva-Bartoll, O., Maravé-Vivas, M., & Gil-Gómez, J. (2023). Service-learning in physical education teacher education: A retrospective exploratory study to examine its challenges. *Teaching and Teacher Education, 135*, 104350. DOI: 10.1016/j.tate.2023.104350

Sánchez-Ruiz, L. M., López-Alfonso, S., Moll-López, S., Moraño-Fernández, J. A., & Vega-Fleitas, E. (2022). Educational digital escape rooms footprint on students' feelings: A case study within aerospace engineering. *Information (Basel), 13*(10), 478. DOI: 10.3390/info13100478

Santos Rego, M. Á., Lorenzo Moledo, M., & Sáez Gambín, D. (2024). *University & Service-Learning: It's Quality that matters*. Narcea.

Schultes, M.-T., Graf, D., Holzer, J., Schober, B., & Spiel, C. (2025). Implementation and evaluation of service-learning at higher education institutions. *Evaluation and Program Planning, 112*, 102622. DOI: 10.1016/j.evalprogplan.2025.102622 PMID: 40543380

Screpnik, C., Negre-Bennasar, F., & Salinas, J. (2024). Inclusive education with serious games and user centered design, exploring the intersection of accessibility and usability. *RELATEC. Latin American Journal of Educational Technology, 23*(2), 27–50. DOI: 10.17398/1695-288X.23.2.27

Shohel, M. M. C., Weller, S., & Brooks, R. (2025). Academics' learning attitudes and readiness for generative AI in higher education: The role of responsible decision-making. *Cogent Education, 12*(1), 2514933. DOI: 10.1080/2331186X.2025.2514933

Singun, A. J. (2025). Unveiling the barriers to digital transformation in higher education institutions: A systematic literature review. *Discover Education, 4*(37), 37. Advance online publication. DOI: 10.1007/s44217-025-00430-9

Sousa, A. E., & Cardoso, P. (2025). Use of generative AI by higher education students: Perspectives on perceived benefits and challenges. *Electronics (Basel), 14*(7), 1258. DOI: 10.3390/electronics14071258

Sperling, K., Stenberg, C.-J., McGrath, C., Åkerfeldt, A., Heintz, F., & Stenliden, L. (2024). In search of artificial intelligence (AI) literacy in teacher education: A scoping review. *Computers and Education Open*, *6*, 100169. DOI: 10.1016/j.caeo.2024.100169

Stojanov, A., Liu, Q., & Koh, J. H. L. (2024). University students' self-reported reliance on ChatGPT for learning: A latent profile analysis. *Computers and Education: Artificial Intelligence*, *6*, 100243. DOI: 10.1016/j.caeai.2024.100243

Tagare, D., Karki, T., & Yu, W. (2025). K-12 teachers' ethical competencies for AI literacy: Insights from a systematic literature review. *Computers & Education*, *239*, 105435. DOI: 10.1016/j.compedu.2025.105435

Tinterri, A., Pelizzari, F., Di Padova, M., Palladino, F., Vignoli, G., & Dipace, A. (2024). Automating board-game based learning: A comprehensive study to assess reliability and accuracy of AI in game evaluation. *Intelligenza Artificiale*, *18*(1), 103–119. DOI: 10.3233/IA-240030

Tlili, A., Adarkwah, M. A., Lo, C. K., Bozkurt, A., Burgos, D., Bonk, C. J., Costello, E., Mishra, S., Stracke, C. M., & Huang, R. (2024). Taming the monster: How can open education promote the effective and safe use of generative AI in education? *Journal of Learning for Development*, *11*(3), 398–413. DOI: 10.56059/jl4d.v11i3.1657

Tsirantonaki, S., & Vlachou, A. (2025). AI-driven inclusive practices: Innovative approaches to differentiated teaching and educational inclusion. *European Journal of Inclusive Education*, *4*(1), 134–146. DOI: 10.7146/ejie.v4i1.156613

Veldkamp, A., van de Grint, L., Knippels, M. C. P. J., & van Joolingen, W. R. (2020). Escape education: A systematic review on escape rooms in education. *Educational Research Review*, *31*, 100364. Advance online publication. DOI: 10.1016/j.edurev.2020.100364

Veytia Bucheli, M. G., Gómez-Galán, J., Cáceres Mesa, M. L., & López Catalán, L. (2024). Digital technologies as enablers of universal design for learning: Higher education students' perceptions in the context of SDG4. *Discover Sustainability*, *5*(1), 473. Advance online publication. DOI: 10.1007/s43621-024-00699-0

Viberg, O., Mutimukwe, C., Hrastinski, S., Cerratto-Pargman, T., & Lilliesköld, J. (2024). Exploring teachers' (future) digital assessment practices in higher education: Instrument and model development. *British Journal of Educational Technology*, *55*(6), 2597–2616. DOI: 10.1111/bjet.13462

Viudes-Carbonell, S. J., Gallego-Durán, F. J., Llorens-Largo, F., Molina-Carmona, R., & Mengual-Andrés, S. (2021). Towards an iterative design for serious games. *Sustainability (Basel)*, *13*(6), 3290. DOI: 10.3390/su13063290

Vlachopoulos, D., & Makri, A. (2017). The effect of games and simulations on higher education: A systematic literature review. *International Journal of Educational Technology in Higher Education*, *14*(1), 22. DOI: 10.1186/s41239-017-0062-1

Wan, K., Woo, Y. Y., & Ho, G. T. S. (2025). Enhancing service-learning through generative AI: A mixed-methods study on educational game design in a finance course. *Cogent Education*, *12*(1), 2592370. DOI: 10.1080/2331186X.2025.2592370

Wang, S., Wang, F., Zhu, Z., Wang, J., Tran, T., & Du, Z. (2024). Artificial intelligence in education: A systematic literature review. *Expert Systems with Applications*, *252*, 124167. DOI: 10.1016/j.eswa.2024.124167

Zainuddin, Z., Chu, S. K. W., Shujahat, M., & Perera, C. J. (2020). The impact of gamification on learning and instruction: A systematic review of empirical evidence. *Educational Research Review*, *30*, 100326. DOI: 10.1016/j.edurev.2020.100326

Zhai, X., Chu, X., Chai, C. S., Jong, M. S. Y., Istenic, A., Spector, J. M., Liu, J.-B., Yuan, J., & Li, Y. (2021). A review of artificial intelligence (AI) in education from 2010 to 2020. *Complexity*, *8812542*(1), 8812542. Advance online publication. DOI: 10.1155/2021/8812542

Žilak, M., & Car, Ž. (2025). A framework for improving accessibility of serious games in handheld augmented reality based on user interaction data. *Applied Sciences (Basel, Switzerland)*, *15*(4), 2161. DOI: 10.3390/app15042161

Chapter 6
Designing AI Scaffolds for Game-Based Reading and Writing:
A Cognitive Load Framework for Diverse Literacy Learners

Farrah Zafar
http://orcid.org/0009-0005-8692-4283
The British University in Dubai, UAE

Tendai Charles
http://orcid.org/0000-0002-0253-5960
The British University in Dubai, UAE

ABSTRACT

This chapter develops a cognitive load framework for designing AI-supported game-based literacy environments for diverse learners. Responding to the growing use of large language models, adaptive feedback, and automated scaffolds in reading and writing platforms, the chapter argues that AI features should be evaluated as cognitive-load interventions rather than as neutral enhancements. The chapter links three themes: AI, game-based literacy learning, and diverse learner participation. It synthesizes cognitive load theory, reading-comprehension research, writing-process research, game-based learning, formative feedback, self-regulated learning, Universal Design for Learning, culturally sustaining pedagogy, and automation trust. The central contribution is an Adaptive Scaffolding Matrix that maps AI support families to phases of literacy activity: orientation, comprehension and encoding, composition and revision, and reflection and consolidation. The chapter then develops design propositions, four illustrative scenarios, and a multi-method evaluation agenda.

INTRODUCTION

AI-mediated literacy is no longer restricted to specialist tutoring systems or isolated automated writing-evaluation tools. It now appears inside the ordinary platforms through which learners read, annotate, draft,

DOI: 10.4018/979-8-3373-7472-7.ch006

revise, play, and receive feedback. In game-based literacy environments, the same learner may encounter a quest narrative, a vocabulary hint, an adaptive comprehension check, a generative explanation, and a revision suggestion within a single task sequence. This chapter therefore examines AI not as a separate technological novelty but as a design layer that can either clarify or complicate the literacy work learners are asked to do (Azzam & Charles, 2025; Kasneci et al., 2023; Zawacki-Richter et al., 2019).

The literacy component is central to this argument because reading comprehension involves the active construction of meaning through interactions among reader, text, activity, and sociocultural context, while writing involves recursive planning, translating, reviewing, and revising rather than the linear production of correct sentences (Flower & Hayes, 1981; Kintsch, 1988; RAND Reading Study Group, 2002). In game-based environments, these processes can be strengthened when play mechanics make comprehension, evidence use, rhetorical choice, and revision visible. They can also be weakened when the game rewards speed, guesswork, or surface correctness more strongly than meaning making and metacognitive control.

Furthermore, this chapter links the three central themes of AI and game-based literacy learning for diverse learners. The first theme is artificial intelligence as a form of adaptive scaffolding: automated glosses, conversational agents, feedback engines, and generative language supports may reduce barriers to participation, especially when teachers configure them around explicit literacy goals. The second theme is game-based literacy learning: quests, levels, roles, points, narrative dilemmas, and collaborative missions are treated as instructional structures only when they advance reading and writing outcomes. The third theme is diversity: learners differ in prior knowledge, language background, disability status, cultural repertoire, confidence, and digital fluency, and these differences shape the cognitive load imposed by both literacy tasks and AI interfaces (Baker & Hawn, 2022; Bray et al., 2024; Paris, 2012).

From the perspective of cognitive load theory, the practical design question is not whether AI should be present in literacy games. The more precise question is when a support should be visible, what form it should take, how much learner effort it should remove, and what kind of effort it should deliberately preserve. A hover definition may reduce unnecessary decoding burden for a multilingual reader, but a constantly open chatbot may divide attention and create a second task. A revision suggestion may help a novice-writer notice evidence gaps, but a full rewrite may displace the composing decisions that writing instruction is intended to cultivate (Risko & Gilbert, 2016; Shute, 2008; Sweller, 1988).

Crucially, this chapter makes three contributions. First, it offers a phase-sensitive account of how AI supports alter intrinsic, extraneous, and germane load during reading, writing, and reading-to-write synthesis. Second, it proposes an Adaptive Scaffolding Matrix (ASM) that maps families of AI support to literacy phases and cognitive load targets. Third, it outlines design propositions, scenarios, and evaluation measures for educators, researchers, and developers who wish to use AI and game mechanics in ways that preserve learner agency, support diverse learners, and keep literacy learning rather than tool operation at the center of the design.

Positioning the Chapter

The volume's three linked commitments—AI, game-based literacy learning, and diverse learners—are best understood as interdependent design conditions rather than as separate topics. AI features function as literacy supports only when their value is judged by their effects on reading comprehension, composing, revision, and transfer. The goal is not to celebrate automation for its own sake, but to show how automated supports can be pedagogically constrained so that they assist learners without replacing the interpretive and rhetorical work that literacy development requires.

The AI theme is addressed through a design view of LLMs, automated feedback, adaptive glossing, dashboards, and teacher-facing orchestration tools. Recent research suggests that LLMs can provide timely explanations and feedback, but the same literature emphasizes limitations, including bias, hallucination, brittleness, over-reliance, and the need for human oversight (Kasneci et al., 2023; Lee & See, 2004; UNESCO, 2023). For this reason, the chapter treats AI outputs as provisional resources to be evaluated, not as authoritative answers. This stance is particularly important in literacy instruction, where learners must learn to judge evidence, audience, voice, and purpose.

The game-based literacy theme is addressed by examining how game mechanics can either support or distort literacy work. Foundational game-based learning scholarship emphasizes that effective learning games coordinate cognitive, affective, motivational, and sociocultural design dimensions rather than adding points and rewards to ordinary tasks (Gee, 2003; Plass et al., 2015). In a literacy game, mechanics should therefore make reading strategies, source evaluation, vocabulary learning, rhetorical moves, and revision decisions consequential. A game that rewards quick clicking but not explanation may be engaging without being instructionally valid.

The diverse-learner theme is addressed by positioning learner variability as a cognitive-load variable rather than as an accommodation issue added at the end. Multilingual learners, students with disabilities, novice academic writers, and learners with limited digital fluency may experience AI-mediated games differently because they bring different schemas, language repertoires, and interaction histories to the same interface. UDL and culturally sustaining pedagogy therefore inform the framework: learners should encounter multiple means of representation and expression, while multilingual variation should be treated as a resource for rhetorical choice rather than an error state by default (Bray et al., 2024; Canagarajah, 2011; Rao et al., 2014).

CONCEPTUAL FRAMEWORK

Cognitive Load Theory in Reading and Writing

The literacy tasks discussed in this chapter are cognitively complex because they combine lower-level language processing with higher-level meaning making and rhetorical decision-making. A learner reading a game-based environmental science narrative, for example, may need to decode unfamiliar words, infer causal relations, monitor comprehension, compare claims across sources, and decide whether an AI paraphrase preserves the source meaning. Similarly, a learner writing a persuasive game mission may need to plan a stance, select evidence, anticipate an audience, revise for coherence, and decide whether an automated suggestion improves or merely smooths the prose. These interactions explain why cognitive load theory is a useful but demanding lens for AI-mediated literacy design.

Sweller (1988) conceptualised cognitive load theory (CLT) as a learning theory grounded in the limitations of working memory and the centrality of long-term memory schemas. Reading and writing place sustained demands on this architecture because learners must coordinate interacting elements, including lexical decoding, syntactic parsing, discourse integration, genre knowledge, and rhetorical decision-making, often under time and attentional constraints. The intrinsic cognitive load of literacy tasks is therefore variable rather than fixed: it depends on element interactivity and on what learners already know (Sweller et al., 1998). What is manageable for an expert reader or writer may be overwhelming for a novice who has not yet developed relevant schemas.

Van Merriënboer and Sweller (2005) distinguish three analytically useful forms of load. Intrinsic load reflects task-inherent complexity and the number of interacting elements that must be processed simultaneously. Extraneous load reflects avoidable demands induced by suboptimal design, including fragmented interfaces, unclear goals, and poorly timed explanations. Germane load reflects cognitive effort invested in processes that support schema construction, such as self-explanation, deliberate practice, and revision. In literacy contexts, intrinsic load is shaped by text complexity, source integration demands, and genre conventions; it can be moderated through sequencing, segmentation, and the provision of supportive schemas. Extraneous load is frequently amplified by split attention across windows, redundancy, and unnecessary navigation demands (Mayer & Moreno, 2003; Yeung et al., 1998).

Kalyuga et al. (2003) describe the expertise reversal effect, in which supports that benefit novices can become redundant or distracting for more expert learners. AI-mediated environments heighten this risk because assistance can be abundant, immediate, and continuously available, even when learners may benefit more from productive struggle or strategic self-monitoring (Mahapatra, 2024). From a CLT perspective, the critical question becomes how supports can be calibrated to learner expertise and phased demands so that they reduce avoidable load while still generating germane effort directed toward learning rather than mere task completion (Paas et al., 2003).

Literacy Processes as the Core Learning Target

A literacy-centred framework must distinguish target outcomes from the technologies used to pursue them. The intended outcomes are not simply more efficient completion of game tasks, higher engagement, or smoother use of AI. The intended outcomes are deeper comprehension, more strategic reading, stronger academic and multimodal writing, improved revision quality, and greater capacity to transfer literacy strategies beyond the game. This distinction matters because AI can improve immediate task performance while weakening learning if learners outsource core processes such as inference, planning, evidence selection, or revision judgment.

In reading, AI scaffolds are most defensible when they help learners move from surface access to situation-model construction. Vocabulary glosses, paraphrases, annotation prompts, and question generators should support the integration of ideas across sentences, sources, and modalities rather than merely translate difficult words into easier ones. Kintsch's (1988) construction-integration model is useful here because it clarifies why comprehension demands more than decoding; learners must connect propositions, activate prior knowledge, suppress irrelevant interpretations, and build a coherent mental model. When AI supports these processes through focused prompts, it can reduce unnecessary barriers while preserving interpretive work.

In writing, AI scaffolds should support planning, drafting, reviewing, and revising without turning composing into acceptance of machine-generated prose. Flower and Hayes (1981) conceptualize writing as a recursive cognitive process in which writers set goals, generate content, translate ideas, and review emerging text. Graham and Perin's (2007) synthesis of writing instruction further highlights the value of strategy instruction, summarization, peer assistance, goal setting, and process-oriented approaches. AI-mediated literacy games can use these findings by rewarding planning notes, evidence integration, revision depth, and reflection rather than only grammatical accuracy or final-product polish.

Integrated reading-to-write tasks are especially important for the book's literacy emphasis because they require learners to coordinate comprehension, source evaluation, synthesis, attribution, and audience awareness. These tasks also reveal why cognitive load is not a purely technical construct. A learner who is reading in an additional language, negotiating unfamiliar disciplinary vocabulary, and composing for a formal audience is managing linguistic, rhetorical, cultural, and interface demands simultaneously. AI and game mechanics should therefore be sequenced so that they support this coordination instead of adding unnecessary switching, alerts, or choices at the most demanding moment of the literacy task.

AI-Mediated Scaffolding, Feedback, and Self-Regulated Learning

AI tools are most relevant to literacy when they provide contingent support for decisions that readers and writers must learn to make. In reading, these decisions include whether to reread, annotate, infer from context, consult a gloss, question an explanation, or connect the text to prior knowledge. In writing, they include whether to reorganize an argument, clarify audience, strengthen evidence, reject a surface-level correction, or preserve a multilingual rhetorical choice. The educational value of AI feedback therefore depends not only on whether the feedback is accurate, but also on whether learners are required to interpret and act on it in ways that build self-regulation.

Empirical work on AI-supported writing points to this balanced view. Studies of LLM-generated feedback report potential benefits for revision, motivation, and access to timely support, while studies comparing human and AI feedback caution that generative systems may vary in accuracy, prioritization, and criteria alignment (Meyer et al., 2024; Steiss et al., 2024). Research with ESL writers also indicates that generative feedback can be useful when students are prepared to use it dialogically rather than passively (Mahapatra, 2024). These findings support a design principle used throughout the chapter: AI should create occasions for judgment, not remove judgment from the learner.

Panadero (2017) characterises self-regulated learning as a cyclical process of planning, monitoring, and evaluating one's learning. AI-mediated supports in literacy commonly operate at three interrelated levels: linguistic assistance that clarifies language and vocabulary, strategic guidance that externalises task structure, and evaluative support that provides feedback on comprehension or writing quality. When aligned with learner needs and task phases, such supports can reduce intrinsic load by externalising complex schemas and can reduce extraneous load by providing relevant information at the moment of need (van Merriënboer & Sweller, 2005).

Zawacki-Richter et al. (2019) note that AI systems often shift the learner's work from performing a task to managing an interaction with a system. In LLM-mediated settings, this interaction management can include generating prompts, comparing multiple outputs, and judging output reliability under time pressure. The cognitive cost of verification and calibration becomes part of the learning environment, particularly when model outputs are fluent yet inaccurate. These costs are not inherently undesirable, but they should be treated as design variables: if verification is not an intended learning objective, the interface should minimize unnecessary verification burdens through constrained outputs, transparency cues, and opportunities to consult sources.

Wirth et al. (2020) argue that cognitive load and metacognitive control interact dynamically as learners regulate effort and strategy use. From a scaffolding perspective, AI functions are most educationally defensible when they operate as temporary supports that enable performance beyond current competence while maintaining a trajectory toward learner independence. AI can strengthen self-regulated learning when it prompts goal articulation, strategy selection, confidence judgments, and justification of revisions.

Conversely, AI can weaken self-regulated learning when it displaces monitoring and decision-making, encouraging cognitive offloading rather than learning (Risko & Gilbert, 2016).

Shute (2008) synthesises evidence that formative feedback is most effective when it is timely, specific, and aligned with explicit criteria. Writing instruction is often constrained by the time required to provide high-quality feedback at scale; AI can expand feedback availability, but the quality of feedback varies and requires careful governance. Steiss et al. (2024) report that human feedback often outperforms ChatGPT feedback on several dimensions of formative quality even when AI feedback is usable and time-saving. At the same time, Meyer et al. (2024) show that LLM-generated, theory-based feedback can improve revision outcomes, motivation, and positive emotions relative to no-feedback conditions. Taken together, these findings position AI feedback as a potentially valuable augmentation layer when anchored in teacher-defined criteria and when learners are required to interpret, prioritize, and justify uptake decisions (Ranalli et al., 2021).

Parasuraman and Riley (1997) distinguish misuse, disuse, and abuse of automation, highlighting that the central problem is not mere use but the appropriateness of reliance. Lee and See (2004) similarly conceptualise trust in automation as a calibration problem: learners should rely on AI in proportion to its demonstrated capabilities and contextual fit. Design features such as transparency cues, uncertainty markers, source links, and verification prompts can reduce the cognitive cost of calibration and promote safer, more educationally productive interaction patterns.

Game-Based Literacy as a Dual-Task Context

Game-based literacy should be understood as a literacy environment rather than as a motivational wrapper. In well-designed games, learners read rules, interpret signs, follow narratives, evaluate claims, negotiate roles, compose messages, and use feedback to adapt their strategies. These activities are literacy practices, not peripheral activities. De la Hera et al. (2024) show that digital literacy games have been studied in relation to multiple competencies, including information literacy and technological literacy, and they identify design considerations such as clear goals, feedback, and challenge-skill balance. The chapter builds on this literature by asking how AI can support such practices while minimizing unnecessary load.

The dual-task character of literacy games is not inherently harmful. Games can make literacy purposes concrete by embedding reading and writing in consequential situations: a learner reads a clue to unlock a path, evaluates a source to challenge a misleading claim, or revises a message to persuade a non-player character. The risk arises when the mechanics compete with the literacy purpose. Cognitive load theory therefore offers a diagnostic language for deciding when mechanics are productive, when they should be simplified, and when AI supports should be delayed until the learner has first attempted the relevant literacy strategy.

Alotaibi (2024) reports that game-based learning (GBL) can enhance engagement and persistence, but outcomes depend strongly on alignment between mechanics and learning objectives. In literacy games, learners must manage comprehension or composition processes while simultaneously attending to gameplay rules, feedback systems, and time-bound decisions. Evidence from a UAE national online programming program also indicates that learner engagement in visually structured, game-like digital tasks depends not only on task appeal but also on navigational clarity, technical access, and timely trainer support (Elsawah & Charles, 2023). When mechanics are tightly aligned with learning objectives, they can function productively by encouraging retrieval, application, and self-explanation. When alignment is weak, mechanics operate primarily as extraneous load, diverting attention from reading and writing processes.

Cai et al. (2022) find in a meta-analysis that scaffolding is a decisive factor in whether digital game-based learning yields consistent benefits, including effects on cognitive load. A CLT-informed implication is that phases with high intrinsic literacy demand, such as first exposure to complex texts or initial construction of arguments and source integration, should not be coupled with high-arousal game elements such as dense audiovisual stimulation or strict time pressure. Instead, designers can separate phases by using calmer segments for deep reading and drafting, and reserving higher-arousal segments for retrieval practice, consolidation, or application. Barzilai and Blau (2014) similarly highlight that scaffolding within game environments can reduce perceived load and improve learning when it helps learners focus attention on task-relevant information.

Equity, Accessibility, and Text Complexity as Load Moderators

Diversity in literacy classrooms includes more than proficiency level. Learners differ in home languages, dialects, genre familiarity, disability status, access to digital tools, confidence with games, and prior exposure to AI systems. These differences influence cognitive load because the same task may require different amounts of working-memory coordination for different learners. An interface that appears intuitive to a digitally fluent student may impose high extraneous load on another learner; an AI correction framed as neutral may unintentionally privilege dominant varieties of English or suppress culturally meaningful voice.

Equity-oriented AI design therefore requires both inclusive options and evidence of differential impact. It is not enough to claim that an AI literacy game is adaptive if its benefits accrue mainly to learners who already have high English proficiency, high digital fluency, or stable access to devices. Evaluation should disaggregate outcomes and interaction patterns, examine whether feedback quality varies across language varieties, and invite educator and learner review of automated decisions (Baker & Hawn, 2022; UNESCO, 2023). This is why the later evaluation agenda includes bias auditing and UDL uptake indicators alongside cognitive load and literacy outcomes.

Baker and Hawn (2022) argue that algorithmic bias in education can manifest in training data, model behavior, interface design, and evaluation criteria, with downstream consequences for opportunity to learn. These concerns intersect with language and literacy: multilingual learners may be disadvantaged by models trained primarily on dominant varieties of English, and by interfaces that presume high levels of digital fluency. At the institutional level, ethical leadership is therefore central to AI integration because policies on access, data protection, and digital inclusion shape which learners benefit from advanced tools (Charles & Papadaki, 2025). Equity-oriented design therefore requires evaluation not only of average effects but also of differential impacts across learner groups.

Rao et al. (2014) position Universal Design for Learning (UDL), as a framework for ensuring multiple means of representation, action and expression, and engagement. Bray et al. (2023) show in a systematic review that technology-mediated UDL implementations are most effective when accessibility features are aligned with learner variability and context rather than treated as compliance afterthoughts. For AI-mediated literacy, this implies deliberate choices about pacing controls, multimodal representations, and alternative input modes that reduce avoidable barriers without lowering cognitive demand in ways that undermine learning goals.

Paris (2012) argues that culturally sustaining pedagogy requires sustaining learners' linguistic and cultural repertoires rather than assimilating them to a single norm. In writing instruction, translanguaging and codemeshing can be teachable strategies that enrich academic writing development when integrated into pedagogy (Canagarajah, 2011). For AI-mediated literacy, this implies that systems should not treat multilingual variation as error by default; instead, they should support purposeful language choices and provide explicit options for audience, register, and genre conventions. Such options can reduce extraneous load by making expectations explicit while also supporting identity-affirming participation.

Graesser et al. (2004) introduce Coh-Metrix as a computational tool that provides indices of cohesion and language that can approximate aspects of comprehensibility and integration demands. From a CLT perspective, text complexity indices are not merely descriptive; they can inform adaptive sequencing, targeted glossing, and cautious use of simplification or paraphrase generation. When text selection and adaptation are informed by linguistic features such as lexical frequency and syntactic density, as well as cohesion and genre structure, designers can better manage intrinsic load while avoiding over-simplification that reduces opportunities for germane processing. Taken together, CLT, scaffolding research, self-regulated learning models, game-based learning principles, and equity-oriented design converge on a central claim: AI-mediated supports are most defensible when they reduce avoidable extraneous load, manage intrinsic load through sequencing and schema support, deliberately generate germane load through explanation and justification, and preserve learner agency. The next section operationalizes this claim through the Adaptive Scaffolding Matrix.

THE ADAPTIVE SCAFFOLDING MATRIX

Purpose and Structure

The ASM also functions as a communication tool for interdisciplinary teams. Literacy educators can use it to specify the reading or writing process that a support is meant to assist; game designers can use it to decide when mechanics should heighten challenge and when they should recede; developers can use it to constrain AI outputs; and researchers can use it to generate testable hypotheses. This shared vocabulary is important because AI features are often introduced as platform capabilities before their pedagogical function has been clarified.

Van Merriënboer and Sweller (2005) emphasize that instructional supports should be justified in relation to cognitive architecture rather than added as generic enhancements. The Adaptive Scaffolding Matrix (ASM), is proposed as a design heuristic for aligning AI supports with literacy phases and cognitive load targets in game-based reading and writing environments. The framework responds to a persistent problem in AI-enhanced learning design: feature availability often expands faster than principled guidance about when a feature should be enabled, how it should be framed, and when it should be constrained or withdrawn.

Lee and See (2004) argue that abundant automation can increase both capability and the need for calibrated reliance; this tension is especially visible in generative AI that can produce fluent text with variable accuracy. Accordingly, the ASM treats AI supports as modular scaffolds rather than as a monolithic tutor, and it assumes that cognitive load is dynamic, varying not only across learners but also across phases within a single activity. The ASM is motivated by four design aims: reducing extraneous load by minimizing interface fragmentation and prompt overhead, managing intrinsic load by aligning supports to phase-specific bottlenecks such as decoding or synthesis, stimulating germane load through self-explanation and reflective decision-making, and increasing practical actionability by providing a mapping logic that designers and educators can use to justify feature enablement, restriction, or fading.

Mapping Supports to Literacy Phases

The four-phase model below is deliberately practical. It does not claim that literacy unfolds in a fixed sequence; skilled readers and writers move recursively among orienting, comprehending, composing, revising, and reflecting. The model instead provides a way to prevent all supports from appearing at once. If the phase is orientation, the most valuable support may be goal clarification. If the phase is deep comprehension, the interface should protect time on text. If the phase is revision, AI feedback should be criteria-referenced and limited. If the phase is consolidation, the design should ask learners to name strategies they can reuse without the game.

Kalyuga et al. (2003) demonstrate that guidance can become redundant as expertise increases, which implies that scaffolds should be optional, configurable, and fadeable. Along one axis, the ASM distinguishes four functional families of AI support. Linguistic Support Aids (LSA), provide in-context language assistance such as definitions, paraphrases, examples, and optional translation intended to reduce decoding and production barriers. Design Guidance Scaffolds, hereafter DGS, externalise task structure through genre templates, rhetorical move cues, and criteria-aligned checklists. Process Management tools, hereafter PM, support pacing and coordination through segmentation, dashboards, and version control, primarily targeting extraneous load caused by multitasking and fragmentation. Metacognitive Reflection prompts, hereafter MR, elicit planning, monitoring, evaluation, and justification, functioning as germane-load generators linked to self-regulated learning (Panadero, 2017; Wirth et al., 2020).

Sweller et al. (1998) treat learning as schema construction supported by careful sequencing and practice, which highlights the importance of phase-sensitive design. Along the second axis, the ASM assumes a four-phase model of literacy activity that can be instantiated for reading, writing, and integrated tasks. The phases include Orientation, defined as goal setting and task interpretation; Comprehension and Encoding, defined as reading, vocabulary, and integration; Composition and Revision, defined as drafting, reorganising, editing, and source integration; and Reflection and Consolidation, defined as self-assessment and transfer planning. Phases are often recursive rather than linear, but the model supports explicit reasoning about bottlenecks and trade-offs when configuring AI supports.

Table 1 presents the Adaptive Scaffolding Matrix. Each cell indicates typical functions and example AI features that can be deployed in a given phase, together with the intended cognitive load target. The matrix should not be interpreted as a prescription to add more AI; in many contexts, the most defensible decision is to hide or constrain a feature to protect learners from avoidable load or premature cognitive offloading.

Table 1. Adaptive Scaffolding Matrix: Mapping AI Supports to Literacy Phases and Cognitive Load Targets

AI Support Family	Orientation	Comprehension / Encoding	Composition / Revision	Reflection / Consolidation
LSA: Linguistic	Preview key words; clarify task language.	Hover definitions; one-sentence paraphrase; examples; optional translation.	Lexical and phrasing options; error explanations, not automatic corrections.	Personal word list; spaced retrieval; contrastive notes for transfer.
DGS: Task and Genre	Purpose, audience, criteria; exemplar; outline starter.	Schema cues such as cause-effect and compare-contrast; annotation template; question stems.	Argument and synthesis frames; move checklist; citation prompts.	Schema recap; strategy reflection; plan next task; reduce reliance settings.
PM: Workflow	Single-page brief; goal dashboard; progressive tool enablement.	Segmented text; co-located questions; notes panel; reduced pop-ups.	Version control; change tracking; limited feedback queue; focus mode.	Summary dashboard; progress view; export artifacts; teacher review panel.
MR: Metacognitive	Goal setting; difficulty prediction; confidence rating; strategy choice.	Self-explanation prompts; comprehension checks; uncertainty labelling.	Justify feedback uptake; explain revisions; evaluate evidence use.	Post-task reflection; error analysis; transfer prompts; reliance calibration.

Figure 1 visualises the design logic that underpins the Adaptive Scaffolding Matrix before the detailed matrix is presented. It should be read from top to bottom: literacy phases establish the learner's immediate task demands; AI support families are then exposed through progressive disclosure; and the intended effect is judged in relation to intrinsic, extraneous, and germane cognitive load. The side panels make explicit that teacher orchestration and equity-oriented accessibility governance surround the entire activity system rather than functioning as optional additions. This structure is consistent with the chapter's argument that AI features in game-based literacy should be treated as phase-sensitive scaffolds rather than generic enhancements (Kalyuga et al., 2003; Mayer & Moreno, 2003).

Figure 1. Phase-Aligned AI Scaffolding Logic for Game-Based Literacy

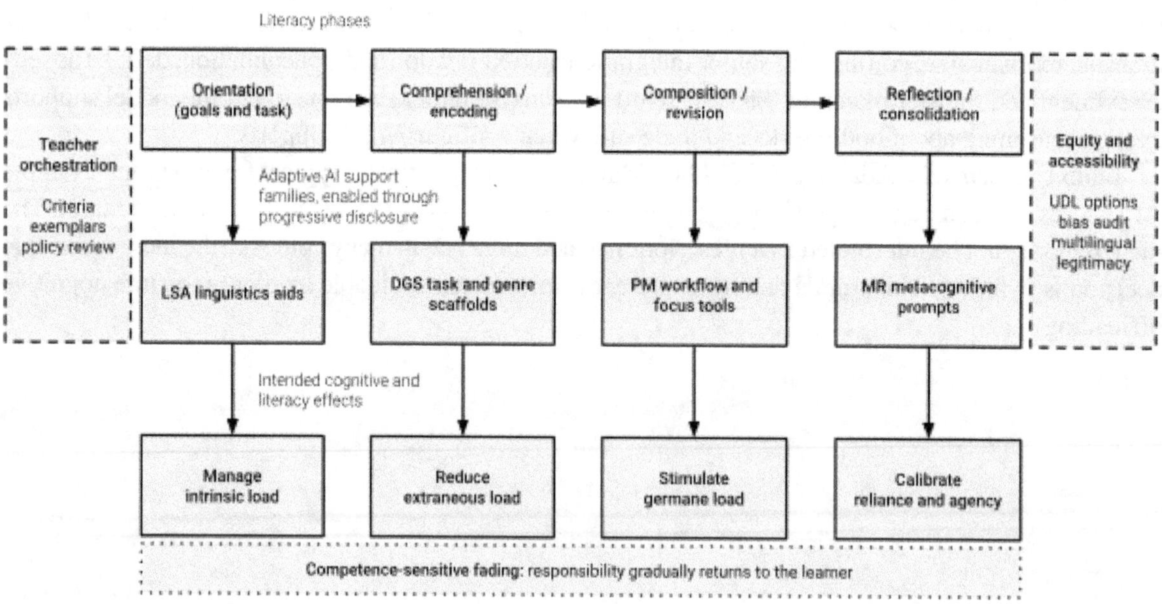

Note. LSA = Linguistic Support Aids; DGS = Design Guidance Scaffolds; PM = Process Management; MR = Metacognitive Reflection.

Progressive Disclosure, Fading, and Teacher Orchestration

Teacher orchestration is also the point at which the chapter's three themes come together in practice. The teacher decides which literacy outcome matters, which game mechanic can make that outcome meaningful, which AI support can reduce barriers, and which supports should be hidden to preserve productive effort. This professional judgment cannot be delegated entirely to a model because it depends on curricular aims, classroom norms, learners' histories, assessment expectations, and ethical constraints. The ASM is therefore designed to augment teacher judgment rather than replace it.

Mayer and Moreno (2003) synthesise multimedia learning principles showing that learners benefit when interfaces minimize unnecessary attention shifts and redundant information. A central implication of the ASM is progressive disclosure: learners should be shown only those AI functions that are relevant to the current phase, and assistance should default to on-demand rather than always-on delivery. Progressive disclosure reduces extraneous load by limiting attentional competition and preventing the interface from behaving as a second task. It also supports agency by making assistance a choice rather than an imposition.

Kalyuga et al. (2003) emphasize that fading should be tied to competence rather than to time-on-task. In literacy, plausible indicators include stable comprehension accuracy, increasing revision depth with growth in higher-order revisions, and improved self-explanation quality. Systems can operationalize fading through rule-based thresholds, educator-configured settings, or hybrid approaches that combine analytics with professional judgement. Fading is most defensible when learners demonstrate stable inferential comprehension and increasingly make higher-order, criteria-aligned revisions without heavy reliance on supports.

Ranalli et al. (2021) show that trust and engagement with automated feedback are shaped by how criteria and accountability are structured in the learning environment. Teacher orchestration therefore remains essential in AI-mediated literacy for at least three reasons. First, educators define interpretive frames by clarifying the difference between using AI for support and using AI to replace thinking. Second, educators provide criteria and exemplars that anchor feedback and reduce ambiguity, thereby reducing extraneous load. Third, educators provide accountability and ethical oversight, including decisions about privacy, data use, and fairness. The ASM therefore treats teacher-facing controls, such as enabling or disabling specific supports and configuring feedback constraints, as integral design components rather than ancillary administrative features.

DESIGN PROPOSITIONS

Paas et al. (2003) argue that cognitive load research advances when design claims are framed as testable hypotheses linked to both process measures and learning outcomes. Using the ASM as a heuristic, this section advances a set of design propositions intended to guide system design and empirical evaluation in AI-mediated, game-based literacy. The propositions are framed as hypotheses about how particular configurations of AI support are expected to influence cognitive load, learner agency, and literacy outcomes.

Interface and Phase Alignment

These propositions are deliberately framed as design hypotheses rather than universal prescriptions. A support that reduces load for one group may increase load for another; a mechanic that motivates retrieval practice may distract from initial comprehension; a feedback routine that helps novice writers may frustrate advanced writers. The propositions should therefore be tested with attention to both average effects and subgroup patterns, particularly for multilingual learners and learners with disabilities.

Mayer and Moreno (2003) describe split-attention effects in multimedia learning, in which learning is hindered when learners must integrate related information presented in separate locations. Proposition 1 predicts that, in reading tasks, in-context linguistic aids such as hover definitions and concise paraphrases will reduce extraneous load relative to off-screen or separate-window supports, especially for novices and multilingual learners (Yeung et al., 1998).

Shute (2008) emphasizes that feedback is most effective when it is actionable and aligned with criteria, which suggests that more feedback is not necessarily better feedback. Proposition 2 predicts that constrained AI outputs, operationalized as feedback aligned with explicit criteria and limited to a small number of prioritized actions, will reduce extraneous load and increase uptake compared with unconstrained, verbose feedback streams (Steiss et al., 2024).

Cai et al. (2022) report that cognitive load is sensitive to the presence and timing of scaffolding in digital game-based learning. Proposition 3 predicts that coupling complex reading or initial drafting with strict time pressure or dense stimulation will increase extraneous load and reduce comprehension and composition quality; separating high-intrinsic literacy phases from high-arousal game phases is expected to improve outcomes.

Expertise-Sensitive Scaffolding and Self-Regulated Learning

Kalyuga et al. (2003) show that guidance can become redundant as learners develop expertise, which implies that scaffolding should be optional and fadeable. Proposition 4 predicts that design guidance scaffolds such as templates and rhetorical move prompts will have the strongest positive effects for novices and diminishing or negative effects for more expert learners if not faded or made optional.

Panadero (2017) highlights that self-regulation improves when learners explicitly plan, monitor, and evaluate their performance. Proposition 5 predicts that metacognitive reflection prompts that elicit goal setting, confidence ratings, and justification will increase germane load and improve transfer, particularly when paired with feedback cycles that require learners to interpret and prioritize suggestions (Wirth et al., 2020).

Lee and See (2004) conceptualise trust as a calibration process that can be supported through transparency and feedback about system performance. Proposition 6 predicts that transparency cues, including source links, uncertainty markers, and concise rationales, will reduce misuse and disuse by supporting appropriate reliance (Parasuraman & Riley, 1997).

Ranalli et al. (2021) demonstrate that engagement with automated feedback is shaped by learners' need to judge credibility and by the accountability structures surrounding uptake. Proposition 7 therefore predicts that AI-generated feedback will be most effective when integrated into teacher-defined criteria and when learners are required to decide on uptake and justify decisions in relation to audience, purpose, and rubric dimensions (Meyer et al., 2024).

Equity, Multilingual Legitimacy, and Intrinsic-Load Diagnostics

Baker and Hawn (2022) argue that educational technologies can amplify inequities when they advantage learners with higher prior proficiency or greater digital fluency. Proposition 8 predicts that AI-mediated supports can exacerbate disparities if they primarily benefit already-advantaged learners; designs that implement UDL options and bias auditing are expected to reduce differential impact (Bray et al., 2023; Rao et al., 2014).

Paris (2012) argues that culturally sustaining pedagogy requires sustaining learners' linguistic repertoires rather than enforcing assimilation to a single norm. Proposition 9 predicts that systems that allow purposeful translanguaging and distinguish between register choices and errors will better support identity-affirming participation and rhetorical development than systems that enforce monolingual norms by default (Canagarajah, 2011).

Graesser et al. (2004) show that computational indices can approximate cohesion and language features related to comprehensibility. Proposition 10 predicts that incorporating text complexity indices and cohesion diagnostics will enable better matching of texts to learners and more targeted glossing or cautious simplification, thereby reducing cognitive overload and supporting transfer.

DESIGN SCENARIOS FOR GAME-BASED LITERACY

Barzilai and Blau (2014) argue that the effectiveness of game-based learning depends on the design of scaffolding and its alignment with learning objectives. To illustrate how the ASM can be operationalized, this section elaborates four design scenarios representative of common game-based literacy task types. Each scenario specifies a task structure, a phase-aligned configuration of AI supports, and anticipated implications for cognitive load, learner agency, and equity. The scenarios are illustrative rather than exhaustive, and they are intended to support principled design reasoning and the derivation of testable hypotheses in future empirical work (Cai et al., 2022).

Scenario A: Quest-Based Reading Comprehension With Adaptive Vocabulary Support

The central literacy outcome in this scenario is inferential comprehension, not vocabulary lookup frequency. Learners should be rewarded for using vocabulary support strategically, explaining how a word or phrase changes the meaning of a passage, and revising an interpretation when new evidence appears. The AI support therefore operates as a temporary bridge from access to meaning, while the game mechanics make explanation and evidence use consequential.

Yeung et al. (1998) show that explanatory notes can either support or hinder learning depending on how they are integrated with reading tasks. In this scenario, learners progress through a narrative quest in which each level requires comprehension of a short informational or narrative text, followed by inference questions and a brief retell. Game rewards are tied to comprehension accuracy and to reflective explanations rather than speed, thereby limiting the likelihood that time pressure will operate as extraneous load during deep reading.

Mayer and Moreno (2003) argue that reducing split attention can free cognitive resources for comprehension and integration. Consistent with the ASM, the design emphasizes Comprehension and Encoding supports by delivering Linguistic Support Aids, abbreviated as LSA, through in-text hover definitions and one-sentence paraphrases that are constrained in length. Optional examples and translation are available through progressive disclosure rather than being displayed by default. Process Management tools (PM), segment the text into meaningful chunks and co-locate questions, text segments, and a notes panel to minimize window switching.

Panadero (2017) indicates that self-explanation prompts can strengthen monitoring and comprehension when they are strategically placed. Metacognitive Reflection prompts (MR), appear after each chunk and require learners to write a one-sentence gist statement and to rate confidence in their understanding. These prompts are intended to stimulate germane load by eliciting integration and monitoring rather than superficial response selection.

Cai et al. (2022) note that scaffolding can be designed to support learning while still promoting learner autonomy. To reduce dependence, LSA use is logged and progressively faded through delayed availability for repeatedly requested words, paired with prompts that require an initial inference attempt before support is revealed. Equity and accessibility are addressed through UDL-aligned options such as adjustable font, audio support, alternative input modes, and pacing controls (Rao et al., 2014; Bray et al., 2023). Evaluation analytics can examine whether particular learner groups rely disproportionately on LSA and whether performance gaps persist, supporting iterative refinement and bias auditing (Baker & Hawn, 2022).

Scenario B: Writing Mission With AI-Supported Revision Cycles

The writing mission is designed around improvement rather than replacement. AI may identify a weak claim, an unsupported reason, or a confusing transition, but it does not produce the final persuasive letter. The learner must decide which suggestion to accept, revise the text, and explain the decision in relation to audience, purpose, and criteria. This structure makes revision literacy visible and creates a record that teachers can use to discuss authorship and learning.

Shute (2008) argues that writing improvement is supported when feedback cycles are repeated, criteria-referenced, and oriented toward revision rather than correction. In this scenario, learners complete a mission to write a persuasive letter to a community stakeholder based on a contextualised problem. The task is structured around drafting, receiving feedback, revising, and submitting, with rewards tied to improvement between drafts and to the quality of evidence use rather than to a single final score.

Wirth et al. (2020) highlight that regulation requires planning prompts that make goals and criteria explicit. During Orientation, MR prompts require learners to specify audience, purpose, stance, and anticipated challenges, thereby externalising planning and reducing ambiguity-related extraneous load. During Composition and Revision, Design Guidance Scaffolds (DGS), provide an argument frame organised around claim, reasons, evidence, and counterargument, alongside a checklist aligned to a rubric.

Steiss et al. (2024) note that excessive or low-quality feedback can overwhelm learners and shift attention toward superficial edits. AI feedback is therefore constrained to three prioritized suggestions that explicitly reference rubric dimensions, and PM tools provide version control and highlighting of changes between drafts. Learners must annotate which suggestions were accepted or rejected and provide a brief justification linked to audience and criteria, converting feedback interpretation into germane load rather than passive correction (Ranalli et al., 2021).

Canagarajah (2011) argues that multilingual resources can be used strategically when language choices are treated as rhetorical rather than purely corrective. Equity is supported by offering register and language-variety options and by positioning language choice as a rhetorical decision. For multilingual learners, linguistic aids are available during drafting but paired with noticing prompts that encourage learning rather than direct copy-paste adoption. Teacher-facing dashboards allow review of anonymised feedback logs to identify learners who may be over-relying on AI or receiving inconsistent suggestions, supporting governance and differentiated support (Baker & Hawn, 2022).

Scenario C: Teacher-Orchestrated Co-Authoring Studio in Higher Education

In higher education, the scenario also addresses academic integrity by treating AI use as an accountable composing practice. Students are not asked simply to avoid AI or to use it invisibly. They are asked to document how it shaped planning, phrasing, source interpretation, and revision. This approach is consistent with a literacy view of AI: the important question is not merely whether AI was used, but whether students can explain and defend the textual decisions that remain their responsibility.

Risko and Gilbert (2016) describe cognitive offloading as the use of external aids that can reduce immediate cognitive demands while potentially weakening learning if core processing is displaced. Scenario C adopts a workshop model in which students compose sections of an academic report and use AI to generate alternative phrasings, propose outlines, or summarise sources. Game elements are intentionally minimal and focus on collaborative challenges and reflection badges rather than continuous scoring, thereby prioritising deep processing over stimulation.

Lee and See (2004) emphasize that appropriate reliance requires transparency and accountability structures. The educator configures the system to provide DGS supports such as discipline-relevant genre moves, PM supports such as outline and source mapping, and MR prompts that require source credibility checks and confidence ratings. Linguistic support remains available on demand, but co-authoring is constrained: the AI may propose alternatives, yet students must select an option and provide a rationale linked to audience and disciplinary criteria.

Ranalli et al. (2021) show that automated feedback becomes more educationally valuable when learners are required to evaluate and justify uptake rather than accept suggestions uncritically. The design mitigates cognitive offloading by requiring selection and justification, by foregrounding source evaluation, and by encouraging triangulation of AI suggestions with course readings and credible sources. Trust calibration is supported through transparency cues such as uncertainty markers and source links, reducing the verification burden while maintaining accountability (Parasuraman & Riley, 1997).

Paris (2012) argues that culturally sustaining pedagogy can be operationalized by legitimising diverse linguistic repertoires and positioning dominant norms as negotiable rather than neutral. A culturally sustaining stance is implemented by allowing students to position their writing for different audiences and by treating language variety as a rhetorical resource. The educator can also surface how AI systems may privilege dominant discourse norms and use AI outputs as objects of critical discussion rather than as unquestioned authorities, thereby supporting critical digital literacy and equitable participation (Baker & Hawn, 2022).

Scenario D: Integrated Reading-to-Write Synthesis Quest for Source-Based Writing

This scenario is particularly relevant for diverse learners because source-based writing often compounds multiple demands. Students must understand the source, interpret the task, manage citation conventions, paraphrase accurately, and compose for an academic audience. AI support can reduce barriers by making criteria and attribution expectations visible, but it must not turn synthesis into automated summary. The sentence-labelling routine preserves the learner's responsibility for evidence and inference.

Graesser et al. (2004) highlight that integration demands increase when learners must coordinate information across multiple sources with varying modalities. In this scenario, learners complete a synthesis quest that requires reading two short sources, such as an infographic and an article, and writing a brief evidence-based explanation or argument. The task emphasizes integration and citation rather than summary alone, and points are awarded after reflection and revision rather than immediately after first-draft production.

Mayer and Moreno (2003) show that integration costs increase when related information is separated across locations, which motivates interface designs that reduce navigation. During Comprehension and Encoding, PM supports provide a dual-pane view that keeps sources and notes visible without frequent switching, and LSA provide limited paraphrase and vocabulary support. During Composition and Revision, DGS provide a synthesis frame organised around compare-contrast, claim-evidence reasoning, and explicit source attribution prompts.

Paas et al. (2003) argue that germane load is strengthened when learners engage in schema-relevant activity rather than surface performance. MR prompts require learners to label each sentence in the draft as originating from Source A, Source B, or inference, and to rate confidence in attribution. These prompts are intended to generate germane load by forcing attention to evidence use and inference, supporting transferable academic literacy practices and reducing plagiarism risk.

Rao et al. (2014) emphasize that UDL-aligned options support engagement without prescribing a single pathway to competence. Equity is supported through topic choice that connects to learners' community contexts and through explicit instruction on citation norms paired with paraphrase-as-meaning-making prompts. Differentiation can be operationalized by allowing novices to use more structured frames while enabling advanced learners to opt into a more open-ended mode, thereby reducing redundancy for experts while sustaining support for novices (Kalyuga et al., 2003).

MEASUREMENT AND EVALUATION AGENDA

Leppink et al. (2013) argue that cognitive load research requires instruments that differentiate intrinsic, extraneous, and germane load rather than treating load as a single undifferentiated construct. Although the ASM is a conceptual design tool, its practical value depends on empirical evaluation that links phase-aligned support configurations to cognitive load profiles, interaction processes, and literacy outcomes. This section outlines a multi-method measurement agenda that combines differentiated self-report measures, performance indicators, and trace data, while also attending to trust calibration, bias, and accessibility (Baker & Hawn, 2022; Lee & See, 2004).

Measuring Cognitive Load and Learning Processes

A phase-sensitive evaluation design can reveal patterns that a single post-task load rating would obscure. For example, learners may report low load during drafting because AI generated fluent suggestions, but delayed transfer may reveal limited growth in independent writing strategies. Conversely, learners may report higher germane load during reflection because they are explaining revision decisions, yet this effort may predict better transfer. These distinctions are essential for judging whether an AI literacy game is efficient, educationally productive, or merely convenient.

Leppink et al. (2013) provide a validated approach to measuring different types of cognitive load through differentiated self-report scales. Such measures are particularly important in AI-mediated literacy because a feature may reduce one form of load while increasing another. For example, in-context vocabulary support may reduce intrinsic load during decoding yet increase extraneous load if it triggers disruptive pop-ups or prompts excessive switching between text and tool.

Paas et al. (2003) recommend triangulating subjective ratings with performance and process indicators to strengthen inference about cognitive mechanisms. Process measures in AI-mediated literacy can include interaction traces such as tool-switching frequency, time-on-text relative to time-on-AI, interruption patterns, and feedback queue depth. Combining these indicators with learning outcomes can help distinguish efficiency gains, operationalized as reduced extraneous load, from superficial performance gains that reflect cognitive offloading rather than schema construction (Risko & Gilbert, 2016).

Sweller et al. (1998) emphasize that evidence of learning should include delayed retention and transfer, not merely immediate task performance. To support this distinction, evaluations should include delayed post-tests and transfer tasks that require reading or writing without AI support, alongside analysis of revision depth, self-explanation quality, and the stability of strategy use across tasks.

Outcomes, Trust Calibration, and Equity Indicators

Trust calibration is also a literacy outcome when learners are expected to read and use AI-generated explanations. Students need to learn that fluency is not the same as reliability, that an answer may sound plausible while misrepresenting a source, and that automated suggestions should be checked against purpose, audience, evidence, and task criteria. For this reason, evaluation should include evidence of verification behavior and reflective justification, not only acceptance rates.

Shute (2008) suggests that outcome measures should capture both task performance and the quality of learning processes elicited by feedback. For reading, relevant indicators include literal and inferential comprehension accuracy, retell quality, and annotation quality. For writing, rubric-based assessment can be complemented with process indicators such as revision depth and the distribution of revisions across higher- and lower-level concerns, including evidence integration and source attribution accuracy.

Lee and See (2004) argue that reliance is adaptive when it is calibrated to system capability and context. Because AI outputs are probabilistic, evaluation should include reliance and calibration measures such as acceptance rates, verification behaviors such as opening source links, and survey or interview measures probing perceived credibility (Parasuraman & Riley, 1997). Patterns of engagement with automated feedback, including what learners accept, reject, or verify, are often as informative as final scores (Ranalli et al., 2021).

Baker and Hawn (2022) recommend disaggregating both outcomes and interaction patterns across learner groups to identify differential impacts and potential bias. Equity auditing can examine differential error rates, differential feedback quality, and differential alignment with learners' language varieties. UDL indicators, including availability and uptake of multiple representations and expression modes, provide additional evidence of inclusive design (Bray et al., 2023; Rao et al., 2014).

Evaluation Designs and a Multi-Method Matrix

Meyer et al. (2024) demonstrate that randomised classroom-based designs can be used to test the impact of LLM-generated feedback when feedback principles are clearly operationalized. Evaluation can proceed through a sequence of designs: laboratory-based experiments to isolate interface and support effects, classroom-based quasi-experiments to examine ecological validity, and design-based research cycles to iteratively refine ASM implementations. In game-based contexts, randomisation at class or cohort level may be necessary to reduce contamination across conditions.

Paas et al. (2003) note that multi-method approaches strengthen causal inference when subjective, behavioral, and outcome measures converge. Table 2 summarises candidate measures for cognitive load, literacy outcomes, engagement, trust calibration, and equity. The matrix is intended as a planning artefact for designers and researchers, and it can be used to ensure that evaluation plans address both learning outcomes and responsible deployment considerations.

Table 2. Multi-Method Evaluation Matrix for AI-Mediated, Game-Based Literacy

Construct	Examples of Measures	Rationale for AI-Mediated Literacy
Intrinsic load	Text complexity indices; task element-interactivity rating; prior knowledge checks; perceived intrinsic load scale (Leppink et al., 2013).	Separates task difficulty from design issues; supports adaptive text selection and sequencing.
Extraneous load	Perceived extraneous load scale (Leppink et al., 2013); interface analytics such as window switches and clicks; interruption frequency; redundant information exposure.	Detects overload caused by fragmented interfaces, prompt overhead, and feedback clutter.
Germane load	Perceived germane load scale (Leppink et al., 2013); self-explanation quality; reflection depth; strategy reports.	Captures productive effort devoted to schema construction, monitoring, and transfer.
Reading outcomes	Comprehension accuracy, literal and inferential; retell quality; time on meaningful reading; annotation quality.	Evaluates whether AI supports improve understanding rather than only speed or superficial recall.
Writing outcomes	Rubric-based quality; revision depth and distribution; evidence integration; source attribution accuracy.	Tests whether AI feedback produces learning-oriented revisions and transferable writing competence.
Trust and reliance	Acceptance rates of suggestions; verification behaviors; calibration surveys; interviews (Lee & See, 2004).	Distinguishes misuse from disuse and supports safe deployment.
Equity and accessibility	Disaggregated performance; differential feedback quality; UDL access logs; learner choice metrics; bias audits (Baker & Hawn, 2022).	Ensures benefits are not limited to high-proficiency or high-digital-fluency learners.

Figure 2 translates the measurement agenda into an evaluation logic model for empirical and design-based studies. The model begins with an ASM-configured intervention and then asks whether observed learner interaction patterns and literacy outcomes are consistent with the intended cognitive-load mechanisms. It separates process evidence from performance evidence so that improved products are not mistaken for durable learning when gains are produced mainly through cognitive offloading. The final stage returns to trust calibration, equity, and accessibility, signalling that evaluation should feed iterative redesign rather than operate only as a summative judgment (Baker & Hawn, 2022; Lee & See, 2004; Leppink et al., 2013; Paas et al., 2003; Risko & Gilbert, 2016).

Figure 2. Evaluation Logic Model for AI-Mediated, Game-Based Literacy Design

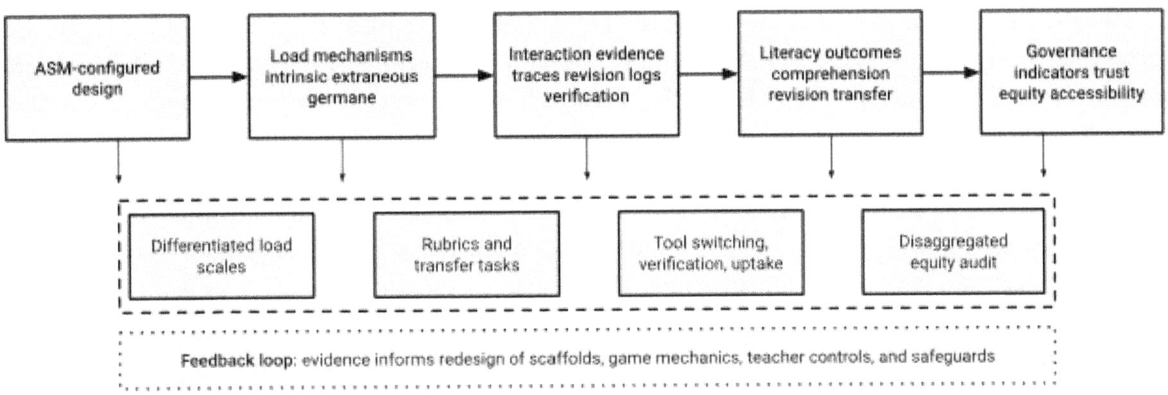

Note. ASM = Adaptive Scaffolding Matrix.

PRACTICAL IMPLEMENTATION GUIDANCE

Implementation should begin with a literacy design brief rather than a feature list. Teachers and designers can first specify the target practice, such as inferential reading, rhetorical audience awareness, source integration, or revision depth. They can then select the game mechanic that makes the practice meaningful and the AI support that reduces avoidable barriers. This sequence prevents a common error in educational technology design: beginning with an available feature and then searching for a pedagogical justification.

Mayer and Moreno (2003) argue that interface design can either support learning by reducing unnecessary processing or impose avoidable demands that compete with essential processing. This section translates the ASM and associated propositions into implementation guidance for designers and educators, foregrounding interaction design and governance mechanisms intended to reduce avoidable cognitive load while preserving learner agency, integrity, and equity (Baker & Hawn, 2022; Lee & See, 2004).

Yeung et al. (1998) demonstrate that split attention and redundancy effects are sensitive to how explanatory supports are integrated with reading materials. Designers should therefore prioritize low-friction interfaces in which reading, note-taking, and writing occur with minimal window switching and with co-located task information. Consolidated dashboards can plausibly reduce extraneous load by keeping goals, rubrics, and progress indicators visible in a single space, thereby reducing navigation and memory burden (Mayer & Moreno, 2003). In reading contexts, long AI explanations should not be presented by default; brief, just-in-time supports with an option to expand are more consistent with coherence-oriented design.

Shute (2008) argues that feedback must be aligned with explicit criteria to support revision rather than correction. When AI is used for feedback, governance should prioritize criterion alignment, restraint, and interpretability. Constrained feedback routines, such as limiting output to two or three rubric-referenced actions and staging feedback across drafts, can reduce extraneous load and increase uptake compared with feedback dumps containing many low-priority suggestions (Steiss et al., 2024). Where possible, educators can provide exemplars and rubrics that anchor AI feedback and reduce ambiguity about what counts as improvement.

Panadero (2017) suggests that prompting should be treated as part of learners' strategic repertoire rather than as a purely technical skill. Prompting demands can constitute extraneous load when learners must craft long, idiosyncratic prompts simply to access basic support. Systems can reduce this burden through structured prompt menus, exemplars, and constrained interaction modes that foreground audience, purpose, and criteria. When prompting is taught explicitly, framing it rhetorically in terms of constraints, audience, and genre can align the practice with literacy learning rather than tool manipulation.

Parasuraman and Riley (1997) argue that inappropriate reliance is more likely when automation use is not governed by clear norms and accountability. Educators should define clear policies for AI use, including what counts as acceptable assistance versus academic misconduct. Such policies should be framed as ethical leadership practices, not merely compliance rules, because technology integration involves decisions about equity, privacy, agency, and institutional responsibility (Charles & Papadaki, 2025). However, policy statements are often insufficient on their own; integrity is more reliably supported when task and interface designs make authorship and decision-making visible. A defensible baseline is to treat AI as a scaffold for understanding and decision-making rather than as a generator of submit-ready text.

Ranalli et al. (2021) indicate that requiring justification can transform feedback interpretation into a learning opportunity rather than an act of passive correction. In writing tasks, a practical integrity routine is to require learners to select or reject AI suggestions, provide a brief rationale linked to audience or rubric criteria, and complete a source-attribution check for any sentence that relies on external information. Lightweight provenance logs can support reflective learning and educator review without turning integrity into surveillance.

Canagarajah (2011) argues that multilingual writers benefit when language choices are treated as rhetorical resources rather than as errors to be eliminated. For multilingual writers, AI can provide valuable linguistic resources, but it can also exert pressure toward dominant norms. A culturally sustaining stance supports experimentation with voice and register while explicitly discussing audience expectations and institutional conventions (Paris, 2012). Accessibility-by-design is equally important: UDL-aligned options, including multiple representations, flexible expression modes, and adjustable pacing, should be integrated from the outset rather than retrofitted (Bray et al., 2023; Rao et al., 2014).

Baker and Hawn (2022) recommend ongoing monitoring of differential interaction costs and outcomes to detect bias and inequity in educational technologies. System-level analytics can be used to monitor differential reliance on AI supports and to identify whether particular groups experience inconsistent feedback or higher interaction costs. Such monitoring is most defensible when combined with transparent communication to learners, clear data governance policies, and opportunities for educators and learners to contest or contextualise automated outputs.

Table 3 summarises common anti-patterns observed in AI-mediated literacy design, explains why they are problematic from a cognitive load and ethics perspective, and lists mitigation strategies grounded in the ASM.

Table 3. Common AI-Mediated Literacy Design Anti-Patterns and Mitigation Strategies

Design Anti-Pattern	Why It Is Problematic for Load and Equity	Mitigation Grounded in ASM and CLT
Always-on chatbot overlay during reading	Competes with the text for attention, increases extraneous load, and can encourage off-task dialogue.	Use on-demand micro-supports through LSA and provide a separate ask mode; segment interactions by phase through PM.
Unbounded generative rewriting of student drafts	Encourages cognitive offloading, reduces agency, increases plagiarism risk, and may normalize dominant discourse norms.	Constrain outputs to feedback and options; require justification through MR; enable educator oversight and criteria anchoring.
Feedback dumps with many low-priority suggestions	Overwhelms working memory, reduces uptake, and shifts focus toward surface edits.	Prioritise two or three criterion-aligned actions; stage feedback across drafts through PM; link suggestions explicitly to the rubric through DGS.
Rigid templates that cannot be bypassed	Becomes redundant for expert learners and can trigger the expertise reversal effect.	Make templates optional; fade guidance based on competence indicators; offer an open-ended mode through PM.
Opaque AI outputs with no rationale or sources	Weakens trust calibration and increases misuse; makes verification cognitively costly.	Add transparency cues, source links, and uncertainty markers; teach verification routines through MR.
One-size-fits-all language correction enforcing monolingual norms	May penalise multilingual repertoires, risks cultural assimilation, and can create inequity.	Offer register options and audience settings; support purposeful translanguaging; explicitly discuss norms and choices.

Limitations

This chapter advances a conceptual synthesis rather than reporting a new empirical intervention, and that boundary should be explicit. The ASM is a design and evaluation heuristic, not a validated instrument. Its value depends on whether future studies can show that phase-aligned AI support improves literacy outcomes while managing cognitive load more effectively than unstructured or always-on assistance. The propositions therefore invite empirical testing across age groups, language backgrounds, genres, platforms, and levels of game complexity.

A second limitation concerns the rapid development of generative AI. Model capability, interface design, institutional policy, and learner familiarity are changing quickly. A support that currently appears unreliable may improve; a support that currently appears engaging may become ordinary and less motivating; a risk that appears technical may become ethical or regulatory as institutions refine expectations for privacy, authorship, and assessment. For this reason, the chapter emphasizes design principles rather than tool-specific recommendations.

A third boundary concerns the measurement of cognitive load. Self-report instruments, interaction traces, and performance measures each provide partial evidence. High time-on-task may indicate productive effort, confusion, or distraction. Frequent AI use may indicate strategic support seeking, overreliance, or unclear task design. Evaluation should therefore combine measures and interpret them in relation to literacy outcomes, learner interviews, and teacher judgment. Without this triangulation, design conclusions can overstate what the data can support.

Future Research and Design Priorities

Three research priorities follow from the chapter's argument. First, researchers should compare phase-aligned AI support with generic AI access in literacy games. This would clarify whether the ASM's central design claim, that support timing matters as much as support availability, holds empirically. Second, studies should examine delayed transfer to non-game and low-support literacy tasks. Immediate performance gains are useful, but literacy education requires learners to carry strategies into new contexts. Third, researchers should examine differential effects for multilingual learners, learners with disabilities, and learners with varying levels of digital fluency.

Design research is particularly well suited to this agenda because AI-mediated literacy games involve complex interactions among pedagogy, interface, learner agency, and institutional policy. Iterative classroom studies can examine how teachers configure scaffolds, how learners interpret AI feedback, how game mechanics influence reading and writing decisions, and how equity concerns emerge in practice. Prior evidence from UAE online programming contexts similarly suggests that implementation studies should include learner perceptions, platform navigation, technical difficulties, and support structures as outcome-relevant evidence rather than background conditions (Elsawah & Charles, 2023). Such studies can refine the ASM from a conceptual framework into a more robust set of design patterns, warnings, and implementation guidelines.

CONCLUSION

Sweller (1988) argues that instructional designs should be evaluated by how effectively they manage working memory constraints while promoting schema construction. AI-mediated supports can meaningfully improve access to feedback, language resources, and strategic guidance in reading and writing, including within engaging game-based environments. Yet these benefits are not automatic: AI features function as load interventions that can either free cognitive resources for learning or consume those resources through interaction overhead and miscalibrated reliance.

Van Merriënboer and Sweller (2005) highlight that effective supports reduce extraneous load, manage intrinsic load, and promote germane processing. The Adaptive Scaffolding Matrix advanced in this chapter offers a principled approach for aligning supports with literacy phases and learner expertise. Its core commitments, progressive disclosure, competence-sensitive fading, and metacognitive reflection, are intended to preserve learner agency while sustaining germane load and self-regulated learning (Panadero, 2017; Wirth et al., 2020). Importantly, the ASM is designed to support defensible restriction as well as enablement: hiding or constraining a feature can be pedagogically appropriate when it prevents premature cognitive offloading or reduces avoidable interface costs.

Baker and Hawn (2022) note that responsible deployment requires attention to differential impacts and the governance of data and decision-making. Future research should test the ASM propositions in diverse settings, examine differential effects across learner groups, and develop trustworthy interfaces that promote appropriate reliance through transparency and accountability structures (Lee & See, 2004; Parasuraman & Riley, 1997). As AI capabilities evolve, the value of cognitive and learning theories is likely to increase, providing a stable foundation for responsible integration of powerful but imperfect tools into literacy education.

REFERENCES

Alotaibi, M. S. (2024). Game-based learning in early childhood education: A systematic review and meta-analysis. *Frontiers in Psychology, 15*, 1307881. Advance online publication. DOI: 10.3389/fpsyg.2024.1307881 PMID: 38629045

Azzam, A., & Charles, T. (2025). K-12 STEM teachers' experiences with artificial intelligence. *TEM Journal, 14*(1), 463-468. https://doi.org/DOI: 10.18421/TEM141-41

Baker, R. S., & Hawn, A. (2022). Algorithmic bias in education. *International Journal of Artificial Intelligence in Education*, *32*(4), 1052–1092. DOI: 10.1007/s40593-021-00285-9

Barzilai, S., & Blau, I. (2014). Scaffolding game-based learning: Impact on learning achievements, perceived learning, and game experiences. *Computers & Education*, *70*, 65–79. DOI: 10.1016/j.compedu.2013.08.003

Bray, A., Devitt, A., Banks, J., Sanchez Fuentes, S., Sandoval, M., Riviou, K., Byrne, D., Flood, M., Reale, J., & Terrenzio, S. (2024). What next for Universal Design for Learning? A systematic literature review of technology in UDL implementations at second level. *British Journal of Educational Technology*, *55*(1), 113–138. DOI: 10.1111/bjet.13328

Cai, Z., Mao, P., Wang, J., He, J., Chen, X., & Fan, X. (2022). Effects of scaffolding in digital game-based learning on student's achievement: A three-level meta-analysis. *Educational Psychology Review*, *34*(2), 537–574. DOI: 10.1007/s10648-021-09655-0

Canagarajah, S. (2011). Codemeshing in academic writing: Identifying teachable strategies of translanguaging. *Modern Language Journal*, *95*(3), 401–417. DOI: 10.1111/j.1540-4781.2011.01207.x

Charles, T., & Papadaki, M. (2025). Ethical leadership in technology integration and digital education. In Soles, B., & Meyerott, T. (Eds.), *Diverse leadership perspectives in education: From K-12 to higher education* (pp. 437–454). IGI Global Scientific Publishing., DOI: 10.4018/979-8-3693-6115-3.ch016

De la Hera, T., Cañete Sanz, L., Navarro Sierra, N., Jansz, J., Kneer, J., Glas, R., & van Vught, J. (2024). Digital literacy games: A systematic literature review. *Frontiers in Communication*, *9*, 1407532. Advance online publication. DOI: 10.3389/fcomm.2024.1407532

Elsawah, W., & Charles, T. (2023). Investigating Emirati students' practices of learning block-based programming in an online learning context: Evidence from a UAE national program. In K. Al Marri, F. Mir, S. David, & A. Aljuboori (Eds.), *BUiD Doctoral Research Conference 2022* (Lecture Notes in Civil Engineering, Vol. 320, pp. 131-142). Springer. https://doi.org/DOI: 10.1007/978-3-031-27462-6_12

Flower, L., & Hayes, J. R. (1981). A cognitive process theory of writing. *College Composition and Communication*, *32*(4), 365–387. DOI: 10.58680/ccc198115885

Gee, J. P. (2003). What video games have to teach us about learning and literacy. [CIE]. *Computers in Entertainment*, *1*(1), 20–24. DOI: 10.1145/950566.950595

Graesser, A. C., McNamara, D. S., Louwerse, M. M., & Cai, Z. (2004). Coh-Metrix: Analysis of text on cohesion and language. *Behavior Research Methods, Instruments, & Computers, 36*(2), 193–202. DOI: 10.3758/BF03195564 PMID: 15354684

Graham, S., & Perin, D. (2007). A meta-analysis of writing instruction for adolescent students. *Journal of Educational Psychology, 99*(3), 445–476. DOI: 10.1037/0022-0663.99.3.445

Kalyuga, S., Ayres, P., Chandler, P., & Sweller, J. (2003). The expertise reversal effect. *Educational Psychologist, 38*(1), 23–31. DOI: 10.1207/S15326985EP3801_4

Kasneci, E., Sessler, K., Küchemann, S., Bannert, M., Dementieva, D., Fischer, F., Gasser, U., Groh, G., Günnemann, S., Hüllermeier, E., Krusche, S., Kutyniok, G., Michaeli, T., Nerdel, C., Pfeffer, J., Poquet, O., Sailer, M., Schmidt, A., Seidel, T., & Kasneci, G. (2023). ChatGPT for good? On opportunities and challenges of large language models for education. *Learning and Individual Differences, 103*, 102274. DOI: 10.1016/j.lindif.2023.102274

Kintsch, W. (1988). The role of knowledge in discourse comprehension: A construction-integration model. *Psychological Review, 95*(2), 163–182. DOI: 10.1037/0033-295X.95.2.163 PMID: 3375398

Lee, J. D., & See, K. A. (2004). Trust in automation: Designing for appropriate reliance. *Human Factors, 46*(1), 50–80. DOI: 10.1518/hfes.46.1.50.30392 PMID: 15151155

Leppink, J., Paas, F., van der Vleuten, C. P. M., van Gog, T., & van Merriënboer, J. J. G. (2013). Development of an instrument for measuring different types of cognitive load. *Behavior Research Methods, 45*(4), 1058–1072. DOI: 10.3758/s13428-013-0334-1 PMID: 23572251

Mahapatra, S. (2024). Impact of ChatGPT on ESL students' academic writing skills: A mixed methods intervention study. *Smart Learning Environments, 11*(1), 9. DOI: 10.1186/s40561-024-00295-9

Mayer, R. E., & Moreno, R. (2003). Nine ways to reduce cognitive load in multimedia learning. *Educational Psychologist, 38*(1), 43–52. DOI: 10.1207/S15326985EP3801_6

Meyer, J., Jansen, T., Schiller, R., Liebenow, L. W., Steinbach, M., Horbach, A., & Fleckenstein, J. (2024). Using LLMs to bring evidence-based feedback into the classroom: AI-generated feedback increases secondary students' text revision, motivation, and positive emotions. *Computers and Education: Artificial Intelligence, 6*, 100199. DOI: 10.1016/j.caeai.2023.100199

Paas, F., Tuovinen, J. E., Tabbers, H., & van Gerven, P. W. M. (2003). Cognitive load measurement as a means to advance cognitive load theory. *Educational Psychologist, 38*(1), 63–71. DOI: 10.1207/S15326985EP3801_8

Panadero, E. (2017). A review of self-regulated learning: Six models and four directions for research. *Frontiers in Psychology, 8*, 422. DOI: 10.3389/fpsyg.2017.00422 PMID: 28503157

Parasuraman, R., & Riley, V. (1997). Humans and automation: Use, misuse, disuse, abuse. *Human Factors, 39*(2), 230–253. DOI: 10.1518/001872097778543886

Paris, D. (2012). Culturally sustaining pedagogy: A needed change in stance, terminology, and practice. *Educational Researcher, 41*(3), 93–97. DOI: 10.3102/0013189X12441244

Plass, J. L., Homer, B. D., & Kinzer, C. K. (2015). Foundations of game-based learning. *Educational Psychologist*, *50*(4), 258–283. DOI: 10.1080/00461520.2015.1122533

Ranalli, J. (2021). L2 student engagement with automated feedback on writing: Potential for learning and issues of trust. *Journal of Second Language Writing*, *52*, 100816. DOI: 10.1016/j.jslw.2021.100816

RAND Reading Study Group. (2002). *Reading for understanding: Toward an R&D program in reading comprehension*. RAND Corporation. https://www.rand.org/pubs/monograph_reports/MR1465.html

Rao, K., Ok, M. W., & Bryant, B. R. (2014). A review of research on Universal Design Educational Models. *Remedial and Special Education*, *35*(3), 153–166. DOI: 10.1177/0741932513518980

Risko, E. F., & Gilbert, S. J. (2016). Cognitive offloading. *Trends in Cognitive Sciences*, *20*(9), 676–688. DOI: 10.1016/j.tics.2016.07.002 PMID: 27542527

Shute, V. J. (2008). Focus on formative feedback. *Review of Educational Research*, *78*(1), 153–189. DOI: 10.3102/0034654307313795

Steiss, J., Tate, T., Graham, S., Cruz, J., Hebert, M., Wang, J., Moon, Y., Tseng, W., Warschauer, M., & Olson, C. B. (2024). Comparing the quality of human and ChatGPT feedback of students' writing. *Learning and Instruction*, *91*, 101894. DOI: 10.1016/j.learninstruc.2024.101894

Sweller, J. (1988). Cognitive load during problem solving: Effects on learning. *Cognitive Science*, *12*(2), 257–285. DOI: 10.1207/s15516709cog1202_4

Sweller, J., van Merriënboer, J. J. G., & Paas, F. (1998). Cognitive architecture and instructional design. *Educational Psychology Review*, *10*(3), 251–296. DOI: 10.1023/A:1022193728205

UNESCO. (2023). *Guidance for generative AI in education and research*. UNESCO. https://unesdoc.unesco.org/ark:/48223/pf0000386693

van Merriënboer, J. J. G., & Sweller, J. (2005). Cognitive load theory and complex learning: Recent developments and future directions. *Educational Psychology Review*, *17*(2), 147–177. DOI: 10.1007/s10648-005-3951-0

Wirth, J., Stebner, F., Trypke, M., Schuster, C., & Leutner, D. (2020). An interactive layers model of self-regulated learning and cognitive load. *Educational Psychology Review*, *32*(4), 1127–1149. DOI: 10.1007/s10648-020-09568-4

Yeung, A. S., Jin, P., & Sweller, J. (1998). Cognitive load and learner expertise: Split-attention and redundancy effects in reading with explanatory notes. *Contemporary Educational Psychology*, *23*(1), 1–21. DOI: 10.1006/ceps.1997.0951 PMID: 9514686

Zawacki-Richter, O., Marín, V. I., Bond, M., & Gouverneur, F. (2019). Systematic review of research on artificial intelligence applications in higher education: Where are the educators? *International Journal of Educational Technology in Higher Education*, *16*(1), 39. Advance online publication. DOI: 10.1186/s41239-019-0171-0

Chapter 7
Designing Culturally Responsive Literacy Ecosystems for Multilingual and Neurodiverse Learners:
Equity-Centered AI and Game-Based Multiliteracies

Ashraf Alam
http://orcid.org/0000-0001-6178-1187
Department of Education, National Institute of Technology Calicut, India

ABSTRACT

This chapter theorises AI-infused, game-based literacy environments as equity-centered multiliteracies ecosystems rather than technocentric novelties. It synthesises autonomous, sociocultural, multiliteracies, critical literacy, Universal Design for Learning, translanguaging, neurodiversity, and design justice constructs to re-specify how multilingual and neurodiverse learners are positioned within algorithmically orchestrated games. AI functionalities are reframed as sociotechnical infrastructures whose affordances, risks, and safeguards co-determine epistemic inclusion. The chapter articulates literacy-first, pedagogy-first design blueprints, neurodiversity-sensitive interfaces, and culturally responsive narrative architectures that preserve teacher agency and learner dignity. A polycentric governance matrix distributes responsibilities across students, families, educators, developers, researchers, and regulators. Collectively, these architectures delineate how AI-GBL systems can be re-engineered as infrastructures for critical, culturally grounded, plurilingual literacies.

DOI: 10.4018/979-8-3373-7472-7.ch007

INTRODUCTION

Global Literacy Precarity in an Algorithmically Game-Saturated Epoch

Contemporary literacy ecologies are marked by a paradox of unprecedented schooling expansion coexisting with pervasive deficits in meaningful reading and writing proficiency (Kim et al., 2023; Kirom & Rosyida, 2024). Large proportions of children complete primary and lower secondary schooling without attaining basic comprehension, vocabulary depth, or inferential reasoning, while adults in many regions remain excluded from functional literacy in dominant and minoritised languages alike. These structural deficits intersect with multilingualism, migration, poverty, gender inequities, disability, and conflict, producing layered regimes of exclusion for learners who navigate multiple languages and atypical cognitive profiles. Education systems are being inundated with Artificial Intelligence (AI) infused tutoring platforms, adaptive reading applications, and game-based environments that are marketed as instruments of personalisation and engagement. These systems frequently encode narrow psychometric conceptions of skill, opaque algorithmic classifications, and homogenised narrative templates that align poorly with the lived semiotic repertoires of multilingual, bilingual, and neurodiverse learners. Without deliberate design and governance, the convergence of AI and game-based infrastructures risks intensifying learning poverty and epistemic marginalisation under the appearance of digital innovation.

Central Argument for Equity-Centred AI-Game Multiliteracies Architectures

The central argument of this chapter is that literacy ecosystems within AI enabled, game saturated environments must be architected as equity-centred *multiliteracies* systems in which literacy remains the epistemic and pedagogical nucleus and technological artefacts operate as contingent mediating infrastructures. Literacy is conceptualised here as a dense constellation of semiotic, cognitive, affective, and sociopolitical practices that unfold across languages, modalities, and institutional sites rather than as an isolated set of decontextualised micro skills (Alnuaim, 2024; Dai & Zhang, 2025; Ventsel et al., 2024). AI models, learning analytics pipelines, narrative engines, and game mechanics are therefore treated as infrastructural assemblages that can either amplify or attenuate these practices. The chapter contends that constructs such as *multiliteracies*, *critical literacy*, *translanguaging pedagogy*, *Universal Design for Learning*, *neurodiversity*, *design justice*, and *AI as sociotechnical infrastructure* can be braided into a coherent design and governance framework. This framework treats multilingual, bilingual, dyslexic, autistic, and otherwise neurodiverse learners as the primary reference point for system configuration, curriculum alignment, and evaluative judgement, such that inclusivity is not a retrofitted accommodation but the foundational design logic.

Key Constructs and Conceptual Vocabulary

The conceptual vocabulary mobilised in this narrative review is intentionally expansive in order to capture the multiplex character of literacy in AI mediated gameful ecologies. Literacy is understood as encompassing decoding, automaticity, comprehension, composition, argumentation, and *critical literacy* practices that are enacted through print, screen, embodied interaction, and data rich interfaces (Chen, 2024; Fitriah et al., 2023). The construct of *multiliteracies* highlights the interweaving of linguistic, visual, auditory, gestural, spatial, and algorithmic modes and foregrounds learners as designers who continually redesign meaning across media and languages. *Digital literacy* and *media literacy* are framed as capacities for navigation, multimodal production, and critical appraisal within saturated information ecologies, while *AI literacy* and *algorithmic literacy* emphasise the ability to interrogate data driven classifications, automated feedback, recommendation logics, and generative outputs (Ariani & Afnita, 2024; Gkintoni et al., 2025). Equity, accessibility, inclusion, *cultural responsiveness*, and *epistemic justice* are treated as non-negotiable design imperatives rather than optional features. The chapter adopts the *neurodiversity* paradigm, which frames dyslexia, autism, attention differences, and related profiles as natural variations in cognition, perception, and sensory integration. The lexicon of *decolonial design* is used to interrogate whose languages, stories, and epistemologies are legitimised within AI game infrastructures and whose are systematically erased or caricatured.

Guiding Interrogatives and Conceptual Methodology

The narrative review proceeds through a set of guiding interrogatives that orient the conceptual synthesis toward concrete design and governance practice. A first interrogative asks how different paradigms of literacy, including autonomous, cognitive, sociocultural, *multiliteracies*, and *critical literacy* perspectives, reconfigure what counts as legitimate AI and game design for literacy and how these paradigms conceptualise constructs such as skill, deficit, proficiency, and agency (Bengel & Peter, 2024; Bhat & Long, 2024; Nazara et al., 2025). A second interrogative examines how multilingualism, translanguaging, and neurodiversity can be encoded into technical architectures, narrative grammars, and game mechanics such that learners' full semiotic repertoires are treated as resources rather than deviations. A third interrogative explores how teacher agency, student voice, and community knowledge can be preserved and expanded through *human in the loop* and *teacher in command* configurations. A fourth interrogative scrutinises how assessment, learning analytics, and data governance can support equitable interpretation, formative feedback, and dignified learner profiling instead of deterministic labelling. Methodologically, the chapter undertakes a conceptual integration of theories and constructs across literacy studies, game studies, learning sciences, human computer interaction, disability studies, AI ethics, and governance scholarship in order to assemble a coherent architecture for practice.

THEORETICAL FOUNDATIONS OF LITERACY, MULTILITERACIES, AND GAME-BASED LEARNING

Paradigmatic Constellations of Literacy and their Design Repercussions

Literacy can be conceptualised through several paradigmatic constellations that carry radically different implications for AI-mediated, game-based learning ecologies. An autonomous literacy paradigm frames reading and writing as decontextualised, standardised micro skills, decomposed into discrete units and measured through psychometric instrumentation, which aligns easily with adaptive drills and algorithmic progression rules (Arkan & Bal, 2025; Chu et al., 2025; Vahedian-Movahed & Martin, 2025). A sociocultural literacy paradigm understands literacy as situated participation in socially organised practices, where texts, tools, and identities are co configured within communities of practice, which foregrounds dialogic interaction, narrative immersion, and collaborative problem solving in game worlds (Gao et al., 2024; Ma et al., 2023). A *multiliteracies* framework extends this view by treating linguistic, visual, auditory, gestural, and spatial modes as interdependent semiotic resources, which fits naturally with audiovisual, interactive, and spatial aspects of serious games. A *critical literacy* perspective foregrounds power, ideology, and representation, which requires that AI feedback and game narratives be treated as objects of critique rather than neutral scaffolds. These divergent paradigms, which are synthesised in Table 1, shape what counts as legitimate task design, narrative framing, and assessment logic within AI enabled literacy games.

Digital, Media, AI, and Data Literacies for Algorithmic Pedagogies

Contemporary literacy ecologies demand an expanded repertoire of digital, media, AI, and data literacies that operate in tandem with conventional decoding and comprehension capacities. Digital literacy involves the navigational, productive, and participatory competencies required to engage with hyperlinked, multimodal, and networked environments, including platform specific conventions, interface grammars, and privacy controls (Liu et al., 2025; Tiwari, 2025). Media literacy focuses on critical interpretation of symbolic artefacts, including recognition of narrative framing, semiotic stereotyping, commercial logics, and persuasive strategies embedded in audiovisual and interactive media. *AI literacy* and *algorithmic literacy* require learners and educators to understand in principle how data are collected, how models infer patterns, how recommendation engines prioritise content, and how automated feedback may misclassify or misinterpret non normative behaviours. Data literacy involves reading and critiquing dashboards, metrics, and visualisations, and connecting these to lived experience rather than treating them as ontological truths. When layered onto the paradigms assembled in Table 1, these literacies configure AI game environments not as black boxes but as epistemic artefacts that can be interrogated, negotiated, and redesigned.

Game-Based Learning, Player Experience, and Semiotic Orchestration

Game-based learning environments enact particular theories of mind, motivation, and knowledge that materially shape literacy opportunities (Akhmetova et al., 2025; Droujkov et al., 2025; Liu & Shadiev, 2025). Constructivist and constructionist perspectives treat learners as active builders of mental models and external artefacts, which resonates with sandbox games, modding ecosystems, and creative writing quests where players compose narratives, design levels, or script dialogue. Situated learning and communities of practice foreground legitimate peripheral participation in shared enterprises, which is mirrored in guild structures, collaborative missions, and affinity spaces around literacy rich games. *Self Determination Theory* highlights autonomy, competence, and relatedness as core psychological nutrients, which can be operationalised through meaningful choice architectures, scaffolded challenge calibration, and socially embedded storylines. *Flow theory* emphasises optimal experience where challenge and skill are finely balanced, which can be used to align text complexity, puzzle difficulty, and feedback timing. Cognitive load theory warns against overloading working memory through excessive interface clutter, superfluous animations, or dense textual overlays, which is especially salient for emergent readers and neurodivergent learners. Within the paradigmatic matrix of Table 1, these constructs guide the orchestration of mechanics, dynamics, and aesthetics in literacy-oriented games.

Inclusive Pedagogical Architectures for Multilingual and Neurodiverse Learners

Inclusive pedagogical architectures for AI mediated literacy games require deliberate integration of *Universal Design for Learning*, *culturally sustaining pedagogy*, *translanguaging pedagogy*, neurodiversity, and intersectional equity constructs. *Universal Design for Learning* advocates multiple means of representation, engagement, and expression, which in a game context translates into adjustable text displays, audio narration, alternative input modes, and varied performance modalities such as oral storytelling or visual composition (Abrams & Hanghøj, 2025; Alam & Mohanty, 2024; Chang & Wong, 2025). *Culturally sustaining pedagogy* insists that curricula affirm and extend learners' linguistic and cultural repertoires rather than subsume them into homogenised norms, which calls for game narratives that embed local histories, vernacular expressions, and community knowledge. *Translanguaging* pedagogy conceptualises bilingualism and multilingualism as fluid, dynamic repertoires rather than separate codes, which suggests mechanics that reward cross linguistic resourcefulness and permit mixed language dialogue. Neurodiversity frameworks treat dyslexia, autism, and attention differences as differences in processing and sensory integration, which motivates flexible pacing, predictable structures, and sensory modulation options. Intersectional equity perspectives highlight how language status, disability, gender, caste, and race compound each other, underscoring the need for the paradigmatic combinations in Table 1 to be operationalised with explicit attention to structural power.

Literacy Paradigms and AI-Game Design Implications

The conceptual apparatus elaborated above can be rendered more actionable through a comparative matrix that juxtaposes literacy paradigms, learner assumptions, semiotic orientations, and AI game design implications (Göle & Temel, 2024; Schabas, 2023; Tseng et al., 2024). Table 1 organises six influential paradigmatic formations and cross walks them with how learners are construed, how language and text are conceptualised, how AI infused game ecologies are positioned, and what concrete design consequences follow for equity-centred AI game based multiliteracies environments. The matrix is deliberately compact and analytic, intended to function as a design heuristic for educators, developers, and policymakers who must adjudicate between competing logics when procuring or constructing AI enabled literacy platforms.

Table 1. Literacy Paradigms and AI-Game Design

Paradigmatic Formation	Learner Ontology and Agency Assumptions	Construal of Language, Text, and Multimodality	Stance toward AI-Game Learning Ecologies	Design Consequences for Equity-Centred AI-GBL
Autonomous Literacy Paradigm	Learner as individual cognitive processor, deficits located intrapsychically, proficiency reducible to decontextualised skill hierarchies	Language as stable code, text as linear print artefact, multimodality treated as embellishment rather than constitutive meaning resource	AI games seen as efficient drill engines and progression trackers, primarily valued for scalability and fine-grained error capture	Design skews toward repetitive micro tasks, narrow mastery metrics, limited narrative richness, high risk of pathologizing multilingual and neurodiverse learners
Sociocultural Literacy Paradigm	Learner as participant in communities of practice, agency distributed across people, tools, and practices, identity co-constructed through interaction	Language as situated social action, text as artefact of activity systems, multimodality as routine feature of communicative repertoires	AI games viewed as cultural tools embedded in local ecologies, emphasis on collaborative quests, peer interaction, and dialogic meaning making	Design foregrounds collaborative missions, shared authorship, contextualised tasks, and in game spaces for reflection on practice and identity
Multiliteracies Framework	Learner as designer and redesigner of semiotic ensembles, agency enacted through recombination and transformation of modes	Language integrated with visual, auditory, gestural, and spatial resources, text as multimodal ensemble spanning print and screen	AI games treated as multimodal design environments that orchestrate soundscapes, visual grammars, spatial layouts, and interactive scripts	Design privileges rich multimodal authoring, player-controlled representations, and adaptive interfaces that respect sensory preferences and cultural aesthetics
Critical Literacy Perspective	Learner as critical analyst and transformative agent, agency oriented toward interrogation of power, ideology, and representation	Language as site of struggle, text as saturated with discourse, multimodality as vehicle for naturalising or contesting dominant narratives	AI games regarded as socio political artefacts whose narratives, reward structures, and classifications must be questioned and repurposed	Design embeds counter narratives, problematises stereotypes, includes meta dialogic prompts, and creates mechanics for rewriting and subverting storylines and system outputs
Universal Design for Learning	Learner as variability rich organism, agency supported through flexible pathways, engagement dependent on alignment with strengths and interests	Language and text configured flexibly across formats, multimodality used to optimise access and expression for diverse sensory and cognitive profiles	AI games seen as platforms for customisable representations, scaffolded engagement, and diverse action expression channels	Design incorporates configurable fonts and layouts, optional audio supports, alternative input modalities, and multiple performance artefacts such as oral, visual, and kinaesthetic outputs
Translanguaging and Neurodiversity Approach	Learner as plurilingual and neurologically diverse agent, agency enacted through fluid language use and idiosyncratic processing strategies	Language as integrated repertoire spanning named codes, text as translanguaged and potentially nonlinear, multimodality as extension of diverse cognitive styles	AI games conceptualised as spaces that legitimise mixed language practices and atypical interaction patterns, with strong emphasis on sensory regulation	Design rewards cross linguistic problem solving, permits mixed language interfaces, offers pacing and sensory controls, and avoids deficit labels while foregrounding strengths-based profiles

Table 1 crystallises the conceptual terrain by exposing the often implicit ontological, semiotic, and technological commitments that undergird AI enabled literacy games. When decision makers adopt an autonomous paradigm without interrogation, they tend to privilege high frequency drills, fine grained error counting, and standardised dashboards that compress learners into narrow proficiency scores.

Once decision makers foreground sociocultural and *multiliteracies* frameworks, they are more likely to commission or design narrative rich, collaborative, and multimodal environments that respect local language ecologies. As *critical literacy*, *Universal Design for Learning*, and translanguaging neurodiversity constructs guide procurement and development, AI game platforms are more likely to incorporate configurable accessibility features, mixed language scripts, and mechanics that invite critique, remixing, and counter storying.

AI IN LITERACY AND GAME-BASED ECOSYSTEMS WITH CAPABILITIES, CONSTRAINTS, AND CRITIQUES

Typological Cartography of AI Functionalities in Literacy-Game Ecologies

AI in literacy-oriented game ecologies can be conceptualised as a heterogeneous ensemble of computational functionalities that interact with texts, speech, behaviour traces, and narrative structures in highly differentiated ways (Anggela et al., 2025; Heinmäe et al., 2025; Khanchai et al., 2025). Natural language processing modules parse orthography, morphology, syntax, discourse organisation, and semantic cohesion in order to flag errors, classify genres, estimate proficiency, and generate feedback on learner writing. Speech technologies transduce acoustic signals into text and text into synthesised voice, thereby enabling oral reading, expressive narration, and pronunciation practice within interactive story worlds. Adaptive engines monitor response patterns and latencies, recalibrating difficulty levels and scaffolds across vocabulary, decoding, and comprehension tasks. Recommendation systems curate texts, quests, and game levels that ostensibly align with learner profiles and emerging preferences. Generative models co-author characters, dialogues, and branching storylines, while analytics backends compute indices of engagement, persistence, and risk. This typology, which is subsequently systematised in Table 2, undergirds the pedagogical and ethical affordances discussed later in the chapter.

Conceptual Frameworks for AI as Sociotechnical Literacy Infrastructure

These AI functionalities cannot be treated as disembodied tools, but must be framed within sociotechnical theories that foreground infrastructures, institutions, and power (Alam & Mohanty, 2023; Laila et al., 2025). A sociotechnical systems perspective conceptualises AI literacy platforms as assemblages of data pipelines, models, interfaces, organisational routines, and policy regimes that co-produce educational realities. *Actor network theory* further extends this lens by treating students, teachers, engineers, algorithms, curricula, devices, and standards as heterogeneous actants whose interactions stabilise or disrupt literacy practices. *Human in the loop* and *teacher in command* constructs insist that professional judgment and pedagogical intention remain central in configuring AI responses, curating content, and interpreting analytics. *Value sensitive design* frames AI literacy systems as moral artefacts that must embed values such as equity, transparency, and linguistic justice in their architectures. These frameworks, when read alongside the typology synthesised in Table 2, reposition AI game ecosystems from neutral conduits of content toward contested infrastructures that must be governed through explicit normative commitments.

Pedagogical Affordances and Literacy Potentials of AI-Game Integrations

From an instructional design perspective, AI mediated game environments afford granular feedback, fine-tuned differentiation, and novel semiotic experiences that are difficult to orchestrate through analogue resources alone (Eybers & Muller, 2024; Gu & Ericson, 2025; Shen & Ab Jalil, 2025). Natural language processing can highlight spelling, grammar, and discourse features in learner texts in near real time, enabling micro revisions and iterative drafting cycles embedded within quests. Speech recognition and synthesis provide multimodal entry points into texts, allowing emergent readers to hear fluent models, practice oral reading, and transform spoken stories into written artefacts. Adaptive difficulty engines maintain a dynamic equilibrium between challenge and competence, which can sustain *flow* in decoding and comprehension tasks for learners with disparate proficiency levels. Generative narrative agents can personalise story arcs, side quests, and character interactions that resonate with learner interests and cultural backgrounds, which amplifies intrinsic motivation. When aligned with the design imperatives enumerated in Table 2, these affordances can support complex multiliteracies development rather than merely accelerating rote practice.

Systemic Risks, Algorithmic Biases, and Ethical Precarities in Literacy AI

The same AI capabilities that expand pedagogical repertoires also introduce systemic risks that can profoundly distort literacy trajectories if left ungoverned (Hassan et al., 2024; Katanosaka et al., 2025). Algorithmic bias in natural language and speech modules can misrecognise minoritised dialects, non-standard accents, and translanguaged utterances, thereby labelling legitimate linguistic practices as erroneous or deficient. Predictive analytics that flag learners as at risk based on partial data traces can entrench deficit expectations and self-fulfilling prophecies, particularly when intersecting with histories of marginalisation. Recommendation engines tuned mainly to engagement metrics can trap learners in narrow content silos, under exposing them to cognitively demanding texts and critical perspectives. Generative models trained on corpora imbued with stereotypes and colonial imaginaries can reproduce harmful narratives and character tropes in game storylines. Extensive behavioural data extraction can normalise surveillance, erode trust, and commodify children's literacy practices. Table 2 therefore juxtaposes functional affordances with equity vulnerabilities and safeguards in order to foreground ethical design and governance as intrinsic to AI literacy strategy.

AI Functions, Affordances, Risks, and Safeguards

To operationalise the conceptual discussion, Table 2 condenses the principal AI modalities observable in literacy games into a compact matrix that links each modality to its core pedagogical affordances, its specific relevance for multilingual and neurodiverse learners, its characteristic equity ethics vulnerabilities, and illustrative safeguards at the levels of design and policy (Hassan et al., 2024; Katanosaka et al., 2025). This matrix is not a static taxonomy, but a heuristic device that can be used by educators, designers, and regulators when auditing existing platforms or commissioning new AI mediated literacy environments, and it complements the paradigm-oriented mapping elaborated in Table 1.

Table 2. AI Functions, Affordances, and Equity Safeguards

AI Functional Modality	Pedagogical-Literacy Affordances	Sensitivity for Multilingual-Neurodiverse Learners	Principal Equity-Ethics Vulnerabilities	Illustrative Design-Policy Safeguards
Natural Language Processing Feedback Engines	Fine grained analysis of orthography, syntax, cohesion, and genre features, rapid formative feedback within writing tasks, automated hint generation for revision and extension	Can surface recurring error patterns, provide vocabulary and structure prompts in multiple languages, scaffold explicit metalinguistic awareness for dyslexic learners when calibrated carefully	Risk of over correction of non-standard varieties, suppression of translanguaging, deficit framing of divergent text structures, opacity of scoring criteria	Multilingual error grammars, transparent feedback rationales, configurable norm settings, explicit recognition of alternative discourse conventions, teacher override controls
Speech Recognition and Text-to-Speech Systems	Support for oral reading fluency, pronunciation modelling, listening comprehension, and oral storytelling, multimodal access to texts for emergent readers	Enable auditory entry points for dyslexic and visually impaired learners, accommodate varied orthographies and scripts, facilitate bilingual oral reading when trained on multiple phonological systems	Accent bias penalising certain phonetic profiles, misrecognition of code switching, potential ridicule or stigma when errors are surfaced publicly, exclusion of low resource languages	Diverse accent corpora, offline processing options, private practice modes, explicit translanguaging tolerance thresholds, inclusion of community recorded voice models
Adaptive Difficulty and Mastery Engines	Dynamic calibration of task difficulty, personalised pacing of decoding, vocabulary, and comprehension challenges, maintenance of optimal challenge-skill balance	Can prevent boredom for advanced readers and cognitive overload for struggling learners, accommodate fluctuating attention profiles, support gradual exposure to complex texts in multiple languages	Reinforcement of narrow skill taxonomies, over reliance on correctness metrics, invisibilisation of higher order literacies, potential for opaque tracking of learner trajectories	Multi-dimensional proficiency models, inclusion of critical and creative tasks in mastery maps, transparency of adaptation logic, periodic human review of learner profiles
Recommendation and Content Curation Algorithms	Curation of texts, quests, and levels aligned with inferred interests and reading levels, support for sustained engagement and progressive complexity	Potential to surface culturally resonant texts in learners' languages, provide alternative entry points for reluctant readers, highlight resources attuned to neurodiverse preferences	Formation of filter bubbles that restrict exposure, amplification of commercial or dominant cultural content, marginalisation of minoritised literatures, algorithmic steering toward low challenge materials	Diversity constraints in recommendation logic, quotas for local and minoritised content, explicit controls for exploring outside recommended sets, periodic curriculum aligned audits

continued on following page

Table 2. Continued

AI Functional Modality	Pedagogical-Literacy Affordances	Sensitivity for Multilingual-Neurodiverse Learners	Principal Equity-Ethics Vulnerabilities	Illustrative Design-Policy Safeguards
Generative Narrative and Dialogue Agents	Creation of personalised storylines, adaptive dialogue, and branching plots, opportunities for co-authored narratives and role play, expansion of expressive possibilities	Can instantiate characters that speak in multiple languages, mirror diverse identities, and respond to atypical interaction patterns, support alternative expressive modes for neurodiverse players	Propagation of stereotypes embedded in training corpora, generation of harmful or biased content, erosion of learner authorship when AI dominates narrative production	Curated and filtered training data, constrained generation templates, learner inspection and editing of AI outputs, explicit prompts for counter narratives, robust safety filters
Learning Analytics and Predictive Risk Modellers	Aggregation of behavioural, performance, and engagement data, identification of patterns in error profiles, time on task, and strategy use, support for targeted interventions	Can reveal hidden struggles among quiet or compliant learners, track growth trajectories for diverse groups, inform differentiated supports for multilingual and neurodiverse students	Premature labelling of learners as low potential, surveillance normalisation, opaque category construction, exacerbation of structural bias when proxies correlate with disadvantage	Clear data minimisation norms, rights for learners and families to access and contest profiles, use of indicators as inquiry prompts not labels, independent algorithmic audits, explicit sunset clauses for stored data

Table 2 highlights that AI functionality, pedagogical affordance, equity vulnerability, and governance safeguard are inseparable dimensions of a single design space rather than separable technical and ethical layers. When educators and developers treat natural language processing, speech technologies, adaptive engines, recommendation algorithms, generative narrative agents, and analytics dashboards as neutral utilities, they risk reproducing linguistic hierarchies, disability stigma, and structural exclusions at scale (Alam & Mohanty, 2022; Palmquist et al., 2025). When these modalities are instead interrogated through constructs such as *sociotechnical systems*, *value sensitive design*, *data justice*, and *design justice*, and when safeguards such as multilingual corpora, transparent adaptation logic, participatory audits, and teacher override mechanisms are institutionalised, AI game based literacy ecosystems can begin to function as infrastructures that expand rather than constrict the semiotic, cognitive, and political horizons of multilingual and neurodiverse learners.

DESIGNING EQUITY-CENTERED AI-GBL MULTILITERACIES ENVIRONMENTS FOR DIVERSE LEARNERS

Literacy-First and Pedagogy-First Design Architectures

Equity-centred AI game based multiliteracies environments must begin from a literacy-first, pedagogy-first design architecture rather than from a technology-first procurement impulse (Alam & Mohanty, 2022; Palmquist et al., 2025). A literacy-first orientation treats *multiliteracies* constructs, such as decoding, fluency, deep comprehension, critical interrogation, and multimodal composition, as the non-negotiable anchor, and only subsequently considers which AI engines and ludic mechanics can mediate these outcomes. Technological Pedagogical Content Knowledge (TPACK) is a framework explaining how effective teaching with technology depends on integrating three knowledge domains: *content* (what is taught), *pedagogy* (how it is taught), and *technology* (digital tools and platforms). Teachers need balanced, context-sensitive TPACK to plan meaningful, engaging, and learner-centred technology-enhanced lessons in classrooms today. A pedagogy-first stance aligns Artificial Intelligence – Game-Based Learning (AI-GBL) features with explicit instructional models such as inquiry cycles, workshop pedagogies, dialogic teaching, and *scaffolded apprenticeship*, so that game quests, challenges, and reward structures mirror purposeful learning progressions. Within this architecture, frameworks analogous to an expanded *TPACK* are operationalised to incorporate AI-specific and game-specific knowledge domains, ensuring that mechanical complexity and narrative exuberance remain subordinate to didactic clarity. When cross-referenced with the paradigmatic constellations already assembled in Table 1 and with the functional affordances articulated in Table 2, this literacy-pedagogy nexus delineates a principled space for subsequent equity-oriented design choices.

Design Logics for Multilingual and Bilingual Learner Ecologies

Designing AI-GBL multiliteracies environments for multilingual and bilingual learners requires an explicit commitment to *translanguaging* as a core epistemological and interactional principle rather than as a tolerated exception. Interfaces, narrative scripts, and feedback channels must permit fluid movement across languages, scripts, and registers, such that learners can mobilise their full linguistic repertoires when solving puzzles, composing narratives, or negotiating quests (Bora et al., 2025; DiPaola et al., 2023; Ng et al., 2024). Game mechanics can reward cross linguistic ingenuity, for instance by unlocking clues when players translate idioms, match proverbs across languages, or reconstruct fragmented bilingual texts, thereby valorising practices often marginalised in monolingual classrooms. Characters and non-player agents can be configured to speak in different combinations of community languages and *lingua francas*, with subtitling and code meshing options that respect local sociolinguistic hierarchies. The design matrix in Table 3 systematises such multilingual design logics across varied learning ecologies, demonstrating how translanguaging, *culturally sustaining pedagogy*, and *AI literacy* can converge to generate powerful multiliteracies trajectories.

Neurodiversity-Sensitive Design for Dyslexic and Heterogeneous Cognitive Profiles

Dyslexic and neurodivergent learners experience literacy not as a linear attainment trajectory but as a complex negotiation of visual, auditory, attentional, and working memory demands, which AI game environments can either exacerbate or ameliorate (Alam, 2023a; Chang & Wang, 2025; Wijayanti et al., 2024). Equity-centred design treats the *neurodiversity* paradigm as foundational, conceptualising dyslexia, autism, and attention differences as natural variants in cognitive architecture that warrant flexible, dignity affirming supports. Interfaces thus provide granular control over typographic features, spacing, colour contrast, motion intensity, and auditory load, enabling learners to calibrate their own sensory envelopes. Mechanics privilege predictable structures with optional novelty, generous time windows, and non-punitive retries, which stabilise engagement for those with fluctuating attention or processing speed. Alternative expressive channels, such as oral storytelling captured through speech recognition, visual sequencing of events, or symbolic in game actions mapped to narrative arcs, enable literacy demonstration without over reliance on extended print production. In Table 3, such neurodiversity-sensitive principles are cross walked with contextual ecologies to foreground design configurations that normalise variability rather than pathologise it.

Narrative-Driven, Culturally Responsive, and Critically Reflexive Game Worlds

Narrative is the primary semiotic engine through which many literacy games operate, and equity-centred AI-GBL environments therefore treat story worlds as sites of cultural affirmation, ethical reflection, and critical literacy rather than as neutral entertainment backdrops (Sperling et al., 2025; Subrata et al., 2025; Yim & Wegerif, 2024). *Narrative theory* highlights plot structures, character arcs, focalisation, and temporal manipulation as resources for scaffolding inferential comprehension and perspective taking, while *critical literacy* insists that these same devices be interrogated for their ideological freight. Culturally responsive narrative design populates games with characters who embody local names, dialects, kinship patterns, and everyday dilemmas, and situates quests within geographies and histories that resonate with learners' lived realities. AI driven dialogue agents can be constrained by *design justice* principles so that they avoid exoticizing communities or reproducing deficit tropes, and instead open space for counter narratives and moral ambiguity. When positioned alongside the contextualised design patterns in Table 3, such narrative architectures enable literacy tasks that simultaneously exercise decoding, comprehension, and critical consciousness within culturally legible worlds.

Design Justice and Participatory Co-Construction of Multiliteracies Games

Equity-centred AI game based multiliteracies environments become truly transformative only when their architectures are co-constructed with those most affected by structural inequities, which is the central tenet of *design justice* (Tahir & Wang, 2024; von Gillern et al., 2025; Yim & Su, 2025a). This requires participatory design processes in which students, families, teachers, and community knowledge holders collaborate with developers and instructional designers across the full lifecycle of ideation, prototyping, testing, and iteration. Youth can co-author characters, storylines, quests, and linguistic repertoires, thereby embedding their own imaginaries, humour, and critique into the ludic fabric. Teachers articulate granular curricular demands, classroom constraints, and assessment pressures, while community elders and local artists contribute oral histories, proverbs, and visual motifs. Table 3 distils these participatory and justice-oriented commitments into a compact matrix that links specific learner ecologies with theoretical lenses, interface-narrative patterns, mechanics-feedback priorities, and multiliteracies targets.

Table 3. Equity-Centred Design for Diverse Literacy Learners in Games

Contextual Learner Ecology	Dominant Theoretical Lenses	Game Interface-Narrative Configurations	Mechanics-Feedback Design Priorities	Targeted Multiliteracies Outcomes
Multilingual Urban Classrooms	*Translanguaging, culturally sustaining pedagogy, AI literacy*	Bilingual menus, code-meshed dialogue, localised avatars, urban spatial metaphors, chat channels supporting mixed-language text	Cross-linguistic puzzles, vocabulary trading, peer-mediated hints, analytics suppressing punitive error counts, teacher-adjustable scaffolds	Decoding across scripts, inferential comprehension, critical reading of urban issues, bilingual writing, multimodal remixing of street texts
Rural Low-Resource Schools	*Universal Design for Learning, community of practice, place-based education*	Low-bandwidth visual assets, offline story bundles, icons referencing agrarian lifeworlds, audio narration for intermittent electricity	Asynchronous quests, cooperative missions on shared devices, minimal interface clutter, feedback compressible into offline printable summaries	Basic decoding fluency, oral comprehension, locally grounded informational writing, visual-literacy integration, collaborative meaning-making
Dyslexic Learners in Inclusive Classrooms	*Neurodiversity, cognitive load theory, multimodal learning*	Customisable fonts and spacing, reduced motion, optional colour overlays, text-to-speech toggles, calm auditory soundscapes	Flexible timing, chunked tasks, non-punitive retries, multimodal answer options, feedback emphasising strategies rather than deficits	Automaticity in word recognition, prosodic reading through audio pairing, structured narrative planning, confidence in composing short texts, metacognitive awareness
Indigenous Language Revitalisation Contexts	*Decolonial design, epistemic justice, orality-literacy continuum*	Interfaces foregrounding Indigenous scripts and motifs, characters speaking community languages first, storylines rooted in local cosmologies	Retrieval quests based on oral histories, collaborative reconstruction of traditional narratives, elders' voiceovers as guidance, feedback co-signed by community representatives	Phonemic-graphemic mapping in endangered languages, intergenerational story transcription, critical appreciation of colonisation narratives, bilingual anthologising of myths
Refugee and Migrant Learning Settings	*Trauma-informed pedagogy, socioemotional learning, funds of knowledge*	Soft colour palettes, non-triggering imagery, avatars reflecting diverse diasporic identities, optional anonymised usernames	Low-stakes exploratory missions, narrative branching away from graphic violence, feedback validating resilience, flexible progression to accommodate mobility	Re-establishment of print routines, narrative reconstruction of journeys, vocabulary for rights and services, expressive writing for emotion regulation, multimodal identity texts

By externalising these ecologies, lenses, and design patterns in Table 3, design teams and institutional decision makers can resist one size fits all templates and instead choreograph AI-GBL configurations that are deeply attuned to local sociolinguistic, cultural, and neurological realities. The matrix demonstrates that equity is not an abstract aspiration but a set of concrete technical and narrative decisions about fonts, voices, pacing, plotlines, metrics, and feedback grammars that either expand or constrain the multiliteracies repertoires of diverse learners. When these decisions are governed by *design justice*, *translanguaging*, *Universal Design for Learning*, and *decolonial* constructs, AI mediated game environments can function as emancipatory literate spaces rather than as algorithmic amplifiers of existing hierarchies, thereby creating a robust foundation for the analytics and governance architectures.

LEARNING ANALYTICS, ASSESSMENT, AND TEACHER AGENCY IN AI-GBL LITERACY ECOSYSTEMS

Conceptual Architectures of Assessment in Game-Infused Literacy Ecologies

Assessment in AI game-based literacy ecosystems can be conceptualised as a multidimensional architecture that integrates measurement, interpretation, and pedagogical decision making into a single dynamic system (Alam, 2023b; Sari et al., 2026; Teke & Baş, 2025). Within this architecture, assessment of learning aggregates performance evidence for accountability and certification, assessment for learning generates real time diagnostics that feed into adaptive scaffolding and instructional adjustment, and assessment as learning cultivates metacognitive self-regulation as learners engage with their own data traces. A sociocultural framing views literacy performance as emergent from participation in activity systems rather than as a fixed individual trait, which means that scores and indicators must be read in relation to contexts, tools, and identities. Evidence-centred design constructs provide a formal language for linking claims about decoding, comprehension, narrative production, and *critical literacy* to observable behaviours within AI-GBL environments. These claims, observations, and interpretations are never neutral; therefore they must be aligned with the equity-oriented paradigms and infrastructural logics articulated in Tables 1, 2, and 3.

Learning Analytics Frameworks and Data Epistemologies for Literacy

Learning analytics within AI mediated game ecologies transform clickstreams, dwell times, error patterns, hint usage, chat logs, and narrative choices into structured indicators that purportedly represent literacy phenomena (Lin et al., 2025; Rahayu & Subekti, 2025; Sayangan, 2024). From an epistemological standpoint, this transformation involves modelling assumptions about what counts as evidence of decoding, vocabulary growth, inferential comprehension, narrative sophistication, and *multiliteracies* engagement. Descriptive analytics render patterns in distributions visible, diagnostic analytics attempt to infer latent strategies and misconceptions, predictive analytics extrapolate likely trajectories, and prescriptive analytics propose interventions. These strata of analysis are powerful yet inherently reductive, since they compress complex semiotic, affective, and social processes into numerical or categorical abstractions. Frameworks informed by *multimodal learning analytics* and *data justice* constructs insist that such abstractions be made contestable and interpretable rather than presented as incontrovertible truths. Within this conceptual frame, the interpretive matrix presented in Table 4 becomes crucial, since it explicitly links common literacy analytics indicators to plausible inferences, misinterpretive pitfalls, inquiry questions, and context sensitive responses.

Teacher Data Literacy, Interpretive Judgment, and Analytics-Informed Pedagogy

Teacher data literacy in AI-GBL literacy ecosystems is not simply a technical aptitude for reading dashboards, but a complex amalgam of statistical reasoning, pedagogical content knowledge, equity consciousness, and ethical discernment (Tang et al., 2025; Voulgari et al., 2025; Wu et al., 2024). Teachers must be able to move fluidly between micro level indicators, such as reading rate, error clusters, or quest completion times, and macro level understandings of learners' identities, home literacies, linguistic repertoires, and emotional states. Interpretive judgment involves treating indicators as hypotheses rather than verdicts, triangulating them with classroom observations, student self-reports, artefact analysis, and family narratives. Table 4 operationalises this interpretive stance by mapping representative literacy analytics indicators to plausible learner inferences, recurrent misinterpretive traps, generative inquiry questions, and responsive action repertoires. Used in this way, analytics become catalysts for professional dialogue and reflective planning rather than prescriptive scripts, and teacher agency remains central in deciding which signals to amplify, which to bracket, and which to contest or nullify.

Table 4. Interpretive Matrix for Literacy Analytics Indicators and Actions

Analytics Indicator	Plausible Learner Inference	Common Misinterpretive Pitfalls	Guiding Inquiry Questions	Responsive Pedagogical-Relational Actions
Reading Fluency Speed-Accuracy Profile	Emerging automaticity in decoding or strategic slowing for comprehension monitoring	Equating slow reading with low intelligence, ignoring unfamiliar vocabulary, scripts, or anxiety	Under what conditions does pacing change, how does the learner describe their own reading experience	Provide repeated reading with audio support, pre-teach key vocabulary, normalise flexible pacing, use one-to-one conferences to reframe reading identity
Vocabulary Growth and Lexical Diversity Index	Expanding word repertoire, experimentation with varied lexis and stylistic play	Treating low lexical diversity as laziness, overlooking multilingual transfer, penalising risk taking with new words	Which domains or languages show richer vocabulary, how does topic familiarity interact with lexical choice	Embed word study in meaningful texts, draw explicit connections across languages, celebrate inventive usage, co-construct personal glossaries
Comprehension Pattern and Item Response Profile	Strengths or vulnerabilities in inference making, integration, or critical evaluation	Reducing comprehension to multiple-choice correctness, ignoring guessing patterns or language barriers, pathologising unfamiliar background knowledge	Which item types are most difficult, what background information or language resources are required, what strategies does the learner report	Model think-aloud strategies, build schema through multimodal inputs, use small-group text discussions, design alternative demonstrations of understanding
Narrative Choice and Pathway Signature	Preference for certain moral positions, identities, or complexity levels in story branches	Over reading moral character from in-game choices, ignoring curiosity or experimentation, neglecting trauma triggers	What attracts the learner to specific branches, how safe do they feel exploring alternative roles, how do they narrate their decisions	Facilitate reflective debriefs, invite rewriting of key scenes, offer narratives with multiple culturally resonant perspectives, ensure optionality around sensitive content
Persistence, Engagement, and Help-Seeking Trajectory	Patterns of grit, frustration tolerance, or strategic disengagement, orientation to collaboration or autonomy	Interpreting low persistence as lack of motivation, overlooking interface friction, home constraints, or emotional distress	When and why does the learner disengage, what supports do they use or avoid, how do external conditions shape access	Adjust challenge levels, streamline interfaces, schedule supportive check-ins, co-design engagement goals, involve families in discussing constraints
Error Cluster and Hint Utilisation Signature	Recurring misconceptions, productive struggle, or over dependence on external scaffolds	Labelling repeated errors as fixed deficits, treating hint use as cheating, ignoring linguistic or neurocognitive profiles	Which errors persist across contexts, how does the learner explain their approach, how does hint behaviour vary by task type	Provide explicit micro-instruction on targeted concepts, model strategic hint use, employ peer tutoring, redesign tasks to surface underlying reasoning

The interpretive grammar encoded in Table 4 repositions analytics from surveillance-oriented instruments into dialogic artifacts that invite inquiry, humility, and co-interpretation. When teachers approach indicators as structured prompts for curiosity rather than as deterministic labels, they are more likely to surface the structural, linguistic, and affective factors that shape performance, especially for multilingual and neurodiverse learners (Alnuaim, 2024; Dai & Zhang, 2025; Ventsel et al., 2024). This stance also creates space for students and families to participate in data conversations, reframing dashboards as shared tools for goal setting and narrative reconstruction rather than unilateral judgments imposed by opaque systems. In such cases, analytics enhance rather than erode professional agency, and the relational dimension of literacy instruction is foregrounded rather than subordinated to numerical abstraction.

Ethics of Datafication, Algorithmic Governance, and Learner Dignity

The proliferation of analytics in AI-GBL literacy ecosystems generates profound ethical questions concerning datafication, algorithmic governance, and the preservation of learner dignity (Alam, 2023c; Kim et al., 2025; Tsai et al., 2025). Datafication converts rich, situated literacy practices into portable data objects that can travel far beyond their original pedagogical contexts, which raises questions about ownership, consent, and secondary use. *Algorithmic governance* constructs draw attention to how thresholds, categories, and triggers embedded in models can shape access to resources, remediation, or opportunities, sometimes in ways that entrench existing inequities. From a *children's rights* and *data justice* perspective, learners must have intelligible explanations of what data are collected, how they are processed, and what consequences follow, and families must have meaningful avenues for contestation. Ethical architectures therefore require data minimisation, clear retention limits, participatory oversight bodies, and enforced firewalls between educational and commercial uses. When read in conjunction with the interpretive and action-oriented lens of Table 4, such governance arrangements help ensure that data serve pedagogical flourishing rather than institutional convenience.

Synergising Assessment, Analytics, and Agency for Transformative Literacy

The ultimate promise of learning analytics in AI-GBL literacy ecosystems lies not in finer calibration of surveillance, but in the synergistic integration of assessment, analytics, and agency that can catalyse transformative multiliteracies trajectories (Pavloff-Pelkonen et al., 2025; Sabatini et al., 2023; Zheng et al., 2024). Assessment architectures grounded in *multiliteracies*, *critical literacy*, and *Universal Design for Learning* provide the conceptual scaffolding for deciding which constructs to measure and how to evidence them, while analytics infrastructures provide high resolution, time sensitive glimpses into learners' engagements with texts, tasks, and narratives. Teacher agency, informed by robust data literacy and ethical reflexivity, weaves these elements into coherent instructional narratives that honour learners' linguistic repertoires, neurocognitive profiles, and cultural identities. When tables such as the paradigmatic map in Table 1, the functional matrix in Table 2, the design blueprint in Table 3, and the interpretive schema in Table 4 are used as living tools rather than static diagrams, they support multi stakeholder dialogue about what counts as successful literacy development in AI games, who decides, and on what grounds. In this way, assessment and analytics cease to be external impositions and become integral components of a justice-oriented literacy ecosystem that will be further situated within broader governance logics, later in this chapter.

MULTI-LEVEL GOVERNANCE, POLICY, AND CROSS-SECTOR COLLABORATION

Ecosystemic Governance View of AI-GBL Literacy Initiatives

AI game based multiliteracies initiatives operate within complex, multi-level ecosystems that extend far beyond individual classrooms or software products (Bhimavarapu, 2025; Ding & Holland, 2025; Fadhli et al., 2023). An ecosystemic governance perspective conceptualises schools, families, communities, markets, and regulatory bodies as interdependent nodes within a dynamic, complex adaptive system. Decisions about curriculum standards, platform procurement, connectivity infrastructure, language policies, and disability accommodations reverberate across this system, shaping how the paradigms in Table 1, the AI functionalities in Table 2, the design logics in Table 3, and the analytics configurations in Table 4 are instantiated in practice. *Multi-level governance* constructs highlight the vertical entanglement of classroom practice, school leadership, district administration, national policy, and transnational guidance, while *polycentric governance* emphasises overlapping centres of authority across public, private, and civil society actors. Within this frame, AI-GBL literacy ecosystems must be treated as long term socio technical transformations that require coordinated stewardship rather than as isolated innovation pilots.

Policy Architectures and Regulatory Normativity for AI-GBL Literacy

Policy architectures for AI enabled, game infused literacy environments encompass curriculum frameworks, assessment regimes, procurement rules, interoperability standards, and data protection norms that jointly define the parameters of legitimate practice (Bang & Siebert-Evenstone, 2025; Pu et al., 2024; Zhang et al., 2025). Curriculum and assessment policies determine whether multimodal, game mediated literacy artefacts can be recognised as valid evidence of learning or remain invisible at the point of certification. Procurement and accreditation procedures decide whether platforms must satisfy accessibility, multilingual, and transparency requirements or can prioritise proprietary lock in and narrow metrics. Data protection and AI ethics regulations specify what forms of learner data may be collected, how long they may be retained, and under what conditions they may be shared across agencies or with vendors. Standards for interoperability, inclusive design, and open licensing can either enable a pluralistic ecosystem of AI-GBL tools aligned with the equity paradigms in Tables 1 to 4 or consolidate platform power. These policy choices are later crystallised in the governance matrix of Table 5.

Stakeholder Roles, Capacities, and Cross-Sector Synergies

Multi-level governance of AI game-based multiliteracies requires a granular understanding of the differentiated roles, responsibilities, and capacities of diverse stakeholder configurations (Alam, 2022; Fiorentini et al., 2025; Yim & Su, 2025b). Teachers and school leaders function as pedagogical gatekeepers who translate policy scripts and platform affordances into daily practice, exercising professional judgment about alignment with *multiliteracies*, *Universal Design for Learning*, and *critical literacy* constructs. System administrators orchestrate funding flows, infrastructural investments, and accountability frameworks that can incentivise equity aligned experimentation or penalise deviation from standardised metrics. Developers and vendor consortia make thousands of micro design decisions about interfaces, algorithms, business models, and data practices that directly shape learners' experiences.

Researchers and intermediary organisations convene evidence, facilitate design-based partnerships, and mediate between global discourses and local realities. Students and families carry situated knowledge about how AI-GBL literacies intersect with identity, language, and aspiration. Table 5 synthesises these distributed functions, responsibilities, capacities, and failure risks into a compact governance map for equity-centered ecosystems.

Implementation, Scaling, and Sustainability Logics for AI-GBL Ecosystems

Implementation and scaling of AI-GBL literacy initiatives are not linear roll outs but emergent processes shaped by organisational culture, path dependence, and power relations (Ma et al., 2025; Ng et al., 2024; Rianti et al., 2025). Perspectives from *implementation science*, *diffusion of innovation*, and *complex change management* illuminate why ostensibly promising pilots often succumb to fragmentation, abandonment, or superficial adoption. Without sustained professional learning, time allocations, and technical support, teachers may experience AI-GBL tools as additional burdens rather than as resources for *multiliteracies* enrichment. If attention is not paid to infrastructural inequities, scaling can deepen divides between well connected schools and those with intermittent electricity or limited devices. Sustainability requires not only financial planning for licences, maintenance, and connectivity, but also governance arrangements for continuous upgrading of models, content, and accessibility features. When the stakeholder functions in Table 5 are activated in a coordinated manner, with clear equity commitments and feedback loops across levels, scaling trajectories can move from episodic pilotitis toward durable, justice-oriented transformation.

Governance for Equity-Centred AI-GBL Literacy Ecosystems

Earlier, the chapter has emphasized that governance of AI game based multiliteracies environments is distributed across multiple stakeholder constellations, each with distinct yet interdependent functions, responsibilities, capacities, and risk profiles. To render these relationships more tractable for policy design and institutional planning, Table 5 articulates a governance matrix that cross walks six composite stakeholder configurations with their primary functions, equity linked responsibilities, required literacies, and consequences when commitments are neglected. This matrix complements the conceptual maps in Tables 1 to 4 by shifting the analytic focus from paradigms, technologies, and designs to the human and institutional actors who must steward these systems over time.

Table 5. Governance for Equity-Centred AI-GBL Literacy Ecosystems

Stakeholder Configuration	Primary Governance Functions	Equity-Linked Responsibilities	Required Literacies and Capacities	Risks when Commitments are Neglected
Students and Families	Articulate experiential feedback, co-design narrative content, monitor impacts on identity, language, and wellbeing	Insist on linguistic respect, accessibility, data dignity, and culturally resonant story worlds, contest harmful classifications	Foundational and digital-literacy, *AI literacy*, rights awareness, participatory communication, intercultural negotiation	Technocratic imposition of tools, erosion of trust, exacerbation of stigma for multilingual and neurodiverse learners, disengagement from formal schooling
Teachers and School Leaders	Curate platforms, frame classroom use, interpret analytics, mediate between policy scripts and learner realities	Enact *Universal Design for Learning*, protect instructional time from platform overreach, foreground *critical literacy* and student agency	Pedagogical-content knowledge, data and assessment literacy, *AI literacy*, change management skills, reflexive equity consciousness	Algorithm driven pacing displacing pedagogy, narrowing of literacies to what is measurable, teacher deskilling, reproduction of existing inequities
System-Level Administrators	Allocate resources, set implementation priorities, define accountability metrics, broker partnerships across sectors	Prioritise underserved schools, mandate accessibility and multilingual coverage, align incentives with inclusion and public value	Strategic planning, budgeting, policy analysis, organisational learning, capacity to read equity disaggregated dashboards	Concentration of resources in already advantaged sites, procurement focused on cost rather than justice, unsustainable pilots divorced from systemic reform
Developers and Vendor Consortia	Design AI-GBL platforms, define data architectures, set business models, maintain and update technical stacks	Embed *value sensitive design*, avoid exploitative monetisation, respect Indigenous data sovereignty, ensure algorithmic transparency	Human-computer interaction expertise, *sociotechnical* awareness, inclusive design skills, ethical risk assessment, collaborative disposition	Platform lock in, surveillance capitalism, propagation of biased models, exclusion of minoritised languages and disabilities, weak interoperability
Researchers and Intermediary Organisations	Generate conceptual frameworks, conduct independent evaluations, facilitate design-based partnerships, translate knowledge	Examine equity impacts, foreground voices of marginalised communities, support capacity building for practitioners and policymakers	Methodological versatility, transdisciplinary synthesis, facilitation of research-practice partnerships, communication for mixed audiences	Dominance of narrow effectiveness trials, absence of critical scrutiny, fragmentation of learning across projects, limited uptake of insights in policy arenas
Policymakers and Regulators	Set legal norms, coordinate multi-level actors, regulate data and AI practices, steward long term public value	Enshrine linguistic and disability rights, require transparency and accessibility, create mechanisms for grievance redress and redressal	Policy design, legal literacy, systems thinking, engagement with civil society, ability to interpret technical and ethical briefs	Regulatory capture by vendors, permissive data regimes, misalignment with rights frameworks, entrenchment of inequitable platform ecologies

Table 5 demonstrates that equitable governance of AI-GBL literacy ecosystems is not reducible to a single ministry directive or platform feature, but emerges from the interplay of student and family voice, pedagogical leadership, administrative stewardship, technical design, research mediation, and regulatory oversight. When any node in this governance matrix fails to enact its equity linked responsibilities, risks cascade through the system in the form of intensified exclusion, narrowed literacies, and algorithmic harm. Conversely, when stakeholders cultivate the literacies and capacities enumerated in the matrix, and when their interactions are structured through participatory, transparent, and reflexive processes, AI game based multiliteracies infrastructures can be aligned with public value, linguistic justice, and neurodiversity affirming practice. This systemic alignment provides the backdrop against which the concluding part of this chapter can synthesise the conceptual argument and articulate a forward-looking agenda for globally relevant, justice-oriented literacy futures.

CONCLUSION

Implications, Boundary Conditions, and Conceptual Limitations

The conceptual architecture advanced in this chapter generates differentiated implications for multiple audiences while remaining bounded by explicit conditions of applicability. For educators and instructional leaders, the tables and matrices function as heuristic tools for interrogating platforms, designing locally grounded AI-GBL tasks, and orchestrating analytics informed, dignity preserving assessment cycles that honour *multiliteracies*, *neurodiversity*, and *translanguaging* practices. For developers and engineering teams, the framework specifies design constraints in relation to accessibility, language coverage, explainability, and *value sensitive design*, thereby repositioning engagement metrics within a wider public value calculus. For policymakers, system administrators, and regulators, the governance matrix offers a scaffold for crafting procurement rules, accountability indicators, and data regimes aligned with linguistic justice and disability rights. At the same time, the chapter is limited by its conceptual status, the absence of empirical instantiation, and a focus on formal and non-formal education systems, which may not fully capture informal, peer organised literacies in volatile contexts.

Future-Oriented Agenda for Research, Design, and Praxis

A future oriented agenda for AI game-based multiliteracies must weave together research, design, and praxis in iterative, participatory cycles. Methodologically, comparative design-based studies with long horizon perspectives are required to test and refine the paradigmatic, technological, and governance constructs articulated here across diverse linguistic, cultural, and infrastructural settings, with particular attention to Indigenous communities, conflict affected zones, and digitally marginalised populations. Design trajectories should prioritise open, modular, and interoperable AI-GBL platforms grounded in *design justice*, *data justice*, and *decolonial* principles, with communities exercising meaningful control over narrative assets, language resources, and data governance. Practice oriented initiatives should cultivate cross sector coalitions that bring together educators, youth, technologists, and policymakers to co create game worlds that function as laboratories for *critical literacy* and collective imagination. Through such aligned efforts, AI and game-based environments can be harnessed not as engines of standardisation, but as infrastructures for cultivating critical, joyful, and culturally grounded readers and writers.

REFERENCES

Abrams, S. S., & Hanghøj, T. (2025). Reflexive AI literacies: Conceptualizing a model for learners' critical engagement with generative AI. *Pedagogies*, •••, 1–20. DOI: 10.1080/1554480X.2025.2561972

Akhmetova, A. I., Seitenova, S. S., Khodjaev, B. K., Jamoldinova, O. R., Yerkebaeva, S. Z., & Kazybayeva, K. U. (2025). Evolution of game-based learning research: A cross-database bibliometric analysis and visualization study (2015-2024). *Contemporary Educational Technology*, *17*(3), ep585. DOI: 10.30935/cedtech/16451

Alam, A. (2022). Impact of university's human resources practices on professors' occupational performance: empirical evidence from India's higher education sector. In *Inclusive businesses in developing economies: Converging people, profit, and corporate citizenship* (pp. 107–131). Springer International Publishing., DOI: 10.1007/978-3-031-12217-0_6

Alam, A. (2023a). Media multitasking with M-learning technology in real-time classroom learning: Analysing the dynamics in formal educational settings for the future of E-learning in India. In *2023 2nd International Conference on Smart Technologies and Systems for Next Generation Computing (ICSTSN)* (pp. 1-6). IEEE. https://doi.org/DOI: 10.1109/ICSTSN57873.2023.10151509

Alam, A. (2023b). The secret sauce of student success: Cracking the code by navigating the path to personalized learning with educational data mining. In *2023 2nd International Conference on Smart Technologies and Systems for Next Generation Computing (ICSTSN)* (pp. 1-8). IEEE. https://doi.org/DOI: 10.1109/ICSTSN57873.2023.10151558

Alam, A. (2023c). Intelligence unleashed: An argument for AI-enabled learning ecologies with real world examples of today and a peek into the future. In *International Conference on Innovations in Computer Science, Electronics & Electrical Engineering*-2022 (Vol. 2717, No. 1, p. 030001). AIP Publishing LLC. https://doi.org/DOI: 10.1063/5.0129803

Alam, A., & Mohanty, A. (2022, December). Facial analytics or virtual avatars: competencies and design considerations for student-teacher interaction in AI-powered online education for effective classroom engagement. In *International Conference on Communication, Networks and Computing* (pp. 252-265). Cham: Springer Nature Switzerland. https://doi.org/DOI: 10.1007/978-3-031-43145-6_21

Alam, A., & Mohanty, A. (2023, January). Learning on the move: a pedagogical framework for state-of-the-art mobile learning. In *International Conference on Data Management, Analytics & Innovation* (pp. 735-748). Singapore: Springer Nature Singapore. https://doi.org/DOI: 10.1007/978-981-99-1414-2_52

Alam, A., & Mohanty, A. (2024). Integrated constructive robotics in education (ICRE) model: A paradigmatic framework for transformative learning in educational ecosystem. *Cogent Education*, *11*(1), 2324487. DOI: 10.1080/2331186X.2024.2324487

Alnuaim, A. (2024). The impact and acceptance of gamification by learners in a digital literacy course at the undergraduate level: Randomized controlled trial. *JMIR Serious Games*, *12*, e52017. DOI: 10.2196/52017 PMID: 39177662

Anggela, A. F. P., Setiawan, D. A., & Rahutami, R. (2025). Magbox Games to Improve Literacy of Grade VI Elementary School Students on Short Story Materials. *Jurnal Pedagogi dan Pembelajaran, 8*(2), 364-372. https://doi.org/DOI: 10.23887/jp2.v8i2.98363

Ariani, F., & Afnita, N. (2024). The Influence of Digital-Based Gamification on Student Engagement and Language Literacy Skills: A Study at Madrasah Tsanawiyah. *Jurnal Komunikasi Pendidikan, 8*(2), 141–156. DOI: 10.32585/jurnalkomdik.v8i2.5036

Arkan, Z., & Bal, M. (2025). The relationship between school-age students' literacy skills and digital well-being: A systematic review. *BMC Psychology, 13*(1), 1240. DOI: 10.1186/s40359-025-03573-4 PMID: 41214781

Bang, H. J., & Siebert-Evenstone, A. (2025). Evaluation of a Personalized Game-Based Learning app for Developing Young Children's Reading Skills. *Journal of Educational Technology Systems, 54*(1), 88–118. DOI: 10.1177/00472395251337095

Bengel, P., & Peter, C. (2024). Promoting technological literacy through virtual game-based field trips: Effects on knowledge, attitudes, and gender. *European Journal of Geography, 15*(2), 120–134. DOI: 10.48088/ejg.p.ben.15.2.120.134

Bhat, M., & Long, D. (2024, July). Designing interactive explainable AI tools for algorithmic literacy and transparency. In *Proceedings of the 2024 ACM Designing Interactive Systems Conference* (pp. 939-957). https://doi.org/DOI: 10.1145/3643834.3660722

Bhimavarapu, U. (2025). AI-Enabled Learning Environments Evaluating Literacy Outcomes Through Machine Learning. In *Rethinking Literacy in the Era of Sustainability and Artificial Intelligence* (pp. 133–160). IGI Global Scientific Publishing., DOI: 10.4018/979-8-3373-0725-1.ch005

Bora, D., Patel, P., Psyridou, M., Ruotsalainen, J., Richardson, U., & Torppa, M. (2025). Foundational English literacy development in India: A randomised-control trial using phonics instruction and GraphoLearn. *Reading and Writing, 38*(5), 1309–1335. DOI: 10.1007/s11145-024-10551-6

Chang, C. H., & Wang, R. S. M. (2025, July). Finance Literacy Thematic Board Game Development and Game-based Learning Evaluation. In *2025 IEEE Gaming, Entertainment, and Media Conference (GEM)* (pp. 1-6). IEEE. https://doi.org/DOI: 10.1109/GEM66882.2025.11155504

Chang, X., & Wong, G. K. (2025). A systematic review of how educators integrate ethics into artificial intelligence curriculum. *Journal of Research on Technology in Education*, •••, 1–18. DOI: 10.1080/15391523.2025.2551112

Chen, J. J. (2024). A scoping study on AI affordances in early childhood education: Mapping the global landscape, identifying research gaps, and charting future research directions. *Journal of Artificial Intelligence Research, 81*, 701–740. DOI: 10.1613/jair.1.16882

Chu, H. C., Wang, C. C., Hwang, G. J., Kuo, F. R., & Chen, Y. H. (2025). Trends of Game-Based Learning in the Mobile Era: A Review of the Top 100 Highly Cited Empirical Studies. *Wangji Wanglu Jishu Xuekan, 26*(5), 653–661. DOI: 10.70003/160792642025092605008

Dai, Y., & Zhang, J. (2025). Serious Games: A Study on Digital Literacy and Skill Improvement of Architecture Students in China Vocational Institute. In *Integrating Technology in Problem-Solving Educational Practices* (pp. 27-58). IGI Global. https://doi.org/DOI: 10.4018/979-8-3693-6745-2.ch002

Ding, L., & Holland, S. (2025). AI Odyssey: Designing and Evaluating a Board Game for Family-Based AI Literacy. *International Journal of Serious Games, 12*(4), 121–145. DOI: 10.17083/dnza4k90

DiPaola, D., Shen, J., Hu, R., Alghowinem, S., & Breazeal, C. (2023, August). Dronescape: Designing an educational escape room for adult ai literacy. In *2023 IEEE Conference on Games (CoG)* (pp. 1-8). IEEE. https://doi.org/DOI: 10.1109/CoG57401.2023.10333148

Droujkov, D., Emerson, A., Carpenter, D., Tian, X., Azevedo, R., & Barnes, T. (2025, July). Investigating the Impact of Confusion and Agency on Motivation in a Game-Based Learning Environment. In *International Conference on Artificial Intelligence in Education* (pp. 177-189). Cham: Springer Nature Switzerland. https://doi.org/DOI: 10.1007/978-3-031-98420-4_13

Eybers, O. O., & Muller, A. (Eds.). (2024). *AI Approaches to Literacy in Higher Education*. IGI Global., DOI: 10.4018/979-8-3693-1054-0

Fadhli, M., Kuswandi, D., Utami, P. S., & Sartika, S. B.Mohamad Hardyman bin Barawi. (2023). Game-Based Learning and Children's Digital Literacy to Support Pervasive Learning: A Systematic Reviews. *Jurnal Teknologi Pendidikan, 25*(3), 386–393. DOI: 10.21009/jtp.v25i3.38388

Fiorentini, J. P., Leif, S. A., Fasching-Varner, K. J., & McCreery, M. P. (2025). Learning to Read or Reading to Learn: A Narrative Literature Review of Literacy within Digital Game-Based Learning Environments. *Technology, Knowledge and Learning*, 1-20. https://doi.org/DOI: 10.1007/s10758-025-09851-9

Fitriah, N., Degeng, M. D. K., Degeng, I. N. S., & Praherdhiono, H. (2023). Enhancing Early Childhood Financial Literacy Through FinSOLEkid Indonesia: A Comparative Study of Digital Platforms. *Golden Age: Jurnal Ilmiah Tumbuh Kembang Anak Usia Dini, 8*(3), 171–181. DOI: 10.14421/jga.2023.83-06

Gao, H., Huai, H., Yildiz-Degirmenci, S., Bannert, M., & Kasneci, E. (2024, October). Datalivr: Transformation of data literacy education through virtual reality with chatgpt-powered enhancements. In *2024 IEEE International Symposium on Mixed and Augmented Reality (ISMAR)* (pp. 120-129). IEEE. https://doi.org/DOI: 10.1109/ISMAR62088.2024.00026

Gkintoni, E., Magriplis, E., Vantaraki, F., Skoulidi, C. M., Anastassopoulos, P., Cornea, A., Inchaurraga, B., Santurtun, J., Mancha, A. C., Giorgakis, G., Kouppas, K., Timotheou, S., Moreno Juan, M. J., Muñagorri, M., Harasiuk, M., Lopez, A. G., Skoulidi, E., & Vantarakis, A. (2025). Designing for Engagement in Primary Health Education Through Digital Game-Based Learning: Cross-National Behavioral Evidence from the iLearn4Health Platform. *Behavioral Sciences (Basel, Switzerland), 15*(7), 847. DOI: 10.3390/bs15070847 PMID: 40723631

Göle, M. O., & Temel, F. (2024). The Effect of Digital Game-Based and Different Education Programs on Phonological Awareness Skills of 60-72 Months-Old Children. *Journal of Theoretical Educational Science, 17*(1), 202–235. DOI: 10.30831/akukeg.1358837

Gu, X., & Ericson, B. J. (2025, August). AI literacy in K-12 and higher education in the wake of generative AI: An integrative review. In *Proceedings of the 2025 ACM Conference on International Computing Education Research* V. 1 (pp. 125-140). https://doi.org/DOI: 10.1145/3702652.3744217

Hassan, N. H., Rahim, N. A. A., Hoong, A. L. S., & Mostafa, K. (2024, August). A Conceptual Study on Utilization of Artificial Intelligence (AI), Virtual Reality (VR) and Augmented Reality (AR) on Green Education: Effectiveness and Engagement. In *International Conference on Intelligent Manufacturing and Robotics* (pp. 270-278). Singapore: Springer Nature Singapore. https://doi.org/DOI: 10.1007/978-981-96-3949-6_20

Heinmäe, E., Puksand, H., & Kollom, K. (2025). AI in Action: Pedagogical Advice Using Artificial Intelligence as a Digital Resource in Early Childhood Education. *AI in Early Education: Integrating Artificial Intelligence for Inclusive and Effective Learning*, 41-58. https://doi.org/DOI: 10.1002/9781394352821.ch03

Katanosaka, T., Khan, M. F. F., & Sakamura, K. (2025, March). Experiential Learning of SNS Etiquette through a Digital Cooperative Game. In *2025 1st International Conference on Consumer Technology (ICCT-Pacific)* (pp. 1-4). IEEE. https://doi.org/DOI: 10.1109/ICCT-Pacific63901.2025.11012867

Khanchai, S., Worragin, P., Ariya, P., Intawong, K., & Puritat, K. (2025). Toward Sustainable Digital Literacy: A Comparative Study of Gamified and Non-Gamified Digital Board Games in Higher Education. *Education Sciences*, *15*(8), 966. DOI: 10.3390/educsci15080966

Kim, G. M., Johnson, L. L., & Nash, B. (2023). Games to promote empathy as a literacy practice: A new teacher's playful practice. *English Education*, *56*(1), 20–43. DOI: 10.58680/ee202356120

Kim, Y. J., Kim, G., & Stoiber, A. (2025). Playful design for AI Literacy: Creating inclusive learning and assessment opportunities. *International Journal of Human-Computer Studies*, *199*, 103508. DOI: 10.1016/j.ijhcs.2025.103508

Kirom, S., & Rosyida, D. A. (2024). Educational Game" Sianting" to Improve Literacy and Anti-Bullying Education Using Problem-Solving Approach. *Al-Adzka: Jurnal Ilmiah Pendidikan Guru Madrasah Ibtidaiyah*, *14*(2), 189–205. DOI: 10.18592/aladzkapgmi.v14i2.14031

Laila, L., Wardi, L. Z., & Deta, U. A. (2025). Opportunities to Implement Traditional Games as Contextualized Physics Learning Innovations. *Reog: Journal of Ecoethnoscience Education*, *1*(1), 24–31. DOI: 10.58706/reog.v1n1.p24-31

Lin, Z., Dai, Y., & Ng, O. L. (2025). Constructionism in K-12 AI Literacy Education: A Systematic Review of Pedagogical Designs, Student Outcomes, and Learning Mechanisms. *Journal of Educational Computing Research*, *07356331251360442*(7-8), 1748–1781. Advance online publication. DOI: 10.1177/07356331251360442

Liu, J., & Shadiev, R. (2025). A review of empirical research on game-based digital citizenship education. *Education and Information Technologies*, *30*(14), 1–53. DOI: 10.1007/s10639-025-13549-x

Liu, J., Shadiev, R., & Cao, M. (2025). Effects of digital citizenship educational game on teenagers' learning achievement, motivation, cognitive load, and behavioral patterns. *Education and Information Technologies*, *30*(11), 1–54. DOI: 10.1007/s10639-025-13399-7

Ma, Q., Jain, A., Kim, J., Chai, M., & Kaufman, G. (2025, April). ImaginAItion: Promoting Generative AI Literacy Through Game-Based Learning. In *Proceedings of the Extended Abstracts of the CHI Conference on Human Factors in Computing Systems* (pp. 1-9). https://doi.org/DOI: 10.1145/3706599.3719844

Ma, R., Sanusi, I. T., Mahipal, V., Gonzales, J. E., & Martin, F. G. (2023, March). Developing machine learning algorithm literacy with novel plugged and unplugged approaches. In *Proceedings of the 54th ACM Technical Symposium on Computer Science Education* V. 1 (pp. 298-304). https://doi.org/DOI: 10.1145/3545945.3569772

Nazara, D. K., Mustapa, N., Hendriawan, D., & Mahabbati, A. (2025). The Influence of Digital Learning Media in Stimulating Literacy Skills of Children Aged 5-6 Years. PAUDIA, 791-811. https://doi.org/DOI: 10.26877/paudia.v14i4.2271

Ng, D. T. K., Su, J., & Chu, S. K. W. (2024). Fostering secondary school students' AI literacy through making AI-driven recycling bins. *Education and Information Technologies*, *29*(8), 9715–9746. DOI: 10.1007/s10639-023-12183-9

Ng, D. T. K., Xinyu, C., Leung, J. K. L., & Chu, S. K. W. (2024). Fostering students' AI literacy development through educational games: AI knowledge, affective and cognitive engagement. *Journal of Computer Assisted Learning*, *40*(5), 2049–2064. DOI: 10.1111/jcal.13009

Palmquist, A., Sigurdardottir, H. D. I., & Myhre, H. (2025). Exploring interfaces and implications for integrating social-emotional competencies into AI literacy for education: A narrative review. *Journal of Computers in Education*, •••, 1–37. DOI: 10.1007/s40692-025-00354-1

Pavloff-Pelkonen, E., Hakkarainen, K., & Korhonen, T. (2025). Educational design and implementation of game literacy in a multiliteracy learning environment. *Journal of Research on Technology in Education*, •••, 1–19. DOI: 10.1080/15391523.2025.2487284

Pu, L., Liang, J., Wang, J., Zhang, N., & Zhong, W. (2024). Impact of AI-Based Learning, Digital Literacy, Information Stewardship on Learning Outcomes. *El Profesional de la Información*, *33*(5). Advance online publication. DOI: 10.3145/epi.2024.ene.0515

Rahayu, W. A., & Subekti, P. (2025). Implementation of" E-Lens" inquiry-based learning game to improve literacy and numeracy skills. *Jurnal Cakrawala Pendidikan*, *44*(3), 510–522. DOI: 10.21831/cp.v44i3.76930

Rianti, S. S., Chamalah, E., Kusumadewi, R. F., & Passat, S. A. (2025). Implementation of AI-Based Educational Games to Improve Early Reading Skills of Elementary School Students. *EduBase: Journal of Basic Education*, *6*(1), 146–156. DOI: 10.47453/edubase.v6i1.3227

Sabatini, J., Graesser, A. C., Hollander, J., & O'Reilly, T. (2023). A framework of literacy development and how AI can transform theory and practice. *British Journal of Educational Technology*, *54*(5), 1174–1203. DOI: 10.1111/bjet.13342

Sari, H. P., Primasari, Y., Supriyono, S., & Herminingsih, D. I. (2026). Gleaming English game for youth, an android-based game for English literacy improvement: Research and development. [EduLearn]. *Journal of Education and Learning*, *20*(1), 485–496. DOI: 10.11591/edulearn.v20i1.23119

Sayangan, Y. V. (2024). Digital Picture Card Media Based on Mother Tongue Assisted with Artificial Intelligence in Literacy Learning for Early Grades. *International Journal of Elementary Education, 8*(3), 461–471. Advance online publication. DOI: 10.23887/ijee.v8i3.84158

Schabas, A. (2023). Game-based science learning: What are the problems with teachers practicing it in class? *Assyfa Learning Journal, 1*(2), 89–103. DOI: 10.61650/alj.v1i2.128

Shen, Y., & Ab Jalil, H. (2025). Exploring lifelong literacy learning in digital gameplay among midlife-to-older adults. *Educational Gerontology*, •••, 1–19. DOI: 10.1080/03601277.2025.2495275

Sperling, K., Stenliden, L., Mannila, L., Hallström, J., Nordlöf, C., & Heintz, F. (2025). Perspectives on AI literacy in Middle School Classrooms: An Integrative Review. *Postdigital Science and Education, 7*(3), 1–31. DOI: 10.1007/s42438-025-00560-1

Subrata, H., Judijanto, L., Aeni, C., Ali, A., & Amir, A. S. (2025). Implementation of Multimedia-assisted Collaborative Game-Based Learning to Improve Competitive Spirit and Problem Solving Ability in Literacy Learning for Elementary Students. *Jurnal Pendidikan Progresif, 15*(2), 1415–1430. DOI: 10.23960/jpp.v15i2.pp1415-1430

Tahir, R., & Wang, A. I. (2024). Evaluating the effectiveness of game-based learning for teaching refugee children Arabic using the integrated LEAGUÊ-GQM approach. *Behaviour & Information Technology, 43*(1), 110–138. DOI: 10.1080/0144929X.2022.2156386

Tang, J. T., Chu, S. T., & Chang, T. F. (2025). Enhancing English alphabet handwriting skills in preschool children through digital game-based learning approach. *Innovation in Language Learning and Teaching, 19*(4), 297–315. DOI: 10.1080/17501229.2024.2352791

Teke, N., & Baş, T. (2025). Early Literacy Skills in Digital Games. *European Journal of Education, 60*(3), e70173. DOI: 10.1111/ejed.70173

Tiwari, S. (2025). Designing ethical AI characters for children's early learning experiences. *AI. Brain and Child, 1*(1), 1–17. DOI: 10.1007/s44436-025-00015-1

Tsai, S. K., Chuang, T. Y., & Lin, Z. J. (2025). Enhancing Environmental Literacy Through Digital Game-Based Learning: A Technology-Integrated Attitude Change Approach. *Sustainability (Basel), 17*(16), 7416. DOI: 10.3390/su17167416

Tseng, Y. J., Yadav, G., Hou, X., Wu, M., Chou, Y. S., Chen, C. C., . . . Koedinger, K. R. (2024, September). Activeai: The effectiveness of an interactive tutoring system in developing k-12 ai literacy. In *European Conference on Technology Enhanced Learning* (pp. 452-467). Cham: Springer Nature Switzerland. https://doi.org/DOI: 10.1007/978-3-031-72315-5_31

Vahedian-Movahed, S., & Martin, F. (2025, June). From Play to Pedagogy: Discovering the Ecosystem of AI Educational Tools and Curricula. In *Proceedings of the 30th ACM Conference on Innovation and Technology in Computer Science Education* V. 1 (pp. 333-339). https://doi.org/DOI: 10.1145/3724363.3729068

Ventsel, A., Hansson, S., Rickberg, M., & Madisson, M. L. (2024). Building resilience against hostile information influence activities: How a new media literacy learning platform was developed for the Estonian defense forces. *Armed Forces and Society, 50*(4), 1021–1041. DOI: 10.1177/0095327X231163265 von Gillern, S., Gould, H., & Pérez Cortés, L. (2025). Preservice teachers' perceptions on digital game-based learning in elementary English language arts. *Journal of Digital Learning in Teacher Education, 41*(4), 1–14. DOI: 10.1080/21532974.2025.2540638

Voulgari, I., Naoum, E., & Sfyroera, M. (2025). Fostering AI Literacy in Early Childhood: Designing Educational Activities for Preschoolers. *AI in Early Education: Integrating Artificial Intelligence for Inclusive and Effective Learning*, 21-40. https://doi.org/DOI: 10.1002/9781394352821.ch02

Wijayanti, A., Dwiningrum, S. I. A., & Saptono, B. (2024). Digital literacy in elementary schools post COVID-19: A systematic literature review. *International Journal of Learning. Teaching and Educational Research, 23*(12), 96–112. DOI: 10.26803/ijlter.23.12.6

Wu, D., Chen, M., Chen, X., & Liu, X. (2024). Analyzing K-12 AI education: A large language model study of classroom instruction on learning theories, pedagogy, tools, and AI literacy. *Computers and Education: Artificial Intelligence, 7*, 100295. DOI: 10.1016/j.caeai.2024.100295

Yim, I. H. Y., & Su, J. (2025a). Artificial intelligence (AI) learning tools in K-12 education: A scoping review. *Journal of Computers in Education, 12*(1), 93–131. DOI: 10.1007/s40692-023-00304-9

Yim, I. H. Y., & Su, J. (2025b). Artificial intelligence literacy education in primary schools: A review. *International Journal of Technology and Design Education, 35*(5), 1–30. DOI: 10.1007/s10798-025-09979-w

Yim, I. H. Y., & Wegerif, R. (2024). Teachers' perceptions, attitudes, and acceptance of artificial intelligence (AI) educational learning tools: An exploratory study on AI literacy for young students. *Future in Educational Research, 2*(4), 318–345. DOI: 10.1002/fer3.65

Zhang, M., Ran, C., Liu, F., Yin, M., Cui, S., Li, C., & Li, B. (2025). Hello! AI: An Interactive Rhyme-Based Game for Children AI Literacy Education. *International Journal of Human-Computer Interaction*, •••, 1–26. DOI: 10.1080/10447318.2025.2574514

Zheng, Y., Zhang, J., Li, Y., Wu, X., Ding, R., Luo, X., Liu, P., & Huang, J. (2024). Effects of digital game-based learning on students' digital etiquette literacy, learning motivations, and engagement. *Heliyon, 10*(1), e23490. Advance online publication. DOI: 10.1016/j.heliyon.2023.e23490 PMID: 38187224

Chapter 8

Differentiating Instruction Using Game-Based Learning and AI:

Supporting Literacy Instruction in Secondary Inclusive ELA Classroom

Ashleigh Bridges
http://orcid.org/0009-0000-1899-3934
Texas A&M University-Texarkana, USA

ABSTRACT

Differentiation in secondary English Language Arts classrooms is essential for equitable literacy outcomes, especially in inclusive settings where students with and without disabilities learn together. Integrating artificial intelligence (AI) and game-based learning (GBL) offers teachers tools to individualize instruction, boost engagement, and align learning with students' diverse needs. Using Universal Design for Learning (UDL) and T-TESS Dimension 2.4: Differentiation, this chapter examines how AI and GBL support differentiation through adaptive feedback, multimodal learning, and interactive storytelling. Additionally, by drawing on research and utilizing a classroom case study, it explores how these technologies enhance literacy, inclusion, and equity in secondary ELA. The findings suggest that combining AI's adaptive features with GBL's motivational elements creates accessible, responsive learning aligned with T-TESS 2.4. The chapter concludes with implications for instruction, co-teaching, and policy in diverse classrooms.

INTRODUCTION

In inclusive secondary English Language Arts (ELA) classrooms, differentiating instruction presents a challenge for teachers who are seeking to meet the diverse academic, cognitive, and emotional needs of their students (Deunk et al., 2018; Jager et al., 2025). These teachers must balance the rigorous literacy standards (i.e. text analysis, argumentative writing, and inferring) while ensuring that students who vary widely in their reading proficiency, learning profiles, and motivation can have access to the grade level curriculum (Applebee & Langer, 2013; Dalton & Proctor, 2007). Students receiving special education services in inclusive settings face additional barriers including difficulties with decoding, comprehension, and written expression (Hall et al., 2004; Hehir et al., 2016). When the curriculum is not purposefully

DOI: 10.4018/979-8-3373-7472-7.ch008

designed, the traditional one-size-fits-all instruction can negatively impact these disparities, which limits equitable access to complex literacy tasks (CAST, 2018).

There are two emerging instructional technologies that offer complimentary pathways for addressing these challenges. The first is artificial intelligence (AI), and it supports differentiation by providing adaptive feedback and data-driven insights that identify each student's individual strengths and learning needs (Holmes et al., 2019). The second is game-based learning (GBL), which enhances engagement and student motivation through narrative experiences and interactive challenges to make abstract concepts accessible and meaningful (Gee, 2007; Plass et al, 2015). When used together in designing literacy curriculum, AI and GBL can support an inclusive classroom model by creating engagement and cognitive adaptability to shift the teacher's role towards being a facilitator while expanding opportunities for student participation and mastery of the content. This chapter examines how AI and GBL can be integrated into secondary ELA classrooms to support differentiation and inclusive literacy instruction that is grounded in the Universal Design for Learning (UDL) framework and aligned to the Texas Teacher Evaluation and Support System (T-TESS) Dimension 2.4: Differentiation.

DEFINING THE CORE CONCEPTS

Defining Inclusion

Inclusion represents a legal mandate and a pedagogical commitment to ensure that students with disabilities and diverse learners can learn alongside their peers in the general education setting (United States Department of Education, 2025). The Individuals with Disabilities Education Act (IDEA) of 2004 and the Least Restrictive Environment (LRE) requirement guarantees that students with disabilities have access to the general curriculum and can fully participate to the maximum extent appropriate (United States Department of Education, 2025), which makes inclusion extend far beyond the physical classroom placement. Inclusion is about belonging, participation, and equitable access to meaningful learning opportunities (Florian & Black-Hawkins, 2011). Inclusive classrooms view diversity as an asset. For example, teachers design instruction that responds to student needs rather than perceiving their differences as deficits. Florian and Black-Hawkins (2011) and Hehir et al. (2016) demonstrate that inclusion benefits all students by fostering empathy, collaboration, and academic achievement. For literacy, these benefits are meaningful because a student's reading and writing development are foundational to their academic success (Applebee & Langer, 2013).

Defining Differentiation

Differentiation is a responsive approach to teaching that recognizes and plans for the diverse learning needs of the students in the classroom. Tomlinson (2017) defines differentiation as a way to tailor classroom instruction to meet individual needs. This can be completed through modifications in content, process, product, and learning environment. Rather than delivering a uniform lesson, teachers can adjust the depth, pacing, and mode of instruction based on students' readiness, interests, and learning profiles (Tomlinson, 2017). With differentiation, it is not about simplifying the instruction or lowering the expectations; instead, it is about providing equitable access to rigor and adjusting instruction to promote students' growth in their learning (Ouyang & Ye, 2023). In secondary ELA, students are reading complex test and constructing evidence-based writing, which is why having an intentional responsiveness to student needs is necessary to help them reach mastery.

Frameworks that Support Differentiation in Inclusive Classrooms

T-TESS Dimension 2.4: Differentiation

Within Texas public schools, differentiation is embedded in the Texas Teacher Evaluation and Support System (T-TESS), a statewide framework designed to assess and guide effective teaching practices. Dimension 2.4: Differentiation assesses a teacher's ability to adjust instruction for individual students based on readiness, interests, and learning profiles while maintaining high expectations for all students (Texas Education Agency, 2022). This standard reflects a commitment to upholding an inclusive, student-centered instruction, and it makes explicit to teachers about what they may already understand. In the context of secondary ELA, Dimension 2.4: Differentiation supports the teacher's role in designing flexible literacy experiences that accommodates diverse students, including those with disabilities, through purposeful scaffolding, adaptive tools, and responsive feedback. Therefore, integrating AI and GBL directly supports the use of differentiation to be data-driven and support engagement across a range of abilities in the classroom.

Other Differentiation Tools

While T-TESS provides the framework in the state of Texas, adjusting instruction to meet diverse student needs is a national and global expectation for teacher effectiveness. There are major frameworks used across the United States and internationally. The Framework for Teaching (FFT) by Charlotte Danielson (2011) and the Australian Professional Standards for Teachers (APST, 2017) similarly embed the principle of differentiation in their observation tools. The Danielson Framework's components (2011), particularly Domain 1: Planning and Preparation of demonstrating knowledge of students and Domain 3: Instruction for demonstrating flexibility and responsiveness, requires teachers to adjust the content, process, and product for student readiness, their interests, and their learning profiles. The APST outlines that teachers are expected to design and implement effective instruction using their knowledge of student learning and knowledge of content, and they are to incorporate differentiated strategies that address the diverse learning needs of students across the range of abilities in the classroom (Australian Institute for Teaching and School Leadership, 2017). Even though this specific chapter is referencing the T-TESS, the strategies of AI and GBL integration are not just a response to a Texas mandate, but a practical application of a universal best practice in inclusive, student-centered education that is expected world-wide.

Differentiation as a Support

No matter the content area, differentiation is not optional. It is essential because students' learning variability is present in every classroom, and instruction must be adapted to provide an equitable access to learning (CAST, 2018; Tomlinson, 2017). But in secondary ELA, differentiation can be perceived as more complex. Students must be able to engage with challenging texts to synthesize ideas and express their understanding through writing, which are both tasks that require significant demands on decoding, vocabulary, and background knowledge. Yet, teachers often find that achieving meaningful differentiation in practice is difficult due to time constraints, class sizes, and curriculum pacing demands (Jager et al., 2025). Now, AI and GBL have emerged as tools that can support aspects of differentiation, provide adaptive scaffolds, and enhance engagement in literacy learning that once seemed difficult.

AI and GBL share a common goal: to personalize the learning experience and increase access for all students. AI supports differentiation through adaptive feedback and data-driven insights that identify each student's strengths and needs (Holmes et al., 2019), and GBL enhances engagement and motivation through narrative immersion and interactive challenges that make abstract literacy concepts tangible (Gee, 2007; Plass et al., 2015). When used together, these tools offer a model of inclusive literacy instruction that combines emotional engagement with cognitive adaptability, which is where the teacher acts as a facilitator of the learning by integrating the technology to expand opportunities for student participation and their mastery of the content.

Universal Design for Learning (UDL)

The Universal Design for Learning (UDL) framework provides the foundation for equitable and inclusive literacy instruction in secondary classrooms. It is based on the understanding that a student's learning variability is predictable and should be anticipated in the design of the instruction. Rather than be it being addressed through individual accommodations after barriers have already occurred, UDL promotes a proactive planning that ensures all students, regardless of their ability, background, or learning style, can access and engage with grade-level content (CAST, 2018). It has three guiding principles: (a) multiple means of engagement to support motivation and persistence by providing choices, relevance, and appropriate challenge levels; (b) multiple means of representation to ensure that key concepts are presented in a variety of formats; and (c) multiple means of action and expression to allow students the ability to demonstrate their understanding through diverse formats (CAST, 2018).

UDL and differentiation intersect in inclusive literacy instruction where teachers design multiple opportunities for students to engage with complex texts, process the information, and express their understanding. Thousand et al. (2006) describes differentiation to ensure meaningful participation for all students by aligning learning goals and materials to diverse abilities. Florian and Black-Hawkins (2011) defines it as extending what would ordinarily be available to all students, making it seem as being proactive and equitable rather than reactive. UDL also complements T-TESS Dimension 2.4: Differentiation where it focuses on designing instruction from the start to minimize barriers, but differentiation is a teacher's responsive adjustments to meet student needs (Texas Education Agency, 2022). Together, they create a learning environment that is both accessible and adaptive for all students.

Constructivism

Constructivism is grounded in the work of Lev Vygotsky and Jerome Bruner, who understood that learning as something that happens between people through interactions, dialogue, and reflection rather than in isolation. Vygotsky's (1978) described the Zone of Proximal Development (ZPD) as the gap between what a student can do independently and what they can achieve with guidance from a teacher or a peer. That gap is where real learning lived, and dialogue was how one could close that gap. Bruner (1996) expanded on these ideas with the concept of scaffolding, which emphasizes that teachers provide structured support to help students master complex concepts, gradually releasing those supports as student independence increases. Bruner argued that the teacher's job is not to simplify the content but provide the supports necessary and slowly scale them back as the student gains independence.

This translates in secondary ELA where the gap between what a struggling reader can do independently and what they can accomplish with support is significant. Close reading, literary analysis, and various types of writing are all cognitively demanding where most students who struggle cannot master it alone. Applebee and Langer (2013) found that instructional approaches that focused on scaffolded discussion produced higher literacy achievement across diverse student populations because of the support the student was provided to work the challenging curriculum. Similarly, Hammond (2015) emphasizes that culturally responsive teaching allows teachers to build on a student's cultural and linguistic background to deepen engagement and cognitive rigor. Students think deeper about texts that they can connect with.

The UDL framework complements constructivism by encouraging a proactive lesson design that anticipates student variability rather than reacting to it in the moment (CAST, 2018). Tomlinson's (2017) differentiated instruction model applies these frameworks into the classroom by promoting teachers to plan variations in the content, process, and product based on student readiness, interest, and learning profile. Together, these frameworks create a foundation for an equitable and high-engagement instructional learning environment where AI and GBL can serve as meaningful extensions of a constructivist pedagogy in literacy classrooms.

DIFFERENTIATION AND INCLUSION IN LITERACY INSTRUCTION

The evolution of differentiation as an instructional approach parallels the rise of inclusive education. As schools became more diverse in student ability, language, background, and lived experiences, a uniform curriculum became more difficult to ignore. The teachers in the classrooms found that delivering the same lesson in the same way to every student caused some students to become left behind or even under-challenged (Florian & Black-Hawkins, 2011; Hall et al., 2004). It became clear that an equitable access to the curriculum required more than placing students in the same classroom. Equitable access instruction to instruction required flexibility in how the content is taught and how students engage with it (Hehir et al., 2016; Tomlinson, 2017).

With the implementation of IDEA (1990; 2004), which emphasized that all students must have access to the general curriculum, differentiation became recognized as being essential to provide an equitable instruction. Hall et al. (2004) describes differentiation as a proactive strategy that aligns closely with UDL anticipating student diversity rather than reacting to it. Similarly, Vygotsky's (1978) concept of ZPD and Bruner's (1996) work on the concept of scaffolding established the theoretical foundation for flexible instruction that adjusts as students gain independence. Together, these concepts led to Tomlinson's (2017) development of practical models of differentiation that emphasized differentiation does not require multiple curricula; instead it is a variation of components within the one curriculum.

Across the literature, differentiation is consistently framed as a practice of equity because it recognizes learner variability, and the teacher must adapt their instruction to ensure meaningful access for all students (CAST 2018; Tomlinson, 2017). Differentiation ensures that all students engage in challenging, meaningful learning tailored to their unique pathways toward mastery (Florian & Black-Hawkins, 2011). Additionally, inclusion and differentiation are mutually reinforcing practices. Inclusion provides the context of diverse students learning together while differentiation provides the method of intentional, responsive instruction that allows every student to thrive (Hall et al., 2004; Hehir et al., 2016). Together, they establish the pedagogical and moral foundation for leveraging emerging tools such as AI and GBL to create classrooms that are both inclusive and adaptive.

Using Technology for Differentiation in Inclusive Literacy Classrooms

Differentiation, Engagement, and Adaptivity

The evolution of differentiation from traditional instruction to a technology-supported adaptation illustrates a clear path towards personalized instruction. However, engagement and adaptivity often remain disconnected in practice. Traditional adaptive platforms allow for the adjustment of the content difficulty but do not intrinsically motivate or engage students with the content (Gee, 2007; Plass et al., 2015). On the other hand, game-based tools engage students but lack personalization. The integration of AI and GBL addresses this divide by merging cognitive responsiveness with emotional engagement for students. In secondary ELA, the combination of AI and GBL allows teachers to scaffold literacy skills. AI analyzes an individual's reading behaviors, vocabulary acquisition, and comprehension trends (Holmes et al., 2019), while GBL places those skills within narrative contexts that foster persistence and curiosity (Gee, 2003, 2007). This integration reflects the core of UDL principles, which is to provide multiple pathways for engagement representation and expression (CAST, 2018), and T-TESS Dimension 2.4: Differentiation, which is to support teachers in providing responsive instruction that maintains authentic student engagement (Texas Education Agency, 2022). The partnership between AI and GBL illustrates how differentiation extends beyond adjusting content; it centers on sustaining high expectations with the curriculum through adaptive and student-centered practices (Tomlinson, 2017). By using adaptive feedback and immersive storytelling, teachers can personalize both the learning process and the final products of literacy instruction.

Technology and Literacy Engagement

As digital tools began to enter classrooms, literacy instruction evolved beyond print-based models. Early applications of educational technology in reading and writing such as multimedia texts, online annotation tools, and digital storytelling offered opportunities for engagement and multimodal learning. Dalton and Proctor (2007) demonstrated that technology-enhanced reading instruction supports strategy use and comprehension by providing visual, auditory, and interactive elements that scaffold meaning-making. Similarly, Leu et al. (2013) found that online reading comprehension requires unique skills (i.e. evaluating digital sources and integrating multimedia information) that extend beyond traditional literacy instruction into new dimensions.

In ELA classrooms, technology-based literacy tasks allow for student choice and collaboration, which aligns with differentiation. Digital annotation platforms enable teachers to track reading comprehension in real time, and collaborative writing tools support peer feedback across ability levels (Dalton & Proctor, 2007). However, much of this early technology relied on a static design where teachers had to manually differentiate the assignments. As a result, even though engagement increased, personalization remained limited (Leu et al., 2013).

The emergence of adaptive technology learning systems marked a significant shift in how technology could support differentiation. Platforms such as *Newsela* began using algorithms to match students with reading materials at their individualized Lexile levels and track their comprehension progress (Zawacki-

Richter et al., 2019). Gee (2003, 2007) argues that video games mirror the optimal learning conditions by embedding feedback, narratives, and incremental challenges for the individual. Educational games extended these features into academic contexts by allowing students to apply literacy skills within problem-solving narratives. Despite their promises, early implementations of GBL in literacy often targeted elementary students and general education populations, which left students with disabilities behind. Steinkuehler (2018) highlights how game-based environments support reading comprehension and analytical thinking for students. Yet, there are few studies that examined their application within inclusive or secondary special education contexts. Therefore, this gap shows the need to explore how GBL and the use of AI can provide both engagement and adaptivity for diverse students.

Technology Integration and Co-Teaching

The success of technology-enhanced differentiation depends on teacher implementation and collaboration. Research on technology integration has shown that teachers' beliefs, self-efficacy, and professional learning shape whether technology enhances or distracts from instructional goals (Ertmer & Ottenbreit-Leftwich, 2010). One key collaborative structure that strengthens differentiated instruction in inclusive ELA settings is co-teaching. Brendle et al. (2017) found that co-teaching fosters differentiated instruction by enabling flexible grouping. In co-teaching, two teachers share the instructional responsibilities to support the learning of all students, using one of six widely recognized models: (1) one teach/one assist, (2) one teaches/one observes, (3) station teaching, (4) alternative teaching, (5) parallel teaching, and (6) team teaching (Scruggs et al., 2007). When technology is added to this mix, collaboration becomes even more powerful because teachers can interpret digital data together and align their interventions to best support students through the collaborative teaching strategies and technology.

However, professional development often falls behind technological innovations. Research reveals that many teachers feel underprepared to integrate AI into literacy instruction (Holmes et al., 2019). Without structured training in AI integration, teachers risk using technology superficially rather than as a tool. Professional Learning Communities (PLCs) have proven effective for building capacity in adaptive technology integration, especially when they emphasize data interpretation, ethical considerations, and student-centered design (Darling-Hammond et al., 2020). These PLCs provide teachers with structured opportunities to reflect on instructional practices, analyze student performance data generated by AI and game-based platforms, and co-design differentiated learning experiences that align with UDL principles and integrate AI and/or GBL. By fostering a culture of continuous improvement, PLCs can empower teachers to move beyond the use of surface-level technology and towards a pedagogically sound integration that supports diverse students (Trust, 2012).

In summary, the research demonstrates that while differentiation and technology-enhanced learning are well-established in education, the combined use of AI and GBL in inclusive literacy instruction remains underexplored (Gee, 2007; Holmes et al., 2019). Existing research shows that effective differentiation requires intentional design that responds to students' learning needs (Tomlinson, 2017), and the UDL framework provides accessibility, engagement, and rigor for all students (CAST, 2018). However, there is limited support on how to implement this in daily instructional practices along with AI and GBL in secondary ELA classrooms. So, building on the theoretical foundations of UDL and constructivism, this chapter will explore how to fill that gap by examining how these emerging technologies can carry out differentiation in secondary ELA classrooms by promoting both access and rigor for all students to demonstrate how AI and GBL can extend these evidence-based practices in literacy instruction.

DIFFERENTIATION IN ACTION IN THE INCLUSIVE CLASSROOM

Differentiation is key to equitable literacy instruction in inclusive classrooms because students vary in reading proficiency, interests, levels of background knowledge, and how they approach learning (Tomlinson, 2017). In secondary ELA, where students are engaging in complex reading, analysis, and writing tasks, the student diversity is vast (Applebee & Langer, 2013). Inclusive settings require instructional design that provides access to grade-level content while supporting varied literacy needs (Hall et al., 2004; Hehir et al., 2016). T-TESS Dimension 2.4: Differentiation utilizes Tomlinson's (2017) explanation of differentiation of tailoring instruction to student readiness, interests, and learning profiles while maintaining rigorous expectations and requires teachers to implement it within the classroom (Texas Education Agency, 2022). This ensures that teachers know that all students can demonstrate mastery of state standards through individualized pathways and adaptive supports.

Differentiation in literacy requires variation in the content, process, and product of student learning (Tomlinson, 2017). In secondary ELA classrooms, differentiation of the content may include adapted texts, visual summaries, or audio supports (CAST, 2018). Differentiation of the process involves flexible grouping, guided questioning, or scaffolded reading activities that help students engage with complex texts in ways aligned to their needs (Applebee & Langer, 2013). Differentiation of the product allows students to demonstrate comprehension through essays, discussions, or creative media, which ensures students have multiple pathways for expression (CAST, 2018; Hall et al., 2004). Tomlinson (2017) emphasizes that differentiation must maintain academic rigor. The goal is not to simplify learning but to make complex literacy accessible to all students (CAST, 2018). Research confirms the effectiveness of differentiation in inclusive classrooms when supported by collaborative teaching and ongoing assessment. For example, Brendle, Lock, and Piazza (2017) found that co-teaching models enhance differentiation by allowing teachers to flexibly group students and provide real-time feedback. Co-teachers can divide responsibilities, where one teacher is focusing on whole-group literary analysis, and the other is providing targeted instruction for students requiring additional scaffolding. This collaboration aligns with Vygotsky's (1978) vision of social learning as a driver of cognitive development and aligns with the adaptive principles in T-TESS Dimension 2.4: Differentiation.

Challenges

Despite its vast importance, differentiation remains one of the most difficult instructional practices to implement consistently. Teachers often state that limited time, large class sizes, and inconsistent resources as barriers to individualized instruction, and while the teachers recognize the value of differentiation, their instructional decisions are often shaped by contextual constraints and personal beliefs about student ability (Jager et al. 2025). Deunk et al. (2018) highlights that successful differentiation depends on professional learning and collaborative structures that sustain reflective practice. Similarly, Onyishi and Sefotho (2020) found that while teachers value differentiation, they often need clearer models and tools to apply it effectively. These findings show the growing role of technology, like AI and GBL, supports individualized learning. Furthermore, the integration of AI and GBL directly supports the four components of T-TESS Dimensions 2.4 Differentiation: (1) adjusting instruction for diverse leaners, (2) providing varied paths to mastery, (3) using data to modify content and process, and (4) supporting high expectations. These components not only reflect the best practices of instruction but also look at the deeper purpose of differentiation.

Differentiation as Equity

Differentiation is not only an instructional approach but also a matter of educational equity as it ensures that all students have meaningful access to rigorous learning opportunities (CAST, 2018; Tomlinson, 2017). Students with disabilities often face systemic barriers in literacy, including inaccessible materials and instructional approaches that do not account for diverse learning profiles (Hall et al., 2004; Hehir et al., 2016). Differentiated instruction addresses these barriers by offering multiple means of access and expression (CAST, 2018). Florian and Black-Hawkins (2011) argue that inclusive pedagogy transforms student diversity; they see it as a foundation for effective teaching rather than a limitation. Equitable differentiation also involves culturally responsive practices. Teachers who integrate diverse texts, multimodal materials, and adaptive technology ensure that literacy instruction reflects and values all students' backgrounds (CAST 2018; Hammond, 2015). This approach aligns with federal and state priorities emphasizing equity and accessibility in education (United States Department of Education, 2023). By designing flexible instruction grounded in UDL and differentiation, teachers uphold every student's right to meaningful participation in literacy learning.

Case Study: Differentiation in an 8th Grade Inclusion ELA Classroom

This case study utilizes *Amplify Reading* as the foundational curriculum for an 8th-grade inclusive English Language Arts classroom. The platform uses an adaptive, narrative-based design to provide a differentiated reading experience (Amplify Education, 2023). While *Amplify Reading* is primarily designed for K–8 students, it can be an effective tool for supporting literacy differentiation in a middle school setting and beyond because of its emphasis on artificial intelligence-driven personalization and story-based personalization. Additionally, *Amplify Reading* is recognized as a high-quality instructional material (HQIM) by the Texas Education Agency (TEA), reinforcing its alignment with state standards and inclusive instructional practices. This case study is designed to support the curriculum for *Romeo and Juliet* in the curriculum found in *Amplify Reading*.

In an eighth grade ELA inclusion classroom, two co-teachers design a unit on Shakespeare's *Romeo and Juliet* aligned with TEKS §110.36(b)(2), §110.36(b)(4), and §110.36(b)(6), which emphasize reading comprehension, analysis of the literary elements, and writing (Texas Education Agency, 2017). The class includes 22 students, where six of those students receive special education services for reading comprehension and written expression. Using the T-TESS Dimension 2.4: Differentiation, the co-teachers begin by using diagnostic reading assessments to identify each student's readiness and literacy profile. The instruction is differentiated across content, process, and product as students access the text through modern English adaptations, audio dramatizations, and visual scene summaries. During reading, students are grouped by readiness to analyze character motivations and figurative language. The writing tasks are tiered to provide varied paths to mastery where some students compose character analysis paragraphs using sentence frames, and others write literary essays comparing themes of fate and free will across acts. Throughout the unit, teachers use data to inform instruction by reviewing daily reading exit tickets and adjusting small group lessons. They maintain high expectations by ensuring all students analyze soliloquies and cite textual evidence as required by the TEKS. By embedding flexible scaffolds and maintaining academic rigor, the co-teachers exemplify the intent of T-TESS 2.4: Differentiation.

GAME-BASED LEARNING (GBL) IN LITERACY INSTRUCTION

GBL merges pedagogy and play to create immersive, student-centered learning environments where students actively construct meaning through interaction and problem-solving (Gee, 2003, 2007). Extending the theories outlined earlier in the chapter, GBL situates literacy learning within interactive, story-driven contexts that sustain student engagement and support differentiated pathways towards comprehension and analysis (CAST, 2018; Holmes et al., 2019). In secondary ELA where engagement and critical thinking are essential, GBL can make literacy skills tangible by transforming abstract concepts such as theme, symbolism, and character development into experiential challenges that deepen understanding (Gee, 2007; Tomlinson, 2017). GBL's effectiveness is rooted in its alignment with intrinsic motivation principles. Malone and Lepper (1987) identify challenge, curiosity, and fantasy as key drivers of engagement, all of which are elements that are central to well-designed educational games. Prensky (2001) and Sitzmann (2011) further validate GBL's impact on learning outcomes, particularly in literacy development.

Theoretical Connections in GBL

Gee (2003, 2007) argues that video games holds principles of effective learning. In a GBL environment, students engage within a structured yet flexible system that mirrors Bruner's (1996) concept of scaffolding where the supports that are embedded within the learning experience and are gradually removed as mastery develops. Similarly, Deci and Ryan's (2000) Self-Determination Theory highlights three motivational needs: autonomy, competence, and relatedness. These psychological needs are essential for fostering intrinsic motivation and sustained engagement in learning environments. In the context of GBL, having well-designed educational games naturally fulfills these needs by offering students choice and control over their learning paths, which is that autonomy piece (Deci & Ryan, 2000). And embedding these incremental challenges that build mastery and adding a narrative-driven or collaborative element creates that sense of relatedness in which students need to promote their skill development in the learning process (Gee, 2003; Malone & Lepper, 1987; Steinkuehler, 2018). This makes GBL a powerful tool for engaging diverse learners in inclusive literacy classrooms and aligns with UDL by providing multiple means of engagement (CAST, 2018).

GBL and Literacy in Secondary ELA Inclusion

GBL supports literacy development by embedding reading and writing tasks within interactive narratives that promote meaning-making and deeper engagement (Gee, 2003, 2007; Steinkuehler, 2018). In ELA classrooms, games can assist students in contextualizing comprehension, vocabulary, and writing through story-based experiences to promote critical analysis (Clark et al., 2016; Plass et al., 2015). Narrative-driven games can require students to interpret the text, infer meaning from the text, and make decisions grounded in evidence (Steinkuehler, 2018). Clark, Tanner-Smith, and Killingsworth (2016) found that GBL environments outperform the traditional methods in promoting motivation and academic achievement. This is significant in an inclusive classroom where student engagement and differentiation to content are essential. For students with learning disabilities, GBL also reduces performance anxiety by framing literacy as exploration of the learning material rather than an evaluation, which transforms reading from a solitary task to a collaborative one that fosters peer interaction and shared meaning (Papastergiou, 2019; Steinkuehler, 2018).

Additionally, GBL supports T-TESS 2.4: Differentiation by offering multiple pathways for student engagement and mastery. Through interactive storytelling, challenge levels, and multimodal supports, GBL allows students to demonstrate literacy understanding in diverse ways (CAST 2018; Steinkuehler, 2018). This flexibility empowers teachers to vary their instructional processes and products, which, in turn, is fulfilling the T-TESS expectation of tailoring instruction to student interests and learning profiles (Plass et al., 2015; Tomlinson, 2017). By integrating GBL into an inclusive ELA classroom, teachers can maintain high expectations while ensuring that all students, including those with disabilities, are engaging in the rigor of the curriculum.

Differentiating with GBL

In inclusive classrooms, GBL serves as a tool for differentiation by providing multiple means of engagement and representation, two key elements of the UDL framework (CAST, 2018). When using GBL, students can progress at their own pace, receive individualized feedback, and choose pathways that align with their strengths and interests. For struggling readers or students with disabilities, multimodal supports such as narration, visual cues, and adaptive feedback can help enhance their comprehension and sustain motivation in GBL environments (Dalton & Proctor, 2007; Plass et al., 2015). For advanced students, open-ended tasks and narrative branching can provide deeper analytical challenges (Gee, 2003, 2007; Malone & Lepper, 1987). Overall, the GBL structure allows teachers to adjust content, process, and product that aligns with differentiation and UDL (CAST, 2018; Tomlinson, 2017). For example, a teacher can differentiate by content or by selecting games that are aligned with literacy standards and text. The process can be differentiated by students progressing through levels or story branches at their own pace. And lastly, the product is differentiated where students can demonstrate mastery through creative outputs such as digital journals, reflection essays, or narrative reconstructions. This structure parallels the T-TESS Dimension 2.4: in response to instruction to maintain high expectations for all students (Texas Education Agency, 2022) through multimodal supports, adaptive feedback, and narrative challenges. GBL allows teachers to vary the content, process, and product in ways that reflect the principles of differentiation and UDL by providing accessible entry points for struggling readers and extensions for advanced learners and uses responsive instruction in inclusive ELA settings to ensure that all students can engage meaningfully in rigorous literacy tasks (CAST, 2018; Tomlinson, 2017).

Case Study: Game-Based Learning for Literacy Differentiation in an 8th Grade Inclusion Classroom

In the eighth grade ELA inclusion classroom, the co-teachers use a GBL platform to enhance engagement during their *Romeo and Juliet* unit. The game is designed as an interactive simulation, and it is aligned to TEKS §110.36(b)(4)(A): analyzing character relationships and conflicts (Texas Education Agency, 2017). The game also supports T-TESS 2.4: Differentiation by allowing students to make narrative decisions that mirror Shakespeare's themes. Students assume character roles to navigate moral and social dilemmas like those in the play. The game's branching storylines adjust instruction dynamically to offer differentiated reading passages and vocabulary scaffolds. Students who need fluency support use built-in text-to-speech and visual summaries, while advanced students explore alternate endings that require textual evidence to justify their narrative choices. Teachers monitor the in-game analytics to identify comprehension trends and regroup students for targeted discussions. These data points help them inform instruction and provide feedback aligned to student progress. Throughout this process, students experience various paths to mastery to demonstrate their understanding through gameplay reflection journals, character diaries, or analytical discussions. By maintaining high expectations for literary interpretation and evidence-based reasoning, the co-teachers ensure engagement for all students and show how GBL utilizes differentiation through motivation, adaptivity, and analysis to support the rigor of the curriculum.

ARTIFICIAL INTELLIGENCE IN LITERACY INSTRUCTION

AI is redefining literacy instruction by enabling adaptive and data-driven differentiation that responds to students' unique learning profiles in real time. Unlike traditional instructional models that rely on standardized instruction, AI tools can analyze student performance to personalize their learning, adjust the content complexity, and provide immediate and target feedback (Holmes et al., 2019). While GBL enhances student engagement and motivation (Gee, 2003; Plass et al., 2015), AI focuses on personalization and providing individualized feedback, pacing, and scaffolding. When integrated together, AI and GBL can extend a teacher's capacity to respond to student diversity in inclusive ELA settings to support access and rigor to the curriculum (CAST, 2018; Texas Education Agency, 2022).

AI Tools and Platforms

AI supports differentiation through continuous data collection and real-time analysis of student performance to allow teachers to make timely instructional adjustments (Holmes et al., 2019; Luckin et al., 2016). Adaptive systems use algorithms to adjust reading difficulty, writing feedback, and instructional pacing to match the student's need (Maity & Deroy, 2024). Holmes, Bialik, and Fadel (2019) describe AI in education as a partnership between students, teachers, and machines. It is a tool that personalizes learning while enhancing a teacher's effectiveness. In literacy classrooms, AI enhances reading comprehension and writing development by identifying student needs and offering precise feedback. Tools such as *NoRedInk* and *Grammarly* provide automated writing analysis, while platforms like *Newsela* adjust text complexity dynamically, which reflect broad findings that AI supports adaptive learning pathways and personalized instruction (Holmes et al., 2019; Luckin et al., 2016). For reading, AI-based platforms assess comprehension and engagement, modifying tasks or offering supports such as definitions, summaries, or text-to-speech for struggling readers (Zawacki-Richter et al., 2019). These adaptive mechanisms directly reflect the UDL principle of multiple means of representation and expression (CAST, 2018). Students can access text in varied formats such as audio, simplified summaries, or interactive annotations while still expressing understanding through digital responses or creative projects.

AI's capacity to analyze student data and provide individualized scaffolds directly aligns with T-TESS Dimension 2.4: Differentiation and emphasizes the use of assessment data to inform instruction and meet diverse student needs (Texas Education Agency, 2022). Through adaptive algorithms, AI platforms can continuously monitor student performance in areas such as reading comprehension, vocabulary acquisition, and writing fluency, offering real-time insights that help teachers tailor instruction (Holmes et al., 2019). These insights allow teachers to adjust the pacing of the lesson, modify the content complexity, and personalize feedback to the students to ensure that each student receives instruction aligned with their readiness level, interests, and learning profile without compromising the academic rigor (Luckin et al., 2016).

Moreover, AI transforms literacy instruction from the standard instruction model into a dynamic system of feedback and adaptation (Holmes et al., 2019; Luckin et al., 2016). This shift supports the UDL framework by offering multiple means of representation and expression, particularly for students with disabilities or those requiring additional scaffolds to support their learning (CAST, 2018). When used ethically and intentionally, AI empowers teachers to become more responsive facilitators of learning to ensure that differentiation is not only possible but also sustainable in inclusive secondary ELA classrooms (Williamson & Eynon, 2020).

Teacher Roles

The adoption of AI in education does not replace teachers; rather, it enhances their ability to differentiate their instruction efficiently. Teachers can use AI-generated insights to contextualize feedback and make informed instructional decisions. Luckin et al. (2016) emphasizes that AI should be a co-pilot, where it is augmenting instructional decision making. They argue that AI is most effective when it supports teachers' professional judgement by providing insights that help refine instruction rather than replace human expertise. In co-taught inclusion settings, AI supports the shared planning and reflection between both teachers. Data dashboards allow both the teachers to track student progress across skills such as vocabulary, comprehension, and writing fluency (Brendle et al, 2017; Holmes et al, 2019; Luckin et al., 2016). This shared data fosters intentional grouping, targeted mini-lessons, and individualized interventions, which are core elements of T-TESS Dimension 2.4: Differentiation. When paired with GBL, AI can also inform how teachers scaffold narrative challenges or reading passages to ensure accessibility for all students (Holmes et al., 2019; Plass et al., 2015).

Ethical Considerations

Many teachers express uncertainty about interpreting data or integrating AI ethically (Holmes et al., 2019). Algorithms trained on non-representative data may unintentionally continue inequities, particularly for students with disabilities (Williamson & Eynon, 2020). Teachers must critically evaluate the AI tools for transparency and fairness to ensure that they enhance and not constrain student agency (Williamson & Eynon, 2020). Ethical implementation of AI also involves maintaining a balance between generated and human feedback. While AI can efficiently assess surface-level writing mechanics, such as grammar and syntax (Holmes et al., 2019), it is the teachers who provide the responses that foster voice, creativity, and critical thinking (Hammond, 2015). The United States Department of Education (2023) recommends that AI should always operate within a framework of human oversight, inclusion, and equity because it is essential to ensure that AI tools are used ethically and do not replace anyone's professional judgement. When AI is implemented with these principles in mind, it can serve as a powerful tool to support differentiation by promoting and maintaining high expectations in inclusive classrooms.

Differentiating with AI

Effective AI integration depends on teacher readiness and professional learning as educators must understand how to interpret and apply AI in meaningful ways (Darling-Hammond et al., 2017, 2020). In inclusive ELA classrooms, co-teaching teams can use AI insights to guide flexible grouping, develop tiered supports, and track literacy growth over time. (Brendle et al., 2017; Scruggs et al., 2007). Ultimately, AI's impact depends on thoughtful human design and reflection (Holmes et al., 2019). Luckin et al. (2016) states that AI can amplify what a teacher values the most, which is understanding what the students are learning. When used intentionally, AI empowers teachers to make differentiation possible and sustainable, and it can be differentiated across all areas of the content, process, and product. Zawacki-Richter et al. (2019) notes that adaptive AI systems can improve reading comprehension. For students with disabilities, these supports reduce barriers to grade-level participation and foster independence.

Case Study: AI-Supported Differentiation in an 8th Grade Inclusion ELA Classroom

In the eighth grade ELA inclusion classroom, co-teachers can integrate an AI-driven literacy platform to personalize reading and writing instruction during a *Romeo and Juliet* unit. The lesson aligns with TEKS §110.36(b)(5): analyzing author's craft and word choice (Texas Education Agency, 2017). T-TESS 2.4: Differentiation can align by using AI feedback to tailor instruction to student readiness. Students can interact with adaptive reading tasks where AI is continuously adjusting the instruction based on comprehension data. One student with dyslexia can access the text using text-to-speech and adaptive summaries of Act III, while an advanced student receives an extended interpretive prompt comparing the imagery in Romeo's soliloquy to Shakespeare's Sonnet 18. Weekly AI-generated reports allow the co-teachers to use data to inform instruction, which allows them to form flexible reading groups and design scaffolded writing conferences moving forward. The teachers maintain high expectations by ensuring all students practice citing textual evidence, interpreting figurative language, and analyzing character motivations. By leveraging AI's adaptivity with teacher-led reflection, differentiation becomes fluid in the classroom. The integration of AI transforms the instruction of *Romeo and Juliet* into an inclusive experience where every student progresses toward mastery at an appropriate pace.

Integrating AI and GBL for Inclusive Literacy

Together, AI and GBL offer an innovative and effective model for differentiated literacy instruction in inclusive secondary ELA classrooms by enhancing personalization, sustaining engagement, and supporting flexible learning (Clark et al., 2016; Holmes et al., 2019; Plass et al., 2015). While GBL provides engagement through interactive narrative and contextualized challenges, AI personalizes instruction through adaptive data and responsive feedback (Gee, 2003; Plass et al., 2015). Integrated together, they form a framework that aligns with the UDL and T-TESS Dimension 2.4: Differentiation, both of which ensure that instruction is equitable and rigorous (CAST, 2018; Texas Education Agency, 2022). By combining GBL with AI, teachers can be responsive to the learning needs of their students in the classroom environment to promote engagement and academic rigor.

Instructional Synergy

AI and GBL complement each other pedagogically by helping teachers address both engagement and adaptivity (Holmes et al., 2019; Luckin et al., 2016). GBL motivates students through meaningful play and narrative immersion, while AI ensures that literacy tasks remain within each student's ZPD (Vygotsky, 1978). Plass et al. (2015) describes this dynamic as a closed learning loop where motivation drives persistence, data informs adjustment, and adaptive feedback sustains learning over time. AI-enhanced GBL systems like *Amplify Reading* can create a dynamic learning environment in which differentiation occurs through ongoing adaptive feedback and personalized pathways (Amplify Education, 2023; Holmes et al., 2019; Luckin et al., 2016). Within these contexts, the teacher's role may shift from primarily delivering direct instruction to serving as a facilitator and learning designer who is interpreting data, modeling strategies, and guiding student reflection. This aligns with the collaborative principles of co-teaching, where co-teachers share the instructional responsibility and decision-making (Brendle et al., 2017). AI and GBL expand this collaboration by providing shared, real-time insights into student learning patterns. AI-powered narrative games adjust reading levels and writing prompts based on the student input (Clark et al., 2016; Plass et al., 2015). Lin et al. (2023) emphasizes how adaptive feedback mechanisms sustain student engagement and support literacy growth.

Pedagogical Implications

In differentiated literacy instruction, engagement alone may be insufficient as it often needs to be paired with adaptivity and accessible design to support the diverse learning needs of students. AI can contribute to the adaptivity by providing personalized scaffolding and feedback based on ongoing student data (Holmes et al., 2019; Luckin et al., 2016), while GBL can offer motivating and meaningful contexts that promote sustained engagement and deepen comprehension (Clark et al., 2016; Plass et al., 2015). Lu et. al's (2022) meta-analysis confirms that game-based learning significantly improves students' computational thinking, especially when role-playing and adaptive elements are included. Similarly, Holmes, Bialik, and Fadel (2019) highlights that AI enables continuous differentiation by tailoring instruction based on student behavior rather than predetermined pathways. This integrated approach supports UDL's call for multiple means of engagement, representation, and expression (CAST, 2018). And therefore, these systems produce a classroom that is responsive by design: one where differentiation is both planned and enacted.

Case Study: Integrating AI and GBL for Differentiation in an 8th Grade Inclusion Classroom

In the eighth grade ELA classroom, co-teachers can merge AI and GBL using an adaptive reading game based on *Romeo and Juliet* to foster engagement and comprehension. The lesson demonstrates T-TESS 2.4: Differentiation through dynamic, personalized instruction and aligns with TEKS §110.36(b)(7): analyzing theme and archetypes (Texas Education Agency, 2017). As students navigate through the interactive storylines that mirror the Capulet and Montague feud, the AI program adjusts reading complexity and feedback in real time. Meanwhile, the GBL structure motivates students through the challenges that require them to provide textual evidence to advance. The co-teachers plan the varied paths to mastery to allow some students to reconstruct scenes through digital storytelling and others to complete thematic essays. By using AI analytics, the co-teachers inform instruction through weekly data reviews and restructured small groups, and they collaborate to maintain high expectations to ensure that all students demonstrate mastery of inferencing, theme analysis, and textual synthesis at grade level.

Professional Development and Teacher Preparation

Even though the use of AI and GBL for differentiation in literacy instruction has been researched, the success of these innovations ultimately depends on the teacher's readiness and professional learning. Research emphasizes that teachers serve as the bridge between technology and the classroom reality (Darling-Hammond et al., 2017; Trust, 2012). However, research consistently shows that most teachers receive limited training in applying these emerging technologies for differentiation (Ertmer & Ottenbreit-Leftwich, 2010). Effective integration requires an intentional and sustained professional development (PD) that supports both technical proficiency and pedagogical transformation. Darling-Hammond et al. (2017) and Trust (2012) emphasize that high-quality PD is essential in preparing teachers to implement AI and GBL in ways that support differentiation in inclusion. When teachers are equipped to implement, interpret the learning data, design differentiated tasks, and maintain high expectations for all students, they are able to meet the expectation of T-TESS Dimension 2.4: Differentiation (Texas Education Agency, 2022). Aligning technology with instruction is key to ensuring that differentiation becomes sustainable and equitable practice in inclusive ELA classrooms (Holmes et al., 2019).

Professional Development (PD) Needs

Traditional PD formats such as one-time workshops or demonstrations rarely produce lasting changes in instructional practice. Darling-Hammond et al. (2017) found that effective PD must be continuous, collaborative, and directly connected to classroom application. For AI and GBL, teachers need time to explore these new technologies, and then reflect on the student data and adapt lesson designs in the moment. Holmes et al. (2019) emphasize that AI's educational potential can only be realized when teachers understand how algorithms generate insights and how to interpret those results ethically and pedagogically.

This preparation is crucial in inclusive ELA settings where teachers must balance the rigor of the content with accessibility. Special education teachers and general educations teachers alike require targeted training on using AI-driven analytics to differentiate reading and writing instruction while upholding UDL principles (CAST, 2018). For example, teachers might learn how to analyze comprehension dashboards from an adaptive reading program or how to design GBL tasks that support multiple modes of expression. PD should help teachers move beyond the basic understanding of familiarity and towards pedagogical fluency, which is understanding not only how to use technology, but why and when to use it to support diverse students (Trust, 2012).

Coaching and Mentorship

Beyond formal PD sessions, ongoing coaching and mentorship are essential for sustaining change in the classroom. Research on effective professional learning emphasizes that job-embedded coaching and continuous feedback lead to stronger implementation of new practices (Darling-Hammond et al., 2017; Desimone, 2009). Instructional technology coaches can model classroom integration, assist in lesson planning, and provide real-time support which can increase teacher confidence and effective use of digital tools (Ertmer & Ottenbreit-Leftwich, 2010). According to Darling-Hammond et al. (2017), coaching significantly increases transfer of learning from PD to classroom practice. With schools adopting AI and GBL systems, coaches can also serve as mediators between teachers and data to help the teachers interpret the analytics meaningfully (Holmes et al., 2019). Over time, this approach creates communities of practice where the use of technology evolves through a collective inquiry rather than isolated effort (Trust, 2012). This culture embodies the inclusive and collaborative elements of differentiated instruction (Brendle et al., 2017). As teachers grow more fluent in both the tools and the theories that guide their use of AI and GBL in the classrooms, they are able to create the inclusive literacy environments where AI and GBL amplify the art of teaching (Luckin et al, 2016).

Professional Learning Communities

The most effective PD models for AI and GBL integration are collaborative and reflective. PLCs provide an ideal structure for teachers collaborate and reflect when analyzing data, sharing teaching strategies, and evaluating the impact of adaptive tools on student outcomes. Additionally, PLCs can foster teacher agency and innovation because they emphasize inquiry, experimentation, and allow for peer feedback when planning instruction (Trust, 2012). In inclusive classrooms, teachers can use PLCs to align differentiation strategies, interpret AI analytics, and adapt GBL activities to meet specific literacy goals, which mirrors the T-TESS Dimension 2.4: Differentiation expectation that the teachers are to use ongoing assessment to adjust instruction for individual students (Texas Education Agency, 2022). By embedding AI and GBL integration into PLC routines, districts can ensure that differentiation remains data-informed, and it promotes the concept of horizontal learning, where teachers are learning from each other's successes and challenges rather than the top-down training that may not address real classroom contexts (Holmes et al. 2019; Trust, 2012).

Leadership and Policy Implications

School and district leaders play a crucial role in shaping professional learning for AI and GBL integration. Leadership support determines whether technology adoption becomes a sustainable innovation or a short-term initiative (Darling-Hammond et al., 2017; Trust, 2012). Administrators can model reflective technology use by engaging in data discussions with teachers, providing release time for collaborative planning, and recognizing experimentation as part of professional growth. Equity must remain central in leadership decisions as access to inclusive instructional practices (Hehir et al., 2016). Without strategic planning, technology can intensify any existing inequities in access and support (Williamson & Eynon, 2020). Leaders should ensure that all teachers have access to the necessary tools, adequate time, and coaching to explore adaptive learning. Aligning these efforts with UDL and state standards ensures that innovation directly supports inclusive literacy outcomes rather than existing as an isolated initiative.

Ethical Frameworks

As AI becomes embedded more in literacy instruction, having an ethical understanding must be part of teacher preparation. Teachers should know how the algorithms collect, interpret, and store student data, and the teachers must be trained to recognize any potential bias in adaptive systems. UNESCO (2023) advises that teacher education programs include explicit instruction in AI literacy to understand, critique, and ethically use AI in educational settings. Teachers who develop this awareness can make informed decisions about when to rely on AI feedback and when to apply their professional judgment.

Additionally, reflection is equally important. PD programs should include opportunities for teachers to analyze case studies, discuss ethical dilemmas, and evaluate how AI and GBL affect student agency and identity. Research emphasizes that meaningful teacher learning requires inquiry, collaboration, and opportunities to examine the impact of instructional decisions on diverse learners (Darling-Hammond et al., 2017; Trust, 2012). Reflecting on how technology shapes access, engagement, and equity is critical when implementing AI because it introduces new considerations for responsible data use and student autonomy (UNESCO, 2023; United States Department of Education, 2023). This reflective cycle reinforces the idea that differentiation is an evolving practice (Holmes et al. 2019), and it moves professional learning beyond compliance and toward professional inquiry, which helps teachers see themselves as co-designers of ethical, inclusive learning environments.

CONCLUSION

The integration of AI and GBL represents a transformative step towards providing differentiation in secondary inclusive ELA classrooms. Research shows that AI can provide adaptive, data-driven feedback to support personalized learning pathways (Holmes et al., 2019; Luckin et al., 2016), while GBL can enhance student engagement and deepen comprehension through the immersive and interactive storytelling (Clark et al., 2016; Plass et al., 2015). Together, these tools address two of the most persistent challenges in literacy instruction, engagement, and accessibility by merging adaptive feedback with immersive storytelling. Grounded in the UDL framework and aligned with T-TESS Dimension 2.4: Differentiation, AI and GBL allows teachers to design learning experiences that are responsive to individual needs (CAST, 2018; Texas Education Agency, 2022).

Differentiation in inclusive secondary ELA classrooms requires more than instructional variety; it demands an intentional, systemic design that acknowledges and celebrates student diversity (Florian & Black-Hawkins, 2011; Hehir et al., 2016). The combination of AI and GBL offers teachers a pathway to achieve the goal of uniting personalization with engagement. However, technology alone cannot ensure inclusion; it must be guided by reflective, empathetic teachers who understand that data and design serve people, not the reverse. As classrooms continue to evolve, AI and GBL will play increasingly important roles in shaping equitable literacy experiences (Darling-Hammond et al., 2017; UNSECO, 2023). When used ethically and strategically, they empower teachers to move beyond accommodation and towards transformation, making literacy accessible, relevant, and inspiring for every student to achieve literary success (United States Department of Education, 2025).

GAPS IN THE RESEARCH

Despite promising findings across the literature, several important gaps remain in research on AI and GBL integration for differentiated literacy instruction in inclusive secondary settings. First, there is limited scholarship focused specifically on secondary special education and inclusive ELA classrooms. Much of the existing work centers on elementary populations or in higher education, and there are few studies that examine how AI and GBL work together to support differentiated instruction for students with diverse literacy needs (Clark et al., 2016; Williamson & Eynon, 2020; Zawacki-Richter et al., 2019). This gap limits the current findings for practitioners who teach older students navigating increasingly complex literacy demands.

Second, there is a continued need for research on teacher training and professional learning. Studies indicate that many teachers lack adequate preparation to interpret AI-generated data or to integrate adaptive or game-based tools in ways that enhance literacy development (Darling-Hammond et al., 2017; Holmes et al., 2019; Trust, 2012). Existing professional development models frequently emphasize the technical skill acquisition but do not always provide the sustained, collaborative, and practice-based learning necessary for aligning technology use with differentiation principles. Therefore, future research could explore professional learning structures that include co-teaching models, reflective inquiry, and alignment with frameworks such as UDL and T-TESS.

Third, the ethical and equity considerations remain insufficiently studied. Researchers and scholars have noted that AI systems may reproduce biases if not designed, implemented, and monitored thoughtfully (UNESCO, 2023; United States Department of Education, 2023; Williamson & Eynon, 2020). Few studies examine how adaptive technologies affect students with disabilities, emergent bilingual learners, or students with limited access to digital resources. As a result, frameworks for equitable and inclusive AI and GBL design are still emerging and require further empirical and policy-focused investigation.

Finally, questions continue about the long-term impacts of AI and GBL instruction on literacy outcomes. Much of the existing research emphasizes short-term measures such as engagement, motivation, or immediate comprehension gains rather than sustained literacy development (Clark et al., 2016; Plass et al., 2015). There is limited evidence examining how AI and GBL environments influence the growth in students' writing proficiency, critical reading, independent strategy use, or literacy self-efficacy over extended periods (Williamson & Eynon, 2020; Zawacki-Richter et al., 2019). Addressing these gaps is essential for developing a more comprehensive evidence base to guide practitioners and policymakers in implementing equitable and sustainable AI and GBL practices in the classroom. Future research should include longitudinal investigations, mixed-methods studies capturing teacher and student perspectives, and examinations of organizational conditions that support responsible, inclusive technology integration in secondary ELA classrooms.

IMPLICATIONS FOR INSTRUCTIONAL PRACTICE

Effective integration of AI and GBL in secondary ELA classrooms benefits from intentional instructional design that prioritizes flexibility, reflection, and collaboration. Teachers can embed differentiation into lesson structures by incorporating adaptive technologies and choice-driven activities that anticipate student variability and allow learners to engage with texts at appropriate challenge levels while maintaining agency (CAST, 2018; Hall et al., 2004). AI-generated analytics may also support reflective differentiation by helping teachers interpret learning data, form flexible groups, and adjust instruction in ways that are responsive to student needs (Holmes et al., 2019; Luckin et al., 2016). These practices align with T-TESS Dimension 2.4: Differentiation and with broader professional frameworks such as the Framework for Teaching and international teacher standards including the Australian Professional

Standards for Teachers (Danielson Group, 2011; Australian Institute for Teaching and School Leadership, 2017; Texas Education Agency, 2022).

Collaborative instructional models may further enhance the implementation of AI and GBL by enabling teachers to share roles, analyze data together, and ensure that differentiated supports remain both pedagogically sound and student-centered (Brendle et al., 2017; Scruggs et al., 2007). Districts and schools can strengthen this work by providing ongoing training aligned with inclusive pedagogy and ethical technology use to help teachers apply AI-generated insights responsibly and connect them meaningfully to literacy goals (Darling-Hammond et al., 2017; UNESCO, 2023; United States Department of Education, 2023).

LOOKING FORWARD

As technology continues to shape literacy instruction, the teacher's role becomes even more central. They are not merely as a user of AI and GBL tools, but now a professional who applies their human judgment to ensure these innovations are used equitably and responsibly. While AI and GBL platforms can contribute to enhancing differentiation and accessibility, teachers remain the primary decision-makers who interpret learning data, scaffold meaning, and sustain the relationships that support student growth (Holmes et al., 2019; Luckin et al., 2016). Effective differentiation requires educators to integrate digital insights with professional expertise so that instruction reflects the values of inclusion, equity, and high expectations articulated in frameworks such as T-TESS Dimension 2.4: Differentiation and national or international standards like the Framework for Teaching and the Australian Professional Standards for Teachers (Australian Institute for Teaching and School Leadership, 2017; Danielson Group, 2011; Texas Education Agency, 2022).

Looking ahead, the future of inclusive literacy instruction may depend on a balanced partnership between human expertise and intelligent systems where technology amplifies, rather than replaces, the teacher's ability to design learning experiences grounded in empathy, intentionality, and pedagogical precision. Ensuring ethical and equitable implementation will require continued professional learning and reflective practice (UNESCO, 2023; United States Department of Education, 2023). When thoughtfully integrated, AI and GBL can support teachers in advancing inclusive, engaging, and rigorous literacy environments for all learners.

REFERENCES

Amplify Education. (2023). *Amplify Reading* [Adaptive literacy platform]. https://www.amplify.com/programs/amplify-reading

Applebee, A. N., & Langer, J. A. (2013). *Writing instruction that works: Proven methods for middle and high school classrooms*. Teachers College Press.

Australian Institute for Teaching and School Leadership. (2017). *Australian professional standards for teachers* (Revised). https://www.aitsl.edu.au/docs/default-source/national-policy-framework/australian-professional-standards-for-teachers.pdf

Brendle, J., Lock, R., & Piazza, K. (2017). A Study of Co-Teaching Identifying Effective Implementation Strategies. *International Journal of Special Education*, *32*(3). https://files.eric.ed.gov/fulltext/EJ1184155.pdf

Bruner, J. (1996). *The culture of education*. Harvard University Press. DOI: 10.4159/9780674251083

CAST. (2018). *Universal Design for Learning guidelines version 2.2*. CAST. https://udlguidelines.cast.org

Clark, D. B., Tanner-Smith, E. E., & Killingsworth, S. S. (2016). Digital games, design, and learning: A systematic review and meta-analysis. *Review of Educational Research*, *86*(1), 79–122. DOI: 10.3102/0034654315582065 PMID: 26937054

Dalton, B., & Proctor, C. P. (2007). Reading as thinking: Integrating strategy instruction in a universally designed digital literacy environment. In McNamara, D. S. (Ed.), *Reading comprehension strategies: Theories, interventions, and technologies* (pp. 421–440). Lawrence Erlbaum Associates Publishers.

Danielson Group. (2011). *The framework for teaching evaluation instrument*. The Danielson Group.

Darling-Hammond, L., Hyler, M. E., & Gardner, M. (2017). *Effective teacher professional development*. Learning Policy Institute. DOI: 10.54300/122.311

Darling-Hammond, L., Hyler, M. E., & Gardner, M. (2020). *Preparing teachers for deeper learning*. Harvard Education Press.

Deci, E. L., & Ryan, R. M. (2000). The "what" and "why" of goal pursuits: Human needs and the self-determination of behavior. *Psychological Inquiry*, *11*(4), 227–268. DOI: 10.1207/S15327965PLI1104_01

Deunk, M. I., Smale-Jacobse, A. E., de Boer, H., Doolaard, S., & Bosker, R. J. (2018). Effective differentiation practices: A systematic review and meta-analysis of studies on the cognitive effects of differentiation in primary education. *Educational Research Review*, *24*(1), 31–54. DOI: 10.1016/j.edurev.2018.02.002

Ertmer, P. A., & Ottenbreit-Leftwich, A. T. (2010). Teacher technology change: How knowledge, confidence, beliefs, and culture intersect. *Journal of Research on Technology in Education*, *42*(3), 255–284. DOI: 10.1080/15391523.2010.10782551

Florian, L., & Black-Hawkins, K. (2011). Exploring inclusive pedagogy. *British Educational Research Journal*, *37*(5), 813–828. DOI: 10.1080/01411926.2010.501096

Gee, J. P. (2003). *What video games have to teach us about learning and literacy*. Palgrave Macmillan. DOI: 10.1145/950566.950595

Gee, J. P. (2007). *Good video games + good learning: Collected essays on video games, learning, and literacy*. Peter Lang. DOI: 10.3726/978-1-4539-1162-4

Hall, T., Vue, G., Strangman, N., & Meyer, A. (2004). *Differentiated instruction and implications for UDL implementation*. CAST.

Hammond, Z. (2015). *Culturally responsive teaching and the brain: Promoting authentic engagement and rigor among culturally and linguistically diverse students*. Corwin.

Hehir, T., Schifter, L., Grindal, T., Ng, M., & Eidelman, H. (2016). *A summary of the evidence on inclusive education*. Abt Associates.

Holmes, W., Bialik, M., & Fadel, C. (2019). *Artificial intelligence in education: Promises and implications for teaching and learning*. Center for Curriculum Redesign.

Jager, L., Denessen, E., Cillessen, A. H. N., & Meijer, P. C. (2025). Instructional differentiation in secondary education: Teachers' actions and reasoning. *Teaching and Teacher Education, 159*(1), 105009. DOI: 10.1016/j.tate.2025.105009

Leu, D., Kinzer, C., Coiro, J., Castek, J., & Henry, L. (2013). New Literacies: A Dual-Level Theory of the Changing Nature of Literacy, Instruction, and Assessment. In *Theoretical Models and Processes of Reading* (pp. 1150-1181).

Lu, Z., Chiu, M. M., Cui, Y., Mao, W., & Lei, H. (2022). Effects of Game-Based Learning on Students' Computational Thinking: A Meta-Analysis. *Journal of Educational Computing Research, 61*(1), 235–256. DOI: 10.1177/07356331221100740

Luckin, R., Holmes, W., Griffiths, M., & Forcier, L. B. (2016). *Intelligence unleashed: An argument for AI in education*. Pearson.

Maity, S., & Deroy, A. (2024). Generative AI and its impact on personalized intelligent tutoring systems. *arXiv preprint arXiv:2410.10650*. https://arxiv.org/abs/2410.10650

Malone, T. W., & Lepper, M. R. (1987). *Making learning fun: A taxonomy of intrinsic motivations for learning*. In R. E. Snow & M. J. Farr (Eds.), *Aptitude, learning, and instruction: Vol. 3. Conative and affective process analyses* (pp. 223–253). Lawrence Erlbaum.

Onyishi, C. N., & Sefotho, M. M. (2020). Teachers' perspectives on the use of differentiated instruction in inclusive classrooms: Implication for teacher education. *International Journal of Higher Education, 9*(6), 136–150. DOI: 10.5430/ijhe.v9n6p136

Ouyang, J., & Ye, N. (2023). Differentiated instruction: Meeting the needs of all students. *Curriculum and Teaching Methodology, 6*(11), 57–61.

Papastergiou, M. (2019). Exploring the potential of computer and video games for health and physical education: A literature review. *Computers & Education, 53*(3), 603–622. DOI: 10.1016/j.compedu.2009.04.001

Plass, J. L., Homer, B. D., & Kinzer, C. K. (2015). Foundations of game-based learning. *Educational Psychologist*, *50*(4), 258–283. DOI: 10.1080/00461520.2015.1122533

Prensky, M. (2001). *Digital game-based learning*. McGraw-Hill.

Scruggs, T. E., Mastropieri, M. A., & McDuffie, K. A. (2007). Co-teaching in inclusive classrooms: A metasynthesis of qualitative research. *Exceptional Children*, *73*(4), 392–416. DOI: 10.1177/001440290707300401

Steinkuehler, C. (2018). Video games and digital literacies. *Journal of Adolescent & Adult Literacy*, *62*(1), 83–87. DOI: 10.1598/JAAL.54.1.7

Texas Education Agency. (2017). *Texas Essential Knowledge and Skills for English Language Arts and Reading, High School (19 TAC §110.36).* https://texas-sos.appianportalsgov.com/rules-and-meetings?$locale=en_US&interface=VIEW_TAC_SUMMARY&queryAsDate=11%2F17%2F2025&recordId=196164

Texas Education Agency. (2022). *Texas Teacher Evaluation and Support System (T-TESS) rubric.* https://teachfortexas.org/resource_files/Guides/T-TESS_Rubric.pdf

Thousand, J. S., Nevin, A. I., McNeil, M., & Liston, A. (2006). Differentiating instruction in inclusion in inclusive classrooms: Myth or reality? https://files.eric.ed.gov/fulltext/ED493953.pdf

Tomlinson, C. A. (2017). *How to differentiate instruction in academically diverse classrooms* (3rd ed.). ASCD.

Trust, T. (2012). Professional Learning Networks Designed for Teacher Learning. *Journal of Digital Learning in Teacher Education*, *28*(4), 133–138. DOI: 10.1080/21532974.2012.10784693

UNESCO. (2023). *Guidance for generative AI in education and research.* UNESCO. https://www.unesco.org/en/articles/guidance-generative-ai-education-and-research

United States Department of Education. (2023). *Artificial intelligence and the future of teaching and learning: Insights and recommendations.* https://www.ed.gov/sites/ed/files/documents/ai-report/ai-report.pdf

United States Department of Education. (2025). *Individuals with disabilities education act (IDEA)*. U.S. Department of Education. https://www.ed.gov/laws-and-policy/individuals-disabilities/idea

Vygotsky, L. S. (1978). *Mind in society: The development of higher psychological processes*. Harvard University Press.

Williamson, B., & Eynon, R. (2020). Historical threads, missing links, and future directions in AI in education. *Learning, Media and Technology*, *45*(3), 217–235. DOI: 10.1080/17439884.2020.1798995

Zawacki-Richter, O., Marín, V. I., Bond, M., & Gouverneur, F. (2019). Systematic review of research on artificial intelligence applications in higher education. *International Journal of Educational Technology in Higher Education*, *16*(1), 39. DOI: 10.1186/s41239-019-0171-0

Chapter 9
From AI Scenario Design to Video Simulation:
Advancing Intercultural and Global Literacies in Teacher Education

Nabat Erdogan
http://orcid.org/0009-0001-1439-2717
University of Central Missouri, USA

Michelle L. Conrad
http://orcid.org/0009-0001-9841-1099
University of Central Missouri, USA

Yuankun Yao
University of Central Missouri, USA

ABSTRACT

This chapter presents the design and development of AI-generated classroom scenarios and video simulations created to advance intercultural and global literacies in teacher education. Grounded in culturally responsive pedagogy, intercultural and global competence frameworks, and experiential learning theory, the project treats competence as a reflective, action-oriented literacy. AI was used to draft scenarios and videos, while all pedagogical and ethical decisions were guided through a human-centered, iterative process. Fifty scenarios aligned with six intercultural and four global competencies were created, extensively reviewed and edited, and transformed into video simulations with accompanying instructional guides. The simulations were then integrated into teacher preparation courses and professional development settings. The chapter demonstrates how AI can support experiential, scenario-based learning while human expertise ensures ethical representation and instructional quality, offering a scalable model for preparing educators to teach in diverse classrooms.

DOI: 10.4018/979-8-3373-7472-7.ch009

INTRODUCTION

As United States classrooms continue to grow more culturally and linguistically diverse (Krasnoff, 2016; Leider et al., 2024; Yoon, 2023), preparing educators to respond effectively to this diversity remains a pressing priority. In today's globalized world, teaching increasingly involves developing not only intercultural communication skills but also the literacies needed to interpret, engage, and act within global and multilingual contexts (Dzerviniks et al., 2024; Shliakhovchuk, 2021; Uzum et al., 2024). These literacies, broadly defined as the capacity to read, understand, and respond to cultural and communicative diversity, are foundational to culturally responsive and globally competent teaching.

Building on a project funded by the Longview Foundation and the MoExcels Workforce Initiative, this chapter describes the design and development of intercultural and global classroom scenarios that are transformed into Artificial Intelligence (AI)-generated video simulations. A step-by-step process of conceptualizing, drafting, validating, and producing these simulations is presented, with attention to their potential to cultivate intercultural and global literacies in teacher education. The chapter situates this innovation within established frameworks of culturally responsive pedagogy, intercultural and global competence, experiential learning, and AI-supported teacher training.

CONCEPTUAL FRAMING: FROM COMPETENCY TO LITERACY

The project expands traditional understandings of intercultural competence to include intercultural and global literacies, which encompass "meaning-making across cultural contexts" (Virgona et al., 2025, p. 5). Where competence emphasizes skill and behavior, literacy emphasizes interpretation, reflection, and critical awareness, the ability to *read* cultural situations, analyze perspectives, and act with sensitivity and adaptability (Shliakhovchuk, 2021). In teacher education, intercultural literacy involves interpreting cultural cues, understanding linguistic diversity, recognizing how culture influences communication and learning, and interacting effectively and respectfully with people from different cultural backgrounds. Global literacy, in turn, entails examining global issues, understanding diverse perspectives, and taking action for collective well-being and sustainable development (Jing, 2023). Both literacies are deeply intertwined and essential for teachers navigating classrooms that are becoming increasingly more culturally and linguistically diverse.

By engaging with AI-generated scenario videos, teacher candidates practice these literacies through guided observation, analysis, and reflection on authentic intercultural interactions. The videos make visible the nuances of communication, such as tone, emotion, gesture, and language use, allowing participants to develop not just cognitive understanding but also the interpretive sensitivity that underpins intercultural and global literacy. This process supports the development of pedagogical judgment, enabling future teachers to respond more thoughtfully and effectively in culturally and linguistically diverse classroom contexts.

THEORETICAL FOUNDATIONS

The project this chapter is based on is grounded in several intersecting bodies of research: culturally responsive pedagogy, intercultural communication competence, global competence, experiential learning theory, and the use of AI in teacher preparation.

Culturally Responsive Pedagogy and Intercultural Competence

Culturally responsive pedagogy, as defined by Gay (2018) and Ladson-Billings (1995), emphasizes the importance of affirming students' cultural identities in the learning process and connecting curriculum and instruction to students' lived experiences. Ladson-Billings' concept of culturally relevant teaching argues that effective educators must not only promote academic success but also help students maintain cultural integrity and develop critical consciousness to challenge inequities in the education system. Gay (2018) further elaborates on how teachers can do this through intentional instructional practices, relationship-building, and high expectations grounded in cultural awareness. This pedagogical framework serves as a foundation for the AI-driven scenarios, which are intentionally designed to present dilemmas and opportunities where these principles can be applied and practiced.

Intercultural competence represents a fundamental professional requirement in contemporary teacher education, equipping educators with the necessary capacities to foster equitable and productive learning environments in increasingly diverse classrooms. In educational contexts, intercultural competence refers to the integrated constellation of knowledge, skills, attitudes, and awareness that enables teachers to interact both effectively and appropriately with students, colleagues, and families from varied cultural and linguistic backgrounds (Deardorff, 2006). Deardorff's model emphasizes self-awareness, empathy, openness, and the ability to adapt behavior as essential components of intercultural communication competence. The ultimate objective of cultivating this competence extends beyond mere interpersonal harmony; it aims to create classrooms where all students feel valued and are systemically empowered to achieve their full academic potential (Gay, 2018). This AI-driven project incorporates intercultural competence by designing scenarios where teachers must navigate misunderstandings, demonstrate empathy, and adapt their responses to help their students navigate challenges in ways that promote equity, belonging, and academic growth.

Dimensions of Intercultural Competence

Intercultural competence is not a singular trait but a multifaceted, developmental capacity synthesized from several interdependent domains. For educators, this competence is most comprehensively conceptualized through a tripartite model (see Figure 1) encompassing cognitive, affective, and behavioral dimensions (Bennett, 2008; Deardorff, 2006). The Cognitive Domain encompasses the knowledge and awareness facets of IC. This involves an understanding of key cultural concepts and frameworks, a clear recognition of one's own cultural worldview and its inherent biases, and possession of specific, contextual knowledge about the cultural practices, communication styles, and historical backgrounds of the students and communities one serves (Banks, 2015). This domain includes meta-cognitive awareness, the understanding that one's own perspective is culturally constructed and not a universal standard (Bennett, 1993). The Affective Domain concerns the internal dispositions, attitudes, and mindsets that predispose an individual toward effective intercultural engagement. Foundational attitudes include genuine respect for difference, curiosity and openness toward other cultures, empathy, and a disciplined willingness to suspend judgment (Byram, 1997). The Behavioral Domain refers to the actionable ability to apply knowledge and attitudes in practice. It encompasses a suite of practical skills, including effective verbal and non-verbal communication across cultural lines, the flexibility to adapt one's teaching style and classroom management approaches appropriately, skills for mediating cross-cultural misunderstandings, and the capacity to design, implement, and assess an inclusive curriculum and pedagogy (Ladson-Billings, 1995).

In professional practice, true intercultural competence is evidenced by the synergy of these domains. For instance, a teacher's respectful attitude, reflecting the affective dimension, together with knowledge of a student's cultural norm of collective rather than individual recognition, representing the cognitive dimension, should lead to the adaptation of classroom participation structures to include group-based response opportunities as a behavioral expression of this competence. This integrated application is the hallmark of pedagogically sound intercultural competence.

Figure 1. Dimensions of Intercultural Competence (created using Google Flow AI)

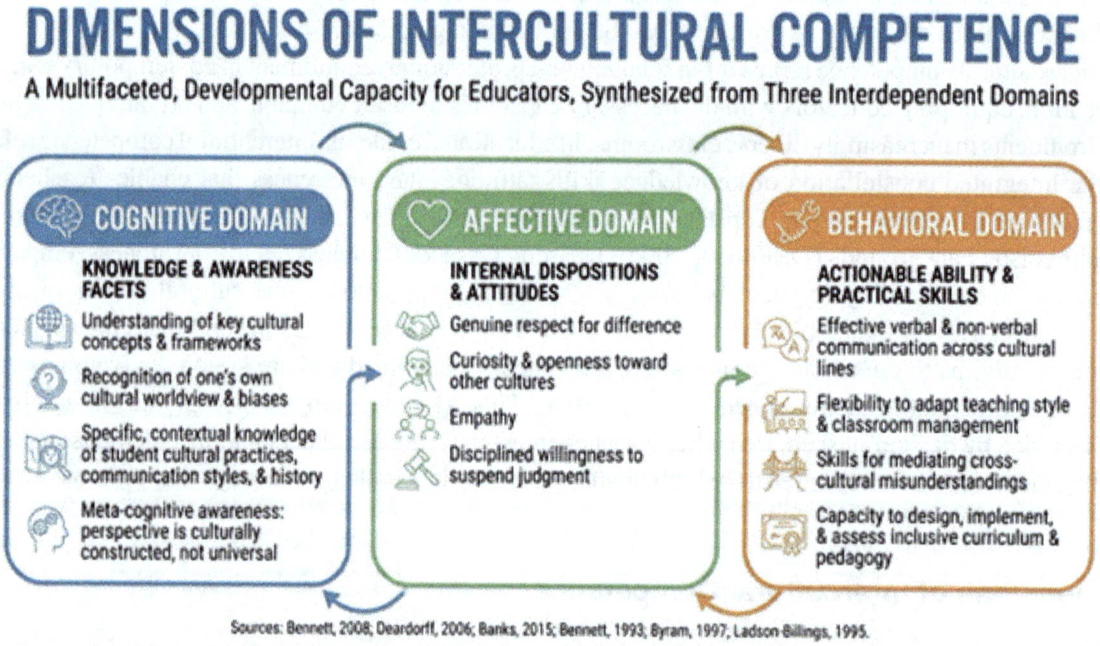

Global Competence

The world is ever more interconnected with rapid technological, economical, and social changes. Integrated with the ideas of intercultural literacy is the need for students to be prepared to participate in the global workforce. The Organization for Economic Cooperation and Development (OECD, 2018) through the Programme for International Student Assessment (PISA) "seeks to determine what is important for citizens to know and be able to do" in modern societies (p. 13). Global competence is defined as "the capacity and disposition to understand and act on issues of global significance" (Mansilla & Jackson,

2011, p. xiii). Adopting a framework of global competence from Mansilla and Jackson (See Figure 2), the OECD conceptualizes global competence as a multidimensional and lifelong learning goal. Within this perspective, schools are seen as uniquely positioned to help students understand their place in the community and world, while also strengthening their ability to make judgments and take action (OECD, 2018). The framework for developing global competence includes four domains: investigate the world, understand diverse perspectives, communicate ideas, and take action.

Figure 2. Dimensions of Global Competence (OECD, 2018)

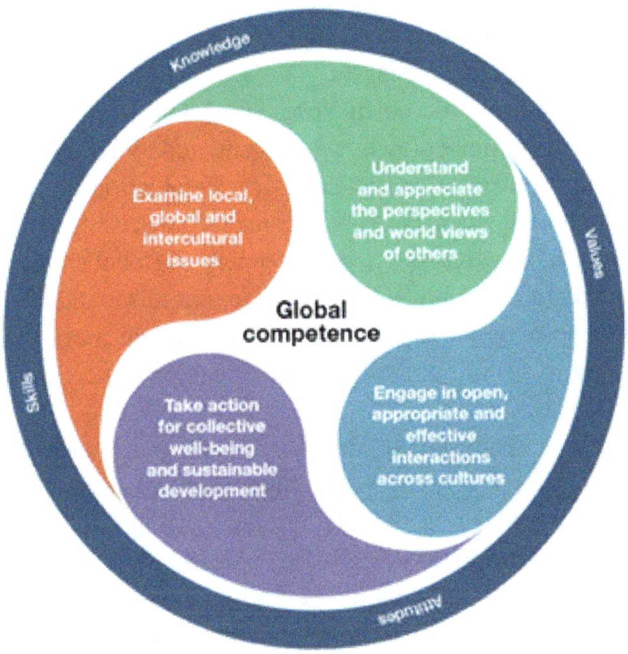

Investigating the world, understanding perspectives, communicating ideas, and taking action operate as interconnected dimensions of global competence that guide how students engage with local and global issues. Investigating the world invites educators to design learning environments where students pose globally relevant questions, explore solutions to significant issues through locally grounded inquiries, and draw on information from local, national, and international sources to connect community problems with broader global concerns (Mansilla & Jackson, 2011). Understanding perspectives emphasizes students' ability to recognize that individuals interpret the world differently, articulate and weigh diverse viewpoints respectfully, and demonstrate empathy as they integrate multiple perspectives into their own evolving understandings (Mansilla & Jackson, 2011).

Communicating ideas highlights students' capacity to use effective verbal and non-verbal communication in culturally diverse settings and to collaborate with peers and professionals across borders in written and visual formats, including email, social media, and other digital tools, as they navigate the complexity of global communication and competitiveness (Mansilla & Jackson, 2011). Taking action focuses on students' belief that they can positively influence their communities and the wider world by recognizing opportunities, applying their learning to take ethical and creative action, and evaluating how their decisions shape both local and global contexts (Mansilla & Jackson, 2011). Together, these four domains support global leadership by preparing students to participate as informed, responsible global citizens.

Building on this foundation, organizations such as the Asia Society and Digital Promise have translated global competence frameworks into practical tools for schools. The Asia Society offers Global Leadership Performance Outcomes that include *I can* statements and rubrics to help educators and students articulate, practice, and assess global leadership skills (Asia Society, 2025). Digital Promise provides complementary educator resources, such as project ideas, student online learning modules, and global career readiness examples that embed global competence into everyday instruction (Digital Promise, 2024). These tools underscore the parallel need for educators themselves to develop global literacy if they are to mentor students as global citizens.

Globally literate teachers cultivate their own global competence while also creating classroom environments that affirm diversity, promote global engagement, and integrate content-aligned explorations of worldwide issues into disciplinary learning (Longview Foundation & Learn NC, n.d.). They facilitate international and intercultural partnerships and conversations, design opportunities for students to collaborate across borders, and assess students' development of global competence alongside academic outcomes (Longview Foundation & Learn NC, n.d.). To support this work, teacher preparation programs must purposefully develop pedagogical skills that enable future educators to embed global dimensions into their subject areas and to sustain globally oriented, equity-focused practice across their careers (Longview Foundation, 2025).

In a ten-year literature review on global competence in higher education by Jiaxin et al. (2024), findings suggested that exposure to cross-cultural online programs and communication, as well as an internationalized curriculum, were two factors that influenced global competence. They also suggested that incorporating cross-cultural education designed to expand students' cultural awareness and sensitivity was best accomplished through a combination of teaching methods. Specifically focused on teacher preparation, Nopas and Kerdsomboon (2024) found that there were limited opportunities for experiential learning. They suggest teacher training programs should foster global competence by emphasizing experiential learning and cross-cultural communication skills.

Experiential Learning Framework

Building intercultural and global development concepts into learning should be student-centered and allow students to fully engage in the learning process. Experiential, scenario-based learning is grounded in Kolb's (1984) experiential learning theory to provide a key pedagogical rationale for this project. In experiential learning, ideas are continuously formed and reformed through experience. The theory is built on six propositions (Kolb & Kolb, 2005):

- Learning is a process; therefore, the focus should be on engaging students in the process to enhance learning.
- All learning is relearning. Students' beliefs and ideas should be examined, tested, and reintegrated with new ideas.
- Conflict and differences drive the learning process, causing students to resolve conflicts to adapt to the world.

- Learning is a holistic process of adapting to the world. Learning involves the integration of the whole person's thoughts, feelings, perceptions, and behaviors.
- Learning results from interactions between the individual and the environment, bringing new experiences into existing concepts.
- Learning is a process of constructing new knowledge.

The experiential learning process is cyclical, with four modes of transforming and integrating new experiences to promote active engagement and learning, as shown in Figure 3 (Kolb, 1984). The four modes are Concrete Experience (students are actively engaged in learning experiences), Reflective Observation (students observe and reflect on those experiences), Abstract Conceptualization (students draw conclusions or generalizations from them), and Active Experimentation (students apply what they have learned to new activities or situations; Kolb & Kolb, 2005).

Figure 3. Kolb's Experiential Learning Cycle (created using Google Flow AI)

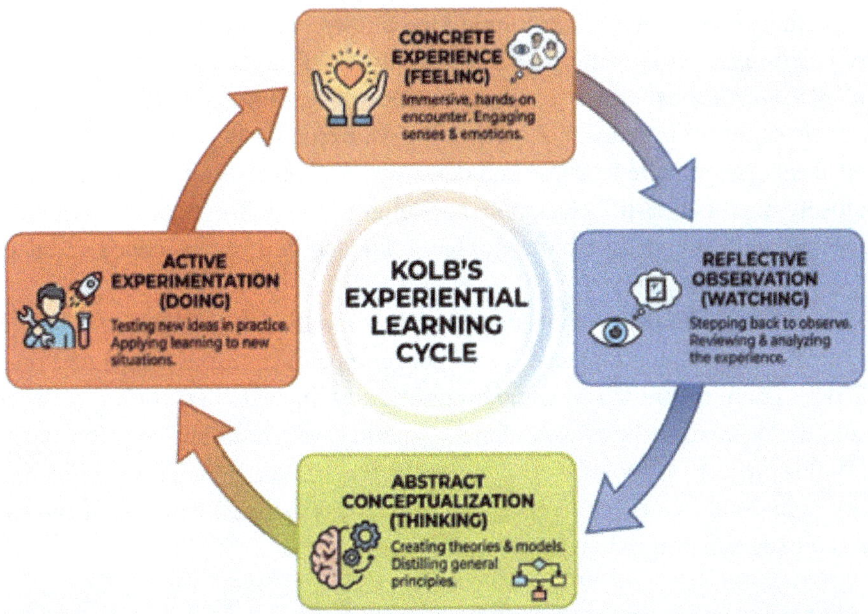

Kolb's (1984) learning cycle, comprising concrete experience, reflective observation, abstract conceptualization, and active experimentation, frames the AI video simulations as experiential learning tools. These simulations are designed to provide educators with concrete intercultural and global experiences in a virtual format. Each experience is followed by structured reflection and application tasks such as journaling, collaborative discussions, and lesson planning. Together, these elements help pre-service and in-service teachers internalize culturally responsive practices through authentic, contextualized experiences. Through this process, intercultural and global literacies become embodied practices rather than abstract understandings.

Game-Based Learning and AI Integration

Both game-based learning (GBL) and AI strategies help students to "transcend their immediate reality" to learn and develop (Plass et al., 2015, p. 259). These approaches allow students to learn from immersive, experiential experiences where activities could be difficult or even dangerous to practice in reality, such as in engineering or healthcare (Mikrouli et al., 2024). These strategies also allow students in any field to engage in coursework, increasing learner motivation, focus, and memory (Hartt et al., 2020). Using games, however, should still take into account the learning objectives, goals of the game, and the learner preferences, while also allowing students to use past knowledge in new ways (Hartt et al., 2020).

While these may be new instructional strategies for educators, these approaches allow students to learn to make choices and plan for complex career situations. This can minimize the possibility of mistakes when students enter the real-world (Hartt et al., 2020; Manzano-León et al., 2021; Mikrouli et al., 2024; Squire & Jenkins, 2003). The military has historically viewed games and simulations as valuable tools for teaching and assessing skills that cannot be safely or practically practiced in real-world settings (Squire & Jenkins, 2003). AI and games allow for multiple chances to practice, adjust for mistakes, and collaborate with others (Dahalan et al., 2023; Zebek & Saygi, 2024).

Finally, the integration of AI in teacher training has shown promise in creating scalable, interactive, and personalized learning environments. Research by Zawacki-Richter et al. (2019) highlights the potential of AI to enhance educational processes through adaptive learning systems, intelligent tutoring, and simulation-based learning environments. AI technologies, particularly when combined with immersive simulations and scenarios, provide teacher candidates with the opportunity to engage in practice-based learning that closely mirrors real-life classroom challenges, especially those involving diverse student populations. This not only supports skill development but also builds confidence and decision-making capacity in a low-risk setting.

Utilizing AI-developed simulation tools can provide a multisensory experience where students are able to think critically about situations and hone their competence through repeated practice of skills (Moyer et al., 2017). Training through AI simulations imitates the real interactions "between the task, the environment, and the behavior" allowing students to modify responses and improve outcomes (Lateef, 2010, p. 349). In this project, AI tools do not replace the teacher educator's role but extend experiential opportunities by generating realistic, diverse, and ethically grounded learning scenarios that can be revisited across courses and professional contexts.

Developing Intercultural and Global Competencies in School and Classroom Settings

The translation of intercultural and global competencies from theoretical construct to professional practice requires pedagogical approaches that move beyond passive knowledge transmission to active, reflective application. In the presented project, the same experiential learning processes (Kolb, 1984) that support students' development (concrete experience, reflective observation, abstract conceptualization, and active experimentation) are intentionally applied to teachers' own professional learning. Teacher education and professional development, therefore, employ several key experiential methodologies that position educators as learners who iteratively interpret, test, and refine their practice.

Reflective practice serves as the cornerstone of professional development in this area. It engages educators in a continuous cycle of critically examining their own cultural identities, implicit biases, and assumptions, and analyzing how these factors influence their expectations, interactions, and instructional decisions (Howard, 2003). Structured reflective tools such as cultural autobiographies, guided journaling in response to classroom interactions, and collaborative analysis of teaching portfolios make this internal process explicit and transformative, moving teachers through reflective observation and abstract conceptualization toward more intentional action.

Experiential and immersive learning provides teachers with concrete experiences of diversity that can then be systematically reflected on and translated into new practices. While long-term cultural immersion programs are highly impactful, meaningful experiences can also be integrated into preparation programs through community-based learning projects, structured home visits, or partnerships with schools serving demographics different from a teacher candidate's own background (Sleeter, 2008). These experiences offer concrete referents for theoretical knowledge, surface implicit assumptions, and create opportunities for teachers to plan, try out, and refine new responses in subsequent classroom interactions.

Scenario-Based Learning (SBL) has emerged as a particularly effective pedagogy for bridging theory and practice within the controlled, low-risk environment of teacher preparation. SBL presents pre- and in-service teachers with nuanced, realistic narratives of professional dilemmas endemic to diverse school settings, for example, a conflict rooted in cultural misinterpretation between students, a challenging parent conference where communication styles clash, or a dilemma regarding the selection of culturally representative curricular materials (Darling-Hammond, 2017).

Engaging with a scenario requires teachers to holistically activate their intercultural and global competencies by analyzing situational dynamics through cognitive knowledge, examining their emotional and attitudinal responses within the affective domain, and formulating, justifying, and sometimes role-playing actionable strategies that reflect behavioral skill development. The facilitated debriefing that follows is critical, allowing for deeper reflection, exposure to multiple perspectives from peers, and the consolidation of learning across all three domains, thereby fostering a more integrated competence (Kegan & Lahey, 2009).

A Persistent Challenge of Developing and Implementing Scenario-Based Learning

Despite a strong theoretical and empirical consensus on the efficacy of active pedagogies like SBL, a significant practical barrier routinely limits their widespread, consistent, and high-quality implementation. This barrier is the resource-intensive nature of creating and curating high-quality training materials (Cushner & Mahon, 2009). Developing a repository of realistic, culturally nuanced, and pedagogically sound scenarios requires a significant investment of expert time in research, writing, and validation. The challenge is compounded when seeking to create multi-modal resources, such as written cases, video vignettes, audio recordings, etc., to enhance authenticity, as these involve production costs and technical expertise. Consequently, many teacher education programs are constrained to using a small, static set of commercially available or locally developed case studies. These may lack relevance to specific local contexts, fail to represent emerging demographic trends, or provide insufficient variety to address the full spectrum of developmental readiness among educators (Hitchcock et al., 2002). This gap between the pedagogical ideal and the practical limitations of resources constitutes a significant impediment to advancing intercultural and global competency development at scale.

Educators' competence in intercultural and global domains is a critical, complex, and integrated professional capacity. Its development requires moving from an abstract understanding to reflective practice through pedagogies such as scenario-based learning, which uniquely bridges knowledge, attitude, and skill. The persistent practical challenge of creating high-quality, diverse scenario materials systematically constrains the field's ability to prepare teachers effectively for diverse classrooms (Banks, 2015). By evaluating the potential of generative AI as a practical tool to support the creation of these vital resources, this study seeks to address a concrete implementation barrier by offering pragmatic insights that may enhance teacher education programs' capacity to systematically and effectively develop the intercultural competence essential to 21st-century teaching.

DESIGN AND DEVELOPMENT PROCESS

This project employed an iterative design process to develop AI-powered classroom scenarios and video-based simulations that advance intercultural and global literacies in teacher education. Three researchers from a Midwestern university, who were involved in a Longview Foundation-funded project, collaboratively designed the scenarios, drawing on their expertise in literacy education, intercultural competence, and teacher preparation. Although AI tools were used to generate draft text, dialogue, and video simulations, all pedagogical, linguistic, and ethical decisions were guided by theory, educator expertise, and systematic human review. AI functioned as a generative and technical support rather than an instructional authority.

The design process did not follow a linear path from idea to finished product. Instead, it unfolded through repeated cycles of drafting, reviewing, and revising materials. Each phase revealed new considerations related to cultural representation, language use, pedagogical clarity, and inclusivity. These insights informed subsequent revisions. The research team took detailed notes as they designed scenarios, which captured AI prompts, researcher reflections, revisions, and decision rationales. In this chapter, those notes are treated as design data and used as evidence of how AI-generated materials were refined into pedagogically sound, ethically grounded instructional tools. The following sections describe each phase of the development process in detail, demonstrating how theoretical principles were translated into concrete design, prompting, and editing practices, as well as video simulations and instructional materials.

Identifying Intercultural and Global Competencies

The design and development process began with the deliberate identification of core intercultural and global competencies that would anchor all subsequent scenario design, AI prompting, editing, and revisions. This initial phase was foundational, as it established the project's conceptual boundaries and ensured that all AI-generated materials aligned with recognized educational goals rather than surface-level representations of culture. Grounded in this commitment to clearly defined educational purposes, the project was situated within broader global education goals. Specifically, it explicitly supports the United Nations' Sustainable Development Goal 4, which emphasizes inclusive, equitable, and quality education, as well as the promotion of lifelong learning opportunities for all (United Nations, 2024). In alignment with this goal, the research team prioritized competencies that enable teachers to interpret cultural complexity, engage ethically with linguistic and cultural diversity, and act in ways that promote equity and collective well-being in classroom settings. To develop a coherent and theoretically grounded competency set, the research team reviewed and synthesized widely recognized international frameworks, including the OECD Global Competence Framework (OECD, 2018), UNESCO's intercultural education guidelines (UNESCO, 2006), and Deardorff's (2006) intercultural competence model. Rather than adopting a single framework wholesale, elements from each were intentionally integrated to reflect both the interpersonal demands of culturally responsive teaching and the broader civic and global responsibilities of educators.

Through this synthesis process, the team identified ten competencies, six intercultural and four global, that together represent a balanced, practice-oriented model of intercultural and global literacy for teachers. Selection criteria emphasized competencies that are observable in classroom interactions, require interpretation and judgment rather than rule-following, and can be meaningfully practiced through scenario-based and experiential learning.

The six Intercultural Competencies focus on teachers' capacity to navigate everyday classroom interactions with cultural and linguistic awareness:

1. **Cultural Self-Awareness** – Understanding one's own cultural identity, values, and biases and how they shape instructional decisions and interactions.
2. **Curiosity and Openness** – Demonstrating genuine interest in and respect for cultural differences without judgment or defensiveness.
3. **Empathy and Perspective-Taking** – Recognizing, validating, and responding to the emotions, experiences, and viewpoints of others.
4. **Cultural Communication Skills** – Navigating differences in verbal and non-verbal communication styles, including silence, eye contact, and participation norms.
5. **Conflict Resolution Across Cultures** – Managing misunderstandings and tensions in culturally respectful and relationship-sustaining ways.
6. **Adapting Behavior in Diverse Settings** – Adjusting instructional approaches and interactional strategies appropriately in multicultural contexts.

The four Global Competencies extend this interpersonal focus to broader social, ethical, and civic dimensions of teaching:

1. **Investigating the World** – Demonstrating curiosity and the ability to explore local and global issues, questions, or challenges that shape students' lives.
2. **Recognizing Perspectives** – Identifying, articulating, and critically evaluating multiple viewpoints, including one's own.
3. **Communicating Ideas Effectively Across Cultures** – Expressing ideas clearly, respectfully, and responsibly with diverse audiences in varied cultural contexts.
4. **Taking Action for Collective Well-Being** – Applying knowledge, skills, and empathy to contribute positively to classrooms, communities, and society.

These ten competencies functioned as *design anchors* throughout the project. Each scenario and its corresponding teacher response, video simulation, and instructional guide were explicitly mapped to a single primary competency, ensuring conceptual coherence across the materials. Importantly, framing these competencies as literacies, rather than static skills, positioned them as practices that require ongoing interpretation, reflection, and adaptation. Viewing competencies as literacies informed the development of scenarios that prioritize meaning-making and ethical decision-making rather than the identification of correct or incorrect responses. By establishing this competency framework at the outset, the project ensured that AI-supported scenario generation remained tightly aligned with international standards, pedagogical theory, and the broader goal of preparing teachers for culturally and globally complex classrooms.

Identifying Culturally and Linguistically Relevant Classroom Dilemmas Within Each Intercultural and Global Competence

The second phase focused on identifying classroom dilemmas that reflect authentic intercultural and global challenges teachers encounter in multilingual and multicultural classrooms and align with the identified intercultural and global competencies. The aim was to design scenarios that represent moments of uncertainty, misunderstanding, tension, or conflict that require teachers to interpret students' experiences, consider multiple perspectives, and make thoughtful pedagogical decisions. During initial scenario generation, however, the research team noticed a lack of diversity in the scenarios: they tended to focus on surface-level cultural topics and did not address more critical or complex intercultural elements that teachers encounter in everyday classrooms. For example, while examining the central topics of the early AI-generated scenarios, the team observed that most were very similar, focusing primarily on holidays and traditions. While holidays and cultural celebrations can be useful instructional entry points, an overreliance on them risks presenting culture as static, celebratory, and disconnected from everyday classroom practice. In response, the research team intentionally shifted the focus of scenario design. The scope moved beyond surface-level cultural elements such as food and holidays to emphasize situations that teachers commonly encounter in multilingual classrooms. AI was purposefully prompted to generate scenario topics addressing deeper intercultural challenges, including navigating classroom routines, responding to student silence or withdrawal, supporting emotional well-being, and working with Students with Limited or Interrupted Formal Education (SLIFE). To broaden the range of issues represented and ensure that concerns not initially identified by the research team were also reflected, AI was explicitly instructed to offer scenario topics with other unique issues that an interculturally competent teacher might need to address (Researcher Notes, 2025). This led to scenarios involving confusion about homework, unfamiliarity with classroom technology, uncertainty about participation norms, anxiety about peer interaction, and so on. These situations are common in diverse classrooms yet are often misinterpreted as a lack of motivation or engagement. By grounding scenarios in these authentic dilemmas, intercultural and global competencies were framed as an everyday teaching practice rather than a special-topic lesson. This phase established the conceptual foundation for all subsequent design work.

Drafting Initial Scenarios Using AI Tools

Once key competencies and classroom dilemmas were identified, an AI-assisted text-generation tool, ChatGPT, was used to draft initial versions of scenarios. This tool allowed the research team to generate multiple narrative possibilities efficiently and to explore a wide range of classroom contexts. As the AI was used to generate and edit scenarios, the research team made sure that each scenario followed a consistent structure:

- A narrator's introduction describing the student's linguistic, cultural, and educational background
- A short student utterance that presents the intercultural or global dilemma

- Four possible teacher responses, only one of which reflects the most culturally and globally competent action

One of the finalized scenarios on intercultural competence, with a focus on *Curiosity and Openness*, is provided below. All finalized scenarios followed this standard template.

Narrator Introduction:

This is Danylo, a 6th-grade student who moved from Ukraine two years ago. He speaks Ukrainian at home, but his English has become conversational. He is attentive and sometimes reflects on how schoolwork is organized differently across countries.

Student Dialogue (Danylo):

"In Ukraine, teachers give one big test at the end. Here… many small quizzes every week. I feel surprised… so many grades all the time."

What is the most interculturally competent way for the teacher to respond?
Teacher Response Options:

A. "That's a thoughtful observation, Danylo. Schools organize learning in different ways. Here we use smaller quizzes to help students practice often. Would anyone else like to share experiences with different grading systems?"
B. "That's a thoughtful observation, Danylo. Schools organize learning in different ways. Here we use smaller quizzes to help students practice often. You will get used to our grading system over time."
C. "That's a thoughtful observation, Danylo. Schools organize learning in different ways. Here we use smaller quizzes to help students practice often. We believe this approach helps students manage stress better."
D. "That's a thoughtful observation, Danylo. Schools organize learning in different ways. Here we use smaller quizzes to help students practice often. Please try to follow our system in class going forward."

Following this template, a total of 50 scenarios, five for each intercultural and global competency, were drafted, edited, and finalized. This ensured systematic coverage of all targeted global and intercultural competencies and consistency in scenario structure. The standardized design also supported reliable implementation across teacher education and professional development contexts.

Applying Rigorous Editing and Quality Principles to AI-Generated Scenarios

Across all phases of development, the project applied a consistent set of editing and quality principles. This helped ensure accuracy of cultural and linguistic representation, authenticity of scenarios and teacher-student dialogues within those scenarios, ethical integrity, and pedagogical usefulness. These principles functioned as an internal validation framework guiding all revisions of AI-generated content.

Fact-checking was foundational to the scenario development process. All scenarios were systematically reviewed to verify cultural references and factual details in order to ensure accuracy and avoid misrepresentation. For example, one scenario involved an Arabic student from Egypt responding to a teacher's request to "draw a picture of what a normal American breakfast looks like". The original student dialogue stated: *"Ms. Carter... I wasn't sure what to draw. We usually eat flatbread, cheese, and beans in the morning. I didn't grow up with cereal or pancakes... so I didn't know what you meant by 'normal.'"* Because the research team did not have direct cultural or culinary expertise related to Egyptian or broader Arabic breakfast practices, additional research was conducted to confirm the accuracy of this representation. After verifying that flatbread, cheese, and beans are commonly consumed at breakfast in Egypt, the dialogue was used in the finalized scenario.

Since each scenario included a brief introduction to the student's background, including linguistic and cultural context, the research team also verified the accuracy of all references to students' language backgrounds based on their country of origin and ethnic identity. During this review, several inaccuracies were identified, such as grouping multiple African language varieties together and referring to them as a single language or referring to a dialect as a separate language. In one instance, a generated scenario indicated that a student spoke Twi. Further fact-checking revealed that, while Twi is often referred to as a language due to its large number of speakers and its role as a lingua franca in Ghana, it is linguistically classified as a dialect of Akan, the principal language of the Akan people. To avoid potential confusion or misrepresentation, the student's linguistic and ethnic background in this scenario was revised to reflect a different, more clearly defined context.

During the review process, the research team also addressed instances in which AI-generated responses were factually accurate but conceptually incomplete. For example, in a scenario targeting the global competency *Investigating the World*, Marisol, a 4th-grade student from El Salvador, reflects on differences in language support across school systems. The initially generated "correct" teacher response attributed these differences primarily to the availability of teachers and resources. The correct response stated: *"That's a wonderful question, Marisol. In some countries, schools have more teachers and programs to help students who speak different languages, but in others, they don't have enough resources. Let's look at a few examples of how schools around the world help students learn in more than one language."* Upon review, the researchers determined that this explanation overlooked a critical factor: in the United States, language support for English learners is not only a matter of resources but is also shaped by federal and state policies that require schools to provide English as a Second Language (ESL) services, as mandated by Title VI of the Civil Rights Act of 1964, the Supreme Court decision in Lau v. Nichols (1974), and subsequent federal and state education policies. To correct this incompleteness, the research team prompted ChatGPT to revise the teacher responses to reflect both structural resources and policy-based mandates. The revised teacher response option read as follows: *"Good question, Marisol. In the U.S., there are laws and programs that make sure students who speak other languages get help learning English. In some other countries, schools may not have those rules or enough teachers trained to help. Let's look at how different countries support students who speak more than one language and why it's so important."* This revision ensured that the scenario more accurately represented the systemic factors influencing language support in schools and strengthened its alignment with global competence learning goals.

Linguistic authenticity and language appropriateness were another central concern throughout the scenario editing process. Student dialogues were carefully revised to reflect realistic English proficiency levels based on age, time in U.S. schools, and prior educational experiences. This alignment was considered essential to accurately represent language proficiency and instructional credibility.

Early AI drafts often included syntactic structures that exceeded plausible proficiency levels. For example, one of the scenarios introduced a 3rd-grade student, Aarav, who recently moved from Nepal. The introduction explicitly stated that Aarav's family speaks Nepali and that he is still in the early stages of learning English. However, the initially generated speech for Aarav included a sentence with an adverbial clause: *"Teacher, in my country, students stand up when the teacher comes to class"*. This sentence structure seemed too advanced for a 3rd-grade language learner who was recently exposed to the target language, so the researchers asked the AI to revise the student's speech by simplifying the sentence structure and possibly adding some grammatical errors to the student's speech. As a result, Aarav's speech was revised to: "Teacher… in my country… teacher come to class, … and students stand up. Here… students sit. Why different?" The revised version preserved meaning while reflecting early-stage English development. Similar revisions were applied across all AI-generated scenarios.

The researchers' assumption was that effective teachers should consider their students' language proficiency levels and tailor their speech accordingly to support their English learners' comprehension. Following this premise, teacher language was also revised to match students' receptive abilities. For example, one of the scenarios generated for the intercultural competence focus area *Cultural Self-Awareness* involved a 6th-grade student, Layla, whose family immigrated from Egypt three years ago. The initially generated correct response for this scenario included a more advanced word, such as *"appreciate"*, abstract vocabulary such as *"perspective"*, and complex phrasing like *"open to sharing"*, as it said: *"Thank you for telling me, Layla. I didn't realize my wording assumed one experience. I really appreciate your perspective. Would you be open to sharing it with the class tomorrow?"* Such words and phrases were removed from the teacher's speech to demonstrate the teacher's understanding of language acquisition stages and the importance of adjusting their speech appropriately for each language proficiency level. As a result, the teacher response option was revised as *"Thank you for telling me, Layla. I didn't realize my words assumed only one experience. I am glad you shared your idea. Would you like to share it with the class tomorrow?"* Such changes reinforced the idea that adapting language is a pedagogical act central to intercultural competence.

Scenario diversity guided representation decisions. As discussed in Phase 2, when early drafts repeatedly focused on holidays and traditions, the research team intentionally redirected development toward deeper classroom dilemmas involving students from varied linguistic, cultural, and migration backgrounds, including SLIFE. As development progressed, scenario topics were intentionally diversified to align with six intercultural competencies and four global competencies. Intercultural scenarios addressed communication styles (such as verbal and non-verbal, direct vs. indirect, etc.), emotional expression, humor, silence, eye contact, personal space, turn-taking norms, etc. Global competence scenarios addressed broader issues such as educational access, migration, displacement, and language policy. The design process addressed the need for accurate contextualization, particularly in global scenarios, to avoid reinforcing simplistic explanations of inequality. This ensured that teacher candidates learned to interpret student experiences within broader social and structural contexts. The researchers also intentionally prompted ChatGPT to create scenarios representing diverse student populations. For example, the AI was instructed: *"I already have countries such as Mexico, Syria, Egypt, Somalia, Japan, Ukraine, Nepal, Italy, and Croatia. Please include some other countries. Please add more context to the narrator introduction, also provide diversity in scenarios"*. To ensure relevance for educators across K-12 settings, the research team also ensured that the created scenarios included situations involving students of different age groups and grade levels. These approaches helped generate a wide range of student backgrounds, languages, and cultural experiences, while also expanding the depth of the narrators' introductions to include family structure, prior schooling, language proficiency, and personal interests.

Bias awareness informed multiple rounds of ethical review throughout the scenario development process. One recurring issue identified in early drafts was the tendency for scenarios to portray U.S. students as mean or dismissive toward peers from other countries. To address this, scenarios were carefully revised to frame interpersonal conflict as misunderstanding rather than intentional cruelty. For example, ChatGPT-generated student dialogues initially included experiences such as:

- ***João (Brazil):*** *"Teacher... I say story of Festa Junina... kids laugh... they say it sound silly... but in Brazil... it is happy."*
- ***Hana (Ethiopia):*** *"Ms. Lee... kids say my voice sound funny... They copy me when I read... I don't want read loud."*
- ***Jiwon (South Korea):*** *"Teacher... kids laugh when I bring kimchi... They say it smell strong... I feel embarrassed."*

In response, the research team revised or removed such scenarios to avoid portraying U.S. peers as consistently teasing or dismissive. The goal was to represent cultural differences in ways that reflect misunderstanding, curiosity, or learning moments rather than negative intent. While such cases also exist in real classrooms, they are not as frequent as the AI-generated scenarios suggested. By eliminating these exaggerated portrayals, the team ensured that the scenarios reflected more realistic and nuanced intercultural interactions, allowing teachers to focus on understanding cultural differences and developing responsive pedagogical strategies.

Bias awareness also prompted careful attention to how students' backgrounds were introduced. Early AI-generated introductions sometimes included deficit framing, such as: *"This is Jordan, a 9th-grade student born and raised in the U.S. He identifies as White and speaks only English. Jordan is generally respectful but hasn't had many experiences with cultural diversity. After reading a short story from Nigeria in English class, he seems confused and raises his hand."* Such monolingual student portrayals were reviewed and adjusted to avoid implying limitations or lack of competence. Language was carefully modified to ensure neutral, factual, and respectful representations; for example, "speaks only English" was revised to "speaks English as his first language". Besides removing deficit language, such introductions were also revised to emphasize curiosity and engagement and provide more accurate, neutral descriptions, as follows: *"This is Jordan, a 9th-grade student born and raised in the U.S. He identifies as White and speaks English as his first language. Jordan is curious and engaged in learning. He is generally respectful, but hasn't had many experiences with cultural diversity. After reading a short story from Nigeria in English class, he seems confused and raises his hand."* Across all revisions, the research team sought to balance authenticity, clarity, and inclusivity, reinforcing ethical standards and promoting intercultural understanding.

Balance, clarity, and pedagogical depth were enforced across all teacher response options. All options were revised to be similar in length, tone, and complexity so that culturally responsive choices emerged from interpretation rather than surface cues. While ChatGPT was effective in generating initial draft text, early outputs often included teacher responses that varied substantially in length, making the correct response easily identifiable because it was consistently the longest. To address this issue, ChatGPT was prompted to standardize the length of all responses. Also, some responses lacked pedagogical depth, relying on vague encouragement, such as *Good job* or *Nice try*, or on rule enforcement, such as *You must learn fast and complete the assignment like other students*, rather than instructional strategies that support the development of teachers' intercultural competence. This limitation was addressed by prompting the AI to revise responses to include concrete, pedagogically meaningful instructional strategies, particularly in the correct responses.

As a result, teacher responses were rewritten to model explicit explanation of classroom norms, emotional validation, instructional scaffolding, and inclusive participation strategies. Incorrect responses were also revised to reflect realistic but limited teaching practices rather than exaggerated errors. This practice demonstrates that AI-generated content served as a draft requiring human pedagogical judgment. Together, these principles ensured that AI-generated scenarios were transformed into ethically sound, linguistically authentic, and pedagogically meaningful learning tools.

Transforming Text Into AI-Generated Video Simulations

Once the written scripts of the scenarios were finalized, they were transformed into short video simulations using AI-based text-to-video tools. This phase introduced a new set of design challenges related to selecting and effectively using appropriate technologies, including ensuring accurate pronunciation in AI-generated speech, maintaining clear narrative flow and pacing, and selecting images and visuals that accurately and appropriately represented each scenario and student context. As these issues arose, they were addressed systematically and carefully, ensuring that each element of the videos met the design goals.

The first step in this phase was to identify AI tools capable of producing realistic and pedagogically appropriate video simulations. The research team selected multiple tools to support different aspects of video creation. Still images for narrators were generated using Google Gemini, which enabled the creation of diverse visual characters representing different racial backgrounds. These images were then uploaded to D-ID (De-Identification), an AI-driven video generation platform specializing in realistic lip-syncing and facial animation. D-ID enables users to produce short talking-head videos by animating static images and synchronizing them with text scripts or audio input.

Using this platform, the research team animated the narrator images by inputting the finalized text scripts for the narrators' speech, resulting in short video simulations that visually and audibly presented each scenario. Throughout this process, the researchers encountered several challenges, particularly related to pronunciation accuracy. Some AI-generated audio failed to correctly pronounce student names, especially those from diverse cultural and linguistic backgrounds. For example, the Somali name *Hassan* is correctly pronounced with stress on the second syllable. However, the avatar consistently placed stress on the first syllable.

Addressing these pronunciation issues required creative solutions. To correct the problem, the researchers modified the spelling of the name from *Hassan* to *Hassaan* by adding an additional *a* to the second syllable. This adjustment aligned more closely with English phonological patterns and enabled the AI to place stress on the correct syllable. Because the written script beneath the avatar's speech is not visible to viewers, this spelling *tweak* successfully corrected the pronunciation without affecting the authenticity of the written scenario text.

Speech pacing also required careful adjustment. In several cases, commas and other punctuation marks introduced unnecessary pauses in the narration. By removing or modifying punctuation from text-to-video scripts, the research team reduced these pauses and improved the overall narrative flow, resulting in clearer and more natural-sounding video simulations. Throughout this iterative review and revision process to address issues such as pronunciation accuracy, pacing, and visual alignment with the scenario content, the researchers ensured that the narrator videos were suitable for use in teacher education and professional development contexts. These revisions highlight that video simulation design requires linguistic and technical expertise in addition to pedagogical judgment.

After creating narrator videos introducing each context, the research team focused on developing authentic AI-generated videos depicting students and their dialogues. Flow, Google's AI-powered filmmaking platform, which leverages the Veo 3 model for video generation was used for this purpose. Veo's text-to-video feature enables the creation of high-quality 1080p video clips up to 8 seconds long from text prompts. Student dialogues for all 50 scenarios were generated using Veo within the Flow platform. One advantage of Veo is its ability to accurately portray student appearances when sufficient descriptive information is provided, including skin tone, hair, facial features, and clothing. In addition, Veo can adjust students' English accents to align with their reported linguistic and cultural backgrounds when such information is provided. For example, students from Latin American countries can be represented with Hispanic-accented English, and students from Russia or Ukraine can be represented with Slavic-accented English. These features contributed to more realistic and culturally responsive student representations, which enhanced the authenticity of the video simulations. However, it should be noted that generating authentic videos required careful, intentional prompting. For instance, in the text-to-video scripts, the researchers explicitly specified the desired accent for each student, such as: *"With his Spanish accent of English, facing the screen, Jose says..."* Such detailed instructions were essential not only for linguistic accuracy but also for conveying cultural nuance, intonation patterns, and speech rhythms that reflect real-world diversity. Without this level of specificity, the resulting videos sometimes produced generic native-English speech that could potentially undermine the instructional goals of intercultural competence. By combining AI capabilities with deliberate, human-guided scripting, the project ensured that student portrayals were both linguistically authentic and pedagogically meaningful, supporting educators' ability to observe, interpret, and respond to culturally diverse classroom interactions.

Once the narrator's introduction and student dialogue videos were created, the next goal was to integrate these components within a platform that would also allow for the inclusion of teacher response options for each scenario. Canva and Canva AI were selected for this purpose. Canva was used as the primary presentation tool, while Canva AI was utilized to create clickable teacher response options. These interactive features enabled educators to practice their intercultural and global competence skills by reviewing and responding to all 50 scenarios.

Figures 4 and 5 are provided below to give the reader visual examples of the final instructional product.

Figure 4. Narrator Introduction Slide for Intercultural Competence 1: Cultural Self-Awareness (Scenario 3)

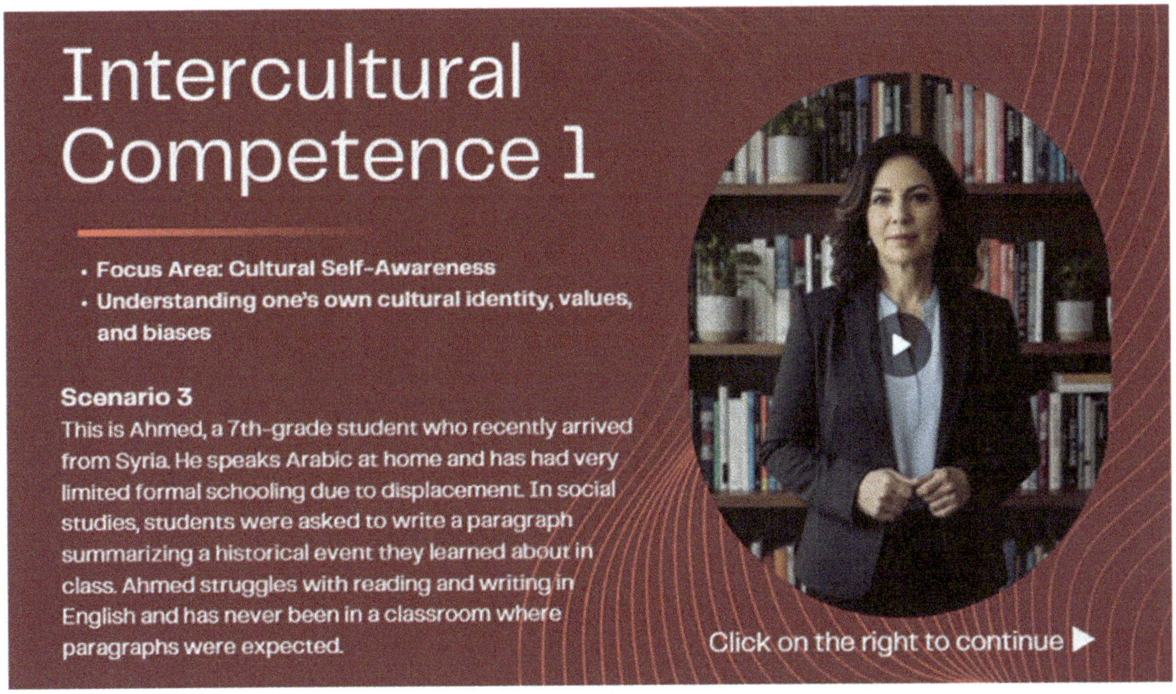

Figure 5. Student Dialogue and Clickable Teacher Responses Slide for Intercultural Competence 1: Cultural Self-Awareness (Scenario 3)

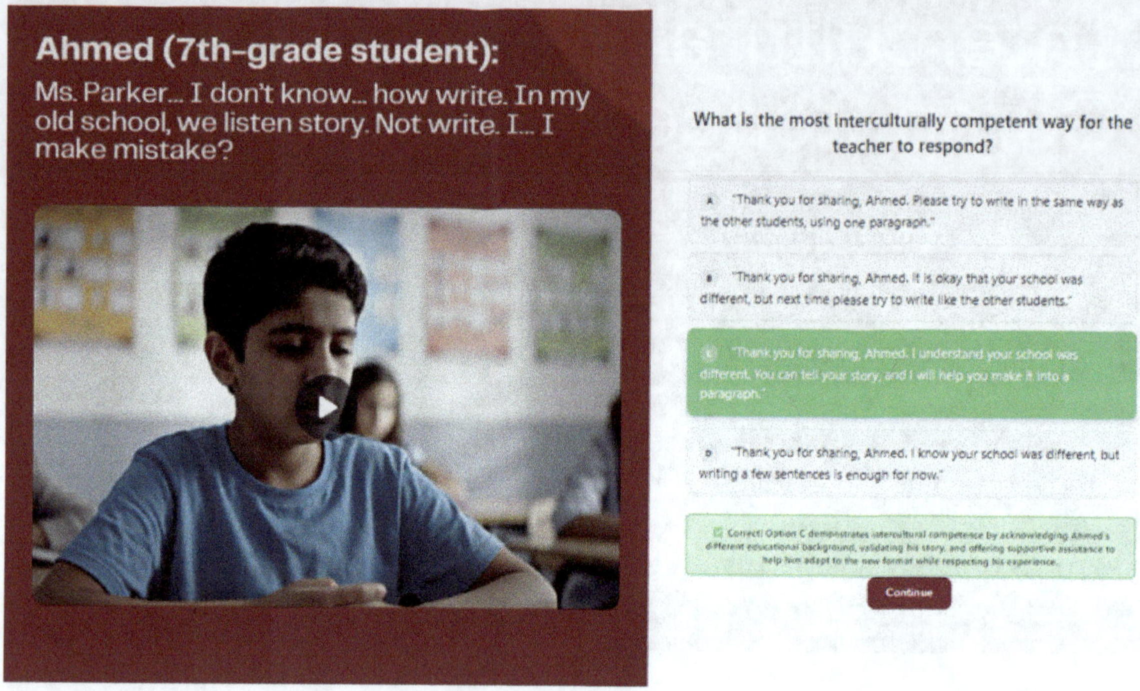

Developing Faculty and Teacher Guides

Once written scenarios and interactive video simulations were created, each scenario was embedded within a broader instructional module through the development of Faculty Guides and Teacher Guides. In total, 20 instructional guides were created to support the implementation of the modules: 10 Faculty Guides and 10 Teacher Guides, each aligned with one of 10 competencies, including six intercultural competencies and four global competencies. More particularly, each competency was supported by a matched pair of guides, with the Faculty Guides designed for teacher educators in higher education settings and the Teacher Guides designed for pre-service and in-service teachers working in K-12 classrooms. These guides were developed to ensure that the scenarios function as intentional learning tools rather than standalone artifacts, supporting structured engagement, reflection, and application across teacher education and K-12 contexts.

Both Faculty and Teacher Guides share a common foundational structure. Each guide includes a competence overview that defines the intercultural or global competence and situates it within educational practice, essential questions that prompt critical reflection, and scenario summaries that connect the interactive video simulations to real-world classroom situations. This shared structure ensures conceptual coherence across audiences and reinforces consistent understandings of each competence.

Despite these shared elements, the purpose and content of the guides differ intentionally based on the audience. Faculty Guides are designed for teacher educators who prepare pre-service teachers in higher education settings. In addition to the competence overview, essential questions, and scenario descriptions, Faculty Guides include faculty facilitation notes and assignments that support deep analysis of each competency. Introduced assignments position the scenarios as tools for metacognitive reflection and critical dialogue. Faculty notes provide guidance on how to further the discussion of the topic with teacher candidates.

In contrast, Teacher Guides are designed for in-service and pre-service teachers who work directly with K-12 students. While they maintain the same competence focus and scenario alignment, Teacher Guides translate abstract competencies into classroom-ready learning activities and include student-facing reflection questions, implementation strategies, and teacher reflection prompts that support ongoing professional growth. Thus, Teacher Guides emphasize practical application, helping teachers foster students' intercultural and global competencies while simultaneously reflecting on their own instructional practices. Together, the Faculty and Teacher Guides create a coherent instructional ecosystem that supports the development of intercultural and global competence across the teacher preparation continuum, which is essential for preparing educators to effectively navigate and teach in diverse, interconnected classrooms.

Integration Into Teacher Education and Professional Development

Finally, the scenarios, video simulations, and guides were integrated into teacher preparation courses at the research team's institution and professional development workshops provided to neighboring school districts. The project and created materials are intended to engage participants in structured cycles of viewing simulations, discussing teacher responses using intercultural competence rubrics, reflecting individually and collaboratively, and designing lesson plans that incorporate intercultural and global strategies. Through these cycles, participants practice reading, interpreting, and responding to culture, which are core practices of intercultural and global literacies. This project is currently ongoing and is planned to positively impact both teacher candidates and in-service educators by enhancing their ability to recognize cultural nuances, adapt instructional practices to diverse learners, and foster inclusive classroom environments. Ultimately, the initiative aims to cultivate a more culturally responsive teaching workforce, improve student engagement across diverse populations, and contribute to broader educational goals of equity, global awareness, and intercultural understanding.

CONCLUSION

This chapter has described the design and development of AI-powered classroom scenarios and video simulations created to advance intercultural and global literacies in teacher education. Grounded in culturally responsive pedagogy, intercultural competence, global competence, and experiential learning, the project shows that preparing educators for diverse classrooms requires more than awareness of cultural difference; teachers need structured opportunities to interpret complex situations, reflect on multiple perspectives, and make thoughtful instructional decisions.

A key insight from this work is that AI does not serve as a pedagogical decision-maker. Instead, it functions as a tool that can expand experiential learning opportunities when used within clear theoretical, linguistic, and ethical boundaries. AI-generated materials were only the starting point. Transforming them into meaningful instructional resources required sustained human judgment to ensure authenticity, accuracy, inclusivity, and alignment with educational goals. This process highlights that intercultural and global literacies do not emerge automatically from technology; they must be intentionally designed, modeled, and taught.

The resulting simulations position intercultural and global competence as lived classroom practice, leveraging game-based learning principles to create interactive, engaging scenarios. By navigating realistic challenges in a structured, playful environment, educators rehearse how to read cultural dynamics, consider diverse viewpoints, and choose contextually responsive actions. This approach moves teacher preparation beyond abstract discussions of diversity toward practice-based learning that reflects the complexity of real classrooms. More broadly, the chapter offers a model for responsible AI integration in teacher education, demonstrating that technology, including AI-driven, game-based simulations, is most valuable when it strengthens, rather than replaces, the reflective, ethical, and relational work at the heart of teaching.

REFERENCES

Asia Society. (2025). *Global competence outcomes and rubrics.* https://asiasociety.org/education/leadership-global-competence

Banks, J. A. (2015). *Cultural diversity and education: Foundations, curriculum, and teaching* (6th ed.). Routledge. DOI: 10.4324/9781315622255

Bennett, M. J. (1993). Towards ethnorelativism: A developmental model of intercultural sensitivity. In Paige, R. M. (Ed.), *Education for the intercultural experience* (pp. 21–71). Intercultural Press.

Bennett, M. J. (2008). Transformative training: Designing programs for culture learning. In Moodian, M. A. (Ed.), *Contemporary leadership and intercultural competence* (pp. 95–110). Sage.

Byram, M. (1997). *Teaching and assessing intercultural communicative competence.* Multilingual Matters.

Cushner, K., & Mahon, J. (2009). Intercultural competence in teacher education: Developing the intercultural competence of educators and their students. In Deardorff, D. K. (Ed.), *The SAGE handbook of intercultural competence* (pp. 304–320). Sage. DOI: 10.4135/9781071872987.n17

Dahalan, F., Alias, N., & Shaharom, M. S. N. (2023, January 12). Gamification and game based learning for vocational education and training: A systematic literature review. *Education and Information Technologies, 29*(2), 1279–1317. DOI: 10.1007/s10639-022-11548-w

Darling-Hammond, L. (2017). Teacher education around the world: What can we learn from international practice? *European Journal of Teacher Education, 40*(3), 291–309. DOI: 10.1080/02619768.2017.1315399

Deardorff, D. K. (2006). Identification and assessment of intercultural competence as a student outcome of internationalization. *Journal of Studies in International Education, 10*(3), 241–266. DOI: 10.1177/1028315306287002

Digital Promise. (2024). *Global education.* https://digitalpromise.org/initiative/global-education/

Dzerviniks, J., Ušča, S., Tarune, I., & Vindaca, O. (2024). Intercultural competence of teachers to work with newcomer children. *Education Sciences, 14*(8), 802. DOI: 10.3390/educsci14080802

Gay, G. (2018). *Culturally responsive teaching: Theory, research, and practice.* Teachers College Press.

Hartt, M., Hosseini, H., & Mostafapour, M. (2020, June 16). Game on: Exploring the effectiveness of game-based learning. *Planning Practice and Research, 35*(5), 589–604. DOI: 10.1080/02697459.2020.1778859

Hitchcock, C., Meyer, A., Rose, D., & Jackson, R. (2002). Providing new access to the general curriculum: Universal design for learning. *Teaching Exceptional Children, 35*(1), 8–17. DOI: 10.1177/004005990203500201

Howard, G. R. (2003). *We can't teach what we don't know: White teachers, multiracial schools* (2nd ed.). Teachers College Press.

Jiaxin, G., Huijuan, Z., & Hasan, H. M. (2024). Global competence in higher education: A ten-year systematic literature review. *Frontiers in Education, 9*, 1404782. Advance online publication. DOI: 10.3389/feduc.2024.1404782

Jing, H. (2023). Global awareness, intercultural communicative competence, and global citizenship. In *Developing Global Awareness for Global Citizenship Education: English Language Teachers' Beliefs and Practices in China* (pp. 25–53). Springer Nature Singapore. DOI: 10.1007/978-981-99-4179-7_2

Kegan, R., & Lahey, L. L. (2009). *Immunity to change: How to overcome it and unlock the potential in yourself and your organization*. Harvard Business Press.

Kolb, A. Y., & Kolb, D. A. (2005). Learning styles and learning spaces: Enhancing experiential learning in higher education. *Academy of Management Learning & Education*, *4*(2), 193–212. https://www.jstor.org/stable/40214287. DOI: 10.5465/amle.2005.17268566

Kolb, D. A. (1984). *Experiential learning: Experience as the source of learning and development*. Prentice-Hall, Inc.

Krasnoff, B. (2016). *A guide to evidence-based practices for teaching all students equitably: Culturally responsive teaching*. Region X Equity Assistance Center at Education Northwest.

Ladson-Billings, G. (1995). Toward a theory of culturally relevant pedagogy. *American Educational Research Journal*, *32*(3), 465–491. DOI: 10.3102/00028312032003465

Lateef, F. (2010). Simulation-based learning: Just like the real thing. *Journal of Emergencies, Trauma and Shock*, *3*(4), 348–352. DOI: 10.4103/0974-2700.70743

Lau v. Nichols, 414 U.S. 563 (1974). https://supreme.justia.com/cases/federal/us/414/563/

Leider, C. M., Tigert, J., & Norova, N. (2024). Teaching culturally and linguistically diverse learners: A content analysis of teacher professional organizations' position statements. *Teachers College Record*, *126*(3), 54–85. DOI: 10.1177/01614681241252502

Longview Foundation. (2025). Internationalizing teacher preparation. https://longviewfdn.org/programs/internationalizing-teacher-prep/

Longview Foundation & Learn NC. (n.d.). *The globally competent teaching continuum*. https://www.nafsa.org/sites/default/files/ektron/files/underscore/2016colloquia/2016_teachered_GCTC.pdf

Mansilla, J. B., & Jackson, A. (2011). *Educating for global competence: Preparing our youth to engage the world.* Asia Society. https://asiasociety.org/files/book-globalcompetence.pdf

Manzano-León, A., Camacho-Lazarraga, P., Guerrero, M. A., Guerrero-Puerta, L., Aguilar-Parra, J. M., Trigueros, R., & Alias, A. (2021). Between level up and game over: A systematic literature review of gamification in education. *Sustainability (Basel)*, *13*(4), 2247. DOI: 10.3390/su13042247

Mikrouli, P., Tzafilkou, K., & Protogeros, N. (2024). Applications and learning outcomes on game based learning in education. *International Educational Review*, *2*(1), 25–54. DOI: 10.58693/ier.212

Moyer, R., Snodgrass, J., Klein, S., & Tebben, C. (2017). *Simulation work-based learning: Instructional approaches and noteworthy practices.* U.S. Department of Education. https://files.eric.ed.gov/fulltext/ED583035.pdf

Nopas, D., & Kerdsomboon, C. (2024). Fostering global competence in teacher education: Curriculum integration and professional development. *Higher Education Studies, 14*(2). https://ccsenet.org/journal/index.php/hes/article/view/0/49853

Organization for Economic Cooperation and Development (OECD). *(2018). PISA 2018 assessment and analytical framework.* https://www.oecd.org/content/dam/oecd/en/publications/reports/2019/04/pisa-2018-assessment-and-analytical-framework_d1c359c7/b25efab8-en.pdf

Plass, J. L., Homer, B. D., & Kinzer, C. K. (2015). Foundations of game-based learning. *Educational Psychologist, 50*(4), 258–283. DOI: 10.1080/00461520.2015.1122533

Researcher Notes. (2025). *Notes taken by the researchers while creating scenarios for the Longview Project* [Unpublished research notes].

Shliakhovchuk, E. (2021). After cultural literacy: New models of intercultural competency for life and work in a VUCA world. *Educational Review, 73*(2), 229–250. DOI: 10.1080/00131911.2019.1566211

Sleeter, C. E. (2008). Preparing White teachers for diverse students. In Cochran-Smith, M., Feiman-Nemser, S., & McIntyre, D. J. (Eds.), *Handbook of research on teacher education* (3rd ed., pp. 559–582). Routledge. DOI: 10.4324/9780203938690-69

Squire, K., & Jenkins, H. (2003). Harnessing the power of games in education. *Insight, 3*, •••. https://plato.acadiau.ca/courses/engl/saklofske/download/digital%20gaming%20education.pdf

United Nations Department of Economic and Social Affairs. (2024). *The sustainable development goals report 2024*. United Nations. https://unstats.un.org/sdgs/report/2024/

United Nations Educational, Scientific and Cultural Organization. (2006). *UNESCO guidelines on intercultural education*. UNESCO.

Uzum, B., Yazan, B., Akayoglu, S., & Keles, U. (2024). Teacher candidates' intercultural communication in telecollaboration: Locating acts of positioning in translingual negotiations. *Journal for Multicultural Education, 18*(1-2), 53–66. DOI: 10.1108/JME-09-2023-0096

Yoon, B. (2023). Research synthesis on culturally and linguistically responsive teaching for multilingual learners. *Education Sciences, 13*(6), 557. DOI: 10.3390/educsci13060557

Zawacki-Richter, O., Marín, V. I., Bond, M., & Gouverneur, F. (2019). Systematic review of research on artificial intelligence applications in higher education–where are the educators? *International Journal of Educational Technology in Higher Education, 16*(1), 1–27. DOI: 10.1186/s41239-019-0171-0

Zebek, N., & Saygi, E. (2024). Gamification in education: Why where, when, and how? - A systematic review. *Games and Culture, 19*(2), 237–264. DOI: 10.1177/15554120231158625

Chapter 10
Game-Based Review Strategies to Support Multilingual Learners in Secondary Science Classrooms

Carrie Elizabeth May
http://orcid.org/0009-0006-3439-2227
George Mason University, USA

Alexandra Maria Patzak
http://orcid.org/0000-0002-6043-9029
George Mason University, USA

ABSTRACT

This chapter examines how Game-Based Learning (GBL) can be used as an equity-oriented instructional approach for supporting multilingual learners (MLs) in secondary science classrooms. Drawing on Second Language Acquisition theory (SLA) and Self-Determination Theory (SDT), it argues that review activities can function as powerful, literacy-rich, and motivational learning spaces when intentionally designed. The chapter demonstrates how GBL supports language development, scientific literacy, and student motivation. Review game design guidelines are outlined following SLA and SDT principles. The chapter presents classroom-based examples of both non-digital and digital review games, detailing materials, setup, gameplay, and reflections on their alignment with SLA and SDT principles. It also explores the role of AI, future directions, and instructional implications.

INTRODUCTION

"Oh wait! That rock is breaking, is that weathering or erosion?!" A student exclaims to their group as they try to identify the process in the picture and provide justification. Each team debates their answer, some students switching between English and their native language as they work to identify what they are seeing and explain how they know. Other students are flipping through their notebooks, re-reading notes and checking their spelling. The teams are racing to get the answer written first, as each student

DOI: 10.4018/979-8-3373-7472-7.ch010

is required to state the term and provide an explanation on their whiteboard. Once an entire table has a correct answer, they can race to the board to fill in their game piece for *Connect 4* (1974). It is through this game-based classroom review that students are displaying their science understanding, increasing their English literacy, and helping to build a strong classroom culture. Just a few weeks earlier at the start of the year, this same classroom was quiet. Students were slow to speak, hesitant to express their ideas in English, and working on communicating their thoughts. Now, they are leading the conversation, engaged with the content, and using literacy tools to show their understanding.

In this example, the classroom population consists primarily of multilingual learners (MLs), students who come to school with two or more languages and emerging English proficiency (Goodall et al., 2024). Within this instructional context, the teacher's role extends beyond the teaching of the subject to include the cultivation of a learning environment in which students learn literacy alongside content and feel linguistically and intellectually safe (Meng, 2021). Game-based learning (GBL) offers low-stakes, interactive opportunities that reduce the linguistic pressure frequently associated with conventional classroom tasks for MLs (Plass et al., 2015). Such review practices represent a departure from traditional test preparation models and illustrate a more effective, student-centered approach. When designed through the perspective of Second Language Acquisition (SLA) for MLs, GBL can integrate content review with literacy development through repetition and automaticity of vocabulary (Laksanasut, 2025; Meng, 2021).

For teachers of ML classrooms, planning effective content reviews presents a persistent challenge, particularly when reinforcing complex content and simultaneously supporting students who are still developing proficiency in the language of instruction (Scherzinger & Brahm, 2023). Traditional approaches to literacy instruction and content review often prioritize accuracy and recall, inadvertently increasing anxiety and limiting engagement and motivation for MLs (Rajendran et al., 2025). GBL review activities can create motivating learning environments by applying Self-Determination Theory (SDT) principles of autonomy, competence, and relatedness (Hafiza & Pratolo, 2024; Kalogiannakis et al., 2021; Plass et al., 2015; Ryan & Deci, 2000). When met, these three tenets increase the intrinsic motivation of MLs to practice reading, writing, and academic vocabulary (Hafiza & Pratolo, 2024; Rajendran et al., 2025). In addition, GBL fosters social interaction and collaboration, creating opportunities for peer scaffolding, shared problem-solving, and negotiation of meaning, processes that are essential for both literacy development and conceptual understanding (Szilágyi et al., 2025). It is through SDT that GBL can motivate ML students when designed intentionally.

As secondary schools serve increasingly linguistically diverse populations, educators are called to design instruction that advances both content learning and literacy development in the classroom (de Oliveira et al., 2024; Goodall et al., 2024). Teaching science in this context presents unique challenges, as students must simultaneously engage with complex concepts and specialized academic language (Lee et al., 2019). Secondary science content often includes abstract concepts, specialized vocabulary, and multiple forms of representation, such as diagrams, graphs, and symbolic notation, all of which can be challenging for students to access without intentional language support (Tang, 2023). In the United States, the Next Generation Science Standards (NGSS) articulate expectations for science learning among students aged 5–18 that emphasize practices which are inherently language-intensive (Lee et al., 2019). They emphasize discussion, argumentation, and explanation, practices that rely heavily on students' proficiency in the English language (Lee, 2020). These demands can create significant cognitive and linguistic barriers that affect engagement, comprehension, and motivation for MLs.

This chapter argues that GBL review activities can be powerful, equity-oriented spaces that reinforce literacy principles to MLs when intentionally designed through the perspective of Second Language

Acquisition (SLA) and Self-Determination Theory (SDT). Rather than positioning review as a neutral recap of content, this chapter reframes GBL reviews as a literacy-rich, motivational context in which MLs can meaningfully engage with academic language, disciplinary practices, and peer interaction in low-stakes, supportive environments. Drawing on theory, research, and classroom-based examples, the chapter first examines SLA and SDT foundations, then illustrates how GBL strategies can be intentionally designed to support content understanding, literacy development, and motivation for MLs in secondary science classrooms.

THEORETICAL FOUNDATIONS: SECOND LANGUAGE ACQUISITION AND LITERACY DEVELOPMENT

SLA research provides a foundational lens for understanding how MLs develop proficiency in an additional language while simultaneously engaging with academic content. Language acquisition is most effective when students are exposed to comprehensible input that extends slightly beyond their current proficiency and are supported with opportunities to produce language, receive feedback, and negotiate meaning through interaction (Ibarra-Balarezo & Guaman-Luna, 2025; Krashen, 1981). For MLs, literacy development is further strengthened by instructional approaches that integrate visual scaffolds, collaborative dialogue, translanguaging, and contextually rich tasks (Rajendran et al., 2025; Wang et al., 2025). These approaches enable students to negotiate meaning across languages and connect new academic concepts to existing linguistic knowledge (Cummins, 2000). The following section outlines key SLA hypotheses, examines their application in multilingual science classrooms, and highlights their alignment with GBL strategies.

Second Language Acquisition Hypotheses

Stephen Krashen's (1982) theory of SLA is grounded in five central hypotheses that explain how individuals acquire an additional language. These hypotheses, the Acquisition–Learning Hypothesis, the Comprehensible Input Hypothesis, the Monitor Hypothesis, the Affective Filter Hypothesis, and the Natural Order Hypothesis, have had a lasting influence on language acquisition research and instructional practice. Collectively, Krashen's framework emphasizes the importance of meaningful, low-anxiety exposure to language, a perspective that is particularly relevant in content-area classrooms where MLs must develop academic literacy while engaging with complex disciplinary concepts. Consideration of each hypothesis underscores how theoretical perspectives on language acquisition can inform its implications for classroom instruction.

The Acquisition–Learning Hypothesis distinguishes between two processes of language development: acquisition and learning. Krashen (1982) explains that acquisition is a subconscious process that occurs through meaningful interaction in the target language, whereas learning is a conscious process focused on the formal properties of language, such as grammatical rules. Bakhtin's Dialogic Theory extends this idea by emphasizing the role of social interaction and dialogue in language development, supporting a social constructivist view of acquisition (Shirkhani et al., 2015). In classroom contexts, content-based instruction that incorporates discussion, interaction, and meaning-focused activities is particularly effective in promoting language acquisition (Charos, 2024).

Closely related to acquisition is the Comprehensible Input Hypothesis, which proposes that students make progress when they are exposed to language input that is slightly beyond their current proficiency level, commonly referred to as *i + 1* (Abukhattala, 2013). For acquisition to occur, this input must be both meaningful and understandable, underscoring the importance of authentic and contextualized language use (Goodall et al., 2024). This principle is especially critical for MLs, as access to content learning is limited when instruction relies on language that students cannot comprehend (Stairs-Davenport & Skotarczak, 2018). This work is supported by Long's (1980) Interaction Hypothesis, which posits that conversational interaction facilitates language acquisition by providing opportunities for learners to negotiate meaning, receive feedback, and make input more comprehensible. In practice, teachers can support comprehensible input through scaffolding, use of visuals, gestures, modeling, and peer interactions that allow students to engage with new language while remaining appropriately challenged (Goodall et al., 2024; Ibarra-Balarezo & Guaman-Luna, 2025).

The same support of peer interaction is especially important to the Monitor and Output Hypothesis. The Monitor Hypothesis explains how the unconscious language acquisition pertains to language fluency, while the conscious learning of grammar is used only to monitor language output (Krashen, 1982). Supporting this view, Swain's (1995) Output Hypothesis argues that opportunities to produce spoken and written language allow students to notice gaps in their linguistic knowledge, test hypotheses, and refine their understanding of the target language (Goodall et al., 2024). In classroom settings, these theories suggest that excessive focus on error correction may inhibit fluency. Instead, teachers should provide opportunities for students to communicate freely, using explicit correction strategically rather than interrupting communication constantly (Li, 2025).

Emotional factors influencing literacy learning are addressed in the Affective Filter Hypothesis, which posits that students' emotional states can either facilitate or impede language acquisition (Krashen, 1982). Negative affective factors such as anxiety, fear, or embarrassment raise the affective filter, preventing comprehensible input from being fully processed (Fortuna, 2025). Conversely, positive emotions, motivation, and supportive classroom environments lower the affective filter and increase students' openness to language input (Abukhattala, 2013). While attending to individual emotional needs can be challenging in classroom settings, teachers can design lessons and activities that promote motivation, confidence, and a sense of belonging, offering individualized support when possible (Luo, 2024).

One way to support positive emotions in the classroom is to scaffold lessons based on The Natural Order Hypothesis (Krashen, 1982). This hypothesis explains that language structures are acquired in a predictable sequence that is consistent across students, regardless of instructional methods or explicit teaching. This suggests that instruction cannot alter the natural order of acquisition, emphasizing the importance of aligning teaching practices with students' developmental readiness. Teachers must therefore maintain realistic expectations and foster supportive learning environments where errors are viewed as a natural part of language development and growth, supporting positive emotions in the classroom (Goodall et al., 2024; Li, 2025).

Together, these hypotheses suggest that language and literacy development is most effective when instruction prioritizes meaningful communication, active engagement, emotional safety, and opportunities for both input and output (Goodall et al., 2024). In content-area classrooms such as science, these principles are particularly critical, as MLs must simultaneously acquire academic literacy and engage with complex disciplinary concepts. The following section explores how SLA principles can be operationalized in science classrooms to promote both conceptual understanding and literacy development for MLs.

Application of Second Language Acquisition in a Multilingual Science Classroom

The SLA hypotheses described above provide a clear rationale for instructional design that embed language use within meaningful, low-pressure activities, such as GBL. As such, these hypotheses build an important foundation for understanding how language learning can be supported in secondary science classrooms (Goodall et al., 2024). Contemporary approaches to teaching MLs emphasize that language instruction should be purposeful and embedded within disciplinary practices, a concept often described as *language-in-use* (Lee, 2020). Science classrooms can support literacy by incorporating multimodal representations, providing structured opportunities for student dialogue, and implementing intentional scaffolding strategies. These tools will be discussed through both SLA hypothesis and NGSS science standards.

Scientific literacy develops not only from reading and writing but also from evaluating multimodal representations. In science classrooms, MLs must interpret diagrams, graphs, data tables, and models (Tang, 2023). For example, during laboratory investigations, students must comprehend procedural texts, analyze visual data, and communicate findings using academic language and symbolic representations. These practices align with NGSS practices, particularly developing and using models, and analyzing and interpreting data, both of which place significant literacy demands on students (Lee, 2020). By engaging students with multimodal representations, science instruction supports language acquisition consistent with the Acquisition–Learning and Comprehensible Input Hypotheses.

Literacy development in science also emerges through collaborative sensemaking and academic discourse among students and teachers (Gibbons, 2015). NGSS emphasizes practices such as constructing explanations and engaging in argument from evidence, which require structured opportunities for student talk and interaction (Lee, 2020). These interactions support literacy development by allowing MLs to rehearse scientific language orally, either in English or their native languages (Cummins, 2000). Translanguaging practices, which encourage students to discuss content in their native language before translating to English, further enhances comprehension and engagement without detracting from content learning (Rajendran et al., 2025; Wang et al., 2025). Such social interaction supports SLA Output Theory principles related to monitoring output, lowering affective filters, and respecting natural language and literacy development (Swain, 1995).

Given the cognitive and linguistic demands of secondary science, MLs benefit from scaffolded instructional strategies that maintain academic rigor while supporting comprehension and participation (Nutta et al., 2010). Research-supported practices include visual scaffolds such as diagrams and data displays, dialogue during investigations and analysis, and contextually rich tasks grounded in real-world phenomena (Lyon et al., 2016). Applying SLA theory to multilingual science instruction therefore requires intentional planning that integrates language scaffolds, hands-on inquiry, collaborative discussion, and supportive classroom environments (Castañeda & Bautista, 2011). Together, these approaches operationalize SLA principles in alignment with NGSS language demands and support MLs' development of both scientific understanding and disciplinary literacy (Lee, 2020).

Alignment of Second Language Acquisition in Game-Based Learning

One way science teachers can create interaction with multimodal content, increase opportunities for student dialogue, and scaffold learning is through GBL strategies. GBL refers to the use of game principles in education, where teachers intentionally change activities to engage students in meaningful learning experiences that include gaming components like teams, points, challenges, and feedback (Laksanasut, 2025; Plass et al., 2015). In science classrooms, GBL in reviews can reinforce conceptual understanding, promote academic discourse, and support MLs equitably by embedding language use within purposeful, engaging contexts (Hafiza & Pratolo, 2024). SLA theory provides a strong theoretical rationale for the use of GBL in multilingual science classrooms, as GBL naturally incorporates comprehensible input through visual and contextualized cues, meaningful output through collaboration and problem-solving, and lowered affective filters by framing learning as playful, low-risk, and engaging (Fortuna, 2025; Ibarra-Balarezo & Guaman-Luna, 2025).

From a SLA perspective, instructional strategies that lower anxiety and increase motivation support greater language and literacy uptake by reducing the affective filter (Fortuna, 2025; Krashen, 1982). GBL fosters a positive classroom climate and minimizes performance risk, allowing students to engage more fully with input and participate more confidently in language use (Hafiza & Pratolo, 2024). In addition, GBL promotes literacy development by engaging students in multimodal learning experiences (Rajendran et al., 2025). GBL Review activities that integrate visuals, movement, dialogue, symbols, and text provide MLs with opportunities to practice reading, writing, and academic vocabulary in meaningful, context-rich ways. Such practices align with Krashen's Acquisition–Learning and Comprehensible Input Hypotheses by embedding language development within authentic scientific contexts and offering scaffolded access to disciplinary language (Abukhattala, 2013).

Moreover, GBL fosters social interaction and collaboration, enabling peer scaffolding, shared problem-solving, and negotiation of meaning processes that are critical for both language development and conceptual understanding (Szilágyi et al., 2025). Peer interaction within games promotes oral language development, linguistic risk-taking, feedback, and clarification, all of which support the negotiation of meaning essential to SLA (Hafiza & Pratolo, 2024). The frequent opportunities for language input and output are inherent in collaborative gameplay aligned with the Monitor Hypothesis, as students are able to test ideas, reflect on their understanding, and adjust both content knowledge and literacy in real time.

Overall, GBL supports literacy development through SLA by creating interactive, meaningful, and low-stakes opportunities for MLs to engage with language across multiple modes (Hafiza & Pratolo, 2024). Literacy-focused questions, peer interaction, and immediate feedback embedded within games promote language development, conceptual understanding, and student motivation (Rajendran et al., 2025). When intentionally designed, GBL leverages SLA principles to support literacy, positioning games as a powerful instructional approach rather than a supplemental activity in multilingual science classrooms.

MOTIVATIONAL FOUNDATIONS OF GAME BASED LEARNING FOR MULTILINGUAL LEARNERS

While SLA theory explains how MLs develop literacy through meaningful input, interaction, and supportive learning environments, it does not fully account for the motivational processes that influence sustained engagement in learning tasks. SDT offers such a framework by examining how students' motivation is shaped by the fulfillment of three basic psychological needs: autonomy, competence, and relatedness (Ryan & Deci, 2000). In educational contexts, SDT posits that when learning environments support students' sense of choice, provide meaningful feedback that fosters competence, and promotes social connection, students are more likely to engage deeply and sustain effort in the learning task.

In the context of literacy development for MLs, these needs are often challenged by linguistic barriers, rigid classroom activities, limited opportunities for peer communication, and pacing pressures (Rajendran et al., 2025). For MLs in secondary classrooms, these motivational supports are especially important, as students must navigate both linguistic and cognitive challenges simultaneously (Meng, 2021). The following section introduces SDT and examines how its core principles align with GBL strategies to enhance motivation, participation, and equitable access to learning for MLs.

Motivational Challenges for Multilingual Learners

Ryan & Deci (2000) outlined the essential psychological needs that an individual requires to be self-motivated through the SDT. These needs include autonomy, relatedness, and competence. Autonomy includes the need for people to have choice and feel in control of their goals. Relatedness is the feeling of connection and belonging to a group. Competence is the feeling of being capable and effective in class. When these needs are supported in educational contexts, MLs are more likely to participate actively, take linguistic risks, and sustain effort despite the challenges of learning in an additional language (Tripp & Waight, 2024).

Autonomous supportive learning environments allow for choices around learning, provide explanations when choice is constrained, and encourage students to make choices based on their personal goals (Ryan & Deci, 2000). For MLs, classrooms that support student autonomy by offering meaningful choices in topics, tasks, languages, or modes of expression are associated with higher levels of motivation and engagement (Ahmed & Hossain, 2024). Research shows that when MLs feel they have student autonomy they are more willing to use the target language and persist in complex tasks (Laksanasut, 2025). Autonomy is particularly important for MLs, as rigid, teacher-controlled instruction can heighten anxiety and reduce opportunities for authentic language use (Alamer et al., 2025). It was found that autonomy increased intrinsic motivation served as a protective factor against language anxiety.

Relatedness refers to the need to feel socially connected and valued within a learning community (Ryan & Deci, 2000). The classroom culture and interactions experienced by students within science classrooms contribute to a student's motivation and commitment to learning (Velayutham & Aldridge, 2013). For MLs, feelings of belonging are closely tied to participation and literacy development (Tripp & Waight, 2024). Research demonstrates that positive relationships with teachers and peers, collaborative learning structures, and inclusive classroom practices promote engagement and reduce anxiety for language students (Meng, 2021). Relatedness is especially critical for MLs who may experience marginalization or isolation due to language differences (Laksanasut, 2025). Classrooms that affirm students' linguistic identities and encourage peer interaction create conditions that support both motivation and literacy growth.

Competence involves students' beliefs about their ability to succeed and make progress. MLs often face academic tasks that simultaneously demand content knowledge and advanced literacy skills, which can undermine their sense of competence if adequate support is not provided (Rajendran et al., 2025; Tripp & Waight, 2024). Studies indicate that competence-supportive practices, such as scaffolded instruction, formative feedback, and opportunities for success in low-stakes settings, enhance MLs' confidence and willingness to engage in language production (de Oliveira et al., 2024). When students are recognized for their hard work and celebrated for their successes, they perceive that they are capable of meeting linguistic and academic demands and are more likely to persist and take risks necessary for literacy acquisition (McInerney, 2023).

Together, autonomy, competence, and relatedness interact to shape MLs' motivation and engagement (Laksanasut, 2025). When these psychological needs are met, students are more likely to participate in academic discourse, persist through linguistic challenges, and view themselves as capable language users (Alamer et al., 2025). Research suggests that instructional approaches such as collaborative learning, scaffolded tasks, and GBL environments are particularly effective in supporting intrinsic motivation for MLs by addressing all three needs of SDT simultaneously (Plass et al., 2015).

Enhancing Motivation through Game Based Learning in Review Games

GBL in multilingual science classrooms provides a promising instructional context for supporting the diverse needs of MLs (Hafiza & Pratolo, 2024). By shifting review activities from prescriptive worksheets to interactive, student-centered experiences, GBL fosters increased engagement, persistence, and literacy development (Laksanasut, 2025). Research indicates that when GBL is implemented with clear pedagogical intent, it can serve as a powerful tool for supporting intrinsic motivation through autonomy, competence, and relatedness (Kalogiannakis et al., 2021).

Within the framework of SDT, GBL in classroom reviews support autonomy by allowing students to make meaningful choices and take academic and linguistic risks. These choices may include selecting roles within a team, choosing strategies to solve problems, or determining how to respond to questions using oral, written, or multimodal formats (Kalogiannakis et al., 2021). Such opportunities position students as active participants in their learning rather than passive recipients of information (Laksanasut, 2025). This shift from teacher-directed review to student-centered participation increases student ownership and supports sustained engagement and persistence, outcomes closely associated with autonomy-supportive learning environments (Noels et al., 2000).

GBL also supports the SDT need for competence by fostering feelings of mastery and progress. Well-designed games provide immediate, formative feedback that helps students quickly identify what they understand and where additional support is needed (Li et al., 2024). This feedback loop is particularly valuable for MLs, who benefit from timely clarification of both content knowledge and language use (Hafiza & Pratolo, 2024). In addition, games typically offer repeated opportunities for success, enabling students to practice literacy and content skills across varied contexts. By emphasizing progress and strategy use rather than accuracy alone, GBL reduces anxiety around literacy tasks such as reading scientific texts, using academic vocabulary, or constructing explanations (Li, 2025). As a result, MLs are more likely to develop confidence in their abilities and engage more willingly in language production, reinforcing both motivation and skill development (Ryan & Deci, 2000; Plass et al., 2015). However, research cautions that certain game features, such as competitive leaderboards or point systems, may unintentionally emphasize extrinsic motivation, potentially discouraging students who struggle or shifting focus from learning to winning (Kalogiannakis et al., 2021).

The social nature of GBL directly supports the SDT need for relatedness, defined as the desire to feel connected and valued within a learning community (Ryan & Deci, 2000). Review games frequently incorporate collaborative structures such as teams, shared goals, and collective problem-solving, which promote meaningful peer interaction (Kalogiannakis et al., 2021). Through these interactions, MLs build relationships with classmates and develop a stronger sense of belonging in the classroom. Social engagement during GBL also creates authentic opportunities to practice academic language in supportive contexts, where reading, writing, and vocabulary become social practices rather than isolated tasks (Hafiza & Pratolo, 2024). As students explain reasoning, negotiate meaning, and co-construct understanding with peers, they gain confidence in using academic language and experience the classroom as a safe space for participation.

When aligned with equitable and inclusive science instruction, GBL review activities create accessible opportunities for MLs to engage with disciplinary literacy, participate confidently in scientific practices, and persist in learning (Kalogiannakis et al., 2021). As a result, motivation becomes a central component of effective science instruction, and GBL functions as a strategic tool for supporting both literacy and conceptual understanding (Hafiza & Pratolo, 2024). By fostering engagement through meaningful choices, collaborative problem-solving, and low-stakes practice, GBL not only reinforces content knowledge but also provides a practical context for applying principles of SLA and SDT (Laksanasut, 2025).

Implementation of Game Based Learning for Multilingual Learners

Together, SLA and SDT highlight the importance of intentional instructional design when implementing GBL review activities for MLs that target literacy. Review games based in GBL function not only as engaging activities but as motivational scaffolds that support autonomy, competence, and relatedness while simultaneously utilizing literacy development for language use (Hamari et al., 2016). To be effective, GBL review activities, both digital and non-digital, should be deliberately designed to offer meaningful choice, provide timely and formative feedback, and promote collaboration through shared goals and peer interaction (Dichev & Dicheva, 2017). These design features ensure that review games support literacy development, conceptual understanding, and student motivation without reducing academic rigor (Nutta et al., 2010). To translate SLA and SDT principles into classroom practice, teachers can use the ten following design guidelines when creating or adapting GBL review activities for MLs: align games with clear learning objectives, provide scaffolds for literacy, balance challenge and support, incorporate collaboration and peer interaction, use immediate constructive feedback, support autonomy through choice, promote low-stakes engagement, reflect and debrief after gameplay, leverage technology thoughtfully, and design for cultural and linguistic inclusivity.

Align Games with Clear Learning Objectives

To maximize their instructional value, review games must be intentionally aligned with clear content and literacy learning objectives rather than functioning as stand-alone or purely motivational activities (Plass et al., 2015). When games are explicitly designed to reinforce targeted scientific concepts, academic vocabulary, or literacy practices such as constructing explanations, interpreting data, or applying Claim, Evidence, and Reasoning (CER) frameworks, gameplay becomes a meaningful extension of instruction rather than a distraction (Lee, 2020). This alignment ensures that students are engaging with the same disciplinary literacy and practices emphasized in core instruction, supporting continuity in learning.

From a motivational perspective, alignment with learning objectives supports students' sense of competence. When students can clearly see how game tasks connect to instructional goals, they are more likely to perceive progress and experience success, which strengthens confidence and persistence (Ryan & Deci, 2000). For MLs in science classrooms, this clarity is especially important, as it helps reduce cognitive overload and allows students to focus on both content understanding and language use (Hafiza & Pratolo, 2024). Well-aligned review games thus serve as instructional scaffolds that reinforce conceptual understanding and language development while fostering motivation and engagement (Plass et al., 2015).

Provide Scaffolds for Literacy

For MLs, successful participation in GBL depends on access to instructional scaffolds that support literacy, comprehension, and language production (Nutta et al., 2010). Without intentional language support, GBL review activities risk privileging students with higher English proficiency rather than promoting equitable participation. Strategies such as visual supports, sentence frames, translanguaging opportunities, and multimodal cues help MLs engage meaningfully with game tasks by making academic language accessible and reducing linguistic barriers (Gibbons, 2015; Wang et al., 2025). These scaffolds enable students to interpret instructions, process content, and communicate ideas with greater confidence.

From an SLA perspective, literacy scaffolds ensure that review games provide comprehensible input and opportunities for meaningful output, both of which are essential for language acquisition (de Oliveira et al., 2024; Ibarra-Balarezo & Guaman-Luna, 2025). At the same time, scaffolding supports students' sense of competence by allowing them to experience success while using academic language in authentic contexts. By embedding literacy scaffolds into GBL, teachers create inclusive learning environments that promote both literacy development and conceptual understanding for MLs (Laksanasut, 2025).

Balance Challenge and Support

Effective review games maintain an optimal balance between cognitive challenge and instructional support, ensuring that tasks are sufficiently demanding to promote learning while remaining accessible to students at varying proficiency levels (Chan & Lo, 2024). Well-designed games situate learning at desirable difficulty, or within a range where students can succeed with appropriate scaffolding (Vygotsky, 1978). When challenge levels are too high, MLs may experience frustration or disengagement; when too low, opportunities for growth and motivation are diminished.

To sustain engagement and persistence, teachers can adjust game pacing, offer hints or strategic prompts, and encourage working as a team. These design features help ensure that students remain challenged without becoming overwhelmed, reinforcing a sense of competence and encouraging continued participation (Arip & Hashim, 2024). For MLs in science classrooms, balancing challenge and support also reduces anxiety around language use, enabling students to focus on meaning-making and problem-solving (Li, 2025). By carefully calibrating difficulty and scaffolding, review games can promote sustained engagement, equitable participation, and deeper learning across diverse proficiency levels (Nutta et al., 2010).

Incorporate Collaboration and Peer Interaction

Incorporating collaboration and peer interaction into review games is essential for supporting both literacy development and student motivation. Games that require teamwork, shared decision-making, and collective problem-solving create opportunities for students to negotiate meaning, clarify understanding, and co-construct knowledge with peers. These social interactions are central to SLA, as they provide meaningful contexts for language use and promote feedback, clarification, and adjustment of literacy in real time (Rajendran et al., 2025).

From the perspective of SDT, collaborative game structures support the psychological need for relatedness, fostering a sense of belonging and connection within the classroom community (Ryan & Deci, 2000). For MLs, peer interaction reduces isolation and creates a supportive environment in which students feel more comfortable using academic language (Arip & Hashim, 2024). Collaborative gameplay also encourages linguistic risk-taking and sustained engagement, as students rely on one another to achieve shared goals. By embedding collaboration into GBL, teachers can leverage social interaction as both a motivational support and a mechanism for developing literacy.

Use Immediate, Constructive Feedback

Immediate and constructive feedback is a critical component of effective GBL, particularly for MLs (Arip & Hashim, 2024). Feedback provided during gameplay should emphasize progress, strategy use, and learning opportunities rather than focusing solely on correctness. Such feedback helps students understand what they are doing well and how they can improve, supporting the development of metacognitive awareness and self-regulation (Hattie & Timperley, 2007). When feedback is timely and specific, it not only reinforces content knowledge and academic literacy but also encourages risk-taking and sustained engagement, creating a supportive environment in which MLs can confidently practice and refine both disciplinary skills and language proficiency.

From a SDT perspective, timely and supportive feedback strengthens students' sense of competence by making growth visible and achievable (Ryan & Deci, 2000). For MLs, immediate feedback also supports language acquisition and literacy by clarifying meaning, reinforcing academic vocabulary, and guiding appropriate language use in context (Hafiza & Pratolo, 2024). When feedback is embedded naturally within gameplay using hints, prompts, or opportunities to revise responses, students are more likely to remain engaged, take linguistic risks, and persist in learning. Accordingly, GBL feedback serves as both an instructional scaffold and a source of motivation, supporting improved learning outcomes for diverse students.

Support Autonomy through Choice

Supporting student autonomy through meaningful choice is a key design principle in effective GBL. Providing students with options, such as selecting teammates, assuming different roles within a game, choosing strategies, topics, or response formats, positions students as active agents in their learning rather than passive recipients of instruction (Reeve, 2012). These choices promote a sense of ownership and personal relevance, which are essential for fostering intrinsic motivation (Ryan & Deci, 2000).

For MLs, autonomy-supportive practices also encourage linguistic risk-taking and sustained engagement. When students are given flexibility in how they participate, for example by responding orally, in writing, or through multimodal representations, they can draw on their linguistic strengths while gradually expanding their academic language repertoire (Kalogiannakis et al., 2021; Vaughn et al., 2025). By valuing student choice, GBL environments create inclusive spaces that respect students' identities and experiences, reduce anxiety, and support deeper participation in both literacy and content learning (Li, 2025; Noels et al., 2000).

Promote Low-Stakes Engagement

Promoting low-stakes engagement is essential in GBL, particularly for MLs who may experience anxiety around language use and academic performance. When games are designed to be playful, exploratory, and non-punitive, students are more likely to take literacy risks, experiment with academic literacy, and engage meaningfully without fear of failure (Rajendran et al., 2025). Low-stakes environments lower affective barriers to learning, allowing students to focus on communication and understanding rather than on avoiding errors (Fortuna, 2025).

From a motivational perspective, low-stakes gameplay supports intrinsic motivation by reducing pressure associated with grades, public evaluation, or competition (Ryan & Deci, 2000). Instead of emphasizing winning or correctness alone, effective review games prioritize participation, collaboration, and progress. For MLs, this approach encourages repeated practice of reading, writing, speaking, and listening skills in authentic contexts. By maintaining a playful and supportive tone, GBL creates safe spaces for literacy experimentation, sustained engagement, and deeper learning across diverse proficiency levels (Plass et al., 2015).

Reflect and Debrief After Gameplay

Reflection and debriefing are critical components of GBL, providing opportunities for students to consolidate learning, surface misconceptions, and connect game experiences to broader literacy and content goals (Chang, 2019). Structured reflection allows MLs to process both conceptual knowledge and academic literacy, reinforcing vocabulary, sentence structures, and strategies encountered during gameplay. Teachers can guide debriefing by prompting students to discuss the strategies they used, the literacy choices they made, and the collaborative experiences within their teams.

From a SDT perspective, reflection supports both relatedness and competence. Discussing ideas with peers fosters social connection and a sense of belonging, while evaluating one's own understanding and performance reinforces confidence in learning and literacy (Ryan & Deci, 2000). For MLs, guided reflection encourages metacognitive engagement, helps clarify linguistic and scientific misunderstandings, and provides meaningful opportunities to practice literacy in a supportive, low-stakes environment (Hafiza & Pratolo, 2024). By embedding structured reflection into GBL, teachers can extend the motivational and literacy benefits of gameplay, ensuring that the activity contributes to sustained engagement, deeper comprehension, and transferable literacy skills.

Leverage Technology Thoughtfully

Digital platforms, such as Blooket, Kahoot, Wayground, and Gimkit, can enhance engagement in GBL by providing interactive, visually rich, and data-informed experiences that support both motivation and learning (Chang, 2021). These tools can reinforce vocabulary development, support multimodal comprehension, and allow students to practice literacy in meaningful contexts, making them particularly valuable for MLs. Platforms that integrate Figures, audio, and immediate feedback not only increase interactivity but also provide comprehensible input and opportunities for meaningful output, supporting literacy alongside content learning (Ibarra-Balarezo & Guaman-Luna, 2025).

From a pedagogical perspective, technology must be selected thoughtfully to ensure alignment with learning objectives, accessibility, and inclusivity (Wang & Tahir, 2020). Considerations include whether the platform accommodates students at varying literacy levels, allows for multiple modes of response, and promotes collaboration and social interaction. When thoughtfully implemented, digital review games can amplify motivation by supporting autonomy through choice, competence through timely feedback, and relatedness through collaborative features, while simultaneously scaffolding language and literacy development in equitable ways.

Design for Cultural and Linguistic Inclusivity

Effective GBL should intentionally validate and integrate students' cultural and linguistic backgrounds, creating an inclusive environment that affirms students' identities. Incorporating translanguaging practices, which allow students to use their home languages alongside English, and embedding culturally responsive examples within game content helps MLs connect new concepts to their prior knowledge and experiences (Jasmaniah et al., 2024; Wang et al., 2025). Such practices not only support comprehension and participation but also foster a sense of relatedness, a key component of SDT, by signaling that students' identities and linguistic repertoires are valued within the classroom (Ryan & Deci, 2000). By designing review games that honor language diversity and cultural knowledge, teachers can enhance motivation, engagement, and meaningful learning for all students.

From a literacy perspective, culturally and linguistically inclusive game design provides multiple access points for learning, encouraging participation in both academic discourse and content mastery (Arip & Hashim, 2024). For instance, students can explain reasoning, construct arguments, or respond to prompts in their preferred language or a combination of languages, scaffolding both comprehension and expression (Gibbons, 2015). By embedding inclusive practices, teachers can promote engagement, motivation, and belonging while simultaneously supporting language acquisition and content understanding, ensuring that GBL is equitable, relevant, and meaningful for all students (Arip & Hashim, 2024). These strategies highlight how thoughtful integration of language, culture, and content can transform review activities into powerful opportunities for both learning and identity affirmation, setting the stage for the application of SLA principles and SDT in classroom game design.

Drawing from the first author's experience as a science teacher working with MLs, the following section presents a range of GBL review activities. These include non-digital games in which students respond to teacher-generated questions, non-digital games in which students create their own questions or clues, and digital games that structure interactive review. Although these activities were developed and implemented in a science classroom, each can be adapted for use across content areas. Each example includes a description of required materials, setup, gameplay, and reflection on how the activity supports principles of SLA and SDT. The combination of collaboration, choice, and visible success supports both literacy and intrinsic motivation, aligning closely with research on SLA and SDT.

REVIEW GAME EXAMPLES: NON-DIGITAL GAMES

Connect 4

Adapted from the popular kids' game, *Connect 4* (1974), this review activity has students answer questions in teams while racing to connect four squares on a class board. This game can be used as a full-class review or, with a little more preparation, adapted for students to review in smaller groups as the teacher rotates throughout the room. In both versions, students answer questions to earn the opportunity to place their game pieces on the game board while trying to get four game pieces in a row.

Supplies: Student whiteboards, dry-erase markers and erasers, review questions in a slide presentation or on pieces of paper, and a game board

Full Class Activity

Set-Up: Students should be placed into groups, with at least four teams total. Each team needs a different color to represent their game piece. For example, a pad of sticky notes or a different-colored dry-erase marker. On each slide, there is an 8x8 grid (or larger if there are more groups) that does not change position from slide to slide (as seen in Figure 1 and 2).

Figure 1. Slide 1 Question-

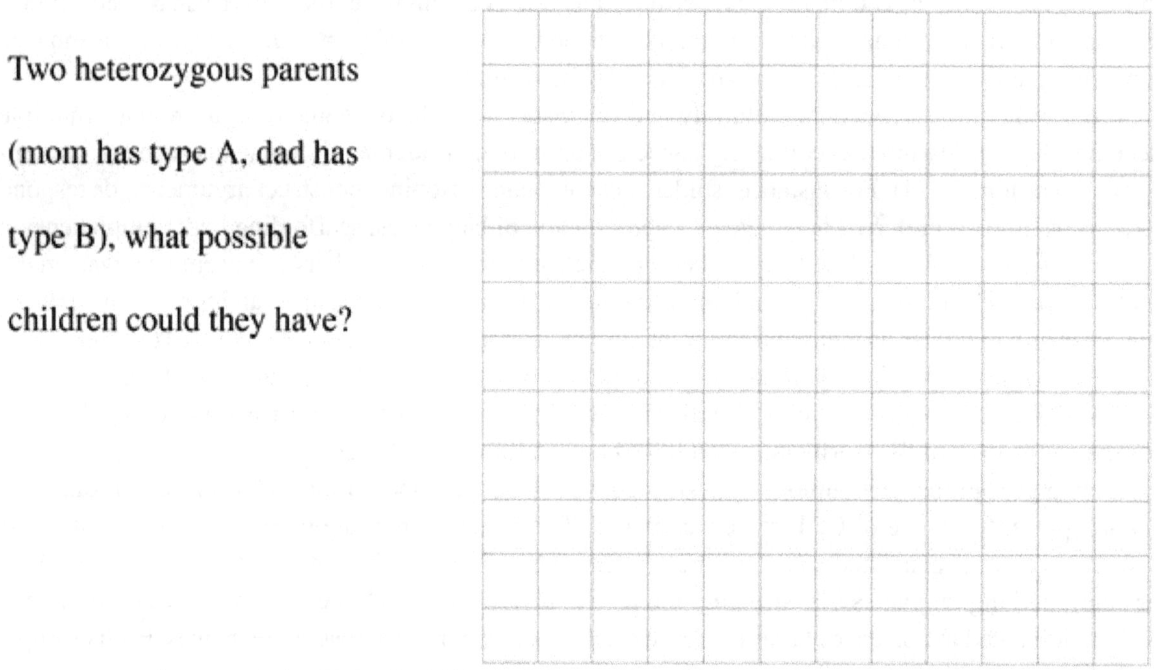

Figure 2. Slide 2 Question-

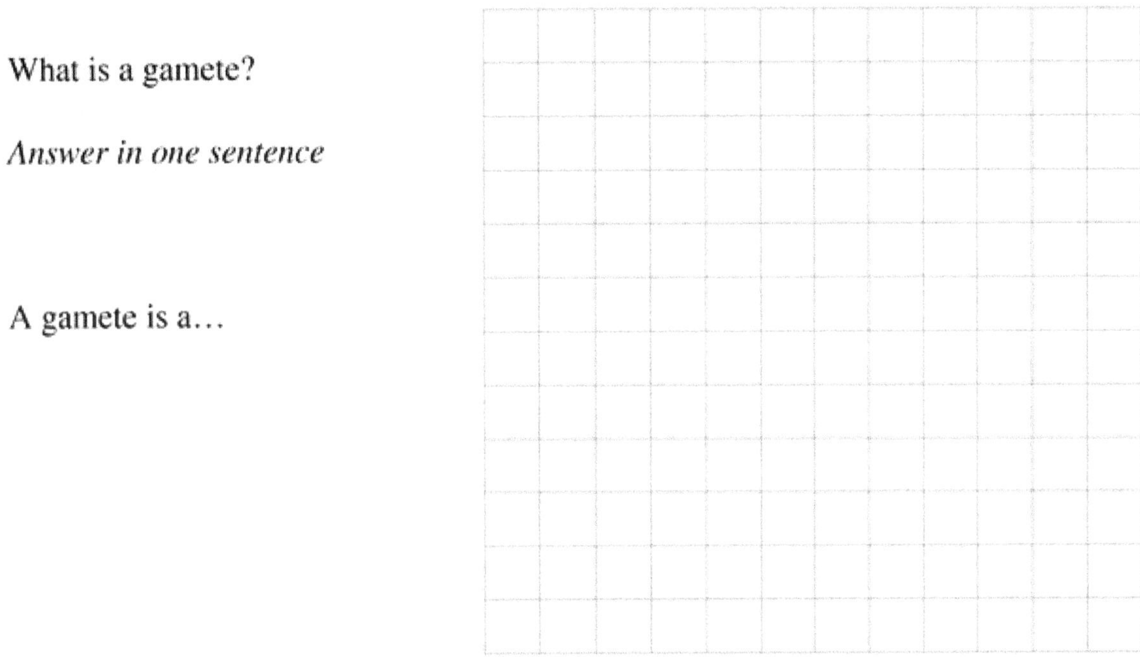

Gameplay: On each slide, a question is presented for the groups to answer. Every person in the group must have the correct answer written on their whiteboard to earn credit for the question. Once every member of the group has the correct answer, one representative from that group can run to the board and place their game piece by either coloring in a square or placing a sticky note. All teams have a chance to answer every question and place a game piece in a square. Standard Connect 4 rules apply: students must start at the bottom of the board, once a square is placed it cannot be moved, and the team that gets four in a row horizontally, vertically, or diagonally wins.

After a team wins, different rules can be applied to maintain engagement.

For example-

- **Erase or Place:** Teams may choose to erase another teams square instead of placing their own
- **Anti-Gravity**: Students may place a square anywhere on the grid, it does not have to fall to the bottom
- **2x2**: A 2x2 square also counts as a win

Small Group

Set-Up: Students are placed into groups of two or more, with each student using a different-colored marker, sticky note, or game piece. Each group will have a cup or envelope filled with review questions and a game board grid on a piece of paper.

Gameplay: Students take turns. On each turn, a student selects a question and answers it. If the answer is correct, the student may place their color or game piece on the game board. The next student then takes their turn. This continues until one student can get 4 pieces in a row. After, the board can be cleared, and play can continue for multiple rounds until all review questions have been answered.

Second Language Acquisition

Connect 4 supports SLA by operationalizing key principles from established SLA theories. Consistent with Krashen's (1982) Comprehensible Input Hypothesis, the game provides repeated exposure to academic vocabulary and content-specific literacy within a structured and meaningful context. Students engage in both written and oral literacy as they collaboratively answer questions, discuss possible responses, and justify their reasoning, creating opportunities for comprehensible input and output of language in a low-anxiety environment (Shirkhani et al., 2015). The collaborative nature of the game also aligns with Bakhtin's Dialogic Theory, as students negotiate meaning, clarify misunderstandings, and co-construct understanding through peer discussion. Additionally, the low-stakes, game-based format reduces performance pressure, supporting Krashen's Affective Filter Hypothesis by encouraging risk-taking and sustained language use (Abukhattala, 2013; Fortuna, 2025). Through these combined mechanisms, Connect 4 creates an instructional setting that promotes literacy development while reinforcing disciplinary content.

Self-Determination Theory

Connect 4 reinforces competence in SDT by allowing students to see their progress visually on the game board, reinforcing a sense of effectiveness and mastery (Li et al., 2024). Autonomy is promoted through strategic decision-making, such as choosing where to place tokens and engaging with optional rule variations (Kalogiannakis et al., 2021). Relatedness is fostered through team-based decision-making and collective problem-solving, as students collaborate toward shared goals.

Grudgeball

This high-intensity review game strongly motivates students by incorporating competition between groups and creating interactive dynamics in which correct responses allow teams to influence other teams' scores (Haiken, 2017). The game has become a staple in many classrooms, with students demonstrating high levels of enthusiasm and engagement. Once the mechanics are understood, it can be easily adapted for use in a variety of classroom contexts and levels. Although the game is widely used as a review activity, several modifications to traditional Grudgeball rules have been introduced to ensure sustained participation and motivation among all teams.

Supplies: Student whiteboards, dry-erase markers and erasers, review questions in a slide, a trashcan or basketball hoop, and two balls to shoot.

Set-Up: Place students into teams of four to five, with every student having their own whiteboard and marker. Each team will compete against all the others. The basic goal is that when student teams answer questions correctly, they earn opportunities to remove Xs from opposing teams. Alliances and grudges tend to form between teams, increasing student buy-in and motivation.

On the board, each team starts with 10 Xs. The team with the most Xs at the end of the game wins. For example:

The Rowdy Rudibegos: X X X X X X X X X X Capybaras: X X X X X X X X X X
Owala Monsters: X X X X X X X X X X Busy Bees: X X X X X X X X X X

Gameplay

Answering Questions: Every team will take a turn answering a question. When it is their turn, they have 30 seconds to answer. Every person in the group must have the correct answer written on their whiteboard to earn credit for the question. When this happens, that team automatically will be able to remove 2 Xs from any other team or teams. These Xs do not have to come from the same team; they may be divided between teams.

For all teams who are off turn, there is also a chance to answer the question and earn a single X to remove. For this opportunity, the first team in which every member writes the correct answer earns the ability to remove 1 X from any other team.

Additional Xs: For each of these teams, they will choose one student to come up and shoot the ball for additional Xs to remove. The shooter can choose to shoot from close range for 1 additional X, from farther away for 3 additional Xs, or from the back of the room for 10 Xs. If it is a team's turn and they successfully answer the question and then make a close-range basket, they can remove a total of 3 Xs (2 Xs for the question + 1 X for the shot = 3 Xs). If the shooter misses the basket, the team only removes the Xs earned from answering the question correctly.

No-Elimination: When a team has all their Xs removed, they are not removed from the game. Instead, whenever they earn an X or take their turn, they may choose either to continue removing Xs from other teams or to add Xs back to their own total.

Winning the Game: Game play lasts between 30–45 minutes, depending on how many questions are included. At the end of that time, the team with the most Xs remaining wins. To maintain motivation during the final two or three questions, the teacher can remove turns so that only the first two teams to answer correctly get to shoot. This can dramatically change the outcome of the game, especially if high-value shots are made.

Second Language Acquisition

Grudgeball supports literacy by incorporating several principles from established SLA theories. Through repeated engagement with content-related questions, students are exposed to academic vocabulary and literacy in meaningful contexts, aligning with Krashen's (1982) Comprehensible Input Hypothesis (Ibarra-Balarezo & Guaman-Luna, 2025). The requirement to collaboratively negotiate answers encourages both comprehensible output and interaction, as students clarify meaning, provide feedback, and refine their language use through peer discussion (Swain, 1995). Additionally, the fast-paced yet low-stakes competitive structure promotes spontaneous language production while minimizing anxiety, thereby supporting Krashen's Affective Filter Hypothesis (Li, 2025). Collectively, these features create a dynamic learning environment that fosters active literacy and development alongside content review.

Self-Determination Theory

Grudgeball supports the three tenants of SDT that foster a supportive and motivating learning environment. (Ryan & Deci, 2000). This game supports competence by allowing students to demonstrate mastery through correct answers and strategic decisions (Laksanasut, 2025). Relatedness is fostered through team collaboration, alliances, and shared goals, promoting social engagement and a sense of belonging. Autonomy is supported as teams choose which opponents to target and how to use earned points, providing students with meaningful choices and a sense of control over gameplay.

Jeopardy Jenga

This game is a new twist on a classic, *Jeopardy!* (1964) combined with *Jenga* (1986) to create more competition and require greater strategy from students. Not only does the *Jeopardy*! game board allow students to choose content questions, but the *Jenga* component also requires students to evaluate their own understanding as they decide which level of question to attempt. This game has been used with many levels of students and in different content areas, and it consistently creates a highly engaging classroom environment.

Supplies: Student whiteboards, dry-erase markers and erasers, 1–3 Jenga towers, depending on class size, Jeopardy game board questions

Jeopardy Jenga Set-Up: Place students into groups of three to four players while keeping an even number of teams. Each player should have their own whiteboard and marker. Each pair of teams should sit across from each other with a Jenga tower between them, as seen in Figure 3. Team names will be written on the board and scores tracked there, while the Jeopardy board slides are projected.

Figure 3. Classroom set-up of teams with Jenga towers between them.

Gameplay

Answering Questions: Teams will rotate turns selecting which question they want to answer from the board. Once a question is presented, each team competes only against the team seated across from their Jenga tower. For example, teams 1 and 2 compete against each other, Teams 3 and 4 compete, and Teams 5 and 6 compete. Whichever teams have all group members answer correctly first earn the points. For example, if it is a 100-point question and Teams 1, 4, and 6 answer correctly first within their respective pairings, they each receive 100 points.

Jenga Twist: The teams that did not earn the points (Teams 2, 3, and 5) will each send one player to their Jenga tower to remove blocks corresponding to the Jeopardy point value. For a 100-point question, the losing team removes one block; for a 500-point question, they remove five blocks. For this portion, standard Jenga rules apply: players may not use more than one hand, must place removed blocks back on top, and may not remove blocks from the top three rows.

Tower Falls: When a tower falls, the Team responsible loses 1,000 points. At that point, rotate teams so students can face new opponents. If Team 3 causes their tower to fall, they rebuild the tower, and Teams 2, 4, and 6 rotate to a different tower/team pairing. Then, continue playing!

Winning the Game: A 5x5 Jeopardy board typically takes about 45 minutes to complete. Once all questions are answered, the team with the most points wins.

Second Language Acquisition

Jeopardy Jenga reinforces SLA through repeated exposure to content and vocabulary across varying levels of difficulty, supporting Krashen's Comprehensible Input Hypothesis by providing accessible yet progressively challenging literacy input (Abukhattala, 2013). The requirement for students to assess question difficulty and select appropriate prompts promotes metalinguistic awareness, as learners reflect on their understanding of both literacy and content (Stairs-Davenport & Skotarczak, 2018). Collaborative decision-making and discussion among teammates further align with Long's (1980) Interaction Hypothesis by creating opportunities for negotiation of meaning, clarification, and peer feedback. These interactions, combined with the structured and low-pressure game format, support sustained language use and development in a supportive classroom context (Abukhattala, 2013).

Self-Determination Theory

Jeopardy Jenga supports SDT through the different game mechanics. The choice of question values and content supports autonomy, as students decide which risks to take (Kalogiannakis et al., 2021). Competence is developed through immediate feedback and visible progress via scoring (Hafiza & Pratolo, 2024). Relatedness emerges through team collaboration and shared responsibility, especially when managing the Jenga component together (Kalogiannakis et al., 2021).

The Unfair Game

Created to keep every student engaged, the Unfair Game tracks points, but those points are awarded at random. This results in students competing to answer questions in order to qualify for the *chance* to earn points, ensuring that no team loses motivation by falling too far behind. The use of the random point values ensures every team's chance of winning always remains within reach. The randomness of points also decouples language and content proficiency from outcome, which is powerful for MLs.

Supplies: Student whiteboards, dry-erase markers and erasers, review questions in a slide, and a randomized point system

Set-Up: Place students into teams of four to five, with every student having their own whiteboard and marker. Each team competes against all other teams. The setup for this game depends on how the teacher chooses to create the randomized point system. This can be done using cards labeled #1–__, depending on the number of questions, with point values hidden behind each number. Another option is using a wheel–style spinner with point values on it.

Gameplay

Answering Questions: When a question is presented on the board, teams race to be the first to answer correctly. Every student must write an answer on their whiteboard. The first team to answer correctly, this can include multiple teams if tied, then spins the wheel or selects a number to reveal the points they earn.

Points Value: The point system can include an even mix of positive and negative values, along with random modifiers to increase engagement and excitement for students.

For example-

- **Reverse the Point Value:** Take whatever point value a team has and reverse the sign (500 becomes -500, or -300 becomes 300)
- **Switch with another:** The Team must switch point values with a team of their choice
- **Bankruptcy**: Team loses all their points, returning their score to zero
- **Dance to avoid bankruptcy:** If the team does a dance, they will not lose their points

Second Language Acquisition

The Unfair Game supports SLA by creating sustained opportunities for meaningful language use through continuous team participation, regardless of point totals. Students are required to process questions, articulate responses, and negotiate meaning within their teams, aligning with Long's (1980) Interaction Hypothesis by promoting clarification, feedback, and co-construction of understanding. The unpredictable point system reduces emphasis on correctness and performance outcomes, thereby lowering anxiety and supporting Krashen's (1982) Affective Filter Hypothesis (Fortuna, 2025). By encouraging risk-taking in literacy within a low-stakes environment, the game also provides opportunities for comprehensible output consistent with Swain's (1995) Output Hypothesis, supporting ongoing literacy development alongside content review.

Self-Determination Theory

The Unfair Game supports SDT by incorporating game play mechanics that support intrinsic motivation (Ryan & Deci, 2000). The game strongly supports relatedness by maintaining participation from all teams. Competence is emphasized through earning opportunities rather than fixed outcomes, helping students feel capable even when outcomes are uncertain (Laksanasut, 2025). Autonomy is present as students engage willingly without fear of permanent failure, allowing them to make meaningful choices and take risks in a low-stakes environment Noels et al., 2000).

Fly Swatter Game

This game can be used as a longer review or as a quick closing ticket at the end of class. Having this game-board slide created provides many opportunities to increase engagement in class no matter the amount of time available. Once the slide is created, it can be reused multiple times. Designed to target vocabulary recognition, this whole-class review is a fast-paced game that can include the entire class or be played individually (Suhendra, 2023).

Supplies: Game board (figure 4), fly swatter

Figure 4. Game board slide that has vocabulary, Figures, and/or definitions placed randomly

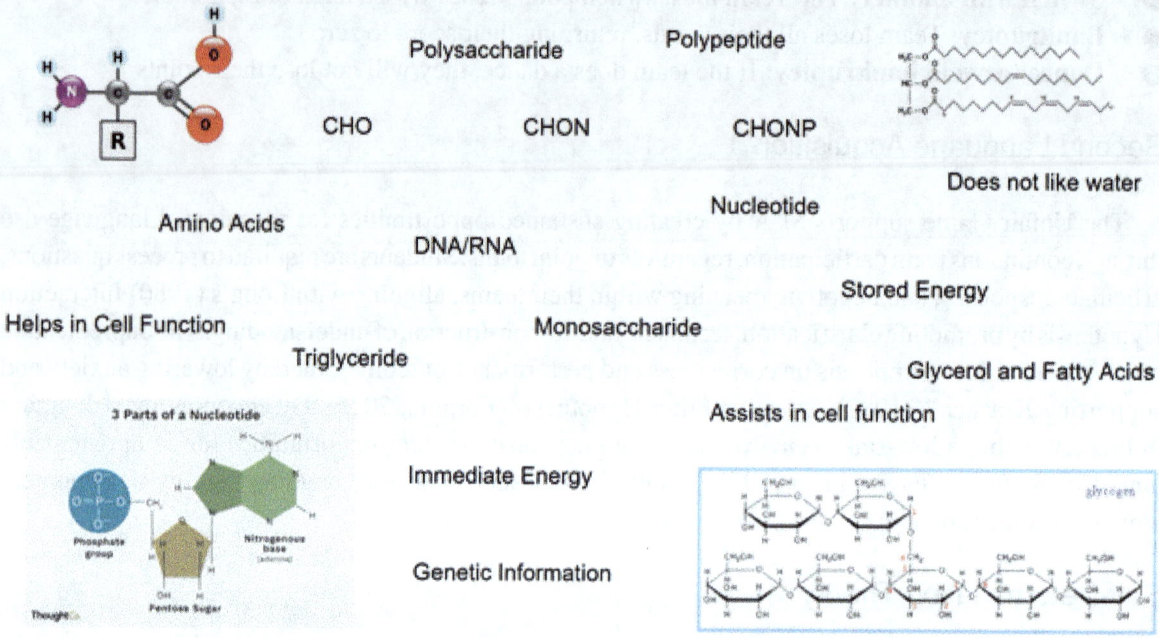

Set-Up: Split the class into 2-4 teams.

Gameplay

For each team, one representative stands at the board holding a fly swatter. As questions are asked, the first player to hit and hold the correct term, definition, or Figure earns a point for their team. Rotate players at the board every couple questions.

Teacher Questions: The teacher provides the questions that students race to answer at the board.

Team Questions: As students' literacy and language skills increase, the teacher can require them to write questions based on the game board. This can be done ahead of time or during the game. If done ahead of time, project the game board and give students time to write review questions and submit them to the teacher. This can be completed individually, in pairs, or as a team. The teacher can then randomly select from these questions during gameplay. If done during the game, alternate between teams, giving them the opportunity to ask questions to the students at the board.

Scaffolding: Provide question stems for students as they write the questions

Second Language Acquisition

This game emphasizes SLA through rapid vocabulary recognition and listening comprehension (Laksanasut, 2025). Students must process spoken definitions and connect them to written or visual representations, strengthening literacy connections. The fast pace encourages automaticity in language processing, providing repeated opportunities for comprehensible input and output in a low-anxiety context, which supports literacy development consistent with Krashen's (1982) Comprehensible Input Hypothesis and Swain's (1985) Output Hypothesis.

Self-Determination Theory

The Fly Swatter Game promotes motivation and engagement by addressing the three tenets identified in SDT (Ryan & Deci, 2000). Competence is developed through quick feedback and successful identification. Relatedness is built through team-based play and shared excitement. Autonomy is supported through rotating roles and increasing student-generated questions as literacy grows.

Hot Seat

Hot Seat is a whole-class review game that can be modified and adapted in many ways to accommodate different student and class needs. Whether used as a whole-class review, a class competition, or an extension activity for students who finish work early, Hot Seat provides many opportunities for students to practice both content knowledge and literacy skills. The premise for all variations is that students give clues by forming sentences that describe class vocabulary while other students try to identify the correct terms.

Supplies: Prepared slide-deck or vocabulary cards (Figure 5)

Figure 5. Slide-deck or vocabulary card

Whole Class

Set-Up: Split the class into two teams. Project the prepared vocabulary slide deck onto the board.

Gameplay: Each team sends one representative to the board, facing the class and unable to see the projected word. When it is Team A's turn, students on that team raise their hands and offer clues to the representative at the board. The team may provide up to three clues, after which the student at the board guesses the projected term. If the guess is correct, the team earns a point, and the next teammate comes to the board. If the guess is incorrect, the other team may give one additional clue, and their representative has the opportunity to steal the point. Rotate students at the board every round or after multiple rounds.

To enhance student engagement: Instructors may incorporate unexpected elements such as random words like pickle in Figure 5, references to celebrities, or the inclusion of class members as part of the game content.

Partner Slide-Deck

Set-Up: Students stand in pairs with one partner facing the board with the projected slide deck, and the other facing another direction.

Game-Play: When a term is projected, the partner facing the board gives clues while the other partner guesses the term. Once the correct term is stated, pairs may raise their hand or sit down to indicate they have completed the round. In the next round, partners switch positions. To increase engagement, each round can be treated as a race to see which pair guesses the term the fastest, followed by a discussion of the clues that led to a quick guess.

Small Group Vocabulary Cards

Set-Up: Have students stand in small groups or pairs with vocabulary cards

Game-Play: In each group, one student draws a vocabulary card and provides clues while the other group members guess the term. To make the activity more game-like, groups can race against each other to see who can guess the terms the fastest, or a timer can be used to see how many terms each group identifies in one minute.

Scaffolding: Figures or sentence stems are included with the vocabulary to help students give clues.

Second Language Acquisition

Hot Seat directly supports SLA by requiring students to produce descriptive language, paraphrase meanings, and use circumlocution when exact vocabulary is unknown. The activity emphasizes listening, speaking, and vocabulary development, while scaffolds such as sentence stems and visual supports provide additional guidance (Li, 2025). By engaging in meaningful language production and collaborative interaction, students receive comprehensible input and practice output, aligning with Krashen's (1982) Comprehensible Input Hypothesis, Monitor Hypothesis, and Swain's (1985) Output Hypothesis.

Self-Determination Theory

Hot Seat fosters motivation and supports the psychological needs identified in SDT by allowing students to generate clues, communicate meaning, and work together. Autonomy is supported through student-generated clues and multiple gameplay formats, providing opportunities for students to use authentic language (Alamer et al., 2025). Competence grows as students successfully communicate meaning and guess terms in a low-stake setting (Tripp & Waight, 2024). Relatedness is emphasized through cooperative clue-giving and peer interaction (Meng, 2021).

Battleship

Adapted from the *Battleship* (1967) board game, this version is designed to target vocabulary use and identification. Although it requires one-time preparation to create the game board, the materials can be reused. This game is for small groups of students and can easily be used as a review activity or as supplemental material for students who finish work early.

Supplies: Laminated game-board (Figure 6) in folders, paperclips, dry-erase markers and erasers

Figure 6. Battleship vocabulary game-board

Macromolecule and Enzyme Battleship

In the Nucleus	Hydrophobic	Nucleic Acids	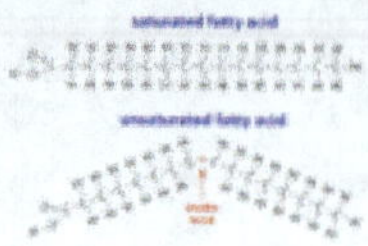	Dehydration Synthesis (Polymerization)
Active Site	Found in butter and oil	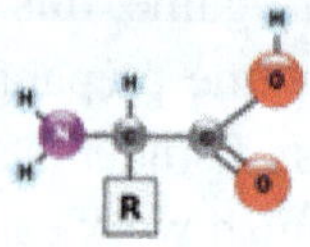	Unsaturated Fatty Acid	Monosaccharide
Amino Acids	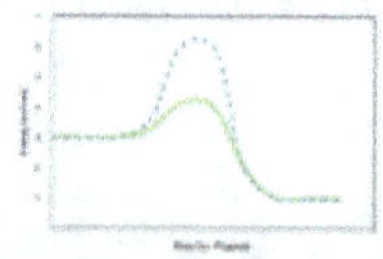	H Bond	Build Muscle and help with cell functioning	Stored Energy
Free Floating DNA	Polysaccharide	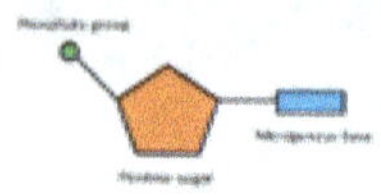	Protein	Found in all living things
Found in fruit, bread, and pasta	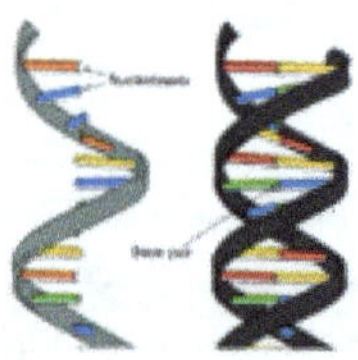	Polypeptide Bond	Found in Meat and Beans	Codes for traits

Set-Up: To create the game board, make one 5x5 grid filled with vocabulary terms. Using a paper folder, laminate a game board onto each side of the folder so that each student has two boards, one to place their ships and one to mark their guesses. In pairs, place the folders back-to-back and secure the tops together with a paper clip so they stand upright. Have students fill in their ships using dry-erase markers. On a 5x5 grid, this includes ships that are 2x1, 3x1, and 4x1. With an expanded grid, more ships or larger ships can be used.

Gameplay: To play Battleship, students take turns firing shots, attempting to sink their opponent's ships by correctly identifying squares on the grid. Students take turns firing shots by giving the definition or description of the square they want to target. Each student uses one game board to place their own ships and the other to track guesses and mark hits or misses. The game continues until one player has sunk all of their opponent's ships.

Second Language Acquisition

Vocabulary Battleship promotes SLA through precise literacy by requiring students to give accurate definitions or descriptions to *fire* at a target term. Repetition and corrective feedback support retention, while peer interaction provides opportunities for clarification and negotiation of meaning. These features align with Krashen's (1982) Comprehensible Input Hypothesis, Swain's (1985) Output Hypothesis, and Long's (1980) Interaction Hypothesis, providing students with meaningful opportunities for literacy development in an engaging, low-anxiety context.

Self-Determination Theory

Vocabulary Battleship enhances student engagement by providing meaningful choices, opportunities to demonstrate skill, and collaborative interaction, reflecting the principles of SDT. Autonomy is supported through strategic targeting of vocabulary terms, as students choose which terms to guess and how to give the proper clue (Ahmed & Hossain, 2024). Competence is reinforced as students track progress and experience mastery through successful clues and hits (McInerney, 2023). Relatedness develops through full class participation and structured peer interaction in pairs (Tripp & Waight, 2024).

REVIEW GAME EXAMPLES: DIGITAL GAMES

Blooket

Blooket (2026) offers multiple game modes built around answering content questions, allowing students to engage in different styles of play while reviewing the same material. Students earn points, rewards, or advantages depending on the game mode selected. Blooket is flexible, highly motivating, and effective for both whole-class and independent review.

Second Language Acquisition

Blooket supports SLA by providing repeated exposure to vocabulary and content language across a variety of game modes. The diversity of gameplay formats sustains engagement while reinforcing literacy through repetition and contextualized use, supporting Krashen's (1982) Acquisition–Learning Hypothesis by promoting subconscious literacy development through meaningful, content-based interactions. Additionally, the low-stakes, individualized GBL environment helps reduce anxiety and supports Krashen's (1982) Affective Filter Hypothesis, encouraging sustained participation and risk-taking in language use (Luo, 2024).

Self-Determination Theory

In Blooket, the design of the site and games provides opportunities for students to make choices, demonstrate skills, and collaborate, reflecting the key constructs of SDT. Blooket supports autonomy by allowing choice of game modes and pacing (Alamer et al., 2025). Competence is developed through scoring and progression systems (Rajendran et al., 2025), and relatedness is fostered during whole-class or team-based play (de Oliveira et al., 2024).

Gimkit

Gimkit (n.d.) combines quiz-based learning with game mechanics such as earning virtual currency, power-ups, and upgrades. Students answer questions to gain resources that affect gameplay, encouraging repeated practice and strategic thinking. Gimkit emphasizes mastery through repetition and is especially effective for sustained review sessions and vocabulary practice.

Second Language Acquisition

Gimkit promotes SLA by requiring repeated exposure to academic vocabulary and content language through retrieval practice tied to earning in-game currency. This repetition strengthens vocabulary retention and fluency, while the strategic decision-making component encourages deeper processing of both literacy and content. The low-stakes, game-based format also supports Krashen's (1982) Comprehensible Input and Affective Filter Hypotheses by providing meaningful input in an engaging environment that reduces anxiety and promotes sustained language use (Fortuna, 2025).

Self-Determination Theory

In Gimkit, students' motivation is enhanced through SDT as the game structure intentionally supports autonomy, competence, and relatedness, supporting (Ryan & Deci, 2000). Gimkit strongly supports autonomy by allowing students to choose upgrades and strategies. Competence is reinforced through mastery-based progression, and relatedness is supported through shared gameplay experiences and optional team modes.

Google Form Scavenger Hunts

Although the initial setup for this activity requires significant preparation, once developed it can be reused for multiple years and consistently generates high levels of student engagement. To prepare the activity, the teacher creates a series of Google Forms with multiple-choice questions that students complete in pairs or small groups. In the answer key for each correct response, feedback is embedded to provide a clue directing students to the next location in the scavenger hunt. After the forms are created, QR codes or links are generated for each form and placed at designated locations, forming a continuous loop. Students begin the activity by scanning the QR code or accessing the link to the first form. Upon submitting a correct response, students receive a feedback clue that guides them to the next location, and the process continues until all locations have been completed. This structure supports self-paced learning, promotes critical thinking and collaboration, and emphasizes the application of knowledge rather than speed-based competition.

Second Language Acquisition

Google Form Scavenger Hunts support SLA by emphasizing comprehension, application, and extended literacy processing rather than speed. Students engage with language and content appropriate written prompts, Figures, and real-world contexts, supporting academic literacy and deeper comprehension (Laksanasut, 2025). These features align with Krashen's (1982) Comprehensible Input Hypothesis by providing accessible, meaningful input, while the self-paced structure helps reduce anxiety and supports the Affective Filter Hypothesis (Fortuna, 2025). The use of teams and collaboration as students complete the scavenger hunt reinforces Bakhtin's Dialogic Theory as social interactions support literacy development (Shirkhani et al., 2015).

Self-Determination Theory

This review creates conditions that encourage sustained participation and intrinsic motivation by meeting the psychological needs of students outlined in the SDT. Google Form Scavenger Hunts supports autonomy through self-paced progression and allows students to choose different strategies to solve problems (Kalogiannakis et al., 2021). Competence is reinforced through successful completion of questions and immediate feedback as questions are answered (Li et al., 2024). Relatedness can be supported through the partner or small-group collaboration as students navigate reading, writing, and vocabulary as social practices (Hafiza & Pratolo, 2024).

Kahoot

Kahoot is a fast-paced quiz platform that promotes engagement through timed multiple-choice questions and immediate feedback (Kahoot, n.d.). Students respond individually using their devices while questions are projected for the class. The competitive leaderboard encourages participation and excitement, making Kahoot effective for quick reviews, formative assessments, and activating prior knowledge. Different variations in game settings allows students to work in groups, giving time to speak to teammates before answering questions. Additional games are also available that introduce different game mechanics while students still answer questions.

Second Language Acquisition

Kahoot supports SLA through repeated exposure to academic vocabulary and sentence structures within a highly engaging, game-based format. Students develop listening comprehension as questions are read aloud and reading comprehension as they process answer choices (Laksanasut, 2025). Immediate feedback reinforces correct language forms, while the fast pace promotes automaticity in language processing. These features align with Krashen's (1982) Comprehensible Input Hypothesis and support literacy development in a low-anxiety learning environment consistent with the Affective Filter Hypothesis (Ibarra-Balarezo & Guaman-Luna, 2025).

Self-Determination Theory

Kahoot enhances student engagement by providing opportunities for meaningful collaboration and skill demonstration, aligning with the principles of SDT (Laksanasut, 2025). Kahoot supports competence through visible scores and immediate feedback that provide many opportunities for success (Hafiza & Pratolo, 2024). Relatedness is fostered by shared class participation and excitement, with game options that increase collaboration and team problem-solving (Ryan & Deci, 2000). While autonomy is limited, engagement remains high due to time-bound challenges and competitive elements.

Quizlet Live

Quizlet Live is a collaborative game that requires students to work together to match terms with definitions, concepts, or Figures (Quizlet, n.d.). Students are placed into randomized teams and must communicate to succeed, reinforcing academic literacy and teamwork. In this game, each player on a team has 4 vocab terms presented on their screen. All members of the team will receive the definition at the top of their screen, and the team members must work together to identify which player has the correct term and select it. This platform is particularly effective for vocabulary acquisition and peer-supported learning.

Second Language Acquisition

Quizlet Live supports SLA by emphasizing collaborative vocabulary learning that requires sustained peer interaction. Students communicate with teammates to match terms and definitions accurately, promoting negotiation of meaning, clarification, and peer scaffolding (Laksanasut, 2025). These features align with Long's (1980) Interaction Hypothesis and Swain's (1995) Output Hypothesis. The opportunity for translanguaging between students in this game also helps students access prior knowledge and clarify meaning of content alongside processing the information in English (Gibbons, 2015; Wang et al., 2025).

Self-Determination Theory

In Quizlet Live, the game structure promotes autonomy, competence, and relatedness, creating a collaborative environment that encourages engagement and sustained participation (Ryan & Deci, 2000). This tool strongly supports relatedness through mandatory teamwork (Kalogiannakis et al., 2021). Competence develops as teams successfully match terms and receive immediate feedback, seeing a progress scale on their screen (Li et al., 2024). Autonomy is limited but present through student-centered participation and collaborative decision-making (Noels et al., 2000).

Wayground

Wayground (2026) is a self-paced or live quiz platform that allows students to work through questions individually while receiving instant feedback. Unlike Kahoot, questions appear on students' screens, reducing cognitive load and supporting accessibility. Wayground is well-suited for differentiation, homework, asynchronous learning, and low-pressure review activities. The use of AI settings allows the teacher to opt-in to AI feedback for students, giving additional explanations when students answer incorrectly. Optional game play allows students to choose power-ups and interactions with other players as well.

Second Language Acquisition

Wayground supports SLA by presenting questions directly on students' devices, which reduces cognitive load and allows learners to process language at their own pace. The platform supports reading comprehension, vocabulary recognition, and language accuracy, while immediate corrective feedback reinforces learning (Laksanasut, 2025). These features align with Krashen's (1982) Comprehensible Input Hypothesis and support the Affective Filter Hypothesis by providing accessible input and feedback in a low-pressure learning environment (Fortuna, 2025).

Self-Determination Theory

In Wayground, the game structure promotes engagement by providing opportunities for student choice, skill development, and collaborative problem-solving, reflecting the principles of SDT (Ryan & Deci, 2000). Wayground strongly supports autonomy through self-paced options and flexible settings. Competence is reinforced through feedback and progress tracking (de Oliveira et al., 2024), while relatedness can be supported through optional team modes, power-ups, or class discussions of results (Tripp & Waight, 2024).

INCORPORATING ARTIFICIAL INTELLIGENCE INTO GAME BASED LEARNING

Artificial intelligence (AI) offers a flexible tool for enhancing GBL without undermining the interactive, student-centered elements that make these activities effective. When used intentionally, AI can increase engagement, support differentiation, and improve instructional efficiency across all phases of gameplay, including preparation, implementation, and reflection (Fitria, 2021). Both teacher-directed and student-mediated uses of AI provide opportunities to increase the pedagogical value of review games while maintaining teacher control and instructional purpose.

Teacher Use of AI

One of the most accessible applications of AI occurs during teacher preparation and content generation. AI can rapidly produce extensive banks of review questions in multiple formats, including multiple-choice, short-answer, and application-based prompts, as well as tiered questions at varying levels of difficulty (Celik et al., 2022). This could include student-friendly vocabulary definitions, non-examples, and extension tasks for students. These capabilities allow teachers to reuse familiar game structures while updating content, targeting specific literacy goals, and being responsive to specific class needs. The use of AI as a tool for teachers in preparing GBL review activities can significantly reduce preparation time and increase instructional efficiency (Chen & Chang, 2024). AI-supported preparation can also enhance differentiation in literacy for MLs by generating questions at multiple reading levels, providing sentence stems, or creating scaffolded prompts (Park & Kim, 2025). In content, AI can also be a tool used to create higher-order or application-based challenges for students. During gameplay, AI can further increase engagement and support instruction by functioning as a teacher-controlled facilitator (Chen & Chang, 2024). This can be done by utilizing AI to introduce surprise challenge questions, bonus rounds, or follow-up tasks when teams respond quickly or demonstrate mastery of content and literacy. In this role, the use of AI for preparation, content generation, and instructional support enhances novelty and engagement while allowing teachers to retain full control over pacing and instructional goals.

Student Use of AI

Teachers can also incorporate AI use for students into lesson plans as a way for students to reflect before and after GBL review activities (Klamma et al., 2020). Before an activity, students could prepare by using AI to quiz themselves on vocabulary, practice explaining concepts, explore examples and non-examples, or identify areas where they need additional support (de Oliveira et al., 2024). For MLs, this additional guided practice can build confidence in content and literacy, leading to active participation during GBL review activities. Another way that AI can support GBL preparation is to assist students in generating review game questions (Chen & Chang, 2024). AI can be used to help MLs revise, refine, and extend their original question prompts instead of generating content independently, scaffolding access to content and building literacy. When used in this manner, AI increases rigor, encourages attention to misconceptions, and strengthens literacy skills while preserving the student-driven nature of the activity (Park & Kim, 2025). Following gameplay, AI can function as a tool for reflection and formative assessment, enabling students to identify challenging concepts, generate targeted practice questions, or summarize key ideas from the review. These preparatory and reflective applications help transform GBL reviews from a standalone activity into an integrated learning experience that supports ongoing content understanding and literacy growth (Yuan & Hu, 2025).

When integrated thoughtfully, AI enhances the effectiveness of GBL by supporting teacher preparation, facilitating differentiation, enriching gameplay, and promoting student preparation and reflection (Fitria, 2021). Rather than replacing instructional decision-making, AI can function as a flexible support that amplifies existing pedagogical practices (Celik et al., 2022). If used with clear purpose and appropriate parameters for students, AI can extend the reach of GBL for MLs, making review activities more inclusive, efficient, and responsive to these diverse learners while preserving the engagement of these activities.

IMPLICATIONS AND FUTURE DIRECTIONS

GBL has the potential to redefine how literacy is experienced and supported in ML classrooms. By shifting away from traditional worksheet-based activities and assessment models toward interactive, formative, and collaborative approaches, educators can capture a more authentic picture of student learning (Black & Wiliam, 2009). GBL review activities embed feedback within play, helping both teachers and students monitor progress of content and literacy in real time while reducing performance anxiety (Plass et al., 2015). Additional research should consider how learners of different cultures respond to varying GBL techniques (Laksanasut, 2025).

Looking ahead, emerging technologies, particularly AI-driven adaptive feedback and learning analytics, offer new avenues for customizing learning experiences, personalizing vocabulary and literacy practice, and tracking progress across languages (Holmes et al., 2019). When thoughtfully implemented, these tools can complement GBL by providing timely feedback, targeted support, and data-informed insights that help teachers respond to students' evolving linguistic and conceptual needs.

For teacher development, this chapter encourages practitioners to embrace creative, flexible, and equity-oriented pedagogies that center student agency and linguistic diversity (Darling-Hammond et al., 2020; Vaughn et al., 2025). By intentionally aligning GBL with principles from SLA and SDT, teachers can design learning environments that are both academically rigorous and emotionally supportive. Ultimately, the integration of GBL, SLA, and SDT represents a forward-looking model for inclusive literacy instruction, one that fosters motivation, community, and confidence among MLs while redefining the culture of science learning as collaborative, accessible, and linguistically affirming.

REFERENCES

Abukhattala, I. (2013). Krashen's Five Proposals on Language Learning: Are They Valid in Libyan EFL Classes. *English Language Teaching*, *6*(1), 128–131. DOI: 10.5539/elt.v6n1p128

Ahmed, M. K., & Hossain, K. I. (2024). Nurturing learner autonomy to enhance motivation and academic achievement for the L2 learners in ESL contexts. *IUBAT Review*, *7*(2), 176–196. DOI: 10.3329/iubatr.v7i2.78809

Alamer, A., Robat, E. S., Shirvan, M. E., & Ryan, R. (2025). Self-Determination Theory and Language Learning: A Multilevel Meta-Analysis. *Educational Psychology Review*, *37*(2), 59. DOI: 10.1007/s10648-025-10038-y

Arip, A. J., & Hashim, H. (2024). Gamification in English as second language (ESL) learning: A systematic review. *International Journal of Academic Research in Progressive Education and Development*, *13*(4), 2837–2853. DOI: 10.6007/IJARPED/v13-i4/24069

Battleship [Board game]. (1967). Milton Bradley.

Black, P., & Wiliam, D. (2009). Developing the theory of formative assessment. *Educational Assessment, Evaluation and Accountability*, *21*(1), 5–31. DOI: 10.1007/s11092-008-9068-5

Blooket. (2026). *Blooket.* https://blooket.com/

Castañeda, M., & Bautista, N. (2011). Teaching science to ELLs, part II. *Science Teacher (Normal, Ill.)*, *78*(3), 40.

Celik, I., Dindar, M., Muukkonen, H., & Järvelä, S. (2022). The promises and challenges of artificial intelligence for teachers: A systematic review of research. *TechTrends*, *66*(4), 616–630. DOI: 10.1007/s11528-022-00715-y

Chan, S., & Lo, N. (2024). Enhancing EFL/ESL instruction through gamification: a comprehensive review of empirical evidence. In *Frontiers in Education* (Vol. 9, p. 1395155). Frontiers Media SA. https://doi.org/DOI: 10.3389/feduc.2024.1395155

Chang, B. (2019). Reflection in learning. *Online Learning : The Official Journal of the Online Learning Consortium*, *23*(1), 95–110. DOI: 10.24059/olj.v23i1.1447

Chang, X. Game-Based Learning in ESL Classrooms: A Focus on Gimkit and Other Apps (May 01, 2021). http://doi.org/DOI: 10.2139/ssrn.5106362

Charos, K. (2024). Effective ways of incorporating Krashen's hypothesis into ESL instructional practices. *University Research Base*, 153-161. Retrieved from https://scholar.kokanduni.uz/index.php/rb/article/view/303

Chen, C. H., & Chang, C. L. (2024). Effectiveness of AI-assisted game-based learning on science learning outcomes, intrinsic motivation, cognitive load, and learning behavior. *Education and Information Technologies*, *29*(14), 18621–18642. DOI: 10.1007/s10639-024-12553-x

Connect 4 [Board game]. (1974). Milton Bradley.

Cummins, J. (2000). *Language, power, and pedagogy: Bilingual children in the crossfire* (Vol. 23). Multilingual matters.

Darling-Hammond, L., Flook, L., Cook-Harvey, C., Barron, B., & Osher, D. (2020). Implications for educational practice of the science of learning and development. *Applied Developmental Science*, *24*(2), 97–140. DOI: 10.1080/10888691.2018.1537791

de Oliveira, L. C., Avalos, M. A., & Blair, A. (2024). Expanding teacher understanding of scaffolding for multilingual learners using a language-based approach to content instruction. *TESOL in Context*, *33*(1), 25–42. DOI: 10.21153/tesol2024vol33no1art2008

Dichev, C., & Dicheva, D. (2017). Gamifying education: what is known, what is believed and what remains uncertain: a critical review. *International Journal of Educational Technology in Higher Education*, *14*(1), 9. DOI: 10.1186/s41239-017-0042-5

Fitria, T. N. (2021). Artificial intelligence (AI) in education: Using AI tools for teaching and learning process. In *Presiding seminar national & call for paper STIE AAS* (pp. 134-147).

Forms, G. (n.d.). *Google Forms*. https://docs.google.com/forms/u/0/

Fortuna, R. S.Roniel Sanchez Fortuna. (2025). Lowering the filter: The role of attitude in English language acquisition. *International Journal of English Pedagogy*, *10*(2), 111–125. DOI: 10.30574/wjarr.2025.25.3.1020

Gibbons, P. (2015). *Scaffolding language, scaffolding learning: Teaching English language learners in the mainstream classroom* (2nd ed.). Heinemann.

Gimkit. (n.d.). *Gimkit: Play and Learn*. https://www.gimkit.com/

Goodall, M. V., Gomez, M., & Webster, D. W. (2024). Effective instruction: The intersection of structured literacy and second-language acquisition for multilingual learners. *The Reading League Journal*, *5*(2), 30–37. https://www.thereadingleague.org/wp-content/uploads/2024/06/the-reading-league-journal-may-2024-effective-instruction.pdf

Hafiza, A. F., & Pratolo, B. W. (2024). A systematic review of the effectiveness of game-based learning in English language teaching. *International Journal on E-Learning*, *6*(2), 56–64. DOI: 10.31763/ijele.v6i2.1312

Haiken, M. (2017). *Gamify Literacy: Boost Comprehension, Collaboration and Learning*. ASCD.

Hamari, J., Shernoff, D. J., Rowe, E., Coller, B., Asbell-Clarke, J., & Edwards, T. (2016). Challenging games help students learn: An empirical study on engagement, flow and immersion in game-based learning. *Computers in Human Behavior*, *54*, 170–179. DOI: 10.1016/j.chb.2015.07.045

Hattie, J., & Timperley, H. (2007). The power of feedback. *Review of Educational Research*, *77*(1), 81–112. DOI: 10.3102/003465430298487

Holmes, W., Bialik, M., & Fadel, C. (2019). *Artificial intelligence in education: Promises and implications for teaching and learning*. Center for Curriculum Redesign. https://curriculumredesign.org/wp-content/uploads/AIED-Book-Excerpt-CCR.pdf

Ibarra-Balarezo, S. C., & Guaman-Luna, M. M. (2025). The use of comprehensible input to improve listening comprehension in high school EFL sudents: A literature review. *Revista Mexicana de Investigación e Intervención Educativa, 4*(S1), 171–182. DOI: 10.62697/rmiie.v4iS1.160

Jasmaniah, J., Nurhayati, N., & Zuhra, F. (2024). Game-Based Learning Model with A Culturally Responsive Teaching Approach to Enhance Student Motivation in Learning Mathematics. *Jurnal Ilmiah Sekolah Dasar, 8*(4), 708–717. DOI: 10.23887/jisd.v8i4.86595

Jenga [Board game]. (1986). Hasbro Gaming.

Jeopardy! [Board game]. (1964). Milton Bradley.

Kahoot. (n.d.). *Kahoot!* https://kahoot.com/

Kalogiannakis, M., Papadakis, S., & Zourmpakis, A. I. (2021). Gamification in science education. A systematic review of the literature. *Education Sciences, 11*(1), 22. DOI: 10.3390/educsci11010022

Klamma, R., Lange, P. de, Neumann, A. T., Hensen, B., Kravcik, M., Wang, X., & Kuzilek, J. (2020). Scaling Mentoring Support with Distributed Artificial Intelligence. *Intelligent Tutoring Systems*, 38–44. https://doi.org/DOI: 10.1007/978-3-030-49663-0_6

Krashen, S. D. (1982). *Principles and practice in second language acquisition*. Pergamon Press.

Laksanasut, S. (2025). Gamification in ESL/EFL education: Transforming language learning and teaching through play. *TESOL and Technology Studies, 6*(1), 16–29. DOI: 10.48185/tts.v6i1.1562

Lee, O. (2020). Science and language instructional shifts with second-language learners. *Asia-Pacific Science Education, 6*(2), 263–284. DOI: 10.1163/23641177-BJA10005

Lee, O., Miller, E. C., & Januszyk, R. (2019). *NGSS for all students*. National Science Teaching Association Press.

Li, H. (2025). Exploring the relationship between language anxiety and the monitor hypothesis in ESL learners. *Literature. Language and Cultural Studies, 1*(1), 133–138. DOI: 10.63313/LLCS.9019

Li, L., Hew, K. F., & Du, J. (2024). Gamification enhances student intrinsic motivation, perceptions of autonomy and relatedness, but minimal impact on competency: A meta-analysis and systematic review. *Educational Technology Research and Development, 72*(2), 765–796. DOI: 10.1007/s11423-023-10337-7

Long, M. H. (1980). *Input, interaction, and second language acquisition*. University of California.

Luo, Z. (2024). A review of Krashen's input theory. *Journal of Education. Humanities and Social Sciences, 26*(1), 130–135. DOI: 10.54097/3fnf5786

Lyon, E. G., Tolbert, S., Solís, J., Stoddart, P., & Bunch, G. C. (2016). *Secondary science teaching for English learners: Developing supportive and responsive learning contexts for sense-making and language development*. Bloomsbury Publishing PLC.

McInerney, K. (2023). Perceptions from newcomer multilingual adolescents: Predictors and experiences of sense of belonging in high school. In *Child & youth care forum* (Vol. 52, No. 5, pp. 1041-1072). New York: Springer US. https://doi.org/DOI: 10.1007/s10566-022-09723-8

Meng, Y. (2021). Fostering EFL/ESL Students' State Motivation: The Role of Teacher-Student Rapport. *Frontiers in Psychology*, *12*, 754797. DOI: 10.3389/fpsyg.2021.754797 PMID: 34589039

Noels, K. A., Pelletier, L. G., Clément, R., & Vallerand, R. J. (2000). Why are you learning a second language? Motivational orientations and self-determination theory. *Language Learning*, *50*(1), 57–85. DOI: 10.1111/0023-8333.00111

Nutta, J., Bautista, N. U., & Butler, M. B. (2010). *Teaching science to English language learners*. Routledge. DOI: 10.4324/9780203850572

Park, S., & Kim, O. (2025). Scaffolding with Generative AI in Language Classrooms: A Critical Thinking Framework. , (77), 349-372. https://doi.org/DOI: 10.17002/sil..77.202510.351

Plass, J. L., Homer, B. D., & Kinzer, C. K. (2015). Foundations of game-based learning. *Educational Psychologist*, *50*(4), 258–283. DOI: 10.1080/00461520.2015.1122533

Quizlet. (n.d.). *Quizlet*. https://https://quizlet.com/

Rajendran, M., Srinivasan, V., Ilangovan, A., Singh, A. B., & Bakhromdjanovna, M. Z. (2025). Exploring anxiety among english learners: A comprehensive literature review. *Multidisciplinary Reviews*, *8*(9), 2025270. DOI: 10.31893/multirev.2025270

Reeve, J. (2012). A self-determination theory perspective on student engagement. In Christenson, S. (Eds.), *Handbook of research on student engagement* (pp. 149–172). Springer. DOI: 10.1007/978-1-4614-2018-7_7

Ryan, R. M., & Deci, E. L. (2000). Self-determination theory and the facilitation of intrinsic motivation, social development, and well-being. *The American Psychologist*, *55*(1), 68–78. DOI: 10.1037/0003-066X.55.1.68 PMID: 11392867

Scherzinger, L., & Brahm, T. (2023). A systematic review of bilingual education teachers' competences. *Educational Research Review*, *39*, 100531. DOI: 10.1016/j.edurev.2023.100531

Shirkhani, F., Nesari, A. J., & Feilinezhad, N. (2015). Bakhtinian dialogic concept in language learning process. *Procedia: Social and Behavioral Sciences*, *205*, 510–515. DOI: 10.1016/j.sbspro.2015.09.060

Stairs-Davenport, A., & Skotarczak, B. (2018). Improving comprehensible input for ELLs through technology. *TESL-EJ*, *22*(3), 1-12. https://www.tesl-ej.org/pdf/ej87/int.pdf

Suhendra, K. K. A. (2023). The Effect of Fly Swatter Game Toward Students' Vocabulary Mastery. [TATEFL]. *The Art of Teaching English as a Foreign Language*, *4*(2), 37–44. DOI: 10.36663/tatefl.v4i2.613

Swain, M. (1995). Three functions of output in second language learning. In Cook, G., & Seidlhofer, B. (Eds.), *Principle and practice in applied linguistics* (pp. 125–144). Oxford University Press.

Szilágyi, S., Palencsár, E., Körei, A., & Török, Z. (2025). Examining the effectiveness of non-digital game-based learning among university computer science students on the topic of improper integrals. *Education Sciences*, *15*(2), 132. DOI: 10.3390/educsci15020132

Tang, K. S. (2023). The characteristics of diagrams in scientific explanations: Multimodal integration of written and visual modes of representation in junior high school textbooks. *Science Education, 107*(3), 741–772. DOI: 10.1002/sce.21787

Tripp, J. N., & Waight, N. (2024). Co-creating a community of belonging and presence: Multilingual learners' experiences of science and language learning at an urban, inclusive STEM-focused high school. *Science Education, 108*(1), 25–62. DOI: 10.1002/sce.21827

Vaughn, M., Lammert, C., Carrizales, D., & Arlington, K. C. (2025). Multilingual learners and possibilities for agency. *Peabody Journal of Education, 100*(4), 482–494. DOI: 10.1080/0161956X.2025.2535921

Velayutham, S., & Aldridge, J. M. (2013). Influence of psychosocial classroom environment on students' motivation and self-regulation in science learning: A structural equation modeling approach. *Research in Science Education, 43*(2), 507–527. DOI: 10.1007/s11165-011-9273-y

Vygotsky, L. S. (1978). *Mind in society: The development of higher psychological processes*. Harvard University Press.

Wang, A. I., & Tahir, R. (2020). The effect of using Kahoot! for learning–A literature review. *Computers & Education, 149*, 103818. DOI: 10.1016/j.compedu.2020.103818

Wang, X., Xia, C., Zhao, Q., & Chen, L. (2025). Enhancing second language motivation and facilitating vocabulary acquisition in an EFL classroom through translanguaging practices. *Applied Linguistics Review, 16*(5), 2183–2216. DOI: 10.1515/applirev-2024-0292

Wayground. (2006). *Wayground*. https://wayground.com/

Yuan, B., & Hu, J. (2025, December). Generative AI as a tool for enhancing reflective learning in students. In *2025 IEEE International Conference on Teaching, Assessment, and Learning for Engineering (TALE)* (pp. 1-6). IEEE. https://doi.org/DOI: 10.1109/TALE66047.2025.11346600

Chapter 11
Reimagining Literacy Through Play and Algorithms:
AI-Driven Storytelling, Adaptive Games, and the Future of Critical Literacy Education

Hemlata Parmar
http://orcid.org/0009-0009-1438-5427
Manipal University Jaipur, India

Utsav Krishan Murari
http://orcid.org/0009-0007-1606-6775
Manipal University Jaipur, India

Fakira Mohan Nahak
http://orcid.org/0000-0003-1665-2460
Manipal University Jaipur, India

Atul Arora
Sharda University, India

ABSTRACT

In this chapter, the AI-driven storytelling and adaptive game-based learning are explored as the methods to make literacy education an inclusive, critical, and culturally responsive practice. It theorizes AI-generated narratives and adaptive literacy games as dynamic scaffolds and personalize learning, maintains interest, and promotes vocabulary, fluency, writing, and critical literacy among diverse learner groups, based on the multiliteracies theory, socio-constructivism, and digital game-based learning. The chapter presents the findings of recent empirical studies and systematic reviews, discusses ethical and accessibility issues (authorship, bias, surveillance, and equity), and suggests principles of pedagogical design and an equitable AI literacy practice model based on the idea of cultural responsiveness, explainability, and learner agency.

DOI: 10.4018/979-8-3373-7472-7.ch011

1. INTRODUCTION: REFRAMING LITERACY IN THE AGE OF ALGORITHMS

Literacy as an academic phenomenon has undergone paradigm shifts over the past 3 decades. Literacy is now interpreted as a socialized, multimodal and culturally contingent practices that encompass reading, writing and critically decoding meaning in image, sound, gesture, interface and algorithmically negotiated production, since it has been traditionally perceived as the ability to decode and encode printed text (New London Group, 1996; Street, 1995). This expanded concept, sometimes known as multiliteracies, is the idea that meaning is made in the new technologically saturated, culturally heterogeneous worlds where texts are interactive, hybrid and more co-constructed with the algorithmic agents (Cope and Kalantzis, 2015). The meeting point of artificial intelligence and education has made it a pressing and challenged change.

The advent of AI-driven narrative systems and dynamic digital games within educational settings is a never-before-see but indeed complicated prospect to teachers. On the one hand, these technologies can offer the personalization-at-scale: adaptive platforms have the potential to scale text complexity, pacing and feedback based on individual learner profiles in a way that cannot be reliably reproduced by human teachers in heterogeneous classrooms (Wang et al., 2024). On the other hand, other, more concrete, pedagogical risks exist within the same systems: the algorithms reproduce language hierarchies, the surveillance systems gather learner data without meaningful consent, and the literacy is promoted as interpretive richness and authorial agency of language (U.S. Department of Education, 2023; Selwyn, 2022).

Emerging empirical literature from 2020 provides initial, context-specific evidence of what these technologies can and cannot do to accomplish literacy. Reviews of digital games-based learning indicate moderate, practically meaningful, impact on cognitive, motivational, and engagement preconditions of long-term literacy practice, specifically when games are used as part of coherent instructional cycles, but not when they are used as novelty supplements (Alotaibi, 2024; Garzón, 2025). Parallel experiments of AI-enhanced writing systems have shown that when automated feedback is provided in parallel with explicit teacher scaffold and revision routines, revision frequency, organizational coherence, and genre awareness improve (Zhang, 2025; Bircan, 2025). The inference of latent literacy constructs by micro-behavioral traces during gameplay is an innovative research area that is currently under investigation as a promising diagnostic technique but has yet to be validated against established external measures (Lu, 2025).

The evidence base is limited to three important limitations. To begin with, there are limited longitudinal and extensive randomized controlled trials investigating transfer and retention and equity outcomes, especially among linguistic and socioeconomic subgroups (Wang et al., 2024; Garzón, 2025). Second, the studies that focus on learners with reading disabilities, English learners, and translanguaging learners are poorly developed in comparison to the heterogeneity of the current classroom. Third, the unanswered questions that these gaps necessitate are not merely methodological but political: who do AI-enabled literacy environments benefit, and in which institutional circumstances do such benefit fairly disseminate (AILit Framework, OECD and European Commission, 2025)?

This chapter is based on the belief that AI-based narrative and play environments can no longer be regarded as a natural technical extension of the current educational infrastructure. Instead, they are intentionally created learning environments that need to be interrogated critically regarding their assumptions regarding language, culture, authorship, and knowledge. It is within this context that the chapter aims to accomplish three interrelated objectives: (a) synthesize theoretical and empirical knowledge on AI-driven storytelling and adaptive game-based learning as literacy practices critically; (b) to determine the equity, ethical, and pedagogical circumstances under which such settings could facilitate authentic literacy development; and (c) to propose practical design principles and an original pedagogical model, the EQUITY- The chapter is structured in ten parts, traversing between theoretical bases, empirical review, equity analysis, and methodological advice, to a synthesizing conclusion.

2. CONCEPTUAL AND THEORETICAL FOUNDATIONS

2.1 Multiliteracies Theory and Algorithmically Mediated Meaning-Making

The multiliteracies theoretical framework initially developed by the New London Group (1996) and later by Cope and Kalantzis (2015) is a conceptualization of literacy as a socially constructed, multimodal process instead of a single cognitive ability of reading print. The framework was formed because of two overlapping forces: the growing cultural and linguistic diversity of the learner population and the revolution of communications technologies, which began to transform the production, distribution, and interpretation of texts. In this context, literacy involves the management of various semiotic resources, i.e. linguistic, visual, auditory, gestural and spatial and involves the ability to negotiate dynamic, interactive and culturally encoded texts.

Artificial intelligence-based narrative space and dynamically driven game platforms represent paradigmatic examples of the texts that the multiliteracies theory predicts. They are inherently multimodal: a combination of written text and animation, sound, branching narrative structure, and pathways that are determined algorithmically. They also essentially break the traditional authorship: AI-generated or adapted texts are not objects written by a single human author but are instead emergent products of the interactions between learner inputs, training data, and design parameters. This fluidity is not a deficiency in a multiliteracies approach but a pedagogical provocation to what Cope and Kalantzis (2015) describe as design awareness, the critical consciousness of the processes that constitute texts through social, cultural and technical power. Learners who read the AI-created narratives are, in the most profound way, learning to interpret the algorithm as a co-author with ideological commitments of its own (Mills, 2024).

The extension of multiliteracies to AI settings, suggested by Mills (2024), posits that the new literacy education needs to foster what she terms algorithmic design literacy - the ability not only to apply AI tools but also to critically examine and redesign the algorithms of textual meaning production and distribution. This is the expansion of the initial concept of multiliteracies called Transformed Practice - learning through critical application and redesign - into the experience of AI, where the learners are the seekers of the technological conditions of their own meaning-making. This idea shift is the key to the discussion that is built in this chapter.

2.2 Socio-Constructivist Perspectives: Scaffolding, Zone of Proximal Development, and AI Mediation

The second underlying theory is Vygotskian socio-constructivism that cognitive development is essentially social and that learning takes place within Zone of Proximal Development (ZPD) the distinction between what students can do on their own and what they can do with the assistance of a more competent peer or teacher (Vygotsky, 1978). Further elaboration of scaffolding by Bruner (1986) applied this understanding to formal pedagogy, which requires instructional assistance but only up to a point when the learner can absorb the competencies, and never to the point of reliance.

In principle, adaptive AI systems operationalize scaffolding at scale: they scale task difficulty based on real-time learner performance, provide differentiated feedback, and can keep a learner in a productive challenge range throughout long sequences of practice. Empirical studies of adaptive literacy platforms indicate that the vocabulary and writing quality gains can be observed when AI scaffolding works as an adjunct and not a replacement of teacher judgment, in controlled conditions (Wang et al., 2024; Lu, 2025). More importantly, though, the original model of Bruner demands that the scaffolding provided should be decipherable and eventually removable: the learner should be capable of internalization, not just reliance, of the assistance given. Opaque automated feedback - feedback that informs learners what to modify but not why, or feedback that is measured in terms that learners cannot measure or query - risks inducing compliance, as opposed to understanding. Through socio-constructivist theory, the justification of AI scaffolding is therefore presented, as well as the parameters through which it should be held accountable.

2.3 Play, Situated Cognition, and Game-Based Literacy Learning

The third theoretical basis of this chapter is the scholarship of play and situated cognition, as discussed in Gee (2003) seminal text of video games and literacy and Shaffer (2006) analysis of epistemic games. Gee states that good games reflect the principles of learning that are not always practiced in school, such as placing practice within purposeful agency, just-in-time feedback based on performance, and repeated practice in different contexts, as well as allowing learners to perform in different identities such as characters, roles, and positions that widen their interpretive and expressive repertoires. Particularly narrative-based games generate what Gee describes as projective identity - a fruitful confusion between the identity of the learner and identity of the character - that creates strong emotional investment in meaning-making.

This analysis can be extended by Shaffer (2006) in his notion of epistemic games, which states that games have the capacity of immersing the learner in the real activities - ways of thinking, acting and knowing - of specific communities of practices. In the context of literacy education, this is particularly important: a game, where the players are situated as journalists, historians, or storytellers, is not only a way of practicing comprehension skills within a gamified package, but of inviting students to the epistemological practices according to which various forms of text are created. By overlaying adaptive AI over game-based worlds, a new layer is added: the ability to personalize not just difficulty but narrative path and produce stories that are responsive to individual learner decision-making, providing the lasting interpretive experience that literacy development needs (Alotaibi, 2024).

All these three theoretical frameworks narrow down to a single implication where technology does not have a stand-alone effect of leading to literacy gains. Critically reflective, socially mediated practice is engaged with purposeful tools to learn literacy. Instructional designs should thus incorporate AI systems that uphold equity, interpretability, and learner agency. This theoretical synthesis guides the empirical review and pedagogical proposals that ensue.

3. AI-DRIVEN STORYTELLING AS LITERACY PEDAGOGY

3.1 Defining AI-Driven Storytelling in Educational Contexts

Educational AI-driven storytelling can be defined as the utilization of computational models, such as rule-based narrative engines or large language models (LLMs), to create, edit, extend, or co-create narratives based on input from learners and pedagogical requirements. In contrast to fixed digital texts, AI-generated stories are dynamic: they can be followed down the plot, modified to lexical complexity, customized to the tastes of the learner, or confined to pedagogically defined vocabulary lists and genre norms (Lo, 2025; Sánchez-López, 2025). This dynamism is what makes AI storytelling better than the previous generations of digital reading platforms and makes it a qualitatively new sort of literacy environment.

An important difference between the literature lies in the fact that open generative systems (where the text generation procedure is relatively free) and pedagogically constrained systems (where curriculum-relevant parameters, e.g. target vocabulary, readability thresholds, genre templates, inferential prompts) influence the AI outputs to attain quantifiable learning outcomes (Wang et al., 2024). In the context of literacy education, the latter are more practically applicable and can be more easily applied in assessment practice. In the lens of multiliteracies, the two kinds would be viewed as a kind of participatory design-oriented meaning-making - the learners are not only consumers of texts but also engage with algorithmic agents in the creation of texts, that is, the learners are both readers and co-designers of narrative.

3.2 Empirical Affordances: Vocabulary, Fluency, and Narrative Competence

3.2.1 Vocabulary Development

Vocabulary knowledge plays a central role in the development of literacy and there is strong evidence that vocabulary breadth and depth are directly related to reading comprehension, academic performance, and quality writing (Beck et al., 2013). AI-based narrative provides long-term, contextual exposure to target vocabulary in the form of narrative embedding - words that are found in more than one episode of a story in a semantically meaningful context are more easily learned and remembered than words found in a decontextualized list (Nation, 2001). Adaptive systems may also be used to recycle words between narrative arcs, creating semantic depth by increasing complexity.

There is growing empirical evidence that AI narrative environments have the potential to generate small, yet significant gains in both receptive and expressive vocabulary in younger learners and English language learners when implemented as part of sustained instructional interventions and not novelty exposures (Garzón, 2025). Importantly, though, scholars highlight that exposure is not a determinant of vocabulary acquisition: explicit focus on word meaning, teacher-mediated reflexivity, and the ability to produce target vocabulary by the learner are significant mediating variables (Wang et al., 2024). Good AI storytelling designs thus incorporate metacognitive vocabulary tasks, such as noticing, defining negotiation, and useful use, instead of thinking that narrative immersion is the sole acquisition strategy.

3.2.2 Reading Fluency and Comprehension

Reading fluency - the ability to read correctly, quickly and with the right amount of prosody - has long-standing links to reading comprehension, in part because automaticity in the decoding level relieves a cognitive load on higher-order meaning-making processes (Rasinski, 2010). AI-based storytelling systems can facilitate the development of fluency by showing texts scaffolded to the current level of decoding and understanding, allowing the learner to read extensively without becoming bored, and, with the use of branching narrative, encouraging the learner to reread on their own, which is a high-fluency-building activity. According to Zhang (2025), adaptive literacy interventions that include individualized text leveling demonstrate high gains in reading speed and comprehension monitoring with explicit fluency instruction and teacher feedback, but with smaller effect sizes when using AI tools without teacher interference.

At the reading comprehension stage, AI stories that incorporate inferential requests within plot lines, where learners must use existing knowledge of the text to make predictions or answer narrative ambiguities, demonstrate specific opportunities in the development of higher-order comprehension strategies (Lu, 2025). The pedagogical condition that is critical in this case is that inferential demands should be scaffolded and explicit and not incidentally embedded, which is a design feature that involves close collaboration between AI system developers and literacy educators.

3.2.3 Narrative Competence and Co-Authorship

In addition to decoding and comprehension, literacy education is becoming more a foreground to narrative competence - the ability to recognize, create and judge stories in a variety of genres and media. AI-based story-telling offers group writing activities wherein students are liberated to revise narrative structures, challenge genre conventions, and explore authorial possibilities in low-stakes situations. These two studies on the teaching of AI-aided writing indicate that the positive outcome (in the form of narrative structure, coherence, and genre awareness) was attained when the students were not perceived as passive users of the AI-generated text but as editors and co-creators (Bircan, 2025; Lo, 2025). Such profits, most importantly, are attributed not to the automated feedback itself but to the dialogic quality of the co-authorship process - the productive tension of intentions of the machine-generated suggestions and learners.

The idea of AI co-authorship, specifically, poses pedagogically generative inquiries regarding agency, originality, and ownership that do not have an easy solution yet are fertile grounds to develop critical literacy. Bircan (2025) discovered that pre-service teachers who embraced reflective co-authorship behaviors of explicitly annotating, critiquing, and selectively revising AI-generated story drafts exhibited notably stronger narrative competence and metacognitive awareness of writing as a purposeful, revisable process compared to those who accepted AI outputs uncritically. This observation implies that AI storytelling can be of pedagogical significance not so much due to its technological nature but rather due to the reflective and critical practices that it can support when incorporated into well-considered instructional frameworks.

4. ADAPTIVE GAME-BASED LEARNING AND LITERACY ACQUISITION

4.1 Conceptualizing AGBL: From Play to Personalized Literacy Practice

Adaptive Game-Based Learning (AGBL) names digitally mediated learning environments where instructional content, pacing, feedback and narrative flow are personalized in real time by the interaction of gameplay mechanics and adaptive algorithms. Contrary to fixed-difficulty educational games, AGBL systems learners not only analyze learner behavior, such as response latency, error patterns, hint use, navigation choices, but also dynamically modify the learning environment to sustain productive challenge (Garzón, 2025). In the context of literacy education, AGBL systems are usually created to scaffold core competencies (phonological awareness, decoding, vocabulary, fluency, reading comprehension, and writing) using contextualized meaningful practice within narrative or problem-solving game worlds.

Theoretically, AGBL incorporates three established frameworks. It is claimed that learning is best achieved when practice is provided within real contexts of activity, not on decontextualized tasks; situational cognition (Brown et al., 1989; Gee, 2003) suggests that games provide learning opportunities by placing literacy tasks within the context of meaningful narrative action (quests, challenges, dialogue decisions). Self-determination theory (Deci and Ryan 2000) is the theory of motivation that states that motivation is maintained when the learner perceives competence, autonomy, and relatedness, which adaptive games can offer via calibrated challenge, meaningful choice, and narrative social worlds. The theory of formative assessment (Black and Wiliam, 1998, 2009) describes feedback as the key component of the learning process; the adaptive games implementation of this concept is based on continuous, embedded, game-state-dependent feedback instead of post-hoc test scores.

4.2 Design Features of Effective Literacy-Focused Adaptive Games

The studies of effective AGBL design are united around some important features. It is based on adaptive difficulty calibration, the dynamic adaptation of text complexity, lexical density and task demands based on performance. Lu (2025) shows that stealth assessment models that are trained on micro-behavioral game traces can detect latent vocabulary knowledge and inferential reasoning skills with validity coefficients that are as high as traditional tests and allows real-time difficulty adjustment based on real literacy constructs instead of proxy measures of engagement.

A second important design aspect is context-sensitive feedback. Garzon (2025) research affirms that embedded feedback in the gameplay either in the form of narrative consequences, visualization of progress, or even in-story hints is more effective at supporting engagement and transfer compared to post-game external correction. Importantly, feedback specificity and interpretability are relevant: ambiguous signals of success or failure generate less learning than feedback that points out the literacy strategy or construct onto which the learner is to direct their attention.

A third important factor is narrative immersion - how deeply the players are emotionally and interpretively engaged with the game world and the characters. A meta-analysis by Alotaibi (2024) established that narrative-immersive games had larger effect sizes on comprehension and vocabulary scores compared to non-narrative game formats, especially with younger learners, which indicates that story engagement has the potential to create cognitive and motivational conditions that support literacy practice. This goes in line with the theoretical argument put forward by Gee (2003) that the concept of identity projection into the game characters intensifies interpretation investment in the textual meaning.

4.3 Stealth Assessment: Promise, Practice, and Limits

One of the most pedagogically important affordances of AGBL is stealth assessment - the assessment of literacy skills based on behavioral traces in the course of playing the game instead of on explicit testing (Lu, 2025). Micro-level data in literacy-based games can be analyzed using machine learning models to draw inferences about underlying constructs like vocabulary knowledge, inferential reasoning, and monitoring of comprehension. This includes response latency, error rate, rereading, navigation, reliance on hints, etc. Since stealth evaluation is integrated into the learning activity stream, it removes the psychic punishment related to traditional testing and allows more predictive inferences to be made.

The recent investigation by Lu (2025) confirms this methodology in a cascade of game-based reading conditions and shows that the models of predicting behavior in inferential comprehension are highly correlated with external standardized measures when the models are well-validated. Borrella (2025) builds on these results to learn analytics dashboards, revealing that explainable analytics, dashboards that transform behavioral data into interpretable instructional indicators, support more effective formative decision-making by teachers as compared to dashboards that display decontextualized performance scores. This pedagogical implication is that the usefulness of stealth assessment requires the interpretability of its results to teachers and learners, rather than its underlying models being sophisticated.

Significant limitations remain. Most stealth assessment validation research uses small, homogenous samples; cross-cultural, and cross-linguistic validity are not determined. Ethical issues surrounding the ongoing behavioral monitoring that stealth assessment suggests are also serious: learners might not be informed that all their gameplay choices are being used to draw inferences to educational conclusions, which prompts ethical concerns of informed consent and ownership of data not sufficiently answered elsewhere in the research literature (U.S. Department of Education, 2023).

4.4 Effectiveness Across Learner Groups: What the Evidence Shows

In primary school and early childhood, meta-analyses prove that game-based literacy interventions can enhance phonological awareness, vocabulary and early reading at educationally significant effect sizes (Alotaibi, 2024). Adaptivity seems especially useful with young learners, as it helps to avoid the frustration caused by fixed levels of difficulty and allows the learners to keep engaged throughout a long practice. In the case of upper primary and adolescent students, adaptive inferential comprehension and writing-organization games have smaller yet significant effects, and it was found that teacher-mediated reflection is a reliable effect size moderator (Garzón, 2025).

There is still partial evidence of multilinguals and learners with learning disabilities. Preliminary research indicates that English language learners might experience less of a barrier to comprehension with multimodal adaptive games, which feature audio narration, visual scaffolding, and adjustable pacing, and start acquiring vocabulary more quickly than in text-only conditions (Wang et al., 2024). The body of research on learners with a dyslexia or other reading disorder is especially limited; systematic reviews have no large, well-powered studies on the effectiveness of AGBL in neurodiverse populations (Garzón, 2025). The point of difference is not just methodological but an underscoring of how long AI literacy tool development has been historically focused on neurotypical, English-dominant learner models, a structural injustice that design practice and funding priorities need to tackle.

5. AI-POWERED FEEDBACK, WRITING INSTRUCTION, AND FORMATIVE ASSESSMENT

5.1 The Architecture of AI Feedback in Writing

Feedback is one of the most effective variables in the development of writing competence, and decades of studies have confirmed that timely, specific and action-oriented feedback leads to a significantly better development of writing as compared to delayed or generic feedback (Hattie and Timperley, 2007). The AI-based feedback systems increase the bandwidth and immediacy of feedback learners obtain, automating the response on the levels of linguistic complexity that were previously available only in a one-on-one tutoring. Modern AI applications in education usually provide feedback on three simultaneous registers: surface-level feedback that focuses on orthography, grammar, punctuation, and syntactic accuracy; discourse-level feedback that focuses on cohesion, paragraph structure, topic development, and genre conventions; and strategic/metacognitive feedback that reminds learners of audience, purpose, and argumentative clarity (Wang et al., 2024).

The most widely studied and longest history of evidence on the accuracy of automated writing evaluation is surface-level feedback. The more pedagogically ambitious and empirically promising is discourse-level feedback: Lo (2025) finds that AI feedback systems that focus on structural coherence and genre awareness are more effective in enhancing the overall quality of student writing, especially with writers in middle and secondary school who are already beyond the basic decoding issues. Strategic feedback is the most technically difficult and pedagogical contingent: Bircan (2025) discovers that AI-prompted strategic hints enhance writing quality, but only when teachers mediate the interaction between the learner and the hint, eliciting a clear response of whether and why the suggestions apply to the writer communicative purpose.

5.2 Iterative Revision and Process-Oriented Writing Instruction

The modern theory of writing views composition as a recursive act of planning, writing, revising and editing, where revision is not an end-of-the-line corrective action but a generative aspect of writing evolution (Flower and Hayes, 1981). This orientation is structurally compatible with AI feedback systems: a feedback system can offer quick formative feedback at various points in the composing process, allowing an iterative cycle of revision, which a teacher cannot maintain at scale. In a randomized controlled trial by Zhang (2025), students who performed on AI-generated feedback combined with teacher-led revision workshops demonstrated a significantly more significant improvement in argumentative coherence estimated by using validated analytic rubrics compared to those who only received AI feedback or only received conventional instruction, with moderate-range effect sizes (d = 0.48).

The learning outcomes on literacy education are not limited to the cognitive ones. Computer-assisted revision can alleviate anxiety levels in writers confronting high-stakes writing activities by making revision a routine instead of a performance, keeping the writer engaged through less waiting time, and establishing an environment where writers with low confidence in their revisioning skills gain revision experience that they would not in the absence of AI assistance (Lo, 2025). The researchers have continued to warn, though, that motivational benefits depend on whether learners are placed in the position of critical users of AI feedback instead of passive consumers: when AI recommendations are not evaluated and instead accepted as true, the metacognitive benefits of revision (reflection on own writing decisions) are lost (Wang et al., 2024; Mills, 2024).

5.3 Learning Analytics and Formative Assessment in Literacy

Learning analytics dashboards (LADs) - AI systems that combine and visualize patterns in writing behavior of learners over time - are becoming increasingly popular in literacy classrooms. In the case of literacy instruction, the metrics such as revision frequency, lexical diversity, sentence complexity, genre adherence and correspondence to rubric criteria are relevant. These dashboards, when interpretively designed, can facilitate the cycles of formative assessment by allowing teachers to diagnose learning needs, distinguish patterns within the classroom, and focus on an instructional intervention (Borrella, 2025).

A research into explainable learning analytics dashboards by Khelifi (2024) concluded that systems that delivered interpretive guidance, i.e., informing about the meaning of patterns, the reasons why they are important in the development of literacy, and what instructional actions the patterns imply, yielded far more effective teacher decision-making and learner self-regulation than those that only reported uncontextualized metrics. This result relates to more general principles of formative assessment theory: feedback, whether to teachers or learners, must be actionable - related to concrete, revisable practices - to bring about learning change (Black and Wiliam, 2009).

The validity is also questionable with the incorporation of AI analytics and formative assessment. Writing dimensions that are quantifiable and are represented by automated metrics, such as sentence length, lexical frequency, cohesion markers, and consistently do not measure dimensions that are qualitatively central to literacy: voice, creativity, cultural appropriateness, and rhetorical situational judgment (Wang et al., 2024). Policy guideline by large learning institutions, therefore, indicates the presence of human-in-the-loop assessment systems, in which AI provides diagnostic support and instructors continue to have interpretive authority over high-stakes teaching and assessment options (U.S. Department of Education, 2023). This division of labor is not merely a precautionary measure but the pedagogical necessity: the devaluation of writing analysis to quantifiable proxies is sure to result in learners who will be maximizing towards algorithmic acceptance rather than actual communicative capacity.

6. EQUITY, ACCESSIBILITY, AND CULTURAL RESPONSIVENESS IN AI LITERACY TOOLS

6.1 Algorithmic Bias as a Literacy Issue

Equity concerns take center stage in any serious academic interest in AI-enabled literacy learning, particularly, given that generative and adaptive systems are developed based on training data in a social world that encapsulates the trends, assumptions, and exclusions of that social world. The analysis of AI bias in education has repeatedly revealed that these systems are aimed at upholding the discourse of the dominant languages and language norms, including Standard American English, Western narrative conventions, and academic register, not to mention that they also pathologize deviant dialects and minority language use (Wang et al., 2024; Sánchez-López, 2025). This bias is exhibited within the framework of literacy as error-correction feedback that cuts vernacular African American English forms of expression into wrongs rather than rightly recognized as varieties of systematically rule-constrained variety; in the narrative generation systems that fail on culturally constrained protagonist representations; and in adaptive algorithms that direct learners with underprivileged backgrounds to simplified contents, according to the partial behavioral proxy.

It is not just a technical issue that should be addressed by improving the training data, although data diversification is required. It is a socio-political issue that is based on the fact that knowledge communities are endowed with the resources, institutional power, and cultural authority to influence the development of AI (Selwyn, 2022; Pangrazio and Selwyn, 2019). The systematic review by Garzón (2025) notes that the bias of educational AI is embedded in the optimization goals of the models to provide results on test benchmarks based on the dominant cultural norms, i.e., unless explicitly counter-designed, algorithmic systems will replicate and intensify the linguistic hierarchies that they are trained on. In the case of literacy education, where culturally normalized and linguistic gatekeeping has traditionally been a domain of power, the stakes are especially high.

Critical literacy scholarship provides a fruitful answer: instead of viewing algorithmic bias as the technical flaw that is minimized, educators can make it a pedagogical asset. By asking students to name instances of AI systems misrepresenting their language use, generating stereotyped figures, or silencing non-dominant forms of narration, students are performing exactly the type of ideological textual analysis defining critical literacy (Freire and Macedo, 1987; Luke and Freebody, 1997). Pangrazio and Selwyn (2019) contend that the ability to critically interpret how digital systems collect, categorize, and operate on information about people, dubbed personal data literacies, ought to be considered part of modern literacy education; AI bias provides a practical and ready-to-use argument.

6.2 Multilingual Learners and Translanguaging Practices

The presence of multilingual classrooms is not an exception, but the rule in most national education systems, and most AI tools focused on literacy are based on monolingual, English-dominant environments. This discrepancy has significant pedagogical implications on learners, whose literacy practices are based on the idea of translanguaging - the mobile movement among languages, registers and modalities to create and convey meaning (García and Wei, 2014). AI systems which punish code-switching, fail to acknowledge the legitimacy of multilingual expression, or give feedback tuned only to the standards of monolingual writing risk suppressing the entire linguistic repertoire of learners instead of capitalizing on it.

Recent studies indicate that AI storytelling systems could facilitate multilingual literacy when configured with adjustable settings to enable the integration of heritage languages, give students culturally familiar narrative prompts, and offer multimodal aids that ease the linguistic burden on students yet to master proficiency in the target language (Garzón, 2025). Sánchez-López (2025) reports that culturally specific narrative frameworks applied to AI storytelling platforms generated greater engagement and more textual output among multilingual secondary learners compared to culturally generic ones, indicating the significance of designing content locally. These results confirm the position of García and Wei (2014), who argue that the effective multilingual literacy pedagogy supports and implements the entire range of translanguaging repertoire instead of the need to assimilate to the norms of a single language.

6.3 Universal Design for Learning and Accessibility

An essential aspect of equity in AI-driven literacy teaching is accessibility. Readers with reading disorders, attention challenges, sensory and motor challenges often face obstacles in digital settings that are speed-focused, focused on text density and limited input modalities. The Universal Design of Learning (UDL) framework (CAST, 2018) answers these questions by endorsing multiple ways of representation, expression, and engagement - principles of design that are evident in the development of AI-based literacy tools.

The UDL principles can be implemented in AI adaptive systems using the text-to-speech feature, customizable font size and spacing, dyslexic-friendly typeface, multiple types of multimodal input (voice recognition, touch-based interaction), and dynamically adaptable pacing. The review by Alotaibi (2024) reports significant accessibility gains when these features are not provided as a set of optional accessibility accommodations but instead implemented as part of the core of the game or narrative structure. The design ethic is that accessibility features must augment learner autonomy - augmenting what learners may do unaided - not to replace the cognitive work that generates literacy development. Garzon (2025) warns against adaptivity that is not designed well, and which accidentally increases the cognitive load or stigmatizes learners by sending them to content simplified to the point of not generating productive cognitive activity.

6.4 Designing for Inclusion: Participatory and Community-Based Approaches

The literature further concludes that AI literacy tools that have been designed, rather than to marginalized groups, are more culturally suited, more easily adopted, and more equitable in their results than top-down tool design (Garzón, 2025; AILit Framework, OECD and European Commission, 2025). Participatory design strategies, where teachers, learners, families and community members are involved in the design process at early stages, allowing the needs of contexts, cultural mismatch, and barriers to accessibility during their design phase. They also provide a sense of ownership and trust that is a precondition to the type of critical, reflective interaction with AI tools that this chapter recommends.

Turning the above into practical design choices, inclusive AI literacy tool development must: be grounded in the multilingual expression; not apply retrofitting to multilingual expression; base narrative content on narratives traditions that are culturally diverse (not biased to Western linear narrative forms); establish participatory content creation processes that enable learners and teachers to add locally relevant texts and characters; and undertake continuous iterative evaluation using disaggregated outcome data, In this frame, inclusivity is not an appendix but a design philosophy that re-organizes the whole development process.

7. CRITICAL AI LITERACY: ETHICS, AUTHORSHIP, AND LEARNER AGENCY

7.1 Extending Critical Literacy into Algorithmic Environments

The widespread presence of AI-generated texts in modern classrooms creates a need to fundamentally expand the critical literacy tradition into the realm of algorithms. Theorized by Freire and Macedo (1987), Luke and Freebody (1997), and more recently Janks (2010), critical literacy focuses education on the analysis of power, ideology and representation in texts - who has a voice, in whose interest, and whose knowledge is counted. Algorithms systems: narrative generators, adaptive games, feedback machines, recommendation engines are not neutral as they are active agents of cultural ordering that both condition the kinds of texts that learner's study, the kind of linguistic forms that are prized and whose voices are suppressed or enhanced.

Modern theories of AI literacy conceptualize the construct as multidimensional including conceptual knowledge (how AI systems work technically), procedural skills (how to use and query them), and ethical dispositions (how to assess bias, accountability, and social impact) (Mills, 2024; AILit Framework, OECD and European Commission, 2025). What the critical literacy tradition has added is the necessity of the ethical dispositions component not being an appendix but the guiding center: learners need to learn the habit of the skeptical, curious, ethically oriented approach to the reading of AI-generated texts not as the authority or the neutrality algorithm. The argument by Selwyn (2022) that education should not only equip students to use AI but ask and oppose its colonization of learning spaces aligns with this orientation and provides the political urgency to what otherwise could be an agenda of technical skills.

7.2 Authorship, Co-Creation, and the Pedagogy of Revision

The co-authorship of AI provokes philosophically challenging and pedagogically generative questions of originality, intent, and ownership. By co-writing texts with AI systems, the agency of humans and machine in the generation of meaning is less demarcated, making traditional assessment practices and cultural expectations of creative authorship challenging (Mills, 2024). Instead of seeing this blurring as something that needs to be legislated out, recent scholarship suggests that co-authorship should be embraced as a pedagogical possibility - as a place where the writing process itself becomes observable, debatable and pedagogical (Bircan, 2025; Zhang, 2025).

This stand is supported by empirical research. Zhang (2025) established that students who practiced reflective co-authorship (formally annotating, critiquing and selectively revising AI-generated text snippets) exhibited much greater metacognitive awareness of writing as a rewritable purposeful process, and much greater control over narrative structure than students who used AI assistance without critically reflecting. Bircan (2025) finds similar results with pre-service teachers; she claims that reflective co-authorship produces what she calls authorial agency literacy - an advanced sense of writing as a form of consequence construction and not machine-like production. The findings are directly applicable to the pedagogy of writing: AI must not be presented as the creator of student work, but rather as a generative interlocutor that fosters, challenges, and encourages explicit authorial judgments.

7.3 Developing Learner Agency: Conditions and Classroom Practices

The driving purpose of multiliteracies pedagogy and critical AI literacy is learner agency, or the ability to act intentionally, reflectively and self-directedly within the learning context. The research of self-regulated learning confirms that agency is developed when the learner has real options regarding his/her learning process, when he/she realizes the tools and standards according to which his/her work is organized, when he/she feels that he/she is an active meaning-creator and not an active recipient of the instruction (Zimmerman, 2002; Borrella, 2025). These conditions should be explicitly designed in the context of AI-mediated literacy environments, since, unless redesigned as pedagogical, the default architecture of many AI tools, opaque algorithms, fixed adaptive pathways, automated assessment, etc. can weaken, not support agency.

Examples of concrete classroom practices that build agency in AI literacy situations are: structured reflection guidelines wherein students explicitly assess and justify their interaction with AI feedback;

comparative text analysis exercises wherein learners analyze human-written and AI-written versions of the same type of text and explain the difference; collaborative critical discussion where students discuss whose perspective AI narratives focus on and whose it marginalizes; and goal-setting activities using learning analytics data in accessible formats (Mills, Mills (2024) records that such practices not only enhance quantifiable writing achievements but also cultivate more nuanced critical dispositions toward the algorithmic technology - dispositions that can be of civic worth far beyond the literacy classroom. In this framing, agency is not merely a motivational variable, but a democratic competency.

8. PEDAGOGICAL MODELS AND DESIGN PRINCIPLES: THE EQUITY-AI FRAMEWORK

8.1 From Isolated Tools to Integrated Pedagogical Systems

The common conclusion of the empirical studies reviewed in this chapter is that learning potential of AI-enabled literacy tools lies not in the level of technological sophistication but in the quality of pedagogical integration, the extent to which the AI systems are integrated in coherent instructional sequences in line with explicit literacy goals, formative assessment, and critical reflection (Wang et al., 2024; Garzón, 2025; Lu, Single AI systems that are implemented in the absence of curricular contextualization, teacher mediation, and access to critical reflection always yield superficial results compared to those of systems in which the technology is used, and not replaced by, pedagogically based teaching. The discovery creates the main design argument of this chapter: the answer of literacy educators is not whether to use AI but how to form the instructional ecology in which AI functions.

8.2 Core Design Principles

Based on the theoretical frameworks and empirical evidence derived above, it is possible to describe five interconnected design principles to an equitable, rigorous AI-enabled literacy pedagogy.

The curriculum consistency and the pedagogical congruency dictate that AI tools must be created in accordance with rigorously justified literacy objectives as opposed to generic performance measures. Adaptive logic must be adjusted to the literacy constructs - inferential comprehension, vocabulary depth, argument structure - that can be readable by teachers and learners and be connected to curriculum standards. Both Wang et al. (2024) and Lu (2025) note that the specificity of alignment is a more suitable predictor of learning gain than the complexity of the AI system in general.

Learning analytics, adaptive decision-making and AI feedback must be displayed in a way that is interpretable and actionable, and available to teachers and learners. This research project by Khelifi (2024) demonstrates that, compared to opaque performance scores, explainable analytics or analytics in which behavioral data is compared to literacy constructs and specific instructional responses are suggested can result in much greater pedagogical effectiveness. Transparency also is ethically a surveillance check: by making adaptive logic transparent and visible, both learners and educators can question the power of algorithms rather than accept it unquestioningly.

Human-in-the-loop governance demands educators to maintain interpretive control over the assessment decisions, instructional choices and ethical judgments. AI is used as a diagnostic and scaffolding tool; the teacher interprets, contextualizes and takes actions based on the information produced by AI without losing oversight of the overall educational experience of the learner. Both the empirical data on the limitations of AI and the ethical reasoning that the consequences of such decisions on the educational path of learners must include human judgment support this principle (U.S. Department of Education, 2023).

Cultural responsiveness and inclusivity demand that AI literacy products be designed to support linguistic diversity and support non-dominant narrative traditions and have accessibility features designed in, not as an add-on. The architecture must both incorporate UDL principles (CAST, 2018) and not be an optional accessibility accommodation. The best way to attain authentic cultural responsiveness is through participatory design processes, which include stakeholders in the community (Garzón, 2025).

The integration of AI literacy implies that AI-based literacy pedagogy needs to explicitly develop the ability of students to question the functioning of algorithmic systems: what they assume, what their biases are, and what impacts whose voices and knowledge are appreciated. Instead of positioning critical AI literacy as a discrete curricular strand, the most successful applications incorporate critical inquiry into daily literacy practices: comparative text analysis, bias detection, reflective co-authorship, and organized discussion of the social and political aspects of AI (Mills, 2024; Selwyn, 2022).

8.3 The EQUITY-AI Pedagogical Model

This chapter presents the EQUITY-AI Pedagogical Model as an innovative integrative framework to support the application of AI-enabled literacy instructions in equitable, critically based, and pedagogically consistent fashions. The model applies the above five design principles into a working acronym system of six interdependent components:

E—Embed: AI applications into explicit literacy aims and teaching series to make certain that adaptive reasoning is applied to particular, confirmed learning aims, instead of general performance indicators.

Q — Qualify: content and feedback in teacher mediated and contextual judgement, retaining human control over the meaning of analytics and the customization of AI recommendations to the needs of individual learners.

U—Unpack: algorithmic processes, authorship suppositions, and representational biases by structuring critical discussion, making AI-generated texts a location of ideological analysis instead of a location of delivery of neutral information.

I—Include: various languages, cultures and access requirements by using participatory design, UDL integration and culturally responsive content management that authenticates non-dominant narrative practices.

T — Transparency: in analytics, adaptive logic, data use, making sure learners and teachers can understand how AI systems make decisions, use learner data and influence learning space.

Y — Yield authority: to high-stakes instructional and assessment decisions on the part of human educators and to authentic choices on the part of learners, without agency being sacrificed as a democratic right or a pedagogical by-word.

The EQUITY-AI model places AI-enabled story telling and adaptive games not in opposition to human literacy pedagogy but as pedagogical companions whose usefulness is achieved based on the quality of the human educational ecosystem in which they are found. The classroom implementation according to this model has a cyclic structure: explicit literacy goals are introduced, an AI-driven practice is provided, either by telling stories or playing a game; a teacher-mediated reflection, followed by focused instruction based on the analytics data, formative assessment, and critical inquiry into AI processes embedded into the literacy practice. It is an iterative cycle, in which the analytics data and teacher observation inform further instructional choices.

8.4 Teacher Professional Development and Institutional Conditions

The effectiveness of the EQUITY-AI model depends solely on the professional knowledge of the implementing educators and the support of the institutions. Studies have repeatedly reported that AI tools are either under- or overused when not supported by ongoing, context-oriented professional development: teachers do not just need help with the technical functionality of platforms but with the interpretive literacy to understand analytics critically, provide pedagogical mediation of AI feedback, and incorporate critical AI literacy into current curriculum frameworks (Digital Promise, 2024; Wang et al., 2024).

The AI literacy framework of teachers in AI-enabled settings presented by Digital Promise (2024) includes three domains of teacher professional learning: conceptual knowledge about how AI systems operate, their constraints; pedagogical knowledge about how to design AI-based learning experiences; critical disposition, which involves the ability to assess AI tools in terms of bias, equity, and alignment with educational values. The framework is partitioned into three parts, which are designed to correspond to the competencies that the EQUITY-AI model demands and recommend that teacher education programs and school-based professional development systems be redesigned to consider all three domains, rather than the first one.

9. METHODOLOGICAL FRAMEWORK FOR EVALUATING AI-ENABLED LITERACY INTERVENTIONS

9.1 The Current State of the Evidence Base

The rate of proliferation of AI-enabled tools in literacy education has far exceeded the creation of rigorous, longitudinal, and equity-oriented evaluation studies. One of the most extensive systematic reviews and bibliometric analyses of AI in education studies by Wang et al. (2024) finds that such a methodological limitation as short intervention periods, limited sample sizes, lack of outcome variety, and insufficient consideration of the varying impact on different classes of learners are persistent. A parallel review of adaptive literacy learning systems by Garzon (2025) agrees with these results, providing some remarkable lack of real randomized controlled trials with sufficient power and pre-registration.

The limitations are consequential in that they restrict the claims that can be made about AI-enabled literacy tools that can be legitimately made about their effectiveness and about their implications of equity. Systematic reviews have the potential to determine regularities in the evidence available, but they cannot address the systematic lack of this kind of study to generate causal arguments about the long-term learning outcomes of different populations. To develop a more sufficient evidence base, researchers and funders need to invest in the methodology.

9.2 Recommended Research Designs

The most robust study design to make causal assertions about AI literacy interventions is cluster randomized controlled trials in which classes or schools are placed in varied conditions rather than individual students and does not interfere with natural groupings in instruction and does not contaminate. Where the practicality of true randomization is not met, there are reasonable causal leverage in quasi-experimental designs using propensity score matching and interrupted time-series designs (Wang et al., 2024). Of note, experimental designs will be pre-registered with hypotheses and primary outcomes, publicly share attrition and adherence to implementation, and long enough to assess learning, preferably at least a full academic year, to assess learning that is not simply short-term.

Longitudinal follow-up assessments - determining the effects of interventions on literacy several months after intervention completion - are needed to determine whether improvements in vocabulary, fluency, or writing quality are maintained and applied to new types of texts and situations. This is especially crucial to AI-driven personalization, which can yield engagement benefits and transient performance gains without yielding the long-lasting restructuring of cognition that comes with lasting literacy competence (Garzón, 2025).

9.3 Outcome Measures, Equity Analysis, and Ethical Governance

The intensive assessment will demand a set of results that would reflect the multidimensionality of the development of literacy as introduced in this chapter. Interactions between measures of engagement, self-regulated learning and critical AI literacy and standardized and curriculum-based measures of reading fluency, vocabulary breadth and depth, and writing quality (with analytic rubrics with proven inter-rater reliability and cultural diversity sensitivity) should be complemented. The latter is especially significant considering the arguments of this chapter: performance-based assessments where learners evaluate AI-generated texts, detect algorithmic bias, and justify authorship and data usage are the direct manifestations of the critical literacy outcomes that are at the center of the theoretical framework promoted in this chapter.

Equity-oriented assessment should not be added as an after-thought sub-group analysis to research design. By language background, socioeconomic status, learning difference, and gender, disaggregated analyses are crucial to detecting the presence of differentiated effects that may be obscured by aggregate statistics (Wang et al., 2024). The interpretive richness required to comprehend how AI tools mediate with learner identities, cultural practices, and classroom interactions in a manner that cannot be measured with quantitative outcome measures is offered by qualitative methods - classroom observation, teacher and learner interviews, discourse analysis of student texts.

The ethical management of assessment studies must be strictly observed in relation to informed consent, data reduction, information disclosure of data use, and the right of the participants, especially when children are involved, and data to play behavioral games are recorded over a long period of time. Scholars should log and analyze instances of adaptive systems steering learners towards easier material or produce representations that can promote deficit perceptions of marginalized learners, which should be publicly recorded and not hidden in aggregate results (U.S. Department of Education, 2023).

10. CONCLUSION: TOWARD PEDAGOGICAL ECOSYSTEMS FOR ALGORITHMIC LITERACY FUTURES

The chapter sought to take a critically based, empirically based examination of how AI-driven storytelling and adaptive game-based learning may be created, employed, and assessed to contribute to equitable, critical, and culturally responsive literacy development in a wide range of learner populations. The argument presented in ten sections can be summarized in three main claims, which all have implications regarding research, policy, and practice.

To start with, AI-powered literacy spaces introduce real pedagogical affordances: personalization, dynamically scaffolded, iterative feedback, and ongoing formative assessment on scale and frequency that human instructors cannot always deliver. The empirical data are consistent with moderate, and context-dependent impacts on vocabulary learning, reading fluency and writing quality when the introduction of these tools is pedagogical, i.e. when they are woven into a coherent series of curricular activities, mediated by competent teachers, and supplemented by the ability to reflect critically. These affordances are factual, yet conditional: the research literature provides no data on the benefits that can be linked to technology, regardless of the instructional ecosystem within which it is used.

Second, AI-enabled literacy spaces are associated with severe equity threats, which should be handled as a design concern, but not as issues to be resolved once the system is live. The effect of dominant linguistic and cultural norms on algorithmic bias, the modeling of surveillance as an optimization strategy instead of education, and the systematic underrepresentation of multilingual, neurodiverse and culturally marginalized learners in design and research processes are not only technical issues but also socio-political, based on the structure of power that education has long echoed and reinforced. Critical literacy scholarship offers conceptual tools to engage in pedagogy that minimize these dangers as opposed to merely mitigating them.

Third, and most essentially, no human versus machine agency decision is available to the future of literacy education in algorithmically mediated spaces but the building of pedagogical ecosystems where technological affordances can support human learning, creativity, and democratic participation. The EQUITY-AI Pedagogical Model developed in this chapter conceptualizes this belief into a model that insists on critical AI literacy, builds the human agency over consequential pedagogical choices, and designs towards the full diversity of learner populations instead of the idealized center of the distribution.

This argument suggests a research agenda that is challenging. There is a need to conduct longitudinal, adequately powered, equity-disaggregated studies across the whole range of learner populations to which AI literacy tools are being applied. To measure the complexity of the interactions between AI tools and pedagogical settings, learner identities, and cultural practices, methodological innovation, a combination of experimental rigor and learning analytics with qualitative inquiry, is needed. And most crucially, researchers, educators, and creators of AI need to collaborate more closely, with communities and learners at the table since the earliest design phases, in case the tools currently being developed to support literacy education are to be truly useful to the full spectrum of students to which they are aimed.

Literacy has been a place of contestation about whose voices are heard, whose wisdom is deemed important and who has the authority to define competence. This is not a new fact altered by AI, but it does increase the stakes: literacy environments mediated by algorithms are at a scale, pace, and obscurity that both complicates and makes increasingly important the necessity of critical engagement. The pedagogical and academic urgency of this time is to make sure that the architecture of such spaces becomes the product of the values of education equity, agency, criticality and inclusion, as opposed to being left to the technical and commercial logic of the systems that generate them.

REFERENCES

AILit Framework (OECD & European Commission). (2025). Empowering learners for the age of AI: An AI literacy framework for primary and secondary education (Review draft). https://ailiteracyframework.org/wp-content/uploads/2025/05/AILitFramework_ReviewDraft.pdf

Alotaibi, M. S. (2024). Game-based learning in early childhood education: Effects on cognition, social and emotional outcomes. *Frontiers in Psychology*. Advance online publication. DOI: 10.3389/fpsyg.2024.1307881 PMID: 38629045

Beck, I. L., McKeown, M. G., & Kucan, L. (2013). *Bringing words to life: Robust vocabulary instruction* (2nd ed.). Guilford Press.

Bircan, M. A. (2025). The effect of STEM-themed story writing training with artificial intelligence on preservice teachers' digital literacy and narrative competence. *Education and Information Technologies*. Advance online publication. DOI: 10.1007/s10639-025-13625-2

Black, P., & Wiliam, D. (1998). Assessment and classroom learning. *Assessment in Education: Principles, Policy & Practice*, *5*(1), 7–74. DOI: 10.1080/0969595980050102

Black, P., & Wiliam, D. (2009). Developing the theory of formative assessment. *Educational Assessment, Evaluation and Accountability*, *21*(1), 5–31. DOI: 10.1007/s11092-008-9068-5

Borrella, I. (2025). Design principles and impact of a learning analytics dashboard to support student self-regulation. *Applied Sciences (Basel, Switzerland)*, *15*(21), 11493. DOI: 10.3390/app152111493

Brown, J. S., Collins, A., & Duguid, P. (1989). Situated cognition and the culture of learning. *Educational Researcher*, *18*(1), 32–42. DOI: 10.3102/0013189X018001032

Bruner, J. (1986). *Actual minds, possible worlds*. Harvard University Press. DOI: 10.4159/9780674029019

CAST. (2018). Universal design for learning guidelines version 2.2. http://udlguidelines.cast.org

Cope, B., & Kalantzis, M. (2015). *A pedagogy of multiliteracies: Learning by design*. Palgrave Macmillan., DOI: 10.1057/9781137539724

Deci, E. L., & Ryan, R. M. (2000). The "what" and "why" of goal pursuits: Human needs and the self-determination of behavior. *Psychological Inquiry*, *11*(4), 227–268. DOI: 10.1207/S15327965PLI1104_01

Digital Promise. (2024). AI literacy: A framework to understand, evaluate, and use emerging technology. https://digitalpromise.org/wp-content/uploads/2024/06/24cLSR0009-Exec-Summary-AI-Literacy-Framework-Paper_FINAL.pdf

Flower, L., & Hayes, J. R. (1981). A cognitive process theory of writing. *College Composition and Communication*, *32*(4), 365–387. DOI: 10.58680/ccc198115885

Freire, P., & Macedo, D. (1987). *Literacy: Reading the word and the world*. Bergin & Garvey.

García, O., & Wei, L. (2014). *Translanguaging: Language, bilingualism and education*. Palgrave Macmillan., DOI: 10.1057/9781137385765

Garzón, J., Patiño, E., & Marulanda, C. (2025). Systematic review of artificial intelligence in education. *Multimodal Technologies and Interaction*, *9*(8), 84. DOI: 10.3390/mti9080084

Gee, J. P. (2003). *What video games have to teach us about learning and literacy*. Palgrave Macmillan. DOI: 10.1145/950566.950595

Hattie, J., & Timperley, H. (2007). The power of feedback. *Review of Educational Research*, *77*(1), 81–112. DOI: 10.3102/003465430298487

Janks, H. (2010). *Literacy and power*. Routledge.

Khelifi, T. (2024). EX-LAD: An explainable learning analytics dashboard. *Proceedings of the Learning Analytics and Knowledge Conference*.

Lo, J. (2025). Assessing an AI-driven feedback system for extended writing. Computers and Education: Artificial Intelligence. https://doi.org/DOI: 10.1016/j.caeai.2025.100170

Lu, W. (2025). Game-based learning prediction model construction: Stealth assessment in adaptive game-based learning. Journal of Learning Analytics. https://learning-analytics.info/index.php/JLA/article/view/8105

Luke, A., & Freebody, P. (1997). Shaping the social practices of reading. In Muspratt, S., Luke, A., & Freebody, P. (Eds.), *Constructing critical literacies* (pp. 185–225). Hampton Press.

Mills, K. (2024). *AI literacy: A framework to understand, evaluate, and use*. Digital Promise / EDUCAUSE.

Nation, I. S. P. (2001). *Learning vocabulary in another language*. Cambridge University Press. DOI: 10.1017/CBO9781139524759

New London Group. (1996). A pedagogy of multiliteracies: Designing social futures. *Harvard Educational Review*, *66*(1), 60–92. DOI: 10.17763/haer.66.1.17370n67v22j160u

Pangrazio, L., & Selwyn, N. (2019). "Personal data literacies": A critical literacies approach to enhancing understandings of personal digital data. *New Media & Society*, *21*(2), 419–437. DOI: 10.1177/1461444818799523

Rasinski, T. V. (2010). *The fluent reader: Oral and silent reading strategies for building fluency, word recognition and comprehension* (2nd ed.). Scholastic.

Sánchez-López, I. (2025). AI storytelling and narrative evolution in creative industries: A systematic review. *Research Square*. DOI: 10.21203/rs.3.rs-7318246/v1

Selwyn, N. (2022). *Should robots replace teachers? AI and the future of education*. Polity Press.

Shaffer, D. W. (2006). *How computer games help children learn*. Palgrave Macmillan. DOI: 10.1057/9780230601994

Street, B. V. (1995). *Social literacies: Critical approaches to literacy in development, ethnography and education*. Longman.

U.S. Department of Education, Office of Educational Technology. (2023). Artificial intelligence and the future of teaching and learning: Insights and recommendations. https://www.ed.gov/ai-report/ai-report.pdf

Vygotsky, L. S. (1978). *Mind in society: The development of higher psychological processes.* Harvard University Press.

Wang, S., Wang, F., Zhu, Z., Wang, J., Tran, T., & Du, Z. (2024). Artificial intelligence in education: A systematic literature review and bibliometric analysis. *Information Processing & Management.* Advance online publication. DOI: 10.1016/j.ipm.2024.103923

Zhang, K. (2025). Enhancing critical writing through AI feedback: A randomized controlled trial. *Behavioral Sciences (Basel, Switzerland), 15*(5), 600. Advance online publication. DOI: 10.3390/bs15050600 PMID: 40426378

Zimmerman, B. J. (2002). Becoming a self-regulated learner: An overview. *Theory into Practice, 41*(2), 64–70. DOI: 10.1207/s15430421tip4102_2

Chapter 12
Designing Serious Games for Multidimensional Literacy Across Safety, Energy, STEM, and Health:
A Design-Based, AI-Ready Instructional Framework

Carolina L. Recio-Colmenares
Universidad de Guadalajara, Mexico

Roxana B. Recio-Colmenares
Universidad de Guadalajara, Mexico

César Alejandro García García
http://orcid.org/0000-0002-8781-575X
Universidad de Guadalajara, Mexico

ABSTRACT

This chapter examines the role of serious games in supporting the development of multidimensional literacies across safety, energy, STEM, and health domains. Literacy is understood as a situated practice that involves interpreting information, making decisions, and reflecting on outcomes within specific contexts. The chapter presents a design-based synthesis of four case studies, including simulations of emergency evacuation, energy systems, chemical reasoning, and health decision-making. These cases illustrate how structured game environments can support the application of disciplinary knowledge through interaction and feedback. While artificial intelligence is not fully implemented, the designs are prepared for future adaptive extensions. The chapter discusses implications for instructional design, inclusive educational practice, and the use of simulation-based environments to support applied learning.

DOI: 10.4018/979-8-3373-7472-7.ch012

INTRODUCTION

Literacy in contemporary education extends beyond the acquisition of reading and writing skills and is increasingly understood as a situated, multidimensional practice involving the interpretation, application, and evaluation of disciplinary knowledge within specific contexts (Lankshear & Knobel, 2011). In domains such as safety management, energy systems, scientific reasoning, and health decision-making, literacy entails the capacity to navigate uncertainty, reason under constraints, and act upon contextual information rather than rely solely on declarative knowledge. This perspective aligns with research that frames literacy as a form of meaning-making embedded in social, technical, and professional practices (Gee, 2008; Shanahan & Shanahan, 2014).

Traditional instructional approaches often provide limited support for this form of literacy development, particularly when learning involves dynamic systems, risk-sensitive decisions, or procedural reasoning. Learners are frequently exposed to theoretical constructs without sufficient opportunities to observe how these operate under real-world conditions, which can result in fragmented understanding and reduced transferability (Brown et al., 1989). In response, serious games have been explored as instructional environments that situate learners within simulated contexts where disciplinary reasoning can be enacted, tested, and revised through interaction (Clark et al., 2016; de Freitas, 2018).

Serious games integrate simulation, rule-based mechanics, and feedback systems to create environments in which learners engage with complex problems through iterative decision-making. When designed with instructional alignment, these environments can translate abstract disciplinary constructs—such as evacuation dynamics, energy trade-offs, stoichiometric relationships, or clinical protocols—into tasks that require interpretation, judgment, and reflection. Prior research indicates that such simulations can support deeper cognitive engagement when learning activities reflect the epistemic practices of professional domains (Shaffer, 2006; Hamari et al., 2016).

Recent developments in educational technology have also highlighted the potential contribution of artificial intelligence (AI) to game-based learning, particularly in relation to personalization, adaptive feedback, and learning analytics (Baker & Siemens, 2014; Holmes et al., 2022). However, the integration of AI in serious games for literacy development remains uneven, with many implementations still at prototype or early deployment stages. In this chapter, AI is therefore approached from an AI-ready perspective, where systems are designed with structural conditions—such as decision points, feedback loops, and data capture mechanisms—that enable future adaptive integration without assuming its current implementation.

The purpose of this chapter is to examine how serious games, grounded in instructional design principles and conceived as AI-ready environments, can support the development of multidimensional literacies across four applied domains: safety, energy, STEM, and health. A design-based and conceptual case synthesis approach is used to analyze four interventions developed in different educational contexts: an evacuation simulation addressing safety literacy (see Figure 1), an energy system simulation focused on sustainability-oriented reasoning (see Figure 2), a card-based game supporting stoichiometric reasoning in STEM education (see Figure 3), and game-based interventions for oral hygiene and maternal oral health education (see Figure 4).

Across these cases, literacy is treated as situated reasoning that emerges through interaction with simulated systems, constraints, and feedback. The instructional coherence of the interventions is supported by the Dick and Carey model, which provides a structured approach for aligning learning objectives, gameplay mechanics, formative feedback, and assessment processes (Dick & Carey, 2015). Rather than reporting empirical outcomes, the chapter focuses on design rationale and on how game mechanics operationalize literacy processes within evolving instructional systems.

The remainder of the chapter presents a conceptual framework integrating literacy theory, serious game design, and AI readiness, followed by the methodological orientation of the design-based synthesis. The four case studies are then examined, leading to a cross-case thematic analysis, a discussion of implications for inclusive educational practice, and directions for future research. Through this structure, the chapter positions serious games as a viable pathway for supporting contextually grounded literacy development in complex learning environments.

CONCEPTUAL FRAMEWORK

Literacy in this chapter is approached as a situated and multidimensional practice that emerges through interaction with disciplinary systems rather than through the passive acquisition of content. From this standpoint, literacy involves interpreting contextual cues, applying procedural and symbolic knowledge, and making decisions within dynamic environments (Lankshear & Knobel, 2011). This position is consistent with situated cognition, where knowledge is constructed through participation in meaningful activity rather than through decontextualized instruction (Brown et al., 1989).

In domains such as safety, energy, STEM, and health, literacy extends beyond conceptual understanding to include strategic reasoning, risk evaluation, and adaptive judgment. Learners must operate under uncertainty, weigh trade-offs, and respond to feedback within constraints that resemble those found in real-world practice. Research on disciplinary literacy reinforces this view by emphasizing that expert reasoning is enacted through domain-specific activity rather than through familiarity with terminology or isolated procedures (Shanahan & Shanahan, 2014).

Serious games provide environments that are well aligned with this conception of literacy. By integrating simulation, rule-based mechanics, and feedback systems, they allow learners to engage with complex systems through goal-directed action and iterative decision-making (Gee, 2008; Clark et al., 2016). Within these environments, game mechanics function as mediating structures: abstract disciplinary constructs are translated into tasks that require interpretation, evaluation, and adjustment. When these mechanics are aligned with instructional objectives, they support forms of engagement that resemble disciplinary practice (Shaffer, 2006).

Simulation fidelity plays a central role in this process. Fidelity, in this context, does not imply exhaustive realism but the preservation of the functional relationships that define a system. Whether representing evacuation dynamics, energy allocation, chemical interactions, or clinical decision pathways, simulations provide conditions in which learners can observe consequences, test alternatives, and refine strategies through feedback. Literacy, therefore, can be understood as the capacity to reason within these modeled systems rather than the ability to recall isolated information.

Artificial intelligence (AI) is positioned here as a design-oriented extension rather than as a fully implemented component. The interventions analyzed are conceived as AI-ready systems, meaning that their structures incorporate decision points, feedback parameters, and data capture mechanisms that could support future adaptive functionality. This framing allows the analysis to focus on how literacy develops through simulation and instructional alignment, while maintaining a clear path toward later integration of personalization, learning analytics, and adaptive scaffolding (Baker & Siemens, 2014; Holmes et al.,

2022). In this sense, AI functions as a potential layer of responsiveness rather than a prerequisite for instructional effectiveness.

Instructional design provides the coherence necessary to align these elements. The Dick and Carey model serves as the primary framework guiding the interventions examined in this chapter (Dick & Carey, 2015). It supports alignment among learning objectives, instructional strategies, feedback structures, and assessment processes, ensuring that gameplay mechanics reinforce targeted literacy practices instead of operating as superficial additions. The model also foregrounds formative evaluation, enabling iterative refinement based on observed learner interaction.

Taken together, this framework conceptualizes literacy development as emerging from the interaction of three components: simulation-based engagement, instructional alignment, and AI readiness. Serious games provide the environment in which disciplinary reasoning is enacted; instructional design ensures coherence and intentionality; and AI readiness establishes the conditions for future adaptivity. This structure guides the analysis of the case studies that follow, allowing for a consistent examination of how serious games support literacy across safety, energy, STEM, and health domains.

DESIGN ANALYSIS AND CONCEPTUAL CASE-BASED SYNTHESIS

This chapter adopts a design-oriented, conceptual case-based synthesis to examine how serious games support the development of multidimensional literacies across applied domains. Rather than functioning as an empirical multi-case study, the analysis centers on instructional design decisions, simulation structures, and gameplay mechanics through which literacy processes are enacted. This orientation aligns with design-based research, where learning environments are treated as evolving systems shaped through iterative refinement rather than as fixed interventions subjected solely to experimental validation (Brown, 1992; Yin, 2018).

The cases are drawn from ongoing and prior development projects in safety, energy, STEM, and health education. Each intervention was designed using established instructional principles, with the Dick and Carey model providing a common structure for aligning objectives, strategies, feedback, and assessment (Dick & Carey, 2015). The emphasis of the analysis is therefore placed on how design choices translate disciplinary reasoning into interactive tasks that support literacy as situated practice.

The analysis is informed by multiple sources, including design documentation, prototype behavior, formative observations, and alignment with relevant literature. This combination supports analytical inference regarding how literacy develops through simulation-based interaction, while acknowledging that empirical validation remains beyond the scope of the present work.

A key characteristic of the interventions is their iterative development. Formative evaluation played a central role in refining gameplay mechanics to better support disciplinary reasoning. For example, in early testing of the *Molecular Duelist* game, learners tended to combine atom cards based on visual similarity rather than stoichiometric compatibility. In response, the feedback system was modified so that invalid combinations triggered a stability indicator grounded in bonding principles instead of a generic rejection. This adjustment redirected attention toward quantitative relationships, strengthening the alignment between gameplay and the intended literacy process.

Comparable refinements were observed across the remaining cases. In safety simulations, adjustments to crowd behavior parameters improved the visibility of decision-relevant risk cues. In the energy simulation, changes to resource constraints and feedback timing shifted attention toward long-term system consequences. In health-related interventions, progression systems were recalibrated to balance behavioral reinforcement with interpretive decision-making. These modifications illustrate how the interventions evolved through interaction with learners rather than remaining fixed at initial design stages.

Two criteria guided case selection. First, each intervention frames literacy as a context-dependent process requiring interpretation, judgment, and adaptation. Second, each design demonstrates alignment between instructional objectives and gameplay interaction, while incorporating structural elements that could support future adaptive functionality. These elements include decision nodes, feedback systems, and data structures that enable potential personalization without altering the instructional core.

The analysis is therefore interpretative. The cases are examined as design exemplars that illustrate how serious games can operationalize literacy through simulation, rule-based interaction, and feedback-driven refinement. While the findings do not constitute empirical validation, they provide a structured basis for understanding how instructionally aligned, AI-ready serious games may support literacy development in complex domains.

ETHICAL CONSIDERATIONS IN AI-ENHANCED GAME-BASED LITERACY

The integration of artificial intelligence into game-based learning environments introduces ethical considerations that extend beyond technical implementation and must be addressed alongside instructional design decisions. In AI-enhanced or AI-ready serious games for literacy development, responsibility involves not only data protection but also issues related to transparency, equity, learner agency, and pedagogical alignment. As these environments increasingly simulate complex decision-making scenarios in domains such as safety, energy, STEM, and health, the ethical implications of adaptive systems become more pronounced.

Data collection and learner privacy represent an initial point of concern. AI-ready systems depend on structured interactions, decision logs, and performance indicators that may later support personalization and learning analytics. While such data can enhance feedback and scaffolding, they also require clear policies regarding consent, ownership, and use. Ethical implementation demands that learners and institutions understand what information is collected, how it is stored, and how it may be analyzed. In educational settings, this clarity is necessary to maintain trust and ensure compliance with data protection standards.

A related issue involves the transparency of adaptive processes. When systems modify scenarios, adjust difficulty, or influence progression, these changes are often governed by mechanisms that are not directly visible to learners. In literacy-oriented environments, this opacity can shift attention away from disciplinary reasoning toward system-oriented behavior. For this reason, adaptive elements should remain interpretable and clearly connected to instructional objectives, allowing both learners and educators to understand the basis of system responses.

Concerns about equity and bias also emerge in the design of AI-ready environments. Systems built on limited or unrepresentative data may favor particular patterns of interaction or misinterpret learner performance. In domains such as health or safety, this can have implications for how risk or appropriate action is understood. Addressing this requires careful consideration of how diversity is represented within the system, how performance is evaluated, and how feedback avoids reinforcing deficit-based assumptions.

Learner agency is another dimension that requires attention. While adaptive systems can support engagement and personalization, excessive automation risks reducing opportunities for independent judgment. In the context of literacy development, this is particularly relevant, as learners must interpret information, evaluate alternatives, and make decisions under uncertainty. Adaptive features should therefore be designed to support decision-making processes rather than replace them.

Ethical considerations also extend to the broader instructional intent of these systems. Serious games designed for literacy development should not equate engagement with learning effectiveness or present adaptive technologies as inherently beneficial. Positioning AI as a potential extension of the design—rather than as a defining feature—helps maintain focus on instructional alignment and simulation-based reasoning. In this chapter, AI readiness is treated as a structural condition that enables future adaptability without determining current educational value.

In summary, ethical considerations in AI-enhanced game-based literacy involve data governance, transparency, equity, learner agency, and instructional responsibility. Addressing these elements during the design process is essential to ensure that future AI integration strengthens, rather than compromises, the educational purpose of serious games. Embedding ethical reflection within instructional and simulation design supports the development of environments that remain both pedagogically coherent and responsive to diverse learners.

ALGORITHMIC BIAS AND THE PURSUIT OF EDUCATIONAL EQUITY

Algorithmic bias poses a substantive challenge for AI-enhanced educational systems, particularly when these environments aim to support equitable literacy development. In serious games conceived as AI-ready platforms, adaptive mechanisms are designed to personalize feedback, regulate difficulty, and scaffold learning trajectories. Without explicit safeguards, however, these same mechanisms can reproduce or amplify existing inequities rather than reduce them.

A primary source of bias lies in the data that inform adaptive logic. Interaction logs, performance histories, and behavioral patterns capture more than cognitive processes; they also reflect prior educational access, language use, and socio-cultural context. When these signals are treated as neutral indicators of ability, adaptive systems may encode deficit-oriented interpretations of performance. In literacy-focused games, this can surface as early task simplification, constrained progression paths, or uneven distributions of corrective feedback across learner groups.

Addressing this issue requires that AI-ready designs make their assumptions about learner diversity explicit. Instead of optimizing solely for efficiency or short-term performance, adaptive mechanisms should be oriented toward growth, treating learning as iterative and responsive to support. This stance is consistent with views of literacy as situated practice, where competence develops through interaction with disciplinary systems rather than as a fixed attribute.

Bias can also enter through the construction and evaluation of simulated scenarios. In safety or health contexts, adaptive rules may embed simplified or skewed assumptions about behavior and risk, shaping what counts as an effective decision. In STEM and energy simulations, similar distortions can limit exposure to complex problem spaces for some users. In both cases, the concern is not only accuracy but access: who is given opportunities to engage with higher-order challenges.

Mitigation strategies include maintaining a human-in-the-loop structure in which educators retain interpretive oversight. Practically, this can involve configurable parameters, transparent indicators of system decisions, and mechanisms that allow learners to question or revise automated feedback. These features help position adaptive systems as supports for reasoning rather than as opaque evaluators.

Design choices at the interface level also matter. Multimodal representations—combining visual, procedural, and strategic forms of interaction—reduce dependence on narrow performance metrics that may privilege specific learner profiles. At the same time, they provide a richer basis for interpreting learner activity, which can inform more balanced adaptive responses over time.

In summary, addressing algorithmic bias is integral to aligning AI-enhanced serious games with the goal of educational equity. AI readiness should be understood not only as technical capacity but as a commitment to responsible adaptation that accounts for variation in learner experience. When equity is treated as a design constraint rather than a post hoc correction, game-based literacy environments can expand access to complex forms of reasoning and support more inclusive participation.

DATA PRIVACY AND THE GRANULARITY OF BEHAVIORAL TRACKING

The use of artificial intelligence in game-based literacy environments depends on the collection and analysis of detailed learner interaction data. In AI-ready serious games, behavioral tracking enables the identification of patterns in decision-making, strategy use, and reflection that can inform adaptive instructional design. At the same time, increasing data granularity raises concerns related to privacy, consent, and proportionality, particularly in systems intended for diverse educational contexts.

Behavioral data in these environments may include decision sequences, response times, error patterns, navigation paths, and interaction frequency. Although such information can support future personalization, its use is not neutral. Extensive tracking can shift the character of the learning environment, moving it away from exploration toward continuous evaluation. This shift is relevant for literacy development, where risk-taking, revision, and reflection play a central role. When learners perceive that every action is monitored, their willingness to experiment may be reduced.

Not all forms of behavioral data contribute equally to instructional insight. From a literacy perspective, tracking should focus on indicators that reflect interpretation, strategy, and conceptual change. Indiscriminate data collection adds limited pedagogical value while increasing the scope of potential intrusion. Designing AI-ready systems therefore involves selecting what to measure as much as how to measure it. This principle of proportionality helps balance analytical usefulness with respect for learner privacy.

Concerns become more pronounced in contexts involving minors or sensitive domains such as health and safety. In these cases, data practices must prioritize minimization, anonymization, and clearly defined governance structures. It is not sufficient for learners and educators to be informed that data are collected; they must also understand how those data contribute to instructional processes and what limits are placed on their use. Such clarity is central to maintaining trust in digitally mediated learning environments.

Consent mechanisms require similar attention. Formal agreement alone does not ensure meaningful consent. Explanations of data use, retention, and potential secondary applications must be accessible and proportionate to the audience. Where feasible, systems should allow users to decline non-essential data collection without losing access to core learning functions. This flexibility acknowledges variability in user expectations and supports learner autonomy.

The question of long-term data storage further complicates the ethical landscape. While aggregated datasets may support research and system improvement, reuse must remain consistent with the original educational purpose. AI-ready design therefore benefits from explicit governance frameworks that define access conditions, retention periods, and permissible forms of analysis.

In summary, the use of behavioral tracking in AI-enhanced serious games requires careful calibration. The goal of adaptive personalization must be balanced with proportional data practices that preserve trust and support meaningful engagement. When tracking is limited to pedagogically relevant signals and implemented with transparency, it can contribute to literacy development without compromising ethical standards.

ALGORITHMIC TRANSPARENCY AND THE BLACK BOX PROBLEM

As artificial intelligence is incorporated into game-based literacy environments, questions of algorithmic transparency become directly relevant to instructional design. In educational settings, adaptive systems may influence how learner actions are interpreted, how feedback is produced, and how progression pathways are structured. When these processes are not visible, it becomes difficult to understand the relationship between learner behavior and system response, with implications for both trust and pedagogical coherence.

The so-called black box problem refers to cases in which the internal logic of an algorithm—often associated with complex machine learning models—cannot be readily interpreted. In AI-ready serious games, this lack of interpretability can weaken the connection between action and consequence. If learners cannot infer why a particular response occurs, opportunities for reflection, strategy adjustment, and metacognitive development are reduced.

From the standpoint of literacy, this issue is not only technical. Literacy development depends on the ability to interpret systems, identify patterns, and reason about cause and effect. When adaptive mechanisms operate without explanation, learners may begin to treat the system as an external authority rather than as a structure that can be understood and engaged with. This shifts the role of the learner away from active interpretation toward passive acceptance, which is inconsistent with the goals of simulation-based learning.

Transparency is equally relevant for educators and designers. Without some level of visibility into how adaptive decisions are generated, it is difficult to assess whether system behavior aligns with instructional goals or disciplinary expectations. Interpretability supports the identification of unintended patterns, including bias or misalignment, and allows adjustments that preserve the integrity of the learning experience.

For these reasons, AI-ready design benefits from approaches that favor interpretability, particularly in early stages of implementation. Rule-based adaptations, explicit decision criteria, and accessible analytics can provide a level of transparency that supports both instructional evaluation and learner understanding. These mechanisms do not eliminate complexity, but they make the relationship between data and response more observable.

Learner-facing transparency is also relevant. Providing concise explanations of how actions influence feedback or progression can support reflective engagement without requiring technical detail. When learners can relate their decisions to system behavior, the adaptive environment becomes part of the reasoning process rather than an opaque constraint.

In summary, addressing the black box problem is necessary for maintaining both ethical accountability and pedagogical coherence in AI-enhanced serious games. Transparent systems make it possible to relate learner action, system response, and instructional intent, supporting literacy development as a process of interpretation rather than compliance. As AI-ready environments evolve, transparency should be treated as a design requirement rather than an optional feature.

CRITICAL AI LITERACY AS A NEW EDUCATIONAL MANDATE

As artificial intelligence becomes more integrated into educational technologies, the need for critical AI literacy becomes increasingly evident. Using AI-enabled tools is no longer sufficient; learners must also be able to understand, question, and evaluate how algorithmic systems influence decisions and shape access to information. In AI-ready serious games, this form of literacy serves both as a learning objective and as a safeguard that helps maintain the learner's role as an active interpreter of the system.

Critical AI literacy involves recognizing when algorithmic processes are present, understanding in broad terms how data inform system behavior, and assessing the implications of those processes for learning. This includes awareness of how interaction data are collected, how feedback is generated, and how certain forms of reasoning may be privileged within the system. In this sense, critical AI literacy extends existing notions of digital and disciplinary literacy to include the ability to engage with algorithmic mediation.

Game-based environments offer specific opportunities to support this development. Design strategies can make system behavior more visible and open to reflection—for example, by providing explanations for adaptive changes, allowing comparison of alternative decision paths, or prompting learners to examine how outcomes are shaped by underlying rules. When these elements are present, the system itself becomes part of the learning object, rather than remaining an invisible mechanism.

Framing critical AI literacy as an instructional goal also has implications for equity. Learners who are unaware of how algorithmic systems operate may be more vulnerable to opaque or biased feedback, particularly in contexts where prior educational experiences differ. By contrast, learners who can interpret and question adaptive responses are better positioned to identify limitations and engage with the system more critically. This contributes to more balanced and inclusive learning environments.

The role of educators and designers is therefore central. Supporting critical AI literacy requires alignment between curricular objectives, instructional strategies, and system design. Serious games are well suited to this task, as their interactive structure allows learners to encounter and examine system behavior within controlled settings.

In summary, critical AI literacy can be understood as an extension of contemporary literacy education in contexts shaped by algorithmic systems. Embedding opportunities for learners to interpret and reflect on AI-mediated processes helps ensure that adaptive technologies support, rather than constrain, learner agency. In AI-ready serious games, this orientation reinforces the broader goal of literacy as informed and active participation within complex systems.

INCLUSIVE DESIGN AND THE PREVENTION OF THE PARTICIPATION GAP

The incorporation of artificial intelligence and serious games into literacy education introduces new possibilities for personalization, but also raises concerns regarding equitable participation. AI-ready environments can support diverse learners; however, without deliberate design choices, they may reproduce existing disparities in access and engagement. For this reason, inclusive design is not an auxiliary consideration but a central condition for ensuring that these systems benefit a broad range of learners.

The participation gap involves more than access to technology. It also includes differences in how learners engage with content, interpret system feedback, and benefit from adaptive processes. Learners from under-resourced contexts, multilingual backgrounds, or with diverse cognitive and physical needs may encounter difficulties when game mechanics or interfaces assume uniform prior knowledge or modes of interaction. Under these conditions, adaptive systems risk reinforcing disparities by responding more effectively to already dominant patterns of behavior.

Designing for inclusion requires attention to multiple dimensions of learner diversity, including language, cultural context, prior experience, and accessibility. In practice, this involves offering varied forms of interaction—such as visual, procedural, and narrative elements—that provide alternative entry points into disciplinary tasks. Adaptive mechanisms should also be sensitive to different expressions of competence, avoiding reliance on narrow performance indicators that may privilege specific learner profiles.

From a literacy perspective, inclusive design supports the understanding of knowledge as situated and context-dependent. When learners are able to approach problems through different strategies, the system acknowledges that disciplinary reasoning does not follow a single path. This flexibility helps prevent exclusion by validating multiple ways of engaging with complex content.

AI readiness introduces additional considerations. Adaptive systems must be developed and evaluated using data that reflect diverse learner populations. Without this, there is a risk that certain groups receive limited feedback, reduced challenge, or constrained opportunities for progression. Inclusive design therefore requires ongoing evaluation and adjustment, rather than a one-time implementation of accessibility features.

Educators remain essential in this process. Their role includes identifying barriers that may not be evident through system data and supporting learners in interpreting adaptive feedback. Communication about how the system operates, combined with opportunities for learner input, can help ensure that participation remains equitable.

In summary, addressing the participation gap in AI-enhanced game-based literacy environments requires intentional design that considers access, representation, and adaptive fairness. When diversity is treated as a foundational design parameter, serious games can expand participation and support literacy development across a wider range of learners.

INFORMED CONSENT AND GOVERNANCE FRAMEWORKS

The use of AI-enhanced and AI-ready serious games in literacy development requires clear approaches to informed consent and institutional governance. As these environments rely on learner data to support adaptive functionality, questions of transparency and accountability extend beyond system design and into the policies that regulate their use. Consent and governance, in this context, are not procedural add-ons but conditions that shape how these systems are experienced and trusted.

Informed consent involves more than formal acknowledgment of data collection. Learners—and, where relevant, their guardians—should be able to understand what data are collected, how they are used, and how they relate to the learning process. This includes explaining behavioral tracking, the role of algorithmic analysis, and the extent to which data contribute to feedback or future system development.

When these elements are communicated clearly, participation becomes an informed choice rather than a default condition.

Governance frameworks provide the structure needed to support these practices. They define who can access learner data, under what conditions it may be shared, and how long it is retained. In AI-ready systems, this is particularly relevant, as future functionality may expand the scope of data use. Establishing clear boundaries helps ensure that subsequent developments remain aligned with the original educational purpose.

From a literacy perspective, transparency in data use contributes to sustained engagement. When learners understand how their interactions influence system responses, they are better positioned to reflect on their own learning processes. In contrast, unclear or opaque practices can weaken confidence in both the system and its instructional intent.

Additional safeguards are necessary for vulnerable populations, including minors and participants in sensitive domains such as health or safety simulations. In these cases, governance mechanisms should incorporate stricter data minimization practices and oversight procedures. Institutional review bodies or equivalent structures play a role in evaluating whether consent processes are appropriate and whether data practices limit potential harm.

Governance should also be treated as an ongoing process. As adaptive capabilities evolve, consent procedures and oversight mechanisms may need to be revised to account for new forms of data use and decision-making. Static policies are unlikely to remain adequate in systems that are designed to change over time.

In summary, informed consent and governance frameworks are integral to the responsible deployment of AI-ready serious games. By clarifying data practices and establishing accountability, they support learner agency and help maintain alignment between technological development and educational objectives.

CONCLUSION OF ETHICAL PERSPECTIVES

Ethical considerations in AI-enhanced and AI-ready serious games are closely tied to their role in supporting multidimensional literacy development. As these environments incorporate data-driven mechanisms and adaptive features, ethical design becomes part of the instructional structure rather than an external constraint. The issues discussed—bias, privacy, transparency, inclusion, and governance—point to a shared requirement: aligning technological capabilities with clearly defined educational purposes.

Across these dimensions, a consistent concern is that adaptive systems may shift the balance between learner interpretation and automated decision-making. When algorithmic processes are opaque, disproportionate, or misaligned with instructional goals, they can limit opportunities for reflection and reduce learner agency. Maintaining a focus on literacy requires that systems support interpretation, reasoning, and evaluation, rather than replacing them.

Transparency plays a central role in this alignment. When learners and educators can relate system responses to underlying processes, adaptive behavior becomes part of the learning environment rather than an external imposition. Similarly, inclusive design ensures that variation in learner background, experience, and ability is reflected in how systems respond, avoiding narrow definitions of competence.

Governance and consent provide the structural conditions that sustain these practices. Clear policies regarding data use, access, and oversight help ensure that system evolution remains consistent with its original educational intent. This is particularly relevant in contexts involving minors or sensitive domains, where the consequences of misalignment are more pronounced.

Taken together, these considerations suggest that the effectiveness of AI in serious game–based literacy environments depends less on algorithmic complexity and more on the coherence of design decisions. When ethical principles are integrated into instructional design, AI-ready systems can support engagement, reflection, and equitable participation. Achieving this requires ongoing coordination among educators, designers, and institutions, ensuring that technological development remains grounded in pedagogical objectives.

CASE STUDY: SAFETY LITERACY IN EMERGENCY SIMULATIONS

Safety literacy can be understood as the ability to interpret environmental risk indicators, evaluate protective alternatives, and make context-sensitive decisions aimed at reducing harm during emergency situations (Bird & Menz, 2022). In educational contexts, its development benefits from immersive environments that allow learners to engage with high-risk scenarios under controlled conditions. When simulations incorporate behavioral variability, environmental constraints, and time pressure, learners move beyond procedural memorization toward a more situated understanding of risk.

This form of literacy involves interpreting non-linear cues such as crowd density gradients, alarm signals, visibility limitations, and architectural bottlenecks. Such demands are difficult to address through traditional instruction alone. Serious games provide an alternative by situating learners within interactive systems that require ongoing problem solving, hypothesis testing, and situational reasoning (Gee, 2008).

Within these environments, learners shift from passive recipients of safety procedures to active interpreters of dynamic conditions. The ALFIL simulation was designed following the Dick and Carey (2015) model to ensure alignment between learning objectives and system components, including scenario structure, agent behavior, and feedback mechanisms. The simulation models crowd behavior using agent-based dynamics that generate emergent patterns, requiring learners to anticipate how local changes—such as exit accessibility or alarm timing—affect collective outcomes.

Learners experiment with evacuation strategies under varying conditions of panic, density, and constraint. This process supports iterative reasoning, as outcomes must be analyzed and strategies adjusted accordingly. Safety literacy is thus constructed as a situated practice: learners do not simply locate exits, but begin to understand why certain routes fail under specific conditions.

The capacity of simulations to reproduce variability and constraint is central to their instructional value (de Freitas, 2018). An extension of the ALFIL framework applied these principles to the News Divine nightclub incident, incorporating spatial configurations and behavioral features derived from documented reports. In this case, learners engage with a representation of a real event shaped by restricted visibility, crowd congestion, and structural limitations.

Here, the interpretative task is anchored in a historically grounded scenario rather than an abstract model. Learners must evaluate how human behavior, architectural design, and emergency conditions interact, reinforcing safety literacy as context-dependent reasoning. The simulation highlights that effective decision-making depends on understanding system dynamics rather than following fixed procedures.

Although artificial intelligence is not yet fully implemented, the system is structured to capture detailed behavioral data, including response timing, route selection, and strategy changes. These data provide a basis for future adaptive functionality. As noted by Holmes et al. (2022), such infrastructures can support personalized feedback and scenario variation. Similarly, Baker and Siemens (2014) emphasize the role of learning analytics in linking observed behavior to instructional adaptation.

Engagement with the simulation also supports the development of disciplinary perspectives. Learners begin to approach problems from the standpoint of safety professionals, balancing factors such as evacuation speed, congestion risk, and crowd behavior (Shaffer, 2006). This shift contributes to the transferability of learning beyond the simulated environment.

The progression from functional to critical literacy is reinforced through repeated interaction. As described by Nutbeam (2000), critical literacy involves understanding why systems behave as they do. In ALFIL, learners often revise initial assumptions—for example, recognizing that the widest exit may become unsafe under panic conditions. These revisions emerge through iterative engagement rather than direct instruction.

The safe-failure structure of the simulation is central to this process. Learners can observe the consequences of ineffective decisions, such as incomplete evacuations, and reattempt scenarios with revised strategies. Feedback tools, including heatmaps and evacuation metrics, support this cycle of reflection and adjustment (Gee, 2008).

Social dimensions are also embedded in the model. Simulated agents exhibit varied behaviors, including dependency, hesitation, or aggressive movement, requiring learners to consider diverse responses in emergency contexts (Sørensen et al., 2012). Multimodal feedback further supports accessibility by allowing different forms of interaction with the system.

Overall, this case illustrates how serious games, when aligned with instructional design principles and structured for future adaptivity, can support the development of safety literacy as a form of situated reasoning. By engaging learners in dynamic simulations of risk, these environments bridge the gap between theoretical instruction and applied decision-making (see Figure 1).

Figure 1. Conceptual representation of safety literacy development through serious game simulation in ALFIL and the News Divine case. The model illustrates how learners progress from interaction within a risk-based virtual environment to interpretation, decision-making, and reflective reasoning that support safety literacy formation. Figure by authors.

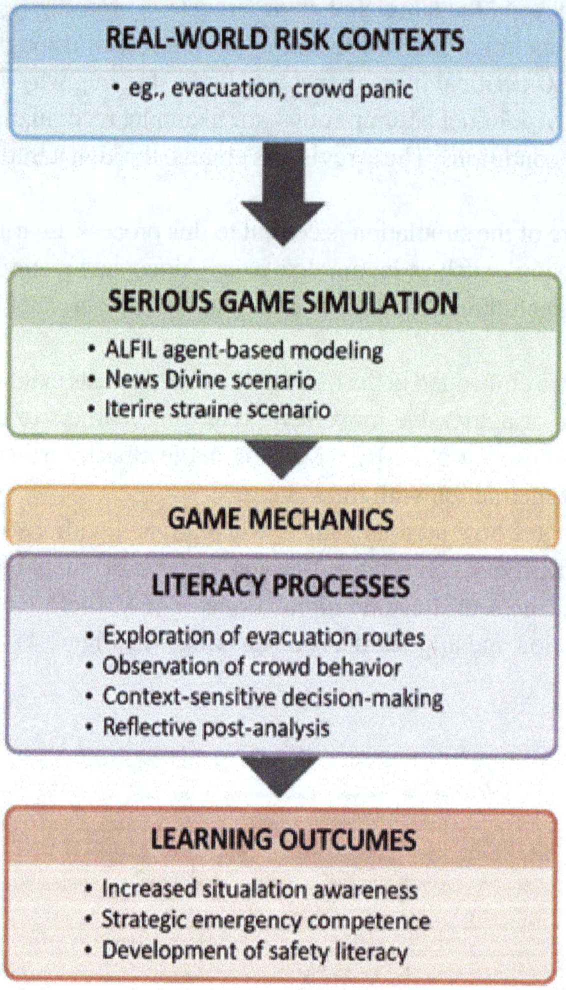

CASE STUDY: ENERGY LITERACY IN SUSTAINABILITY SIMULATIONS

Energy literacy is commonly understood as a multidimensional construct that extends beyond knowledge of energy concepts to include the ability to reason about sustainability, resource allocation, and the long-term implications of decisions within complex socio-technical systems (DeWaters & Powers, 2013). This challenge is often framed through the energy trilemma, which highlights tensions among energy security, social equity, and environmental sustainability. When instruction remains abstract and disconnected from systemic consequences, learners tend to struggle with evaluating trade-offs and policy implications (Cotton et al., 2017).

Serious games provide an alternative by placing learners within simulated environments where economic, environmental, and social variables interact dynamically. In these settings, energy systems are experienced as evolving structures shaped by competing priorities and delayed effects, rather than as static models (Katsaliaki & Mustafee, 2015). This shift supports the development of systems-level reasoning and encourages learners to engage with sustainability as an applied problem.

The Power Grid serious game was designed following the instructional alignment principles of Dick and Carey (2015), linking gameplay mechanics to specific outcomes related to strategic resource management. Learners assume the role of regional energy managers responsible for balancing investments in renewable and non-renewable sources within constrained systems. Decision-making involves allocating capital, responding to simulated disruptions—such as supply fluctuations or regulatory changes—and evaluating the cumulative effects of these actions over time.

A central feature of the simulation is the tension between short-term optimization and long-term system stability. Through repeated gameplay cycles, learners encounter delayed and compound consequences, which highlights the concept of path dependency. Early decisions influence later possibilities, reinforcing the idea that energy planning is shaped by constraints that evolve over time. In this context, literacy emerges as iterative reasoning rather than the identification of optimal solutions.

The simulation operates as a controlled microworld in which learners can test strategies without real-world consequences. Feedback mechanisms—such as emissions trajectories, public approval indicators, and financial metrics—support reflection and adjustment. These feedback loops encourage learners to refine their understanding of how socio-technical systems respond to intervention.

From an AI-readiness perspective, the system captures detailed patterns of decision-making that can inform future adaptive functionality. Although artificial intelligence is not currently implemented, the underlying data structures enable extensions aligned with learning analytics (Baker & Siemens, 2014). Potential developments include adaptive scenario variation, dynamic policy constraints, and feedback tailored to recurring misconceptions. In this framework, AI is conceptualized as a support for interpretation rather than as a decision-making authority.

Inclusive design considerations further strengthen the model. Principles associated with Universal Design for Learning emphasize multiple forms of representation and engagement (Rose & Meyer, 2002). The simulation incorporates visual indicators, procedural interaction, and narrative elements, allowing learners to approach complex concepts through different modalities. For those who find abstract modeling difficult, visual representations of environmental impact can serve as more accessible entry points.

This approach broadens participation by reducing reliance on prior technical expertise. As a result, energy literacy becomes more accessible across diverse learner groups, which is particularly relevant given the societal implications of energy decision-making.

The game also supports the development of disciplinary perspectives. By engaging with trade-offs, constraints, and long-term outcomes, learners begin to adopt reasoning patterns associated with energy policy and environmental analysis (Shaffer, 2006). This contributes to the transfer of learning beyond the simulation context.

As the system evolves, considerations related to transparency become more prominent. Adaptive interventions should remain interpretable, allowing learners to understand the relationship between system changes and underlying conditions. Maintaining this clarity supports critical engagement with the simulation and prevents the system from functioning as an opaque mechanism.

In summary, the Power Grid case illustrates how serious games can support energy literacy by embedding learners in interactive systems that require strategic reasoning and reflection. When aligned with instructional design principles and structured for future adaptivity, such environments provide a coherent framework for understanding sustainability challenges (see Figure 2).

Figure 2. Conceptual representation of energy literacy development through serious game simulation using the Power Grid model. The diagram illustrates how learners engage with contextual sustainability challenges, simulate policy and resource allocation decisions, and apply reflective reasoning to support the development of energy literacy. Figure by authors.

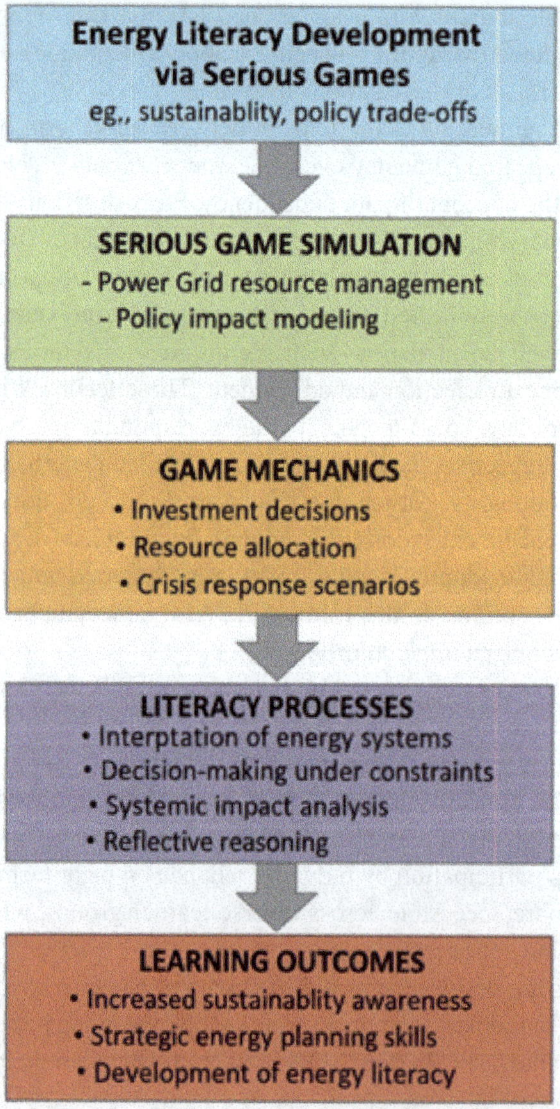

CASE STUDY: STEM LITERACY IN CHEMICAL EDUCATION SIMULATIONS

STEM literacy involves the ability to interpret symbolic representations, apply quantitative reasoning, and model scientific phenomena within context-specific situations (Bybee, 2013). In chemistry education, this competence is difficult to develop due to the cognitive gap between macroscopic observations, sub-microscopic interactions, and symbolic representations such as equations and formulas. This "triplet relationship" often leads to fragmented understanding when instruction emphasizes notation without supporting connections across representational levels.

Without tools that bridge symbolic abstraction and physical interpretation, learners may struggle to construct coherent models of chemical processes, limiting transfer beyond the classroom. Serious games provide an alternative by allowing learners to manipulate variables at the sub-microscopic level while observing the symbolic consequences of their actions. In this context, literacy shifts from recalling formulas to interpreting and applying the internal logic of chemical systems.

Game-based environments support this integration by enabling iterative experimentation and feedback (Qian & Clark, 2016). Chemical formulas become operational rules rather than static expressions, requiring learners to test and refine their understanding through interaction. This approach reinforces literacy as a form of applied reasoning.

The Molecular Duelist serious game was developed following the instructional alignment principles of Dick and Carey (2015), linking gameplay mechanics to stoichiometric reasoning and chemical bonding. The game uses a trading-card–based system in which each card represents an atom or reaction component. Players must combine cards, manage energy constraints, and construct valid molecular structures according to rules of compatibility and conservation.

This mechanic reflects the combinatorial and resource-based reasoning inherent to stoichiometry. Valid card combinations require processes analogous to balancing equations, ensuring that learners engage with underlying chemical constraints rather than superficial pattern recognition. Through repeated interaction, concepts such as valence, molar ratios, and reaction feasibility become operational within the gameplay.

The duel structure introduces immediate consequences for incorrect decisions. Failed reactions result in tactical setbacks, prompting learners to reassess their reasoning and attempt alternative strategies. This process supports the development of epistemic frames associated with scientific practice, as learners begin to approach problems with attention to accuracy, efficiency, and constraint management (Shaffer, 2006).

Scaffolding is provided through progressive complexity and guided tutorials, allowing learners to transition from supported exploration to independent problem solving. This structure reinforces conceptual development through iteration, with feedback closely tied to disciplinary rules.

The system is also designed to capture detailed interaction data, including error patterns and progression trajectories. Although artificial intelligence is not currently implemented, this infrastructure supports future adaptive functionality (Holmes et al., 2022). Potential extensions include identifying specific areas of difficulty and adjusting task complexity accordingly. In this framework, AI functions as a support for interpretation rather than as an autonomous decision-maker.

Inclusive design principles further enhance accessibility. Following Universal Design for Learning (Rose & Meyer, 2002), the game integrates multiple forms of representation, including symbolic notation, color-coded elements, animations, and procedural interaction. This allows learners to engage with chemical concepts through different modalities. For example, visual matching of card elements may provide an initial pathway for understanding stoichiometric relationships before formal mathematical representation.

This multimodal approach broadens access to STEM reasoning by accommodating varied learning profiles. Literacy development, in this context, emerges through interaction with symbolic systems in meaningful settings (Lankshear & Knobel, 2011).

As shown in Figure 3, the progression within Molecular Duelist moves from symbolic interpretation to computational reasoning and strategic adjustment. By aligning gameplay with scientific constraints, the system integrates engagement with disciplinary accuracy, supporting the development of transferable STEM literacy.

Figure 3. Conceptual representation of STEM literacy development through serious gameplay using Molecular Duelist. The diagram highlights how learners interpret chemical symbolism, apply computational reasoning to model reactions, and engage in reflective strategy adjustment, contributing to the development of STEM literacy. Figure by authors.

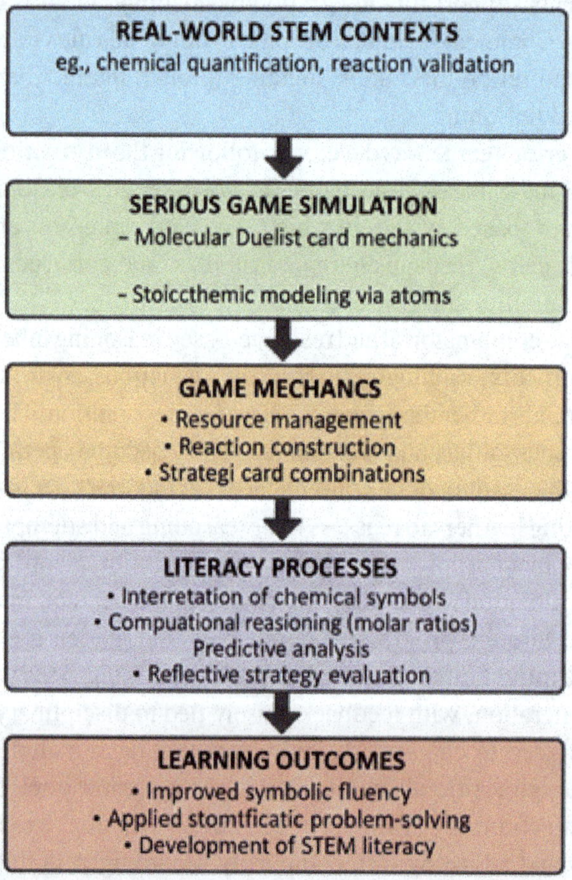

CASE STUDY: HEALTH LITERACY IN BEHAVIORAL AND CLINICAL SIMULATIONS

Health literacy can be understood as the ability to access, interpret, and apply health-related information in ways that support individual and public well-being (Nutbeam, 2000). This construct extends beyond factual knowledge to include behavioral regulation, risk awareness, and the capacity to apply guidelines within changing personal and clinical contexts. Nutbeam's distinction between functional, interactive, and critical literacy provides a useful framework for examining how educational interventions support progressively more complex forms of understanding.

Serious games and simulation-based environments offer particular advantages for developing health literacy by placing learners in contexts where decisions can be practiced and evaluated without real-world consequences. These environments translate abstract recommendations into actionable experiences, reducing the gap between knowing what constitutes appropriate behavior and consistently applying it.

A central feature of such environments is the opportunity for safe failure. Learners can test actions, observe outcomes, and revise their strategies without irreversible effects (Fleming et al., 2020). The Super Sonrisas Digitales serious game illustrates this approach in the context of oral hygiene education for primary school learners. Within a narrative setting, players address bacterial accumulation through simulated brushing actions defined by timing, sequence, and coverage.

This structure reinforces routine behaviors through repeated interaction. By embedding brushing practices within gameplay, the system supports the transition from recognizing correct actions to performing them consistently. Health literacy, in this context, develops as procedural competence, where learners connect biological rationale with practical execution.

The design follows the instructional alignment principles of Dick and Carey (2015), ensuring that gameplay elements correspond to defined learning objectives. Visual indicators, progression systems, and feedback mechanisms are mapped to oral health standards, allowing learners to refine technique through iterative practice. The system functions as a consistent feedback environment, complementing instruction that may be less structured in everyday settings.

A second intervention addresses a more advanced context: oral health management during pregnancy. This simulation-based platform is designed for dental students and focuses on decision-making within clinically relevant scenarios. Rather than presenting guidelines directly, the system requires learners to evaluate patient conditions and apply evidence-based protocols.

In this setting, learners engage in interpretative reasoning, considering factors such as medication safety, treatment timing, and maternal–fetal health. This supports the transition toward critical health literacy, where decision-making involves analysis, judgment, and contextual adaptation (Silk et al., 2017).

From an equity perspective, simulation-based approaches can reduce barriers associated with traditional health education. Multimodal interaction—combining visual, procedural, and narrative elements—provides accessible entry points for learners with different backgrounds and levels of prior knowledge (Sørensen et al., 2012). In the primary-level game, narrative framing supports engagement across linguistic and cultural contexts. In the clinical simulation, standardized exposure ensures that all learners encounter complex cases, regardless of variation in real-world practice opportunities.

Both interventions are structured to support future adaptive functionality. Although artificial intelligence is not currently implemented, the systems are designed to capture interaction data that can inform later extensions (Holmes et al., 2022). Potential applications include analyzing brushing patterns to adjust difficulty or identifying recurring clinical errors to guide feedback. In this framework, AI supports interpretation and refinement rather than replacing professional judgment.

These environments also contribute to the development of disciplinary perspectives. Learners begin to adopt roles associated with health practice, whether as individuals responsible for personal care or as professionals making clinical decisions (Shaffer, 2006). This alignment supports the integration of knowledge, behavior, and values within meaningful contexts.

As shown in Figure 4, health literacy in these interventions develops through a progression from information interpretation to action and reflection. By situating learners within interactive systems, serious games support literacy as an evolving capability grounded in practice rather than information retention.

Figure 4. Conceptual representation of health literacy development through serious games and simulation-based instructional design. The diagram illustrates how learners interpret health-related information, apply decision pathways aligned with professional guidelines, and engage in reflective practice, contributing to the formation of health literacy. Figure by authors.

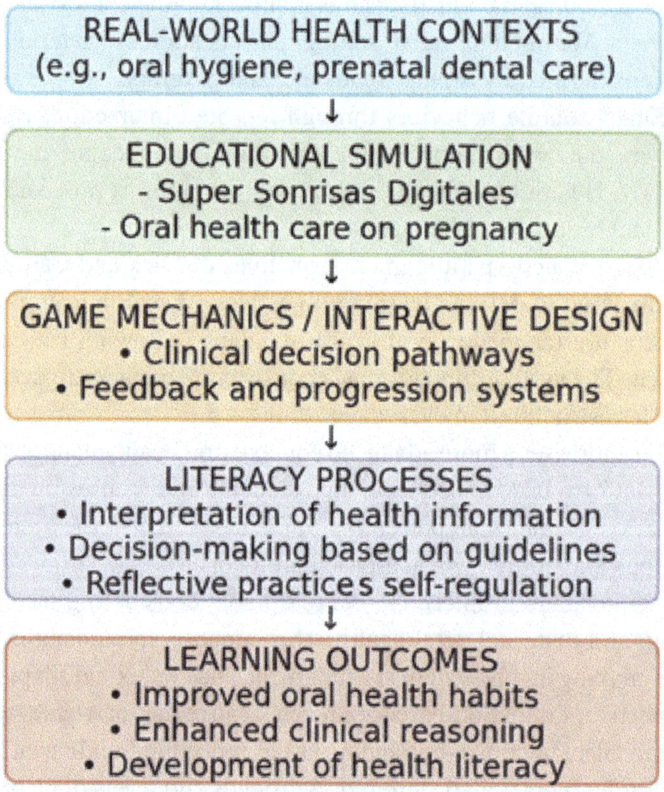

CROSS-CASE INTEGRATION AND THEMATIC SYNTHESIS

Across the four cases—safety, energy, STEM, and health—a consistent pattern emerges: serious games support literacy development most effectively when disciplinary reasoning is embedded within simulations of real-world systems. In all cases, literacy is not treated as the acquisition of isolated knowledge, but as a process involving interpretation, decision-making, and iterative refinement. This perspective aligns with situated cognition, where understanding develops through engagement with meaningful contexts.

Viewed collectively, the cases suggest that literacy is better understood as an adaptive competence than as a fixed outcome. Learners improve their ability to navigate uncertainty, identify relevant signals, and make decisions under constraint through repeated interaction with complex systems. In this sense, literacy develops through use rather than accumulation.

Three interrelated themes can be identified across the interventions. First, simulation functions as a mediating structure for literacy development. In each case, learners interact with systems in which knowledge is embedded within relationships and constraints. Whether the task involves evacuation planning, energy allocation, chemical modeling, or clinical reasoning, the simulation provides a context in which disciplinary logic becomes visible through action. Importantly, fidelity is not defined by visual realism, but by the coherence of the underlying model.

Second, game mechanics translate disciplinary concepts into actionable processes. Rule-based interactions require learners to plan, test, and revise strategies, often under conditions of uncertainty or limitation. This introduces cognitive tension, which encourages deeper engagement with the system. Rather than following predefined procedures, learners explore alternative possibilities and evaluate their consequences, supporting the development of more robust mental models.

Third, feedback structures play a central role in supporting reflection. All cases incorporate feedback—through system responses, performance indicators, or scenario outcomes—that allows learners to assess their decisions and adjust accordingly. While artificial intelligence is not fully implemented, the systems are designed to capture meaningful interaction data. This creates the basis for future adaptive functionality, where feedback could be tailored to individual patterns of reasoning.

These themes do not operate independently. Simulation provides context, mechanics enable action, and feedback supports reflection. Together, they form a coherent structure in which literacy emerges through interaction rather than instruction alone. AI readiness adds a forward-looking dimension, allowing these environments to evolve toward more responsive and personalized systems without altering their core instructional logic.

Overall, the synthesis indicates that serious games can support literacy development when design elements are aligned and grounded in disciplinary reasoning. Under these conditions, learners are not positioned as recipients of information, but as participants in systems that require interpretation and judgment. This shift increases the likelihood that literacy gains extend beyond the simulated environment into professional and real-world contexts.

DISCUSSION

Current research suggests that serious games, when grounded in instructional design frameworks and conceived with adaptive potential, can support literacy as a situated and multidimensional practice rather than as the acquisition of isolated information (Gee, 2008; Holmes et al., 2022). Across the four cases examined, literacy emerged as a cognitive and strategic process shaped through interaction with simulated environments. This aligns with perspectives from situated cognition and the New Literacy Studies, which frame literacy as meaning-making enacted through participation in disciplinary contexts (Brown et al., 1989; Lankshear & Knobel, 2011).

A key contribution of the analyzed interventions lies in their use of simulation to expose learners to the consequences of decision-making before these manifest in real-world contexts. Across domains, learners engaged with uncertainty by interpreting signals, evaluating constraints, and adjusting strategies over time. These conditions support what has been described as productive failure, where initial difficulty within complex problems contributes to deeper understanding when combined with feedback and reflection (Kapur, 2008). Literacy, in this sense, develops through cycles of action and revision rather than through direct instruction.

Game mechanics played a central role by translating abstract concepts into rule-governed interaction. Learners engaged in hypothesis testing, resource management, and iterative refinement, reinforcing literacy as an applied process. This pattern is consistent with research on epistemic engagement, where learning is strengthened when individuals adopt reasoning practices associated with professional domains (Shaffer, 2006; Clark et al., 2016). By operating within these roles, learners begin to internalize disciplinary logics in ways that extend beyond formal instruction.

Although artificial intelligence is not yet fully implemented, its conceptual integration influenced system design and highlights opportunities for future adaptation. The AI-ready structure allows for the potential incorporation of personalized feedback, scenario variation, and learner modeling, consistent with developments in learning analytics (Baker & Siemens, 2014; Long & Magerko, 2020). In this framework, AI is positioned as a support mechanism rather than a replacement for learner reasoning.

Several limitations should be noted. The interventions remain at varying stages of development, and the present analysis is primarily design-oriented rather than empirical. Scalability depends on both technical feasibility and instructional coherence, particularly in relation to accessibility and maintenance. In addition, digital inequities may limit the reach of such systems if infrastructural conditions are not addressed. Finally, literacy outcomes are inferred from design and interaction patterns rather than longitudinal data, indicating the need for further validation.

Despite these constraints, the findings suggest that serious games can support engagement with complex systems when aligned with literacy-focused objectives. By providing environments for interpretation, decision-making, and reflection, these interventions offer a basis for transferable reasoning. Future work should incorporate empirical evaluation, including comparisons with traditional instruction and analysis of long-term retention and transfer.

Overall, the results support the integration of simulation, instructional alignment, and adaptive potential as complementary elements in literacy-oriented education. Serious games are best understood not as replacements for conventional methods, but as structured environments for practice that extend learning into applied contexts.

Implications for Practice and Inclusive Education

Simulation-based learning environments, when aligned with instructional objectives, can broaden access to disciplinary reasoning by allowing learners to engage with complex systems regardless of prior background (Holmes et al., 2022). The interventions analyzed suggest that literacy development is strengthened when learning occurs within contextualized challenges rather than abstract exercises, increasing both accessibility and transferability.

From a design perspective, serious games are most effective when integrated as complements to traditional instruction. They provide opportunities for situated practice in which learners test assumptions, observe outcomes, and refine strategies. This shift repositions the educator as a facilitator of learning experiences rather than solely a transmitter of content. Achieving this requires alignment between literacy objectives, game mechanics, and feedback systems from the outset.

In terms of inclusion, serious games offer advantages through multimodal representation. By combining visual, procedural, and experiential elements, they create alternative entry points for learners with diverse needs. Learners who may struggle with text-based instruction can engage through interaction, using procedural success as a foundation for conceptual understanding. The iterative structure of gameplay also supports differentiated pacing and resilience.

Although AI is not yet fully implemented, the AI-ready design of these systems suggests future potential for personalized support. Adaptive feedback, dynamic difficulty adjustment, and diagnostic insights could enhance learning by responding to individual needs. When applied carefully, these features may reduce inequities by providing targeted support that is not always available in traditional settings.

At the same time, implementation requires attention to accessibility, data practices, and transparency. Systems must be usable across diverse contexts, and data collection must be clearly communicated and ethically managed. Adaptive features should remain aligned with instructional goals, avoiding reliance on opaque or unjustified automation. Addressing infrastructural disparities is also essential to ensure that access to these environments is not uneven.

In summary, serious games designed with instructional coherence and adaptive potential offer a viable pathway for supporting inclusive literacy development. By enabling learners to engage with disciplinary systems through structured interaction, these environments extend learning beyond content acquisition toward meaningful participation in practice.

CONCLUSION

This chapter examined how serious games, when designed through evidence-based instructional alignment and conceived with AI-ready potential, may support the development of multidimensional literacies across safety, energy, STEM, and health domains. Rather than framing literacy as the accumulation of discrete knowledge, the cases illustrate how it emerges through sustained interaction with simulated environments in which learners interpret contextual signals, make decisions, and refine their understanding through feedback. This perspective aligns with contemporary views of literacy as a situated and dynamic practice embedded in disciplinary activity.

Across the cases, serious games functioned as cognitively immersive environments that translated disciplinary challenges into interactive problem spaces. Within these environments, learners engaged in procedural reasoning, decision-making under constraint, and reflective analysis of outcomes. Although the level of technological development varied, the underlying design structures—grounded in frameworks such as the Dick and Carey model—maintained alignment among learning objectives, game mechanics, and formative feedback. This ensured that gameplay operated as the primary mechanism for literacy development rather than as a supplementary feature.

Artificial intelligence was not fully implemented in the analyzed interventions, but it was consistently positioned as a future extension to support adaptivity and personalization. The AI-ready orientation of these systems allows for the integration of learner modeling, automated feedback, and scenario modulation without altering the core instructional logic. In this sense, AI readiness functions as a design condition that anticipates future enhancement while preserving current pedagogical validity.

Several limitations should be acknowledged. The analysis is primarily conceptual and design-based, with limited empirical validation across contexts. In addition, the scalability of serious game interventions depends on technical infrastructure, accessibility, and institutional support, particularly as adaptive and data-driven components are introduced. These constraints highlight the need for longitudinal research examining the transfer of literacy from simulated environments to real-world practice.

Despite these limitations, the synthesis suggests that serious games designed with instructional coherence and adaptive potential can support engagement with complex disciplinary systems. By enabling learners to interpret, reason, and reflect within structured simulations, these environments provide a basis for transferable literacy aligned with real-world demands. Rather than replacing traditional instruction, they extend it by offering opportunities for applied, experiential learning.

In increasingly complex educational and professional contexts, the ability to navigate and act within dynamic systems is becoming central to literacy. The findings presented here indicate that serious games—when designed with instructional rigor and ethical consideration, and prepared for adaptive extension—offer a viable pathway for supporting these capabilities. Continued progress will depend on iterative design, responsible integration of data-driven approaches, and sustained interdisciplinary collaboration.

Future Research Directions

Future research should extend the design-based insights presented in this chapter through empirical validation and longitudinal analysis to assess the effectiveness of serious games and AI-informed adaptivity in supporting disciplinary literacy across diverse learner populations. As most of the cases discussed remain at conceptual or prototype stages, further studies are required to evaluate outcomes in authentic educational, professional, and clinical contexts. This transition is necessary to establish ecological validity and determine whether literacy gains observed during gameplay persist under real-world conditions.

One relevant direction involves the integration of adaptive artificial intelligence to adjust simulation complexity, generate diagnostic feedback, and model learner performance. Research on AI-enabled learning analytics may clarify how personalization influences engagement, misconception correction, and transfer beyond simulated environments. In particular, the "human–AI loop" warrants examination, focusing on how learners and educators interpret and use AI-generated recommendations. This line of inquiry is essential to ensure that adaptive systems support, rather than displace, human judgment and reflective practice.

Further research should also address scalability across educational levels, from primary education to higher education and professional training. Longitudinal studies are needed to evaluate the durability of literacy gains and the extent to which learners can generalize strategies to novel contexts. Mixed-method approaches—combining performance data, process-tracing, and qualitative perspectives—may provide a more comprehensive understanding of how literacy develops through sustained interaction with simulation-based systems. Additionally, the maintenance and updating of serious games should be considered, particularly in rapidly evolving domains such as STEM and health, to prevent instructional obsolescence.

Pedagogical and equity dimensions require continued attention. Future studies should examine how learners with diverse linguistic, cognitive, and socio-economic backgrounds engage with simulation-based environments compared to conventional instruction. This includes exploring design strategies that account for variability in how risk, evidence, and decision-making are interpreted across contexts. Ethical considerations related to data governance, transparency, and informed consent should remain central, particularly as adaptive systems become more prevalent. Empirical research on algorithmic accountability will be necessary to ensure that predictive models do not reinforce existing inequities.

In summary, advancing research in serious games and AI-ready literacy environments requires a shift from conceptual analysis toward systematic, inclusive, and ethically grounded evaluation. Progress will depend on collaboration among instructional designers, domain experts, technologists, and policymakers. Open and transparent research practices will be critical for building a robust evidence base that supports the responsible development of simulation-based and adaptive educational tools.

REFERENCES

Baker, R. S., & Siemens, G. (2014). Educational data mining and learning analytics. In Sawyer, K. (Ed.), *The Cambridge handbook of the learning sciences* (pp. 253–274). Cambridge University Press. DOI: 10.1017/CBO9781139519526.016

Bird, L., & Menz, R. (2022). Developing safety literacy in built environments: A conceptual approach. *Safety Science*, *145*, 105423. DOI: 10.1016/j.ssci.2021.105423

Brown, J. S., Collins, A., & Duguid, P. (1989). Situated cognition and the culture of learning. *Educational Researcher*, *18*(1), 32–42. DOI: 10.3102/0013189X018001032

Bybee, R. W. (2013). *The case for STEM education: Challenges and opportunities*. NSTA Press.

Clark, D. B., Tanner-Smith, E. E., & Killingsworth, S. S. (2016). Digital games, design, and learning: A systematic review and meta-analysis. *Review of Educational Research*, *86*(1), 79–122. DOI: 10.3102/0034654315582065

Cotton, D., Miller, W., & Winter, J. (2017). Sustainability in higher education: Challenges and opportunities. *International Journal of Sustainability in Higher Education*, *18*(5), 792–808. DOI: 10.1108/IJSHE-02-2017-0032

de Freitas, S. (2018). Are games effective learning tools? A review of educational games. *Computers & Education*, *128*, 154–164. DOI: 10.1016/j.compedu.2018.09.017

DeWaters, J., & Powers, S. (2013). Energy literacy among middle and high school youth. *Energy Policy*, *59*, 218–228. DOI: 10.1016/j.enpol.2013.03.057

Dick, W., & Carey, L. (2015). *The systematic design of instruction* (8th ed.). Pearson.

Fleming, T. M., Merry, S. N., Stasiak, K., Hopkins, S., Patolo, T., Ruru, S., Latu, M., Shepherd, M., Christie, G., & Goodyear-Smith, F. (2020). Serious games for health: A systematic review. *JMIR Serious Games*, *8*(3), e17123. DOI: 10.2196/17123

Gee, J. P. (2008). *What video games have to teach us about learning and literacy* (2nd ed.). Palgrave Macmillan.

Hamari, J., Shernoff, D., Rowe, E., Coller, B., Asbell-Clarke, J., & Edwards, T. (2016). Challenging games help students learn: An empirical study. *Computers in Human Behavior*, *54*, 170–179. DOI: 10.1016/j.chb.2015.07.045

Holmes, W., Bialik, M., & Fadel, C. (2022). *Artificial intelligence in education: Promises and implications*. Center for Curriculum Redesign.

Kapur, M. (2008). Productive failure. *Cognition and Instruction*, *26*(3), 379–424. DOI: 10.1080/07370000802212669

Katsaliaki, K., & Mustafee, N. (2015). Applications of simulation within the energy sector. *European Journal of Operational Research*, *245*(3), 543–559. DOI: 10.1016/j.ejor.2015.04.020

Lankshear, C., & Knobel, M. (2011). *New literacies: Everyday practices and social learning* (3rd ed.). Open University Press.

Long, D., & Magerko, B. (2020). AI-based adaptive instruction in STEM education. *Computers & Education, 149*, 103113. DOI: 10.1016/j.compedu.2020.103113

Nutbeam, D. (2000). Health literacy as a public health goal. *Health Promotion International, 15*(3), 259–267. DOI: 10.1093/heapro/15.3.259

Qian, M., & Clark, D. B. (2016). Game-based learning and 21st-century skills. *Computers in Human Behavior, 63*, 50–58. DOI: 10.1016/j.chb.2016.05.023

Rose, D. H., & Meyer, A. (2002). *Teaching every student in the digital age: Universal design for learning*. ASCD.

Shaffer, D. W. (2006). Epistemic frames for epistemic games. *Journal of Online Learning and Teaching, 2*(2), 1–6.

Shanahan, T., & Shanahan, C. (2014). Disciplinary literacy strategies. *Journal of Adolescent & Adult Literacy, 57*(9), 628–631. DOI: 10.1002/jaal.297

Silk, H., Douglass, A. B., & Douglass, J. M. (2017). Oral health during pregnancy. *Journal of Dental Research, 96*(8), 823–830. DOI: 10.1177/0022034517708424

Sørensen, K., Van den Broucke, S., Fullam, J., Doyle, G., Pelikan, J., Slonska, Z., & Brand, H. (2012). Health literacy and chronic disease outcomes. *BMC Public Health, 12*(1), 80. DOI: 10.1186/1471-2458-12-80

Yin, R. K. (2018). *Case study research and applications: Design and methods* (6th ed.). SAGE.

Chapter 13
PLANT-A-QUESTION:
Promoting Environmental Education Through a New Engaging Board Game

Andrea Fernandez-Gutierrez
http://orcid.org/0000-0003-1902-4902
University of León, Spain

Raquel Alonso-Redondo
http://orcid.org/0000-0001-8664-2642
University of León, Spain

Aitor Álvarez-Santacoloma
http://orcid.org/0000-0001-5121-0970
University of León, Spain

Sara del Río
http://orcid.org/0000-0002-0733-2150
University of León, Spain

Giovanni-Breogán Ferreiro-Lera
University of León, Spain

Norma-Yolanda Ochoa-Ramos
http://orcid.org/0009-0005-2869-0511
University of León, Spain

Juan J. Gutiérrez-Gonzalez
http://orcid.org/0000-0002-6795-6192
University of León, Spain

Ángel Penas
University of León, Spain

Alejandro González Pérez
http://orcid.org/0000-0001-6431-4226
Universidad Nacional Autónoma de México, Mexico

ABSTRACT

Ensuring sustained student engagement in the biological sciences is an increasing educational challenge, particularly with regard to 'plant blindness' and limited engagement with climate change. This study presents PLANT-A-QUESTION, an analogue board game designed to promote botanical and environmental literacy, and to support SDGs 13 (Climate Action) and 15 (Life on Land). Based on active and GB learning, the game involves players in collaborative problem-solving and covers topics such as biodiversity, climate resilience, and botany.The tool was evaluated with 86 secondary school pupils and validated by 11 subject experts and educators. The results showed that the game was well received. Expert feedback confirmed its value as a motivational and educational resource. Overall, PLANT-A-QUESTION demonstrates the potential of analogue, game-based learning to encourage engagement and promote environmental literacy and ecological understanding, while emphasising the importance of low-tech, interactive strategies in an AI-driven context.

DOI: 10.4018/979-8-3373-7472-7.ch013

INTRODUCTION

Student motivation is a concern in schools, colleges and universities (Rizkallah & Seitz, 2017; Wigfield & Eccles, 2002), encouraging educators and institutions to explore innovative approaches such as motivational strategies and game-based learning (GBL) to address the challenges associated with maintaining student engagement and fostering a positive learning environment (Alsaad & Durugbo, 2021; Patrício et al., 2018). Recognizing that traditional teaching methods alone are not always enough to engage and excite students, there is a growing emphasis on incorporating motivational techniques and gamification elements into education (Cavalcante-Pimentel et al., 2022; Dichev et al., 2014; Matsumoto, 2016). This shift aims to align educational practices more closely with the evolving needs and preferences of learners, ultimately improving the overall educational experience and promoting meaningful academic achievement (Yıldırım & Şen, 2021). Motivation in the context of education refers to the driving force that compels individuals to engage in learning activities, persevere in the face of challenges, and achieve academic goals (Gopalan et al., 2017; Harandi, 2015). It plays a crucial role in shaping students' attitudes, behaviour and overall learning experience.

With regard to plants, which sustain life on Earth through trophic chains and the preservation of ecosystems, they often go unnoticed due to a phenomenon known as Plant Blindness (PB) (Pedrera et al., 2023). In fact, despite their fundamental role, plants receive less attention than animals in both education and public perception (Balas & Momsen, 2014; Fernández-González & Franco-Mariscal, 2021; Stagg & Dillon, 2022). This insufficient awareness constitutes an impediment to the conservation of biodiversity and the achievement of numerous Sustainable Development Goals (SDGs) (IPCC, 2023; Lavorel, 2013). In this sense, a comprehensive understanding of the roles of plants in climate regulation and ecosystem resilience is imperative to foster climate literacy and promote sustainable behaviours (Amedie, 2013; Desta et al., 2012; Di Sacco et al., 2021; Seddon et al., 2020).

Understanding plant adaptations to environmental challenges contributes to informed conservation and sustainable management, particularly to biodiversity conservation, climate resilience, and the achievement of SDGs 13 (Climate Action) and 15 (Life on Land) (IPCC, 2023). Education is therefore essential for equipping younger generations with the knowledge and skills to address global challenges (Caena & Redecker, 2019). In this context, board games have demonstrated to be an effective tool, enhancing awareness about sustainability, climate change, and biodiversity conservation (Arboleya-García & Miralles, 2022; Vázquez-Vílchez et al., 2021).

This chapter introduces PLANT-A-QUESTION, an analogue educational board game designed to enhance environmental and botanical literacy among learners. PLANT-A-QUESTION addresses the phenomenon of PB through the implementation of collaborative, inquiry-based gameplay experience grounded in scientific content related to biodiversity and climate change. In contrast to the current focus on AI-driven educational technologies, this work emphasizes the pedagogical value of low-tech, socially interactive learning environments as complementary tools that foster engagement, critical thinking, and knowledge construction. Furthermore, the chapter presents empirical evidence validating the effectiveness of this approach in improving student's motivation and perception of learning, particularly within diverse educational contexts.

We modelled the game with the following research questions in mind:

- Is it possible to design a board game with botanical content that effectively engages and appeals to teenagers?

- Can GBL theory effectively address PB and raise awareness among young people about environmental issues such as climate change?
- How does the implementation of GBL theory in secondary education impact the teaching of botany, specifically in terms of student motivation and their perception of the learning process?

Game-Based Learning (GBL)

Since the 2010s, GBL has become a preferred method for enhancing student comprehension and learning retention (Jayasinghe & Dharmaratne, 2013; Xu et al., 2023). GBL integrates both digital and physical games for educational purposes to improve learning outcomes (Dahalan et al., 2024). Play and imitation should not be overlooked, as they are fundamental pillars of children's cognitive development (DeVries, 2000; Vygotsky, 1967). According to Piaget's constructivist theory, different forms of play closely align with stages of cognitive development: practical play supports sensory and motor development, symbolic play aligns with the preoperational stage, and rule-based games foster operational thinking (Ifenthaler et al., 2012; Piaget, 1975). Furthermore, play enhances children's social nature, encouraging cooperation and enabling them not only to reinforce existing knowledge but also to learn new concepts from a historical and cultural perspective (Vygotsky, 1978). In this sense, GBL can be understood as "a type of play with defined learning outcomes" that involves affective, motivational, cognitive, and socio-cultural engagement (Plass et al., 2015, p. 259).

Among GBL tools, board game-based approaches are becoming increasingly popular due to their low cost, high flexibility, and accessibility, offering inclusive and adaptable learning environments for students with diverse cognitive, communicative, and motivational needs (da Silva Teixeira et al., 2024; López Polo & Sotoca Orgaz, 2019; Nautiyal et al., 2024). Evidence indicates their effectiveness in improving the acquisition of key concepts related to health, sustainability, and global challenges as well as in developing professional competencies, including nursing (Camacho-Sánchez et al., 2023; Chiang et al., 2022; Santos Almeida et al., 2024; Uribe et al., 2017). Their impact is particularly noticeable among low and average performing students, improving their performance by more than 10% in low-stress learning environments (Chen et al., 2020). Furthermore, these approaches promote environmental and scientific literacy by facilitating the understanding of complex systems while fostering generic and metacognitive skills, including information management and the ability to handle complex situations (Chiarello & Castellano, 2016; Taspinar et al., 2016).

Furthermore, board game-based approaches represent a favourable alternative to digital GBL resources. Digital game learning strategy has been commonly used in the last years to enhance motivation, especially in digital native learners (Khan et al., 2017; Yıldırım & Şen, 2021). Despite the numerous benefits associated with digital GBL in the classroom, which include content acquisition, deep learning and engagement (Crocco et al., 2016), it is important to recognize the potential drawbacks. For example, excessive use of digital games can contribute to increased screen time, raising concerns about potential negative effects on students' physical health and well-being as well as reduced face-to-face interaction (Khan et al., 2017; Pohl et al., 2009). In addition, relationships that are established exclusively through digital environments are often characterized as weaker or less authentic (Juárez Varón et al., 2023; Khan et al., 2017)., it has also been found that online education generates less interest and connection than face-to-face education (Juárez Varón et al., 2023). In contrast, board games played on a shared physical space, constitute a rich and interactive form of educational experience (Boghian et al., 2019; Su et al., 2022). Indeed, educational board games are designed to reinforce specific subjects such as mathematics, language, arts, and science (Randel et al., 1992), while promoting collaboration, communication, and social learning (Lord, 2001; Manninen, 2003; Willis, 2007).

AI-Literacy and AI-Based Learning Approaches

Focusing on student engagement, new technologies have emerged as tools for pedagogical innovation. Artificial intelligence (AI) literacy has gained importance in recent years, with the emergence of appropriate AI tools for different age groups (Ng et al., 2023; Yim, 2024). Specifically, tools powered by Generative AI (GenAI) and Intelligent Tutoring Systems (ITS) are redefining the state of the art in education by offering personalized learning pathways (Kasneci et al., 2023; Ng et al., 2023). Furthermore, advances in Generative AI and Large Language Models (LLMs) enable the generation of complex problem-solving scenarios and adaptive learning content (Kasneci et al., 2023). These AI-powered tools, utilized alongside Natural Language Processing (NLP), facilitate the simulation of real-world environmental challenges, allowing students to explore cause-and-effect relationships in a safe setting (Zhai et al., 2021). However, despite these advances, there is still a limited understanding of the most effective strategies to integrate AI into classroom practice, particularly in ways that foster active, collaborative, and critical learning processes (Chiu, Ahmad, et al., 2024; Yim & Su, 2025).

AI literacy learning has been exhaustively analysed in higher education, but lesser information is available regarding primary school students and general public (Yim, 2024). Furthermore, research points out that the effectiveness of AI literacy learning has great dependency on the computer science background of the learners (Chiu, Moorhouse, et al., 2024).

Application in Biology and Plant Blindness

GBL approaches have been widely used as resources for increasing engagement in different biology subjects. From undergraduate biology learning, where digital games are proven to enhance knowledge retention, although not motivation (Bónus et al., 2024). To specific and more advanced biology subjects, such as genetics or anatomy, in which different GBL techniques proved useful for increasing engagement, highlighting the analog modalities (Beger et al., 2025; Mohd Hussaini & Saleh, 2026; Seddighi-Khavidak et al., 2026). In the specific context of PB and climate issues, board games have demonstrated to be an effective tool in enhancing awareness of sustainability, climate change, and biodiversity conservation (Arboleya-García & Miralles, 2022; Vázquez-Vílchez et al., 2021).

AI literacy has recurrently been set aside in biology education due to the great differences in the curriculum of this subject. Furthermore, the integration of AI literacy into a biology course does not increase the engagement or biology knowledge of students although it enhances their digital skills (Zha et al., 2025). The implementation of AI tools to assist biology lessons has great potential to overcome typical constraints such as infrastructure limitations, scarce teacher training or implementation costs (Telaumbanua, 2025). However, no evidence was found on these methods for plant and environment subjects.

MATERIALS AND METHODS

This work details the design and subsequent implementation of a novel educational board game focused on botanical concepts. A main objective was to analyze student's adaptability to shifting learning environments specific to each round of the game. Likewise, the research sought to rigorously evaluate the game's impact on student's multidimensional development, focusing specifically on the cognitive, affective, and psychomotor domains. This was achieved through mechanisms of active participation, peer-to-peer collaboration, and critical cognitive reflection. Within this framework, learners are compelled to engage in strategic decision-making, complex problem-solving, and the practical application of theoretical knowledge in a dynamic and interactive ludic setting.

Study Methods

The empirical application of PLANT-A-QUESTION was conducted within the context of the Expociencia UNILEON fair, over two consecutive years (2022 and 2023). This significant public engagement event serves as a vital nexus between university researchers and general society, attracting an annual attendance of over 10,000 students. The overarching aim of this initiative is to foster scientific literacy and encourage entrepreneurial thinking, whilst simultaneously serving as a platform for the widespread dissemination of avant-garde research undertaken by the scientific community at the University of León (ULE). This setting provided an optimal environment to facilitate interaction with a diverse cohort of students spanning various educational levels. Upon completion of the gameplay sessions, a representative sample of students was selected via random sampling to participate in a structured evaluation. The primary objective of this survey instrument was to rigorously assess the participants' subjective perceptions regarding the game's design, its overall acceptability as an educational resource, and the perceived acquisition of learning outcomes.

The final study cohort consisted of 86 secondary education students from Spanish institutions. In terms of gender distribution, the sample included 40 females, 44 males, and 2 participants who identified as non-binary or other. Table 1 presents a complete breakdown of the demographic profiles and academic backgrounds of these participants . To complement the student feedback, an independent validation phase was conducted with an expert panel. A Likert-scale questionnaire was administered to assess the pedagogical and scientific soundness of the game mechanics. This expert panel comprised 11 professionals selected for their diverse multidisciplinary backgrounds, including university professors, representatives from the pharmaceutical industry, and experienced secondary school teachers.

Table 1. Basic profiles of participants. (EP: Primary Education, ESO: Obligatory Secondary Education).

Gender	Age range	Course level
Male	10-11	5th EP
	12-13	1st ESO
	14-16	3rd ESO
	15-17	4th ESO
Female	10-11	5th EP
	12-14	1st ESO
	14-15	3rd ESO
	14-17	4th ESO
	16	1st Baccalaureate
Other	12	4th ESO

STUDY INSTRUMENTS

The Board Game PLANT-A-QUESTION

To develop the board game, we first identified the concepts that the students needed to practice and understand. This study considered previous research about the characteristics of board games that are most valuable to regular players. Based on these insights, we established environmental sciences as the game's central theme. To increase its appeal and foster sustained player interest, we designed the game by combining dice and cards. Each round involves shuffling the cards from different categories on the board, as well as generating random numbers to ensure a dynamic gameplay experience.The game is designed to be played in groups, encouraging collaboration and social interaction among participants. To do this, we first reviewed the curricula of primary, secondary and higher education courses in biology and related subjects for their content related to plants, adaptations and climate change (Consejería de Educación Castilla y León, 2015; Ley Orgánica 3/2020; Decreto 38/2022; Decreto 39/2022). After extracting the concepts outlined in these regulations, we categorized the questions into four groups: Adaptations, Biomes and Ecosystems, General Botany and Climate Change (Figure 1).

- **Adaptation:** Included in this category are concepts such as characteristics inherent to plants that enable their taxonomic classification, their role in vegetation communities and their interaction with the environment, such as tropisms, nastic movements, phytohormones, adaptations to water loss, etc.
- **Biomes and Ecosystems:** This category considers the type of vegetation that integrates forests, grasslands, shrubs, etc. and how they are distributed worldwide based on their climate conditions.
- **General Botany:** Covering a broad spectrum, this category includes discussions on plants, their various parts, and general characteristics. It explores nomenclature, types of nutrition, organs, fruits, seeds, and the overall plant cycle.
- **Climate Change:** This category focuses on the characteristics of climate change, the underlying processes and their impact on life. Special emphasis is placed on understanding how plant ecosystems are affected by a changing climate.

Figure 1. Icon Images for the four categories: (a) Adaptations, (b) Biomes and Ecosystems, (c) General Botany, and (d) Climate Change. Source: own elaboration.

(a) (b) (c)

These four categories are thought to reinforce biological and botanical concepts usually learned at school, to spark interest in topics such as science and the environment, and to emphasize climate awareness by using real data on the effect of climate change. We also divided the questions into two levels of difficulty: the first covering the third cycle of primary education to the 3rd year of secondary education (students aged 10 to 15 years, thus an easy level), and the second covering the 4th year of secondary school to the 2nd year of the Baccalaureate or other general education levels (students aged 16 to 22, a medium-difficult level).

PLANT-A-QUESTION was designed to provide a unique and engaging experience in every round, supporting the dynamic and educational objectives of the game. To achieve this, the tokens in each thematic category and their corresponding numbers are randomly assigned at the start of each round, ensuring varied gameplay sessions that enhance replayability and maintain player interest. The combinations players must follow to collect tokens and achieve victory are determined randomly, forcing participants to continually adapt their strategies. The interplay between randomness and strategy not only keeps players entertained but also fosters critical thinking and problem-solving in dynamic scenarios. In addition, the process of assembling and interacting with the board helps players immerse themselves in the learning experience, making complex concepts more accessible (Chiarello & Castellano, 2016). This approach provides teachers with an interactive tool that fosters understanding and encourages self-learning among students (Taspinar et al., 2016).

The board game pieces were initially handcrafted (Figure 2) and then further developed and enhanced with additional design elements (Figure 3) for printing and lamination. We handcrafted all the elements used in the game and used them at the UNILEON science fair in the years 2022 and 2023, with the intention of participating in future editions as well. There, we were able to interact with a wide range of students from different grade levels.

Figure 2. Left: assembled game board with all its handcraft elements: dice, category triangles, numbers, tokens and question cards. Right: a gameplay session at Expociencia UNILEON 2023.

Figure 3. (a) Game rules; (b) game board panel, category triangles, numbers and tokens; (c) question card samples of the four categories.

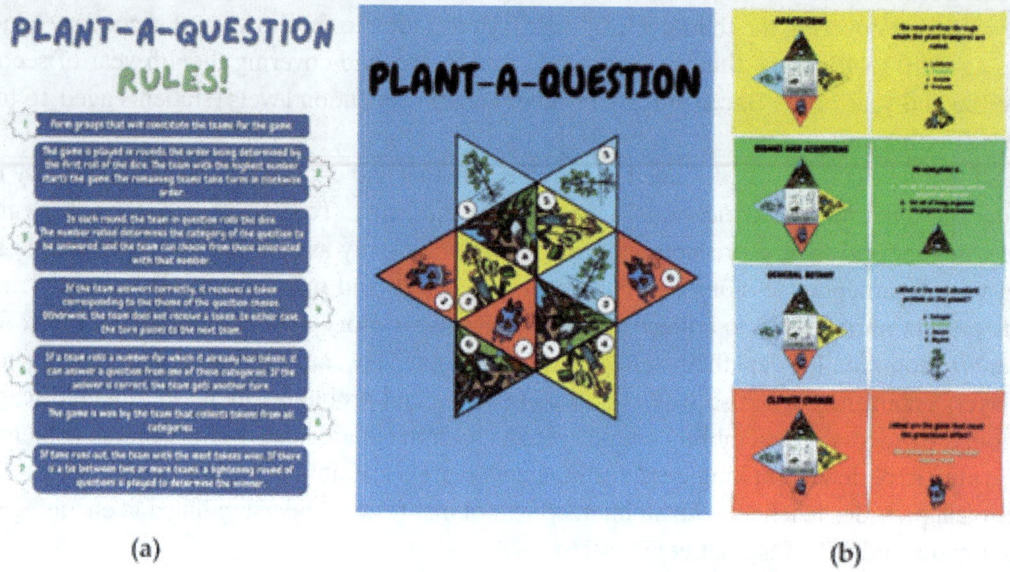

Game rules

The rules of the game were established in order to promote a structured and engaging learning experience for students. These rules were designed to encourage active participation, collaboration, and cognitive reflection, while reinforcing botanical concepts in a playful environment. The game's structure incorporates a series of challenges and learning objectives aligned with educational goals . The rules governing the game are described below:

- Form groups, which will constitute the teams for the game.
- The game is played in rounds, with the order being determined by the first roll of the dice. The team with the highest number starts the game. The remaining teams take turns in clockwise order.
- In each team's turn, the dice is rolled. The resulting number determines the category of the question to be answered. All numbers have 2 different categories associated so that the team can choose one of them.
- Once the question has been read, players of the team have 1 minute to deliberate and choose a unique common answer.
- If the team answers correctly, it receives a token corresponding to the category of the question. Otherwise, the team does not receive a token. In either case, the turn passes to the next team.
- If a team rolls a number for which it already has tokens, it should answer a question from one of these categories. If the answer is correct, the team gets another turn.
- The game is won by the team that collects tokens from all categories.

- If time runs out, the team with the most tokens wins. If there is a tie between two or more teams, a lightning round of questions is played to determine the winner.

Crafting an Effective Survey

A well-designed survey ensures accurate data collection by addressing ambiguity (Anggraeni et al., 2022). It emphasizes data relevance, facilitates analysis and maintains integrity by reducing non-response bias (Evans & Mathur, 2018; Fink, 2011). This meticulous approach improves the overall reliability and validity of statistical conclusions, providing valuable information that aligns with research objectives (Fink, 2011; Widener, 2007). To this end, we first identified the age, grade level and gender. After playing the game, we wanted to know the students' overall impression, their acceptance of the game and whether they felt they had learned anything, so we ask them:

- Rate from 0 to 10 your experience with PLANT-A-QUESTION (0 very bad, 10 excellent).
- Would you play another round of this game?
- If this game was available to purchase, would you buy it to play with friends and family?
- Does playing this game reinforce the knowledge learned in your school or high school? Please rate from 0 to 10 (0 very bad, 10 excellent).
- Finally, to know more about their opinion, we asked them to comment about the experience and the game.

The questionnaire was carried out on a wide range of students, from 5th grade to the first year of Baccalaureate, aged between 10 and 17, during two consecutive years at the UNILEON science fair. For ease of visualization, we summarized the results in histograms and sector diagrams (Arteaga et al., 2012; Fonseca et al., 2015).

In order to further evaluate the competences of PLANT-A-QUESTION, the perspective of botany experts, professors, and teachers was reflected, and a Likert-type assessment survey was designed to consider various aspects of the game. This survey was conducted using the Google Forms platform and consisted of a total of 27 questions, which were divided as follows:

A. Design and Playability:

Q1. Is the estimated time to play adequate for an hour-long educational session?
Q2. Is the level of complexity of the game appropriate for the age and educational level of the players?
Q3. Are the game pieces or elements (pieces, cards, board) of good quality and easy to handle?
Q4. Is the visual design appealing and does it motivate students to participate?
Q5. Does the game offer enough variety of questions to maintain interest throughout the game?

B. Educational Content

Q6. Are the scientific concepts presented correctly explained and contextualised to the educational level of the game?
Q7. Does the game allow for the development of cognitive skills such as analysis, synthesis or problem solving?

Q8. Does the content favour the understanding of the relationship between plants and climate change?
Q9. Does the game provide examples or real-life applications of the topics addressed?
Q10. Do the educational resources of the game (questions, cards, etc.) encourage active learning and curiosity?

C. Impact on Learning

Q11. Do you find that the game helps to consolidate concepts that are often difficult to grasp in a traditional classroom?
Q12. Does the game promote interaction and teamwork among players?
Q13. Does the game encourage students' interest in plants and their importance in ecosystems?
Q14. Does the game include elements of feedback that allow players to learn from their mistakes?
Q15. Do you consider the question of the game to be useful in reducing the phenomenon of 'plant blindness'?

D. Feasibility and Implementation

Q16. Is it easy to prepare the game and explain it to students?
Q17. Could the game be adapted to different educational levels or teaching contexts?
Q18. Is the production cost of the game reasonable for implementation in schools?
Q19. Does the game include a guide to facilitate its use in the classroom?
Q20. Do you consider that the game can be integrated into existing curricula without difficulty?

E. Innovation and Originality

Q21. Does the game bring something new or different compared to other educational resources on plants and the environment?
Q22. Does the playful approach of the game enhance the learning experience compared to traditional methods?
Q23. Does the game include creative elements that make it unique and engaging for students?

F. Suggestions and Open Comments

Q24. What aspects of the game do you think need to be improved?
Q25. What elements of the game do you think are most effective and should be maintained?
Q26. Do you have any recommendations for adapting the game to different cultural or educational contexts?
Q27. Do you think the game could benefit audiences other than students? Who and why?

From Q1 to Q23 the questions consisted in evaluating different game aspects on a scale from 1 to 5, being 1: strongly disagree and 5: strongly agree. The last section, Q24-Q27, was made up of open questions.

Data Analysis

Data were analyzed using descriptive statistical methods to provide an overview of the game's strengths and areas for improvement, based on both student and expert surveys. Metrics such as mean, standard deviation, minimum and maximum, first and third quartiles were calculated for each question to assess central tendency and variability in responses (Prasad, 2023). For example, questions related to the game's ability to enhance understanding of plant-climate relationships and promote the development of cognitive skills received high mean scores, indicating good performance in these areas. A full summary of the basic statistics applied can be found in Tables S1 and S2 of Supplementary Material.

The variability of the scores was examined to identify inconsistencies or outliers, allowing for the identification of areas for improvement. Comparisons were made between questions to explore correlations between different evaluation criteria, such as perceived complexity and adaptability across educational levels. This analysis provided a more comprehensive view of the results, improving the interpretability and robustness of the score assessment.

RESULTS

Students' Survey

A more detailed analysis of the students' survey results (Figure 4) revealed that 88.4% of the participants expressed a desire to play again, while 75.6% indicated their willingness to purchase the game to play with friends or family. In terms of approval, 84.9% of students rated the game between 5 and 10, with 64% assigning it a near-excellent rating, and 33.7% frequently rated it a 9. This consistent rating highlights the consensus amongst students regarding the game's excellence. The results also show that the game is effective in reinforcing and consolidating knowledge, with 100% unanimous agreement and a high rating (9 and 10) of 69.8% (Figure 5).

Figure 4. Sector diagrams of the survey questions regarding whether students would play another game and if the students would purchase the game to play with friends and family.

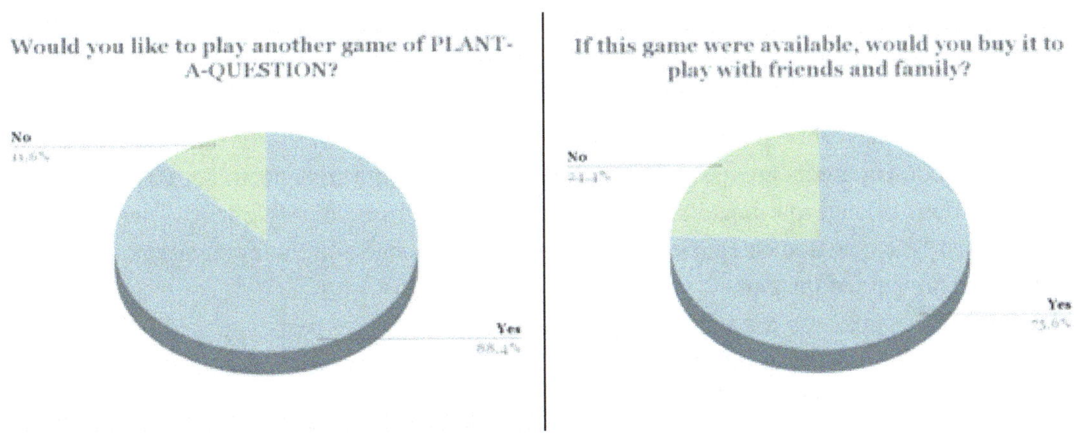

Figure 5. Histograms illustrate the survey questions about the experience of playing PLANT-A-QUESTION (blue, left) and whether the game reinforces the acquisition of knowledge at school/high school (orange, right).

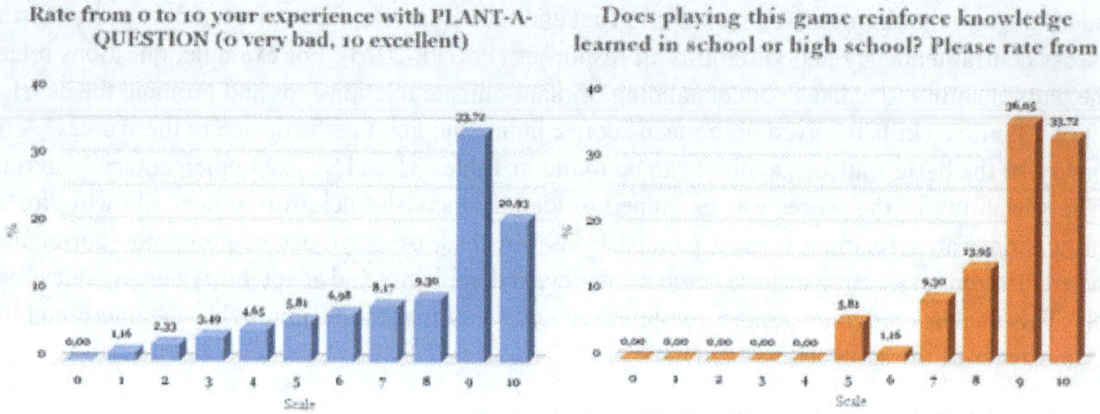

Experts' Survey

Regarding to the expert survey (N=11), the study found that the visual and tactile components of PLANT-A-QUESTION were favourably rated, with Q3, about the quality of components, receiving an average score of 4.2 and Q4, related to the visual design, receiving 4.3 on a five-point scale ranging from strongly disagree to strongly agree (Figure 6). The game's ability to improve understanding of plant-climate relationships was strongly supported, with an average score of 4.6 onQ8. Its potential to facilitate curricular objectives such as critical thinking and ecological awareness was highlighted as a major strength, scoring 4.2 on Q9. Furthermore, the integration of the game into school curricula was strongly supported, as evidenced by the high average score of 4.6 on Q20. The game's playful approach to learning was another aspect that received positive feedback. Question Q22, which assessed the benefits of GBL theory over traditional learning methods, received an average score of 4.7, while Q23, which focused on creative elements, received an average score of 4.5 (Figure 6).

The open-ended responses (questions Q24-Q27), provided a more personalized feedback on PLANT-A-QUESTION. The main points highlighted by respondents were:

- Teamwork and playfulness were often praised by respondents, such as "the teamwork dynamic and its playful content are its greatest strengths", or "they motivate students to actively participate".
- The questions related to climate change were considered to be highly effective, with one expert stating that "the question categories related to climate change and their educational focus should remain a core part of the game".
- Adapting the game was a common suggestion, with several experts suggesting that the game should be digitized: "the design could be digitized for greater appeal and easier distribution, making it accessible to a wider audience".
- Regarding achieving greater participation, it was noted that older learners could benefit from the game: "It would be of particular interest to older adults as a way to keep them active and involved

with environmental issues" and "if the game were slightly modified, it could be adapted for general audiences and even for recreational use in non-educational settings".

Figure 6. Histogram illustrating the average responses of experts to 23 Likert-type survey questions, with values ranging from 1 (strongly disagree) to 5 (strongly agree).

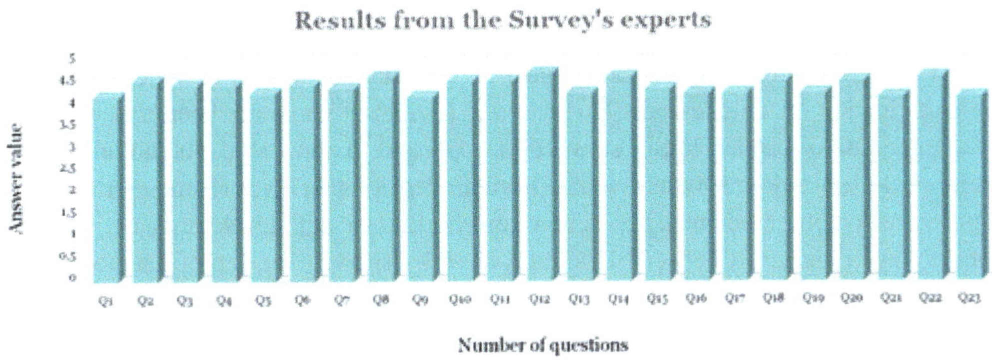

DISCUSSION

GBL and AI literacy have been gaining popularity as useful resources for enhancing motivation and learning outcomes in all teaching environments. Among these resources, physical board games have been increasingly recognized as valuable educational tools, offering a variety of cognitive, psychological, and social benefits (Boghian et al., 2019; Da Silva Teixeira et al., 2024; Nautiyal et al., 2024). Unlike digital interfaces, which often isolate students, board games facilitate face-to-face social interaction, a critical factor for developing communication skills and emotional intelligence (Rogerson et al., 2016). In the context of science related subjects, the learning process has always been considered challenging due to the complex concepts involved. Recent surveys on social perception in Spain indicate that only 12.3% of the population is interested in science and technology and 12.7% in environmental sciences and ecology (FECYT, 2023). Therefore, the main objective of this work was to make a board game related to botany and biology attractive and participatory for students of all ages, combating the supposed aridity of the subject through playful immersion.

With this in mind, the game was designed to be enjoyed in an engaging environment, promoting friendly competition and prioritizing knowledge acquisition through meaningful learning, in line with previous findings (Anggraeni *et al.*, 2022). The game, with its unique board and tokens that players must collect to win, reinforces the idea presented elsewhere (Sezer, 2015; Treher, 2011) that incorporating tools such as dice, coins and points is well-received and popular. These tangible components serve as haptic anchors for memory, allowing students to physically manipulate abstract concepts, which has been shown to improve retention in science education (Zacharia & Olympiou, 2011). This is not trivial, as a recent study has shown that the first impression and aesthetics of a game inevitably influence the final opinion of it (Schlüter *et al.*, 2021). For this reason, achieving an artistic and appealing finish that would capture the public's attention and invite them to play was highly desirable.

The rules of this board game are designed so that individuals of any gender and age can participate equally (Dele-Ajayi *et al.*, 2018). For this, we established two difficulty levels, provided personalized feedback, and offered specific challenges based on the learner's performance (Deeva *et al.*, 2021). This stratification aligns with Flow Theory, which suggests that optimal learning occurs when the level of challenge matches the participant's skill level, thus avoiding both boredom and frustration (Csikszentmihalyi, 1990; Hamari et al., 2016). This adaptability ensures that the learning experience is tailored to the user's specific needs and pace. Each player has an equal opportunity to use their skills, strategic thinking and knowledge, promoting a sense of fairness. Although other studies indicate greater or more noticeable participation by male learners(Farias *et al.*, 2022), our game has been met with unanimous acceptance, regardless of gender. In this sense, it is important to allow students to compete fairly and to prevent more skilled or dominant individuals from hindering others or influencing their decisions, a common phenomenon observed when bonds between children are still developing (Farias *et al.*, 2017). The age of the players, generally between 12 and 15, has been shown to be appropriate for question-and-answer or test-based learning (Brod, 2021).

The survey results have promising implications. The high percentage of participants willing to play again suggests they enjoyed the game, underscoring its appeal for repeated participation. This desire to replay is indicative of intrinsic motivation, driven by the satisfaction of psychological needs for competence, autonomy, and relatedness as described in Self-Determination Theory (Przybylski et al., 2010; Ryan & Deci, 2000). Furthermore, the game's potential commercial success can be inferred from the willingness to purchase it to use it in contexts beyond the classroom and education, denoting both personal enjoyment and suitability in social or family settings. While agreeing on the appeal and adaptability of the design, experts recommended adjustments to the game's complexity to make it more appropriate for different age groups. Simplified question sets for younger students and advanced modules for older players were suggested as practical modifications to broaden its reach.

As Emel'yanenko et al. (2016) suggest, the impact of using games in education is significantly affected by the learner's values and worldview within their specific social context. Furthermore, the gravity of the climate change situation necessitates the creation of a completely new culture that allows students to develop a holistic awareness that reconnects them with their environment (Amran et al., 2019), fostering an ecosocial consciousness (Carbonell-Alcocer et al., 2022). Crucially, gamification offers a safe space to discuss alarming environmental trends, potentially mitigating 'eco-anxiety' by empowering students to simulate positive interventions and solutions (Ojala, 2012; Ouariachi et al., 2020). Therefore, one of the objectives of this work was to assess the feasibility of using board games to raise awareness about environmental issues. Board games and other educational tools have been shown to help improve general knowledge about these topics (Kalogiannakis et al., 2021). Different areas of knowledge and skills have been combined within a single game, allowing learners to develop a holistic understanding of interrelated concepts (Barnett & Jung, 2020; Kriz, 2003).

PLANT-A-QUESTION, according to the experts surveyed, integrates effectively with existing educational frameworks, promoting environmental literacy and interdisciplinary understanding of biology and climatology. It effectively addresses basic concepts such as photosynthesis, carbon sequestration and ecosystem connectivity, presenting these ideas interactively and transcending traditional didactic approaches. Experts highlighted the value of integrating these interactive frameworks to deepen students' understanding and foster an appreciation of real-world ecological dynamics. However, several experts emphasized the need to adapt the content to better meet the diverse needs of local education systems. Indeed, tailoring educational games to specific demographic groups has been shown to significantly enhance their impact (Sandbrook *et al.*, 2015). To increase its relevance, experts suggested including more local examples and thematic modules that reflect the flora, fauna and climate issues specific to each region.

This research analyses the effectiveness of implementing GBL theory in teaching botany and environmental topics in secondary education. Educational games have been recognized as a powerful and innovative learning approach (Noemí & Máximo, 2014), promoting active participation by effectively combining the enjoyment of the game with knowledge acquisition (Londoño Vásquez & Rojas López, 2021). Current research highlights the importance of balancing enjoyment and educational values (Franzwa et al., 2013; Kim et al., 2019), and PLANT-A-QUESTION successfully achieves this balance. Players reported enjoying the experience while simultaneously improving their understanding of the topic.

Through the dynamics of decision-making and problem-solving, the game deepens understanding and facilitates information retention as players directly experience the consequences of their choices (De Freitas, 2018). It also encourages collaborative learning, exploration and critical thinking, and provides opportunities for students to interact meaningfully with the material (Hung et al., 2021). This collaborative element facilitates 'peer scaffolding', where students with greater botanical knowledge assist their peers during the game, thereby reinforcing their own understanding while helping others, a fundamental principle of social constructivist learning (Topping, 2005). During the UNILEON science fair, participants were required to apply their knowledge in a dynamic and interactive environment, which reinforced the game's ability to promote teamwork, communication, and the exchange of ideas.

The deliberate process of answering questions not only reinforces positive leadership behaviours (PSL), which have been linked to long-term benefits in adulthood (Louis & Murphy, 2018) but also promotes social learning. This aspect of shared learning experiences fosters a sense of community, an essential element of effective educational environments (Vlachopoulos & Makri, 2017). Furthermore, study participants responded positively to the rules of the game, reporting a smooth and enjoyable experience without any notable difficulties. These findings illustrate the potential of PLANT-A-QUESTION as a model for the effective integration of GBL in secondary education.

Despite its strengths, the game has room for improvement in several areas. In this regard, expanding the content was a recurring theme, with experts advocating for a broader range of question categories. This diversification would allow the game to cover a wider range of topics, from basic plant biology to advanced climate modelling. The introduction of adaptive question sets categorized by difficulty level, such as easy, medium and advanced, was also recommended to better cater to players' varying skill levels and prior knowledge. The need for cultural and pedagogical adaptability was another critical point. Providing multilingual options or teacher's guides tailored to different cultural contexts could further enhance the game's accessibility and relevance (Alencar & de la Hera Conde-Pumpido, 2018; Talandron-Felipe, 2021). In this point, other learning tools can compensate for the shortcomings of the physical board game. Artificial intelligence can facilitate game personalization to adapt to the specific audience at any given time, while providing explanations tailored to each player without compromising the quality of learning (Tinterri et al., 2024). Additionally, it can provide educators with a powerful tool that enhances their ability to effectively implement individualized learning. The aesthetic and functional aspects of the game could benefit from improvements, representing another area where AI can provide support. For example, experts suggested including dynamic features, such as rotating boards or moving pieces, to increase interactivity. They also suggested integrating visual storytelling elements that evolve as the game progresses and offer an engaging experience for players. Immersive technologies created by AI provide an opportunity to modernize educational procedures that are less engaging for students without eliminating the teacher's role (Bamanger, 2025; Mishra, 2020). In addition, digital resources promote interaction between players and the game's academic content (Bonner & Reinders, 2018). The development of a companion digital app for tech-savvy learners was also suggested to increase overall interactivity (Billy & Anush, 2024), bridging the physical and digital worlds to create a hybrid 'physigital' learning ecosystem. This combination can benefit from the positive aspects of each approach, such as the high motivation provided by analogue games as well as the greater attractiveness and increase in digital skills provided by AI-based resources. Both experts and students agreed on the educational and engaging nature of PLANT-A-QUESTION, highlighting its ability to reinforce knowledge and stimulate interest in science and environmental issues through dynamic and playful learning.

CONCLUSIONS

PLANT-A-QUESTION proved to be an effective educational resource for promoting engagement in environmental sciences through analogue game-based learning. By integrating botanical and environmental content with collaborative and inquiry-driven mechanics, the game successfully addressed key educational challenges, including PB, climate change awareness, and the understanding of plant-environment relationships. The findings demonstrate that board game-based approaches can foster meaningful participation, active learning, and environmental literacy among secondary school students.

PLANT-A-QUESTION is considered an integrative alternative for students, as it involves active learning, cooperative problem-solving, and thematic content related to environmental sciences. The game actively engages students in a meaningful way. Furthermore, it directly addresses several SDGs. The inclusion of different difficulty levels, personalized feedback, and an emphasis on teamwork allows students to gain a comprehensive understanding of interconnected concepts, thus fostering an interactive and dynamic learning experience. This approach recognizes the relationship between learning and enjoyment.

The results obtained from both students and expert evaluators revealed a high level of satisfaction and acceptance. The majority expressed a desire to play again, indicating continued interest and participation. The willingness to purchase the game to play with friends or family suggests that students valued it not only as an educational tool but also as a source of entertainment. Expert assessment further confirmed the game's pedagogical potential, particularly regarding its applicability across educational levels, its adaptability to different learning needs, and its capacity to support both collaborative and individual learning processes.

The inclusive design of PLANT-A-QUESTION constitutes another relevant contribution of this study, allowing participation from people of all genders. By promoting teamwork, communication, and shared problem-solving, the game creates participatory learning environments in which students from diverse backgrounds can actively engage with scientific concepts. In this sense, the study supports the role of analogue game-based learning as a valuable strategy for fostering environmental and scientific literacy through socially interactive educational experiences.

The excellent reviews the game receives for its effectiveness in reinforcing and consolidating knowledge underscore its pedagogical value. Its educational impact not only meets but exceeds expectations in facilitating meaningful learning experiences. The positive correlation between enjoyment and educational effectiveness supports the game's potential as a valuable pedagogical tool.

PLANT-A-QUESTION has proven to be an effective and engaging educational resource that aligns with contemporary educational needs. The game's adaptability, inclusive design, and positive reception position it as a valuable tool for educators seeking innovative ways to enhance student learning experiences in environmental science and related subjects. With the current educational landscape increasingly shaped by AI-driven tools and digital learning environments, this chapter highlights the continuing relevance of low-tech pedagogical approaches that prioritize face-to-face interaction, experiential learning, and collaborative knowledge construction. Future developments may incorporate AI-assisted elements, such as adaptive educational resources or personalized feedback systems, to further improve accessibility and broaden participation while preserving the game's social and interactive foundations.

A survey of experts and professional educators suggests that PLANT-A-QUESTION has great potential as an educational resource, especially due to its ability to be integrated into school curricula, engage students and effectively teach concepts about plants and climate. Experts also highlighted its adaptability to different educational levels and its capacity to offer thematic content, making it a versatile tool to support both individual and collaborative learning.

Despite the promising results, some limitations should be acknowledged. Future improvements could include more diverse samples, objective measures of the learning process, and studies to evaluate the game's long-term impact. Furthermore, improvements in content diversity, cultural adaptability and visual design are needed to maximize its impact. Incorporating hybrid game elements that combine traditional formats with digital tools could also ensure its relevance in today's educational landscape. These refinements would help positioning the game as a tool for fostering environmental awareness and interdisciplinary learning.

ACKNOWLEDGMENTS

The authors would like to thank the financial support given by the following institutions: Spanish Ministry of Science, Innovation and Universities (G.-B.F.-L., FPU21/03022), University of León (A.F.-G. and A.A.-S.), CONACYT-México (N.-Y.O.-R.) and Postdoctoral grant DGAPA-UNAM (A.G.-P.).

Authors would like to thank María Hernández Gordón, Beatriz López Medina and Silvia Muñoz Cano for their collaboration in this research. In turn, we extend our acknowledgement to Bridget Ryder for her advice on English terminology.

Finally, we would like to thank the experts who generously gave their time, expertise and valuable insights to this research. Their commitment and thoughtful responses have been invaluable in the development and refinement of this educational tool. We would also like to express our sincere appreciation to the students who participated in the survey with such enthusiasm and selfless cooperation. Thank you for your commitment and support in moving this research forward.

REFERENCES

Alencar, A., & de la Hera Conde-Pumpido, T. (2018). Gaming in multicultural classrooms: The potential of collaborative digital games to foster intercultural interaction. In *Social interactions in virtual worlds: An interdisciplinary perspective*. DOI: 10.1017/9781316422823.012

Alsaad, F. M., & Durugbo, C. M. (2021). Gamification-as-Innovation: A Review. *International Journal on Management of Innovation & Technology*, *18*(5), 2130002. Advance online publication. DOI: 10.1142/S0219877021300020

Amedie, F. A. (2013). Impacts of Climate Change on Plant Growth, Ecosystem Services, Biodiversity, and Potential Adaptation Measure. Master Thesis in Atmospheric Science with Orientation towards Environmental Science (60 HEC).

Amran, A., Perkasa, M., Satriawan, M., Jasin, I., & Irwansyah, M. (2019). Assessing students 21st century attitude and environmental awareness: Promoting education for sustainable development through science education. *Journal of Physics: Conference Series*, *1157*(2), 022025. DOI: 10.1088/1742-6596/1157/2/022025

Anggraeni, L., Affandi, I., Wahyudin, D., Paramitha, S. T., & Ramadhan, M. G. (2022). Optimization of the Board Game as a Platform for the Concept of Peace Education: A Survey Method Study. *International Journal of Education in Mathematics. Science and Technology*, *10*(2). Advance online publication. DOI: 10.46328/ijemst.2292

Arboleya-García, E., & Miralles, L. (2022). 'The Game of the Sea': An Interdisciplinary Educational Board Game on the Marine Environment and Ocean Awareness for Primary and Secondary Students. Education Sciences 2022, Vol. 12, Page 57, 12(1), 57. DOI: 10.3390/educsci12010057

Arteaga, P., Batanero, C., Contreras, J. M., & Cañadas, G. R. (2012). Understanding statistical graphs: A research survey. *Boletín de Estadística e Investigación Operativa*, *28*(3), 261–277.

Balas, B., & Momsen, J. L. (2014). Attention "blinks" differently for plants and animals. *CBE Life Sciences Education, 13*(3), 437–443. Advance online publication. DOI: 10.1187/cbe.14-05-0080

Bamanger, E. (2025). Augmented reality in EFL education: Transforming high school student achievement through interactive learning tools. *The Journal of Technology Studies, 50*(1), 30–41. DOI: 10.21061/jts.439

Barnett, W. S., & Jung, K. (2020). *Understanding and responding to the pandemic's impacts on preschool education: What can we learn from last spring*. National Institute for Early Education Research.

Beger, A. W., Hannan, S., Patel, R., & Sweeney, E. M. (2025). Virtual escape rooms in anatomy education: Case studies from two institutions. *Advances in Physiology Education, 49*(3), 621–632. DOI: 10.1152/advan.00248.2024

Billy, I., & Anush, H. (2024). The Digital Evolution-need to adapt education for a Tech-Savvy Generation. The Business and Management Review: Conference proceedings of the Centre for Business & Economic Research (ICBED-2024, 15-17th April), 15, 131.

Boghian, I., Cojocariu, V.-M., Popescu, C. V., & Mâţă, L. (2019). Game-based learning: Using board games in adult education. *Journal of Educational Sciences & Psychology, 9*(1), 51–57.

Bonner, E., & Reinders, H. (2018). Augmented and virtual reality in the language classroom: Practical ideas. *Teaching English With Technology, 18*(3), 33–53.

Bónus, L., Antal, E., & Korom, E. (2024). Digital game-based inquiry learning to improve eighth graders' inquiry skills in biology. *Journal of Science Education and Technology, 33*(4), 1–17. DOI: 10.1007/s10956-024-10096-x

Brod, G. (2021). Generative learning: Which strategies for what age? *Educational Psychology Review, 33*(4), 1295–1318. DOI: 10.1007/s10648-020-09571-9

Caena, F., & Redecker, C. (2019). Aligning teacher competence frameworks to 21st century challenges: The case for the European Digital Competence Framework for Educators (Digcompedu). *European Journal of Education, 54*(3), 356–369. Advance online publication. DOI: 10.1111/ejed.12345

Camacho-Sánchez, R., Manzano-León, A., Rodríguez-Ferrer, J. M., Serna, J., & Lavega-Burgués, P. (2023). Game-Based Learning and Gamification in Physical Education: A Systematic Review. *Education Sciences, 13*(2), 183. DOI: 10.3390/educsci13020183

Carbonell-Alcocer, A., Romero-Luis, J., Gértrudix-Barrio, M., & Borges-Rey, E. (2022). Educating for a sustainable future through the Circular Economy: Citizen involvement and social change. *Comunicar: Media Education Research Journal, 30*(73), 21–32. DOI: 10.3916/C73-2022-02

Cavalcante-Pimentel, F. S., Morais-Marques, M., & Barbosa-de-Sales-Junior, V. (2022). Learning Strategies through Digital Games in a University Context. *Comunicar: Media Education Research Journal, 30*(73), 77–86. DOI: 10.3916/C73-2022-07

Chen, S., Jamiatul Husnaini, S., & Chen, J. J. (2020). Effects of games on students' emotions of learning science and achievement in chemistry. *International Journal of Science Education, 42*(13), 2224–2245. DOI: 10.1080/09500693.2020.1817607

Chiang, F. K., Wang, S., & Tang, Z. (2022). Design and Evaluation of a Board Game in Food and Nutrition Education. *Education Sciences*, *12*(3), 162. DOI: 10.3390/educsci12030162

Chiarello, F., & Castellano, M. G. (2016). Board games and board game design as learning tools for complex scientific concepts: Some experiences. *International Journal of Game-Based Learning*, *6*(2), 1–14. Advance online publication. DOI: 10.4018/IJGBL.2016040101

Chiu, T. K. F., Ahmad, Z., Ismailov, M., & Sanusi, I. T. (2024). What are artificial intelligence literacy and competency? A comprehensive framework to support them. *Computers and Education Open*, *6*, 100171. Advance online publication. DOI: 10.1016/j.caeo.2024.100171

Chiu, T. K. F., Moorhouse, B. L., Chai, C. S., & Ismailov, M. (2024). Teacher support and student motivation to learn with Artificial Intelligence (AI) based chatbot. *Interactive Learning Environments*, *32*(7), 3240–3256. DOI: 10.1080/10494820.2023.2172044

Consejería de Educación Castilla y Léon. (2015). Orden EDU/362/2015. Establece el currículo y se regula la implantación, evaluación y desarrollo de la educación secundaria obligatoria en la Comunidad de Castilla y León. Boletín Oficial de Castilla y León, 86(8 de mayo de 2015), 17975–17979. https://www.educa.jcyl.es/es/resumenbocyl/orden-edu-362-2015-4-mayo-establece-curriculo-regula-implan.ficheros/549394-BOCYL-D-08052015-4.pdf

Consejería de Educación Castilla y León. (2015). ORDEN EDU/363/2015. Establece el currículo y se regula la implantación, evaluación y desarrollo del bachillerato en la Comunidad de Castilla y León. Boletín Oficial de Castilla y León, 86(8 de mayo de 2015), 14058–14079. https://www.educa.jcyl.es/es/resumenbocyl/orden-edu-363-2015-4-mayo-establece-curriculo-regula-implan.ficheros/549395-BOCYL-D-08052015-5.pdf

Crocco, F., Offenholley, K., & Hernandez, C. (2016). A Proof-of-Concept Study of Game-Based Learning in Higher Education. *Simulation & Gaming*, *47*(4), 403–422. Advance online publication. DOI: 10.1177/1046878116632484

Csikszentmihalyi, M. (1990). *Flow: The psychology of optimal experience*. Harper & Row.

Da Silva Teixeira, J., Belo Angeluci, A. C., Prates, P.Junior, & Prado Martin, J. G. (2024). 'Let's play?' A systematic review of board games in biology. *Journal of Biological Education*, *58*(2), 251–270. DOI: 10.1080/00219266.2022.2041461

Dahalan, F., Alias, N., & Shaharom, M. S. N. (2024). Gamification and Game Based Learning for Vocational Education and Training: A Systematic Literature Review. *Education and Information Technologies*, *29*, 1279–1317. Decreto 38/2022, de 29 de Septiembre, Por El Que Se Establece La Ordenación y El Currículo de La Educación Primaria En La Comunidad de Castilla y León, Boletín Oficial de Castilla y León (2022).DOI: 10.1007/s10639-022-11548-w

De Freitas, S. (2018). Are games effective learning tools? A review of educational games. *Journal of Educational Technology & Society*, *21*(2).

Decreto 39/2022, de 29 de Septiembre, Por El Que Se Establece La Ordenación y El Currículo de La Educación Secundaria Obligatoria En La Comunidad de Castilla y León, Boletín Oficial de Castilla y León (2022).

Deeva, G., Bogdanova, D., Serral, E., Snoeck, M., & De Weerdt, J. (2021). A review of automated feedback systems for learners: Classification framework, challenges and opportunities. *Computers & Education*, *162*, 104094. Advance online publication. DOI: 10.1016/j.compedu.2020.104094

Dele-Ajayi, O., Strachan, R., Pickard, A., & Sanderson, J. (2018). Designing for All: Exploring gender diversity and engagement with digital educational games by young people. *Proceedings - Frontiers in Education Conference*, 2018-October. DOI: 10.1109/FIE.2018.8658553

Desta, H., Lemma, B., & Fetene, A. (2012). Aspects of climate change and its associated impacts on wetland ecosystem functions-A review. *The Journal of American Science*, *8*(10).

DeVries, R. (2000). Vygotsky, Piaget, and Education: A reciprocal assimilation of theories and educational practices. *New Ideas in Psychology*, *18*(2–3), 187–213. DOI: 10.1016/S0732-118X(00)00008-8

Di Sacco, A., Hardwick, K. A., Blakesley, D., Brancalion, P. H. S., Breman, E., Cecilio Rebola, L., Chomba, S., Dixon, K., Elliott, S., Ruyonga, G., Shaw, K., Smith, P., Smith, R. J., & Antonelli, A. (2021). Ten golden rules for reforestation to optimize carbon sequestration, biodiversity recovery and livelihood benefits. *Global Change Biology*, *27*(7), 1328–1348. Advance online publication. DOI: 10.1111/gcb.15498

Dichev, C., Dicheva, D., Angelova, G., & Agre, G. (2014). From gamification to gameful design and gameful experience in learning. *Cybernetics and Information Technologies*, *14*(4), 80–100. Advance online publication. DOI: 10.1515/cait-2014-0007

Emel'yanenko, V. D., Vetoshko, A. N., Malinnikov, S. G., Malashenko, I. V., & Vetoshko, L. I. (2016). Man's Values and Ideologies as a Basis of Gamification. *International Journal of Environmental and Science Education*, *11*(18), 12576–12592.

Evans, J. R., & Mathur, A. (2018). The value of online surveys: A look back and a look ahead. *Internet Research*, *28*(4), 854–887. Advance online publication. DOI: 10.1108/IntR-03-2018-0089

Farias, C., Hastier, P. A., & Mesquita, I. (2017). Towards a more equitable and inclusive learning environment in sport education: Results of an action research-based intervention. *Sport Education and Society*, *22*(4), 460–476. DOI: 10.1080/13573322.2015.1040752

Farias, C., Segovia, Y., Valério, C., & Mesquita, I. (2022). Does Sport Education promote equitable game-play participation? Effects of learning context and students' sex and skill-level. *European Physical Education Review*, *28*(1), 20–39. DOI: 10.1177/1356336X211013832

FECYT. (2023). FECYT presenta los resultados de la Encuesta de Percepción Social de la Ciencia y la Tecnología: aumenta el interés por la ciencia entre la población española. https://www.fecyt.es/es/noticia/fecyt-presenta-los-resultados-de-la-encuesta-de-percepcion-social-de-la-ciencia-y-la#:~:text=De%20esta%20forma%2C%20el%2047,ecolog%C3%ADa%20(49%2C4%25)

Fernández-González, C., & Franco-Mariscal, A. J. (2021). Teaching the Plant Kingdom Using Cooperative Learning and Plants Elements: A Case Study with Spanish Secondary School Students. *Journal of Turkish Science Education*, *18*(1), 17–31. Advance online publication. DOI: 10.36681/tused.2021.50

Fink, A. (2011). *How to Ask Survey Questions*. How to Ask Survey Questions., DOI: 10.4135/9781412984393

Fonseca, L., Lima, V., & Silva, M. (2015). Utilization of quality tools: Does sector and size matter? *International Journal of Qualitative Research, 9*(4).

Franzwa, C., Tang, Y., & Johnson, A. (2013). Serious game design: Motivating students through a balance of fun and learning. *5th International Conference on Games and Virtual Worlds for Serious Applications (VS-GAMES)*, 1–7. DOI: 10.1109/VS-GAMES.2013.6624239

Gopalan, V., Bakar, J. A. A., Zulkifli, A. N., Alwi, A., & Mat, R. C. (2017). A review of the motivation theories in learning. *AIP Conference Proceedings, 1891*, 020043. Advance online publication. DOI: 10.1063/1.5005376

Hamari, J., Shernoff, D. J., Rowe, E., Coller, B., Asbell-Clarke, J., & Edwards, T. (2016). Challenging games help students learn: An empirical study on engagement, flow and immersion in game-based learning. *Computers in Human Behavior, 54*, 170–179. DOI: 10.1016/j.chb.2015.07.045

Harandi, S. R. (2015). Effects of e-learning on Students' Motivation. *Procedia: Social and Behavioral Sciences, 181*, 423–430. Advance online publication. DOI: 10.1016/j.sbspro.2015.04.905

Hung, I.-C., Chen, C.-C., & Lin, T.-L. (2021). Applying Board Games on Curriculum Design for Elementary School — A Case of Integrative Activities Curriculum. *Knowledge Innovation on Design and Culture*, 81–83.

Ifenthaler, D., Eseryel, D., & Ge, X. (2012). Assessment for Game-Based Learning. In *Assessment in Game-Based Learning: Foundations, Innovations, and Perspectives* (pp. 1–8). Springer., DOI: 10.1007/978-1-4614-3546-4_1

IPCC. (2023). The Sustainable Development Goals Report 2023 Special Edition. In The Sustainable Development Goals Report.

Jayasinghe, U., & Dharmaratne, A. (2013). Game-based learning vs. gamification from the higher education students' perspective. *Proceedings of 2013 IEEE International Conference on Teaching, Assessment and Learning for Engineering, TALE 2013*, January 2016, 683–688. DOI: 10.1109/TALE.2013.6654524

Juárez Varón, D., Bellido-García, I., & Gupta, B. B. (2023). Analysis of stress, attention, interest, and engagement in onsite and online higher education: A neurotechnological study. *Comunicar: Media Education Research Journal, 31*(76), 21–34. DOI: 10.3916/C76-2023-02

Kalogiannakis, M., Papadakis, S., & Zourmpakis, A. I. (2021). Gamification in science education. A systematic review of the literature. *Education Sciences, 11*(1), 22. DOI: 10.3390/educsci11010022

Kasneci, E., Sessler, K., Küchemann, S., Bannert, M., Dementieva, D., Fischer, F., Gasser, U., Groh, G., Günnemann, S., Hüllermeier, E., Krusche, S., Kutyniok, G., Michaeli, T., Nerdel, C., Pfeffer, J., Poquet, O., Sailer, M., Schmidt, A., Seidel, T., & Kasneci, G. (2023). ChatGPT for good? On opportunities and challenges of large language models for education. *Learning and Individual Differences, 103*, 102274. Advance online publication. DOI: 10.1016/j.lindif.2023.102274

Khan, A., Ahmad, F. H., & Malik, M. M. (2017). Use of digital game based learning and gamification in secondary school science: The effect on student engagement, learning and gender difference. *Education and Information Technologies, 22*(6), 2767–2804. Advance online publication. DOI: 10.1007/s10639-017-9622-1

Kim, S. J., Lee, K., & Park, Y. (2019). Balancing Fun and Learning through a User Interface: A Case Study of Wii Game. *KSII Transactions on Internet and Information Systems, 13*(7).

Kriz, W. C. (2003). Creating effective learning environments and learning organizations through gaming simulation design. *Simulation & Gaming, 34*(4), 495–511. Advance online publication. DOI: 10.1177/1046878103258201

Lavorel, S. (2013). Plant functional effects on ecosystem services. *Journal of Ecology, 101*(1), 4–8. Advance online publication. DOI: 10.1111/1365-2745.12031

Londoño Vásquez, L. M., & Rojas López, M. D. (2021). From Games to Gamification: A Proposal for an Integrated Model. *Educación y Educadores, 23*(3).

López Polo, E., & Sotoca Orgaz, P. (2019). "El Catán Motriz" Un juego de mesa con movimiento para educación física. *Revista Digital de Educación Física, 56*, 30–43.

Lord, T. R. (2001). 101 Reasons for using cooperative learning in biology teaching. *The American Biology Teacher, 63*(1), 30–38. Advance online publication. DOI: 10.2307/4451027

Louis, K. S., & Murphy, J. F. (2018). The Potential of Positive Leadership for School Improvement: A Cross-Disciplinary Synthesis. [NJCIE]. *Nordic Journal of Comparative and International Education, 2*(2–3), 165–180. DOI: 10.7577/njcie.2790

Manninen, T. (2003). Interaction forms and communicative actions in multiplayer games. *Game Studies, 3*(1).

Matsumoto, T. (2016). Motivation Strategy Using Gamification. *Creative Education, 07*(10), 1480–1485. Advance online publication. DOI: 10.4236/ce.2016.710153

Ministerio de Educación Cultura y Deporte. (2020). Ley Orgánica 3/2020, de 29 de diciembre, por la que se modifica la Ley Orgánica 2/2006, de 3 de mayo, Educación. *BOE Núm., 340*, 340.

Mishra, N. D. S. (2020). Applications of artificial intelligence in education. In *Artificial intelligence in education: Revolutionizing learning and teaching* (pp. 9–17). DOI: 10.25215/9358094575.02

Mohd Hussaini, H., & Saleh, S. (2026). Enhancing students' motivation in learning genetics through STEM-GBL among Northern Matriculation students. *Jurnal Pemikir Pendidikan, 14*(1), 152–165. DOI: 10.51200/jpp.v14i1.7535

Nautiyal, V. V., Silverio, S. A., & Salvador, E. E. P. (2024). Let's get on-board: A practical framework for designing and implementing educational board games in K-12 classrooms. *Frontiers in Education, 9*, 1420515. Advance online publication. DOI: 10.3389/feduc.2024.1420515

Ng, D. T. K., Lee, M., Tan, R. J. Y., Hu, X., Downie, J. S., & Chu, S. K. W. (2023). A review of AI teaching and learning from 2000 to 2020. *Education and Information Technologies, 28*(7), 8445–8501. DOI: 10.1007/s10639-022-11491-w

Noemí, P.-M., & Máximo, S. H. (2014). Educational Games for Learning. *Universal Journal of Educational Research, 2*(3), 230–238. Advance online publication. DOI: 10.13189/ujer.2014.020305

Ojala, M. (2012). Hope and climate change: The importance of hope for environmental engagement among young people. *Environmental Education Research, 18*(5), 625–642. DOI: 10.1080/13504622.2011.637157

Ouariachi, T., Li, C. Y., & Elving, W. J. (2020). Gamification approaches for education and engagement on pro-environmental behaviors: Searching for best practices. *Sustainability (Basel), 12*(11), 4565. Advance online publication. DOI: 10.3390/su12114565

Patrício, R., Moreira, A. C., & Zurlo, F. (2018). Gamification approaches to the early stage of innovation. *Creativity and Innovation Management, 27*(4), 499–511. Advance online publication. DOI: 10.1111/caim.12284

Pedrera, O., Ortega-Lasuen, U., Ruiz-González, A., Díez, J. R., & Barrutia, O. (2023). Branches of plant blindness and their relationship with biodiversity conceptualisation among secondary students. *Journal of Biological Education, 57*(3), 566–591. Advance online publication. DOI: 10.1080/00219266.2021.1933133

Piaget, J. (1975). *Nachahmung, Spiel und Traum. Die Entwicklung der Symbolfunktion beim Kinde.* Klett-Cotta.

Plass, J. L., Homer, B. D., & Kinzer, C. K. (2015). Foundations of Game-Based Learning. *Educational Psychologist, 50*(4), 258–283. DOI: 10.1080/00461520.2015.1122533

Pohl, M., Rester, M., & Judmaier, P. (2009). Lecture Notes in Computer Science: Vol. 5616. *Interactive game based learning: Advantages and disadvantages.*, , PART 3.DOI: 10.1007/978-3-642-02713-0_10

Prasad, S. (2023). Measures of Central Tendencies. In *Elementary Statistical Methods* (pp. 37–96). Springer Nature Singapore., DOI: 10.1007/978-981-19-0596-4_2

Przybylski, A. K., Rigby, C. S., & Ryan, R. M. (2010). A motivational model of video game engagement. *Review of General Psychology, 14*(2), 154–166. DOI: 10.1037/a0019440

Randel, J. M., Morris, B. A., Wetzel, C. D., & Whitehill, B. V. (1992). The Effectiveness of Games for Educational Purposes: A Review of Recent Research. *Simulation & Gaming, 23*(3), 261–276. DOI: 10.1177/1046878192233001

Rizkallah, E. G., & Seitz, V. (2017). Understanding student motivation: A key to retention in higher education. *Scientific Annals of Economics and Business, 64*(1), 45–57. Advance online publication. DOI: 10.1515/saeb-2017-0004

Rogerson, M. J., Gibbs, M., & Smith, W. (2016). Digitising boardgames: Issues and tensions. *Proceedings of the 2016 Annual Symposium on Computer-Human Interaction in Play*, 400–406. DOI: 10.1145/2967934.2968110

Ryan, R. M., & Deci, E. L. (2000). Self-determination theory and the facilitation of intrinsic motivation, social development, and well-being. *The American Psychologist, 55*(1), 68–78. DOI: 10.1037/0003-066X.55.1.68

Sandbrook, C., Adams, W. M., & Monteferri, B. (2015). Digital games and biodiversity conservation. *Conservation Letters, 8*(2), 118–124. DOI: 10.1111/conl.12113

Santos Almeida, I., Pinto, C., Lima, A., Moreira, T., & Fernandes, C. S. (2024). Game4NurseSupervisor: Development of a board game for nursing mentoring. *Nurse Education in Practice, 76*, 103939. Advance online publication. DOI: 10.1016/j.nepr.2024.103939

Schlüter, A., Waldkirch, M., Burmeister-Lamp, K., & Auernhammer, J. (2021). No second chance for a first impression: The role of aesthetics in early access video games. *International Journal of Innovation Management, 25*(10), 2140002. DOI: 10.1142/S1363919621400028

Seddighi-Khavidak, S., Sanchez, B. N., Chan, S. S. K., & Le-Chan, G. (2026). Game-based learning enhances engagement and comprehension in undergraduate architecture and biology education. *Education Sciences, 16*(1), 9. Advance online publication. DOI: 10.3390/educsci16010009

Seddon, N., Daniels, E., Davis, R., Chausson, A., Harris, R., Hou-Jones, X., Huq, S., Kapos, V., Mace, G. M., Rizvi, A. R., Reid, H., Roe, D., Turner, B., & Wicander, S. (2020). Global recognition of the importance of nature-based solutions to the impacts of climate change. *Global Sustainability, 3*, e15. Advance online publication. DOI: 10.1017/sus.2020.8

Sezer, G. O. (2015). Decreasing Undesired Attitudes of Students in Classroom: Use of Awards. In I. Koleva, R. Efe, E. Atasoy, & Z. B. Kostova (Eds.), Education in the 21st Century: Theory and Practice (pp. 751–758). ST. KLIMENT OHRIDSKI UNIVERSITY PRESS.

Stagg, B. C., & Dillon, J. (2022). Plant awareness is linked to plant relevance: A review of educational and ethnobiological literature (1998–2020). *Plants, People, Planet, 4*(6), 579–592. Advance online publication. DOI: 10.1002/ppp3.10323

Su, Y. D., Mo, Y. H., Dong, X., & Wang, X. (2022). A review of the health education board game in nursing. *Chinese Journal of Nursing Education, 19*(6). Advance online publication. DOI: 10.3761/j.issn.1672-9234.2022.06.018

Talandron-Felipe, M. M. P. (2021). Considerations Towards Culturally-Adaptive Instructional Systems. In Sottilare, R. A., & Schwarz, J. (Eds.), Lecture Notes in Computer Science: Vol. 12792. *Adaptive Instructional Systems. Design and Evaluation. HCII 2021*. Springer., DOI: 10.1007/978-3-030-77857-6_43

Taspinar, B., Schmidt, W., & Schuhbauer, H. (2016). Gamification in education: A board game approach to knowledge acquisition. *Procedia Computer Science, 99*, 101–116. Advance online publication. DOI: 10.1016/j.procs.2016.09.104

Telaumbanua, D. (2025). The role of artificial intelligence in improving the quality of biology learning. *Cognizance Journal of Multidisciplinary Studies, 5*(1), 78–84. DOI: 10.47760/cognizance.2025.v05i01.007

Tinterri, A., Pelizzari, F., Vignoli, G., Palladino, F., & Di Padova, M. (2024). Towards AI-assisted board game-based learning: Assessing LLMs in game personalisation. *Proceedings of the 18th European Conference on Games Based Learning*. DOI: 10.34190/ecgbl.18.1.3055

Topping, K. J. (2005). Trends in peer learning. *Educational Psychology, 25*(6), 631–645. DOI: 10.1080/01443410500345172

Treher, E. N. (2011). *Learning with Board Games*. Learning With Board Game.

Uribe, R. V., Utrilla Cobos, S. A., & Santamaría Ortega, A. (2017). Aprendizaje basado en juegos. Una alternativa viable para la enseñanza significativa de la sustentabilidad. *Revista Electrónica Sobre Educación Media y Superior*, *4*(7), 16.

Vázquez-Vílchez, M., Garrido-Rosales, D., Pérez-Fernández, B., & Fernández-Oliveras, A. (2021). Using a Cooperative Educational Game to Promote Pro-Environmental Engagement in Future Teachers. *Education Sciences*, *11*(11), 691. DOI: 10.3390/educsci11110691

Vlachopoulos, D., & Makri, A. (2017). The effect of games and simulations on higher education: A systematic literature review. *International Journal of Educational Technology in Higher Education*, *14*(1), 22. Advance online publication. DOI: 10.1186/s41239-017-0062-1

Vygotsky, L. S. (1967). Play and Its Role in the Mental Development of the Child. *Social Psychology*, *5*(3), 6–18. DOI: 10.2753/RPO1061-040505036

Vygotsky, L. S. (1978). *Mind in Society: Development of Higher Psychological Processes* (Cole, M., Jolm-Steiner, V., Scribner, S., & Souberman, E., Eds.). Harvard University Press., DOI: 10.2307/j.ctvjf9vz4

Widener, S. K. (2007). An empirical analysis of the levers of control framework. *Accounting, Organizations and Society*, *32*(7–8), 757–788. Advance online publication. DOI: 10.1016/j.aos.2007.01.001

Wigfield, A., & Eccles, J. S. (2002). Students' Motivation During the Middle School Years. I*mproving Academic Achievement.* DOI: 10.1016/B978-012064455-1/50011-7

Willis, J. (2007). Cooperative Learning Is a Brain Turn-On. *Middle School Journal*, *38*(4), 4–13. Advance online publication. DOI: 10.1080/00940771.2007.11461587

Xu, M., Luo, Y., Zhang, Y., Xia, R., Qian, H., & Zou, X. (2023). Game-based learning in medical education. *Frontiers in Public Health*, *11*, 1113682. Advance online publication. DOI: 10.3389/fpubh.2023.1113682

Yıldırım, İ., & Şen, S. (2021). The effects of gamification on students' academic achievement: A meta-analysis study. *Interactive Learning Environments*, *29*(8), 1301–1318. Advance online publication. DOI: 10.1080/10494820.2019.1636089

Yim, I. H. Y. (2024). A critical review of teaching and learning artificial intelligence (AI) literacy: Developing an intelligence-based AI literacy framework for primary school education. *Computers and Education: Artificial Intelligence*, *7*, 100319. Advance online publication. DOI: 10.1016/j.caeai.2024.100319

Yim, I. H. Y., & Su, J. (2025). Artificial intelligence (AI) learning tools in K-12 education: A scoping review. *Journal of Computers in Education*, *12*, 93–131. DOI: 10.1007/s40692-023-00304-9

Zacharia, Z. C., & Olympiou, G. (2011). Physical versus virtual manipulative experimentation in physics learning. *Learning and Instruction*, *21*(3), 317–331. DOI: 10.1016/j.learninstruc.2010.03.001

Zha, S., Bragdon, M. M., Gong, N., Wang, J., Leavesley, S., Eaton, R., & Bosarge, E. (2025). A case study of integrating AI literacy education in a biology class. *International Journal of Artificial Intelligence in Education*, *35*(4), 2453–2477. DOI: 10.1007/s40593-025-00476-8

Zhai, X., Chu, X., Chai, C. S., Jong, M. S. Y., Istenic, A., Spector, M., Liu, J.-B., Yuan, J., & Li, Y. (2021). A Review of Artificial Intelligence (AI) in Education from 2010 to 2020. *Complexity*, *2021*(1), 8812542. Advance online publication. DOI: 10.1155/2021/8812542

Chapter 14
Game, Read, Lead:
Transforming Hospitality Literacy in Higher Education With CESIM Hospitality

Carimo Rassal
University of Algarve, Portugal & CIDEHUS, University of Évora, Portugal

ABSTRACT

This chapter examines the integration of game-based learning (GBL) and artificial intelligenceto advance literacy development in hospitality education. Using the CESIM simulation platform over multiple years in undergraduate and graduate hospitality programs, it reframes literacy as a broad construct encompassing reading, writing, and interpreting complex data. The pedagogical design combines adaptive teaching, flipped classroom, inquiry-based learning, Montessori principles, and technology-enhanced strategies to create an immersive, literacy-centered environment. Findings indicate that this approach increased student engagement and improved literacy outcomes. Implications include enhanced student readiness for industry, a shift in instructor roles toward facilitation, the need for faculty training, and the need for institutional support to implement such innovative approaches. The chapter also acknowledges limitations such as the simulation's scope and context-specific factors, and calls for further research including longitudinal studies on career impacts and deeper AI integration.

INTRODUCTION

In an era characterized by accelerated technological advancement, higher education institutions are increasingly challenged to prepare students for complex, data-driven, and communication-intensive professions (Dogan & Arslan, 2026). Within this evolving educational landscape, hospitality management programs face the dual responsibility of equipping students with both the industry-specific technical knowledge and the broader literacies required for global leadership (Singh, 2026). The emergence of artificial intelligence, game-based learning, and digital simulation tools has created new opportunities to integrate literacy instruction into professional and vocational education in more embedded, experiential ways (Zvereva et al., 2026). As the hospitality industry becomes more reliant on analytics, automation, and customer experience personalization, the corresponding educational response must support students in reading data critically, writing strategically, and engaging with diverse forms of information in multimodal ways (Gawlik-Kobylińska, 2026). These literacies, often considered peripheral in managerial

DOI: 10.4018/979-8-3373-7472-7.ch014

education, are central to professional practice and can be fostered through targeted simulation-based instruction (Bailey et al., 2026).

This chapter explores how the CESIM Hospitality Simulation platform has been used at a Portuguese university in undergraduate and master's hospitality education between 2022 and 2025 to promote literacy through game-based and artificial intelligence (AI) supported learning. The approach reframes literacy not only as reading and writing competence but as the broader ability to interpret, synthesize, and communicate across various forms of text and data. In this context, CESIM is positioned not only as a managerial simulation but also as a learning space where students practice reading operational reports, interpreting financial dashboards, developing team strategies, and engaging critically with AI-generated feedback. The integration of adaptive teaching strategies, Montessori-inspired autonomy, flipped classrooms, and inquiry-based learning creates an ecosystem in which students encounter literacies in authentic, relevant, and high-stakes contexts.

The focus of this chapter is threefold. First, it situates hospitality literacy within contemporary theories of learning and explores how artificial intelligence and game-based environments offer a renewed vision for literacy instruction. Second, it presents a pedagogical framework used in Portugal that incorporates simulation into hospitality curricula to develop academic, digital, and professional literacies. Finally, it offers insights from actual classroom practice, highlighting student outcomes, instructional strategies, and inclusion-based adaptations that have supported multilingual and under-resourced learners. By embedding literacy development into AI-driven hospitality simulations, this approach advances an inclusive, practice-aligned, and literacy-centered vision for higher education.

Theoretical Foundations of Literacy, AI, and Game-Based Learning

Literacy, long associated with the mastery of reading and writing in academic settings, has undergone considerable redefinition over recent decades (Kurniadi et al., 2026). As societies have become increasingly digitized and globally interconnected, literacy has expanded to encompass digital, media, critical, and multimodal literacy (Lloyd et al., 2025). These forms of literacy include the ability to navigate, interpret, evaluate, and produce information across text, visual, numerical, and interactive formats. The concept of multiliteracies (Green & Giblin, 2025), introduced through a pedagogical shift that recognizes the multiplicity of communicative practices, provides a foundation for understanding how students today engage with knowledge not only through books and articles but also through dashboards, interfaces, simulations, and collaborative networks. In professional education contexts, these literacies take on heightened importance (Hong & Hua, 2020). Students are expected to interpret financial reports, communicate with stakeholders, adapt messaging for diverse audiences, and critically assess information sources (Breland, 2026).

AI, particularly in educational technology, has reshaped how literacy is taught, assessed, and practiced (Alshammari et al., 2026). AI tools provide responsive feedback, tailored content recommendations, and real-time analytics to guide students through complex decision-making processes. AI-powered systems are increasingly used to support reading comprehension, offer writing suggestions, generate adaptive quizzes, and provide data-driven insights into learner engagement. These tools allow literacy instruction to move beyond static text analysis toward more dynamic, personalized, and iterative processes (Chen & Alibakhshi, 2026). In simulation environments, AI can highlight discrepancies between student decisions and optimal strategies, suggest areas for further inquiry, and generate narratives based on learner choices

(Wu et al., 2026). These features do not replace human instruction but instead augment the learning process, allowing instructors to provide more nuanced and individualized support.

Game-based learning adds another dimension to this landscape. Educational games and simulations embed learning in meaningful contexts where students must apply knowledge, test hypotheses, and reflect on outcomes (Liang & Kuo, 2026). These environments often present problems that lack clear answers, encouraging players to interpret complex systems, engage in trial-and-error reasoning, and collaborate with peers. In doing so, game-based learning aligns closely with literacy development (Shin & Rowe, 2026). Students must read instructions carefully, synthesize information from multiple sources, interpret real-time feedback, and articulate their strategies. The narrative structures of games often require students to follow storylines, evaluate scenarios, and make meaning across various modalities. In simulation-based games like CESIM, students encounter data in the form of financial tables, performance metrics, and customer satisfaction indexes, all of which demand careful reading and contextual understanding.

Together, AI and game-based learning offer a robust framework for reimagining literacy education. They shift the focus from passive consumption of content to active interpretation, production, and evaluation of information within complex, simulated environments. These environments promote not only traditional academic literacy but also the competencies required for effective participation in professional fields (Chaves-Yuste et al., 2026). In hospitality management, where decision-making, communication, and data analysis are central, this integration becomes especially relevant. Students must move fluently between qualitative and quantitative information, between customer feedback and pricing strategies, and between team collaboration and individual accountability. In this sense, literacy becomes both a foundation and an outcome of the simulation experience.

This reconceptualization of literacy also aligns with constructivist and experiential learning theories (Chew & Da, 2025). Students learn not by memorizing isolated facts but by constructing understanding through engagement with meaningful, situated tasks in real-world contexts. Simulation-based environments enable learners to assume professional roles, confront authentic challenges, and apply interdisciplinary knowledge (Pham & Duong, 2025). The feedback loop inherent in simulations enables students to reflect on their choices, consider alternatives, and revise their approaches, reinforcing metacognitive aspects of literacy. Furthermore, by embedding literacy within decision-making cycles, simulations support the development of critical thinking, argumentation, and evidence-based reasoning. These skills are transferable beyond the classroom and are essential for leadership in hospitality and other complex industries (Lin & Wang, 2025).

AI-enabled simulations also offer opportunities for formative assessment of literacy practices (Trajkovski & Hayes, 2025). Instructors can monitor how students interact with texts, how they write about their strategies, and how they respond to changing scenarios. This enables timely, targeted interventions that support individual learning trajectories. AI-generated reports can be used as discussion tools, prompting students to explain their rationale and revise their thinking. In this way, the simulation itself becomes a literacy text, and student interaction with it becomes a form of reading and writing. These interactions can be scaffolded to support learners at different proficiency levels, making the experience both rigorous and inclusive (Finkelstein & Soffer-Vital, 2025).

The synergy among AI, game-based learning, and literacy development lays the foundation for more engaging, responsive, and practical instruction in higher education (Rye et al., 2025). By treating simulation platforms not only as training tools but as environments for critical literacy practice, educators can better prepare students for the demands of contemporary professional life. In hospitality education, this shift is particularly significant, as students are called to integrate service principles, financial judgment, team coordination, and customer insight, all of which require robust literacies across multiple modes.

Hospitality Education and Multiliteracies

Hospitality management education has traditionally centered on technical competencies such as operations, finance, marketing, and service design (Ngo, 2026). While these domains remain essential, the hospitality professional landscape now demands additional literacies, including data interpretation, digital communication, ethical judgment, and cross-cultural negotiation. The modern hospitality professional is expected to make decisions based on complex data, adapt messaging for international audiences, and manage service experiences increasingly mediated by digital platforms (Liu et al., 2025). As such, the development of literacies must be integral to hospitality curricula rather than supplemental.

Within this evolving context, the concept of multiliteracies becomes especially relevant. Hospitality students must navigate textual materials such as case studies and business reports, but they must also interpret visual content, interactive interfaces, and customer feedback systems. They are required to produce written content ranging from staff communications to marketing briefs, all of which must be clear, professional, and audience-aware (Ni & Lam, 2025). Furthermore, the rise of sustainability practices, ethical service standards, and global citizenship in the hospitality sector has introduced additional layers of complexity that require critical and reflective literacies. Students are expected to evaluate competing values, justify decisions, and anticipate consequences within a globalized service environment (Xinlin et al., 2025).

Despite these demands, literacy instruction in hospitality programs has often been implicit or fragmented. Writing may be addressed in isolated assignments, while reading is assumed to be a prerequisite rather than an instructional goal. This has created gaps in students' ability to apply literacy skills across contexts. Simulation-based learning offers a remedy by embedding literacy into the flow of professional tasks. In CESIM, for example, students read simulation briefs, analyze performance reports, write team strategy statements, and reflect on outcomes in real time. These activities are not standalone exercises but are embedded in the core gameplay and directly impact results. As such, students are motivated to read carefully, write persuasively, and communicate clearly, not just for grades, but also for performance within the simulation environment.

The CESIM platform presents students with challenges that mirror those they will face in actual hotel and restaurant operations. They must manage budgets, interpret trends, balance service quality and profitability, and respond to feedback. All of these tasks require literacy in both academic and applied forms. Reading a balance sheet or a performance dashboard requires numeracy and narrative interpretation. Writing a rationale for a staffing decision requires coherence, justification, and attention to detail. Engaging with a simulated customer complaint requires empathy, precise language, and a professional tone. These are not abstract skills but situated literacies that emerge through practice in context.

Hospitality education in Portugal, as in many parts of the world, has embraced internationalization, drawing students from diverse linguistic and cultural backgrounds. This diversity enriches the learning environment but also creates challenges for literacy instruction (Dewan, 2025). Students may have varying levels of English proficiency, different educational backgrounds, and differing expectations about writing and communication. The use of simulation platforms that support multilingual access, scaffolded learning, and visualized data can help bridge these differences. Instructors can design tasks that validate students' existing literacies while guiding them toward new forms of expression and analysis. Simulation environments can serve as a common ground where students from different backgrounds collaborate, negotiate meaning, and learn from one another.

The integration of multiliteracies into hospitality education through simulation also aligns with inclusive teaching practices (Neina et al., 2025). By providing multiple modes of engagement, such as text, visuals, numbers, and interactive simulations, the program accommodates varied learning preferences and abilities. Students who struggle with dense academic texts may excel at interpreting dashboards or articulating strategies orally. Those with strong writing skills may help their teams craft persuasive rationales. By valuing these diverse contributions, the simulation fosters a learning culture that recognizes multiple forms of expertise. This inclusivity is not only pedagogically sound but also reflects the collaborative and multifaceted nature of hospitality work (Huo et al., 2025).

The application of multiliteracies in hospitality education has implications for curriculum design, faculty development, and student assessment (Rocca, 2024, pp.73-95). Programs should move beyond traditional lecture-based, examination-focused, and content-transmission models, such as theory-dominated hospitality, finance, and management courses, toward pedagogical practices that systematically develop students' communication, interpretation, and reflective capacities throughout the learning process (Zhu et al., 2026). Faculty need to be equipped to guide students in developing these literacies within disciplinary contexts, using tools like CESIM as both instructional and assessment platforms. The evaluation itself must evolve to capture not only outcomes but also the literate processes by which those outcomes are achieved. This includes evaluating students' ability to read reports critically, write strategy documents clearly, and explain their decisions cogently during team discussions and presentations.

Simulation-based literacy instruction also promotes deeper engagement and learner autonomy (Kaplan et al., 2025). Because students experience the consequences of their decisions in a safe, simulated environment, they become more invested in understanding the information they encounter. They are not simply reading for recall or writing to meet a rubric; they are engaging with texts and data to succeed within the simulation. This experiential connection motivates effort, supports retention, and builds confidence (Aris et al., 2025). Instructors can leverage this motivation to introduce more advanced literacy challenges, such as comparing scenarios, analyzing long-term trends, or writing executive summaries. Through sustained engagement, students progressively internalize clear reading, precise writing, and critical analysis as foundational competencies for professional practice.

Game-Based Learning and Literacy in Higher Education

Game-based learning has emerged as a dynamic pedagogical approach that resonates strongly with the needs of contemporary higher education (Lasley, 2017). In contrast to traditional lecture-driven instruction, game-based methods place students in active learning roles through educational games and simulations (Madshaven et al., 2025). These interactive experiences require learners to do rather than merely listen, promoting deeper engagement with course material. As a result, students often show greater motivation and persistence, both of which are crucial to success in complex academic tasks (Shohel et al., 2022). This heightened engagement creates fertile ground for literacy development, as students become eager to read, interpret, and use information to excel in the game environment. In higher education classrooms, where cultivating advanced reading and analytical skills is a priority, game-based learning offers a practical way to engage students and direct their attention toward academic content (Vásquez et al., 2017).

Within this framework, literacy extends beyond the basic ability to read and write; it encompasses the capacity to understand discipline-specific texts, to communicate effectively about complex concepts, and to apply critical thinking to new information (Jain et al., 2022). Game-based learning naturally supports these forms of literacy by embedding them in meaningful contexts. Many educational games present students with rich narratives, case studies, and datasets that must be deciphered to progress. For example, a business strategy game may require students to read market reports and interpret financial statements before making decisions. In doing so, students practice reading comprehension and critical analysis in a situation that mirrors real-world challenges. They learn the terminology and conventions of their field in context, effectively becoming more *literate* in their discipline's language (Khoo et al., 2025). Because success in the game hinges on understanding such content, learners are intrinsically motivated to engage with texts and refine their comprehension skills. This contextualized practice can be especially beneficial in higher education, where students are often expected to master complex academic and professional literacies that go far beyond general reading ability.

Another important aspect is how game-based learning can integrate writing and communication tasks that reinforce literacy (Aslam et al., 2025). Educational games frequently prompt learners to articulate strategies, justify their decisions, or reflect on outcomes. In a classroom setting, this might take the form of written reflections after a simulation round or group discussions to debrief a game scenario. Through these activities, students practice organizing their thoughts and expressing them clearly, strengthening their writing proficiency. The game environment provides an immediate purpose for writing: students may draft a brief to persuade team members of a strategy or compile a report on their game performance to submit for assessment. In doing so, they are not writing in a vacuum; they are writing to communicate ideas that have tangible relevance within the game's narrative. This relevance helps to transform writing from a purely academic exercise into a vital tool for success, thereby increasing student investment in developing clear written communication (Ismaizam et al., 2022). Repeated cycles of planning, action, and reflection in game-based tasks can significantly bolster students' confidence and skill in handling complex texts and expressing their insights, both hallmarks of advanced literacy.

The theoretical underpinnings of game-based learning further illuminate why it is effective for literacy development (Tian & Naufal, 2025). Constructivist learning theories suggest that learners build new knowledge more robustly when they can connect it to concrete experiences (Cadiz et al., 2023). Games and simulations provide precisely this, a concrete experience in which abstract concepts take on active form. A well-designed educational game functions as a micro-world in which players must understand the rules and information to achieve goals. In the process, they actively construct understanding through trial and error and adjustment. This aligns closely with literacy, wherein learners must connect abstract symbols (words, equations, charts) to meaning. In a game scenario, reading a descriptive passage about a challenge or interpreting a chart of outcomes is immediately tied to an action or decision, reinforcing comprehension through application.

Furthermore, scholars (Lane, 2022; Zahra & Neo, 2024) have pointed out that video games cultivate sophisticated problem-solving and *learning-to-learn* skills. Players continually infer, hypothesize, and draw conclusions, cognitive moves akin to those used in critical reading and academic inquiry. Engagement in these decision-making processes within a game-based context strengthens students' ability to interpret information and apply systematic reasoning, supporting the development of advanced academic reading and analytical competencies.

Finally, game-based learning aligns with student-centered and experiential pedagogies that are increasingly prevalent in higher education (Coleman & Money, 2024), particularly in developing 21st-century skills. Literacy today is not only about consuming information but also about navigating digital environments, collaborating with others, and synthesizing knowledge to solve problems (Kumar &

Prajapati, 2025). Multiplayer and simulation games in the classroom often involve teamwork, requiring students to discuss strategies and negotiate decisions. This social dimension means students are regularly practicing oral literacy, speaking, and listening effectively as they play. It also means they must explain their reasoning and understand others' perspectives, thereby deepening their comprehension of the content. As higher education in countries like Portugal adapts to global educational trends, game-based learning can make learning more active and interdisciplinary. Students immersed in these game scenarios become adept at switching between different *literacies,* such as reading an industry report, interpreting a statistical graph, and communicating a plan, all within one unified learning experience. In sum, game-based learning serves as a catalyst for literacy in its broadest sense, transforming passive learners into active participants who read, write, and converse with purpose as part of their journey through higher education.

AI-Mediated Feedback and Literacy Development

The integration of artificial intelligence into education, particularly as a tool for feedback, represents a significant advancement in supporting student literacy development (Daher, 2025). Feedback is a cornerstone of effective learning; students' progress is best when they receive timely, specific insights into their performance (Slimi et al., 2025). In traditional higher education settings, however, providing individualized feedback on frequent tasks, such as writing assignments or case study analyses, can be challenging due to large class sizes and limited instructor time (Barua & Lockee, 2025; Henderson et al., 2019). This is where AI-mediated feedback offers a transformative advantage. AI-driven platforms can rapidly analyze student work and deliver instant suggestions for improvement (Kaliisa et al., 2025). By doing so, they keep the feedback loop short, allowing students to immediately apply corrections and learn from mistakes while the material is still fresh in their minds. When students submit a written reflection or a project report and receive near-instantaneous guidance on grammar, clarity, argument structure, or even content accuracy, they experience a form of one-on-one tutoring at scale. This immediacy and personalization in feedback are directly linked to better literacy outcomes: students become more aware of their writing pitfalls. They can iterate on their drafts more frequently, a key process in developing stronger writing skills.

AI-mediated feedback tools excel in focusing on micro-level literacy skills without tiring or biasing. For instance, an AI writing assistant can underline unclear sentences and suggest rephrasing, point out overuse of the passive voice, or highlight instances where evidence is lacking to support a claim. Through this process, it functions as a continuous writing support mechanism, encouraging students to refine and strengthen their academic writing proficiency. Over time, students who engage with such feedback start to internalize these recommendations. They might begin to anticipate the AI's critiques and adjust their initial writing accordingly, a sign of growing self-regulation and mastery of literacy (Zhan & Yan, 2025). Beyond writing mechanics, AI can also guide higher-order literacy skills. Some advanced systems use natural language processing to evaluate the coherence and cohesion of an argument or to gauge whether a student's explanation demonstrates understanding of a source text. When a student's essay drifts off-topic or lacks a logical flow, AI can flag this and prompt the student to reconsider how their paragraphs connect to the thesis. This fosters critical thinking about structure and content that is essential for academic literacy in higher education. Importantly, the neutrality of AI feedback, delivered without the personal judgment a student might fear from a human teacher, can make constructive criticism easier to accept. In the context of Portuguese higher education, where students may be writing in a second language or coming from diverse educational backgrounds, AI feedback can serve as a consistent and supportive tool to help all students reach a common standard of academic communication.

Another dimension of AI-mediated feedback lies in reading comprehension and the broader interpretive side of literacy. AI-powered tutoring systems can present questions about assigned readings or even allow students to ask questions about a text and receive explanations (Zhan et al., 2025). For example, a student struggling to understand a dense article about hospitality management strategies could query an AI tutor for clarification on specific passages or terms. The AI, drawing on its trained knowledge base, could then provide a simpler rephrasing or an example to illustrate the concept. This interactive dialogue helps the student actively construct meaning rather than passively re-read confusing sections. It mirrors the experience of having a personal tutor guide one through difficult material, making advanced texts more accessible (Lyanda & Owidi, 2025). Such AI tools can also adapt to the student's level. If the student demonstrates a misunderstanding, the system can break down the information further or offer additional background reading. By scaffolding the reading process in this way, AI-mediated feedback tools support the development of comprehension skills. Students become more confident in approaching complex readings because they know they have a safety net to help decode challenging content. As students' understanding deepens through sustained engagement, AI support can be progressively reduced, thereby promoting independent proficiency. This adaptive feedback model aligns with theories of differentiated instruction and Vygotskian scaffolding (Bao, 2025), in which support adjusts to the learner's evolving needs. Still, now technology can provide this support continuously and at scale.

The role of AI in literacy development is not without challenges, and effective pedagogy must address them to maximize its benefits. One concern is ensuring that students remain the drivers of their own learning rather than over-relying on AI corrections. If a writing assistant autocorrects every error, students might accept changes without understanding them (Le et al., 2026). To mitigate this, educators can frame AI feedback as a conversation. Students should be encouraged to review each suggestion critically and implement only those changes they agree will improve their work. This way, AI becomes a partner in learning rather than an editor that replaces the student's agency. Another challenge is the potential lack of nuance in AI feedback.

Human instructors can recognize tone, creativity, and subtle developmental progress in students' expression that algorithmic systems may not fully capture (Sadegh-Zadeh et al, 2026). Therefore, the ideal use of AI-mediated feedback is in a blended model AI handles the routine, immediate feedback, and instructors step in for higher-level guidance and mentorship (Alnemrat et al., 2025). In a course that integrates a simulation like CESIM, for example, an AI might assist by quickly reviewing each student's reflective journal for writing quality and basic understanding. At the same time, the instructor focuses on discussing the strategic insights and leadership aspects that the AI cannot evaluate. This division of labor can significantly enhance the quality and quantity of overall feedback, thereby supporting literacy from multiple angles. By 2025, many higher education institutions in Portugal and beyond are experimenting with such approaches, recognizing that AI tools, when carefully implemented, can democratize the feedback process (Sánchez-Caballé & Santos, 2025). Every student can receive iterative, detailed critiques and support that was once logistically impossible, leading to a classroom environment where continuous improvement in reading, writing, and critical thinking is the norm.

In summary, AI-mediated feedback is a powerful innovation for advancing literacy development in game-based and simulation-enhanced learning (Liu & Fan, 2025). It provides a safety net and a springboard: a safety net that catches errors and misunderstandings before they calcify, and a springboard that challenges students to reach higher levels of clarity and insight. The immediacy of AI feedback keeps students engaged in a loop of action and reflection that mirrors the way proficient readers and writers operate, constantly questioning and refining their understanding (Wiboolyasarin & Jinowat, 2025). As with any tool, its effectiveness lies in how it is used. Educators in the hospitality higher education field are learning to harness AI feedback systems to complement their teaching, ensuring that technology amplifies human pedagogical intentions (Liu et al., 2024). When balanced correctly, AI-mediated feedback not only polishes the mechanics of student work but also helps shape thoughtful, articulate graduates who can autonomously learn true literacy in the information-rich world they will lead (Chang et al., 2026).

Simulation-Based Pedagogy in Hospitality

Simulation-based pedagogy has become a keystone of innovation in hospitality education, merging theoretical knowledge with practical application in a risk-free virtual environment (Xu et al., 2025). In this approach, students assume simulated roles, such as hotel managers or restaurant entrepreneurs, and navigate complex scenarios that mirror real-world operations. A prime example is the use of the CESIM Hospitality simulation (Aguilera-Castillo et al., 2025), which puts learners in charge of running a virtual hotel and restaurant. Through this immersive experience, students must employ skills across a range of domains: analyzing financial reports, adjusting marketing strategies, managing staffing, and responding to customer satisfaction metrics. The simulation thus serves as a capstone of interdisciplinary learning, requiring students to draw on concepts from finance, marketing, human resources, and operations management simultaneously. Through this process, they develop hospitality literacy, the fluency in understanding and using the concepts, terminology, and quantitative information that drive the hospitality industry. Unlike traditional classroom exercises that may isolate topics, a comprehensive simulation forces students to see the interplay between different decisions, for instance, how pricing strategy affects occupancy rates and ultimately financial performance, thereby promoting a holistic understanding that is a hallmark of expert knowledge in the field.

From a pedagogical perspective, the use of simulations in hospitality aligns well with established theories of experiential learning (Grant, 2025). Kolb's experiential learning cycle, which emphasizes concrete experience followed by reflective observation and abstract conceptualization, is vividly brought to life in simulation exercises (Henríquez et al., 2025). Students first experience the consequences of their management decisions in the game, for example, seeing profits decline after choosing an inappropriate pricing strategy for a given market condition. Next, guided by instructors or structured debrief questions, they reflect on why those outcomes occurred. They might realize that they ignored a piece of economic data or misunderstood the relationship between guest satisfaction and repeat business. This reflection stage naturally leads to abstract conceptualization, in which learners connect their experiences to broader theories or principles discussed in class, such as revenue management theory or customer service best practices. Finally, they engage in active experimentation by applying those new insights in the next round of the simulation, hopefully with improved results. This cyclical process deepens learning far more effectively than memorizing facts, because students are actively constructing knowledge and testing it. In terms of literacy, each phase of the cycle involves crucial skills: reading and interpreting simulation data, a form of textual and numerical literacy, communicating reflections and strategies (both written and oral literacy, and internalizing conceptual knowledge from texts or lectures to apply in the game, academic literacy. Simulation-based pedagogy thus creates a rich tapestry of learning activities that collectively strengthen the student's ability to comprehend information and act on it, a defining attribute of literate professionals.

The hospitality context introduces distinctive dimensions to simulation-based learning, reflecting the industry's strong emphasis on human interaction, service quality, and real-time decision-making. Unlike purely technical simulations, hospitality simulations frequently require participants to integrate interpersonal judgment with analytical reasoning. This dual focus mirrors the operational realities of hospitality environments, where professionals must simultaneously interpret quantitative information and respond to human needs. As a result, simulation-based learning in hospitality supports the development of literacy practices that extend beyond technical comprehension to include communication, interpretation, and situational awareness (Şeker, 2026).

Hospitality simulations often present dynamic scenarios that require both analytical competence and effective communication (Rafiddin o'g'li, 2026). For example, a simulated environment may introduce unexpected operational disruptions, such as a sudden increase in guest demand due to a local event or logistical constraints affecting service delivery. In response, students must assess available information, determine appropriate priorities, and formulate strategic responses within a limited timeframe. These activities frequently involve producing written communications, such as internal staff memoranda or external customer announcements. Through these tasks, students develop the capacity to interpret context and produce written content that is both situationally appropriate and professionally structured.

These experiences contribute to the development of written communication skills under conditions that approximate professional pressure (Felicen et al., 2026). Students learn to translate operational challenges into coherent messages that align with organizational goals and stakeholder expectations. This process strengthens their ability to apply disciplinary terminology accurately, organize information logically, and communicate decisions clearly. Such competencies are essential in hospitality environments, where written communication often plays a central role in coordinating operations and maintaining service quality.

Team-based collaboration represents another critical component of hospitality simulations (Abbas et al., 2026). Students typically work in groups to manage their virtual organizations, requiring continuous interaction, coordination, and shared decision-making. This collaborative structure promotes the development of professional communication practices, including articulating strategic perspectives, preparing concise team updates, and negotiating alternative courses of action. Through these interactions, students refine their ability to communicate effectively within professional teams.

Participation in team-based simulation also strengthens interpersonal literacy, which is particularly relevant in hospitality contexts (Hussain et al., 2026). Students learn to interpret peers' perspectives, recognize implicit concerns, and adapt their communication style to different audiences. These experiences support the development of communication strategies that reflect sensitivity to organizational roles, cultural differences, and stakeholder expectations. As a result, students become better prepared to engage in the complex interpersonal interactions characteristic of hospitality management.

The goal-oriented structure of simulation environments further contributes to the development of problem-solving competencies (Heintalu et al., 2025). Students are required to analyze evolving situations, identify relevant information, and formulate appropriate responses to achieve defined objectives. This process encourages systematic reasoning and supports the development of analytical literacy. By engaging with operational data, reviewing available resources, and evaluating alternative strategies, students learn to approach complex challenges in a structured and reflective manner.

Through repeated participation in these activities, students engage in iterative cycles of analysis, decision-making, and evaluation (Küçükersen et al., 2026). This process strengthens their capacity to interpret information, synthesize diverse inputs, and communicate strategic decisions effectively. Over successive simulation rounds, students refine their ability to integrate research, analysis, and planning into coherent action. In doing so, they develop competencies associated with research literacy and strategic thinking, which are essential for effective professional practice in hospitality management.

Between 2022 and 2025, the adoption of simulation-based pedagogy in Portuguese hospitality higher education has reflected a global trend towards more experiential and technology-enhanced learning (Costa et al., 2025). This period has seen educators in Portugal exploring simulations not as ancillary tools but as central components of courses. The rationale is clear: Portugal's tourism and hospitality sector is a major economic pillar, and there is a growing imperative to ensure that graduates enter the workforce with practical competencies and a high level of professional literacy. Simulations provide a way to approximate practical experience, especially when real-world training opportunities such as internships are limited. For example, during the disruptions caused by the COVID-19 pandemic, some Portuguese institutions used virtual hospitality management games to replace on-site training, ensuring that students still gained experience in decision-making and problem-solving. Reports from these implementations suggest that students found the simulations challenging but rewarding, often commenting that they finally understood the complexities of running a hospitality business after seeing all the pieces come together in the game. This kind of feedback underscores the pedagogical value of simulations: they reveal the *big picture* of hospitality operations in a way that segmented coursework struggles to achieve. As a result, there is evidence of improved confidence and work readiness among students who undergo such simulation exercises, as they have practiced not only technical calculations but also the reasoning and communication that surround those tasks.

However, effective simulation-based pedagogy requires thoughtful integration and support to reach its full potential (Levin, 2025). One lesson from recent initiatives is that simply inserting a simulation into a course is not a panacea; the instructor's role remains pivotal. Educators must set clear learning objectives for the simulation, prepare students with the necessary background knowledge, and facilitate reflection sessions that connect the simulation back to theoretical frameworks (Xu et al., 2025). In Portuguese higher education, where some faculty may be new to these methods, professional development and sharing of best practices have become important. Instructors are learning to balance guidance with autonomy, letting students take ownership of decisions in the simulation while remaining available to coach or clarify when confusion arises. The emergence of AI tools, such as CESIM's own AI assistant for instructors, is poised to assist with this integration. These tools can help analyze class performance data from the simulation, suggesting which concepts students struggled with and where discussion might be focused. They might also help generate prompts for student reflection or create supplementary scenario variations to further challenge students. By leveraging such technology, instructors can more easily close the loop between simulation and curriculum, ensuring that experiential learning translates into enduring knowledge gains (Nguyen, 2025).

In conclusion, simulation-based pedagogy in hospitality higher education exemplifies the shift towards a more applied, student-centered learning model. It transforms the educational experience from passive information reception to active problem-solving and continuous learning (Aris et al., 2025). Students emerge from these courses not only with a better grasp of hospitality management concepts but also with honed literacies: they can read industry situations astutely, communicate decisions clearly, and write analytically about business outcomes (Valeri et al., 2025). In a field as multifaceted as hospitality, these abilities are crucial. The period from 2022 to 2025 has demonstrated the viability and benefits of this approach in the Portuguese context, aligning with international best practices. As technology advances and AI integration becomes more seamless, we can expect simulation-based learning to become even more powerful. It represents a confluence of game-based engagement, real-world relevance, and guided reflection ingredients that together cultivate a deeper form of literacy. In empowering students to *game, read,* and ultimately *lead* in their future careers, simulation pedagogy supported by AI and innovative design is transforming hospitality education into a training ground for agile, literate, and reflective professionals (Bisaria et al., 2025).

CESIM as a Literacy Environment

The CESIM Hospitality Simulation serves as more than a managerial training tool (Zhang & Jiang, 2024); it is a complex literacy environment in which students continuously engage with multiple forms of text, data, and symbolic representations. Within the simulation, participants encounter operational reports, financial statements, customer satisfaction indicators, market trends, and strategic briefs that must be read, interpreted, and acted upon. These elements require students to develop fluency in the language of hospitality management, including both narrative and numerical forms of communication (Lestari et al., 2025). The platform thus becomes a site where reading extends beyond traditional prose to include visual dashboards, performance metrics, and scenario-based narratives that evolve with each decision cycle. Students must make meaning from these varied representations to navigate the simulation successfully, positioning literacy as a central driver of learning rather than a peripheral academic skill.

Within the CESIM simulation, each round generates new textual and data-based materials that require careful interpretation. When students receive their performance reports, they must analyze revenue figures, cost structures, occupancy rates, and guest satisfaction scores. These reports are not static; they are dynamically generated based on student actions, making them highly relevant and immediately meaningful. This immediacy reinforces careful reading because misunderstandings have direct consequences for subsequent performance. Misinterpretations of a cash flow statement or a customer index can lead to strategic errors, prompting students to revisit the data and clarify their understanding. Through this iterative process, learners become more adept at reading complex informational texts, a skill essential in professional hospitality environments, where managers regularly evaluate performance reports and make data-informed decisions (Zhang et al., 2024).

The literacy environment of CESIM also includes written and oral communication among team members. Students collaborate in small groups to discuss their interpretation of the data and negotiate strategic choices. These interactions require them to articulate their understanding clearly and to listen critically to others. Team members may propose alternative interpretations of the same set of figures, prompting dialogue that deepens comprehension. This collaborative reading of data mirrors real-world managerial practice, where diverse perspectives contribute to more robust decision-making. The necessity to justify one's interpretation fosters precision in language and attention to evidence, reinforcing academic and professional communication literacies simultaneously.

Writing is another essential component of CESIM as a literacy environment (Aguilera-Castillo, 2020). Many implementations require students to submit written rationales for their decisions, either as brief justifications within the platform or as reflective documents for assessment. These writing tasks compel learners to synthesize information from the simulation and translate it into coherent arguments. Students must explain why they chose a particular pricing strategy, staffing level, or marketing investment, and support their choice with simulation data. This practice aligns closely with academic writing conventions, as it involves presenting a claim, supporting it with evidence, and organizing ideas logically. Over time, repeated engagement in such writing tasks strengthens students' ability to communicate complex ideas succinctly and persuasively (Joshi,2025).

The multimodal nature of CESIM further enriches its role as a literacy environment. Students interact with charts, graphs, tables, and narrative summaries, each of which requires different interpretive skills. For instance, a line graph showing occupancy trends over time demands visual literacy, while a written market report requires textual comprehension. Integrating these modes challenges students to integrate information across representations, a key aspect of advanced literacy. In professional hospitality contexts, managers often encounter similar multimodal documents, such as performance dashboards that combine numerical data with explanatory notes. By practicing these skills within CESIM, students develop transferable literacies that will serve them in real-world managerial roles.

CESIM also supports metacognitive aspects of literacy by encouraging reflection on how information is used (Zsigmond et al., 2025). After each round, students typically engage in debriefing sessions to review their performance and discuss what the data reveal about their strategy. This reflection helps learners become more aware of their own reading and interpretation processes. They begin to recognize patterns in their errors or successes, such as consistently misreading demand indicators or overlooking cost drivers. Through guided discussion and self-assessment, students refine their approach to reading and analyzing information, which enhances their ability to learn independently. In this way, CESIM not only provides content for reading but also cultivates reflective readers who are conscious of how they construct meaning from complex texts.

Adaptive Teaching and Montessori Aligned Design

The pedagogical design surrounding CESIM integrates adaptive teaching principles with elements inspired by Montessori education, creating a learning environment that is both structured and flexible (Swargiary, 2024). Adaptive teaching recognizes that students enter the classroom with diverse backgrounds, prior knowledge, and learning needs. In a CESIM-based course, this diversity can be addressed by adjusting task complexity, the pace of progression, and the level of support provided. Instructors can use simulation analytics to identify which teams or individuals are struggling with particular concepts, such as financial interpretation or market analysis, and then provide targeted guidance. This responsiveness ensures that all students have opportunities to succeed, reinforcing equity and inclusion within the learning environment.

Montessori-inspired principles further shape the design by emphasizing learner autonomy, self-directed exploration, and learning through experience (Sablić et al., 2025). In a CESIM classroom, students are not passive recipients of instruction but active managers of their virtual enterprises. They decide which strategies to pursue, test their ideas through the simulation, and observe the outcomes. This mirrors the Montessori concept of a prepared environment, where learners are given tools and resources but are free to choose their paths within a structured framework. The simulation itself acts as this prepared environment, offering data, feedback, and opportunities for experimentation. Students are encouraged to take ownership of their learning, which fosters intrinsic motivation and deeper engagement with the literacy tasks embedded in the game.

Self-correction is another Montessori-aligned feature of the CESIM approach. When students make suboptimal decisions, the simulation provides immediate feedback through performance metrics and financial results. This feedback allows learners to identify errors and adjust their strategies without external judgment. For example, if a team overinvests in marketing and sees a decline in profitability, the data itself signals the need for revision. Students learn to read these signals and self-correct, developing analytical and reflective literacies. This process encourages resilience and a growth mindset, framing mistakes as opportunities for learning rather than failures.

The instructor's role in this adaptive, Montessori-aligned design is that of a facilitator rather than a director (Montessori, 2013). Instructors guide students by posing questions, highlighting patterns in the data, and encouraging deeper analysis, but they do not dictate specific decisions. This approach respects students' capacity to learn through exploration while ensuring that learning remains aligned with academic objectives. For instance, an instructor might ask a team to explain how their pricing strategy relates to observed demand trends, prompting them to articulate their reasoning and revisit the relevant data. Such interactions reinforce literacy by requiring students to read critically, speak clearly, and write reflectively about their choices.

This combination of adaptive teaching and Montessori-inspired design effectively supports diverse learners. Students who grasp concepts quickly can explore more advanced strategies within the simulation, while those who need more time can revisit data and seek clarification without stigma. The platform's analytics and feedback mechanisms provide a safety net that helps instructors tailor their support. As a result, CESIM-based courses can accommodate varying levels of preparedness, including multilingual students and those with limited prior exposure to business concepts. By allowing each learner to progress at an appropriate pace while engaging with the same core tasks, the design promotes equitable access to complex literacy experiences.

Flipped Classroom and Inquiry Based Learning

The integration of CESIM into a flipped classroom model further enhances its capacity to support literacy and deep learning (del Rocío Fernández-Velásquez et al., 2025). In a flipped classroom, students engage with foundational content outside of class, often through readings, videos, or tutorials, and then apply that knowledge during in-class activities (Sancar-Tokmak & Dagli, 2025). This structure aligns well with simulation-based learning, as it allows class time to be devoted to active problem solving, discussion, and reflection. Students might review theoretical material on revenue management or customer satisfaction before class, then use CESIM during class to apply those concepts in a simulated environment. This approach encourages students to arrive prepared by engaging with the relevant texts beforehand, which supports reading comprehension and information retention.

In the classroom, the simulation serves as the focal point of inquiry-based learning (Arifin et al., 2025). Students are presented with authentic problems that require investigation and reasoning. For example, a decline in guest satisfaction within the simulation prompts questions about service quality, pricing, or staffing. Teams must analyze the available data, discuss possible causes, and test their hypotheses through subsequent decisions. This process mirrors the scientific method, with cycles of observation, hypothesis, experimentation, and evaluation. Such inquiry fosters critical literacy, as students learn to question information, seek evidence, and justify conclusions. Rather than accepting data at face value, they develop habits of skeptical and analytical reading that are essential in both academic and professional contexts.

The flipped and inquiry-based design also supports collaborative literacy practices (Austin, 2025). In-class time is often spent in group discussions where students compare interpretations of the simulation data and debate strategic options. These conversations require careful listening, precise language, and the ability to synthesize multiple viewpoints. Students learn to articulate their ideas clearly and to reference specific evidence from the simulation to support their claims. This collaborative discourse strengthens both oral and written communication skills, as insights from discussions often inform written reflections or reports (Kantanen, 2026). The social nature of inquiry also helps students build confidence in expressing themselves, particularly those who may be less comfortable with formal academic writing.

Reflective activities are a key component of this model (Philippakos et al., 2025). After each simulation round, students are typically asked to reflect on what occurred, why it happened, and what they plan to do next. These reflections can be written or discussed orally, but in either case, they require students to integrate information from multiple sources and present a coherent narrative. Reflection transforms experience into learning by prompting students to connect their actions with underlying principles. It also reinforces metacognitive literacy, as students become more aware of how they interpret information and make decisions. Through sustained engagement in reflective practice, learners develop greater strategic awareness in reading and writing, enhancing their capacity to monitor and regulate their own understanding (Morris, 2025).

The flipped classroom and inquiry-based learning approach also contributes to inclusivity and equity (Curran et al., 2025). By providing foundational materials outside of class, students can engage with them at their own pace and revisit difficult sections as needed. This flexibility benefits students who may require more time to process complex texts, including those for whom English is a second language. In-class inquiry then builds on this preparation, allowing all students to participate meaningfully in discussion and problem-solving (Gomez, 2025). The collaborative nature of the simulation ensures that no single student bears the full burden of understanding, as teams pool their knowledge and support one another (Kapici, 2026).

Together, the flipped classroom and the inquiry-based learning framework transform CESIM into a powerful tool for literacy development. Students read and interpret preparatory materials, engage with dynamic simulation texts, discuss and debate their findings, and write reflections that consolidate learning. This integrated cycle ensures that literacy is not treated as an isolated skill but as an essential component of professional practice. By embedding reading, writing, and critical thinking into the heart of hospitality simulation, this pedagogical design prepares students to navigate the information-rich environments they will encounter as future leaders.

Implementation of Game-Based Learning in Portugal

Game-based learning (GBL) has gained noteworthy traction in Portuguese higher education as institutions seek to enhance student engagement and practical competencies (Zarandi et al., 2024). At the University of Algarve, GBL was introduced to modernize traditional hospitality management education. Specifically, a hospitality business simulation game (CESIM) was implemented in the Hotel Management undergraduate program (Course Unit: Accommodation Management) and the master's in hospitality management and administration (Course Unit: Advanced Management of Accommodation Units). This simulation immerses students in managing virtual hotel operations, requiring them to apply theoretical concepts to realistic scenarios. The adoption of CESIM in these programs since 2022 reflects a broader trend in Portugal toward experiential learning, aimed at improving *hospitality literacy* fluency in industry-specific knowledge and decision-making. Faculty champions of this approach saw it as an opportunity to connect classroom theory with the complexities of real-world hotel management, thereby preparing students for the dynamic hospitality sector.

The initial implementation involved carefully aligning the simulation with course objectives and the academic calendar. In 2022, the instructor piloted the CESIM simulation within a controlled framework: students formed teams to run competing virtual hotel businesses over a series of decision-making rounds.

The GBL approach was phased in gradually, complementing lectures and case studies rather than replacing them entirely. By situating the game within the Portuguese higher education context, which traditionally emphasizes theoretical learning, the University of Algarve aimed to create a blended learning environment. The simulation was introduced as a core learning activity, supported by preparatory readings and debriefing sessions to reinforce concepts, allow students to read, and encourage reflection on leadership and teamwork experiences. This structured introduction ensured that both students and the instructor became comfortable with the new tool and that it met learning outcomes aligned with Portugal's national curriculum standards for hospitality management education (Casau et al., 2023).

METHOD

The CESIM simulation used a design-based approach, emphasizing iterative refinement of the teaching approach from 2022 to 2025 (Rassal & Moreira, 2022). Each academic year, data were collected on key metrics, including the number of participating students, team configurations, simulation rounds completed, and student performance outcomes. Third-year Hotel *Management* students typically enrolled in the Accommodation Management undergraduate course, whereas the *Advanced Management of Accommodation Units* master's course catered to graduate students, often with prior industry experience. In both courses, students were organized into teams that managed a virtual hotel, making strategic decisions across front office management, housekeeping, revenue management, and customer service. The number of simulation moves and decision-making rounds was scheduled to fit within the semester: undergraduate students generally completed 9–10 moves per semester, while master's students completed 5–7 moves in 7 weeks, reflecting the different course lengths and depth of content coverage. Each move corresponded to a business cycle in the game, after which instructors facilitated debriefings to discuss results and link game events to hospitality management theories.

Data on student engagement and performance were gathered through the simulation platform and course assessments. The CESIM system tracked quantitative indicators, including Total Time spent by teams in the simulation environment and Total Result, a cumulative performance score representing financial outcomes in the game. Meanwhile, academic performance was measured by Average Student Grade on a 0–20 scale, the standard grading scale in Portugal, and Average Course Grade contribution on a 0–6 scale for the simulation component of the course. Approval rates and pass rates for each course were recorded to gauge overall success. These data were analyzed year over year to assess trends and the impact of iterative changes to the instructional design. For instance, if a given year's cohort showed lower performance or engagement, adjustments were made the next year, such as altering team sizes or providing additional guidance between simulation rounds. Through this continuous improvement approach, the program sought to fine-tune the balance between game autonomy and instructional support, ensuring the simulation remained both challenging and supportive for learning.

LEARNING DESIGN

Designing the learning experience around the CESIM hospitality simulation required blending gameplay with guided learning activities. The learning design evolved from 2022 to 2025 to maximize engagement and educational value. In the classroom, the instructor served as a facilitator or *game master*, introducing real-world scenarios through the simulation and then stepping back to let students collaborate and lead their virtual companies. A typical cycle in the course design involved a pre-game briefing, the simulation move itself, and a post-move debriefing. During briefings, students reviewed key hospitality management concepts from readings and lectures relevant to the upcoming simulation decisions. For example, concepts of yield management before a round, with a focus on pricing decisions. This approach ensured that theoretical reading components directly informed game strategy, reinforcing literacy in financial and operational terminology.

Classroom dynamics during the simulation moves were notably energetic. Students worked in teams of 3 to 5; team sizes varied by year and program, and students practiced leadership and negotiation within their groups. Each team member often took charge of a functional area, for instance, one student focusing on room pricing, another on marketing expenditures, fostering a sense of responsibility and specialization. The rotation of roles was encouraged across different moves so that each student had a chance to lead a segment of the decision-making process, mirroring managerial role rotation in hotel operations. The instructor monitored these interactions and intervened only when necessary to guide discussions or refocus learning objectives. After each move, the class engaged in reflective debrief sessions. In these sessions, teams presented their results, such as occupancy rates or profit margins and analyzed why certain strategies succeeded or failed. The reflective discussions linked game outcomes to core hospitality management concepts, thereby deepening students' conceptual understanding and industry literacy. Over the four-year period, the learning design became progressively student-centered: by 2025, students were largely self-directed during simulation rounds, with the instructor providing feedback primarily during the debriefs. This evolution indicates growing student confidence and competence in autonomously applying hospitality knowledge, a key goal of the Game, Read, Lead approach.

Student Engagement and Literacy Outcomes

The implementation of game-based learning through the CESIM simulation has positively impacted student engagement and learning outcomes, as evidenced by quantitative data collected from 2022 through 2025. Table 1 and Table 2 summarize the yearly data for the undergraduate and master's programs, respectively, highlighting trends in participation and performance. In the undergraduate course, cohort sizes fluctuated from 51 students in 2022 to 30 in 2023, then rising to 42 and 39 in subsequent years, while the master's course saw a gradual decline in enrollment from 24 students in 2022 to 17 by 2025. Despite these variations, both programs maintained a consistent team-based simulation structure. Undergraduate students were typically split into 10–12 teams each year, whereas master's students formed 4–7 teams proportional to their smaller class size. Notably, after the initial pilot year, the undergraduate simulation was standardized to 10 moves per year, reflecting full integration into the semester schedule. In comparison, the master's simulation ranged from 5 to 7 moves, aligning with its shorter, intensive format. These adjustments to the number of moves and teams over time indicate an adaptive approach to pacing and group dynamics: for instance, in 2024, the undergraduate course increased the number of teams to 12 to reduce team size and encourage more active participation per student; this was maintained in 2025 due to positive feedback.

Table 1. Undergraduate Program – CESIM Hospitality Simulation Results (2022–2025)

Year	Students	Simulation Moves	Teams	Total Time (Hours)	Average Grade (0-20)	Approval Rate (%)
2022	51	9	10	677.33	13.21	94
2023	30	10	10	535.21	14.40	100
2024	42	10	12	740.70	12.75	93.18
2025	39	10	12	789.67	13.90	95

Table 2. Master's Program – CESIM Hospitality Simulation Results (2022–2025)

Year	Students	Simulation Moves	Teams	Total Time (Hours)	Average Grade (0-20)	Approval Rate (%)
2022	24	5	5	384.91	14.09	100
2023	23	7	7	456.86	15.81	100
2024	191	6	6	465.04	14.12	100
2025	17	5	4	359.17	12.40	100

Engagement levels, as reflected by the Total Time invested in the simulation, were high in both programs. Undergraduate teams cumulatively spent more time on the platform, from about 535.21 hours in 2023 to 789.67 hours in 2025, suggesting that students in later years dedicated more effort to the game. This rise in total engagement time may be attributed to refined instructional strategies that encouraged deeper involvement, for example, more structured debriefs and the competitive motivation of inter-team comparisons. The master's students, despite their shorter course duration, also showed substantial time investment, peaking at 465.04 hours in 2024. The slightly lower total time in 2025, 359.17 hours for the master's cohort might reflect the smaller class size and fewer moves, but even on a per-student basis, the commitment remained strong. The Total Result outcomes in the simulation, a composite score representing financial performance, further illustrate student engagement and learning progression. In the undergraduate course, total results improved notably from 2022 through 2024, reaching a high of about 5.51 million euros in simulation currency in 2024, before slightly dropping in 2025. This peak corresponds to the year with the most teams, suggesting that increased competition and smaller team sizes may have driven better overall performance. Master's students achieved an exceptional total result in 2023, over 3.11 million euros compared to other years, possibly due to that cohort's particular aptitude or extra rounds of play. Their results, while lower in absolute terms than the undergraduates' owing to different game scenarios and fewer students), showed a generally positive engagement with the simulation. The sustained 100% approval rate in the master's program across all four years is a strong indicator of success; every graduate student met the learning objectives sufficiently each year. In the undergraduate program, approval rates also remained high, reaching 100% in 2023 and staying in the mid-90s percentile in other years. These consistently high pass rates suggest that the integration of the simulation did not hinder academic achievement; with improved student success, as seen in 2023, when all undergraduate students passed, a notable accomplishment for a class of that size.

In terms of student literacy outcomes, the average grades provide insight into how well students mastered the course material over this period. Undergraduate average grades hovered in the low-to-mid range, approximately 12.7 to 14.4, whereas the master's students' averages were slightly higher in the early years, peaking at 15.81 in 2023, before converging toward the 12–14 range by 2025. The overall stability of these averages, with both groups typically scoring in the low-to-mid teens, indicates that students met the learning outcomes at a satisfactory level throughout the simulation's implementation. Notably, the undergraduate average grade rose to 14.40 in 2023, the year with full simulation integration and maximum pass rate, suggesting a positive impact of the GBL approach on student performance. In 2024, a dip in the undergraduate average to 12.75 corresponded with the introduction of more teams and possibly increased difficulty. Still, the following year saw a rebound to 13.90, implying that students and instructors had adapted to the new format. The master's program showed an outstanding average in 2023, likely reflecting a strong cohort and the benefits of the simulation as a capstone-like experience. By 2025, the master's average grade was 12.40, slightly lower than in prior years; this could be due to the smaller cohort, in which each student's performance had a larger effect on the average, or to a more challenging implementation that year. Nevertheless, all master's students passed, and an average above 60% since 12/20 is 60% indicates competent achievement of the course objectives.

Across both programs, the Average Course Grade 0–6 remained high throughout the implementation, typically above 5.0 out of 6.0 each year. This metric, which represents the portion of the course grade derived from the simulation and related assessments, demonstrates that most students performed well in the simulation-based components. In the undergraduate course, the average course grade was highest in 2022, 5.70 and then stabilized around the low-5 range in later years, whereas the master's course saw a peak of 5.88 in 2024. These scores correspond to strong B+ or A-level performance in conventional grading terms, underscoring that most students not only enjoyed the simulation's engaging aspects but also learned the material to a high standard. The small fluctuations in average grades and course scores from year to year are expected in educational settings. They can result from differences in cohort academic preparedness or minor changes in game scenarios. Importantly, there were no severe drops in performance after introducing the simulation; on the contrary, the data suggest that students maintained or improved their mastery of hospitality management concepts. Qualitative observations from instructors reinforce these findings: students in both the undergraduate and master's courses demonstrated enhanced ability to interpret hospitality business data and apply strategic management principles in discussions and written reflections, indicating a deeper literacy in the domain.

In summary, the period from 2022 to 2025 saw the successful implementation of a game-based learning strategy in hospitality management education. Through thoughtful instructional design and continuous refinement, the University of Algarve integrated the CESIM simulation into its curriculum, energizing classroom dynamics and improving learning outcomes. Students became more engaged, as shown by increased time invested and active participation, and achieved high levels of success on their assessments. The combination of *Game, Read, Lead* elements cultivated not only higher performance metrics, grades, and pass rates but also fostered critical thinking, teamwork, and practical decision-making skills. These results support the conclusion that simulation-driven game-based learning can significantly enhance hospitality literacy in higher education, preparing students to transition more confidently from the academic environment to leadership roles in the hospitality industry.

CONCLUSIONS

The conclusions drawn from this study reaffirm the transformative potential of game-based learning in hospitality education (Alshammari et al., 2026). By integrating a simulation platform like CESIM into the curriculum, the chapter demonstrates that hospitality students can significantly enhance their conceptual understanding and practical skills (Zhang & Jiang, 2024). The *GAME, READ, LEAD* approach was instrumental in bridging theoretical knowledge with real-world application. Through gameplay, students actively applied hospitality management concepts in a risk-free, immersive environment, while complementary reading and reflection deepened their understanding of the underlying principles. This interaction between experiential learning and critical analysis has led to a measurable improvement in what can be termed hospitality literacy, namely, students' fluency in industry-specific knowledge, terminology, and decision-making processes (Zhang et al., 2024).

A key finding highlighted is that students engaged with the CESIM simulation exhibited greater confidence and competence in handling complex hospitality scenarios. The simulation's interactive nature required participants to interpret financial reports, market data, and operational metrics, thereby strengthening their analytical literacy and business acumen (Austin, 2025). Moreover, the game's competitive yet collaborative setting fostered soft skills such as teamwork, leadership, and communication. Taken together, these outcomes suggest that the method used effectively prepares students for the multifaceted demands of the hospitality industry (Bailey et al., 2026).

This chapter's findings also emphasize that integrating emerging technologies, particularly AI, can further enhance the learning experience (Daher, 2025). The CESIM platform's contemporary developments include AI-driven tools that support instructors and provide real-time feedback. Incorporating such tools aligns with modern educational trends and helps keep instruction relevant in an era where artificial intelligence and data-driven decision-making are increasingly prevalent in industry practice. Thus, an overarching conclusion is that embracing innovative pedagogies, such as simulation games, especially when combined with structured reading and guided leadership opportunities, can profoundly enhance the quality and relevance of hospitality management education (Liu & Fan, 2025). Such an approach cultivates graduates who are not only knowledgeable but also adaptable, analytically skilled, and prepared to lead in a technology-enhanced hospitality landscape.

Implications for Students

The implications of these findings for students are significant. First and foremost, students stand to gain a richer educational experience that goes beyond rote learning of hospitality theories (Slimi et al., 2025). Through the simulation game, learners engage actively with material that would otherwise remain abstract, thereby internalizing concepts more deeply (Şeker, 2026). They learn to read and interpret key performance indicators and financial statements in the game's hotel and restaurant scenarios, thereby building their industry-specific literacy. This indicates that upon entering the workforce, students are more fluent in the language of hospitality management, from understanding occupancy rates and revenue per available room to interpreting customer satisfaction metrics, and can apply this knowledge in practice with greater ease (Grant, 2025).

Additionally, the game-based learning environment nurtures essential soft skills that traditional lecture-based approaches may not fully cultivate (Jain et al., 2022). Students participating in CESIM simulations often work in teams to manage their virtual hospitality businesses, thereby developing their collaboration and communication skills. They must negotiate decisions, delegate responsibilities, and lead their peers in problem-solving tasks under time constraints, paralleling real-life managerial challenges. As a result, students emerge from the course more confident in their leadership capacities and better prepared for the interpersonal demands of the hospitality workplace.

Importantly, this approach also encourages students to adopt an active learning mindset and adaptability. By taking charge of decisions in the simulation, learners shift from passive recipients of knowledge to protagonists in their own education. They experience firsthand the consequences of strategic choices, which instill a deeper understanding of cause and effect in business operations. When mistakes are made in a safe simulation, students can reflect and learn without real-world consequences, fostering resilience and a growth mindset. Furthermore, exposure to the CESIM platform familiarizes students with advanced educational technology and introduces them to the potential of AI-driven feedback tools. In an industry rapidly adopting digital innovations from AI-powered customer service to data analytics in decision-making, students who have honed digital literacy and adaptability through such simulations are likely to navigate their future workplaces more effectively.

Implications for Instructors

For instructors, adopting a CESIM simulation in their teaching practice carries meaningful implications for pedagogy and professional development (Khoo et al., 2025). One significant implication is the transformation of the instructor's role from a traditional lecturer to an experiential learning facilitator. In a simulation-enhanced classroom, instructors guide students through complex decision-making processes rather than simply delivering content. This requires educators to develop new strategies, such as debriefing sessions in which students' game decisions are analyzed and linked to theoretical frameworks (Lane, 2022). By helping students critically *read* the outcomes of their gameplay, instructors can ensure that the simulation's lessons are fully understood and applied.

The introduction of game-based learning also challenges instructors to integrate multiple instructional approaches (Jain et al., 2022). It is beneficial to integrate the simulation with complementary readings, case studies, or mini-lectures that reinforce the concepts at play (Lasley, 2017). In practice, an instructor might assign academic articles or textbook chapters to the *Read* component before or after each simulation round, then lead discussions linking those ideas to the decisions students made in the game. This integrated approach ensures that the simulation does not operate in a vacuum but rather reinforces and is reinforced by the course's overall curriculum. Instructors must therefore be adept at curriculum design, weaving together traditional content and interactive experiences to maximize learning outcomes.

Moreover, the presence of advanced technologies, such as AI, within the CESIM platform offers instructors new tools to enhance teaching effectiveness (Madshaven et al., 2025). For example, an AI-driven analytics tool can help instructors monitor student performance in real time and identify areas where students struggle with the material. Such insights enable targeted intervention, allowing educators to tailor their feedback and support to each team or individual more precisely (Zarandi et al., 2024). However, instructors also face the task of learning to use these tools effectively. Continuous professional development is necessary, as faculty should stay up to date on simulation features and best practices for facilitation. In essence, instructors who embrace this approach become lifelong learners themselves, adapting to evolving educational technology and refining their mentorship skills to help students get the most from the game-based learning environment.

Implications for Higher Education Schools

At the institutional level, the use of simulation-based learning in hospitality programs carries broad implications for higher education schools and faculties. One key implication is the need to invest in and support innovative pedagogical tools (Zhang & Jiang, 2024). Implementing CESIM or similar simulation platforms requires not only financial resources for licensing and technology infrastructure, but also administrative commitment to curricular change. Academic leaders must recognize the value of such tools in equipping graduates with relevant skills and thereby champion their inclusion in program design. By incorporating game-based learning into hospitality curricula, schools can enhance their reputation for providing cutting-edge, industry-aligned education (Sánchez-Caballé & Santos, 2025). This, in turn, can improve student recruitment and satisfaction, as prospective learners increasingly seek experiential and technologically enriched learning environments.

Furthermore, higher education institutions will need to facilitate training and development for faculty to utilize these simulations effectively (Rafiddin o'g'li, 2026). As instructors adapt to new teaching roles, schools should provide workshops, cross-departmental learning communities, or mentorship programs in which faculty can share strategies for integrating the simulation into traditional coursework. Institutional support is crucial for overcoming initial resistance or uncertainty some educators may have about changing their teaching methods. Over time, a culture that encourages pedagogical innovation can flourish, one in which experimenting with game-based learning, AI tools, and other educational technologies is seen as part of continual improvement in teaching practice (Gawlik-Kobylińska, 2026).

The integration of AI and game-based learning in hospitality education also requires schools to ensure that ethical and effective use guidelines are in place (Nguyen, 2025). Institutions should develop policies governing the use of simulations and AI assistants in the classroom, considering data privacy, academic integrity, and equal access. For instance, if AI-driven feedback tools are available, all students and instructors should have access to and be trained to use them to prevent any disparities (Alshammari et al., 2026). Additionally, higher education institutions may consider forming partnerships with simulation providers or hospitality industry stakeholders to keep simulation content current and realistic. By doing so, institutions ensure that the *literacy* students gain remains aligned with the evolving demands of the hospitality sector. In summary, the move towards incorporating CESIM simulations and similar innovations positions higher education institutions as proactive agents of change, aligning academic outcomes with professional realities and setting a precedent for modernized curriculum design.

Limitations

While the outcomes of this approach are largely positive, it is important to acknowledge the limitations inherent in using a simulation-based pedagogy in hospitality education (Aris et al., 2025). One limitation concerns the simulation's scope relative to the complexity of real-world hospitality operations. A simulation like CESIM, despite its sophistication, is a simplified model of reality. It can capture many variables of hotel and restaurant management, such as pricing, marketing, and operations. However, it may not fully replicate the unpredictability of live customer interactions or the nuances of organizational culture. Therefore, students might excel in the simulated environment yet still face a learning curve when encountering the messier, human-driven challenges of actual hospitality workplaces (Kaplan et al., 2025). This limitation underscores that simulations should complement, not completely replace, real-world experiences such as internships or hands-on training.

Another limitation concerns the generalizability of the observed results. The positive findings reported improvements in hospitality literacy, decision-making, and engagement are contingent on the context in which the simulation was implemented. Factors such as class size, instructor expertise with the platform, and the degree of integration with other coursework can influence the simulation's effectiveness. If not well facilitated, some students may treat the simulation as merely a game to win, focusing narrowly on scores rather than on learning outcomes (Levin, 2025). Additionally, not all students respond equally well to competitive or game-based environments; differing learning styles mean that some learners might feel less comfortable or motivated in the simulation.

There are also practical limitations to consider. Running a complex simulation requires reliable technology and sufficient time allocation within an academic term (Lin & Wang, 2025). Technical issues or steep learning curves at the start can detract from the learning experience if not properly managed. Furthermore, using an AI-enhanced platform demands attention to potential pitfalls such as overreliance on AI recommendations or the need to verify that AI-generated feedback is accurate and pedagogically sound. The initial cost and effort required to adopt such tools can be barriers for some institutions. When weighing the adoption of simulation and AI tools, educators and administrators must consider these constraints and plan accordingly, ensuring that support systems and contingency plans are in place to mitigate their impact.

Future Research Avenues

Building on the insights from this chapter, several promising avenues for future research in hospitality education and educational technology emerge. One area ripe for exploration is the longitudinal impact of simulation-based learning on career readiness. Researchers could track graduates who have experienced the *Game, Read, Lead* approach to see how well their hospitality literacy and skills translate into job performance and career progression. Such studies would provide valuable evidence on whether the benefits observed in an academic setting endure and manifest as competitive advantages in the workforce. This could involve comparing cohorts of students who used CESIM in their studies with those who received more traditional training, examining differences in confidence, adaptability, and early-career success.

Another important direction for future inquiry is optimizing the integration of simulation games with other pedagogical elements. Research could investigate the ideal balance between gameplay and instructional support. For instance, how much and what type of pre-simulation reading, or post-simulation debriefing, are most effective for consolidating knowledge. Experimental studies might examine variations of the *Read* component, such as incorporating reflective journals, discussion forums, or concept-mapping exercises, to determine which methods best reinforce learning from the simulation. Additionally, the role of narrative and scenario design within the game warrants exploration; future simulations could be tailored with diverse scenarios, for example, different cultural contexts or crises, to broaden the scope of hospitality literacy imparted.

Given the emerging role of AI in education, further research should also examine the interplay between AI tools and game-based learning. Investigations could assess how AI-driven personalized feedback or adaptive difficulty settings within simulations affect student learning outcomes. For example, an AI tutor could monitor a student's in-game decisions and provide tailored guidance or additional challenges to address specific weaknesses. Understanding the efficacy and student reception of such AI enhancements will be crucial as these technologies become more prevalent. Moreover, scholarly work can address best practices and ethical considerations for deploying AI in simulation pedagogy, ensuring that these tools support, rather than undermine, critical thinking and academic integrity.

Finally, expanding the concept of hospitality literacy itself could be a rich field of study. The industry is evolving with trends such as sustainability, global diversity, and advanced analytics, suggesting that the definition of hospitality literacy will change as well. Future research might explore how simulation-based learning can incorporate these emerging domains, such as integrating sustainability metrics into simulations or designing scenarios that require cross-cultural guest management. By continuously updating and examining what constitutes essential literacy for hospitality professionals, educators can keep their teaching methods aligned with the industry's changing needs. In sum, future research should not only refine the educational strategies introduced in this chapter but also push the boundaries of how games, reading, leadership, and AI together can redefine learning in hospitality and beyond.

FUNDING

This work is funded by national funds through the Foundation for Science and Technology, under the project UID/00057/2025.

CIDEHUS -https://doi.org/10.54499/UID/00057/2025

DISCLOSURE OF DELEGATION TO GENERATIVE AI

The author declares the use of generative AI in the research and writing process. According to the GAIDeT taxonomy (2025), the following tasks were delegated to GAI tools under full human supervision:

- Proofreading and editing

  The GAI tool used was Grammarly version 1.162.2.0.
  Responsibility for the final manuscript lies entirely with the authors.
  GAI tools are not listed as authors and do not bear responsibility for the final outcomes.
  Declaration submitted by: Author
  Additional note: Improve the paper's readability.

REFERENCES

Abbas, M., Hussain, K., Bajwa, S. U., & Rasheed, M. A. (2026). Digital capabilities as a catalyst for team effectiveness: Insights from hospitality. *International Journal of Contemporary Hospitality Management*, *38*(1), 210–227. DOI: 10.1108/IJCHM-03-2025-0434

Aguilera-Castillo, A., Guerrero-Cabarcas, M., Fúquene, C. A., & Rios, W. F. (2020). Simulations in business education: A case study of Cesim™ Global Challenge. In *Teaching, learning, and leading with computer simulations* (pp. 128–158). IGI Global. DOI: 10.4018/978-1-7998-0004-0.ch005

Alnemrat, A., Aldamen, H., Almashour, M., Al-Deaibes, M., & AlSharefeen, R. (2025). AI vs. teacher feedback on EFL argumentative writing: A quantitative study. [). Frontiers Media SA.]. *Frontiers in Education*, *10*, 1614673. DOI: 10.3389/feduc.2025.1614673

Alshammari, S. H., Alshammari, A. E. A., Alghamdi, B. A., Alrashidi, M. E., Rosli, M. S., & Risdianto, E. (2026). Artificial intelligence in educational technology: A systematic review of pedagogical opportunities, implementation challenges, and ethical considerations. *International Journal on Studies in Education*, *8*(1), 17–37. DOI: 10.46328/ijonse.5974

Arifin, Z., Saputro, S., & Kamari, A. (2025). The effect of inquiry-based learning on students' critical thinking skills in science education: A systematic review and meta-analysis. *Eurasia Journal of Mathematics, Science and Technology Education*, *21*(3), em2592. DOI: 10.29333/ejmste/15988

Aris, M., Ludecke, M., & Crawford, R. (2025). Exploring the use of theatre methods within simulation-based teacher education: A scoping review. *Teachers and Teaching*, •••, 1–25. DOI: 10.1080/13540602.2025.2518402

Aslam, F., Rahman, H., Wahid, S. A., Wahid, S. A., & Ali, N. (2025). Enhancing children's learning experience through alphabet AR-game: A usability and acceptability assessment of augmented reality game-based learning. *Multimedia Tools and Applications*, *84*(25), 29183–29205. DOI: 10.1007/s11042-024-20346-0

Austin, M. S. (2025). Innovative pedagogical approaches: Exploring flipped classroom, inquiry-based learning, and project-based learning. *Educator Insights: Journal of Teaching Theory and Practice*, *1*(1), 1–7.

Bailey, R. P., Hoe, T. W., Morrison, G. Z., Ali, A., & Samsudin, N. (2026). Rethinking higher education: Embodied learning and pedagogical transformation. *Higher Education*, •••, 1–21. DOI: 10.1007/s10734-025-01581-2

Bao, P. (2025). Delineating translanguaging: Theoretical distinctions from code-switching and a Vygotskian model of cognitive scaffolding in multilingual classrooms. *International Journal of Multilingualism*, •••, 1–22. DOI: 10.1080/14790718.2025.2575886

Barua, L., & Lockee, B. (2025). Flexible assessment in higher education: A comprehensive review of strategies and implications. *TechTrends*, *69*(2), 301–309. DOI: 10.1007/s11528-025-01039-3

Bisaria, C., Srikanth, R., Al-Nussairi, A. K. J., Ali, A. D., Al-Hussein, R. K. A., & Durairaj, B. (2025, August). Deep reinforcement learning-optimized resource allocation system for agile management. In *2025 International Conference on Recent Innovation in Science Engineering and Technology (ICRISET)* (pp. 1–7). IEEE. DOI: 10.1109/ICRISET64803.2025.11253820

Breland, C. D. (2026). Amplifying assets: Literacy leadership teams, culturally relevant pedagogy, and multiliteracies turn. *Journal of Adolescent & Adult Literacy*, *69*(5), e70039. DOI: 10.1002/jaal.70039

Cadiz, G. S., Lacre, G. J. R., Delamente, R. L., & Diquito, T. J. A. (2023). Game-based learning approach in science education: A meta-analysis. *International Journal of Social Science and Human Research*, *6*(03), 1856–1865. DOI: 10.47191/ijsshr/v6-i3-61

Casau, M., Dias, M. F., & Amorim, M. (2023). Entrepreneurship and game-based learning in higher education: A systematic review. In *European Conference on Games Based Learning*. DOI: 10.34190/ecgbl.17.1.1785

Chang, W., Swift, A. W., & Shulga, L. V. (2026). Artificial intelligence (AI) preparedness in hospitality: A framework and research agenda for building organizational capacities. *International Journal of Contemporary Hospitality Management*, *38*(4), 1–20. DOI: 10.1108/IJCHM-04-2025-0525

Chaves-Yuste, B., de-la-Peña, C., & Candel, E. C. (2026). Digital game-based learning: Does it improve university students' learning in an online context? *Knowledge Management & E-Learning*, *18*(1), 39.

Chen, J., & Alibakhshi, G. (2026). AI-powered applications' effects on English language learners' cognitive, metacognitive, and resource management strategies, and language achievement. *Journal of Computer Assisted Learning*, *42*(1), e70171. DOI: 10.1002/jcal.70171

Chew, P., & Da, L. I. (2025). Bridging the AI literacy gap: A constructivist, no-code AI curriculum for secondary students. *Computational Thinking and STEM Education, 14.*

Coleman, T., & Money, A. G. (2024). Developing a game design framework to embed student-centred learning. *The International Journal of Information and Learning Technology*, *41*(4), 448–469. DOI: 10.1108/IJILT-11-2023-0226

Costa, P. R., Silva, E. J., Figueira, A., & Noversa, D. (2025, September). The impact of artificial intelligence in Portuguese higher education. In *International Conference on Communication and Applied Technologies* (pp. 447–461). Springer Nature Switzerland.

Curran, S. N., Freed, R., & Root, A. M. (2025). Beyond the answer: Exploring question-asking and promoting inclusivity. In *Accessibility, inclusivity and diversity in education and beyond* (pp. 153–168). Springer Nature Switzerland. DOI: 10.1007/978-3-031-81795-3_7

Daher, R. (2025). Integrating AI literacy into teacher education: A critical perspective paper. *Discover Artificial Intelligence*, *5*(1), 217. DOI: 10.1007/s44163-025-00475-7

del Rocío Fernández-Velásquez, J., López-Regalado, O., & Fernández-Hurtado, G. A. (2025). Educational dualism in action: Systematic review of gamification and flipped classrooms' effects on young learners. *Contemporary Educational Technology*, *17*(1).

Dewan, M. S. (2025). Fostering language proficiency through literature: Navigating challenges and opportunities in multilingual and multicultural classrooms. In *The handbook of English language education in Nepal* (pp. 126–137).

Dogan, M., & Arslan, H. (2026). Empowering academics in the digital age: Navigating the transformation of higher education. *European Journal of Education*, *61*(1), e70420. DOI: 10.1111/ejed.70420

Felicen, S. S., Pulhin, J. C. B., Borbon, N. M. D., Apritado, J. M. M., & Ylagan, A. D. (2026, January). Integrating virtual reality technology in tourism and hospitality education: Student learning experiences. In *Proceedings of the 11th International Conference on Frontiers of Educational Technologies 2025: ICFET 2025* (p. 125). Springer Nature. DOI: 10.1007/978-981-95-2521-8_9

Finkelstein, I., & Soffer-Vital, S. (2025). AI as a game changer in inclusive higher education: Bridging educational gaps through formative assessment. *Educational Research and Evaluation*, 1–31.

Gawlik-Kobylińska, M. (2026). Four-dimensional instructional design as a framework for immersive learning to advance inclusive education (SDG 4). *International Journal of Sustainability in Higher Education*, 1–29. DOI: 10.1108/IJSHE-08-2025-0920

Gomez, M. J. (2025). The impact of inquiry-based learning in science education: A systematic review of student engagement and achievement. *Journal of Education, Learning, and Management*, *2*(2), 353–363. DOI: 10.69739/jelm.v2i2.1143

Grant, K. A. (2025). Experiential learning. In *Practical applications of experiential and community-engaged learning methods in business: High-impact teaching practices in business education* (Vol. 1, p. 91).

Green, C., & Giblin, I. (2025). An empty systematic review of the 'pedagogy of multiliteracies' in K-12 since 1996: A generation later, evidence it improves literacy outcomes is lacking from (quasi-) experimental classroom interventions. *Review of Education*, *13*(3), e70118. DOI: 10.1002/rev3.70118

Heintalu, K., Saks, K., Edisherashvili, N., & Dekker, I. (2025). The conceptualisation of goal setting and goal orientation in higher education: A systematic literature review. *Educational Research Review*, *48*, 100709. DOI: 10.1016/j.edurev.2025.100709

Henderson, M., Ryan, T., & Phillips, M. (2019). The challenges of feedback in higher education. *Assessment & Evaluation in Higher Education*, *44*(8), 1237–1252. DOI: 10.1080/02602938.2019.1599815

Henríquez, V. V., Rabanal, I. C., & Abásolo, J. S. (2025). Applying Kolb's experiential learning cycle for deep learning: A systematic literature review. *Social Sciences & Humanities Open*, *12*, 102096. DOI: 10.1016/j.ssaho.2025.102096

Hong, A. L., & Hua, T. K. (2020). A review of theories and practices of multiliteracies in classroom: Issues and trends. *International Journal of Learning. Teaching and Educational Research*, *19*(11), 41–52. doi:10.26803/ijlter.19.11.3

Hussain, S., Soni, G., & Sharma, S. (2026). Workforce readiness: Industry insights on building future-ready talent for hospitality. *Worldwide Hospitality and Tourism Themes*, *18*(1), 1–21. DOI: 10.1108/WHATT-12-2025-0302

Ismaizam, N. M., Rahman, S. F. A., Ahmad, S. N. S. M., Nazri, N. I. I. M., Idris, N. A. A., Ali, N. A., & Aldaba, A. M. A. (2022). An integration of game-based learning in a classroom: An overview (2016–2021). *International Journal of Academic Research in Progressive Education and Development, 11*(1), 1207–1221. DOI: 10.6007/IJARPED/v11-i1/12347

Jain, S. A., Hussaini, N., John, S., Alexander, D., & Sarkar, B. (2022). Game-based learning in higher education: An effective pedagogical tool for enhanced competency building. In *Handbook of research on acquiring 21st century literacy skills through game-based learning* (pp. 138–163). IGI Global Scientific Publishing. DOI: 10.4018/978-1-7998-7271-9.ch008

Joshi, M. (2025). *Foundations of reading, writing, and proving*. Educohack Press.

Kantanen, H. (2026). Active learning in strategic communication: Combining collaborative, flipped and case-based approaches. *Journal of Communication Management (London)*, 1–15. DOI: 10.1108/JCOM-12-2024-0257

Kapici, H. O. (2025). The impact of digital inquiry vs. classroom-based science instruction on learners' outcomes. *Journal of Science Education and Technology, 35*(1), 217-236. doi:10.1007/s10956-025-10246-9.

Kaplan, H., Kalfon, A., Asaf, M., & Yitshaki, N. (2025). Motivational processes involved in simulation-based learning in teacher education: The perspective of self-determination theory. *European Journal of Teacher Education*, 1–20. DOI: 10.1080/02619768.2025.2554684

Khoo, Y. Y., Ramdan, M. R., Abdullah, N. L., Abd Aziz, N. A., & Mahjom, N. (2025). The impacts of game-based learning on thinking and learning in higher education context: A scoping review. *International Journal of Education in Mathematics. Science and Technology, 13*(3), 623–637.

Küçükersen, F., Özemir, P., Dinçer, D., & Demirbilek, O. (2026). Beyond Kolb: Constructing a design learning cycle for the foundation studio. *Journal of Experiential Education, 49*(1), 158–191. DOI: 10.1177/10538259251362141

Kumar, K., & Prajapati, R. P. (2025). The interrelationship of collaboration, digital literacy, and critical thinking in developing problem-solving skills among 21st century students. *International Journal of Innovative Research in Technology, 12*(3), 2692–2701.

Kurniadi, D., Yuliasri, I., Wahyuni, S., & Sakhiyya, Z. (2026). *IT-based integrated skills approach: A theoretical framework for integrating English proficiency and digital literacy*. PT. Sonpedia Publishing Indonesia.

Lane, C. A. (2022). Game-based pedagogy: Educate, collaborate, and engage. In *Handbook of research on acquiring 21st century literacy skills through game-based learning* (pp. 269–288). IGI Global Scientific Publishing. DOI: 10.4018/978-1-7998-7271-9.ch014

Lasley, E. A. (2017). Twenty-first century literacy, game-based learning, project-based learning. *The Journal of Literacy and Technology, 18*(3).

Le, T. H., Huynh, L., Dang, B., Pham, H. H., Nguyen, N. T. V., & Nguyen, A. (2026). Development and evaluation of artificial intelligence literacy training for teacher education students. *British Journal of Educational Technology*, bjet.70047. DOI: 10.1111/bjet.70047

Lestari, D., Ekasani, K. A., Supartini, N. L., & Sulasmini, N. M. A. (2025). An innovative method of teaching English for hospitality: A case in Bali Tourism College, Indonesia. *Journal of Language Teaching and Research, 16*(1), 324–334. DOI: 10.17507/jltr.1601.34

Levin, O. (2025). 'Do not harm': Dealing with teaching-related challenges through the technology of simulation-based learning. *Technology, Pedagogy and Education*, 1–21.

Liang, M. H., & Kuo, S. H. (2026). Systematic review on health literacy through game-based educational interventions in older adults. *Educational Gerontology, 52*(1), 71–84. DOI: 10.1080/03601277.2025.2470273

Lin, Y. L., & Wang, W. T. (2025). Using business simulation games to explore the effects of instructional and technological support on students' psychological needs, cognitive load, and learning achievement. *Journal of Educational Computing Research, 63*(3), 587–626. DOI: 10.1177/07356331241313128

Liu, H., & Fan, J. (2025). AI-mediated communication in EFL classrooms: The role of technical and pedagogical stimuli and the mediating effects of AI literacy and enjoyment. *European Journal of Education, 60*(1), e12813. DOI: 10.1111/ejed.12813

Liu, S. Q., Bilgihan, A., & Kandampully, J. (2025). The intersection of technology, sustainability and consumer experiences in hospitality and tourism for new horizons. *Journal of Hospitality and Tourism Horizons, 1*(2), 87–109. DOI: 10.1108/JHTH-03-2025-0038

Liu, Y., Li, Y., Song, K., & Chu, F. (2024). The two faces of artificial intelligence (AI): Analyzing how AI usage shapes employee behaviors in the hospitality industry. *International Journal of Hospitality Management, 122*, 103875. DOI: 10.1016/j.ijhm.2024.103875

Lloyd, J., Turner, K. H., Rudniy, A., & Jamieson, S. (2025). Building a future with AI: Entry points for reimagining literacy in higher education. In *Reimagining literacy in the age of AI* (pp. 152–169). Chapman and Hall/CRC. DOI: 10.1201/9781003510635-12

Lyanda, J. N., & Owidi, S. O. (2025). Integrating artificial intelligence in micro teaching: The role of ChatGPT for customized feedback and interactive learning. *International Journal of Recent Research in Social Sciences and Humanities, 12*(2), 1–10.

Madshaven, J. M., Omlin, C. W. P., & Spanos, A. (2025). Making historical consciousness come alive: Abstract concepts, artificial intelligence, and implicit game-based learning. *Education Sciences, 15*(9), 1128. DOI: 10.3390/educsci15091128

Montessori, M. (2013). *The Montessori method.* Transaction Publishers.

Morris, D. L. (2025). Rethinking science education practices: Shifting from investigation-centric to comprehensive inquiry-based instruction. *Education Sciences, 15*(1), 73. DOI: 10.3390/educsci15010073

Neina, Q. A., Qomariyah, U. U., & Utomo, A. P. Y. (2025). Community-based multiliteracy assessment as a strategy for strengthening inclusive education. *International Journal of Education and Literature, 4*(1), 134–143. DOI: 10.55606/ijel.v3i3.191

Ngo, T. T. Q. (2026). Hospitality management education in business schools: Insights from Scotland using actor-network theory. *Journal of Teaching in Travel & Tourism*, •••, 1–30. DOI: 10.1080/15313220.2026.2653565

Nguyen, K. V. (2025). The use of generative AI tools in higher education: Ethical and pedagogical principles. *Journal of Academic Ethics*, *23*(3), 1–21. DOI: 10.1007/s10805-025-09607-1

Ni, Y., & Lam, R. (2025). Students' perceptions of multiliteracies development using AI-assisted portfolio assessment. *Pedagogies*, 1–28. DOI: 10.1080/1554480X.2025.2545212

Pham Thi, T. D., & Duong, N. T. (2025). Designing memorable business simulations for learning engagement. *Education and Information Technologies*, *30*(18), 1–36. DOI: 10.1007/s10639-025-13785-1

Philippakos, Z. A. T., Quinn, M., Voggt, A., & Park, Y. (2025). Active literacy learning through a flipped classroom model in teacher preparation programs. *Literacy Research and Instruction*, 1–20.

Rafiddin o'g'li, N. D. (2026). Enhancing the effectiveness of professional training in tourism education through virtual guide simulation systems. *Stanford Database Library of International Journal of Pedagogics, 6*(01), 194–198.

Rassal, C., & Moreira, L. (2022). O ensino do empreendedorismo com recurso à gamificação num curso superior de gestão hoteleira: O caso da Geração Z. In *Atas do 7.º Congresso Nacional de Práticas Pedagógicas no Ensino Superior* (pp. 315–324). UA Editora.

Rocca, S. (2024). Unpacking digital literacies and multiliteracies. In *DIGICOMPASS: Navigating digital multiliteracies in global language education* (pp. 73–95). Springer Nature. DOI: 10.1007/978-3-031-81318-4_4

Rye, S., Sousa, M., & Sousa, C. (2025). Introduction to game-based learning. In *Transformative learning through play: analogue games as vehicles for educational innovation* (pp. 29–68). Springer Nature Switzerland. DOI: 10.1007/978-3-031-78523-8_2

Sablić, M., Mirosavljević, A., & Bogatić, K. (2025). Multigrade education and the Montessori model: A pathway towards inclusion and equity. *International Journal of Educational Research*, *131*, 102600. DOI: 10.1016/j.ijer.2025.102600

Sadegh-Zadeh, S. A., Movahhedi, T., & Bahonar, F. (2026). Emotion AI in the classroom: Ethics of monitoring student affect through facial and vocal analytics. *AI and Ethics*, *6*(1), 37. DOI: 10.1007/s43681-025-00897-0

Sancar-Tokmak, H., & Dagli, Z. (2025). A systematic review of theoretical foundations and learning effects in gamified flipped classroom research. *Evaluation Review*, 0193841X251320438.

Sánchez-Caballé, A., & Santos, C. C. (2025). Perspectives of higher education in Spanish and Portuguese institutions on artificial intelligence: A content analysis. *Edutec. Revista Electrónica de Tecnología Educativa*, (92), 253–269. DOI: 10.21556/edutec.2025.92.3879

Şeker, F. (2026). Simulation modeling. In M. Uysal, O. Icoz, I. çetin, O. Icoz & Y.Bozkurt (Eds.), *Theories and models in tourism and hospitality research* (p. 384-389).Cabi.

Shin, E., & Rowe, J. (2026). Game-based learning for sustainable development: Impacts on students' perceptions by prior knowledge level. *Simulation & Gaming*, *57*(1), 138–162. DOI: 10.1177/10468781251374320

Shohel, M. M. C., Ashrafuzzaman, M., Naomee, I., Tanni, S. A., & Azim, F. (2022). Game-based teaching and learning in higher education: Challenges and prospects. In *Handbook of research on acquiring 21st century literacy skills through game-based learning* (pp. 78–106).

Singh, A. (2026). Cultivating excellence: Learning and development programs in hospitality. In *Talent management in hotels and hospitality* (pp. 401–426). IGI Global Scientific Publishing.

Slimi, Z., Benayoune, A., & Alemu, A. E. (2025). Students' perceptions of artificial intelligence integration in higher education. *European Journal of Educational Research*, *14*(2), 471–484. DOI: 10.12973/eu-jer.14.2.471

Swargiary, K. (2024). *Modern perspectives on Montessori philosophy: Adaptations and applications in the 2020s*. ERA.

Tian, F., & Naufal Umar, I. (2025). Research trends of digital game-based learning for technical vocabulary acquisition: A systematic decennial literature review (2014–2024). *Arab World English Journal, 16*.

Trajkovski, G., & Hayes, H. (2025). AI-assisted formative assessment and feedback. In *AI-assisted assessment in education: Transforming assessment and measuring learning* (pp. 283–312). Springer Nature Switzerland. DOI: 10.1007/978-3-031-88252-4_7

Valeri, F., Nilsson, P., & Cederqvist, A. M. (2025). Exploring students' experience of ChatGPT in STEM education. *Computers and Education: Artificial Intelligence*, *8*, 100360. DOI: 10.1016/j.caeai.2024.100360

Vásquez, S., Peñafiel, M., Cevallos, A., Zaldumbide, J., & Vásquez, D. (2017). Impact of game-based learning on students in higher education. In *EDULEARN17 Proceedings* (pp. 4356–4363). IATED. DOI: 10.21125/edulearn.2017.1942

Wiboolyasarin, K., & Jinowat, N. (2025). AI-powered feedback in second language writing: A systematic scoping review of technological innovations in digital language education. *International Journal of Language Studies*, *19*(4).

Wu, Q., Chen, L., Chen, M., & Huang, Y. (2026). Exploring the impact of artificial intelligence on business talent development in higher education: A systematic literature review and research agenda. *International Journal of Management Education*, *24*(1), 101287. DOI: 10.1016/j.ijme.2025.101287

Xinlin, J., Wenting, L., Shah, K. A. M., Na, M., & Shah Alam, S. (2025). Transforming hospitality decision-making: The impact of generative AI on cognitive alignment and adaptive intelligence. *Journal of Quality Assurance in Hospitality & Tourism*, 1–35. DOI: 10.1080/1528008X.2025.2528044

Xu, Y., Sun, J., & Peng, J. (2025). Present and future trends of virtual simulation in education: A bibliometric analysis. *Education for Information*, *41*(4), 277–301. DOI: 10.1177/01678329251329554

Zahra, I., & Neo, M. (2024). Transforming education with collaborative games: An interactive learning ecosystem to foster students' critical thinking and problem-solving skills. In *ICERI2024 Proceedings* (pp. 2439–2447). IATED.

Zarandi, N., Soares, A. M., & Alves, H. (2024). Student satisfaction and co-creation behavior in game-based learning in the context of higher education. *Journal of Marketing for Higher Education*, 1–22. DOI: 10.1080/08841241.2024.2351118

Zhan, Y., Boud, D., Dawson, P., & Yan, Z. (2025). Generative artificial intelligence as an enabler of student feedback engagement: A framework. *Higher Education Research & Development*, *44*(5), 1289–1304. DOI: 10.1080/07294360.2025.2476513

Zhan, Y., & Yan, Z. (2025). Students' engagement with ChatGPT feedback: Implications for student feedback literacy in the context of generative artificial intelligence. *Assessment & Evaluation in Higher Education*, 1–14. DOI: 10.1080/02602938.2025.2471821

Zhang, F., & Jiang, T. (2024). Influence of blended learning on students' self-efficacy: An empirical study based on CESIM simulation course. *Higher Education and Practice*, *1*(1), 45–52. DOI: 10.62381/H241108

Zhang, Y., Gao, M., Zhuge, J., & Ye, S. (2024). Strategic-oriented multiteam system cohesion and enterprise investment decision: Evidence from CESIM platform online simulation experiment. *International Review of Economics & Finance*, *95*, 103386. DOI: 10.1016/j.iref.2024.103386

Zhu, Z., Hall, C. M., Koupaei, S. N., Lin, F., & Wang, Z. (2026). Influence of AI on usage intention in tourism and hospitality education: The mediating role of perceived trust. *Current Issues in Tourism*, 1–14. DOI: 10.1080/13683500.2026.2622507

Zsigmond, I., Metallidou, P., Misailidi, P., Iordanou, K., & Papaleontiou-Louca, E. (2025). Metacognitive monitoring in written communication: Improving reflective practice. *Education Sciences*, *15*(3), 299. DOI: 10.3390/educsci15030299

Zvereva, G., Hamari, J., Pirkkalainen, H., & Xi, N. (2026). Gamification for ethics literacy. *Journal of Educational Technology & Society*, *29*(1), 291–331.

Chapter 15
Before the Screen:
Game-Based Literacy Learning in Infancy and Toddlerhood

Ross Glen Chandler Nunamaker
http://orcid.org/0000-0002-2126-0528
The Lynda A. Cohen Center for the Study of Child Development, University of Cincinnati, USA

William Arthur Mosier
http://orcid.org/0000-0003-4120-810X
The Lynda A. Cohen Center for the Study of Child Development, University of Cincinnati, USA

ABSTRACT

This chapter reframes early literacy development by centering game-based learning experiences in infancy and toddlerhood, long before children encounter digital technologies or formal reading instruction. Drawing on emergent literacy, sociocultural, and game-based learning theory, it argues that literacy begins at birth through playful, relational interactions embedded in daily routines. These interactions, such as proto-games, narrative play, and responsive feedback, support foundational skills in language, symbolic thinking, and narrative comprehension. The chapter highlights how game-like structures in everyday activities foster motivation, engagement, and meaning-making, providing continuity into later digital and print-based literacy learning. It also emphasizes the importance of recognizing the strengths of family and community-based literacy games. Implications for educator preparation, professional learning, and policy are discussed, urging a shift toward developmentally appropriate and relationship-driven approaches to literacy that begin before the screen.

INTRODUCTION

Literacy development begins long before children encounter structured reading education programs, digital tools, or screen-based technologies. From birth, children engage in meaning-making through responsive interactions, oral language exposure, and participation in socially embedded routines that lay the groundwork for later reading and writing. These early experiences form the foundation upon which later literacy learning is constructed. Understanding literacy as a developmental process that begins in infancy challenges narrow conceptions that position literacy as a skill set acquired only after children

DOI: 10.4018/979-8-3373-7472-7.ch015

begin a structured reading education program (Bus et al., 2015; NAEYC, 2022; Roskos et al., 2023; Teale & Sulzby, 1986; Weiss et al., 2022; Whitehurst & Lonigan, 1998).

Emergent literacy theory has long established that early experiences with language, symbols, and shared meaning are integral to literacy development. Rather than viewing infancy and toddlerhood as a preparatory stage that precedes real literacy learning, emergent literacy frameworks emphasize that children actively construct literacy-related knowledge from their earliest interactions with caregivers and environments (Slot et al., 2020; Teale & Sulzby, 1986; Weiss et al., 2022). Oral language, symbolic play, early narrative understanding, and engagement with books and print all emerge gradually through participation in everyday routines. These foundational competencies are later reorganized and refined as children encounter conventional reading and writing instruction (Gardner-Neblett et al., 2017; Storch & Whitehurst, 2001; Whitehurst & Lonigan, 1998). Contemporary syntheses continue to reaffirm this developmental continuum, emphasizing that literacy learning from birth is shaped by social interactions rather than instruction (NAEYC, 2022; Roskos et al., 2023; Shortridge, 2022).

During infancy and toddlerhood, literacy learning is embedded within daily interactions such as caregiver-child conversations, shared book reading, songs, rhymes, and playful routines. These experiences support the development of oral language, narrative comprehension, and symbolic thinking, all of which are closely associated with later literacy outcomes. Recent empirical research highlights the significance of the first two years of life, demonstrating that the quantity and quality of language exposure during this period are strongly associated with later language, literacy, and socioemotional outcomes (Logan et al., 2019; Slot et al., 2020; Weiss et al., 2022). In particular, back-and-forth conversational exchanges have been shown to support the neural and cognitive foundations necessary for later reading and writing development (Barr, 2013; Salley et al., 2022).

Shared book reading represents one of the most extensively studied early literacy practices, yet it is often underestimated as a literacy activity for infants and toddlers. Research indicates that book-sharing experiences beginning in infancy contribute to measurable gains in vocabulary development, even before children demonstrate conventional expressive language skills (Clemens & Kegel, 2021; Gardner-Neblett et al., 2017; Hsieh, 2025; Murray & Egan, 2014; O'Farrelly et al., 2018). Intervention studies with parents of infants and toddlers further suggest that responsive, interactive book reading supports language growth and early narrative understanding when adults follow children's cues and emphasize shared engagement rather than instruction (Gardner-Neblett et al., 2017; Salley et al., 2022). These findings underscore the importance of early literacy routines that are embedded within caregiving contexts and characterized by warmth, responsiveness, and shared attention.

Despite robust evidence supporting early literacy development, literacy is frequently framed in policy, practice, and public discourse as an activity dependent on formal instruction, academic readiness, or technology-based tools. Such perspectives risk overlooking the rich literacy learning already occurring through play, interaction, and routine-based experiences in the earliest years (Fuller et al., 2020). When literacy is narrowly defined in this way, infants and toddlers are positioned as passive recipients awaiting instruction rather than as active participants in literacy learning. Policy analyses and population-level studies suggest that this disconnect contributes to persistent inequities by obscuring the cumulative impact of everyday language exposure and relational learning opportunities that occur in the first two years of a child's life (Fuller et al., 2020; Logan et al., 2019; NAEYC, 2022; Saracho, 2017).

Reframing literacy as a developmental process rooted in social engagement and symbolic meaning-making invites a broader understanding of how young children construct early knowledge of language and representation. Play-based and game-like experiences offer particularly powerful contexts for this learning, as they allow infants and toddlers to explore roles, narratives, and symbols within emotionally meaningful interactions. Through play, children experiment with communication, negotiate meaning, and engage in early forms of storytelling that parallel the cognitive processes involved in later reading and writing. Recent scholarship emphasizes that these playful interactions are not ancillary to literacy development but central to how young children learn to make meaning (Roskos et al., 2023; Shortridge, 2022).

The concept of *before the screen* provides framing for understanding literacy development in the earliest years as inherently game-based, even in the absence of digital technologies. Before children interact with screens, they interact with people. Before they navigate digital narratives, they participate in shared routines that follow recognizable patterns of initiation, response, and feedback. Games such as peek-a-boo, finger plays, call-and-response songs, and playful naming routines involve anticipation, turn-taking, and repetition. These patterned interactions mirror the structures of formal games and support foundational literacy skills, including vocabulary development, narrative sequencing, and symbolic representation (Barr, 2013; NAEYC, 2022; Teale & Sulzby, 1986; Whitehurst & Lonigan, 1998). Contemporary analyses of play and interaction further highlight how such routines function as early learning systems that organize attention, motivation, and meaning-making (Löhr & Gil, 2015; Roskos et al., 2023).

This chapter builds on these perspectives by examining how game-based approaches to literacy learning can be meaningfully applied to infancy and toddlerhood prior to the introduction of screen-based technologies. By centering literacy development *before the screen*, the chapter emphasizes play, interaction, and routine-based learning as critical pathways for supporting early literacy across diverse early childhood contexts. In doing so, it challenges assumptions about when literacy learning begins and highlights the importance of intentional, developmentally appropriate approaches to literacy that should start at birth.

WHAT *BEFORE THE SCREEN* MEANS FOR LITERACY LEARNING

The phrase *before the screen* is not intended to reject technology outright or to suggest that digital tools have no place in literacy learning. Rather, it serves as a conceptual lens for understanding how literacy develops prior to children's engagement with screen-based media and how those early experiences shape later interactions with digital technologies and games. For infants and toddlers, literacy learning is grounded in relational experiences that occur through play, routine, and interaction. These experiences are not preparatory in a narrow sense. They are literacy learning itself (NAEYC, 2022; Teale & Sulzby, 1986; Whitehurst & Lonigan, 1998). Contemporary scholarship on early literacy and play continues to emphasize that foundational learning systems are established through interaction long before children encounter formal instruction or digital platforms (Roskos et al., 2023; Shortridge, 2022).

In infancy and toddlerhood, literacy can be understood as a process of meaning-making that emerges through social interaction. Long before children decode print or recognize letters, they participate in exchanges that involve listening, responding, anticipating, and expressing intent. Emergent literacy research consistently emphasizes that these early experiences form the foundation for later reading and writing development (Teale & Sulzby, 1986; Whitehurst & Lonigan, 1998). Current research further demonstrates that the quantity and quality of early interaction, particularly conversational turn-taking, is strongly associated with later language and literacy outcomes (Weiss et al., 2022). From this perspective, literacy is not introduced through instruction but constructed through participation in shared activities that carry meaning. Recent syntheses reinforce this view, highlighting how early literacy development is shaped by interactional quality rather than exposure to discrete skills or tools (Roskos et al., 2023).

Literacy as Social Interaction, Not Instruction

For very young children, literacy learning occurs within relationships. Adults and caregivers play a central role in shaping how infants and toddlers experience language and symbols through responsive interaction. Joint attention, turn-taking, imitation, and gestures are not peripheral behaviors. They are core mechanisms through which language and literacy develop (Barr, 2013; NAEYC, 2022; Vygotsky, 1978). Empirical studies of early caregiver-child interaction highlight how contingent, responsive exchanges support neurological and cognitive systems associated with later literacy development, reinforcing the importance of face-to-face social interaction over direct instruction (Weiss et al., 2022). When an adult responds to an infant's vocalization, labels an object a toddler is pointing toward, or repeats a playful sound during a routine, they are engaging in literacy work that is socially mediated and profoundly interactive. Contemporary observational studies of infant-toddler classrooms and home environments continue to document how these micro-interactions support early communication and meaning-making (Hsieh, 2025).

This interactional view of literacy challenges instructional models that prioritize discrete skill acquisition. In the earliest years, literacy does not unfold through direct teaching of letters or sounds. Instead, it emerges through patterns of communication that are repeated and reinforced over time. These patterns often take the form of playful routines that resemble games in their structure. For example, naming games during diaper changes or call-and-response songs during transitions follow predictable sequences that invite participation. The child learns not only words but also how communication works, how meaning is shared, and how narratives unfold. Research on shared reading and dialogic interaction demonstrates that such patterned exchanges increase the quantity and quality of child talk and support early language growth (Clemens & Kegel, 2021; Salley et al., 2022).

Research on early language development underscores the importance of adult responsiveness to infants and toddlers during these interactions. Infants and toddlers learn language most effectively when adults follow the child's lead, expand on their attempts at communication, and provide feedback that is contingent and meaningful (Barr, 2013; Pempek & Lauricella, 2017). Intervention studies demonstrate that when adults are supported in using responsive, dialogic strategies, young children demonstrate stronger language outcomes, even in the toddler years (Heidlage et al., 2020; Salley et al., 2022). These qualities mirror the feedback mechanisms associated with effective game-based learning environments, even though no digital tools are involved. Recent qualitative studies further suggest that educators who intentionally scaffold interaction through play create richer opportunities for literacy learning across diverse early childhood contexts (Hsieh, 2025).

Games Without Gadgets

When game-based learning is discussed in educational contexts, it is often associated with digital platforms, points, levels, or adaptive algorithms. However, game-based learning theory identifies core elements that extend far beyond technology. These include clear structures, repetition, feedback, motivation, and narrative context. When viewed through this lens, many everyday interactions with infants and toddlers can be understood as game-based literacy experiences. Contemporary analyses of play and learning emphasize that these elements are present in early childhood routines regardless of the presence of digital media (Quinn et al., 2018; Roskos et al., 2023).

Consider a simple game such as peek-a-boo. The structure is clear and predictable. There is anticipation, surprise, repetition, and shared enjoyment. Importantly, there is also language embedded in the social interaction. Adults narrate the action, emphasize key words, and respond to the child's reactions. Over time, infants begin to anticipate the sequence and participate more actively. This progression reflects early forms of narrative understanding and symbolic representation, both of which are central to literacy development (Barr, 2013; Karrass & Braungart-Rieker, 2005).

Similarly, finger plays and action songs involve rhythm, repetition, and coordinated movement. These experiences support phonological awareness, vocabulary development, and memory, all while engaging children in a playful format. Research on early literacy highlights the value of such rhythmic and repetitive activities for language acquisition, particularly when they are embedded in warm and responsive social interactions (Roskos et al., 2023; Whitehurst & Lonigan, 1998). Studies examining early play patterns further suggest that these embodied routines organize attention and support early language learning through predictable interactional formats (Löhr & Gil, 2015).

Understanding these routines as games without gadgets reframes how educators and families think about game-based learning. It emphasizes that the motivational and cognitive benefits associated with games do not depend on screens. Instead, they arise from the structure and quality of the interaction. Research comparing digital and non-digital experiences suggests that relational interaction remains the primary driver of learning outcomes in the first two-years of life (Bus et al., 2015; Levine et al., 2019). For infants and toddlers, these non-digital games provide an optimal context for literacy learning because they are aligned with developmental capacities and grounded in social connection.

Equity and Access in Early Literacy Play

Framing early literacy as game-based learning *before the screen* also has significant implications for equity and access. Playful literacy routines are universally available and culturally situated. Every family, regardless of income or access to technology, engages in some form of play, storytelling, or shared routine. These practices may look different across cultural contexts, but they serve comparable developmental functions (Saracho, 2017; Hayes et al., 2025). Contemporary studies of home literacy environments continue to document how routine-based interactions with infants and toddlers support language development across diverse family contexts (Bergman Deitcher et al., 2024; Hayes et al., 2025; NAEYC, 2022).

Research on early literacy has documented wide variation in how families support language and literacy development, often shaped by cultural values and practices (Saracho, 2017; Teale & Sulzby, 1986).

Recent scholarship emphasizes that these variations should be understood as strengths rather than deficits, particularly when viewed through a sociocultural lens that values diverse ways of meaning-making (Brinegar et al., 2024; Miller & Khatib, 2023). Songs, chants, storytelling traditions, and everyday routines all represent genuine and powerful forms of literacy engagement. By valuing these practices, educators can support literacy development in ways that are culturally responsive.

This perspective is particularly important in conversations about innovation in literacy education. When innovation is defined primarily in terms of new technologies, families and communities with limited access to digital tools can be perceived as lacking. A *before the screen* framework counters this narrative by highlighting the richness of early literacy learning that occurs through play and social interaction. It reinforces the idea that foundational literacy development does not depend on technology but on relationships and meaningful one-on-one social interaction (Hayes et al., 2025). Policy analyses suggest that equity-oriented early childhood systems must prioritize relational learning and caregiver support alongside, or even before, investments in technology (Fuller et al., 2020).

At the same time, this framework does not deny the role of digital tools later in development. Instead, it situates technology within a broader continuum of literacy learning tools. Infants and toddlers who have experienced rich, game-based interactions with adults are better positioned to engage meaningfully with digital texts and games as they grow older. Infant and toddler early experiences with narrative, feedback, and shared attention provide the foundation for navigating more complex literacy environments as they grow older (Hsieh, 2025).

By conceptualizing literacy learning *before the screen* as inherently game-based, this establishes a developmental grounding for later discussions of game-based and technology-enhanced literacy (Nunamaker & Mosier, 2021; Roskos et al., 2023). It invites educators and researchers to consider how the principles that guide effective literacy games are already present in early childhood practice. In doing so, it sets the stage for examining the theoretical foundations and practical applications of game-based literacy learning in infancy and toddlerhood.

THEORETICAL FOUNDATIONS OF GAME-BASED LITERACY IN EARLY CHILDHOOD

Understanding game-based literacy learning in infancy and toddlerhood requires a theoretical foundation that accounts for how young children develop language, meaning, and symbolic understanding through social interaction and play. This section draws on three complementary bodies of scholarship: emergent literacy theory, sociocultural theory, and game-based learning theory. Together, these perspectives provide a coherent framework for understanding how playful, game-like experiences function as literacy learning in the earliest years of life. Rather than treating these theories as discrete lenses, this section emphasizes their points of convergence, particularly around the role of one-on-one social interaction, motivation, and participation in a learning experience. Recent scholarship in early literacy and play continues to underscore the importance of integrating these perspectives when examining learning in infancy and toddlerhood (NAEYC, 2022; Roskos et al., 2023; Shortridge, 2022).

Emergent Literacy Theory: Literacy as a Developmental Continuum

Emergent literacy theory offers a foundational lens for understanding literacy development in infancy and toddlerhood. Central to this perspective is the assertion that literacy does not begin with formal reading instruction but develops gradually through young children's early experiences with language, symbols, and print-related exposure (Teale & Sulzby, 1986). Infants and toddlers engage in a range of behaviors that reflect early literacy learning, including listening to language, vocalizing, gesturing, attending to books, and participating in shared routines. Consider an infant who makes an utterance and smiles upon seeing their primary caregiver, or a toddler who brings a book over to an adult who is sitting on the floor. These behaviors are not precursors that must be replaced by *real* literacy later. They are integral components of literacy development along a continuous trajectory (NAEYC, 2022; Roskos et al., 2023).

Research grounded in emergent literacy theory highlights the importance of early oral language experiences for later reading and writing outcomes. Vocabulary growth, phonological awareness, and narrative understanding are all supported through early interactions with caregivers and educators (Whitehurst & Lonigan, 1998). More recent research continues to demonstrate that the quantity and quality of language exposure during the first two years of life are strongly associated with later language and literacy-related outcomes, reinforcing the long-term significance of early interaction (Logan et al., 2019; Salley et al., 2022; Weiss et al., 2022). For infants and toddlers, these interactions are most often playful and routine-based, occurring during caregiving moments such as feeding, diapering, and transitions, such as changing clothing or placing an infant or toddler in a car seat. When adults talk, sing, and respond to children during these moments, they are supporting literacy development in ways that align with the principles of emergent literacy.

From a game-based perspective, these early literacy experiences share important characteristics with games. They are repetitive, predictable, and motivating. Young children learn the rules of social interaction through repeated participation, such as when to vocalize, how to take turns, or how to anticipate what comes next in a familiar routine. Over time, young children become more active participants, contributing sounds, gestures, or words that signal growing linguistic competence. Contemporary analyses of early literacy emphasize that these patterned interactions support engagement and learning precisely because they combine structure with responsiveness; a hallmark of both emergent literacy and game-based learning (Roskos et al., 2023).

Sociocultural Theory and Guided Participation

Sociocultural theory further deepens understanding of how game-based literacy learning unfolds in early childhood. Vygotsky's (1978) work emphasized that learning is fundamentally social and that cognitive development occurs through interaction with more knowledgeable others. Language plays a central role in this process, serving as both a tool for communication and a means of organizing thought. For infants and toddlers, literacy learning is inseparable from social interaction, as young children rely on adults to interpret, model, and extend their communicative attempts. Consider how an adult might label the pictures in a book during lap reading with a toddler. Later, the toddler might emulate labelling those pictures in the same book. This is how a key concept within sociocultural theory, guided participation, applies to literacy learning with very young children. Guided participation describes how adults structure and support children's involvement in activities in ways that gradually increase independence and competence.

In early literacy contexts, guided participation often takes the form of shared reading, joint play, and conversational exchanges. Adults adjust their language, gestures, and expectations in response to a young child's cues, creating an interactive space where learning can occur. Recent studies of caregiver-child interaction highlight how these responsive exchanges support language development and emergent literacy by fostering sustained engagement and meaningful feedback (Salley et al., 2022) and that contingent and consistent adult responses are associated with stronger language and communication outcomes (Barr, 2013; Hsieh, 2025).

Within playful routines, adults often scaffold literacy learning without explicit instruction. For example, when a caregiver narrates a toddler's actions during play or expands on a child's single-word utterance, they are supporting language development through contingent feedback. This feedback is immediate, meaningful, and tailored to the child's level of understanding, which mirrors the feedback mechanisms emphasized in game-based learning theory. Research on dialogic and responsive interaction demonstrates that such contingent feedback is associated with stronger language outcomes in the early years, reinforcing the instructional power of guided participation (Heidlage et al., 2020). Additionally, scaffolding is embedded in everyday practice across early childhood settings, reinforcing literacy development through one-on-one interaction rather than didactic teaching (Cunningham, 2022; NAEYC, 2022; Norris, 2017).

Importantly, sociocultural theory also foregrounds the role of culture and context in learning. The ways in which families and communities engage in play, storytelling, and communication are shaped by cultural norms and values. Recognizing early literacy games as culturally situated practices allows educators to honor diverse forms of literacy engagement and avoid imposing narrow definitions of what counts as literacy learning. Recent work on culturally sustaining approaches to early literacy further emphasizes the importance of validating home-based practices and linguistic diversity in early learning environments (Brinegar et al., 2024; Torr, 2019).

Revisiting Game-Based Learning Theory

Game-based learning theory is typically associated with digital games and formal educational settings. These contexts can make infants and toddlers nearly invisible. Yet if you sit beside a toddler during cleanup time and watch them create a self-invented challenge, such as stacking all of the cups in the same spot, the logic of game-based learning emerges. The core principles of game-based learning are not limited to digital games and formal educational settings. Scholars have described game-based learning as involving active participation, problem-solving, feedback, and engagement within meaningful contexts (Jan & Gaydos, 2016). When these principles are applied developmentally, they offer valuable insights into how infants and toddlers learn through play even in the absence of digital tools.

At its core, game-based learning emphasizes motivation and engagement. Young children are naturally motivated to interact with caregivers and explore their environment. Playful routines capture attention and sustain interest through novelty, repetition, and emotional connection. Research on early play and learning suggests that these intrinsic motivational features support sustained engagement and learning across domains, including language and literacy (Roskos et al., 2023; Shortridge, 2022).

Feedback is another key principle of game-based learning that is readily observable in early childhood contexts. In games, feedback helps players understand the consequences of their actions and guides future behavior. For infants and toddlers, adult responses serve this function. Smiles, verbal affirmations, repetition, and expansion of language all provide feedback that reinforces communication attempts and encourages further interaction. Recent studies highlight that such feedback is most effective when it is immediate, provided consistently, contingent, and embedded within ongoing interaction (Alotaibi, 2024; Barr, 2013; Salley et al., 2022).

Narrative also plays an important role in game-based learning, providing context and purpose for action. Even in infancy, children are exposed to simple narratives through storytelling, songs, and play routines that follow a beginning, middle, and end. As toddlers begin to engage in symbolic play, they create and enact simple stories using objects and actions. These early narrative experiences support comprehension and meaning-making, laying the groundwork for later engagement with more complex texts and games (Karrass & Braungart-Rieker, 2005; O'Farrelly et al., 2018; Roskos et al., 2023).

By revisiting game-based learning theory through a developmental lens, it becomes clear that many of its defining features are present in early childhood play. What differentiates early literacy games from later digital games is not the absence of learning principles but the mode of interaction. In infancy and toddlerhood, games are embodied, relational, and co-constructed, relying on human connection rather than technology. Comparative studies of digital and non-digital learning experiences reinforce that relational interaction remains central to learning in the earliest years (Alotaibi, 2024; Bus et al., 2015; Levine et al., 2019).

Integrating the Theoretical Perspectives

When considered together, emergent literacy theory, sociocultural theory, and game-based learning theory offer a robust framework for understanding literacy learning *before the screen*. Emergent literacy theory establishes that literacy development begins early and unfolds through social interaction. Sociocultural theory explains how these interactions support learning through guided participation and cultural mediation. Game-based learning theory highlights the motivational and structural features that make these interactions effective learning experiences.

This integrated framework supports the central argument of this chapter: that game-based literacy learning is not introduced through technology but is rooted in early play and interaction. Infants and toddlers learn about language, symbols, symbolic reasoning, and narratives through participation in literacy games that are embedded in everyday infant and toddler routines. These experiences provide the foundation for later literacy learning, including engagement with digital and AI-mediated environments.

For educators and researchers, this theoretical grounding underscores the importance of recognizing and supporting game-based literacy learning in the earliest years. It challenges narrow definitions of both literacy and game-based learning and calls for approaches that are developmentally informed, culturally responsive, and grounded in one-on-one relationships. By understanding the theoretical foundations of literacy learning *before the screen*, the field can better design practices and policies that support appropriate literacy development across the lifespan.

THE NATURE OF EARLY LITERACY GAMES IN INFANCY AND TODDLERHOOD

Early literacy games in infancy and toddlerhood are grounded in everyday interactions that are playful, patterned, and socially mediated. These games are not discrete activities set apart from care routines or learning time. Instead, they are embedded within the rhythms of daily life and emerge through repeated participation in shared experiences. Understanding the nature of these early literacy games requires close attention to how infants and toddlers engage with others, how meaning is negotiated through interaction, and how play supports the development of language and symbolic thought. Recent scholarship on early play and literacy emphasizes that these interactions function as powerful learning systems, organizing attention, motivation, and communication in developmentally appropriate ways (NAEYC, 2022; Quinn et al., 2018; Roskos et al., 2023; Shortridge, 2022).

This section examines early literacy games across infancy and toddlerhood, highlighting how game-like structures evolve as children's communicative capacities expand. It focuses on three interrelated features of early literacy games: proto-games in infancy, narrative play in toddlerhood, and the role of feedback and meaning-making across both developmental periods.

Proto-Games in Infancy

In infancy, literacy games take the form of proto-games. These are simple, recurring interactions that follow predictable patterns and invite participation even before children use conventional language. Proto-games rely heavily on turn-taking, anticipation, and repetition, all of which support early communication and cognitive development. Consider an infant who smiles at their caregiver during a diaper change or feeding routine, waiting to see if and how the adult will respond, and even waiting in anticipation for the adult's move. Through repeated engagement in these routines, infants begin to understand the structure of social interaction and their role within it. Research on early social and communicative development demonstrates that such patterned interactions support joint attention, intentional communication, and early language learning (Barr, 2013; Slot et al., 2020).

Peek-a-boo is often cited as a classic example of a proto-game. The game's structure is consistent and recognizable, involving hiding, revealing, and shared delight. Infants learn to anticipate what will happen next, demonstrating early forms of prediction and memory. Caregivers typically narrate the interaction, emphasize key words, and exaggerate intonation, all of which support early language development. Observational studies of adult-infant interaction highlight how these routines foster communicative competence by combining emotional engagement with linguistic input (Barr, 2013; Hsieh, 2025).

Beyond peek-a-boo, proto-games include finger plays, tickling games, and vocal imitation routines. In these interactions, adults often echo infants' sounds or mirror movements, creating a back-and-forth exchange that reinforces the infant's role as an active participant. These exchanges are structured by timing, rhythm, and mutual responsiveness rather than chance. Over time, infants begin to initiate these routines, signaling their understanding of the game's structure and their growing agency within the interaction. Research on early vocal and gestural communication underscores the importance of such reciprocal exchanges for language development in the first year of life (Karrass & Braungart-Rieker, 2005; Slot et al., 2020).

From a literacy perspective, proto-games support foundational skills such as listening, turn-taking, and attention to communicative cues. They also introduce infants to the idea that interactions have meaning and that sounds, gestures, and expressions can be used intentionally. These early experiences with symbolic communication are central to emergent literacy development and illustrate how literacy learning is intertwined with play from the very beginning (Roskos et al., 2023; Teale & Sulzby, 1986).

Narrative Play in Toddlerhood

As children transition into toddlerhood, early literacy games become increasingly complex and narrative in nature. Toddlers begin to use words, gestures, and objects to represent ideas and experiences, allowing for more elaborate forms of play. A toddler might stack up blocks, saying "I stack," then knock them down repeatedly, saying "Uh oh!" each time, then, suddenly, pick up an empty bag, put some blocks and other items in it, then head towards the door while saying, "Bye bye!" as they walk towards it. These actions follow a sequence and even an emerging storyline, which can be viewed as the early roots of narrative construction expressed through play. Narrative play involves sequencing events, assigning roles, and creating simple storylines, all of which support the development of emerging narrative comprehension and expressive language (Quinn et al., 2018; Roskos et al., 2023).

Symbolic play is a key context for narrative literacy games during toddlerhood. When a toddler uses a block as a phone or pretends to feed a doll, they are engaging in representational thinking. Adults can support this play by narrating the child's actions, asking simple questions, or introducing new elements that extend the storyline. Research consistently links symbolic play with language growth and narrative development, particularly when adults engage as responsive partners rather than directors (Quinn et al., 2018; Roskos et al., 2023; Shin, 2021).

Book-related play becomes more prominent during this period. Toddlers may point to pictures, label objects, or repeat familiar phrases from favorite books. Interactive book reading, when approached as a game-like exchange, encourages participation and engagement. Adults may pause to allow the child to fill in a word, ask predictive questions, or use expressive vocalizations to bring the story to life. Empirical studies demonstrate that such interactive strategies support vocabulary growth and narrative understanding more effectively than passive book exposure (Clemens & Kegel, 2021; Gardner-Neblett et al., 2017; Hsieh, 2025; O'Farrelly et al., 2018; Salley et al., 2022; Whitehurst & Lonigan, 1998).

Narrative play in toddlerhood reflects an expansion of early literacy games rather than a departure from them. The core elements remain consistent: repetition, anticipation, and feedback. What changes is the level of symbolic complexity and the child's ability to contribute verbally. Through narrative play, toddlers experiment with language, test ideas, and explore meaning within a supportive, playful context. Recent work on early narrative development highlights how these experiences lay the groundwork for later comprehension and storytelling skills (Roskos et al., 2023; Shortridge, 2022).

Feedback and Meaning-Making

Across both infancy and toddlerhood, feedback plays a critical role in early literacy games. Feedback helps children understand the effects of their communicative attempts and guides future participation. In early literacy games, feedback is provided primarily through adult responses that are immediate, contingent, and meaningful.

For infants, feedback may take the form of smiles, vocal affirmations, imitation, or repetition. When an adult responds enthusiastically to an infant's sound or gesture, they signal that the communication has been noticed and valued. This reinforces the infant's motivation to communicate and supports the development of intentional communication. Research on responsive caregiving emphasizes that such feedback is a key predictor of early language growth (Barr, 2013; Slot et al., 2020). Recent empirical work further demonstrates that sustained, contingent responsiveness predicts later language outcomes, underscoring the developmental significance of early feedback (Weiss et al., 2022).

In toddlerhood, feedback becomes more linguistic and elaborate. Adults may expand on a child's utterance, introduce new vocabulary, or model more complex sentence structures. For example, if a toddler says "dog," an adult might respond, "Oh, a dog! Yes, the dog is running." This type of feedback provides a language model while affirming the child's contribution. Over time, these exchanges support vocabulary growth, syntactic development, and narrative skills (Heidlage et al., 2020; Logan et al., 2019; Salley et al., 2022; Whitehurst & Lonigan, 1998).

Feedback also supports meaning-making by helping children connect language to experience. In literacy games, adults often label emotions, actions, and objects, providing a linguistic framework for understanding the world. These labels are embedded within play, making them more salient and memorable. From a game-based learning perspective, this feedback functions similarly to scaffolding mechanisms that guide learners toward increasingly complex forms of participation (Alotaibi, 2024; Jan & Gaydos, 2016; Roskos et al., 2023).

Importantly, feedback in early literacy games is relational rather than evaluative. Unlike formal assessments or instructional feedback, responses in early play are focused on connection and shared understanding. This relational quality fosters a sense of safety and belonging, which is essential for developmentally appropriate learning in early childhood. Research on early socioemotional development underscores that secure, responsive relationships support children's willingness to explore language and take communicative risks (Miller & Khatib, 2023; Slot et al., 2020; Vernon-Feagans et al., 2013).

Early Literacy Games as Developmental Foundations

Examining the nature of early literacy games highlights how deeply intertwined play and literacy are in infancy and toddlerhood. Proto-games introduce infants to the structure of communication, narrative play allows toddlers to experiment with meaning and representation, and responsive feedback supports ongoing language development. Together, these three elements form a cohesive system of literacy learning that is developmentally appropriate and inherently game-based.

While these early literacy games support immediate language outcomes, they also establish patterns of engagement that influence how children approach learning later in life. Young children who experience responsive and playful interactions with adults are more likely to view communication as meaningful and enjoyable. This orientation toward learning carries forward as children encounter new literacy contexts, including digital games and texts (Hayes et al., 2025). Research examining continuity in learning environments suggests that early one-on-one experiences with adults demonstrating engagement and feedback shape later approaches to literacy and learning (Levine et al., 2019; Roskos et al., 2023; Vernon-Feagans et al., 2013).

By recognizing early literacy games as foundational learning experiences, educators and researchers can better support literacy development from birth. This perspective underscores the importance of intentional, responsive interaction in early childhood settings and highlights the role of play as a powerful context for literacy learning. In doing so, it reinforces the central argument of this chapter: that game-based literacy learning begins before the screen, rooted in the playful interactions that shape early development. Building on this understanding of early literacy games, the next section examines how educators can intentionally support these interactions across diverse early childhood settings.

DESIGNING GAME-BASED LITERACY EXPERIENCES IN EARLY CHILDHOOD SETTINGS

Designing game-based literacy experiences for infants and toddlers requires an understanding of early childhood settings as diverse, relational, and contextually grounded environments. Literacy learning for children from birth to three occurs across a range of settings, including infant-toddler classrooms, family child care homes, Early Head Start programs, and home-based care arrangements. While these settings vary in structure, resources, and expectations, they share a common reliance on routines, relationships, and play as the primary contexts for learning. A *before the screen* perspective emphasizes that game-based literacy learning in these environments is not dependent on formal curricula or digital tools but on intentional interaction and responsive practice (Alotaibi, 2024; Jan & Gaydos, 2016; NAEYC, 2022; Roskos et al., 2023; Shortridge, 2022).

This section explores how educators and caregivers can design and support game-based literacy experiences across early childhood settings by focusing on the environment, the role of the adult within that environment, and the integration of literacy-rich play into everyday routines. Rather than prescribing specific activities, this section highlights principles that can be adapted flexibly to different contexts while remaining developmentally appropriate (Saracho, 2017).

Literacy-Rich Play Environments Across Early Childhood Settings

Early childhood environments play a critical role in shaping opportunities for literacy learning. In game-based literacy learning, the environment functions as a facilitator rather than a director of interaction. Materials, space, and routines invite exploration, repetition, and engagement, creating conditions where literacy games can emerge naturally. Research on early learning environments emphasizes that infants and toddlers benefit most from settings that support sustained interaction, shared attention, and predictable routines rather than overstimulation or constant novelty (Heidlage et al., 2020; Slot et al., 2020; Vernon-Feagans et al., 2013).

Across early childhood settings, literacy-rich play environments often include accessible cloth and board books, familiar objects, open-ended materials, and spaces that support close interaction between adults and children. These environments are designed to be predictable yet flexible, allowing young children to anticipate routines while remaining open to variation. Predictability supports infants' need for a sense of security and toddlers' understanding of sequence, both of which are foundational for literacy development (Gardner-Neblett et al., 2017; NAEYC, 2022; Roskos et al., 2023; Teale & Sulzby, 1986; Weiss et al., 2022).

Importantly, literacy-rich environments do not require specialized or expensive materials. Everyday objects, household items, and culturally meaningful artifacts can all support game-based literacy learning when paired with intentional one-on-one adult-child interaction. Studies of family child care and home-based early learning contexts highlight how ordinary materials are routinely transformed into literacy tools through naming games, storytelling, and pretend play (Clemens & Kegel, 2021; Torr, 2019; Vernon-Feagans et al., 2013; Weiss et al., 2022).

The organization of space also matters. Environments that allow adults and children to interact in close physical proximity support joint attention and shared engagement. Whether in a classroom, a family child care home, or a living room, spaces that encourage face-to-face interaction, shared materials, and uninterrupted play are particularly conducive to early literacy games (Barr, 2013; Slot et al., 2020).

The Role of the Adult as Co-Player and Designer

Across early childhood settings, adults play a central role in designing and sustaining game-based literacy experiences. Rather than acting as instructors who deliver content, adults function as co-players who shape interactions through responsiveness, modeling, and scaffolding. In practice, a teacher may be narrating a toddler's pretend stirring in the dramatic-play area when another child begins to cry, requiring a shift in attention that momentarily disrupts the flow of the original interaction. Yet these imperfect, real-time decisions are part of what makes adult participation meaningful. As co-players, adults observe children's interests and cues, then build literacy games around those interests. For infants, this may involve echoing sounds, mirroring expressions, responding to gestures, or repeating familiar routines. For toddlers, adults may continue those interactions while also extending play by adding more language variety, introducing new vocabulary, or helping children sequence events in simple narratives. This role is consistent across settings, even as specific practices may vary. The adult as a facilitator of learning, rather than teacher, is strongly supported by sociocultural and interactionist theories of early learning (Barr, 2013; NAEYC, 2022; Vygotsky, 1978).

As co-players, adults observe young children's interests and cues, then build literacy games around those interests. For infants, this may involve mirroring sounds, responding to gestures, or repeating familiar routines. For toddlers, adults may extend play by expanding language by introducing new vocabulary or helping children sequence events in simple narratives. Empirical studies of infant-toddler classrooms and home-based care settings show that children's language outcomes are strongest when adults follow children's leads and respond contingently rather than directing adult-child interactions (Heidlage et al., 2020; Hsieh, 2025; Norris, 2017; Vernon-Feagans et al., 2013; Weiss et al., 2022).

Designing literacy games in early childhood settings also involves intentional use of language. Adults narrate actions, label emotions, and model expressive language during play activities. These verbal supports are not scripted but responsive, adapting to the child's level of understanding and engagement. Research on early language development emphasizes that such contingent and meaningful responses are key to supporting vocabulary growth and communicative competence (Torr, 2019; Vernon-Feagans et al., 2013; Whitehurst & Lonigan, 1998). Recent intervention research further confirms that one-on-one dialogic and contingent language strategies support expressive language development in toddlerhood (Salley et al., 2022).

Across all early childhood educational settings, adults also design literacy games by embedding them within routines. Transitions, caregiving moments, and daily rituals provide repeated opportunities for play-based literacy interaction. When adults approach these moments with intentionality, they transform routine care into meaningful literacy experiences. Policy and practice analyses emphasize the importance of recognizing caregiving routines as core learning contexts in infant-toddler programs (Fuller et al., 2020; Recchia et al., 2018; Roskos et al., 2023; Saracho, 2017; Vernon-Feagans et al., 2013).

Examples of Game-Based Literacy Across Settings

Game-based literacy learning can be observed in a wide range of early childhood contexts. In an infant-toddler classroom, a caregiver may use a familiar song during diapering routines, pausing to allow the child to vocalize or gesture in response. Over time, the child anticipates the pauses and participates more actively, demonstrating growing communicative competence. Observational studies of infant-toddler care highlight how such routine-based interactions support language and early literacy development (Alotaibi, 2024; Barr, 2013; Shin, 2021; Slot et al., 2020; Torr, 2019).

In a family child care setting, a provider might incorporate storytelling into meal preparation, naming ingredients, describing actions, and inviting toddlers to echo words or predict what will happen next. These interactions follow game-like structures, with repetition, anticipation, and feedback embedded in everyday activities. Research on home environments document how literacy learning is often woven into practical tasks rather than isolated as a separate instructional activity (Clemens & Kegel, 2021).

Home-based care contexts also offer rich opportunities for literacy games. During playtime, a caregiver and toddler may engage in pretend play using household objects, narrating actions and creating simple storylines. The adult's role is not to direct the play but to support the child's meaning-making through language and shared attention. Studies of symbolic play and early narrative development emphasize the importance of such co-constructed play for language growth (Roskos et al., 2023; Shin, 2021).

Across these examples, the core elements of game-based literacy learning remain consistent. There is a shared focus, predictable structure, responsive feedback, and a sense of enjoyment. These elements support literacy development regardless of the specific setting, underscoring the adaptability of a *before the screen* approach.

Inclusion and Responsiveness in Diverse Contexts

Designing game-based literacy experiences across early childhood settings requires attention to inclusion and responsiveness. Children enter early learning environments with diverse linguistic, cultural, and developmental backgrounds. Game-based literacy learning is particularly well suited for supporting this diversity because it can be adapted to the individual needs, interests, and strengths of each child.

In multilingual settings, adults can incorporate home languages into literacy games, using songs, stories, and routines that reflect children's linguistic backgrounds. Research on early bilingual development indicates that maintaining home languages supports both language and literacy outcomes while affirming cultural identity (Miller & Khatib, 2023; Petrovic & Olmstead, 2001; Ribot et al., 2018). Game-based approaches to literacy learning allow caregivers and early childhood educators to respond flexibly across languages without relying on formal instruction.

Similarly, for children with disabilities or developmental delays, literacy games can be adapted through pacing, repetition, and multimodal approaches to communication. A game-based approach also supports Universal Design for Learning by offering multiple means of engagement and expression. Children can participate through movement, vocalization, gesture, or symbolic play, reducing barriers to access and supporting inclusive practice. This flexibility is particularly important in early childhood settings, where developmental variability is the norm rather than the exception.

Designing With Continuity in Mind

Designing game-based literacy experiences in early childhood settings also involves considering continuity across developmental stages. The playful routines and literacy games that infants and toddlers experience lay the groundwork for later engagement with more formal literacy instruction and digital texts. By recognizing these early experiences as foundational, educators can design learning environments that support smooth transitions across the early childhood years.

A *before the screen* framework encourages educators to view early literacy games not as isolated moments but as part of a broader developmental trajectory. The principles that guide effective game-based learning in later childhood, including motivation, feedback, and narrative engagement, are already present in early childhood practice. Supporting these principles intentionally helps ensure that literacy learning remains coherent and developmentally appropriate (Alotaibi, 2024; Jan & Gaydos, 2016; Shortridge, 2022).

GAME-BASED LITERACY IN HOME AND FAMILY ENGAGEMENT CONTEXTS

Literacy learning for infants and toddlers extends well beyond formal early childhood settings and is deeply embedded in family life. Homes are the primary contexts for early language and literacy development, and families serve as children's first literacy partners. From a *before the screen* perspective, game-based literacy learning in home and family engagement contexts emphasizes everyday routines, culturally grounded practices, and responsive interaction rather than any specialized materials or instructional program. These contexts provide rich opportunities for literacy games that support language, narrative understanding, and symbolic meaning-making from birth (Bergman Deitcher et al., 2024; Hayes et al., 2025; Heidlage et al., 2020; Karrass & Braungart-Rieker, 2005; Logan et al., 2019; NAEYC, 2022; Weiss et al., 2022).

This section examines how game-based literacy learning unfolds within home environments and family engagement initiatives. It highlights the role of everyday routines as literacy games, the importance of strength-based approaches to supporting families, and the ways in which culturally and linguistically diverse practices contribute to early literacy development.

Everyday Routines as Literacy Games

For infants and toddlers, much of their learning occurs during routine moments that are repeated daily. Feeding, bathing, dressing, and transitioning between activities provide predictable structures that lend themselves naturally to game-based literacy learning. When approached intentionally, these routines become opportunities for one-on-one playful interactions, language modeling, and shared meaning-making.

During mealtimes, for example, caregivers often name foods, describe actions, and respond to children's vocalizations or gestures. These interactions follow a game-like pattern, with turn-taking and repetition supporting vocabulary development and comprehension. A caregiver might pause after naming an object, allowing the child to respond, or repeat a familiar phrase that the child anticipates. Longitudinal research of early home language environments demonstrates that such conversational routines are strongly associated with later language and literacy outcomes, particularly when they involve one-on-one back-and-forth interaction (Logan et al., 2019; Weiss et al., 2022).

Similarly, caregiving routines such as diapering or bathing offer opportunities for playful exchanges. Songs, rhymes, and naming games can be incorporated into these moments, creating a sense of anticipation and engagement. Studies of infant-caregiver interaction emphasize that responsive, contingent communication during routine care supports early language development more effectively than isolated instructional activities (Barr, 2013; Slot et al., 2020). When routines are approached as literacy games rather than tasks to be completed, they become powerful contexts for learning.

These routine-based literacy games are especially important because they occur consistently and require no additional time or resources. Families do not need to set aside separate periods for literacy instruction. Instead, literacy learning is woven seamlessly into daily life, reinforcing the idea that early literacy is relational and contextual rather than instructional.

Strength-Based Approaches to Supporting Families

Family engagement initiatives play a critical role in supporting early literacy development, particularly when they adopt strength-based approaches that recognize and build upon existing family practices.

Rather than prescribing specific instructional activities or materials, effective family engagement emphasizes helping caregivers identify the literacy games they are already playing with their children and understand their developmental significance (Bergman Deitcher et al., 2024; Hayes et al., 2025; Miller & Khatib, 2023; Saracho, 2017).

Research on family literacy has documented the wide range of ways families support language and literacy development across cultural contexts (Teale & Sulzby, 1986). More recent scholarship reinforces that storytelling traditions, songs, chants, and conversational styles vary widely yet all can support emergent literacy when they involve interaction, repetition, and shared meaning (Brinegar et al., 2024; Torr, 2019). A game-based lens allows educators and family support professionals to frame these practices as valuable literacy experiences rather than deviations from a normative standard.

Home visiting programs, Early Head Start services, and community-based family literacy initiatives often work directly with families of infants and toddlers. In these contexts, professionals can model responsive interaction, highlight moments of turn-taking, and encourage caregivers to follow children's interests during play. Intervention studies demonstrate that when caregivers receive support focused on interaction quality rather than educational materials, children show significant gains in language and early literacy skills (O'Farrelly et al., 2018; Salley et al., 2022).

Strength-based approaches also support caregiver confidence. When families understand that literacy learning does not depend on purchasing special books, apps, or educational toys, they are more likely to engage in meaningful interactions with their children. This is particularly important for families facing economic constraints or limited access to resources. A *before the screen* framework reinforces the message that families already possess all the tools needed to support early literacy through play and one-on-one interactions (Hayes et al., 2025; Miller & Khatib, 2023).

Cultural and Linguistic Diversity in Family Literacy Games

Game-based literacy learning in home contexts is inherently shaped by culture and language. Families bring their own values, traditions, and communication practices to interactions with young children, influencing how literacy games are played and interpreted. Recognizing and honoring this diversity is essential for equitable early literacy support (Brinegar et al., 2024; Hayes et al., 2025; Heidlage et al., 2020).

In multilingual households, caregivers often engage in literacy games across languages, switching fluidly between home languages and the dominant language of the broader community. For example, a caregiver might soothe an infant in their home language during a feeding routine, then shift into English when an older child enters the room, and back again during a game of peek-a-boo. Toddlers often mirror this fluidity, holding up an object and labeling it first in one language and then later in another. Songs, stories, and routines may be repeated in multiple languages, supporting bilingual language development and reinforcing cultural identity. Research on early bilingualism indicates that maintaining home languages in infancy and toddlerhood supports both linguistic development and later literacy outcomes (Crivello et al., 2016; Jasińska & Petitto, 2017; Petrovic & Olmstead, 2001).

Game-based literacy learning is particularly well suited to multilingual contexts because it relies on interaction rather than formal instruction. Caregivers can respond to children's communication attempts in the language that feels most natural, using gestures, tone, and repetition to convey meaning. These interactions support comprehension and expressive language while affirming the child's cultural and linguistic background (Alotaibi, 2024; Brinegar et al., 2024; Ribot et al., 2018).

Cultural practices also shape the types of games and routines families use. Some families may emphasize oral storytelling, while others prioritize music, movement, or shared caregiving activities. A game-based lens allows educators to view these practices as legitimate and powerful forms of literacy engagement. By recognizing the diversity of literacy games across cultures, early childhood professionals can avoid deficit-based assumptions and support inclusive approaches to family engagement (Alotaibi, 2024; Brinegar et al., 2024; Hayes et al., 2025).

Supporting Access and Equity Through Family-Based Literacy Games

Equity is a central consideration in discussions of literacy innovation. When literacy support is framed primarily around technology, families with limited access to devices or internet connectivity may be positioned as disadvantaged. A *before the screen* approach counters this narrative by highlighting the accessibility of game-based literacy learning rooted in everyday one-on-one interactions with infants and toddlers (Alotaibi, 2024; Hayes et al., 2025; Levine et al., 2019; Ribot et al., 2018).

Family-based literacy games require minimal resources and can be adapted to a wide range of contexts. They rely only on the one-on-one adult-child relationship, responsiveness, and a shared attention rather than specialized teaching tools. This accessibility makes them particularly valuable for families experiencing economic hardship, housing instability, or other barriers to accessing formal early learning programs. Population-level research on early literacy disparities underscores the cumulative impact of everyday interactions in shaping outcomes, independent of access to formal instructional resources (Fuller et al., 2020; Logan et al., 2019).

Family engagement initiatives that emphasize game-based literacy learning can also address equity by focusing on caregiver empowerment. By validating families' existing practices and providing guidance on how to build-on them, professionals support more equitable literacy outcomes. From this perspective, caregivers become active partners in literacy development rather than passive recipients of the advice from experts (Brinegar et al., 2024; Hayes et al., 2025).

Additionally, family-based literacy games support continuity across settings. When caregivers and early childhood educators share an understanding of literacy as play-based and relational, children experience consistent expectations and interactions. This continuity supports smoother transitions between home and early childhood settings, reinforcing literacy learning across contexts (Roskos et al., 2023).

Connecting Home-Based Literacy Games to Lifelong Learning

Game-based literacy learning in home and family engagement contexts lays the groundwork for children's future interactions with literacy across settings and modalities. The playful routines and interactions children experience at home shape their attitudes toward communication and learning. Children who experience literacy as enjoyable and meaningful are more likely to approach new literacy challenges with confidence and curiosity (Bergman Deitcher et al., 2024; Brinegar et al., 2024; Clemens & Kegel, 2021; Roskos et al., 2023).

From a developmental perspective, the literacy games played at home during infancy and toddlerhood support the same underlying principles that guide later game-based and digital literacy learning. Motivation, feedback, narrative, and engagement are present in early family interactions, providing continuity across the lifespan. Research comparing early relational learning with later digital engagement highlights that strong early interactional foundations support more effective engagement with technology when it is introduced later (Bus et al., 2015; Levine et al., 2019).

By foregrounding the role of families and home environments in game-based literacy learning, this section reinforces the central argument of the chapter. Literacy learning begins *before the screen*, within relationships and routines that support meaning-making from birth. Family engagement contexts are not peripheral to this process but central to the development of early literacy foundations that support lifelong learning.

IMPLICATIONS FOR EDUCATOR PREPARATION AND PROFESSIONAL LEARNING

Recognizing game-based literacy learning as foundational in infancy and toddlerhood has important implications for how early childhood educators are prepared and supported in practice. Teacher preparation programs and professional learning initiatives often emphasize literacy instruction as something that occurs once children are developmentally ready for print-based skills. A *before the screen* framework challenges that assumption by positioning literacy learning as an integral, interactive, play-based process that begins at birth and is shaped by adult responsiveness to individual one-on-one interactions across settings.

Preparing educators to recognize, design, and sustain early literacy games requires a shift in how literacy, play, and teaching are conceptualized within early childhood education (Roskos et al., 2023). This shift builds directly on the family- and home-based literacy games described in the previous section, underscoring the need for educators to understand, honor, and extend these practices across early childhood contexts (Miller & Khatib, 2023). This section explores implications for educator preparation and ongoing professional learning, focusing on reframing play as literacy work, supporting educators in designing literacy games, and strengthening continuity across developmental stages and learning contexts.

Reframing Play as Literacy in Educator Preparation

One of the most persistent challenges in early childhood educator preparation is supporting future educators in recognizing play as legitimate and essential literacy work. Despite extensive research on play-based learning, play is sometimes positioned as separate from academic content or as a precursor to more serious instruction. This perception is particularly pronounced in conversations about literacy, where emphasis is often placed on print exposure, phonics, or instructional strategies associated with later schooling (Roskos et al., 2023; Saracho, 2017). Complicating matters, educators may encounter programmatic pressures, such as curriculum pacing guides, assessment demands, or expectations for kindergarten readiness, that make it difficult to trust that play can have central role in literacy development. Even well-prepared teachers may find themselves torn between what they know about developmentally appropriate practice and what they are expected to document or produce (NAEYC, 2022).

A *before the screen* perspective reframes play as central to literacy development rather than peripheral. In educator preparation programs, this requires explicit attention to how playful interactions support emergent literacy skills such as vocabulary development, narrative understanding, symbolic representation, and communicative competence. Coursework and field experiences can help candidates identify literacy learning within everyday routines, shared play, and caregiving moments rather than limiting literacy to designated instructional blocks of time. Analyses of early childhood teacher education programs suggest that early childhood teacher candidates benefit from opportunities to observe and reflect on infant-toddler interactions that highlight the literacy value of play and routine-based communication (Garvis & Manning, 2015). In practice, these reflections often deepen when candidates analyze real video footage of their own and other's practice, observe the subtle timing of infant cues, or struggle through the challenge of following a toddler's lead while simultaneously maintaining safety and classroom flow.

Integrating this perspective into early childhood educator preparation also supports alignment with developmentally appropriate practice. Early childhood educators are trained to consider children's developmental capacities, interests, and social contexts. Viewing literacy learning through a game-based lens reinforces these principles by emphasizing individualized interaction, engagement, and meaning-making over direct instruction. This alignment supports the development of coherent pedagogical approaches that honor both play-based learning and literacy development while remaining responsive to the individual needs of infants and toddlers (NAEYC, 2022; Recchia et al., 2018; Roskos et al., 2023).

Preparing Educators to Design and Support Literacy Games

Beyond recognizing play as literacy-building, early childhood educator preparation and professional learning must support educators in intentionally designing and sustaining game-based literacy experiences. This does not involve creating scripted activities or introducing formal games. Instead, it requires developing professional competencies related to observation, responsiveness to each infant and toddler, and reflective practice.

Early childhood educators working with infants and toddlers benefit from learning how to closely observe children's communicative behaviors and identify opportunities for literacy engagement. Professional learning can focus on noticing children's cues, such as vocalizations, gestures, gaze, or emerging words, and responding in ways that extend positive interactions. For example, when an infant repeatedly bangs a spoon, an educator might narrate the action, introduce descriptive language, or turn the moment into a rhythmic exchange. Research on responsive interaction highlights that such contingent responses support language growth more effectively than directive teaching strategies (Barr, 2013; Laurin et al., 2021; Löhr & Gil, 2015; Shin, 2021; Slot et al., 2020).

Intentional design also involves embedding literacy games within routines. Early childhood educators can be supported in planning for a playful use of language during transitions, caregiving moments, and independent play rather than relying solely on designated literacy instruction. Professional development that emphasizes routine-based planning helps educators see literacy opportunities as integrated throughout the day, reducing pressure to add instructional time. Policy and practice analyses of infant-toddler programs emphasize the importance of recognizing caregiving routines as core learning contexts rather than peripheral activities (Fuller et al., 2020).

Reflective practice is another critical component of designing literacy games. Educators can engage in reflection through documentation, peer discussion, coaching, or video analysis to consider how their interactions support or limit infant and toddler play-based literacy development. Reflecting on questions such as how often children initiate interactions, how adults respond to nonverbal communication, or how language is used during play can deepen educators' understanding of their role in supporting literacy development. Studies of early childhood professional learning suggest that reflective, collaborative approaches are particularly effective in supporting sustained changes in practice, especially when learning is embedded in the early childhood educators' daily routines and supported over time (Appova & Arbaugh, 2018; Garvis & Manning, 2015; Heidlage et al., 2020; Markussen-Brown et al., 2017).

Professional Learning Across Diverse Early Childhood Contexts

Early childhood educators work in a wide range of settings, including infant-toddler classrooms, family child care homes, Early Head Start programs, and home-based services. Professional learning initiatives must be flexible enough to address this diversity while maintaining a consistent theoretical grounding. A game-based literacy framework provides a shared language that can be adapted across contexts without prescribing uniform practices (Alotaibi, 2024).

Professional learning that emphasizes game-based literacy learning can focus on shared principles rather than specific activities. Workshops, coaching, and communities of practice can explore how motivation, feedback, and narrative function in different settings. Educators can share examples of literacy games from their own contexts, highlighting similarities across environments while respecting contextual differences. Research on early childhood professional development underscores the value of practice-based learning that draws on educators' lived experiences rather than abstract prescriptions (Dyment et al., 2014).

This approach also supports collaboration between early childhood educators and families. When early care and education professionals view families as partners in literacy learning, professional learning can include strategies for communicating with caregivers about the importance of play-based learning and one-on-one adult-child interaction. Early childhood educators must learn to share observations, model responsive interaction, and validate family practices in ways that strengthen continuity between home and early childhood settings. Family-centered approaches to professional learning are particularly important in infant-toddler contexts, where learning is deeply relational (Brinegar et al., 2024; Hayes et al., 2025).

Continuity Toward Later Literacy and Digital Learning

An important implication of a *before the screen* framework is its emphasis on continuity across developmental stages. Early childhood educator preparation programs often segment literacy learning by age group, with limited attention to how early experiences connect to later instruction. Viewing early literacy games as foundational helps bridge that gap.

Educators who understand how infants and toddlers learn through play are better positioned to support children's transitions into the pre-kindergarten classroom and beyond. The principles that guide early literacy games, including engagement, feedback, and narrative, continue to shape literacy learning as children encounter print-based and digital texts. Professional learning that highlights this continuity helps educators maintain a literacy-first approach even as technology becomes more prominent in later stages of development (Appova & Arbaugh, 2018).

Importantly, this perspective also informs conversations about digital and AI-mediated literacy learning. Educators who recognize the relational foundations of literacy are more likely to approach technology critically and intentionally. Rather than replacing interaction, digital tools can be viewed as extensions of the same principles that support early literacy games for infants and toddlers. Comparative research on digital media use in early childhood suggests that technology is most effective when it complements, rather than substitutes for, adult-child interaction (Bus et al., 2015; Levine et al., 2019).

Supporting Equity Through Educator Preparation

Equity is a central concern in educator preparation and professional learning. Early childhood educators serve children from diverse cultural, linguistic, and socioeconomic backgrounds, and their practices have significant implications for equity in literacy outcomes. A game-based literacy framework supports equity by emphasizing accessibility, responsiveness, and cultural relevance.

Professional learning can help educators recognize and value diverse forms of literacy engagement, including those rooted in home language and cultural practices. By viewing literacy games as culturally situated, early childhood educators are better equipped to support multilingual learners and avoid deficit-based interpretations of children's communication skills. This perspective aligns with research emphasizing culturally sustaining approaches to early literacy education (Brinegar et al., 2024; Hayes et al., 2025).

Additionally, preparing educators to support literacy learning without reliance on technology helps address inequities in access. Educators working in under-resourced settings can draw on game-based approaches that leverage relationships and routines rather than specialized instructional materials. This focus ensures that high-quality literacy support is not contingent on access to digital tools.

Implications for Policy and Program Design

The implications of game-based literacy learning extend beyond individual educators to program design and policy. Early childhood programs that prioritize relational, play-based literacy learning create conditions that support educator practice. Policies that recognize the importance of one-on-one interaction and play in early literacy development can help align expectations across early childhood systems (Fuller et al., 2020).

Educator preparation programs, accreditation standards, and professional development requirements can all benefit from integrating a *before the screen* perspective. By explicitly acknowledging literacy learning in infancy and toddlerhood, these systems can support more coherent and equitable approaches to literacy education. This alignment helps ensure that early literacy is understood not as a narrow set of skills but as a foundational process that unfolds through play and interaction from birth (Roskos et al., 2023).

CONCLUSION

Literacy learning begins well before children encounter print, formal instruction, or digital technologies. From birth, infants and toddlers intentionally attempt to engage in playful, relational interactions to support meaning-making, communication, and symbolic understanding. These early experiences are not peripheral to literacy development. They are foundational to literacy development. By framing these interactions as game-based literacy learning *before the screen*, this chapter has sought to broaden how literacy, play-based learning, and learning are understood in the earliest years of life (Alotaibi, 2024; Roskos et al., 2023; Shortridge, 2022).

Across infancy and toddlerhood, literacy games emerge through everyday routines and shared experiences. Proto-games in infancy introduce children to the structure of communication through turn-taking, anticipation, and repetition. As children move into toddlerhood, these early interactions evolve into more complex narrative and symbolic play, supporting vocabulary development, storytelling, and comprehension. Throughout this developmental progression, responsive feedback from adults plays a critical role in helping children understand the effects of their communicative attempts and encouraging further participation. Research on early language environments and adult-child interaction consistently demonstrates that these relational experiences shape both immediate language development and longer-term literacy outcomes (Barr, 2013; Logan et al., 2019; Shortridge, 2022; Weiss et al., 2022).

The theoretical perspectives examined in this chapter reinforce the centrality of play and adult-child interaction in early literacy development. Emergent literacy theory emphasizes that literacy unfolds along a continuous developmental trajectory beginning in infancy. Sociocultural theory highlights the role of guided participation, cultural context, and adult mediation in shaping the learning experience. Game-based learning theory, when applied developmentally, helps explain why play-based, structured interactions are so effective in supporting engagement, motivation, and meaning-making. When integrated, these perspectives provide a robust framework for understanding literacy learning as an inherently social and game-like process in the earliest years (Alotaibi, 2024; Roskos et al., 2023; Shortridge, 2022; Vygotsky, 1978).

A *before the screen* framework also brings issues of equity and access to the forefront. Playful literacy games are universally available and culturally situated, making them accessible across diverse family and community contexts. By valuing the literacy practices embedded in everyday routines, this approach challenges deficit-based narratives that equate innovation with technology use alone. It affirms that families and educators already possess powerful tools for supporting early literacy through relationships, language, and play. This perspective is particularly important for supporting multilingual learners, children with disabilities, and families with limited access to digital resources (Brinegar et al., 2024; Quinn et al., 2018; Ribot et al., 2018).

The implications for early childhood education are significant. Educator preparation and professional learning must support educators in recognizing play as an integral part of literacy work and in designing responsive, game-based interactions across all early childhood settings. Rather than viewing literacy as something that begins with instruction or devices, educators are encouraged to see literacy as a developmental process that unfolds through interaction from birth. This shift has the potential to strengthen continuity across early childhood systems and to ensure that literacy learning remains developmentally appropriate, culturally responsive, and inclusive as children grow (Brinegar et al., 2024; Fuller et al., 2020; Hayes et al., 2025; NAEYC, 2022).

Importantly, centering literacy learning *before the screen* does not diminish the role of technology in later development. Instead, it situates digital and AI-mediated literacy learning within a broader developmental continuum. The motivational, narrative, and feedback-driven features that characterize effective digital literacy games are grounded in the same principles that support early literacy games in infancy and toddlerhood. Recognizing this continuity allows educators and researchers to approach technology use with intentionality, ensuring that it extends rather than replaces relational learning (Bus et al., 2015; Heidlage et al., 2020; Levine et al., 2019; Vernon-Feagans et al., 2013).

By expanding the conversation about game-based literacy learning to include infancy and toddlerhood, this chapter contributes a developmental perspective that is often missing from discussions of innovation in literacy education. It invites researchers, practitioners, and teacher educators to reconsider where literacy learning begins and how it is supported across contexts. Ultimately, *before the screen* underscores a simple but powerful idea: the foundations of literacy are built through the games we play together from the very beginning of the human experience. These early interactions shape how children engage with language, stories, and learning throughout their lives, making them central to any effort to promote equitable and meaningful literacy outcomes.

REFERENCES

Alotaibi, M. S. (2024). Game-based learning in early childhood education: A systematic review and meta-analysis. *Frontiers in Psychology, 15*, 1307881. DOI: 10.3389/fpsyg.2024.1307881 PMID: 38629045

Appova, A., & Arbaugh, F. (2018). Teachers' motivation to learn: Implications for supporting professional growth. *Professional Development in Education, 44*(1), 5–21. DOI: 10.1080/19415257.2017.1280524

Barr, R. (2013). Memory constraints on infant learning from picture books, television, and touchscreens. *Child Development Perspectives, 7*(4), 205–210. DOI: 10.1111/cdep.12041

Bergman Deitcher, D., Aram, D., & Abramovich, D. (2024). Parents' literacy beliefs, home literacy activities, and children's early literacy skills: Stability and progress approaching first grade. *Behavioral Sciences (Basel, Switzerland), 14*(11), 1038. DOI: 10.3390/bs14111038 PMID: 39594338

Brinegar, K., Harrison, L., & Hurd, E. (2024). Toward a culturally sustaining science of reading. *Middle School Journal, 55*(3), 2–4. (176635226). DOI: 10.1080/00940771.2024.2332142

Bus, A. G., Takacs, Z. K., & Kegel, C. A. T. (2015). Affordances and limitations of electronic storybooks for young children's emergent literacy. *Developmental Review, 35*, 79–97. DOI: 10.1016/j.dr.2014.12.004

Clemens, L. F., & Kegel, C. A. T. (2021). Unique contribution of shared book reading on adult-child language interaction. *Journal of Child Language, 48*(2), 373–386. DOI: 10.1017/S0305000920000331 PMID: 32524924

Crivello, C., Kuzyk, O., Rodrigues, M., Friend, M., Zesiger, P., & Poulin-Dubois, D. (2016). The effects of bilingual growth on toddlers' executive function. *Journal of Experimental Child Psychology, 141*, 121–132. DOI: 10.1016/j.jecp.2015.08.004 PMID: 26402219

Cunningham, D. (2022). Symbolic representations of preschool children: Relations among block play, picture drawing and emergent literacy. *Critical Questions in Education, 13*(1).

Dyment, J. E., Davis, J. M., Nailon, D., Emery, S., Getenet, S., McCrea, N., & Hill, A. (2014). The impact of professional development on early childhood educators' confidence, understanding and knowledge of education for sustainability. *Environmental Education Research, 20*(5), 660–679. DOI: 10.1080/13504622.2013.833591

Fuller, B., Bridges, M., & Land, A. (2020). What policies advance infants and toddlers? Evidence to inform state and federal options. *Social Policy Report, 33*(1), 1–43. DOI: 10.1002/sop2.6

Gardner-Neblett, N., Holochwost, S. J., Gallagher, K. C., Iruka, I. U., Odom, S. L., & Bruno, E. P. (2017). Books and toddlers in child care: Under what conditions are children most engaged? *Child and Youth Care Forum, 46*(4), 473–493. DOI: 10.1007/s10566-017-9391-4

Garvis, S., & Manning, M. (2015). Do master early childhood teacher education programs provide adequate coverage of infants and toddlers?: A review of content. *The Australian Journal of Teacher Education, 40*(40), 164–175. DOI: 10.14221/ajte.2015v40n8.10

Hayes, C., Murnan, R., & Bequette, S. (2025). Family, culture, and literacy: Unlocking the power of home for early literacy achievement. *Early Childhood Education Journal*. Advance online publication. DOI: 10.1007/s10643-025-01986-9

Heidlage, J. K., Cunningham, J. E., Kaiser, A. P., Trivette, C. M., Barton, E. E., Frey, J. R., & Roberts, M. Y. (2020). The effects of parent-implemented language interventions on child linguistic outcomes: A meta-analysis. *Early Childhood Research Quarterly*, *50*, 6–23. DOI: 10.1016/j.ecresq.2018.12.006

Hsieh, M.-F. (2025). Beginning with books: Tailoring formats and strategies for infant and toddler reading activities in early childhood education centers. *Early Childhood Education Journal*, *53*(7), 2615–2630. DOI: 10.1007/s10643-024-01772-z

Jan, M., & Gaydos, M. (2016). What is game-based learning? Past, present, and future. *Educational Technology*, *56*(3), 6–11.

Jasińska, K. K., & Petitto, L.-A. (2017). Age of bilingual exposure is related to the contribution of phonological and semantic knowledge to successful reading development. *Child Development*, *89*(1), 310–331. DOI: 10.1111/cdev.12745 PMID: 28169419

Karrass, J., & Braungart-Rieker, J. M. (2005). Effects of shared parent–infant book reading on early language acquisition. *Journal of Applied Developmental Psychology*, *26*(2), 133–148. DOI: 10.1016/j.appdev.2004.12.003

Laurin, D. E., Guss, S. S., & Horm, D. (2021). Caregiver–infant and toddler interactions during diapering: Caregiver responsiveness and child well-being and involvement. *Infant Mental Health Journal*, *42*(4), 546–559. DOI: 10.1002/imhj.21933 PMID: 34125959

Levine, L. E., Waite, B. M., Bowman, L. L., & Kachinsky, K. (2019). Mobile media use by infants and toddlers. *Computers in Human Behavior*, *94*, 92–99. DOI: 10.1016/j.chb.2018.12.045

Logan, J. A. R., Justice, L. M., Yumuş, M., & Chaparro-Moreno, L. J. (2019). When Children Are Not Read to at Home: The Million Word Gap. *Journal of Developmental and Behavioral Pediatrics : JDBP*, *40*(5), 383–386. Advance online publication. DOI: 10.1097/DBP.0000000000000657 PMID: 30908424

Löhr, T., & Gil, M. S. C. de A. (2015). Learning by playing: Echo and tact in expanding the verbal repertoire of infants. *Paidéia (Ribeirão Preto)*, *25*(60), 77–84. https://doi.org/DOI: 10.1590/1982-43272560201510

Markussen-Brown, J., Juhl, C. B., Piasta, S. B., Bleses, D., Højen, A., & Justice, L. M. (2017). The effects of language- and literacy-focused professional development on early educators and children: A best-evidence meta-analysis. *Early Childhood Research Quarterly*, *38*, 97–115. DOI: 10.1016/j.ecresq.2016.07.002

Miller, G. E., & Khatib, S. M. (2023). Honoring diverse cultures through family literacy approaches that build family, school, and community partnerships. *The Reading Teacher*, *76*(5), 586–593. DOI: 10.1002/trtr.2181

Murray, A., & Egan, S. M. (2014). Does reading to infants benefit their cognitive development at 9-months-old? An investigation using a large birth cohort survey. *Child Language Teaching and Therapy*, *30*(3), 303–315. DOI: 10.1177/0265659013513813

NAEYC. (2022). *Developmentally appropriate practice in early childhood programs serving children from birth through age 8* (4th ed.). National Association for the Education of Young Children.

Norris, D. J. (2017). Comparing language and literacy environments in two types of infant-toddler child care centers. *Early Childhood Education Journal, 45*(1), 95–101. DOI: 10.1007/s10643-014-0679-9

Nunamaker, R., & Mosier, W. (2021). Infants, toddlers, and technology in early childhood settings: Putting the pieces together. In Burris, J., Rosen, D., & Karno, D. (Eds.), *Handbook of Research on Empowering Early Childhood Educators with Technology* (pp. 206–226). IGI Global., DOI: 10.4018/978-1-7998-6888-0.ch011

O'Farrelly, C., Doyle, O., Victory, G., & Palamaro-Munsell, E. (2018). Shared reading in infancy and later development: Evidence from an early intervention. *Journal of Applied Developmental Psychology, 54*, 69–83. DOI: 10.1016/j.appdev.2017.12.001

Pempek, T. A., & Lauricella, A. R. (2017). The effects of parent-child interaction and media use on cognitive development in infants, toddlers, and preschoolers. In Blumberg, F. C., & Brooks, P. J. (Eds.), *Cognitive development in digital contexts* (pp. 53–74). Elsevier., DOI: 10.1016/B978-0-12-809481-5.00003-1

Petrovic, J. E., & Olmstead, S. (2001). Language, power, and pedagogy: Bilingual children in the crossfire. *Bilingual Research Journal, 25*(3), 405–412. DOI: 10.1080/15235882.2001.10162800

Quinn, S., Donnelly, S., & Kidd, E. (2018). The relationship between symbolic play and language acquisition: A meta-analytic review. *Developmental Review, 49*, 121–135. DOI: 10.1016/j.dr.2018.05.005

Recchia, S. L., Shin, M., & Snaider, C. (2018). Where is the love? Developing loving relationships as an essential component of professional infant care. *International Journal of Early Years Education, 26*(2), 142–158. DOI: 10.1080/09669760.2018.1461614

Ribot, K. M., Hoff, E., & Burridge, A. (2018). Language use contributes to expressive language growth: Evidence from bilingual children. *Child Development, 89*(3), 929–940. DOI: 10.1111/cdev.12770 PMID: 28245341

Roskos, K. A., Tremblay, R. E., Boivin, M., Peters, R., & Smith, P. K. (2023). Play's potential in early literacy development. In *Encyclopedia on early childhood development*. https://www.child-encyclopedia.com/play/according-experts/plays-potential-early-literacy-development

Salley, B., Daniels, D., Walker, C., & Fleming, K. (2022). Shared book reading intervention for parents of infants and toddlers. *Journal of Early Childhood Research, 20*(3), 322–340. DOI: 10.1177/1476718X221091462 PMID: 36092249

Saracho, O. N. (2017). Literacy in the twenty-first century: Children, families and policy. *Early Child Development and Care, 187*(3–4), 630–643. DOI: 10.1080/03004430.2016.1261513

Shin, M. (2021). Exploring multisensory experiences in infants' learning and development in the child care classrooms. *Early Child Development and Care, 191*(13), 2116–2127. DOI: 10.1080/03004430.2019.1695127

Shortridge, H. (2022). Tiny hands, big impact: Play's role in early literacy. *Children & Libraries*, *20*(2), 12–17. DOI: 10.5860/cal.20.2.12

Slot, P. L., Bleses, D., & Jensen, P. (2020). Infants' and toddlers' language, math and socio-emotional development: Evidence for reciprocal relations and differential gender and age effects. *Frontiers in Psychology*, *11*, 580297. Advance online publication. DOI: 10.3389/fpsyg.2020.580297 PMID: 33329234

Storch, S. A., & Whitehurst, G. J. (2001). The role of family and home in the literacy development of children from low-income backgrounds. *New Directions for Child and Adolescent Development*, *2001*(92), 53–72. DOI: 10.1002/cd.15 PMID: 11468866

Teale, W. H., & Sulzby, E. (1986). *Emergent literacy: Writing and reading*. Praeger.

Torr, J. (2019). Infants' experiences of shared reading with their educators in early childhood education and care centres: An observational study. *Early Childhood Education Journal*, *47*(5), 519–529. DOI: 10.1007/s10643-019-00948-2

Vernon-Feagans, L., & Bratsch-Hines, M. E.The Family Life Project Key Investigators. (2013). Caregiver-child verbal interactions in child care: A buffer against poor language outcomes when maternal language input is less. *Early Childhood Research Quarterly*, *28*(4), 858–873. DOI: 10.1016/j.ecresq.2013.08.002 PMID: 24634566

Vygotsky, L. S. (1978). *Mind in society: The development of higher psychological processes* (Cole, M., John-Steiner, V., Scribner, S., & Souberman, E., Eds.). Harvard University Press.

Weiss, Y., Huber, E., Ferjan Ramírez, N., Corrigan, N. M., Yarnykh, V. L., & Kuhl, P. K. (2022). Language input in late infancy scaffolds emergent literacy skills and predicts reading related white matter development. *Frontiers in Human Neuroscience*, *16*, 922552. DOI: 10.3389/fnhum.2022.922552 PMID: 36457757

Whitehurst, G. J., & Lonigan, C. J. (1998). Child development and emergent literacy. *Child Development*, *69*(3), 848–872. DOI: 10.1111/j.1467-8624.1998.tb06247.x PMID: 9680688

Compilation of References

Abbas, M., Hussain, K., Bajwa, S. U., & Rasheed, M. A. (2026). Digital capabilities as a catalyst for team effectiveness: Insights from hospitality. *International Journal of Contemporary Hospitality Management*, *38*(1), 210–227. DOI: 10.1108/IJCHM-03-2025-0434

Abrams, S. S., & Hanghøj, T. (2025). Reflexive AI literacies: Conceptualizing a model for learners' critical engagement with generative AI. *Pedagogies*, •••, 1–20. DOI: 10.1080/1554480X.2025.2561972

Abukhattala, I. (2013). Krashen's Five Proposals on Language Learning: Are They Valid in Libyan EFL Classes. *English Language Teaching*, *6*(1), 128–131. DOI: 10.5539/elt.v6n1p128

Adamopoulou, E., & Moussiades, L. (2020). Chatbots: History, technology, and applications. *Machine Learning with Applications*, *2*, 100006.

Adams, C., Pente, P., Lemermeyer, G., & Rockwell, G. (2023). Ethical principles for artificial intelligence in K–12 education. *Computers and Education: Artificial Intelligence*, *4*, 100131. DOI: 10.1016/j.caeai.2023.100131

Adipat, S., Laksana, K., Busayanon, K., Asawasowan, S., & Adipat, B. (2021). Engaging students in the learning process with game-based learning: The fundamental concepts. *International Journal of Technology in Education*, *4*(3), 542–552. DOI: 10.46328/ijte.169

Aguado-García, J.-M., Alonso-Muñoz, S., & De-Pablos-Heredero, C. (2025). Using Artificial Intelligence for Higher Education: An Overview and Future Research Avenues. *SAGE Open*, *15*(2), 21582440251340350. DOI: 10.1177/21582440251340352

Aguilera-Castillo, A., Guerrero-Cabarcas, M., Fúquene, C. A., & Rios, W. F. (2020). Simulations in business education: A case study of Cesim™ Global Challenge. In *Teaching, learning, and leading with computer simulations* (pp. 128–158). IGI Global. DOI: 10.4018/978-1-7998-0004-0.ch005

Ahmed, M. K., & Hossain, K. I. (2024). Nurturing learner autonomy to enhance motivation and academic achievement for the L2 learners in ESL contexts. *IUBAT Review*, *7*(2), 176–196. DOI: 10.3329/iubatr.v7i2.78809

AILit Framework (OECD & European Commission). (2025). Empowering learners for the age of AI: An AI literacy framework for primary and secondary education (Review draft). https://ailiteracyframework.org/wp-content/uploads/2025/05/AILitFramework_ReviewDraft.pdf

Akgun, S., & Greenhow, C. (2022). Artificial intelligence in education: Addressing ethical challenges in K-12 settings. *AI and Ethics*, *2*(3), 431–440. DOI: 10.1007/s43681-021-00096-7 PMID: 34790956

Akhmetova, A. I., Seitenova, S. S., Khodjaev, B. K., Jamoldinova, O. R., Yerkebaeva, S. Z., & Kazybayeva, K. U. (2025). Evolution of game-based learning research: A cross-database bibliometric analysis and visualization study (2015-2024). *Contemporary Educational Technology*, *17*(3), ep585. DOI: 10.30935/cedtech/16451

Akour, M., Alsghaier, H., & Aldiabat, S. (2020). Game-based learning approach to improve self-motivated students' self-learning. *International Journal of Technology Enhanced Learning*, *12*(2), 146–161. DOI: 10.1504/IJTEL.2020.106283

Aksoy, N., & Kurşun, E. (2024). Behind the scenes: A critical perspective on GenAI and open educational practices. *Open Praxis*, *16*(3), 457–470. Advance online publication. DOI: 10.55982/openpraxis.16.3.674

Aláez, M., Díaz-Iso, A., Eizaguirre, A., García-Feijoo, M., & Roldán, M. (2022). Bridging generation gaps through service-learning in higher education: A systematic review. *Frontiers in Education*, *7*, 841482. DOI: 10.3389/feduc.2022.841482

Alam, A. (2023a). Media multitasking with M-learning technology in real-time classroom learning: Analysing the dynamics in formal educational settings for the future of E-learning in India. In *2023 2nd International Conference on Smart Technologies and Systems for Next Generation Computing (ICSTSN)* (pp. 1-6). IEEE. https://doi.org/DOI: 10.1109/ICSTSN57873.2023.10151509

Alam, A. (2023b). The secret sauce of student success: Cracking the code by navigating the path to personalized learning with educational data mining. In *2023 2nd International Conference on Smart Technologies and Systems for Next Generation Computing (ICSTSN)* (pp. 1-8). IEEE. https://doi.org/DOI: 10.1109/ICSTSN57873.2023.10151558

Alam, A., & Mohanty, A. (2022, December). Facial analytics or virtual avatars: competencies and design considerations for student-teacher interaction in AI-powered online education for effective classroom engagement. In *International Conference on Communication, Networks and Computing* (pp. 252-265). Cham: Springer Nature Switzerland. https://doi.org/DOI: 10.1007/978-3-031-43145-6_21

Alam, A., & Mohanty, A. (2023, January). Learning on the move: a pedagogical framework for state-of-the-art mobile learning. In *International Conference on Data Management, Analytics & Innovation* (pp. 735-748). Singapore: Springer Nature Singapore. https://doi.org/DOI: 10.1007/978-981-99-1414-2_52

Alam, A. (2022). Impact of university's human resources practices on professors' occupational performance: empirical evidence from India's higher education sector. In *Inclusive businesses in developing economies: Converging people, profit, and corporate citizenship* (pp. 107–131). Springer International Publishing., DOI: 10.1007/978-3-031-12217-0_6

Alam, A. (2023c). Intelligence unleashed: An argument for AI-enabled learning ecologies with real world examples of today and a peek into the future. In *International Conference on Innovations in Computer Science, Electronics & Electrical Engineering*-2022 (Vol. 2717, No. 1, p. 030001). AIP Publishing LLC. https://doi.org/DOI: 10.1063/5.0129803

Alam, A., & Mohanty, A. (2023). Educational technology: Exploring the convergence of technology and pedagogy through mobility, interactivity, AI, and learning tools. *Cogent Engineering*, *10*(2), 2283282. DOI: 10.1080/23311916.2023.2283282

Alam, A., & Mohanty, A. (2024). Integrated constructive robotics in education (ICRE) model: A paradigmatic framework for transformative learning in educational ecosystem. *Cogent Education*, *11*(1), 2324487. DOI: 10.1080/2331186X.2024.2324487

Alamer, A., Robat, E. S., Shirvan, M. E., & Ryan, R. (2025). Self-Determination Theory and Language Learning: A Multilevel Meta-Analysis. *Educational Psychology Review*, *37*(2), 59. DOI: 10.1007/s10648-025-10038-y

Alencar, A., & de la Hera Conde-Pumpido, T. (2018). Gaming in multicultural classrooms: The potential of collaborative digital games to foster intercultural interaction. In *Social interactions in virtual worlds: An interdisciplinary perspective*. DOI: 10.1017/9781316422823.012

Alfredo, R., Echeverria, V., Jin, Y., Yan, L., Swiecki, Z., Gašević, D., & Martinez-Maldonado, R. (2024). Human-centred learning analytics and AI in education: A systematic literature review. *Computers and Education: Artificial Intelligence*, *6*, 100215. https://doi.org/https://doi.org/10.1016/j.caeai.2024.100215

Almatrafi, O., Johri, A., & Lee, H. (2024). A systematic review of AI literacy conceptualization, constructs, and implementation and assessment efforts (2019–2023). *Computers and Education Open*, *6*, 100173. DOI: 10.1016/j.caeo.2024.100173

Alnemrat, A., Aldamen, H., Almashour, M., Al-Deaibes, M., & AlSharefeen, R. (2025). AI vs. teacher feedback on EFL argumentative writing: A quantitative study. [). Frontiers Media SA.]. *Frontiers in Education*, *10*, 1614673. DOI: 10.3389/feduc.2025.1614673

Alneyadi, S., Abulibdeh, E., & Wardat, Y. (2023). The Impact of Digital Environment vs. Traditional Method on Literacy Skills; Reading and Writing of Emirati Fourth Graders. *Sustainability (Basel)*, *15*(4), 3418. DOI: 10.3390/su15043418

Alnuaim, A. A., Al-Wabil, A., & Alaqeeli, A. (2024). The impact and acceptance of gamification by learners in a digital literacy course at the undergraduate level. *JMIR Serious Games*, *12*, e52017. DOI: 10.2196/52017 PMID: 39177662

Alotaibi, J. (2025). Digital communication in Middle East cultural institutions: Developing a theoretical framework for the use of digital platforms. *Humanities & Social Sciences Communications*, *13*(1), 51. Advance online publication. DOI: 10.1057/s41599-025-06345-y

Alotaibi, M. S. (2024). Game-based learning in early childhood education: A systematic review and meta-analysis. *Frontiers in Psychology*, *15*, 1307881. Advance online publication. DOI: 10.3389/fpsyg.2024.1307881 PMID: 38629045

Alsaad, F. M., & Durugbo, C. M. (2021). Gamification-as-Innovation: A Review. *International Journal on Management of Innovation & Technology*, *18*(5), 2130002. Advance online publication. DOI: 10.1142/S0219877021300020

Alshammari, S. H., Alshammari, A. E. A., Alghamdi, B. A., Alrashidi, M. E., Rosli, M. S., & Risdianto, E. (2026). Artificial intelligence in educational technology: A systematic review of pedagogical opportunities, implementation challenges, and ethical considerations. *International Journal on Studies in Education*, *8*(1), 17–37. DOI: 10.46328/ijonse.5974

Alsharefeen, R., & Al Sayari, N. (2025). Faculty as street-level bureaucrats: Discretionary decision-making in the era of generative AI. *Frontiers in Education, 10*, 1662657. DOI: 10.3389/feduc.2025.1662657

Alsowat, H. H. (2022). Hybrid learning or virtual Learning? Effects on students' essay writing and digital literacy. *Journal of Language Teaching and Research, 13*(4), 872–883. DOI: 10.17507/jltr.1304.20

Alsswey, A., & Malak, M. (2024). Effect of using gamification of "Kahoot!" as a learning method on stress symptoms, anxiety symptoms, self-efficacy, and academic achievement among university students. *Learning and Motivation, 87*, 101993. DOI: 10.1016/j.lmot.2024.101993

Amedie, F. A. (2013). Impacts of Climate Change on Plant Growth, Ecosystem Services, Biodiversity, and Potential Adaptation Measure. Master Thesis in Atmospheric Science with Orientation towards Environmental Science (60 HEC).

Amplify Education. (2023). *Amplify Reading* [Adaptive literacy platform]. https://www.amplify.com/programs/amplify-reading

Amran, A., Perkasa, M., Satriawan, M., Jasin, I., & Irwansyah, M. (2019). Assessing students 21st century attitude and environmental awareness: Promoting education for sustainable development through science education. *Journal of Physics: Conference Series, 1157*(2), 022025. DOI: 10.1088/1742-6596/1157/2/022025

Anggela, A. F. P., Setiawan, D. A., & Rahutami, R. (2025). Magbox Games to Improve Literacy of Grade VI Elementary School Students on Short Story Materials. *Jurnal Pedagogi dan Pembelajaran, 8*(2), 364-372. https://doi.org/DOI: 10.23887/jp2.v8i2.98363

Anggraeni, L., Affandi, I., Wahyudin, D., Paramitha, S. T., & Ramadhan, M. G. (2022). Optimization of the Board Game as a Platform for the Concept of Peace Education: A Survey Method Study. *International Journal of Education in Mathematics. Science and Technology, 10*(2). Advance online publication. DOI: 10.46328/ijemst.2292

Applebee, A. N., & Langer, J. A. (2013). *Writing instruction that works: Proven methods for middle and high school classrooms.* Teachers College Press.

Appova, A., & Arbaugh, F. (2018). Teachers' motivation to learn: Implications for supporting professional growth. *Professional Development in Education, 44*(1), 5–21. DOI: 10.1080/19415257.2017.1280524

Aramburuzabala, P., & Cerrillo, R. (2023). Service-learning as an approach to educating for sustainable development. *Sustainability (Basel), 15*(14), 11231. DOI: 10.3390/su151411231

Arboleya-García, E., & Miralles, L. (2022). 'The Game of the Sea': An Interdisciplinary Educational Board Game on the Marine Environment and Ocean Awareness for Primary and Secondary Students. Education Sciences 2022, Vol. 12, Page 57, 12(1), 57. DOI: 10.3390/educsci12010057

Ariani, F., & Afnita, N. (2024). The Influence of Digital-Based Gamification on Student Engagement and Language Literacy Skills: A Study at Madrasah Tsanawiyah. *Jurnal Komunikasi Pendidikan, 8*(2), 141–156. DOI: 10.32585/jurnalkomdik.v8i2.5036

Arifin, Z., Saputro, S., & Kamari, A. (2025). The effect of inquiry-based learning on students' critical thinking skills in science education: A systematic review and meta-analysis. *Eurasia Journal of Mathematics, Science and Technology Education, 21*(3), em2592. DOI: 10.29333/ejmste/15988

Arip, A. J., & Hashim, H. (2024). Gamification in English as second language (ESL) learning: A systematic review. *International Journal of Academic Research in Progressive Education and Development, 13*(4), 2837–2853. DOI: 10.6007/IJARPED/v13-i4/24069

Aris, M., Ludecke, M., & Crawford, R. (2025). Exploring the use of theatre methods within simulation-based teacher education: A scoping review. *Teachers and Teaching*, •••, 1–25. DOI: 10.1080/13540602.2025.2518402

Arkan, Z., & Bal, M. (2025). The relationship between school-age students' literacy skills and digital well-being: A systematic review. *BMC Psychology, 13*(1), 1240. DOI: 10.1186/s40359-025-03573-4 PMID: 41214781

Arteaga, P., Batanero, C., Contreras, J. M., & Cañadas, G. R. (2012). Understanding statistical graphs: A research survey. *Boletín de Estadística e Investigación Operativa, 28*(3), 261–277.

Ashwin, P. (2022). The educational purposes of higher education: Changing discussions of the societal outcomes of educating students. *Higher Education, 84*(6), 1227–1244. DOI: 10.1007/s10734-022-00930-9

Asia Society. (2025). *Global competence outcomes and rubrics.* https://asiasociety.org/education/leadership-global-competence

Aslam, F., Rahman, H., Wahid, S. A., Wahid, S. A., & Ali, N. (2025). Enhancing children's learning experience through alphabet AR-game: A usability and acceptability assessment of augmented reality game-based learning. *Multimedia Tools and Applications, 84*(25), 29183–29205. DOI: 10.1007/s11042-024-20346-0

Austin, M. S. (2025). Innovative pedagogical approaches: Exploring flipped classroom, inquiry-based learning, and project-based learning. *Educator Insights: Journal of Teaching Theory and Practice, 1*(1), 1–7.

Australian Institute for Teaching and School Leadership. (2017). *Australian professional standards for teachers* (Revised). https://www.aitsl.edu.au/docs/default-source/national-policy-framework/australian-professional-standards-for-teachers.pdf

Ayanwale, M. A., Adelana, O. P., Molefi, R. R., Adeeko, O., & Ishola, A. M. (2024). Examining artificial intelligence literacy among pre-service teachers for future classrooms. *Computers and Education Open, 6*, 100179. DOI: 10.1016/j.caeo.2024.100179

Azzam, A., & Charles, T. (2025). K-12 STEM teachers' experiences with artificial intelligence. *TEM Journal, 14*(1), 463-468. https://doi.org/DOI: 10.18421/TEM141-41

Baig, M. I., Yadegaridehkordi, E., & Zamani, F. (2024). ChatGPT in the higher education: A systematic literature review and research challenges. *International Journal of Educational Research, 127*, 102411. [REMOVED HYPERLINK FIELD] DOI: 10.1016/j.ijer.2024.102411

Bailey, R. P., Hoe, T. W., Morrison, G. Z., Ali, A., & Samsudin, N. (2026). Rethinking higher education: Embodied learning and pedagogical transformation. *Higher Education*, •••, 1–21. DOI: 10.1007/s10734-025-01581-2

Baker, R. S., & Hawn, A. (2022). Algorithmic bias in education. *International Journal of Artificial Intelligence in Education*, *32*(4), 1052–1092. DOI: 10.1007/s40593-021-00285-9

Baker, R. S., & Siemens, G. (2014). Educational data mining and learning analytics. In Sawyer, K. (Ed.), *The Cambridge handbook of the learning sciences* (pp. 253–274). Cambridge University Press. DOI: 10.1017/CBO9781139519526.016

Balas, B., & Momsen, J. L. (2014). Attention "blinks" differently for plants and animals. *CBE Life Sciences Education*, *13*(3), 437–443. Advance online publication. DOI: 10.1187/cbe.14-05-0080

Baldrich, K., Pérez-García, C., Domínguez-Oller, J. C., & Amo Sánchez-Fortún, J. M. (2024). Gamified experiences in educational academic contexts: A systematic review. *Qualitative Research in Education*, *13*(3), 221–242. DOI: 10.17583/qre.13552

Bamanger, E. (2025). Augmented reality in EFL education: Transforming high school student achievement through interactive learning tools. *The Journal of Technology Studies*, *50*(1), 30–41. DOI: 10.21061/jts.439

Bang, H. J., & Siebert-Evenstone, A. (2025). Evaluation of a Personalized Game-Based Learning app for Developing Young Children's Reading Skills. *Journal of Educational Technology Systems*, *54*(1), 88–118. DOI: 10.1177/00472395251337095

Banks, J. A. (2015). *Cultural diversity and education: Foundations, curriculum, and teaching* (6th ed.). Routledge. DOI: 10.4324/9781315622255

Bao, P. (2025). Delineating translanguaging: Theoretical distinctions from code-switching and a Vygotskian model of cognitive scaffolding in multilingual classrooms. *International Journal of Multilingualism*, •••, 1–22. DOI: 10.1080/14790718.2025.2575886

Barnes, M., & Tour, E. (2025). Teachers' use of generative AI: A 'dirty little secret'? *Language and Education*, •••, 1–16. DOI: 10.1080/09500782.2025.2485935

Barnett, W. S., & Jung, K. (2020). *Understanding and responding to the pandemic's impacts on preschool education: What can we learn from last spring*. National Institute for Early Education Research.

Barrett, A., & Pack, A. (2023). Not quite eye to A.I.: Student and teacher perspectives on the use of generative artificial intelligence in the writing process. *International Journal of Educational Technology in Higher Education*, *20*(1), 59. DOI: 10.1186/s41239-023-00427-0

Barrows, H. S. (1987). *Simulated (Standardized) Patients and Other Human Simulations*. Health Sciences Consortium.

Barr, R. (2013). Memory constraints on infant learning from picture books, television, and touchscreens. *Child Development Perspectives*, *7*(4), 205–210. DOI: 10.1111/cdep.12041

Barua, L., & Lockee, B. (2025). Flexible assessment in higher education: A comprehensive review of strategies and implications. *TechTrends*, *69*(2), 301–309. DOI: 10.1007/s11528-025-01039-3

Barus, O. P., Hidayanto, A. N., Handri, E. Y., Sensuse, D. I., & Yaiprasert, C. (2025). Shaping generative AI governance in higher education: A multi-stakeholder and sustainable approach. *International Journal of Educational Research Open*, *8*, 100452. DOI: 10.1016/j.ijedro.2025.100452

Barzilai, S., & Blau, I. (2014). Scaffolding game-based learning: Impact on learning achievements, perceived learning, and game experiences. *Computers & Education*, *70*, 65–79. DOI: 10.1016/j.compedu.2013.08.003

Battleship [Board game]. (1967). Milton Bradley.

Bawa, P. (2020). Game on! *International Journal of Game-Based Learning*, *10*(3), 16–46. DOI: 10.4018/IJGBL.2020070102

Beck, I. L., McKeown, M. G., & Kucan, L. (2013). *Bringing words to life: Robust vocabulary instruction* (2nd ed.). Guilford Press.

Beger, A. W., Hannan, S., Patel, R., & Sweeney, E. M. (2025). Virtual escape rooms in anatomy education: Case studies from two institutions. *Advances in Physiology Education*, *49*(3), 621–632. DOI: 10.1152/advan.00248.2024

Belda-Medina, J., & Calvo-Ferrer, J. R. (2022). Preservice teachers' knowledge and attitudes toward digital-game-based language learning. *Education Sciences*, *12*(3), 182. DOI: 10.3390/educsci12030182

Bender, E. M., Gebru, T., McMillan-Major, A., & Shmitchell, S. (2021). On the dangers of stochastic parrots: Can language models be too big? FAccT '21: *Proceedings of the 2021 ACM Conference on Fairness, Accountability, and Transparency,* 610–623.https://doi.org/DOI: 10.1145/3442188.3445922

Bengel, P., & Peter, C. (2024). Promoting technological literacy through virtual game-based field trips: Effects on knowledge, attitudes, and gender. *European Journal of Geography*, *15*(2), 120–134. DOI: 10.48088/ejg.p.ben.15.2.120.134

Bennett, M. J. (1993). Towards ethnorelativism: A developmental model of intercultural sensitivity. In Paige, R. M. (Ed.), *Education for the intercultural experience* (pp. 21–71). Intercultural Press.

Bennett, M. J. (2008). Transformative training: Designing programs for culture learning. In Moodian, M. A. (Ed.), *Contemporary leadership and intercultural competence* (pp. 95–110). Sage.

Bergman Deitcher, D., Aram, D., & Abramovich, D. (2024). Parents' literacy beliefs, home literacy activities, and children's early literacy skills: Stability and progress approaching first grade. *Behavioral Sciences (Basel, Switzerland)*, *14*(11), 1038. DOI: 10.3390/bs14111038 PMID: 39594338

Bhat, M., & Long, D. (2024, July). Designing interactive explainable AI tools for algorithmic literacy and transparency. In *Proceedings of the 2024 ACM Designing Interactive Systems Conference* (pp. 939-957). https://doi.org/DOI: 10.1145/3643834.3660722

Bhimavarapu, U. (2025). AI-Enabled Learning Environments Evaluating Literacy Outcomes Through Machine Learning. In *Rethinking Literacy in the Era of Sustainability and Artificial Intelligence* (pp. 133–160). IGI Global Scientific Publishing., DOI: 10.4018/979-8-3373-0725-1.ch005

Billy, I., & Anush, H. (2024). The Digital Evolution-need to adapt education for a Tech-Savvy Generation. The Business and Management Review: Conference proceedings of the Centre for Business & Economic Research (ICBED-2024, 15-17th April), 15, 131.

Bircan, M. A. (2025). The effect of STEM-themed story writing training with artificial intelligence on preservice teachers' digital literacy and narrative competence. *Education and Information Technologies*. Advance online publication. DOI: 10.1007/s10639-025-13625-2

Bird, L., & Menz, R. (2022). Developing safety literacy in built environments: A conceptual approach. *Safety Science*, *145*, 105423. DOI: 10.1016/j.ssci.2021.105423

Bisaria, C., Srikanth, R., Al-Nussairi, A. K. J., Ali, A. D., Al-Hussein, R. K. A., & Durairaj, B. (2025, August). Deep reinforcement learning-optimized resource allocation system for agile management. In *2025 International Conference on Recent Innovation in Science Engineering and Technology (ICRISET)* (pp. 1–7). IEEE. DOI: 10.1109/ICRISET64803.2025.11253820

Black, P., & Wiliam, D. (1998). Assessment and classroom learning. *Assessment in Education: Principles, Policy & Practice*, *5*(1), 7–74. DOI: 10.1080/0969595980050102

Black, P., & Wiliam, D. (2009). Developing the theory of formative assessment. *Educational Assessment, Evaluation and Accountability*, *21*(1), 5–31. DOI: 10.1007/s11092-008-9068-5

Blooket. (2026). *Blooket*. https://blooket.com/

Boeker, M., Andel, P., Vach, W., & Frankenschmidt, A. (2013). Game-Based E-Learning Is More Effective than a Conventional Instructional Method: A Randomized Controlled Trial with Third-Year Medical Students. *PLoS One*, *8*(12), e82328. DOI: 10.1371/journal.pone.0082328 PMID: 24349257

Boghian, I., Cojocariu, V.-M., Popescu, C. V., & Mâţă, L. (2019). Game-based learning: Using board games in adult education. *Journal of Educational Sciences & Psychology*, *9*(1), 51–57.

Bonner, E., & Reinders, H. (2018). Augmented and virtual reality in the language classroom: Practical ideas. *Teaching English With Technology*, *18*(3), 33–53.

Bónus, L., Antal, E., & Korom, E. (2024). Digital game-based inquiry learning to improve eighth graders' inquiry skills in biology. *Journal of Science Education and Technology*, *33*(4), 1–17. DOI: 10.1007/s10956-024-10096-x

Bora, D., Patel, P., Psyridou, M., Ruotsalainen, J., Richardson, U., & Torppa, M. (2025). Foundational English literacy development in India: A randomised-control trial using phonics instruction and GraphoLearn. *Reading and Writing*, *38*(5), 1309–1335. DOI: 10.1007/s11145-024-10551-6

Borrella, I. (2025). Design principles and impact of a learning analytics dashboard to support student self-regulation. *Applied Sciences (Basel, Switzerland)*, *15*(21), 11493. DOI: 10.3390/app152111493

Bouakaz, L., & Khalid, S. (2025). AI in education: A sociological exploration of technology in learning environments. *Frontiers in Education*, *10*, 1700876. DOI: 10.3389/feduc.2025.1700876

Boysen, M. S. W., Lund, O., Jørnø, R. L., & Skovbjerg, H. M. (2023). The role of experience in playful learning activities: A design-based self-study within teacher education aimed at the development of tabletop role-playing games. *Teaching and Teacher Education, 128*, 104128. DOI: 10.1016/j.tate.2023.104128

Bozkurt, A. (2024). GenAI et al.: Cocreation, Authorship, Ownership, Academic Ethics and Integrity in a Time of Generative AI. *Open Praxis, 16*(1), 1–10. https://doi.org/. DOI: 10.55982/openpraxis.16.1.654

Brandl, B., & Schrader, C. (2024). Serious games in higher education in the transforming process to Education 4.0—Systematized review. *Education Sciences, 14*(3), 281. DOI: 10.3390/educsci14030281

Braun, V., & Clarke, V. (2006). Using thematic analysis in psychology. *Qualitative Research in Psychology, 3*(2), 77–101. DOI: 10.1191/1478088706qp063oa

Bray, A., Devitt, A., Banks, J., Sanchez Fuentes, S., Sandoval, M., Riviou, K., Byrne, D., Flood, M., Reale, J., & Terrenzio, S. (2024). What next for Universal Design for Learning? A systematic literature review of technology in UDL implementations at second level. *British Journal of Educational Technology, 55*(1), 113–138. DOI: 10.1111/bjet.13328

Breland, C. D. (2026). Amplifying assets: Literacy leadership teams, culturally relevant pedagogy, and multiliteracies turn. *Journal of Adolescent & Adult Literacy, 69*(5), e70039. DOI: 10.1002/jaal.70039

Brendle, J., Lock, R., & Piazza, K. (2017). A Study of Co-Teaching Identifying Effective Implementation Strategies. *International Journal of Special Education, 32*(3). https://files.eric.ed.gov/fulltext/EJ1184155.pdf

Brinegar, K., Harrison, L., & Hurd, E. (2024). Toward a culturally sustaining science of reading. *Middle School Journal, 55*(3), 2–4. (176635226). DOI: 10.1080/00940771.2024.2332142

Brod, G. (2021). Generative learning: Which strategies for what age? *Educational Psychology Review, 33*(4), 1295–1318. DOI: 10.1007/s10648-020-09571-9

Brom, C., Šisler, V., & Slavík, R. (2010). Implementing digital game-based learning in schools: Augmented learning environment of 'Europe 2045'. *Multimedia Systems, 16*(1), 23–41. DOI: 10.1007/s00530-009-0174-0

Brookhart, S. M. (2013). *How to create and use rubrics for formative assessment and grading*. Association for Supervision and Curriculum Development.

Brown, J. S., Collins, A., & Duguid, P. (1989). Situated cognition and the culture of learning. *Educational Researcher, 18*(1), 32–42. DOI: 10.3102/0013189X018001032

Bruner, J. (1986). *Actual minds, possible worlds*. Harvard University Press. DOI: 10.4159/9780674029019

Bruner, J. (1996). *The culture of education*. Harvard University Press. DOI: 10.4159/9780674251083

Bus, A. G., Takacs, Z. K., & Kegel, C. A. T. (2015). Affordances and limitations of electronic storybooks for young children's emergent literacy. *Developmental Review, 35*, 79–97. DOI: 10.1016/j.dr.2014.12.004

Bybee, R. W. (2013). *The case for STEM education: Challenges and opportunities*. NSTA Press.

Byram, M. (1997). *Teaching and assessing intercultural communicative competence*. Multilingual Matters.

Cadiz, G. S., Lacre, G. J. R., Delamente, R. L., & Diquito, T. J. A. (2023). Game-based learning approach in science education: A meta-analysis. *International Journal of Social Science and Human Research, 6*(03), 1856–1865. DOI: 10.47191/ijsshr/v6-i3-61

Caena, F., & Redecker, C. (2019). Aligning teacher competence frameworks to 21st century challenges: The case for the European Digital Competence Framework for Educators (Digcompedu). *European Journal of Education, 54*(3), 356–369. Advance online publication. DOI: 10.1111/ejed.12345

Cai, Z., Mao, P., Wang, J., He, J., Chen, X., & Fan, X. (2022). Effects of scaffolding in digital game-based learning on student's achievement: A three-level meta-analysis. *Educational Psychology Review, 34*(2), 537–574. DOI: 10.1007/s10648-021-09655-0

Camacho-Sánchez, R., Manzano-León, A., Rodríguez-Ferrer, J. M., Serna, J., & Lavega-Burgués, P. (2023). Game-Based Learning and Gamification in Physical Education: A Systematic Review. *Education Sciences, 13*(2), 183. DOI: 10.3390/educsci13020183

Canagarajah, S. (2011). Codemeshing in academic writing: Identifying teachable strategies of translanguaging. *Modern Language Journal, 95*(3), 401–417. DOI: 10.1111/j.1540-4781.2011.01207.x

Carbonell-Alcocer, A., Romero-Luis, J., Gértrudix-Barrio, M., & Borges-Rey, E. (2022). Educating for a sustainable future through the Circular Economy: Citizen involvement and social change. *Comunicar: Media Education Research Journal, 30*(73), 21–32. DOI: 10.3916/C73-2022-02

Casau, M., Dias, M. F., & Amorim, M. (2023). Entrepreneurship and game-based learning in higher education: A systematic review. In *European Conference on Games Based Learning*. DOI: 10.34190/ecgbl.17.1.1785

CAST. (2018). *Universal Design for Learning guidelines version 2.2.* CAST. https://udlguidelines.cast.org

CAST. (2018). Universal design for learning guidelines version 2.2. http://udlguidelines.cast.org

Castañeda, M., & Bautista, N. (2011). Teaching science to ELLs, part II. *Science Teacher (Normal, Ill.), 78*(3), 40.

Cavalcante-Pimentel, F. S., Morais-Marques, M., & Barbosa-de-Sales-Junior, V. (2022). Learning Strategies through Digital Games in a University Context. *Comunicar: Media Education Research Journal, 30*(73), 77–86. DOI: 10.3916/C73-2022-07

Çayak, S. (2024). Investigating the relationship between teachers' attitudes toward artificial intelligence and their artificial intelligence literacy. *Journal of Educational Technology & Online Learning, 7*(4), 367–383. DOI: 10.31681/jetol.1490307

Celik, I., Dindar, M., Muukkonen, H., & Järvelä, S. (2022). The promises and challenges of artificial intelligence for teachers: A systematic review of research. *TechTrends, 66*(4), 616–630. DOI: 10.1007/s11528-022-00715-y

Cerra, P., Pablo, F. Á., & Humberto, B. P. (2022). Effects of Using Game-Based Learning to Improve the Academic Performance and Motivation in Engineering Studies. *Journal of Educational Computing Research, 60*(7), 1663–1687. DOI: 10.1177/07356331221074022

Cetin, O., & Celen, G. (2025). Investigation of pre-service teachers' artificial intelligence literacy and views on the use of artificial intelligence in education. [JESEH]. *Journal of Education in Science, Environment and Health, 11*(4), 285–304. DOI: 10.55549/jeseh.850

Chan, S., & Lo, N. (2024). Enhancing EFL/ESL instruction through gamification: a comprehensive review of empirical evidence. In *Frontiers in Education* (Vol. 9, p. 1395155). Frontiers Media SA. https://doi.org/DOI: 10.3389/feduc.2024.1395155

Chang, C. H., & Wang, R. S. M. (2025, July). Finance Literacy Thematic Board Game Development and Game-based Learning Evaluation. In *2025 IEEE Gaming, Entertainment, and Media Conference (GEM)* (pp. 1-6). IEEE. https://doi.org/DOI: 10.1109/GEM66882.2025.11155504

Chang, B. (2019). Reflection in learning. *Online Learning : The Official Journal of the Online Learning Consortium, 23*(1), 95–110. DOI: 10.24059/olj.v23i1.1447

Chang, W., Swift, A. W., & Shulga, L. V. (2026). Artificial intelligence (AI) preparedness in hospitality: A framework and research agenda for building organizational capacities. *International Journal of Contemporary Hospitality Management, 38*(4), 1–20. DOI: 10.1108/IJCHM-04-2025-0525

Chang, X. Game-Based Learning in ESL Classrooms: A Focus on Gimkit and Other Apps (May 01, 2021). http://doi.org/DOI: 10.2139/ssrn.5106362

Chang, X., & Wong, G. K. (2025). A systematic review of how educators integrate ethics into artificial intelligence curriculum. *Journal of Research on Technology in Education*, •••, 1–18. DOI: 10.1080/15391523.2025.2551112

Charles, T., & Papadaki, M. (2025). Ethical leadership in technology integration and digital education. In Soles, B., & Meyerott, T. (Eds.), *Diverse leadership perspectives in education: From K-12 to higher education* (pp. 437–454). IGI Global Scientific Publishing., DOI: 10.4018/979-8-3693-6115-3.ch016

Charos, K. (2024). Effective ways of incorporating Krashen's hypothesis into ESL instructional practices. *University Research Base*, 153-161. Retrieved from https://scholar.kokanduni.uz/index.php/rb/article/view/303

Chaves-Yuste, B., de-la-Peña, C., & Candel, E. C. (2026). Digital game-based learning: Does it improve university students' learning in an online context? *Knowledge Management & E-Learning, 18*(1), 39.

Cheah, Y. H., Lu, J., & Kim, J. (2025). Integrating generative artificial intelligence in K-12 education: Examining teachers' preparedness, practices, and barriers. *Computers and Education: Artificial Intelligence, 8*, 100363. DOI: 10.1016/j.caeai.2025.100363

Chen, L., Chen, P., & Lin, Z. (2020). *Artificial Intelligence in Education: a review.* IEEE Journals & Magazine | IEEE Xplore. DOI: 10.1109/ACCESS.2020.2988510

Chen, C. H., & Chang, C. L. (2024). Effectiveness of AI-assisted game-based learning on science learning outcomes, intrinsic motivation, cognitive load, and learning behavior. *Education and Information Technologies, 29*(14), 18621–18642. DOI: 10.1007/s10639-024-12553-x

Chen, J. J. (2024). A scoping study on AI affordances in early childhood education: Mapping the global landscape, identifying research gaps, and charting future research directions. *Journal of Artificial Intelligence Research, 81*, 701–740. DOI: 10.1613/jair.1.16882

Chen, J., & Alibakhshi, G. (2026). AI-powered applications' effects on English language learners' cognitive, metacognitive, and resource management strategies, and language achievement. *Journal of Computer Assisted Learning, 42*(1), e70171. DOI: 10.1002/jcal.70171

Chen, S., Jamiatul Husnaini, S., & Chen, J. J. (2020). Effects of games on students' emotions of learning science and achievement in chemistry. *International Journal of Science Education, 42*(13), 2224–2245. DOI: 10.1080/09500693.2020.1817607

Chen, X., Zou, D., Xie, H., & Cheng, G. (2021). Twenty years of personalized language learning. *Journal of Educational Technology & Society, 24*(1), 205–222.

Chergarova, V., Tomeo, M., Morgan, H., & Andrade, S. (2024). Integrating artificial intelligence (AI) into game development to elevate diverse gameplay elements. *Issues in Information Systems, 25*(2), 408–417. DOI: 10.48009/2_iis_2024_132

Chernikova, O., Heitzmann, N., Stadler, M., Holzberger, D., Seidel, T., & Fischer, F. (2020). Simulation-based learning in higher education: A meta-analysis. *Review of Educational Research, 90*(4), 499–541. DOI: 10.3102/0034654320933544

Chesson, D. (2026, January 13). *Grammarly review: Is Grammarly still worth it in 2026?* Kindlepreneur. https://kindlepreneur.com/grammarly-review-is-grammarly-good/

Chew, P., & Da, L. I. (2025). Bridging the AI literacy gap: A constructivist, no-code AI curriculum for secondary students. *Computational Thinking and STEM Education, 14*.

Chiang, F. K., Wang, S., & Tang, Z. (2022). Design and Evaluation of a Board Game in Food and Nutrition Education. *Education Sciences, 12*(3), 162. DOI: 10.3390/educsci12030162

Chiarello, F., & Castellano, M. G. (2016). Board games and board game design as learning tools for complex scientific concepts: Some experiences. *International Journal of Game-Based Learning, 6*(2), 1–14. Advance online publication. DOI: 10.4018/IJGBL.2016040101

Chiotaki, D., Poulopoulos, V., & Karpouzis, K. (2023). Adaptive game-based learning in education: a systematic review. *Frontiers in Computer Science, Volume 5-2023*.

Chiu, T. K. F. (2024). The impact of generative AI (GenAI) on practices, policies and research direction in education: A case of ChatGPT and Midjourney. *Interactive Learning Environments, 32*(10), 6187–6203. DOI: 10.1080/10494820.2023.2253861

Chiu, T. K. F., Ahmad, Z., Ismailov, M., & Sanusi, I. T. (2024). What are artificial intelligence literacy and competency? A comprehensive framework to support them. *Computers and Education Open, 6*, 100171. Advance online publication. DOI: 10.1016/j.caeo.2024.100171

Chiu, T. K. F., Moorhouse, B. L., Chai, C. S., & Ismailov, M. (2024). Teacher support and student motivation to learn with Artificial Intelligence (AI) based chatbot. *Interactive Learning Environments, 32*(7), 3240–3256. DOI: 10.1080/10494820.2023.2172044

Chu, H. C., Wang, C. C., Hwang, G. J., Kuo, F. R., & Chen, Y. H. (2025). Trends of Game-Based Learning in the Mobile Era: A Review of the Top 100 Highly Cited Empirical Studies. *Wangji Wanglu Jishu Xuekan, 26*(5), 653–661. DOI: 10.70003/160792642025092605008

Chung, J. Y., & Jeong, S.-H. (2024). Exploring the perceptions of Chinese pre-service teachers on the integration of generative AI in English language teaching: Benefits, challenges, and educational implications. *Online Journal of Communication and Media Technologies, 14*(4), e202457. DOI: 10.30935/ojcmt/15266

Clark, D. B., Tanner-Smith, E. E., & Killingsworth, S. S. (2016). Digital games, design, and learning: A systematic review and meta-analysis. *Review of Educational Research, 86*(1), 79–122. DOI: 10.3102/0034654315582065 PMID: 26937054

Clemens, L. F., & Kegel, C. A. T. (2021). Unique contribution of shared book reading on adult-child language interaction. *Journal of Child Language, 48*(2), 373–386. DOI: 10.1017/S0305000920000331 PMID: 32524924

Coleman, T., & Money, A. G. (2024). Developing a game design framework to embed student-centred learning. *The International Journal of Information and Learning Technology, 41*(4), 448–469. DOI: 10.1108/IJILT-11-2023-0226

Compare, C., & Albanesi, C. (2023). Belief, attitude and critical understanding. A systematic review of social justice in Service-Learning experiences. *Journal of Community & Applied Social Psychology, 33*(6), 1234–1258. DOI: 10.1002/casp.2639

Connect 4 [Board game]. (1974). Milton Bradley.

Connolly, T. M., Boyle, E. A., MacArthur, E., Hainey, T., & Boyle, J. M. (2012). A systematic literature review of empirical evidence on computer games and serious games. *Computers & Education, 59*(2), 661–686. DOI: 10.1016/j.compedu.2012.03.004

Consejería de Educación Castilla y Léon. (2015). Orden EDU/362/2015. Establece el currículo y se regula la implantación, evaluación y desarrollo de la educación secundaria obligatoria en la Comunidad de Castilla y León. Boletín Oficial de Castilla y León, 86(8 de mayo de 2015), 17975–17979. https://www.educa.jcyl.es/es/resumenbocyl/orden-edu-362-2015-4-mayo-establece-curriculo-regula-implan.ficheros/549394-BOCYL-D-08052015-4.pdf

Consejería de Educación Castilla y León. (2015). ORDEN EDU/363/2015. Establece el currículo y se regula la implantación, evaluación y desarrollo del bachillerato en la Comunidad de Castilla y León. Boletín Oficial de Castilla y León, 86(8 de mayo de 2015), 14058–14079. https://www.educa.jcyl.es/es/resumenbocyl/orden-edu-363-2015-4-mayo-establece-curriculo-regula-implan.ficheros/549395-BOCYL-D-08052015-5.pdf

Cope, B., & Kalantzis, M. (2015). *A pedagogy of multiliteracies: Learning by design*. Palgrave Macmillan., DOI: 10.1057/9781137539724

Costa, P. R., Silva, E. J., Figueira, A., & Noversa, D. (2025, September). The impact of artificial intelligence in Portuguese higher education. In *International Conference on Communication and Applied Technologies* (pp. 447–461). Springer Nature Switzerland.

Cotton, D., Miller, W., & Winter, J. (2017). Sustainability in higher education: Challenges and opportunities. *International Journal of Sustainability in Higher Education, 18*(5), 792–808. DOI: 10.1108/IJSHE-02-2017-0032

Crivello, C., Kuzyk, O., Rodrigues, M., Friend, M., Zesiger, P., & Poulin-Dubois, D. (2016). The effects of bilingual growth on toddlers' executive function. *Journal of Experimental Child Psychology, 141*, 121–132. DOI: 10.1016/j.jecp.2015.08.004 PMID: 26402219

Crocco, F., Offenholley, K., & Hernandez, C. (2016). A Proof-of-Concept Study of Game-Based Learning in Higher Education. *Simulation & Gaming, 47*(4), 403–422. Advance online publication. DOI: 10.1177/1046878116632484

Crompton, H., Burke, D., & Gregory, K. H. (2017). The use of mobile learning in K–12 education: A systematic review. *Computers & Education, 110*, 51–63. DOI: 10.1016/j.compedu.2017.03.013

Cross, B., Gollek, C., Ai, J., & Hainey, T. (2025). How parents read young learners' digital engagement: a posthumanist inquiry into the temporality of co-evolving learning practices in AI game space. *Early Years*, 1–14.

Csikszentmihalyi, M. (1990). *Flow: The psychology of optimal experience*. Harper & Row.

Culcasi, I., Cinque, M., Manasia, L., & Ianos, G. (2023). Learning virtual services for a higher education system in Europe that is more digital and inclusive. *RIDAS. Ibero-American Journal of Service-Learning, 16*, 159–182. DOI: 10.1344/RIDAS2023.16.10

Cummins, J. (2000). *Language, power, and pedagogy: Bilingual children in the crossfire* (Vol. 23). Multilingual matters.

Cunningham, D. (2022). Symbolic representations of preschool children: Relations among block play, picture drawing and emergent literacy. *Critical Questions in Education, 13*(1).

Curran, S. N., Freed, R., & Root, A. M. (2025). Beyond the answer: Exploring question-asking and promoting inclusivity. In *Accessibility, inclusivity and diversity in education and beyond* (pp. 153–168). Springer Nature Switzerland. DOI: 10.1007/978-3-031-81795-3_7

Cushner, K., & Mahon, J. (2009). Intercultural competence in teacher education: Developing the intercultural competence of educators and their students. In Deardorff, D. K. (Ed.), *The SAGE handbook of intercultural competence* (pp. 304–320). Sage. DOI: 10.4135/9781071872987.n17

Da Silva Teixeira, J., Belo Angeluci, A. C., Prates, P.Junior, & Prado Martin, J. G. (2024). 'Let's play?' A systematic review of board games in biology. *Journal of Biological Education, 58*(2), 251–270. DOI: 10.1080/00219266.2022.2041461

Dahalan, F., Alias, N., & Shaharom, M. S. N. (2023, January 12). Gamification and game based learning for vocational education and training: A systematic literature review. *Education and Information Technologies, 29*(2), 1279–1317. DOI: 10.1007/s10639-022-11548-w

Daher, R. (2025). Integrating AI literacy into teacher education: A critical perspective paper. *Discover Artificial Intelligence, 5*(1), 217. DOI: 10.1007/s44163-025-00475-7

Dai, Y., & Zhang, J. (2025). Serious Games: A Study on Digital Literacy and Skill Improvement of Architecture Students in China Vocational Institute. In *Integrating Technology in Problem-Solving Educational Practices* (pp. 27-58). IGI Global. https://doi.org/DOI: 10.4018/979-8-3693-6745-2.ch002

Dalton, B., & Proctor, C. P. (2007). Reading as thinking: Integrating strategy instruction in a universally designed digital literacy environment. In McNamara, D. S. (Ed.), *Reading comprehension strategies: Theories, interventions, and technologies* (pp. 421–440). Lawrence Erlbaum Associates Publishers.

Danielson Group. (2011). *The framework for teaching evaluation instrument.* The Danielson Group.

Dapena, A., Castro, P. M., & Ares-Pernas, A. (2022). Moving to e-service learning in higher education. *Applied Sciences (Basel, Switzerland), 12*(11), 5462. DOI: 10.3390/app12115462

Darling-Hammond, L. (2017). Teacher education around the world: What can we learn from international practice? *European Journal of Teacher Education, 40*(3), 291–309. DOI: 10.1080/02619768.2017.1315399

Darling-Hammond, L., Flook, L., Cook-Harvey, C., Barron, B., & Osher, D. (2020). Implications for educational practice of the science of learning and development. *Applied Developmental Science, 24*(2), 97–140. DOI: 10.1080/10888691.2018.1537791

Darling-Hammond, L., Hyler, M. E., & Gardner, M. (2017). *Effective teacher professional development.* Learning Policy Institute. DOI: 10.54300/122.311

Darling-Hammond, L., Hyler, M. E., & Gardner, M. (2020). *Preparing teachers for deeper learning.* Harvard Education Press.

Darvishinia, N., Rios, A., & Clark, J. S. (2025). Innovative Pathways in STEM: Virtual Reality for Empowering English Language Learners. *Journal of Interactive Learning Research, 36*(3), 269–292. DOI: 10.70725/141357ylqajb

Dayagbil, F. T., Boholano, H. B., & Sumalinog, G. G. (2025). Are they in or out? Exploring pre-service teachers' knowledge, perceptions, and experiences regarding artificial intelligence (AI) in teaching and learning. *Frontiers in Education, 10*, 1665205. DOI: 10.3389/feduc.2025.1665205

de Freitas, S. (2018). Are games effective learning tools? A review of educational games. *Computers & Education, 128*, 154–164. DOI: 10.1016/j.compedu.2018.09.017

De Freitas, S. (2018). Are games effective learning tools? A review of educational games. *Journal of Educational Technology & Society, 21*(2).

de la Fuente-González, M. C., Armijos-Armijos, P. M., González-González, C. S., Aguilar-Parra, J. M., López-Liria, R., & Roig-Vila, R. (2025). Use of digital tools and digital competence in university students during the COVID-19 pandemic. *Alterity, 20*(1), 85–95. DOI: 10.17163/alt.v20n1.2025.09

De la Hera, T., Cañete Sanz, L., Navarro Sierra, N., Jansz, J., Kneer, J., Glas, R., & van Vught, J. (2024). Digital literacy games: A systematic literature review. *Frontiers in Communication, 9*, 1407532. Advance online publication. DOI: 10.3389/fcomm.2024.1407532 de Oliveira, L. C., Avalos, M. A., & Blair, A. (2024). Expanding teacher understanding of scaffolding for multilingual learners using a language-based approach to content instruction. *TESOL in Context*, *33*(1), 25–42. DOI: 10.21153/tesol2024vol33no1art2008

Deardorff, D. K. (2006). Identification and assessment of intercultural competence as a student outcome of internationalization. *Journal of Studies in International Education*, *10*(3), 241–266. DOI: 10.1177/1028315306287002

Deci, E. L., & Ryan, R. M. (2000). The "what" and "why" of goal pursuits: Human needs and the self-determination of behavior. *Psychological Inquiry*, *11*(4), 227–268. DOI: 10.1207/S15327965PLI1104_01

Decreto 39/2022, de 29 de Septiembre, Por El Que Se Establece La Ordenación y El Currículo de La Educación Secundaria Obligatoria En La Comunidad de Castilla y León, Boletín Oficial de Castilla y León (2022).

Deeva, G., Bogdanova, D., Serral, E., Snoeck, M., & De Weerdt, J. (2021). A review of automated feedback systems for learners: Classification framework, challenges and opportunities. *Computers & Education*, *162*, 104094. Advance online publication. DOI: 10.1016/j.compedu.2020.104094

del Rocío Fernández-Velásquez, J., López-Regalado, O., & Fernández-Hurtado, G. A. (2025). Educational dualism in action: Systematic review of gamification and flipped classrooms' effects on young learners. *Contemporary Educational Technology*, *17*(1).

Dele-Ajayi, O., Strachan, R., Pickard, A., & Sanderson, J. (2018). Designing for All: Exploring gender diversity and engagement with digital educational games by young people. *Proceedings - Frontiers in Education Conference*, 2018-October. DOI: 10.1109/FIE.2018.8658553

Desta, H., Lemma, B., & Fetene, A. (2012). Aspects of climate change and its associated impacts on wetland ecosystem functions-A review. *The Journal of American Science*, *8*(10).

Deunk, M. I., Smale-Jacobse, A. E., de Boer, H., Doolaard, S., & Bosker, R. J. (2018). Effective differentiation practices: A systematic review and meta-analysis of studies on the cognitive effects of differentiation in primary education. *Educational Research Review*, *24*(1), 31–54. DOI: 10.1016/j.edurev.2018.02.002

DeVries, R. (2000). Vygotsky, Piaget, and Education: A reciprocal assimilation of theories and educational practices. *New Ideas in Psychology*, *18*(2–3), 187–213. DOI: 10.1016/S0732-118X(00)00008-8

Dewan, M. S. (2025). Fostering language proficiency through literature: Navigating challenges and opportunities in multilingual and multicultural classrooms. In *The handbook of English language education in Nepal* (pp. 126–137).

DeWaters, J., & Powers, S. (2013). Energy literacy among middle and high school youth. *Energy Policy*, *59*, 218–228. DOI: 10.1016/j.enpol.2013.03.057

Di Sacco, A., Hardwick, K. A., Blakesley, D., Brancalion, P. H. S., Breman, E., Cecilio Rebola, L., Chomba, S., Dixon, K., Elliott, S., Ruyonga, G., Shaw, K., Smith, P., Smith, R. J., & Antonelli, A. (2021). Ten golden rules for reforestation to optimize carbon sequestration, biodiversity recovery and livelihood benefits. *Global Change Biology*, *27*(7), 1328–1348. Advance online publication. DOI: 10.1111/gcb.15498

Dichev, C., & Dicheva, D. (2017). Gamifying education: What is known, what is believed, and what remains uncertain: A critical review. *International Journal of Educational Technology in Higher Education, 14*(1), 9. DOI: 10.1186/s41239-017-0042-5

Dichev, C., Dicheva, D., Angelova, G., & Agre, G. (2014). From gamification to gameful design and gameful experience in learning. *Cybernetics and Information Technologies, 14*(4), 80–100. Advance online publication. DOI: 10.1515/cait-2014-0007

Dick, W., & Carey, L. (2015). *The systematic design of instruction* (8th ed.). Pearson.

Digital Promise. (2024). AI literacy: A framework to understand, evaluate, and use emerging technology. https://digitalpromise.org/wp-content/uploads/2024/06/24cLSR0009-Exec-Summary-AI-Literacy-Framework-Paper_FINAL.pdf

Digital Promise. (2024). *Global education.* https://digitalpromise.org/initiative/global-education/

Ding, M., & Yu, M. (2024). Serious game-based learning and learning by making games: Motivational mechanisms in EFL education. *Computers & Education*, 208, 105075. [REMOVED HYPERLINK FIELD] DOI: 10.1016/j.compedu.2024.105075

Ding, A.-C. E., DuBois, M. J., Asher, S., Mick, K., Fu, W., Ellison, G., & Nair, M. (2025). Let's make a game! A case of co-designing with teachers to develop game-based learning curriculum. *Journal of Research on Technology in Education, 57*(4), 784–799. DOI: 10.1080/15391523.2024.2313619

Ding, L., & Holland, S. (2025). AI Odyssey: Designing and Evaluating a Board Game for Family-Based AI Literacy. *International Journal of Serious Games, 12*(4), 121–145. DOI: 10.17083/dnza4k90

DiPaola, D., Shen, J., Hu, R., Alghowinem, S., & Breazeal, C. (2023, August). Dronescape: Designing an educational escape room for adult ai literacy. In *2023 IEEE Conference on Games (CoG)* (pp. 1-8). IEEE. https://doi.org/DOI: 10.1109/CoG57401.2023.10333148

Dogan, M., & Arslan, H. (2026). Empowering academics in the digital age: Navigating the transformation of higher education. *European Journal of Education, 61*(1), e70420. DOI: 10.1111/ejed.70420

Dotger, B. H. (2015). Core pedagogy: Individual uncertainty, shared practice, formative ethos. *Journal of Teacher Education, 66*(3), 215–226. DOI: 10.1177/0022487115570093

Dotger, B. H., & Chandler-Olcott, K. (2022). *Clinical simulations as signature pedagogy: Educator preparation across the disciplines*. Harvard Education Press.

Drajati, N. A., Cahyaningrum, D., Handayani, E. I. P., & Handayani, A. (2025). Understanding the artificial intelligence literacy between novice and experienced English teachers in Indonesia. *TEFLIN Journal, 36*(1), 44–60. DOI: 10.15639/teflinjournal.v36i1/44-60

Drelick, A. M., Woodfield, C., & Freedman, J. E. (2025). Educational chatbot development informed by clinical simulations. *Interactive Learning Environments, 33*(3), 2044–2055.

Drelick, A. M., Woodfield, C., & Freedman, J. E. (2026). Designing and using custom chatbots to support students with disabilities: An educator's guide. *Journal of Special Education Technology*, •••, 01626434261420392.

Droujkov, D., Emerson, A., Carpenter, D., Tian, X., Azevedo, R., & Barnes, T. (2025, July). Investigating the Impact of Confusion and Agency on Motivation in a Game-Based Learning Environment. In *International Conference on Artificial Intelligence in Education* (pp. 177-189). Cham: Springer Nature Switzerland. https://doi.org/DOI: 10.1007/978-3-031-98420-4_13

Duarte, J., Gerritsen, N., Lourenço, M., Melo-Pfeifer, S., & Pinto, S. (2024). Service learning for linguistic and cultural diversity in higher education: Proposals for pre-service (language) teacher education. *Education Sciences*, *14*(7), 750. DOI: 10.3390/educsci14070750

Dutta, S., Ranjan, S., Mishra, S., Sharma, V., Hewage, P., & Iwendi, C. (2024). Enhancing Educational Adaptability: A Review and Analysis of AI-Driven Adaptive Learning Platforms. In *IEEE* (pp. 1–5). DOI: 10.1109/ICIPTM59628.2024.10563448

Dyment, J. E., Davis, J. M., Nailon, D., Emery, S., Getenet, S., McCrea, N., & Hill, A. (2014). The impact of professional development on early childhood educators' confidence, understanding and knowledge of education for sustainability. *Environmental Education Research*, *20*(5), 660–679. DOI: 10.1080/13504622.2013.833591

Dzerviniks, J., Ušča, S., Tarune, I., & Vindaca, O. (2024). Intercultural competence of teachers to work with newcomer children. *Education Sciences*, *14*(8), 802. DOI: 10.3390/educsci14080802

Dziubaniuk, O., Ivanova-Gongne, M., & Nyholm, M. (2023). Learning and teaching sustainable business in the digital era: A connectivism theory approach. *International Journal of Educational Technology in Higher Education*, *20*(1), 20. DOI: 10.1186/s41239-023-00390-w PMID: 37096023

Edwards, L. (2024, May 22). *NoRedInk: How to use it to Teach writing*. Tech & Learning. https://www.techlearning.com/how-to/noredink-how-to-use-it-to-teach

Eke, D. O. (2023). ChatGPT and the rise of generative AI: Threat to academic integrity? *Journal of Responsible Technology*, *13*, 100060. DOI: 10.1016/j.jrt.2023.100060

Elsawah, W., & Charles, T. (2023). Investigating Emirati students' practices of learning block-based programming in an online learning context: Evidence from a UAE national program. In K. Al Marri, F. Mir, S. David, & A. Aljuboori (Eds.), *BUiD Doctoral Research Conference 2022* (Lecture Notes in Civil Engineering, Vol. 320, pp. 131-142). Springer. https://doi.org/DOI: 10.1007/978-3-031-27462-6_12

Eltahir, M. E., & Babiker, F. M. E. (2024). The Influence of Artificial intelligence Tools on Student Performance in e-Learning Environments: Case study. *Electronic Journal of e-Learning*, *22*(9), 91–110. DOI: 10.34190/ejel.22.9.3639

Emel'yanenko, V. D., Vetoshko, A. N., Malinnikov, S. G., Malashenko, I. V., & Vetoshko, L. I. (2016). Man's Values and Ideologies as a Basis of Gamification. *International Journal of Environmental and Science Education*, *11*(18), 12576–12592.

Emihovich, B. (2024). Game-based learning and systems thinking: An innovative instructional approach for the 21st century. *TechTrends*, *68*(1), 174–185. DOI: 10.1007/s11528-023-00915-0

Engin, R. A. (2023). The effect of designing educational digital games on pre-service teachers' some competencies. *Journal of Pedagogical Sociology and Psychology*, *5*(3), 195–208. DOI: 10.33902/jpsp.202323576

Ertmer, P. A., & Ottenbreit-Leftwich, A. T. (2010). Teacher technology change: How knowledge, confidence, beliefs, and culture intersect. *Journal of Research on Technology in Education*, *42*(3), 255–284. DOI: 10.1080/15391523.2010.10782551

Evans, J. R., & Mathur, A. (2018). The value of online surveys: A look back and a look ahead. *Internet Research*, *28*(4), 854–887. Advance online publication. DOI: 10.1108/IntR-03-2018-0089

Evmenova, A. S., Regan, K., Mergen, R., & Hrisseh, R. (2025). Educational Games and the Potential of AI to Transform Writing Across the Curriculum. *Education Sciences*, *15*(5), 567. DOI: 10.3390/educsci15050567

Eybers, O. O., & Muller, A. (Eds.). (2024). *AI Approaches to Literacy in Higher Education*. IGI Global., DOI: 10.4018/979-8-3693-1054-0

Ezzaim, A., Dahbi, A., Haidine, A., & Aqqal, A. (2023). Enhancing Academic Outcomes through an Adaptive Learning Framework Utilizing a Novel Machine Learning-Based Performance Prediction Method. *Data & Metadata*, *2*, 164. DOI: 10.56294/dm2023164

Fadhli, M., Kuswandi, D., Utami, P. S., & Sartika, S. B.Mohamad Hardyman bin Barawi. (2023). Game-Based Learning and Children's Digital Literacy to Support Pervasive Learning: A Systematic Reviews. *Jurnal Teknologi Pendidikan*, *25*(3), 386–393. DOI: 10.21009/jtp.v25i3.38388

Fan, J., & Zhang, Q. (2024). From literacy to learning: The sequential mediation of attitudes and enjoyment in AI-assisted EFL education. *Heliyon*, *10*(17), e37158. DOI: 10.1016/j.heliyon.2024.e37158 PMID: 39286160

Farias, C., Hastier, P. A., & Mesquita, I. (2017). Towards a more equitable and inclusive learning environment in sport education: Results of an action research-based intervention. *Sport Education and Society*, *22*(4), 460–476. DOI: 10.1080/13573322.2015.1040752

Farias, C., Segovia, Y., Valério, C., & Mesquita, I. (2022). Does Sport Education promote equitable game-play participation? Effects of learning context and students' sex and skill-level. *European Physical Education Review*, *28*(1), 20–39. DOI: 10.1177/1356336X211013832

FECYT. (2023). FECYT presenta los resultados de la Encuesta de Percepción Social de la Ciencia y la Tecnología: aumenta el interés por la ciencia entre la población española. https://www.fecyt.es/es/noticia/fecyt-presenta-los-resultados-de-la-encuesta-de-percepcion-social-de-la-ciencia-y-la#:~:text=De%20esta%20forma%2C%20el%2047,ecolog%C3%ADa%20(49%2C4%25)

Felicen, S. S., Pulhin, J. C. B., Borbon, N. M. D., Apritado, J. M. M., & Ylagan, A. D. (2026, January). Integrating virtual reality technology in tourism and hospitality education: Student learning experiences. In *Proceedings of the 11th International Conference on Frontiers of Educational Technologies 2025: ICFET 2025* (p. 125). Springer Nature. DOI: 10.1007/978-981-95-2521-8_9

Fernández-González, C., & Franco-Mariscal, A. J. (2021). Teaching the Plant Kingdom Using Cooperative Learning and Plants Elements: A Case Study with Spanish Secondary School Students. *Journal of Turkish Science Education, 18*(1), 17–31. Advance online publication. DOI: 10.36681/tused.2021.50

Fernando, P. A., & Premadasa, H. S. (2025). Use of Game-Based Activities in Predicting the Sequential-Global Learning Dimension for Primary Schoolers. *IEEE Access : Practical Innovations, Open Solutions, 13*, 204606–204627. DOI: 10.1109/ACCESS.2025.3637994

Fink, A. (2011). *How to Ask Survey Questions*. How to Ask Survey Questions., DOI: 10.4135/9781412984393

Finkelstein, I., & Soffer-Vital, S. (2025). AI as a game changer in inclusive higher education: Bridging educational gaps through formative assessment. *Educational Research and Evaluation*, 1–31.

Fiorentini, J. P., Leif, S. A., Fasching-Varner, K. J., & McCreery, M. P. (2025). Learning to Read or Reading to Learn: A Narrative Literature Review of Literacy within Digital Game-Based Learning Environments. *Technology, Knowledge and Learning*, 1–20.

Fiorentini, J. P., Leif, S. A., Fasching-Varner, K. J., & McCreery, M. P. (2025). Learning to Read or Reading to Learn: A Narrative Literature Review of Literacy within Digital Game-Based Learning Environments. *Technology, Knowledge and Learning*, 1-20. https://doi.org/DOI: 10.1007/s10758-025-09851-9

Fitria, T. N. (2021). Artificial intelligence (AI) in education: Using AI tools for teaching and learning process. In *Presiding seminar national & call for paper STIE AAS* (pp. 134-147).

Fitriah, N., Degeng, M. D. K., Degeng, I. N. S., & Praherdhiono, H. (2023). Enhancing Early Childhood Financial Literacy Through FinSOLEkid Indonesia: A Comparative Study of Digital Platforms. *Golden Age: Jurnal Ilmiah Tumbuh Kembang Anak Usia Dini, 8*(3), 171–181. DOI: 10.14421/jga.2023.83-06

Fiuza-Asorey, M. J., Sotelino Losada, A., Mella Núñez, I., & Lorenzo Moledo, M. (2022). Service-Learning & Inclusive Education in Teacher Training. Evaluating student satisfaction. *Revista Fuentes, 24*(2), 210–221. DOI: 10.12795/revistafuentes.2022.17611

Fleming, T. M., Merry, S. N., Stasiak, K., Hopkins, S., Patolo, T., Ruru, S., Latu, M., Shepherd, M., Christie, G., & Goodyear-Smith, F. (2020). Serious games for health: A systematic review. *JMIR Serious Games, 8*(3), e17123. DOI: 10.2196/17123

Florian, L., & Black-Hawkins, K. (2011). Exploring inclusive pedagogy. *British Educational Research Journal, 37*(5), 813–828. DOI: 10.1080/01411926.2010.501096

Flower, L., & Hayes, J. R. (1981). A cognitive process theory of writing. *College Composition and Communication, 32*(4), 365–387. DOI: 10.58680/ccc198115885

Fonseca, L., Lima, V., & Silva, M. (2015). Utilization of quality tools: Does sector and size matter? *International Journal of Qualitative Research, 9*(4).

Forms, G. (n.d.). *Google Forms*. https://docs.google.com/forms/u/0/

Fortuna, R. S.Roniel Sanchez Fortuna. (2025). Lowering the filter: The role of attitude in English language acquisition. *International Journal of English Pedagogy, 10*(2), 111–125. DOI: 10.30574/wjarr.2025.25.3.1020

Foster, A., & Shah, M. (2020). Principles for advancing game-based learning in teacher education. *Journal of Digital Learning in Teacher Education, 36*(2), 84–95. DOI: 10.1080/21532974.2019.1695553

Franzwa, C., Tang, Y., & Johnson, A. (2013). Serious game design: Motivating students through a balance of fun and learning. *5th International Conference on Games and Virtual Worlds for Serious Applications (VS-GAMES)*, 1–7. DOI: 10.1109/VS-GAMES.2013.6624239

Freedman, J. E., Drelick, A. M., & Dotger, B. H. (2024). Use of Simulated Discussions of Postsecondary Accommodations to Inform Self-Advocacy Instruction. *Learning Disabilities Research & Practice, 39*(1), 26–36.

Freedman, J. E., Woodfield, C. L., & Dotger, B. H. (2020). Using Simulated Meetings to Practice Advocating for Disability-Related Accommodations (Practice Brief). *Journal of Postsecondary Education and Disability, 33*(4), 387–394.

Freire, P., & Macedo, D. (1987). *Literacy: Reading the word and the world.* Bergin & Garvey.

Fuller, B., Bridges, M., & Land, A. (2020). What policies advance infants and toddlers? Evidence to inform state and federal options. *Social Policy Report, 33*(1), 1–43. DOI: 10.1002/sop2.6

Gameil, A. A., & Al-Abdullatif, A. M. (2023). Using digital learning platforms to enhance the instructional design competencies and learning engagement of preservice teachers. *Education Sciences, 13*(4), 334. DOI: 10.3390/educsci13040334

Ganguly, A., Mehjabin, N., & Malik, A.. (2026). Conversational AI agents in education: An umbrella review of current utilization, challenges, and future directions for ethical and responsible use. *AI and Ethics, 6*(72). Advance online publication. DOI: 10.1007/s43681-025-00916-0

Gao, H., Huai, H., Yildiz-Degirmenci, S., Bannert, M., & Kasneci, E. (2024, October). Datalivr: Transformation of data literacy education through virtual reality with chatgpt-powered enhancements. In *2024 IEEE International Symposium on Mixed and Augmented Reality (ISMAR)* (pp. 120-129). IEEE. https://doi.org/DOI: 10.1109/ISMAR62088.2024.00026

García-Gutiérrez, J., Ruiz-Corbella, M., Chiva-Bartoll, O., & Paz-Lourido, B. (2024). *Service-Learning in Higher Education: Current and Future Challenges* (Working Papers Series No. 1). UNED. https://hdl.handle.net/20.500.14468/24228

García, O., & Wei, L. (2014). *Translanguaging: Language, bilingualism and education*. Palgrave Macmillan., DOI: 10.1057/9781137385765

Gardner-Neblett, N., Holochwost, S. J., Gallagher, K. C., Iruka, I. U., Odom, S. L., & Bruno, E. P. (2017). Books and toddlers in child care: Under what conditions are children most engaged? *Child and Youth Care Forum, 46*(4), 473–493. DOI: 10.1007/s10566-017-9391-4

Garvis, S., & Manning, M. (2015). Do master early childhood teacher education programs provide adequate coverage of infants and toddlers?: A review of content. *The Australian Journal of Teacher Education, 40*(40), 164–175. DOI: 10.14221/ajte.2015v40n8.10

Garzón, J., Patiño, E., & Marulanda, C. (2025). Systematic review of artificial intelligence in education: Trends, benefits, and challenges. *Multimodal Technologies and Interaction*, *9*(8), 84. Advance online publication. DOI: 10.3390/mti9080084

Gawlik-Kobylińska, M. (2026). Four-dimensional instructional design as a framework for immersive learning to advance inclusive education (SDG 4). *International Journal of Sustainability in Higher Education*, 1–29. DOI: 10.1108/IJSHE-08-2025-0920

Gay, G. (2018). *Culturally responsive teaching: Theory, research, and practice*. Teachers College Press.

Gee, J. P. (2003). What video games have to teach us about learning and literacy. [CIE]. *Computers in Entertainment*, *1*(1), 20–24. DOI: 10.1145/950566.950595

Gee, J. P. (2007). *Good video games + good learning: Collected essays on video games, learning, and literacy*. Peter Lang. DOI: 10.3726/978-1-4539-1162-4

Gee, J. P. (2008). *What video games have to teach us about learning and literacy* (2nd ed.). Palgrave Macmillan.

Gerlich, M. (2025). From offloading to engagement: How AI can enhance or replace our thinking. *Data*, *10*(11), 172. DOI: 10.3390/data10110172

Giannakos, M., Azevedo, R., Brusilovsky, P., Cukurova, M., Dimitriadis, Y., Hernandez-Leo, D., Järvelä, S., Mavrikis, M., & Rienties, B. (2024). The promise and challenges of generative AI in education. *Behaviour & Information Technology*, *44*(11), 2518–2544. DOI: 10.1080/0144929X.2024.2394886

Gibbons, P. (2015). *Scaffolding language, scaffolding learning: Teaching English language learners in the mainstream classroom* (2nd ed.). Heinemann.

Gillis, A. S., & Barney, N. (2025, February 24). What is gamification? how it works and how to use it: Definition from TechTarget. Search HR Software. https://www.techtarget.com/searchhrsoftware/definition/gamification

Gimkit. (n.d.). *Gimkit: Play and Learn*. https://www.gimkit.com/

Gkintoni, E., Magriplis, E., Vantaraki, F., Skoulidi, C. M., Anastassopoulos, P., Cornea, A., Inchaurraga, B., Santurtun, J., Mancha, A. C., Giorgakis, G., Kouppas, K., Timotheou, S., Moreno Juan, M. J., Muñagorri, M., Harasiuk, M., Lopez, A. G., Skoulidi, E., & Vantarakis, A. (2025). Designing for Engagement in Primary Health Education Through Digital Game-Based Learning: Cross-National Behavioral Evidence from the iLearn4Health Platform. *Behavioral Sciences (Basel, Switzerland)*, *15*(7), 847. DOI: 10.3390/bs15070847 PMID: 40723631

Gkrimpizi, T., Peristeras, V., & Magnisalis, I. (2024). Defining the meaning and scope of digital transformation in higher education institutions. *Administrative Sciences*, *14*(3), 48. DOI: 10.3390/admsci14030048

Glas, R., van Vught, J., Fluitsma, T., De La Hera, T., & Gómez-García, S. (2023). Literacy at play: an analysis of media literacy games used to foster media literacy competencies. *Frontiers in Communication, Volume 8-2023.*

Gligorea, I., Cioca, M., Oancea, R., Gorski, A., Gorski, H., & Tudorache, P. (2023). Adaptive Learning Using Artificial Intelligence in e-Learning: A Literature review. *Education Sciences*, *13*(12), 1216. DOI: 10.3390/educsci13121216

Göle, M. O., & Temel, F. (2024). The Effect of Digital Game-Based and Different Education Programs on Phonological Awareness Skills of 60-72 Months-Old Children. *Journal of Theoretical Educational Science*, *17*(1), 202–235. DOI: 10.30831/akukeg.1358837

Gómez Niño, J. R., Árias Delgado, L. P., Chiappe, A., & Ortega González, E. (2025). Gamifying learning with AI: A pathway to 21st-century skills. *Journal of Research in Childhood Education*, *39*(4), 735–750. DOI: 10.1080/02568543.2024.2421974

Gomez, M. J. (2025). The impact of inquiry-based learning in science education: A systematic review of student engagement and achievement. *Journal of Education, Learning, and Management*, *2*(2), 353–363. DOI: 10.69739/jelm.v2i2.1143

González-Yubero, S., Mauri, M., Cardoso, M. J., & Palomera, R. (2023). Learning through challenges and enigmas: Educational escape room as a predictive experience of motivation in university students. *Sustainability (Basel)*, *15*(17), 13001. DOI: 10.3390/su151713001

Gooch, D., Vasalou, A., Benton, L., & Khaled, R. (2016). Using gamification to motivate students with dyslexia. In *Proceedings of the 2016 CHI Conference on Human Factors in Computing Systems* (pp. 969–980). ACM. https://doi.org/DOI: 10.1145/2858036.2858231

Goodall, M. V., Gomez, M., & Webster, D. W. (2024). Effective instruction: The intersection of structured literacy and second-language acquisition for multilingual learners. *The Reading League Journal*, *5*(2), 30–37. https://www.thereadingleague.org/wp-content/uploads/2024/06/the-reading-league-journal-may-2024-effective-instruction.pdf

Gopalan, M., Rosinger, K., & Ahn, J. (2020). Use of quasi-experimental research designs in education research: Growth, promise, and challenges. *Review of Research in Education*, *44*(1), 218–243. DOI: 10.3102/0091732X20903302

Gopalan, V., Bakar, J. A. A., Zulkifli, A. N., Alwi, A., & Mat, R. C. (2017). A review of the motivation theories in learning. *AIP Conference Proceedings*, *1891*, 020043. Advance online publication. DOI: 10.1063/1.5005376

Gordillo, A., & López-Fernández, D. (2024). Are educational escape rooms more effective than traditional lectures for teaching software engineering? A randomized controlled trial. *IEEE Transactions on Education*, *67*(3), 245–256. DOI: 10.1109/TE.2024.3403913

Gouseti, A., James, F., Fallin, L., & Burden, K. (2025). The ethics of using AI in K-12 education: A systematic literature review. *Technology, Pedagogy and Education*, *34*(2), 161–182. DOI: 10.1080/1475939X.2024.2428601

Govender, T., & Arnedo-Moreno, J. (2025). Narrative alchemy: Co-creating a game-based extensive reading framework for adult language learners. *Entertainment Computing*, *52*, 100870. DOI: 10.1016/j.entcom.2024.100870

Graesser, A. C., McNamara, D. S., Louwerse, M. M., & Cai, Z. (2004). Coh-Metrix: Analysis of text on cohesion and language. *Behavior Research Methods, Instruments, & Computers, 36*(2), 193–202. DOI: 10.3758/BF03195564 PMID: 15354684

Graham, S., & Perin, D. (2007). A meta-analysis of writing instruction for adolescent students. *Journal of Educational Psychology, 99*(3), 445–476. DOI: 10.1037/0022-0663.99.3.445

Grant, K. A. (2025). Experiential learning. In *Practical applications of experiential and community-engaged learning methods in business: High-impact teaching practices in business education* (Vol. 1, p. 91).

Green, C., & Giblin, I. (2025). An empty systematic review of the 'pedagogy of multiliteracies' in K-12 since 1996: A generation later, evidence it improves literacy outcomes is lacking from (quasi-) experimental classroom interventions. *Review of Education, 13*(3), e70118. DOI: 10.1002/rev3.70118

Groff, J. S. (2018). The potentials of game-based environments for integrated, immersive learning data. *European Journal of Education, 53*(2), 188–201. DOI: 10.1111/ejed.12270

Gujjula, R., & Sanghera, K. (2023). Ethical considerations and data privacy in AI education. *Journal of Student-Scientists' Research, 5*. https://doi.org/DOI: 10.13021/jssr2023.3958

Gupta, S., Mehta, V., Kam, R., Ehmann, C., Orgad, A., Kuang, E., Barrantes, A. C., Posada, M., Shah, S., Prasad, N., Pai, T., Ho, E., Xi, S., Zhou, T., Li, E., Wan, S., Paranjape, S., Dearling, Z., Peng, S., & Muse, A. (2025). A Teacher, a Tutor, a Friend: ChatGPT and the High School Experience. *Qualitative Report, 30*(5), 3686–3719. DOI: 10.46743/2160-3715/2025.7324

Gu, X., & Ericson, B. J. (2025, August). AI literacy in K-12 and higher education in the wake of generative AI: An integrative review. In *Proceedings of the 2025 ACM Conference on International Computing Education Research* V. 1 (pp. 125-140). https://doi.org/DOI: 10.1145/3702652.3744217

Hafiza, A. F., & Pratolo, B. W. (2024). A systematic review of the effectiveness of game-based learning in English language teaching. *International Journal on E-Learning, 6*(2), 56–64. DOI: 10.31763/ijele.v6i2.1312

Haiken, M. (2017). *Gamify Literacy: Boost Comprehension, Collaboration and Learning*. ASCD.

Hall, T., Vue, G., Strangman, N., & Meyer, A. (2004). *Differentiated instruction and implications for UDL implementation*. CAST.

Hamari, J., Shernoff, D. J., Rowe, E., Coller, B., Asbell-Clarke, J., & Edwards, T. (2016). Challenging games help students learn: An empirical study on engagement, flow and immersion in game-based learning. *Computers in Human Behavior, 54*, 170–179. DOI: 10.1016/j.chb.2015.07.045

Hammond, Z. (2015). *Culturally responsive teaching and the brain: Promoting authentic engagement and rigor among culturally and linguistically diverse students*. Corwin.

Harandi, S. R. (2015). Effects of e-learning on Students' Motivation. *Procedia: Social and Behavioral Sciences, 181*, 423–430. Advance online publication. DOI: 10.1016/j.sbspro.2015.04.905

Hartt, M., Hosseini, H., & Mostafapour, M. (2020). Game On: Exploring the Effectiveness of Game-based learning. *Planning Practice and Research, 35*(5), 589–604. DOI: 10.1080/02697459.2020.1778859

Hashim, M., Tlemsani, I., & Matthews, R. (2022). Higher education strategy in digital transformation. *Education and Information Technologies, 27*(3), 3171–3195. DOI: 10.1007/s10639-021-10739-1 PMID: 34539217

Hassan, N. H., Rahim, N. A. A., Hoong, A. L. S., & Mostafa, K. (2024, August). A Conceptual Study on Utilization of Artificial Intelligence (AI), Virtual Reality (VR) and Augmented Reality (AR) on Green Education: Effectiveness and Engagement. In *International Conference on Intelligent Manufacturing and Robotics* (pp. 270-278). Singapore: Springer Nature Singapore. https://doi.org/DOI: 10.1007/978-981-96-3949-6_20

Hattie, J., & Timperley, H. (2007). The power of feedback. *Review of Educational Research, 77*(1), 81–112. DOI: 10.3102/003465430298487

Hayes, C., Murnan, R., & Bequette, S. (2025). Family, culture, and literacy: Unlocking the power of home for early literacy achievement. *Early Childhood Education Journal.* Advance online publication. DOI: 10.1007/s10643-025-01986-9

Hehir, T., Schifter, L., Grindal, T., Ng, M., & Eidelman, H. (2016). *A summary of the evidence on inclusive education.* Abt Associates.

Heidlage, J. K., Cunningham, J. E., Kaiser, A. P., Trivette, C. M., Barton, E. E., Frey, J. R., & Roberts, M. Y. (2020). The effects of parent-implemented language interventions on child linguistic outcomes: A meta-analysis. *Early Childhood Research Quarterly, 50*, 6–23. DOI: 10.1016/j.ecresq.2018.12.006

Heinmäe, E., Puksand, H., & Kollom, K. (2025). AI in Action: Pedagogical Advice Using Artificial Intelligence as a Digital Resource in Early Childhood Education. *AI in Early Education: Integrating Artificial Intelligence for Inclusive and Effective Learning*, 41-58. https://doi.org/DOI: 10.1002/9781394352821.ch03

Heintalu, K., Saks, K., Edisherashvili, N., & Dekker, I. (2025). The conceptualisation of goal setting and goal orientation in higher education: A systematic literature review. *Educational Research Review, 48*, 100709. DOI: 10.1016/j.edurev.2025.100709

He, K., Cervera, K., Levine, J., Xu, Y., Collins, P., & Warschauer, M. (2025). Promoting parent-child shared reading with a bilingual conversational agent. *International Journal of Human-Computer Studies, 199*(103489). Advance online publication. DOI: 10.1016/j.ijhcs.2025.103489

Henderson, M., Ryan, T., & Phillips, M. (2019). The challenges of feedback in higher education. *Assessment & Evaluation in Higher Education, 44*(8), 1237–1252. DOI: 10.1080/02602938.2019.1599815

Henríquez, V. V., Rabanal, I. C., & Abásolo, J. S. (2025). Applying Kolb's experiential learning cycle for deep learning: A systematic literature review. *Social Sciences & Humanities Open, 12*, 102096. DOI: 10.1016/j.ssaho.2025.102096

Hernández, J., & Ramírez, R. (2024). Introducing pre-service teachers to game-based learning. *International Journal of Educational Technology and Learning, 17*(1), 1–8. DOI: 10.55217/101.v17i1.825

Hitchcock, C., Meyer, A., Rose, D., & Jackson, R. (2002). Providing new access to the general curriculum: Universal design for learning. *Teaching Exceptional Children, 35*(1), 8–17. DOI: 10.1177/004005990203500201

Holmes, W., Bialik, M., & Fadel, C. (2019). *Artificial intelligence in education: Promises and implications for teaching and learning.* Center for Curriculum Redesign. https://curriculumredesign.org/wp-content/uploads/AIED-Book-Excerpt-CCR.pdf

Holmes, J. B., & Gee, E. R. (2016). A framework for understanding game-based teaching and learning. *On the Horizon, 24*(1), 1–16. DOI: 10.1108/OTH-11-2015-0069

Holmes, W., Bialik, M., & Fadel, C. (2019). *Artificial intelligence in education: Promises and implications for teaching and learning.* Center for Curriculum Redesign.

Holmes, W., Bialik, M., & Fadel, C. (2022). *Artificial intelligence in education: Promises and implications.* Center for Curriculum Redesign.

Holzinger, A., Plass, M., Kickmeier-Rust, M., Holzinger, K., Crişan, G. C., Pintea, C. M., & Palade, V. (2019). Interactive machine learning: experimental evidence for the human in the algorithmic loop: A case study on Ant Colony Optimization. *Applied Intelligence, 49*(7), 2401–2414.

Hong, A. L., & Hua, T. K. (2020). A review of theories and practices of multiliteracies in classroom: Issues and trends. *International Journal of Learning. Teaching and Educational Research, 19*(11), 41–52. doi:10.26803/ijlter.19.11.3

Horvat, M., Jagušt, T., Veseli, Z. P., Malnar, K., & Čižmar, Ž. (2022). An overview of digital game-based learning development and evaluation models. In *2022 45th Jubilee International Convention on Information, Communication and Electronic Technology (MIPRO)* (pp. 717–722). DOI: 10.23919/MIPRO55190.2022.9803333

Howard, G. R. (2003). *We can't teach what we don't know: White teachers, multiracial schools* (2nd ed.). Teachers College Press.

Hsiao, J.-C., & Chang, J. S. (2024). Enhancing EFL reading and writing through AI-powered tools: Design, implementation, and evaluation of an online course. *Interactive Learning Environments, 32*(9), 4934–4949. DOI: 10.1080/10494820.2023.2207187

Hsieh, M.-F. (2025). Beginning with books: Tailoring formats and strategies for infant and toddler reading activities in early childhood education centers. *Early Childhood Education Journal, 53*(7), 2615–2630. DOI: 10.1007/s10643-024-01772-z

Hsu, H.-P., Mak, J., Werner, J., White-Taylor, J., Geiselhofer, M., Gorman, A., & Torrejon Capurro, C. (2024). Preliminary study on pre-service teachers' applications and perceptions of generative artificial intelligence for lesson planning. *Journal of Technology and Teacher Education, 32*(3), 409–437. DOI: 10.70725/869859beoezu

Hsu, T.-C., & Lao, N. (2025). From Policy to Pedagogy–Building Human-Centered AI Literacy Across Educational Contexts. *Informatics in Education, 24*(4), 645–651. DOI: 10.15388/infedu.2025.00

Hsu, T.-C., & Lin, Y.-T. (2025). Effects of integrating AI image recognition and robot game-based learning on computational thinking. *Journal of Educational Technology & Society, 28*(4), 225–240.

Huang, L., Yu, W., Ma, W., Zhong, W., Feng, Z., Wang, H., Chen, Q., Peng, W., Feng, X., Qin, B., & Liu, T. (2025). A survey on hallucination in large language models: Principles, taxonomy, challenges, and open questions. *ACM Transactions on Information Systems, 43*(2), 3155. Advance online publication. DOI: 10.1145/3703155

Huber, S. E., Kiili, K., Nebel, S., Ryan, R. M., Sailer, M., & Ninaus, M. (2024). Leveraging the potential of large language models in education through playful and game-based learning. *Educational Psychology Review, 36*(1), 25. DOI: 10.1007/s10648-024-09868-z

Hu, H., & Sperling, R. A. (2022). Pre-service teachers' perceptions of adopting digital games in education: A mixed methods investigation. *Teaching and Teacher Education, 120*, 103876. DOI: 10.1016/j.tate.2022.103876

Hung, I.-C., Chen, C.-C., & Lin, T.-L. (2021). Applying Board Games on Curriculum Design for Elementary School — A Case of Integrative Activities Curriculum. *Knowledge Innovation on Design and Culture*, 81–83.

Hussain, S., Soni, G., & Sharma, S. (2026). Workforce readiness: Industry insights on building future-ready talent for hospitality. *Worldwide Hospitality and Tourism Themes, 18*(1), 1–21. DOI: 10.1108/WHATT-12-2025-0302

Ibarra-Balarezo, S. C., & Guaman-Luna, M. M. (2025). The use of comprehensible input to improve listening comprehension in high school EFL sudents: A literature review. *Revista Mexicana de Investigación e Intervención Educativa, 4*(S1), 171–182. DOI: 10.62697/rmiie.v4iS1.160

Ifenthaler, D., Eseryel, D., & Ge, X. (2012). Assessment for Game-Based Learning. In *Assessment in Game-Based Learning: Foundations, Innovations, and Perspectives* (pp. 1–8). Springer., DOI: 10.1007/978-1-4614-3546-4_1

IPCC. (2023). The Sustainable Development Goals Report 2023 Special Edition. In The Sustainable Development Goals Report.

Islam, M., Karimi, A., Ahmad, S., Wani, J. A., Butdisuwan, S., Rahman, M. H., Habiba, U., Islam, M. E., & Rahman, M. O. (2025, December 07). N., Karimi, A., Ahmad, S., Wani, J. A., Butdisuwan, S., Rahman, Md. H., Habiba, U., Islam, Md. E., & Rahman, Md. O. (2025). Gamification and game-based learning in teacher training and education: Quantifying through bibliometric paradigms. *Journal of Education*, 00220574251406241. Advance online publication. DOI: 10.1177/00220574251406241

Ismail, I. A. (2025). Protecting privacy in AI-enhanced education: A comprehensive examination of data privacy concerns and solutions in AI-based learning. In Mutawa, A. (Ed.), *Impacts of generative AI on the future of research and education* (pp. 117–142). IGI Global., DOI: 10.4018/979-8-3693-0884-4.ch006

Ismaizam, N. M., Rahman, S. F. A., Ahmad, S. N. S. M., Nazri, N. I. I. M., Idris, N. A. A., Ali, N. A., & Aldaba, A. M. A. (2022). An integration of game-based learning in a classroom: An overview (2016–2021). *International Journal of Academic Research in Progressive Education and Development, 11*(1), 1207–1221. DOI: 10.6007/IJARPED/v11-i1/12347

Ivanov, S., Soliman, M., Tuomi, A., Alhamar Alkathiri, N., & Al-Alawi, A. N. (2024). Drivers of generative AI adoption in higher education through the lens of the Theory of Planned Behaviour. *Technology in Society*, *77*, 102521. DOI: 10.1016/j.techsoc.2024.102521

Jager, L., Denessen, E., Cillessen, A. H. N., & Meijer, P. C. (2025). Instructional differentiation in secondary education: Teachers' actions and reasoning. *Teaching and Teacher Education*, *159*(1), 105009. DOI: 10.1016/j.tate.2025.105009

Jain, S. A., Hussaini, N., John, S., Alexander, D., & Sarkar, B. (2022). Game-based learning in higher education: An effective pedagogical tool for enhanced competency building. In *Handbook of research on acquiring 21st century literacy skills through game-based learning* (pp. 138–163). IGI Global Scientific Publishing. DOI: 10.4018/978-1-7998-7271-9.ch008

Janks, H. (2010). *Literacy and power*. Routledge.

Jan, M., & Gaydos, M. (2016). What is game-based learning? Past, present, and future. *Educational Technology*, *56*(3), 6–11.

Jasińska, K. K., & Petitto, L.-A. (2017). Age of bilingual exposure is related to the contribution of phonological and semantic knowledge to successful reading development. *Child Development*, *89*(1), 310–331. DOI: 10.1111/cdev.12745 PMID: 28169419

Jasmaniah, J., Nurhayati, N., & Zuhra, F. (2024). Game-Based Learning Model with A Culturally Responsive Teaching Approach to Enhance Student Motivation in Learning Mathematics. *Jurnal Ilmiah Sekolah Dasar*, *8*(4), 708–717. DOI: 10.23887/jisd.v8i4.86595

Jayasinghe, U., & Dharmaratne, A. (2013). Game-based learning vs. gamification from the higher education students' perspective. *Proceedings of 2013 IEEE International Conference on Teaching, Assessment and Learning for Engineering, TALE 2013*, January 2016, 683–688. DOI: 10.1109/TALE.2013.6654524

Jenga [Board game]. (1986). Hasbro Gaming.

Jeopardy! [Board game]. (1964). Milton Bradley.

Jiang, F., & Shangguan, D. (2022). Researching and designing educational games on the basis of "self-regulated learning theory". *Frontiers in Psychology*, *13*, 996403. DOI: 10.3389/fpsyg.2022.996403 PMID: 36438312

Jiang, X., Wang, R., Hoang, T., Ranaweera, C., Dong, C., & Myers, T. (2025). Ai-powered gamified scaffolding: Transforming learning in virtual learning environment. *Electronics (Basel)*, *14*(13), 2732. DOI: 10.3390/electronics14132732

Jiao, D. (2024). AI-Driven Personalization in Higher Education: Enhancing Learning Outcomes through Adaptive Technologies. *Adult and Higher Education*, *6*(6). Advance online publication. DOI: 10.23977/aduhe.2024.060607

Jiaxin, G., Huijuan, Z., & Hasan, H. M. (2024). Global competence in higher education: A ten-year systematic literature review. *Frontiers in Education*, *9*, 1404782. Advance online publication. DOI: 10.3389/feduc.2024.1404782

Jing, H. (2023). Global awareness, intercultural communicative competence, and global citizenship. In *Developing Global Awareness for Global Citizenship Education: English Language Teachers' Beliefs and Practices in China* (pp. 25–53). Springer Nature Singapore. DOI: 10.1007/978-981-99-4179-7_2

Johnston, H., Wells, R. F., Shanks, E. M., Boey, T., & Parsons, B. N. (2024). Student perspectives on the use of generative artificial intelligence technologies in higher education. *International Journal for Educational Integrity, 20*(1), 2. DOI: 10.1007/s40979-024-00149-4

Jose, J., & Vinay, M. (2017). Performance Analysis of gamification over the traditional classroom in Education. *Indian Journal of Science and Technology, 10*(13), 1–5. DOI: 10.17485/ijst/2017/v10i13/109065

Joshi, M. (2023). Adaptive Learning through Artificial Intelligence. SSRN *Electronic Journal.* DOI: 10.2139/ssrn.4514887

Joshi, M. (2025). *Foundations of reading, writing, and proving.* Educohack Press.

Juárez Varón, D., Bellido-García, I., & Gupta, B. B. (2023). Analysis of stress, attention, interest, and engagement in onsite and online higher education: A neurotechnological study. *Comunicar: Media Education Research Journal, 31*(76), 21–34. DOI: 10.3916/C76-2023-02

Junruang, C., & Kanjug, I. (2025). The Relationship between Computational and Creative Thinking in Preschool Children: An Application through Gamification and Artificial Intelligence-supported Constructivist Personalized Learning Environment. *Educational Process: International Journal, 17*, e2025337.

Kahoot. (n.d.). *Kahoot!* https://kahoot.com/

Kaimara, P., Fokides, E., Oikonomou, A., & Deliyannis, I. (2022). Pre-service teachers' views about the use of digital educational games for collaborative learning. *Education and Information Technologies, 27*(4), 5987–6005. DOI: 10.1007/s10639-021-10820-9

Kalogiannakis, M., Papadakis, S., & Zourmpakis, A. I. (2021). Gamification in science education. A systematic review of the literature. *Education Sciences, 11*(1), 22. DOI: 10.3390/educsci11010022

Kalyuga, S., Ayres, P., Chandler, P., & Sweller, J. (2003). The expertise reversal effect. *Educational Psychologist, 38*(1), 23–31. DOI: 10.1207/S15326985EP3801_4

Kantanen, H. (2026). Active learning in strategic communication: Combining collaborative, flipped and case-based approaches. *Journal of Communication Management (London)*, 1–15. DOI: 10.1108/JCOM-12-2024-0257

Kapici, H. O. (2025). The impact of digital inquiry vs. classroom-based science instruction on learners' outcomes. *Journal of Science Education and Technology, 35*(1), 217-236. doi:10.1007/s10956-025-10246-9.

Kaplan, H., Kalfon, A., Asaf, M., & Yitshaki, N. (2025). Motivational processes involved in simulation-based learning in teacher education: The perspective of self-determination theory. *European Journal of Teacher Education*, 1–20. DOI: 10.1080/02619768.2025.2554684

Kapp, K. M. (2012). *The gamification of learning and instruction: Game-based methods and strategies for training and education*. Pfeiffer.

Kapur, M. (2008). Productive failure. *Cognition and Instruction*, *26*(3), 379–424. DOI: 10.1080/07370000802212669

Karrass, J., & Braungart-Rieker, J. M. (2005). Effects of shared parent–infant book reading on early language acquisition. *Journal of Applied Developmental Psychology*, *26*(2), 133–148. DOI: 10.1016/j.appdev.2004.12.003

Kasapidis, V., Petrou, A., Konstantinidi, N., Kostalias, K., & Kakogianni, E. (2025). AI and Data Literacy: Challenges and Opportunities for Teachers and Students. *European Journal of Education and Pedagogy*, *6*(3), 7–11. DOI: 10.24018/ejedu.2025.6.3.957

Kasneci, E., Seßler, K., Küchemann, S., Bannert, M., Dementieva, D., Fischer, F., Gasser, U., Groh, G., Günnemann, S., Hüllermeier, E., Krusche, S., Kutyniok, G., Michaeli, T., Nerdel, C., Pfeffer, J., Poquet, O., Sailer, M., Schmidt, A., Seidel, T., & Kasneci, G. (2023). ChatGPT for good? On opportunities and challenges of large language models for education. *Learning and Individual Differences*, *103*, 102274. DOI: 10.1016/j.lindif.2023.102274

Kassenkhan, A. M., Moldagulova, A. N., & Serbin, V. V. (2025). Gamification and Artificial Intelligence in Education: A Review of Innovative Approaches to Fostering Critical Thinking. *IEEE Access : Practical Innovations, Open Solutions*, *13*, 98699–98728. DOI: 10.1109/ACCESS.2025.3576147

Katanosaka, T., Khan, M. F. F., & Sakamura, K. (2025, March). Experiential Learning of SNS Etiquette through a Digital Cooperative Game. In *2025 1st International Conference on Consumer Technology (ICCT-Pacific)* (pp. 1-4). IEEE. https://doi.org/DOI: 10.1109/ICCT-Pacific63901.2025.11012867

Katsaliaki, K., & Mustafee, N. (2015). Applications of simulation within the energy sector. *European Journal of Operational Research*, *245*(3), 543–559. DOI: 10.1016/j.ejor.2015.04.020

Kegan, R., & Lahey, L. L. (2009). *Immunity to change: How to overcome it and unlock the potential in yourself and your organization*. Harvard Business Press.

Keller, J. M. (1987). Development and use of the ARCS model of instructional design. *Journal of Instructional Development : JID*, *10*(3), 2–10. DOI: 10.1007/BF02905780

Kenwright, B. (2018). *Game-Based Learning in Higher Education The good, the bad and the ugly*. https://www.semanticscholar.org/paper/Game-Based-Learning-in-Higher-Education-The-Good,-Kenwright/b478c377bcbecfedec1f4ee671490f17e958d4e5

Kerr, R. C., & Kim, H. (2025). From prompts to plans: A case study of pre-service EFL teachers' use of generative AI for lesson planning. *English Teaching*, *80*(1), 95–118. DOI: 10.15858/engtea.80.1.202503.95

Kezar, A., Hallett, R. E., Corwin, Z. B., & Hypolite, L. (2025). Moving toward institutional culture change in higher education: An exploration into cross-functional professional learning communities. *Innovative Higher Education*, *50*(2), 687–714. DOI: 10.1007/s10755-024-09753-1

Khalid, J., Chuanmin, M., Shahid Rasheed, M., & Kamdar, I. (2025). Towards an inclusive and equitable future: Transformation of digital learning design in the digital era. *Information Technology & People*, •••, 1–24. DOI: 10.1108/ITP-09-2024-1144

Khan, A., Ahmad, F. H., & Malik, M. M. (2017). Use of digital game based learning and gamification in secondary school science: The effect on student engagement, learning and gender difference. *Education and Information Technologies*, *22*(6), 2767–2804. Advance online publication. DOI: 10.1007/s10639-017-9622-1

Khanchai, S., Worragin, P., Ariya, P., Intawong, K., & Puritat, K. (2025). Toward Sustainable Digital Literacy: A Comparative Study of Gamified and Non-Gamified Digital Board Games in Higher Education. *Education Sciences*, *15*(8), 966. DOI: 10.3390/educsci15080966

Khelifi, T. (2024). EX-LAD: An explainable learning analytics dashboard. *Proceedings of the Learning Analytics and Knowledge Conference.*

Khoo, Y. Y., Ramdan, M. R., Abdullah, N. L., Abd Aziz, N. A., & Mahjom, N. (2025). The impacts of game-based learning on thinking and learning in higher education context: A scoping review. [IJEMST]. *International Journal of Education in Mathematics, Science, and Technology*, *13*(3), 623–637. DOI: 10.46328/ijemst.4776

Khoo, Y. Y., Ramdan, M. R., Abdullah, N. L., Abd Aziz, N. A., & Mahjom, N. (2025). The impacts of game-based learning on thinking and learning in higher education context: A scoping review. *International Journal of Education in Mathematics. Science and Technology*, *13*(3), 623–637.

Khosravi, H., Buckingham Shum, S., Chen, G., Conati, C., Tsai, Y.-S., Kay, J., Knight, S., Martinez-Maldonado, R., Sadiq, S., & Gašević, D. (2022). Explainable Artificial Intelligence in education. *Computers and Education: Artificial Intelligence*, *3*, 100074. DOI: 10.1016/j.caeai.2022.100074

Kılıçkaya, F., & Kic-Drgas, J. (2025). Pre-service language teachers' experiences and perceptions of integrating generative AI in practicum-based lesson study. *Humanities & Social Sciences Communications*, *12*(1), 1478. Advance online publication. DOI: 10.1057/s41599-025-05715-w

Kim, G. M., Johnson, L. L., & Nash, B. (2023). Games to promote empathy as a literacy practice: A new teacher's playful practice. *English Education*, *56*(1), 20–43. DOI: 10.58680/ee202356120

Kim, S. J., Lee, K., & Park, Y. (2019). Balancing Fun and Learning through a User Interface: A Case Study of Wii Game. *KSII Transactions on Internet and Information Systems*, *13*(7).

Kim, Y. J., Kim, G., & Stoiber, A. (2025). Playful design for AI Literacy: Creating inclusive learning and assessment opportunities. *International Journal of Human-Computer Studies*, *199*, 103508. DOI: 10.1016/j.ijhcs.2025.103508

Kintsch, W. (1988). The role of knowledge in discourse comprehension: A construction-integration model. *Psychological Review*, *95*(2), 163–182. DOI: 10.1037/0033-295X.95.2.163 PMID: 3375398

Kirom, S., & Rosyida, D. A. (2024). Educational Game" Sianting" to Improve Literacy and Anti-Bullying Education Using Problem-Solving Approach. *Al-Adzka: Jurnal Ilmiah Pendidikan Guru Madrasah Ibtidaiyah*, *14*(2), 189–205. DOI: 10.18592/aladzkapgmi.v14i2.14031

Klamma, R., Lange, P. de, Neumann, A. T., Hensen, B., Kravcik, M., Wang, X., & Kuzilek, J. (2020). Scaling Mentoring Support with Distributed Artificial Intelligence. *Intelligent Tutoring Systems*, 38–44. https://doi.org/DOI: 10.1007/978-3-030-49663-0_6

Klein, A. (2023). Welcome to the 'walled garden.' Is this education's solution to AI's pitfalls? *Education Week, 43*(2).

Kofinas, A. K., Tsay, C.-H., & Pike, D. (2025). The impact of generative AI on academic integrity of authentic assessments within a higher education context. *British Journal of Educational Technology, 56*(6), 2522–2549. DOI: 10.1111/bjet.13585

Kolb, A. Y., & Kolb, D. A. (2005). Learning styles and learning spaces: Enhancing experiential learning in higher education. *Academy of Management Learning & Education, 4*(2), 193–212. https://www.jstor.org/stable/40214287. DOI: 10.5465/amle.2005.17268566

Kolb, D. A. (1984). *Experiential learning: Experience as the source of learning and development.* Prentice-Hall, Inc.

Köse, A., & Özcan, S. (2025). Effectiveness of escape rooms in nursing education: A systematic review. *Nurse Education Today, 151*, 106745. DOI: 10.1016/j.nedt.2025.106745 PMID: 40250204

Krashen, S. D. (1982). *Principles and practice in second language acquisition*. Pergamon Press.

Krasnoff, B. (2016). *A guide to evidence-based practices for teaching all students equitably: Culturally responsive teaching*. Region X Equity Assistance Center at Education Northwest.

Kriz, W. C. (2003). Creating effective learning environments and learning organizations through gaming simulation design. *Simulation & Gaming, 34*(4), 495–511. Advance online publication. DOI: 10.1177/1046878103258201

Küçükersen, F., Özemir, P., Dinçer, D., & Demirbilek, O. (2026). Beyond Kolb: Constructing a design learning cycle for the foundation studio. *Journal of Experiential Education, 49*(1), 158–191. DOI: 10.1177/10538259251362141

Kuhail, M. A., Alturki, N., Alramlawi, S., & Alhejori, K. (2023). Interacting with educational chatbots: A systematic review. *Education and Information Technologies, 28*(1), 973–1018. DOI: 10.1007/s10639-022-11177-3

Kumar, K., & Prajapati, R. P. (2025). The interrelationship of collaboration, digital literacy, and critical thinking in developing problem-solving skills among 21st century students. *International Journal of Innovative Research in Technology, 12*(3), 2692–2701.

Kurniadi, D., Yuliasri, I., Wahyuni, S., & Sakhiyya, Z. (2026). *IT-based integrated skills approach: A theoretical framework for integrating English proficiency and digital literacy*. PT. Sonpedia Publishing Indonesia.

Kurtz, G., Amzalag, M., Shaked, N., Zaguri, Y., Kohen-Vacs, D., Gal, E., Zailer, G., & Barak-Medina, E. (2024). Strategies for integrating generative AI into higher education: Navigating challenges and leveraging opportunities. *Education Sciences, 14*(5), 503. DOI: 10.3390/educsci14050503

Labadze, L., Grigolia, M., & Machaidze, L. (2023). Role of AI chatbots in education: Systematic literature review. *International Journal of Educational Technology in Higher Education, 20*(1), 56. DOI: 10.1186/s41239-023-00426-1

Ladson-Billings, G. (1995). Toward a theory of culturally relevant pedagogy. *American Educational Research Journal, 32*(3), 465–491. DOI: 10.3102/00028312032003465

Laila, L., Wardi, L. Z., & Deta, U. A. (2025). Opportunities to Implement Traditional Games as Contextualized Physics Learning Innovations. *Reog: Journal of Ecoethnoscience Education, 1*(1), 24–31. DOI: 10.58706/reog.v1n1.p24-31

Laksanasut, S. (2025). Gamification in ESL/EFL education: Transforming language learning and teaching through play. *TESOL and Technology Studies, 6*(1), 16–29. DOI: 10.48185/tts.v6i1.1562

Lankshear, C., & Knobel, M. (2011). *New literacies: Everyday practices and social learning* (3rd ed.). Open University Press.

Lasley, E. A. (2017). Twenty-first century literacy, game-based learning, project-based learning. *The Journal of Literacy and Technology, 18*(3).

Lateef, F. (2010). Simulation-based learning: Just like the real thing. *Journal of Emergencies, Trauma and Shock, 3*(4), 348–352. DOI: 10.4103/0974-2700.70743

Lau v. Nichols, 414 U.S. 563 (1974). https://supreme.justia.com/cases/federal/us/414/563/

Lauricella, S., & Edmunds, T. K. (2022). Ludic pedagogy: Taking a serious look at fun in the COVID-19 classroom and beyond. *Educational Considerations, 48*(1), 7–24. DOI: 10.4148/0146-9282.2324

Laurin, D. E., Guss, S. S., & Horm, D. (2021). Caregiver–infant and toddler interactions during diapering: Caregiver responsiveness and child well-being and involvement. *Infant Mental Health Journal, 42*(4), 546–559. DOI: 10.1002/imhj.21933 PMID: 34125959

Lavery, S., Chambers, D., & Cain, G. (Eds.). (2018). *Service-learning: enhancing inclusive education.* Emerald Group Publishing.

Lavorel, S. (2013). Plant functional effects on ecosystem services. *Journal of Ecology, 101*(1), 4–8. Advance online publication. DOI: 10.1111/1365-2745.12031

Lee, J. D., & See, K. A. (2004). Trust in automation: Designing for appropriate reliance. *Human Factors, 46*(1), 50–80. DOI: 10.1518/hfes.46.1.50.30392 PMID: 15151155

Lee, O. (2020). Science and language instructional shifts with second-language learners. *Asia-Pacific Science Education, 6*(2), 263–284. DOI: 10.1163/23641177-BJA10005

Lee, O., Miller, E. C., & Januszyk, R. (2019). *NGSS for all students.* National Science Teaching Association Press.

Leider, C. M., Tigert, J., & Norova, N. (2024). Teaching culturally and linguistically diverse learners: A content analysis of teacher professional organizations' position statements. *Teachers College Record, 126*(3), 54–85. DOI: 10.1177/01614681241252502

Leitner, M., Greenwald, E., Wang, N., Montgomery, R., & Merchant, C. (2023). Designing game-based learning for high school artificial intelligence education. *International Journal of Artificial Intelligence in Education, 33*(2), 384–398. DOI: 10.1007/s40593-022-00327-w

Lelescu, A., Sava, S., Grosseck, G., & Malita, L. (2025). Exploring trust in generative AI for higher education institutions: A systematic literature review focused on educators. *Humanities & Social Sciences Communications, 12*(1), 1961. Advance online publication. DOI: 10.1057/s41599-025-06253-1

Leppink, J., Paas, F., van der Vleuten, C. P. M., van Gog, T., & van Merriënboer, J. J. G. (2013). Development of an instrument for measuring different types of cognitive load. *Behavior Research Methods, 45*(4), 1058–1072. DOI: 10.3758/s13428-013-0334-1 PMID: 23572251

Lestari, D., Ekasani, K. A., Supartini, N. L., & Sulasmini, N. M. A. (2025). An innovative method of teaching English for hospitality: A case in Bali Tourism College, Indonesia. *Journal of Language Teaching and Research, 16*(1), 324–334. DOI: 10.17507/jltr.1601.34

Lester, J. C., Ha, E. Y., Lee, S. Y., Mott, B. W., Rowe, J. P., & Sabourin, J. L. (2013). Serious games get smart: Intelligent game-based learning environments. *AI Magazine, 34*(4), 31–45. DOI: 10.1609/aimag.v34i4.2488

Lester, J. C., Spires, H. A., Nietfeld, J. L., Minogue, J., Mott, B. W., & Lobene, E. V. (2014). Designing game-based learning environments for elementary science education: A narrative-centered learning perspective. *Information Sciences, 264*, 4–18. DOI: 10.1016/j.ins.2013.09.005

Le, T. H., Huynh, L., Dang, B., Pham, H. H., Nguyen, N. T. V., & Nguyen, A. (2026). Development and evaluation of artificial intelligence literacy training for teacher education students. *British Journal of Educational Technology*, bjet.70047. DOI: 10.1111/bjet.70047

Leu, D., Kinzer, C., Coiro, J., Castek, J., & Henry, L. (2013). New Literacies: A Dual-Level Theory of the Changing Nature of Literacy, Instruction, and Assessment. In *Theoretical Models and Processes of Reading* (pp. 1150-1181).

Levine, L. E., Waite, B. M., Bowman, L. L., & Kachinsky, K. (2019). Mobile media use by infants and toddlers. *Computers in Human Behavior, 94*, 92–99. DOI: 10.1016/j.chb.2018.12.045

Levin, O. (2025). 'Do not harm': Dealing with teaching-related challenges through the technology of simulation-based learning. *Technology, Pedagogy and Education*, 1–21.

Liang, H. Y., Hwang, G. J., Hsu, T. Y., & Yeh, J. Y. (2024). Effect of an AI-based chatbot on students' learning performance in alternate reality game-based museum learning. *British Journal of Educational Technology, 55*(5), 2315–2338. DOI: 10.1111/bjet.13448

Liang, M. H., & Kuo, S. H. (2026). Systematic review on health literacy through game-based educational interventions in older adults. *Educational Gerontology, 52*(1), 71–84. DOI: 10.1080/03601277.2025.2470273

Licorish, S. A., Owen, H. E., Daniel, B., & George, J. L. (2018). Students' perception of Kahoot!'s influence on teaching and learning. *Research and Practice in Technology Enhanced Learning, 13*(1), 9. Advance online publication. DOI: 10.1186/s41039-018-0078-8

Li, H. (2025). Exploring the relationship between language anxiety and the monitor hypothesis in ESL learners. *Literature. Language and Cultural Studies, 1*(1), 133–138. DOI: 10.63313/LLCS.9019

Li, J., Bai, J., Zhu, S., & Yang, H. H. (2024). Game-based assessment of students' digital literacy using evidence-centered game design. *Electronics (Basel), 13*(2), 385. DOI: 10.3390/electronics13020385

Li, L., Hew, K. F., & Du, J. (2024). Gamification enhances student intrinsic motivation, perceptions of autonomy and relatedness, but minimal impact on competency: A meta-analysis and systematic review. *Educational Technology Research and Development*, *72*(2), 765–796. DOI: 10.1007/s11423-023-10337-7

Lim, W. M., Gunasekara, A., Pallant, J. L., Pallant, J. I., & Pechenkina, E. (2023). Generative AI and the future of education: Ragnarök or reformation? A paradoxical perspective from management educators. *International Journal of Management Education*, *21*(2), 100790. https://doi.org/https://doi.org/10.1016/j.ijme.2023.100790. DOI: 10.1016/j.ijme.2023.100790

Lin, X., & Tan, H. (2025). A Systematic Review of Generative AI in K–12: Mapping Goals, Activities, Roles, and Outcomes via the 3P Model. *Systems*, *13*(10), 840. DOI: 10.3390/systems13100840

Lin, Y. L., & Wang, W. T. (2025). Using business simulation games to explore the effects of instructional and technological support on students' psychological needs, cognitive load, and learning achievement. *Journal of Educational Computing Research*, *63*(3), 587–626. DOI: 10.1177/07356331241313128

Lin, Y.-L., Wang, W.-T., & Hsieh, M.-J. (2024). The effects of students' self-efficacy, self-regulated learning strategy, perceived and actual learning effectiveness: A digital game-based learning system. *Education and Information Technologies*, *29*(16), 22213–22245. DOI: 10.1007/s10639-024-12700-4

Lin, Z., Dai, Y., & Ng, O.-L. (2025). Constructionism in K-12 AI Literacy Education: A Systematic Review of Pedagogical Designs, Student Outcomes, and Learning Mechanisms. *Journal of Educational Computing Research*, *63*(7-8), 1748–1781. DOI: 10.1177/07356331251360442

Liu, H., & Fan, J. (2025). AI-mediated communication in EFL classrooms: The role of technical and pedagogical stimuli and the mediating effects of AI literacy and enjoyment. *European Journal of Education*, *60*(1), e12813. DOI: 10.1111/ejed.12813

Liu, J., & Shadiev, R. (2025). A review of empirical research on game-based digital citizenship education. *Education and Information Technologies*, *30*(14), 1–53. DOI: 10.1007/s10639-025-13549-x

Liu, J., Shadiev, R., & Cao, M. (2025). Effects of digital citizenship educational game on teenagers' learning achievement, motivation, cognitive load, and behavioral patterns. *Education and Information Technologies*, *30*(11), 1–54. DOI: 10.1007/s10639-025-13399-7

Liu, L. (2025). Impact of AI gamification on EFL learning outcomes and nonlinear dynamic motivation: Comparing adaptive learning paths, conversational agents, and storytelling. *Education and Information Technologies*, *30*(8), 11299–11338. DOI: 10.1007/s10639-024-13296-5

Liu, S. Q., Bilgihan, A., & Kandampully, J. (2025). The intersection of technology, sustainability and consumer experiences in hospitality and tourism for new horizons. *Journal of Hospitality and Tourism Horizons*, *1*(2), 87–109. DOI: 10.1108/JHTH-03-2025-0038

Liu, Y., Li, Y., Song, K., & Chu, F. (2024). The two faces of artificial intelligence (AI): Analyzing how AI usage shapes employee behaviors in the hospitality industry. *International Journal of Hospitality Management*, *122*, 103875. DOI: 10.1016/j.ijhm.2024.103875

Lloyd, J., Turner, K. H., Rudniy, A., & Jamieson, S. (2025). Building a future with AI: Entry points for reimagining literacy in higher education. In *Reimagining literacy in the age of AI* (pp. 152–169). Chapman and Hall/CRC. DOI: 10.1201/9781003510635-12

Lo, J. (2025). Assessing an AI-driven feedback system for extended writing. Computers and Education: Artificial Intelligence. https://doi.org/DOI: 10.1016/j.caeai.2025.100170

Lo, C. K., Hew, K. F., & Jong, M. S. (2024). The influence of ChatGPT on student engagement: A systematic review and future research agenda. *Computers & Education, 219*, 105100. DOI: 10.1016/j.compedu.2024.105100

Loewen, S., Crowther, D., Isbell, D. R., Kim, K. M., Maloney, J., Miller, Z. F., & Rawal, H. (2019). Mobile-assisted language learning: A Duolingo case study. *ReCALL, 31*(3), 293–311. DOI: 10.1017/S0958344019000065

Logan, J. A. R., Justice, L. M., Yumuş, M., & Chaparro-Moreno, L. J. (2019). When Children Are Not Read to at Home: The Million Word Gap. *Journal of Developmental and Behavioral Pediatrics : JDBP, 40*(5), 383–386. Advance online publication. DOI: 10.1097/DBP.0000000000000657 PMID: 30908424

Löhr, T., & Gil, M. S. C. de A. (2015). Learning by playing: Echo and tact in expanding the verbal repertoire of infants. *Paidéia (Ribeirão Preto), 25*(60), 77–84. https://doi.org/DOI: 10.1590/1982-43272560201510

Londoño Vásquez, L. M., & Rojas López, M. D. (2021). From Games to Gamification: A Proposal for an Integrated Model. *Educación y Educadores, 23*(3).

Long, D., & Magerko, B. (2020). AI-based adaptive instruction in STEM education. *Computers & Education, 149*, 103113. DOI: 10.1016/j.compedu.2020.103113

Long, M. H. (1980). *Input, interaction, and second language acquisition*. University of California.

Longview Foundation & Learn NC. (n.d.). *The globally competent teaching continuum.* https://www.nafsa.org/sites/default/files/ektron/files/underscore/2016colloquia/2016_teachered_GCTC.pdf

Longview Foundation. (2025). Internationalizing teacher preparation. https://longviewfdn.org/programs/internationalizing-teacher-prep/

López Polo, E., & Sotoca Orgaz, P. (2019). "El Catán Motriz" Un juego de mesa con movimiento para educación física. *Revista Digital de Educación Física, 56*, 30–43.

López-Pernas, S., Gordillo, A., Barra, E., & Quemada, J. (2024). Educational escape rooms are effective learning activities across educational levels and contexts: A meta-analysis. *IEEE Transactions on Learning Technologies, 17*, 711–724. DOI: 10.1109/TLT.2023.3328913

Lord, T. R. (2001). 101 Reasons for using cooperative learning in biology teaching. *The American Biology Teacher, 63*(1), 30–38. Advance online publication. DOI: 10.2307/4451027

Louis, K. S., & Murphy, J. F. (2018). The Potential of Positive Leadership for School Improvement: A Cross-Disciplinary Synthesis. [NJCIE]. *Nordic Journal of Comparative and International Education, 2*(2–3), 165–180. DOI: 10.7577/njcie.2790

Lu, W. (2025). Game-based learning prediction model construction: Stealth assessment in adaptive game-based learning. Journal of Learning Analytics. https://learning-analytics.info/index.php/JLA/article/view/8105

Luckin, R., Holmes, W., Griffiths, M., & Forcier, L. B. (2016). *Intelligence unleashed: An argument for AI in education*. Pearson.

Luke, A., & Freebody, P. (1997). Shaping the social practices of reading. In Muspratt, S., Luke, A., & Freebody, P. (Eds.), *Constructing critical literacies* (pp. 185–225). Hampton Press.

Luo, Z. (2024). A review of Krashen's input theory. *Journal of Education. Humanities and Social Sciences, 26*(1), 130–135. DOI: 10.54097/3fnf5786

Lu, Z., Chiu, M. M., Cui, Y., Mao, W., & Lei, H. (2022). Effects of Game-Based Learning on Students' Computational Thinking: A Meta-Analysis. *Journal of Educational Computing Research, 61*(1), 235–256. DOI: 10.1177/07356331221100740

Lyanda, J. N., & Owidi, S. O. (2025). Integrating artificial intelligence in micro teaching: The role of ChatGPT for customized feedback and interactive learning. *International Journal of Recent Research in Social Sciences and Humanities, 12*(2), 1–10.

Lyon, E. G., Tolbert, S., Solís, J., Stoddart, P., & Bunch, G. C. (2016). *Secondary science teaching for English learners: Developing supportive and responsive learning contexts for sense-making and language development*. Bloomsbury Publishing PLC.

M, A., Asdam, M., & Asdar, A. (2024). Investigating students' reading strategies and reading comprehension through digital literacy environment. *AL-ISHLAH Jurnal Pendidikan, 16*(3), 3370–3379. https://doi.org/DOI: 10.35445/alishlah.v16i3.5510

Maddox, P. L., & Trost, J. L. (2025). Who benefits? Building a critical service-learning model. *Teaching Sociology, 53*(1), 31–45. DOI: 10.1177/0092055X241262787

Madshaven, J. M., Omlin, C. W. P., & Spanos, A. (2025). Making historical consciousness come alive: Abstract concepts, artificial intelligence, and implicit game-based learning. *Education Sciences, 15*(9), 1128. DOI: 10.3390/educsci15091128

Mahapatra, S. (2024). Impact of ChatGPT on ESL students' academic writing skills: A mixed methods intervention study. *Smart Learning Environments, 11*(1), 9. DOI: 10.1186/s40561-024-00295-9

Maity, S., & Deroy, A. (2024). Generative AI and its impact on personalized intelligent tutoring systems. *arXiv preprint arXiv:2410.10650*. https://arxiv.org/abs/2410.10650

Makri, A., Vlachopoulos, D., & Martina, R. A. (2021). Digital escape rooms as innovative pedagogical tools in education: A systematic literature review. *Sustainability (Basel), 13*(8), 4587. DOI: 10.3390/su13084587

Malone, T. W., & Lepper, M. R. (1987). *Making learning fun: A taxonomy of intrinsic motivations for learning*. In R. E. Snow & M. J. Farr (Eds.), *Aptitude, learning, and instruction: Vol. 3. Conative and affective process analyses* (pp. 223–253). Lawrence Erlbaum.

Manesis, D. (2020). Barriers to the use of Games-Based learning in Pre-School settings. *International Journal of Game-Based Learning, 10*(3), 47–61. DOI: 10.4018/IJGBL.2020070103

Manninen, T. (2003). Interaction forms and communicative actions in multiplayer games. *Game Studies, 3*(1).

Mansilla, J. B., & Jackson, A. (2011). *Educating for global competence: Preparing our youth to engage the world.* Asia Society. https://asiasociety.org/files/book-globalcompetence.pdf

Manzano-León, A. (2025). *Playful Service-Learning: development of games for social transformation.* University of Almeria. https://editorial.ual.es/libro/aprendizaje-servicio-ludico-elaboracion-de-juegos-para-la-transformacion-social_166197/ (20/01/2026).

Manzano-León, A., Camacho-Lazarraga, P., Guerrero, M. A., Guerrero-Puerta, L., Aguilar-Parra, J. M., Trigueros, R., & Alias, A. (2021). Between level up and game over: A systematic literature review of gamification in education. *Sustainability (Basel), 13*(4), 2247. DOI: 10.3390/su13042247

Manzano-León, A., Rodríguez-Ferrer, J. M., Aguilar-Parra, J. M., Martínez, A. M., Luque de la Rosa, A., Salguero, D., & Fernández, J. M. (2021). Escape Rooms as a Learning Strategy for Special Education Master's Degree Students. *International Journal of Environmental Research and Public Health, 18*(14), 7304. DOI: 10.3390/ijerph18147304 PMID: 34299753

Manzano-León, A., Rodríguez-Rivera, P., Raposo-Rivas, M., & Rodríguez-Ferrer, J. M. (2024). Digital game-based learning for transgender identity awareness: A qualitative study in Spanish social education degree. *Current Psychology, 43*(20), 18065–18073. DOI: 10.1007/s12144-023-05556-3

Mao, W., Cui, Y., Chiu, M. M., & Lei, H. (2022). Effects of game-based learning on students' critical thinking: A meta-analysis. *Journal of Educational Computing Research, 59*(8), 1682–1708. DOI: 10.1177/07356331211007098

Ma, Q., Jain, A., Kim, J., Chai, M., & Kaufman, G. (2025, April). ImaginAItion: Promoting Generative AI Literacy Through Game-Based Learning. In *Proceedings of the Extended Abstracts of the CHI Conference on Human Factors in Computing Systems* (pp. 1-9). https://doi.org/DOI: 10.1145/3706599.3719844

Ma, R., Sanusi, I. T., Mahipal, V., Gonzales, J. E., & Martin, F. G. (2023, March). Developing machine learning algorithm literacy with novel plugged and unplugged approaches. In *Proceedings of the 54th ACM Technical Symposium on Computer Science Education* V. 1 (pp. 298-304). https://doi.org/DOI: 10.1145/3545945.3569772

Maraza-Quispe, B., Choquehuanca-Quispe, W., Rosas-Imán, V. H., Quispe-Flores, L. M., Alcázar-Holguín, M. A., Feliciano-Yucra, G., & Martínez-López, A. C. (2024). Impact of gamification on collaborative learning development: A quantitative experimental approach. *IEEE Revista Iberoamericana de Technologias del Aprendizaje, 19*(1), 51–60. DOI: 10.1109/RITA.2024.3368360

Mariappan, L. (2024). From Boredom to Excitement: Transforming Classroom Activities with Realia-Based Games. *Journal of Electrical Systems, 20*(5s), 1600–1606. DOI: 10.52783/jes.2493

Markussen-Brown, J., Juhl, C. B., Piasta, S. B., Bleses, D., Højen, A., & Justice, L. M. (2017). The effects of language- and literacy-focused professional development on early educators and children: A best-evidence meta-analysis. *Early Childhood Research Quarterly*, *38*, 97–115. DOI: 10.1016/j.ecresq.2016.07.002

Maroto Sánchez, A. (2023). Using digital educational escape rooms as a motivational strategy in higher education. *International Journal of Management Education*, *21*(3), 100852. DOI: 10.1016/j.ijme.2023.100852

Marsden, E., & Torgerson, C. J. (2012). Single group, pre- and post-test research designs: Some methodological concerns. *Oxford Review of Education*, *38*(5), 583–616. DOI: 10.1080/03054985.2012.731208

Martin, F., Zhuang, M., & Schaefer, D. (2024). Systematic review of research on artificial intelligence in K-12 education (2017–2022). *Computers and Education: Artificial Intelligence*, *6*, 100195. DOI: 10.1016/j.caeai.2023.100195

Martín-García, X., Bär-Kwast, B., Gijón-Casares, M., & Puig-Rovira, J. M. (2021). The map of the values of service-learning: An instrument for reflection & improvement. *Alterity*, *16*(1), 10–23. DOI: 10.17163/alt.v16n1.2021.01

Martín-Sánchez, M., González-Gómez, M., & Jeong, J. S. (2024). Service-learning in the education system: Evaluation of the degree of implementation as a teaching strategy for education for sustainable development. *Apex. Journal of Scientific Education*, *8*(2). Advance online publication. DOI: 10.17979/arec.2024.8.2.10682

Matsumoto, T. (2016). Motivation Strategy Using Gamification. *Creative Education*, *07*(10), 1480–1485. Advance online publication. DOI: 10.4236/ce.2016.710153

Maxim, A., & Arnedo-Moreno, J. (2025). Learning by designing games: A scoping review. *JMIR Serious Games*, *13*, e54075. DOI: 10.2196/54075 PMID: 40053743

Mayer, R. E., & Moreno, R. (2003). Nine ways to reduce cognitive load in multimedia learning. *Educational Psychologist*, *38*(1), 43–52. DOI: 10.1207/S15326985EP3801_6

McInerney, K. (2023). Perceptions from newcomer multilingual adolescents: Predictors and experiences of sense of belonging in high school. In *Child & youth care forum* (Vol. 52, No. 5, pp. 1041-1072). New York: Springer US. https://doi.org/DOI: 10.1007/s10566-022-09723-8

McMahon, L. E. (2025, July 22). Guidance on the use of federal grant funds to improve education outcomes using artificial intelligence (AI) [Dear Colleague Letter]. U.S. Department of Education. https://www.ed.gov/media/document/opepd-ai-dear-colleague-letter-7222025-110427.pdf

Memarian, B., & Doleck, T. (2024). Human-in-the-loop in artificial intelligence in education: A review and entity-relationship (ER) analysis. *Computers in Human Behavior: Artificial Humans*, *2*(1), 100053. Advance online publication. DOI: 10.1016/j.chbah.2024.100053

Memarian, B., & Doleck, T. (2024). Teaching and learning artificial intelligence: Insights from the literature. *Education and Information Technologies*, *29*(16), 21523–21546. DOI: 10.1007/s10639-024-12679-y

Meng, Y. (2021). Fostering EFL/ESL Students' State Motivation: The Role of Teacher-Student Rapport. *Frontiers in Psychology*, *12*, 754797. DOI: 10.3389/fpsyg.2021.754797 PMID: 34589039

Meyer, J., Jansen, T., Schiller, R., Liebenow, L. W., Steinbach, M., Horbach, A., & Fleckenstein, J. (2024). Using LLMs to bring evidence-based feedback into the classroom: AI-generated feedback increases secondary students' text revision, motivation, and positive emotions. *Computers and Education: Artificial Intelligence*, *6*, 100199. DOI: 10.1016/j.caeai.2023.100199

Mienye, I. D., Swart, A. J., & Obaido, G. (2024). Fairness metrics in AI healthcare applications: A review. In *2024, IEEE International Conference on Information, Reuse and Integration for Data Science (IRI)* (pp. 284–289). IEEE. https://doi.org/DOI: 10.1109/IRI62200.2024.00065

Mikrouli, P., Tzafilkou, K., & Protogeros, N. (2024). Applications and learning outcomes on game based learning in education. *International Educational Review*, *2*(1), 25–54. DOI: 10.58693/ier.212

Miller, G. E., & Khatib, S. M. (2023). Honoring diverse cultures through family literacy approaches that build family, school, and community partnerships. *The Reading Teacher*, *76*(5), 586–593. DOI: 10.1002/trtr.2181

Mills, K. (2024). *AI literacy: A framework to understand, evaluate, and use*. Digital Promise / EDUCAUSE.

Mills, K. A. (2024). Critical Literacy and Digital Futures: Looking Ahead. In *Text-Critical Classroom*. Scandinavian University Press., DOI: 10.18261/9788215071114-24-17

Ministerio de Educación Cultura y Deporte. (2020). Ley Orgánica 3/2020, de 29 de diciembre, por la que se modifica la Ley Orgánica 2/2006, de 3 de mayo, Educación. *BOE Núm.*, *340*, 340.

Mirmotahari, O., Grun, H. N., & Berg, Y. (2025). Gamification as a transferable pedagogical innovation for technology education: developing 21st-century skills through collaborative game-based learning. Frontiers in Education, Nolan, J., & McBride, M. (2014). Beyond gamification: reconceptualizing game-based learning in early childhood environments. *Information Communication and Society*, *17*(5), 594–608.

Mishra, N. D. S. (2020). Applications of artificial intelligence in education. In *Artificial intelligence in education: Revolutionizing learning and teaching* (pp. 9–17). DOI: 10.25215/9358094575.02

Mishra, P., Warr, M., & Islam, R. (2023). TPACK in the age of ChatGPT and Generative AI. *Journal of Digital Learning in Teacher Education*, *39*(4), 235–251. DOI: 10.1080/21532974.2023.2247480

Mohammadi, M. (2024). Language teachers' assessment literacy in AI-aided adaptive learning environments. *Journal of Research in Applied Linguistics*, *15*(2), 73–88.

Mohd Hussaini, H., & Saleh, S. (2026). Enhancing students' motivation in learning genetics through STEM-GBL among Northern Matriculation students. *Jurnal Pemikir Pendidikan*, *14*(1), 152–165. DOI: 10.51200/jpp.v14i1.7535

Montessori, M. (2013). *The Montessori method*. Transaction Publishers.

Moon, J., Lee, U., Koh, J., Jeong, Y., Lee, Y., Byun, G., & Lim, J. (2025). Generative artificial intelligence in educational game design: Nuanced challenges, design implications, and future research. *Technology. Knowledge and Learning*, *30*(1), 447–459. DOI: 10.1007/s10758-024-09756-z

Moorhouse, B. L., & Kohnke, L. M. A. (2024). The effects of generative AI on initial language teacher education: The perceptions of teacher educators. *System, 122*, 103290. DOI: 10.1016/j.system.2024.103290

Moriña, A., Carballo, R., & Doménech, A. (2025). Faculty training in Universal Design for Learning: A systematic review of the benefits and challenges. *Teaching in Higher Education, 30*(7), 1722–1739. DOI: 10.1080/13562517.2025.2465994

Morris, D. L. (2025). Rethinking science education practices: Shifting from investigation-centric to comprehensive inquiry-based instruction. *Education Sciences, 15*(1), 73. DOI: 10.3390/educsci15010073

Moyer, R., Snodgrass, J., Klein, S., & Tebben, C. (2017). *Simulation work-based learning: Instructional approaches and noteworthy practices.* U.S. Department of Education. https://files.eric.ed.gov/fulltext/ED583035.pdf

Muawanah, U., Marini, A., & Sarifah, I. (2024). The interconnection between digital literacy, artificial intelligence, and the use of E-learning applications in enhancing the sustainability of Regional Languages: Evidence from Indonesia. *Social Sciences & Humanities Open, 10*, 101169. https://doi.org/https://doi.org/10.1016/j.ssaho.2024.101169. DOI: 10.1016/j.ssaho.2024.101169

Murillo-Zamorano, L. R., López-Sánchez, J. Á., López-Rey, M. J., & Bueno-Muñoz, C. (2023). Gamification in higher education: The ECOn+ star battles. *Computers & Education, 181*, 104699. DOI: 10.1016/j.compedu.2022.104699

Murray, A., & Egan, S. M. (2014). Does reading to infants benefit their cognitive development at 9-months-old? An investigation using a large birth cohort survey. *Child Language Teaching and Therapy, 30*(3), 303–315. DOI: 10.1177/0265659013513813

Mustafa, M. Y., Tlili, A., Lampropoulos, G., Huang, R., Jandrić, P., Zhao, J., Salha, S., Xu, L., Panda, S., Kinshuk, , López-Pernas, S., & Saqr, M. (2024). A systematic review of literature reviews on artificial intelligence in education (AIED): A roadmap to a future research agenda. *Smart Learning Environments, 11*(1), 59. Advance online publication. DOI: 10.1186/s40561-024-00350-5

Nadeem, M., Oroszlanyova, M., & Farag, W. (2023). Effect of Digital Game-Based Learning on student engagement and motivation. *Computers, 12*(9), 177. DOI: 10.3390/computers12090177

NAEYC. (2022). *Developmentally appropriate practice in early childhood programs serving children from birth through age 8* (4th ed.). National Association for the Education of Young Children.

Naseer, F., Khan, M. N., Addas, A., Awais, Q., & Ayub, N. (2025). Game Mechanics and Artificial Intelligence Personalization: A framework for Adaptive learning systems. *Education Sciences, 15*(3), 301. DOI: 10.3390/educsci15030301

Nation, I. S. P. (2001). *Learning vocabulary in another language.* Cambridge University Press. DOI: 10.1017/CBO9781139524759

Nautiyal, V. V., Silverio, S. A., & Salvador, E. E. P. (2024). Let's get on-board: A practical framework for designing and implementing educational board games in K-12 classrooms. *Frontiers in Education, 9*, 1420515. Advance online publication. DOI: 10.3389/feduc.2024.1420515

Nazara, D. K., Mustapa, N., Hendriawan, D., & Mahabbati, A. (2025). The Influence of Digital Learning Media in Stimulating Literacy Skills of Children Aged 5-6 Years. PAUDIA, 791-811. https://doi.org/ DOI: 10.26877/paudia.v14i4.2271

Neina, Q. A., Qomariyah, U. U., & Utomo, A. P. Y. (2025). Community-based multiliteracy assessment as a strategy for strengthening inclusive education. *International Journal of Education and Literature, 4*(1), 134–143. DOI: 10.55606/ijel.v3i3.191

Neville, D. O., Shelton, B. E., & McInnis, B. (2009). Cybertext redux: Using digital game-based learning to teach L2 vocabulary, reading, and culture. *Computer Assisted Language Learning*, *22*(5), 409–424. DOI: 10.1080/09588220903345168

New London Group. (1996). A pedagogy of multiliteracies: Designing social futures. *Harvard Educational Review*, *66*(1), 60–92. DOI: 10.17763/haer.66.1.17370n67v22j160u

Newsela. (n.d.). LINCS | Adult Education and Literacy | U.S. Department of Education. https://lincs.ed.gov/professional-development/resource-collections/profile-916

Ng, D. T. K., Lee, M., Tan, R. J. Y., Hu, X., Downie, J. S., & Chu, S. K. W. (2023). A review of AI teaching and learning from 2000 to 2020. *Education and Information Technologies*, *28*(7), 8445–8501. DOI: 10.1007/s10639-022-11491-w

Ng, D. T. K., Leung, J. K. L., Chu, S. K. W., & Qiao, M. S. (2021). AI literacy: Definition, teaching, evaluation and ethical issues. *Proceedings of the Association for Information Science and Technology*, *58*(1), 504–509. DOI: 10.1002/pra2.487

Ng, D. T. K., Su, J., & Chu, S. K. W. (2024). Fostering secondary school students' AI literacy through making AI-driven recycling bins. *Education and Information Technologies*, *29*(8), 9715–9746. DOI: 10.1007/s10639-023-12183-9

Ng, D. T. K., Xinyu, C., Leung, J. K. L., & Chu, S. K. W. (2024). Fostering students' AI literacy development through educational games: AI knowledge, affective and cognitive engagement. *Journal of Computer Assisted Learning*, *40*(5), 2049–2064. DOI: 10.1111/jcal.13009

Ngo, T. T. Q. (2026). Hospitality management education in business schools: Insights from Scotland using actor-network theory. *Journal of Teaching in Travel & Tourism*, •••, 1–30. DOI: 10.1080/15313220.2026.2653565

Nguyen, K. V. (2025). The use of generative AI tools in higher education: Ethical and pedagogical principles. *Journal of Academic Ethics*, *23*(3), 1–21. DOI: 10.1007/s10805-025-09607-1

Ni, Y., & Lam, R. (2025). Students' perceptions of multiliteracies development using AI-assisted portfolio assessment. *Pedagogies*, 1–28. DOI: 10.1080/1554480X.2025.2545212

Noels, K. A., Pelletier, L. G., Clément, R., & Vallerand, R. J. (2000). Why are you learning a second language? Motivational orientations and self-determination theory. *Language Learning*, *50*(1), 57–85. DOI: 10.1111/0023-8333.00111

Noemí, P.-M., & Máximo, S. H. (2014). Educational Games for Learning. *Universal Journal of Educational Research*, *2*(3), 230–238. Advance online publication. DOI: 10.13189/ujer.2014.020305

Nopas, D., & Kerdsomboon, C. (2024). Fostering global competence in teacher education: Curriculum integration and professional development. *Higher Education Studies, 14*(2). https://ccsenet.org/journal/index.php/hes/article/view/0/49853

Norris, D. J. (2017). Comparing language and literacy environments in two types of infant-toddler child care centers. *Early Childhood Education Journal, 45*(1), 95–101. DOI: 10.1007/s10643-014-0679-9

Nunamaker, R., & Mosier, W. (2021). Infants, toddlers, and technology in early childhood settings: Putting the pieces together. In Burris, J., Rosen, D., & Karno, D. (Eds.), *Handbook of Research on Empowering Early Childhood Educators with Technology* (pp. 206–226). IGI Global., DOI: 10.4018/978-1-7998-6888-0.ch011

Nushi, M., & Fadaei, M. H. (2020). Newsela: A Level-Adaptive App to improve reading ability. *Reading in a Foreign Language, 32*(2), 239–247. DOI: 10.64152/10125/67381

Nutbeam, D. (2000). Health literacy as a public health goal. *Health Promotion International, 15*(3), 259–267. DOI: 10.1093/heapro/15.3.259

Nutta, J., Bautista, N. U., & Butler, M. B. (2010). *Teaching science to English language learners*. Routledge. DOI: 10.4324/9780203850572

O'Farrelly, C., Doyle, O., Victory, G., & Palamaro-Munsell, E. (2018). Shared reading in infancy and later development: Evidence from an early intervention. *Journal of Applied Developmental Psychology, 54*, 69–83. DOI: 10.1016/j.appdev.2017.12.001

Odvina, R. A., Baylon, L. A., Ayop, R. M. M., & Evardo, O. J.Jr. (2024). Use of Cybergogy in Improving Reading Comprehension among High School Students: A Systematic Literature Review. *Journal of Digital Learning and Education, 4*(3), 210–222. DOI: 10.52562/jdle.v4i3.1330

Ogunleye, B., Zakariyyah, K. I., Ajao, O., Olayinka, O., & Sharma, H. (2024). A systematic review of generative AI for teaching and learning practice. *Education Sciences, 14*(6), 636. DOI: 10.3390/educsci14060636

Ojala, M. (2012). Hope and climate change: The importance of hope for environmental engagement among young people. *Environmental Education Research, 18*(5), 625–642. DOI: 10.1080/13504622.2011.637157

Oncioiu, I., & Bularca, A. R. (2025). Artificial intelligence governance in higher education: The role of knowledge-based strategies in fostering legal awareness and ethical artificial intelligence literacy. *Societies (Basel, Switzerland), 15*(6), 144. DOI: 10.3390/soc15060144

Onyishi, C. N., & Sefotho, M. M. (2020). Teachers' perspectives on the use of differentiated instruction in inclusive classrooms: Implication for teacher education. *International Journal of Higher Education, 9*(6), 136–150. DOI: 10.5430/ijhe.v9n6p136

Organization for Economic Cooperation and Development (OECD). *(2018). PISA 2018 assessment and analytical framework.* https://www.oecd.org/content/dam/oecd/en/publications/reports/2019/04/pisa-2018-assessment-and-analytical-framework_d1c359c7/b25efab8-en.pdf

Othman, N. I., Mohamed, H., & Mat Zin, N. A. (2023). Serious games accessibility design model for low-vision children. *Advances in Human-Computer Interaction, 13*(52), 1–13. DOI: 10.1155/2023/9528294

Ouariachi, T., Li, C. Y., & Elving, W. J. (2020). Gamification approaches for education and engagement on pro-environmental behaviors: Searching for best practices. *Sustainability (Basel), 12*(11), 4565. Advance online publication. DOI: 10.3390/su12114565

Oubagine, R., Laaouina, L., Jehgal, A., & Tairi, H. (2025). Smart Adaptive Learning Systems in Education: Current state and future Perspectives. In *International Conference on Circuit, Systems and Communication (ICCSC)*. IEEE. https://doi.org/DOI: 10.1109/ICCSC66714.2025.11135254

Ouyang, J., & Ye, N. (2023). Differentiated instruction: Meeting the needs of all students. *Curriculum and Teaching Methodology*, *6*(11), 57–61.

Özdemir, O. (2024). Kahoot! Game-based digital learning platform: A comprehensive meta-analysis. *Journal of Computer Assisted Learning*, *41*(1), e13084. Advance online publication. DOI: 10.1111/jcal.13084

Paas, F., Tuovinen, J. E., Tabbers, H., & van Gerven, P. W. M. (2003). Cognitive load measurement as a means to advance cognitive load theory. *Educational Psychologist*, *38*(1), 63–71. DOI: 10.1207/S15326985EP3801_8

Palha, S., Bouwer, A., Webb, K., van Smaalen, D., & Agterberg, D. (2024). Game-based pedagogy in teacher training. *European Conference on Games Based Learning Proceedings, 18*(1), 677–684. https://doi.org/DOI: 10.34190/ecgbl.18.1.2698

Palmquist, A., Sigurdardottir, H. D. I., & Myhre, H. (2025). Exploring interfaces and implications for integrating social-emotional competencies into AI literacy for education: A narrative review. *Journal of Computers in Education*, •••, 1–37.

Panadero, E. (2017). A review of self-regulated learning: Six models and four directions for research. *Frontiers in Psychology*, *8*, 422. DOI: 10.3389/fpsyg.2017.00422 PMID: 28503157

Pangrazio, L., & Selwyn, N. (2019). "Personal data literacies": A critical literacies approach to enhancing understandings of personal digital data. *New Media & Society*, *21*(2), 419–437. DOI: 10.1177/1461444818799523

Papastergiou, M. (2019). Exploring the potential of computer and video games for health and physical education: A literature review. *Computers & Education*, *53*(3), 603–622. DOI: 10.1016/j.compedu.2009.04.001

Parasuraman, R., & Riley, V. (1997). Humans and automation: Use, misuse, disuse, abuse. *Human Factors*, *39*(2), 230–253. DOI: 10.1518/001872097778543886

Paris, D. (2012). Culturally sustaining pedagogy: A needed change in stance, terminology, and practice. *Educational Researcher*, *41*(3), 93–97. DOI: 10.3102/0013189X12441244

Park, S., & Kim, O. (2025). Scaffolding with Generative AI in Language Classrooms: A Critical Thinking Framework.   , (77), 349-372. https://doi.org/DOI: 10.17002/sil..77.202510.351

Patrício, R., Moreira, A. C., & Zurlo, F. (2018). Gamification approaches to the early stage of innovation. *Creativity and Innovation Management*, *27*(4), 499–511. Advance online publication. DOI: 10.1111/caim.12284

Pavloff-Pelkonen, E., Hakkarainen, K., & Korhonen, T. (2025). Educational design and implementation of game literacy in a multiliteracy learning environment. *Journal of Research on Technology in Education*, •••, 1–19. DOI: 10.1080/15391523.2025.2487284

Pedrera, O., Ortega-Lasuen, U., Ruiz-González, A., Díez, J. R., & Barrutia, O. (2023). Branches of plant blindness and their relationship with biodiversity conceptualisation among secondary students. *Journal of Biological Education, 57*(3), 566–591. Advance online publication. DOI: 10.1080/00219266.2021.1933133

Pelizzari, F., & Garzoni, A. (2024). Gamification in higher education: A systematic literature review. *Italian Journal of Educational Technology, 31*(3), 21–43. DOI: 10.17471/2499-4324/1335

Pempek, T. A., & Lauricella, A. R. (2017). The effects of parent-child interaction and media use on cognitive development in infants, toddlers, and preschoolers. In Blumberg, F. C., & Brooks, P. J. (Eds.), *Cognitive development in digital contexts* (pp. 53–74). Elsevier., DOI: 10.1016/B978-0-12-809481-5.00003-1

Pérez, J., Daradoumis, T., & Marquès Puig, J. M. (2020). Rediscovering the use of chatbots in education: A systematic literature review. *Computer Applications in Engineering Education, 28*(6), 1549–1565. DOI: 10.1002/cae.22326

Petrovic, J. E., & Olmstead, S. (2001). Language, power, and pedagogy: Bilingual children in the cross-fire. *Bilingual Research Journal, 25*(3), 405–412. DOI: 10.1080/15235882.2001.10162800

Pham Thi, T. D., & Duong, N. T. (2025). Designing memorable business simulations for learning engagement. *Education and Information Technologies, 30*(18), 1–36. DOI: 10.1007/s10639-025-13785-1

Philippakos, Z. A. T., Quinn, M., Voggt, A., & Park, Y. (2025). Active literacy learning through a flipped classroom model in teacher preparation programs. *Literacy Research and Instruction*, 1–20.

Piaget, J. (1952). The origins of intelligence in children. In *W W Norton & Co eBooks*. DOI: 10.1037/11494-000

Piaget, J. (1975). *Nachahmung, Spiel und Traum. Die Entwicklung der Symbolfunktion beim Kinde*. Klett-Cotta.

Pinargote Castro, M. A., Solórzano Ortega, C. V., Ruilova Alvarado, N. A., & Bulgarín Sánchez, R. M. (2023). Artificial intelligence in the context of teacher training. *Scientific research journal update of the world of science. RECIAMUC, 7*(4), 153–161. https://doi.org/. (4).Oct.2023.153-161DOI: 10.26820/reciamuc/7

Pinter, R., Bagosi, Z., Abari, K., & Katona, J. (2025). Traditional learning methods versus chatbots. In G. Rózsa, K. Abari, & J. Katona (Eds.), *New solutions based on generative artificial intelligence for human-computer interaction* (Lecture Notes in Networks and Systems, Vol. 1308, pp. 38–49). Springer. https://doi.org/DOI: 10.1007/978-3-031-85561-0_4

Pistono, C., Santos, P., Baptista, A., & São Mamede, H. (2024). Framework for adaptive serious games design. *Computer Applications in Engineering Education, 32*(4), e22731. DOI: 10.1002/cae.22731

Plass, J. L., Homer, B. D., & Kinzer, C. K. (2015). Foundations of game-based learning. *Educational Psychologist, 50*(4), 258–283. DOI: 10.1080/00461520.2015.1122533

Pohl, M., Rester, M., & Judmaier, P. (2009). Lecture Notes in Computer Science: Vol. 5616. *Interactive game based learning: Advantages and disadvantages.*, , PART 3.DOI: 10.1007/978-3-642-02713-0_10

Poole, F. J., & Clarke-Midura, J. (2020). A Systematic review of Digital games in second language learning studies. *International Journal of Game-Based Learning, 10*(3), 1–15. DOI: 10.4018/IJGBL.2020070101

Porat, E., Blau, I., & Barak, A. (2018). Measuring digital literacies: Junior high-school students' perceived competencies versus actual performance. *Computers & Education, 126*, 23–36. DOI: 10.1016/j.compedu.2018.06.030

Prasad, S. (2023). Measures of Central Tendencies. In *Elementary Statistical Methods* (pp. 37–96). Springer Nature Singapore., DOI: 10.1007/978-981-19-0596-4_2

Prensky, M. (2001). *Digital game-based learning*. McGraw-Hill.

Przybylski, A. K., Rigby, C. S., & Ryan, R. M. (2010). A motivational model of video game engagement. *Review of General Psychology, 14*(2), 154–166. DOI: 10.1037/a0019440

Pu, L., Liang, J., Wang, J., Zhang, N., & Zhong, W. (2024). Impact of AI-Based Learning, Digital Literacy, Information Stewardship on Learning Outcomes. *El Profesional de la Información, 33*(5). Advance online publication. DOI: 10.3145/epi.2024.ene.0515

Putri, A. A., & Sekti, B. A. (2026). Human–AI Collaboration in Creativity, Design, and Innovation. In *Redefining Global Creative Sectors Through AI and Human Augmentation* (pp. 273–303). DOI: 10.4018/979-8-3373-7153-5.ch009

Qian, M., & Clark, D. B. (2016). Game-based learning and 21st-century skills. *Computers in Human Behavior, 63*, 50–58. DOI: 10.1016/j.chb.2016.05.023

Qi, Z., & Zhonggen, Y. (2022). Meta-analysis on investigating and comparing the effects on learning achievement and motivation for gamification and game-based learning. *Education Research International, 1519880*, 1–19. Advance online publication. DOI: 10.1155/2022/1519880

Quinn, S., Donnelly, S., & Kidd, E. (2018). The relationship between symbolic play and language acquisition: A meta-analytic review. *Developmental Review, 49*, 121–135. DOI: 10.1016/j.dr.2018.05.005

Quizlet. (n.d.). *Quizlet.* https://https://quizlet.com/

Qurbunova, B., & Yusupova, A. (2024). The Deep investigation of the part of AI integ in the field of Education: A Technical review. In *4th International Conference on Advance Computing and Innovative Technologies in Engineering (ICACITE), Greater Noida, India.* IEEE. https://doi.org/DOI: 10.1109/ICACITE60783.2024.10617224

Rafiddin o'g'li, N. D. (2026). Enhancing the effectiveness of professional training in tourism education through virtual guide simulation systems. *Stanford Database Library of International Journal of Pedagogics, 6*(01), 194–198.

Rahayu, W. A., & Subekti, P. (2025). Implementation of" E-Lens" inquiry-based learning game to improve literacy and numeracy skills. *Jurnal Cakrawala Pendidikan, 44*(3), 510–522. DOI: 10.21831/cp.v44i3.76930

Rajendran, M., Srinivasan, V., Ilangovan, A., Singh, A. B., & Bakhromdjanovna, M. Z. (2025). Exploring anxiety among english learners: A comprehensive literature review. *Multidisciplinary Reviews*, *8*(9), 2025270. DOI: 10.31893/multirev.2025270

Ramanathan, & Tara. (2026, February 12). *Duolingo | App, Languages, Background, & Virality*. Encyclopedia Britannica. https://www.britannica.com/topic/Duolingo

Ranalli, J. (2021). L2 student engagement with automated feedback on writing: Potential for learning and issues of trust. *Journal of Second Language Writing*, *52*, 100816. DOI: 10.1016/j.jslw.2021.100816

RAND Reading Study Group. (2002). *Reading for understanding: Toward an R&D program in reading comprehension*. RAND Corporation. https://www.rand.org/pubs/monograph_reports/MR1465.html

Randel, J. M., Morris, B. A., Wetzel, C. D., & Whitehill, B. V. (1992). The Effectiveness of Games for Educational Purposes: A Review of Recent Research. *Simulation & Gaming*, *23*(3), 261–276. DOI: 10.1177/1046878192233001

Rao, K., Ok, M. W., & Bryant, B. R. (2014). A review of research on Universal Design Educational Models. *Remedial and Special Education*, *35*(3), 153–166. DOI: 10.1177/0741932513518980

Rasinski, T. V. (2010). *The fluent reader: Oral and silent reading strategies for building fluency, word recognition and comprehension* (2nd ed.). Scholastic.

Rassal, C., & Moreira, L. (2022). O ensino do empreendedorismo com recurso à gamificação num curso superior de gestão hoteleira: O caso da Geração Z. In *Atas do 7.º Congresso Nacional de Práticas Pedagógicas no Ensino Superior* (pp. 315–324). UA Editora.

Recchia, S. L., Shin, M., & Snaider, C. (2018). Where is the love? Developing loving relationships as an essential component of professional infant care. *International Journal of Early Years Education*, *26*(2), 142–158. DOI: 10.1080/09669760.2018.1461614

Reeve, J. (2012). A self-determination theory perspective on student engagement. In Christenson, S. (Eds.), *Handbook of research on student engagement* (pp. 149–172). Springer. DOI: 10.1007/978-1-4614-2018-7_7

Resch, K., & Schrittesser, I. (2023). Using the service-learning approach to bridge the gap between theory and practice in teacher education. *International Journal of Inclusive Education*, *27*(10), 1118–1132. DOI: 10.1080/13603116.2021.1882053

Researcher Notes. (2025). *Notes taken by the researchers while creating scenarios for the Longview Project* [Unpublished research notes].

Rianti, S. S., Chamalah, E., Kusumadewi, R. F., & Passat, S. A. (2025). Implementation of AI-Based Educational Games to Improve Early Reading Skills of Elementary School Students. *EduBase: Journal of Basic Education*, *6*(1), 146–156. DOI: 10.47453/edubase.v6i1.3227

Ribeiro, Á., Aramburuzabala, P., & Paz, B. (2021). Reflections on the learning service of European higher education. *RIDAS. Ibero-American Journal of Service-Learning*, *12*(12), 3–12. Advance online publication. DOI: 10.1344/RIDAS2021.12.2

Ribot, K. M., Hoff, E., & Burridge, A. (2018). Language use contributes to expressive language growth: Evidence from bilingual children. *Child Development, 89*(3), 929–940. DOI: 10.1111/cdev.12770 PMID: 28245341

Richardson, V. (1997). *Constructivist teacher education: Building a world of new understandings*. Falmer Press.

Risko, E. F., & Gilbert, S. J. (2016). Cognitive offloading. *Trends in Cognitive Sciences, 20*(9), 676–688. DOI: 10.1016/j.tics.2016.07.002 PMID: 27542527

Rizkallah, E. G., & Seitz, V. (2017). Understanding student motivation: A key to retention in higher education. *Scientific Annals of Economics and Business, 64*(1), 45–57. Advance online publication. DOI: 10.1515/saeb-2017-0004

Rocca, S. (2024). Unpacking digital literacies and multiliteracies. In *DIGICOMPASS: Navigating digital multiliteracies in global language education* (pp. 73–95). Springer Nature. DOI: 10.1007/978-3-031-81318-4_4

Rodríguez-Calzada, L., Paredes-Velasco, M., & Urquiza-Fuentes, J. (2024). The educational impact of a comprehensive serious game within the university setting: Improving learning and fostering motivation. *Heliyon, 10*(16), e35608. DOI: 10.1016/j.heliyon.2024.e35608 PMID: 39220894

Rodríguez-Ferrer, J. M., Manzano-León, A., & Aguilar-Parra, J. M. (2023b). Game-based learning and service-learning to teach inclusive education in higher education. *International Journal of Environmental Research and Public Health, 20*(4), 3285. [REMOVED HYPERLINK FIELD] DOI: 10.3390/ijerph20043285

Rodríguez-Ferrer, J. M., Manzano-León, A., Fernández-Jiménez, C., Luque de la Rosa, A., Fernández-Campoy, J. M., & Aguilar-Parra, J. M. (2023a). Shall we play together? Game-based learning for engagement and classroom climate in Spanish socially deprived communities. *Frontiers in Psychology, 14*, 1163441. DOI: 10.3389/fpsyg.2023.1163441 PMID: 37333587

Rodríguez-Ferrer, J. M., Rodríguez Rivera, P., & Manzano León, A. (2025). Effects of the combination of service-learning and play-based learning on the cooperative competences of university students. *Interuniversity Electronic Journal of Teacher Training, 29*(1), 155–168. DOI: 10.6018/reifop.672301

Rogerson, M. J., Gibbs, M., & Smith, W. (2016). Digitising boardgames: Issues and tensions. *Proceedings of the 2016 Annual Symposium on Computer-Human Interaction in Play*, 400–406. DOI: 10.1145/2967934.2968110

Romero, M. (2025). From Consumption to Co-Creation: A Systematic Review of Six Levels of AI-Enhanced Creative Engagement in Education. *Multimodal Technologies and Interaction, 9*(10), 110. DOI: 10.3390/mti9100110

Rondon, S., Sassi, F. C., & De Andrade, C. R. F. (2013). Computer game-based and traditional learning method: A comparison regarding students' knowledge retention. *BMC Medical Education, 13*(1), 30. DOI: 10.1186/1472-6920-13-30 PMID: 23442203

Rose, D. H., & Meyer, A. (2002). *Teaching every student in the digital age: Universal design for learning*. ASCD.

Rosenthal, J., & Ratan, R. (2022). Balancing learning and enjoyment in serious games: A Kerbal Space Program case study examining the communication mediation model. *Computers & Education, 182*, 104480. DOI: 10.1016/j.compedu.2022.104480

Roskos, K. A., Tremblay, R. E., Boivin, M., Peters, R., & Smith, P. K. (2023). Play's potential in early literacy development. In *Encyclopedia on early childhood development*. https://www.child-encyclopedia.com/play/according-experts/plays-potential-early-literacy-development

Rüth, M. (2022). *Learning and teaching with video games: Toward theoretical progress and educational practice* [Doctoral thesis, Universität zu Köln]. KUPS – Köln University Publication Services. https://kups.ub.uni-koeln.de/52965/

Ryan, R. M., & Deci, E. L. (2000). Intrinsic and Extrinsic Motivations: Classic definitions and new directions. *Contemporary Educational Psychology, 25*(1), 54–67. DOI: 10.1006/ceps.1999.1020 PMID: 10620381

Ryan, R. M., & Deci, E. L. (2000). Self-determination theory and the facilitation of intrinsic motivation, social development, and well-being. *The American Psychologist, 55*(1), 68–78. DOI: 10.1037/0003-066X.55.1.68 PMID: 11392867

Rye, S., Sousa, M., & Sousa, C. (2025). Introduction to game-based learning. In *Transformative learning through play: analogue games as vehicles for educational innovation* (pp. 29–68). Springer Nature Switzerland. DOI: 10.1007/978-3-031-78523-8_2

Sabatini, J., Graesser, A. C., Hollander, J., & O'Reilly, T. (2023). A framework of literacy development and how AI can transform theory and practice. *British Journal of Educational Technology, 54*(5), 1174–1203. DOI: 10.1111/bjet.13342

Sablić, M., Mirosavljević, A., & Bogatić, K. (2025). Multigrade education and the Montessori model: A pathway towards inclusion and equity. *International Journal of Educational Research, 131*, 102600. DOI: 10.1016/j.ijer.2025.102600

Sadegh-Zadeh, S. A., Movahhedi, T., & Bahonar, F. (2026). Emotion AI in the classroom: Ethics of monitoring student affect through facial and vocal analytics. *AI and Ethics, 6*(1), 37. DOI: 10.1007/s43681-025-00897-0

Sailer, M., Hense, J. U., Mayr, S. K., & Mandl, H. (2017). How gamification motivates: An experimental study of the effects of specific game design elements on psychological need satisfaction. *Computers in Human Behavior, 69*, 371–380. DOI: 10.1016/j.chb.2016.12.033

Sailer, M., & Homner, L. (2020). The gamification of learning: A meta-analysis. *Educational Psychology Review, 32*(1), 77–112. DOI: 10.1007/s10648-019-09498-w

Sáiz-Manzanares, M. C., Rodríguez Arribas, S., Pardo Aguilar, C., & Queiruga-Dios, M. Á. (2020). Effectiveness of self-regulation and serious games for learning STEM knowledge in primary education. *Psicothema, 32*(4), 516–524. DOI: 10.7334/psicothema2020.30 PMID: 33073757

Sajja, R., Sermet, Y., Cikmaz, M., Cwiertny, D., & Demir, I. (2023, September 19). *Artificial Intelligence-Enabled Intelligent Assistant for Personalized and Adaptive Learning in Higher Education*. arXiv.org. https://arxiv.org/abs/2309.10892

Salley, B., Daniels, D., Walker, C., & Fleming, K. (2022). Shared book reading intervention for parents of infants and toddlers. *Journal of Early Childhood Research*, *20*(3), 322–340. DOI: 10.1177/1476718X221091462 PMID: 36092249

Salvador-García, C., Chiva-Bartoll, O., Maravé-Vivas, M., & Gil-Gómez, J. (2023). Service-learning in physical education teacher education: A retrospective exploratory study to examine its challenges. *Teaching and Teacher Education*, *135*, 104350. DOI: 10.1016/j.tate.2023.104350

Sancar-Tokmak, H., & Dagli, Z. (2025). A systematic review of theoretical foundations and learning effects in gamified flipped classroom research. *Evaluation Review*, 0193841X251320438.

Sánchez-Caballé, A., & Santos, C. C. (2025). Perspectives of higher education in Spanish and Portuguese institutions on artificial intelligence: A content analysis. *Edutec. Revista Electrónica de Tecnología Educativa*, (92), 253–269. DOI: 10.21556/edutec.2025.92.3879

Sánchez-López, I. (2025). AI storytelling and narrative evolution in creative industries: A systematic review. *Research Square*. DOI: 10.21203/rs.3.rs-7318246/v1

Sánchez-Ruiz, L. M., López-Alfonso, S., Moll-López, S., Moraño-Fernández, J. A., & Vega-Fleitas, E. (2022). Educational digital escape rooms footprint on students' feelings: A case study within aerospace engineering. *Information (Basel)*, *13*(10), 478. DOI: 10.3390/info13100478

Sandbrook, C., Adams, W. M., & Monteferri, B. (2015). Digital games and biodiversity conservation. *Conservation Letters*, *8*(2), 118–124. DOI: 10.1111/conl.12113

Santos Almeida, I., Pinto, C., Lima, A., Moreira, T., & Fernandes, C. S. (2024). Game4NurseSupervisor: Development of a board game for nursing mentoring. *Nurse Education in Practice*, *76*, 103939. Advance online publication. DOI: 10.1016/j.nepr.2024.103939

Santos Rego, M. Á., Lorenzo Moledo, M., & Sáez Gambín, D. (2024). *University & Service-Learning: It's Quality that matters*. Narcea.

Saracho, O. N. (2017). Literacy in the twenty-first century: Children, families and policy. *Early Child Development and Care*, *187*(3–4), 630–643. DOI: 10.1080/03004430.2016.1261513

Sari, H. E., Tumanggor, B., & Efron, D. (2024). Improving Educational Outcomes Through Adaptive Learning Systems using AI. [ITALIC]. *International Transactions on Artificial Intelligence*, *3*(1), 21–31. DOI: 10.33050/italic.v3i1.647

Sari, H. P., Primasari, Y., Supriyono, S., & Herminingsih, D. I. (2026). Gleaming English game for youth, an android-based game for English literacy improvement: Research and development. [EduLearn]. *Journal of Education and Learning*, *20*(1), 485–496. DOI: 10.11591/edulearn.v20i1.23119

Sayangan, Y. V. (2024). Digital Picture Card Media Based on Mother Tongue Assisted with Artificial Intelligence in Literacy Learning for Early Grades. *International Journal of Elementary Education*, *8*(3), 461–471. Advance online publication. DOI: 10.23887/ijee.v8i3.84158

Schabas, A. (2023). Game-based science learning: What are the problems with teachers practicing it in class? *Assyfa Learning Journal, 1*(2), 89–103. DOI: 10.61650/alj.v1i2.128

Scherzinger, L., & Brahm, T. (2023). A systematic review of bilingual education teachers' competences. *Educational Research Review, 39*, 100531. DOI: 10.1016/j.edurev.2023.100531

Schlüter, A., Waldkirch, M., Burmeister-Lamp, K., & Auernhammer, J. (2021). No second chance for a first impression: The role of aesthetics in early access video games. *International Journal of Innovation Management, 25*(10), 2140002. DOI: 10.1142/S1363919621400028

Schultes, M.-T., Graf, D., Holzer, J., Schober, B., & Spiel, C. (2025). Implementation and evaluation of service-learning at higher education institutions. *Evaluation and Program Planning, 112*, 102622. DOI: 10.1016/j.evalprogplan.2025.102622 PMID: 40543380

Screpnik, C., Negre-Bennasar, F., & Salinas, J. (2024). Inclusive education with serious games and user centered design, exploring the intersection of accessibility and usability. *RELATEC. Latin American Journal of Educational Technology, 23*(2), 27–50. DOI: 10.17398/1695-288X.23.2.27

Scruggs, T. E., Mastropieri, M. A., & McDuffie, K. A. (2007). Co-teaching in inclusive classrooms: A metasynthesis of qualitative research. *Exceptional Children, 73*(4), 392–416. DOI: 10.1177/001440290707300401

Seddighi-Khavidak, S., Sanchez, B. N., Chan, S. S. K., & Le-Chan, G. (2026). Game-based learning enhances engagement and comprehension in undergraduate architecture and biology education. *Education Sciences, 16*(1), 9. Advance online publication. DOI: 10.3390/educsci16010009

Seddon, N., Daniels, E., Davis, R., Chausson, A., Harris, R., Hou-Jones, X., Huq, S., Kapos, V., Mace, G. M., Rizvi, A. R., Reid, H., Roe, D., Turner, B., & Wicander, S. (2020). Global recognition of the importance of nature-based solutions to the impacts of climate change. *Global Sustainability, 3*, e15. Advance online publication. DOI: 10.1017/sus.2020.8

Şeker, F. (2026). Simulation modeling. In M. Uysal, O. Icoz, I. çetin, O. Icoz & Y.Bozkurt (Eds.), *Theories and models in tourism and hospitality research* (p. 384-389).Cabi.

Sekti, B. A. (2025a). AI Technology Management Concepts and Strategies. In *AI Technology Management and Value Creation* (pp. 1–32). DOI: 10.4018/979-8-3373-2497-5.ch001

Sekti, B. A. (2025b). Foundations of Artificial Intelligence Ethics. In *Navigating Social Trust in the AI Era* (pp. 23–47). DOI: 10.4018/979-8-3373-7011-8.ch002

Sekti, B. A. (2026). Data Privacy and Cybersecurity in Wind Power Systems. In *AI-Powered Analysis* (pp. 335–366). Modeling, and Monitoring of Wind Energy Systems., DOI: 10.4018/979-8-3373-4159-0.ch009

Selwyn, N. (2022). *Should robots replace teachers? AI and the future of education*. Polity Press.

Setiawan, M. R., & Wiedarti, P. (2020). The effectiveness of Quizlet application towards students' motivation in learning vocabulary. *Studies in English Language and Education, 7*(1), 83–95. DOI: 10.24815/siele.v7i1.15359

Sezer, G. O. (2015). Decreasing Undesired Attitudes of Students in Classroom: Use of Awards. In I. Koleva, R. Efe, E. Atasoy, & Z. B. Kostova (Eds.), Education in the 21st Century: Theory and Practice (pp. 751–758). ST. KLIMENT OHRIDSKI UNIVERSITY PRESS.

Shaffer, D. W. (2006). Epistemic frames for epistemic games. *Journal of Online Learning and Teaching*, *2*(2), 1–6.

Shaffer, D. W. (2006). *How computer games help children learn*. Palgrave Macmillan. DOI: 10.1057/9780230601994

Shanahan, T., & Shanahan, C. (2014). Disciplinary literacy strategies. *Journal of Adolescent & Adult Literacy*, *57*(9), 628–631. DOI: 10.1002/jaal.297

Shen, Y., & Ab Jalil, H. (2025). Exploring lifelong literacy learning in digital gameplay among midlife-to-older adults. *Educational Gerontology*, •••, 1–19. DOI: 10.1080/03601277.2025.2495275

Shin, E., & Rowe, J. (2026). Game-based learning for sustainable development: Impacts on students' perceptions by prior knowledge level. *Simulation & Gaming*, *57*(1), 138–162. DOI: 10.1177/10468781251374320

Shin, M. (2021). Exploring multisensory experiences in infants' learning and development in the child care classrooms. *Early Child Development and Care*, *191*(13), 2116–2127. DOI: 10.1080/03004430.2019.1695127

Shirkhani, F., Nesari, A. J., & Feilinezhad, N. (2015). Bakhtinian dialogic concept in language learning process. *Procedia: Social and Behavioral Sciences*, *205*, 510–515. DOI: 10.1016/j.sbspro.2015.09.060

Shliakhovchuk, E. (2021). After cultural literacy: New models of intercultural competency for life and work in a VUCA world. *Educational Review*, *73*(2), 229–250. DOI: 10.1080/00131911.2019.1566211

Shohel, M. M. C., Ashrafuzzaman, M., Naomee, I., Tanni, S. A., & Azim, F. (2022). Game-based teaching and learning in higher education: Challenges and prospects. In *Handbook of research on acquiring 21st century literacy skills through game-based learning* (pp. 78–106).

Shohel, M. M. C., Weller, S., & Brooks, R. (2025). Academics' learning attitudes and readiness for generative AI in higher education: The role of responsible decision-making. *Cogent Education*, *12*(1), 2514933. DOI: 10.1080/2331186X.2025.2514933

Shortridge, H. (2022). Tiny hands, big impact: Play's role in early literacy. *Children & Libraries*, *20*(2), 12–17. DOI: 10.5860/cal.20.2.12

Shute, V. J. (2008). Focus on formative feedback. *Review of Educational Research*, *78*(1), 153–189. DOI: 10.3102/0034654307313795

Silk, H., Douglass, A. B., & Douglass, J. M. (2017). Oral health during pregnancy. *Journal of Dental Research*, *96*(8), 823–830. DOI: 10.1177/0022034517708424

Singh, A. (2026). Cultivating excellence: Learning and development programs in hospitality. In *Talent management in hotels and hospitality* (pp. 401–426). IGI Global Scientific Publishing.

Singun, A. J. (2025). Unveiling the barriers to digital transformation in higher education institutions: A systematic literature review. *Discover Education, 4*(37), 37. Advance online publication. DOI: 10.1007/s44217-025-00430-9

Si, Q., Hodges, T. S., & Coleman, J. M. (2022). Multimodal literacies classroom instruction for K-12 students: A review of research. *Literacy Research and Instruction, 61*(3), 276–297. DOI: 10.1080/19388071.2021.2008555

Slater-Robins, M. (2025, February 11). *What is Grammarly? Everything we know about the best AI writing assistant.* TechRadar. https://www.techradar.com/pro/what-is-grammarly-everything-we-know-about-the-best-ai-writing-assistant

Sleeter, C. E. (2008). Preparing White teachers for diverse students. In Cochran-Smith, M., Feiman-Nemser, S., & McIntyre, D. J. (Eds.), *Handbook of research on teacher education* (3rd ed., pp. 559–582). Routledge. DOI: 10.4324/9780203938690-69

Slimi, Z., Benayoune, A., & Alemu, A. E. (2025). Students' perceptions of artificial intelligence integration in higher education. *European Journal of Educational Research, 14*(2), 471–484. DOI: 10.12973/eu-jer.14.2.471

Slot, P. L., Bleses, D., & Jensen, P. (2020). Infants' and toddlers' language, math and socio-emotional development: Evidence for reciprocal relations and differential gender and age effects. *Frontiers in Psychology, 11*, 580297. Advance online publication. DOI: 10.3389/fpsyg.2020.580297 PMID: 33329234

Snowe, A., & Snowe, A. (2017). *Exploring the use of NoRedInk as a tool for composition instruction.* DOI: 10.23860/diss-snowe-alyson-2017

Song, Y., Weisberg, L. R., Zhang, S., Tian, X., Boyer, K. E., & Israel, M. (2024). A framework for inclusive AI learning design for diverse learners. *Computers and Education: Artificial Intelligence, 6*, 100212. https://doi.org/https://doi.org/10.1016/j.caeai.2024.100212

Song, Y., Weisberg, L. R., Zhang, S., Tian, X., Boyer, K. E., & Israel, M. (2024). A framework for inclusive AI learning design for diverse learners. *Computers and Education: Artificial Intelligence, 6*, 100212. DOI: 10.1016/j.caeai.2024.100212

Sørensen, K., Van den Broucke, S., Fullam, J., Doyle, G., Pelikan, J., Slonska, Z., & Brand, H. (2012). Health literacy and chronic disease outcomes. *BMC Public Health, 12*(1), 80. DOI: 10.1186/1471-2458-12-80

Sousa, A. E., & Cardoso, P. (2025). Use of generative AI by higher education students: Perspectives on perceived benefits and challenges. *Electronics (Basel), 14*(7), 1258. DOI: 10.3390/electronics14071258

Sperling, K., Stenberg, C.-J., McGrath, C., Åkerfeldt, A., Heintz, F., & Stenliden, L. (2024). In search of artificial intelligence (AI) literacy in teacher education: A scoping review. *Computers and Education Open, 6*, 100169. DOI: 10.1016/j.caeo.2024.100169

Sperling, K., Stenliden, L., Mannila, L., Hallström, J., Nordlöf, C., & Heintz, F. (2025). Perspectives on AI literacy in Middle School Classrooms: An Integrative Review. *Postdigital Science and Education, 7*(3), 1–31. DOI: 10.1007/s42438-025-00560-1

Squire, K., & Jenkins, H. (2003). Harnessing the power of games in education. *Insight*, *3*, •••. https://plato.acadiau.ca/courses/engl/saklofske/download/digital%20gaming%20education.pdf

Stagg, B. C., & Dillon, J. (2022). Plant awareness is linked to plant relevance: A review of educational and ethnobiological literature (1998–2020). *Plants, People, Planet*, *4*(6), 579–592. Advance online publication. DOI: 10.1002/ppp3.10323

Stairs-Davenport, A., & Skotarczak, B. (2018). Improving comprehensible input for ELLs through technology. *TESL-EJ*, *22*(3), 1-12. https://www.tesl-ej.org/pdf/ej87/int.pdf

Stasolla, F., Zullo, A., Maniglio, R., Passaro, A., Di Gioia, M., Curcio, E., & Martini, E. (2025). Deep Learning and Reinforcement Learning for Assessing and Enhancing Academic Performance in university Students: A scoping review. *AI*, *6*(2), 40. DOI: 10.3390/ai6020040

Steinkuehler, C. (2018). Video games and digital literacies. *Journal of Adolescent & Adult Literacy*, *62*(1), 83–87. DOI: 10.1598/JAAL.54.1.7

Steiss, J., Tate, T., Graham, S., Cruz, J., Hebert, M., Wang, J., Moon, Y., Tseng, W., Warschauer, M., & Olson, C. B. (2024). Comparing the quality of human and ChatGPT feedback of students' writing. *Learning and Instruction*, *91*, 101894. DOI: 10.1016/j.learninstruc.2024.101894

Stojanov, A., Liu, Q., & Koh, J. H. L. (2024). University students' self-reported reliance on ChatGPT for learning: A latent profile analysis. *Computers and Education: Artificial Intelligence*, *6*, 100243. DOI: 10.1016/j.caeai.2024.100243

Storch, S. A., & Whitehurst, G. J. (2001). The role of family and home in the literacy development of children from low-income backgrounds. *New Directions for Child and Adolescent Development*, *2001*(92), 53–72. DOI: 10.1002/cd.15 PMID: 11468866

Street, B. V. (1995). *Social literacies: Critical approaches to literacy in development, ethnography and education*. Longman.

Subrata, H., Judijanto, L., Aeni, C., Ali, A., & Amir, A. S. (2025). Implementation of Multimedia-assisted Collaborative Game-Based Learning to Improve Competitive Spirit and Problem Solving Ability in Literacy Learning for Elementary Students. *Jurnal Pendidikan Progresif*, *15*(2), 1415–1430. DOI: 10.23960/jpp.v15i2.pp1415-1430

Suhendra, K. K. A. (2023). The Effect of Fly Swatter Game Toward Students' Vocabulary Mastery. [TATEFL]. *The Art of Teaching English as a Foreign Language*, *4*(2), 37–44. DOI: 10.36663/tatefl.v4i2.613

Su, Y. D., Mo, Y. H., Dong, X., & Wang, X. (2022). A review of the health education board game in nursing. *Chinese Journal of Nursing Education*, *19*(6). Advance online publication. DOI: 10.3761/j.issn.1672-9234.2022.06.018

Swain, M. (1995). Three functions of output in second language learning. In Cook, G., & Seidlhofer, B. (Eds.), *Principle and practice in applied linguistics* (pp. 125–144). Oxford University Press.

Swargiary, K. (2024). *Modern perspectives on Montessori philosophy: Adaptations and applications in the 2020s*. ERA.

Sweller, J. (1988). Cognitive load during problem solving: Effects on learning. *Cognitive Science*, *12*(2), 257–285. DOI: 10.1207/s15516709cog1202_4

Sweller, J., van Merriënboer, J. J. G., & Paas, F. (1998). Cognitive architecture and instructional design. *Educational Psychology Review*, *10*(3), 251–296. DOI: 10.1023/A:1022193728205

Szilágyi, S., Palencsár, E., Kőrei, A., & Török, Z. (2025). Examining the effectiveness of non-digital game-based learning among university computer science students on the topic of improper integrals. *Education Sciences*, *15*(2), 132. DOI: 10.3390/educsci15020132

T, S. T., & B, I. A. S. (2024). Artificial intelligence effects on student learning outcomes in higher education. In *Ninth International Conference on Science Technology Engineering and Mathematics (ICONSTEM), Chennai, India*. DOI: 10.1109/ICONSTEM60960.2024.10568868

Tagare, D., Karki, T., & Yu, W. (2025). K-12 teachers' ethical competencies for AI literacy: Insights from a systematic literature review. *Computers & Education*, *239*, 105435. DOI: 10.1016/j.compedu.2025.105435

Tahir, R., & Wang, A. I. (2024). Evaluating the effectiveness of game-based learning for teaching refugee children Arabic using the integrated LEAGUÊ-GQM approach. *Behaviour & Information Technology*, *43*(1), 110–138. DOI: 10.1080/0144929X.2022.2156386

Talandron-Felipe, M. M. P. (2021). Considerations Towards Culturally-Adaptive Instructional Systems. In Sottilare, R. A., & Schwarz, J. (Eds.), Lecture Notes in Computer Science: Vol. 12792. *Adaptive Instructional Systems. Design and Evaluation. HCII 2021*. Springer., DOI: 10.1007/978-3-030-77857-6_43

Tang, J. T., Chu, S. T., & Chang, T. F. (2025). Enhancing English alphabet handwriting skills in preschool children through digital game-based learning approach. *Innovation in Language Learning and Teaching*, *19*(4), 297–315. DOI: 10.1080/17501229.2024.2352791

Tang, K. S. (2023). The characteristics of diagrams in scientific explanations: Multimodal integration of written and visual modes of representation in junior high school textbooks. *Science Education*, *107*(3), 741–772. DOI: 10.1002/sce.21787

Taspinar, B., Schmidt, W., & Schuhbauer, H. (2016). Gamification in education: A board game approach to knowledge acquisition. *Procedia Computer Science*, *99*, 101–116. Advance online publication. DOI: 10.1016/j.procs.2016.09.104

Tavares, N. (2022). The use and impact of game-based learning on the learning experience and knowledge retention of nursing undergraduate students: A systematic literature review. *Nurse Education Today*, *117*, 105484. DOI: 10.1016/j.nedt.2022.105484 PMID: 35917707

Teale, W. H., & Sulzby, E. (1986). *Emergent literacy: Writing and reading*. Praeger.

Teke, N., & Baş, T. (2025). Early Literacy Skills in Digital Games. *European Journal of Education*, *60*(3), e70173. DOI: 10.1111/ejed.70173

Telaumbanua, D. (2025). The role of artificial intelligence in improving the quality of biology learning. *Cognizance Journal of Multidisciplinary Studies*, *5*(1), 78–84. DOI: 10.47760/cognizance.2025.v05i01.007

Texas Education Agency. (2017). *Texas Essential Knowledge and Skills for English Language Arts and Reading, High School (19 TAC §110.36).* https://texas-sos.appianportalsgov.com/rules-and-meetings?$locale=en_US&interface=VIEW_TAC_SUMMARY&queryAsDate=11%2F17%2F2025&recordId=196164

Texas Education Agency. (2022). *Texas Teacher Evaluation and Support System (T-TESS) rubric.* https://teachfortexas.org/resource_files/Guides/T-TESS_Rubric.pdf

Thousand, J. S., Nevin, A. I., McNeil, M., & Liston, A. (2006). Differentiating instruction in inclusion in inclusive classrooms: Myth or reality? https://files.eric.ed.gov/fulltext/ED493953.pdf

Tian, F., & Naufal Umar, I. (2025). Research trends of digital game-based learning for technical vocabulary acquisition: A systematic decennial literature review (2014–2024). *Arab World English Journal, 16.*

Tinterri, A., Pelizzari, F., Di Padova, M., Palladino, F., Vignoli, G., & Dipace, A. (2024). Automating board-game based learning: A comprehensive study to assess reliability and accuracy of AI in game evaluation. *Intelligenza Artificiale, 18*(1), 103–119. DOI: 10.3233/IA-240030

Tinterri, A., Pelizzari, F., Vignoli, G., Palladino, F., & Di Padova, M. (2024). Towards AI-assisted board game-based learning: Assessing LLMs in game personalisation. *Proceedings of the 18th European Conference on Games Based Learning*. DOI: 10.34190/ecgbl.18.1.3055

Tiwari, S. (2025). Designing ethical AI characters for children's early learning experiences. *AI. Brain and Child, 1*(1), 1–17. DOI: 10.1007/s44436-025-00015-1

Tlili, A., Adarkwah, M. A., Lo, C. K., Bozkurt, A., Burgos, D., Bonk, C. J., Costello, E., Mishra, S., Stracke, C. M., & Huang, R. (2024). Taming the monster: How can open education promote the effective and safe use of generative AI in education? *Journal of Learning for Development, 11*(3), 398–413. DOI: 10.56059/jl4d.v11i3.1657

Tomlinson, C. A. (2017). *How to differentiate instruction in academically diverse classrooms* (3rd ed.). ASCD.

Topping, K. J. (2005). Trends in peer learning. *Educational Psychology, 25*(6), 631–645. DOI: 10.1080/01443410500345172

Torr, J. (2019). Infants' experiences of shared reading with their educators in early childhood education and care centres: An observational study. *Early Childhood Education Journal, 47*(5), 519–529. DOI: 10.1007/s10643-019-00948-2

Trajkovski, G., & Hayes, H. (2025). AI-assisted formative assessment and feedback. In *AI-assisted assessment in education: Transforming assessment and measuring learning* (pp. 283–312). Springer Nature Switzerland. DOI: 10.1007/978-3-031-88252-4_7

Treher, E. N. (2011). *Learning with Board Games*. Learning With Board Game.

Tripp, J. N., & Waight, N. (2024). Co-creating a community of belonging and presence: Multilingual learners' experiences of science and language learning at an urban, inclusive STEM-focused high school. *Science Education, 108*(1), 25–62. DOI: 10.1002/sce.21827

Trust, T. (2012). Professional Learning Networks Designed for Teacher Learning. *Journal of Digital Learning in Teacher Education, 28*(4), 133–138. DOI: 10.1080/21532974.2012.10784693

Tsai, S.-K., Chuang, T.-Y., & Lin, Z.-J. (2025). Enhancing environmental literacy through digital game-based learning: A technology-integrated attitude change approach. *Sustainability (Basel), 17*(16), 7416. DOI: 10.3390/su17167416

Tseng, Y. J., Yadav, G., Hou, X., Wu, M., Chou, Y. S., Chen, C. C., . . . Koedinger, K. R. (2024, September). Activeai: The effectiveness of an interactive tutoring system in developing k-12 ai literacy. In *European Conference on Technology Enhanced Learning* (pp. 452-467). Cham: Springer Nature Switzerland. https://doi.org/DOI: 10.1007/978-3-031-72315-5_31

Tsirantonaki, S., & Vlachou, A. (2025). AI-driven inclusive practices: Innovative approaches to differentiated teaching and educational inclusion. *European Journal of Inclusive Education, 4*(1), 134–146. DOI: 10.7146/ejie.v4i1.156613

U.S. Department of Education, Office of Educational Technology. (2023). *Artificial Intelligence and Future of Teaching and Learning: Insights and Recommendations.* Washington, DC. https://www.ed.gov/sites/ed/files/documents/ai-report/ai-report.pdf

U.S. Department of Education, Office of Educational Technology. (2023). Artificial intelligence and the future of teaching and learning: Insights and recommendations. https://www.ed.gov/ai-report/ai-report.pdf

UNESCO. (2017). Literacy rates continue to rise from one generation to the next global literacy trends today. Retrieved from https://on.unesco.org/literacy-map

UNESCO. (2023). *Guidance for generative AI in education and research.* UNESCO. https://unesdoc.unesco.org/ark:/48223/pf0000386693

UNESCO. (2023). *Guidance for generative AI in education and research.* UNESCO. https://www.unesco.org/en/articles/guidance-generative-ai-education-and-research

United Nations Department of Economic and Social Affairs. (2024). *The sustainable development goals report 2024.* United Nations. https://unstats.un.org/sdgs/report/2024/

United Nations Educational, Scientific and Cultural Organization. (2006). *UNESCO guidelines on intercultural education.* UNESCO.

United States Department of Education. (2023). *Artificial intelligence and the future of teaching and learning: Insights and recommendations.* https://www.ed.gov/sites/ed/files/documents/ai-report/ai-report.pdf

United States Department of Education. (2025). *Individuals with disabilities education act (IDEA).* U.S. Department of Education. https://www.ed.gov/laws-and-policy/individuals-disabilities/idea

Uribe, R. V., Utrilla Cobos, S. A., & Santamaría Ortega, A. (2017). Aprendizaje basado en juegos. Una alternativa viable para la enseñanza significativa de la sustentabilidad. *Revista Electrónica Sobre Educación Media y Superior, 4*(7), 16.

Usher, M., & Barak, M. (2024). Unpacking the role of AI ethics online education for science and engineering students. *International Journal of STEM Education, 11*(1), 35. DOI: 10.1186/s40594-024-00493-4

Uzum, B., Yazan, B., Akayoglu, S., & Keles, U. (2024). Teacher candidates' intercultural communication in telecollaboration: Locating acts of positioning in translingual negotiations. *Journal for Multicultural Education, 18*(1-2), 53–66. DOI: 10.1108/JME-09-2023-0096

Vahedian-Movahed, S., & Martin, F. (2025, June). From Play to Pedagogy: Discovering the Ecosystem of AI Educational Tools and Curricula. In *Proceedings of the 30th ACM Conference on Innovation and Technology in Computer Science Education* V. 1 (pp. 333-339). https://doi.org/DOI: 10.1145/3724363.3729068

Valeri, F., Nilsson, P., & Cederqvist, A. M. (2025). Exploring students' experience of ChatGPT in STEM education. *Computers and Education: Artificial Intelligence, 8*, 100360. DOI: 10.1016/j.caeai.2024.100360

van Merriënboer, J. J. G., & Sweller, J. (2005). Cognitive load theory and complex learning: Recent developments and future directions. *Educational Psychology Review, 17*(2), 147–177. DOI: 10.1007/s10648-005-3951-0

Vásquez, S., Peñafiel, M., Cevallos, A., Zaldumbide, J., & Vásquez, D. (2017). Impact of game-based learning on students in higher education. In *EDULEARN17 Proceedings* (pp. 4356–4363). IATED. DOI: 10.21125/edulearn.2017.1942

Vaughn, M., Lammert, C., Carrizales, D., & Arlington, K. C. (2025). Multilingual learners and possibilities for agency. *Peabody Journal of Education, 100*(4), 482–494. DOI: 10.1080/0161956X.2025.2535921

Vázquez-Vílchez, M., Garrido-Rosales, D., Pérez-Fernández, B., & Fernández-Oliveras, A. (2021). Using a Cooperative Educational Game to Promote Pro-Environmental Engagement in Future Teachers. *Education Sciences, 11*(11), 691. DOI: 10.3390/educsci11110691

Velayutham, S., & Aldridge, J. M. (2013). Influence of psychosocial classroom environment on students' motivation and self-regulation in science learning: A structural equation modeling approach. *Research in Science Education, 43*(2), 507–527. DOI: 10.1007/s11165-011-9273-y

Veldkamp, A., van de Grint, L., Knippels, M. C. P. J., & van Joolingen, W. R. (2020). Escape education: A systematic review on escape rooms in education. *Educational Research Review, 31*, 100364. Advance online publication. DOI: 10.1016/j.edurev.2020.100364

Ventsel, A., Hansson, S., Rickberg, M., & Madisson, M. L. (2024). Building resilience against hostile information influence activities: How a new media literacy learning platform was developed for the Estonian defense forces. *Armed Forces and Society, 50*(4), 1021–1041. DOI: 10.1177/0095327X231163265

Vernon-Feagans, L., & Bratsch-Hines, M. E.The Family Life Project Key Investigators. (2013). Caregiver-child verbal interactions in child care: A buffer against poor language outcomes when maternal language input is less. *Early Childhood Research Quarterly, 28*(4), 858–873. DOI: 10.1016/j.ecresq.2013.08.002 PMID: 24634566

Veytia Bucheli, M. G., Gómez-Galán, J., Cáceres Mesa, M. L., & López Catalán, L. (2024). Digital technologies as enablers of universal design for learning: Higher education students' perceptions in the context of SDG4. *Discover Sustainability, 5*(1), 473. Advance online publication. DOI: 10.1007/s43621-024-00699-0

Viberg, O., Mutimukwe, C., Hrastinski, S., Cerratto-Pargman, T., & Lilliesköld, J. (2024). Exploring teachers' (future) digital assessment practices in higher education: Instrument and model development. *British Journal of Educational Technology*, *55*(6), 2597–2616. DOI: 10.1111/bjet.13462

Villatoro Moral, S., Serra Vives, N., & Capellà Galmés, M. À. (2026). Medieval-Themed Video Games For History Teaching: A Systematic Review. *Electronic Journal of e-Learning*, *24*(1), 45–60. DOI: 10.34190/ejel.24.1.4431

Viudes-Carbonell, S. J., Gallego-Durán, F. J., Llorens-Largo, F., Molina-Carmona, R., & Mengual-Andrés, S. (2021). Towards an iterative design for serious games. *Sustainability (Basel)*, *13*(6), 3290. DOI: 10.3390/su13063290

Vlachopoulos, D., & Makri, A. (2017). The effect of games and simulations on higher education: A systematic literature review. *International Journal of Educational Technology in Higher Education*, *14*(1), 22. DOI: 10.1186/s41239-017-0062-1

Vlieghe, J. (2015). Traditional and digital literacy. The literacy hypothesis, technologies of reading and writing, and the 'grammatized' body. *Ethics and Education*, *10*(2), 209–226. DOI: 10.1080/17449642.2015.1039288

von Gillern, S., Gould, H., & Pérez Cortés, L. (2025). Preservice teachers' perceptions on digital game-based learning in elementary English language arts. *Journal of Digital Learning in Teacher Education*, *41*(4), 1–14. DOI: 10.1080/21532974.2025.2540638

Voulgari, I., Naoum, E., & Sfyroera, M. (2025). Fostering AI Literacy in Early Childhood: Designing Educational Activities for Preschoolers. *AI in Early Education: Integrating Artificial Intelligence for Inclusive and Effective Learning*, 21-40. https://doi.org/DOI: 10.1002/9781394352821.ch02

Vygotsky, L. S. (1978). Mind in Society: the development of higher psychological processes. In *Medical Entomology and Zoology*. https://ci.nii.ac.jp/ncid/BA03570814

Vygotsky, L. S. (1967). Play and Its Role in the Mental Development of the Child. *Social Psychology*, *5*(3), 6–18. DOI: 10.2753/RPO1061-040505036

Vygotsky, L. S. (1978). *Mind in Society: Development of Higher Psychological Processes* (Cole, M., Jolm-Steiner, V., Scribner, S., & Souberman, E., Eds.). Harvard University Press., DOI: 10.2307/j.ctvjf9vz4

Vygotsky, L. S. (1978). *Mind in society: The development of higher psychological processes*. Harvard University Press.

Wang, A. I., Zhu, M., & Sætre, R. (2016). The effect of digitizing and gamifying quizzing in classrooms. *ResearchGate*. https://www.researchgate.net/publication/309292274_The_Effect_of_Digitizing_and_Gamifying_Quizzing_in_Classrooms

Wang, A. I., & Tahir, R. (2020). The effect of using Kahoot! for learning–A literature review. *Computers & Education*, *149*, 103818. DOI: 10.1016/j.compedu.2020.103818

Wang, S., Wang, F., Zhu, Z., Wang, J., Tran, T., & Du, Z. (2024). Artificial intelligence in education: A systematic literature review and bibliometric analysis. *Information Processing & Management*. Advance online publication. DOI: 10.1016/j.ipm.2024.103923

Wang, S., Wang, F., Zhu, Z., Wang, J., Tran, T., & Du, Z. (2024). Artificial intelligence in education: A systematic literature review. *Expert Systems with Applications*, *252*, 124167. https://doi.org/https://doi.org/10.1016/j.eswa.2024.124167. DOI: 10.1016/j.eswa.2024.124167

Wang, X., Xia, C., Zhao, Q., & Chen, L. (2025). Enhancing second language motivation and facilitating vocabulary acquisition in an EFL classroom through translanguaging practices. *Applied Linguistics Review*, *16*(5), 2183–2216. DOI: 10.1515/applirev-2024-0292

Wan, K., Woo, Y. Y., & Ho, G. T. S. (2025). Enhancing service-learning through generative AI: A mixed-methods study on educational game design in a finance course. *Cogent Education*, *12*(1), 2592370. DOI: 10.1080/2331186X.2025.2592370

Wayground. (2006). *Wayground.* https://wayground.com/

Weiss, Y., Huber, E., Ferjan Ramírez, N., Corrigan, N. M., Yarnykh, V. L., & Kuhl, P. K. (2022). Language input in late infancy scaffolds emergent literacy skills and predicts reading related white matter development. *Frontiers in Human Neuroscience*, *16*, 922552. DOI: 10.3389/fnhum.2022.922552 PMID: 36457757

Whitehurst, G. J., & Lonigan, C. J. (1998). Child development and emergent literacy. *Child Development*, *69*(3), 848–872. DOI: 10.1111/j.1467-8624.1998.tb06247.x PMID: 9680688

Wiboolyasarin, K., & Jinowat, N. (2025). AI-powered feedback in second language writing: A systematic scoping review of technological innovations in digital language education. *International Journal of Language Studies*, *19*(4).

Widener, S. K. (2007). An empirical analysis of the levers of control framework. *Accounting, Organizations and Society*, *32*(7–8), 757–788. Advance online publication. DOI: 10.1016/j.aos.2007.01.001

Wigfield, A., & Eccles, J. S. (2002). Students' Motivation During the Middle School Years. I*mproving Academic Achievement.* DOI: 10.1016/B978-012064455-1/50011-7

Wijayanti, A., Dwiningrum, S. I. A., & Saptono, B. (2024). Digital literacy in elementary schools post COVID-19: A systematic literature review. *International Journal of Learning. Teaching and Educational Research*, *23*(12), 96–112. DOI: 10.26803/ijlter.23.12.6

Williamson, B., & Eynon, R. (2020). Historical threads, missing links, and future directions in AI in education. *Learning, Media and Technology*, *45*(3), 217–235. DOI: 10.1080/17439884.2020.1798995

Williams, R. G., Makoul, G., Hawkins, R., Hallock, J. A., Scoles, P., & Reichgott, M. J. (2001). Standardized/simulated patients in medical education. In *Annual Meeting of the American Medical Association Section on Medical Schools*, Chicago. IL.

Willis, J. (2007). Cooperative Learning Is a Brain Turn-On. *Middle School Journal*, *38*(4), 4–13. Advance online publication. DOI: 10.1080/00940771.2007.11461587

Wilson, S. N., Engler, C. E., Black, J. E., Yager-Elorriaga, D. K., Thompson, W. M., McConnell, A., Cecena, J. E., Ralston, R., & Terry, R. A. (2017). Game-Based learning and information literacy. *International Journal of Game-Based Learning*, *7*(4), 1–21. DOI: 10.4018/IJGBL.2017100101

Wirth, J., Stebner, F., Trypke, M., Schuster, C., & Leutner, D. (2020). An interactive layers model of self-regulated learning and cognitive load. *Educational Psychology Review, 32*(4), 1127–1149. DOI: 10.1007/s10648-020-09568-4

Wu, D., Chen, M., Chen, X., & Liu, X. (2024). Analyzing K-12 AI education: A large language model study of classroom instruction on learning theories, pedagogy, tools, and AI literacy. *Computers and Education: Artificial Intelligence, 7*, 100295. DOI: 10.1016/j.caeai.2024.100295

Wu, Q., Chen, L., Chen, M., & Huang, Y. (2026). Exploring the impact of artificial intelligence on business talent development in higher education: A systematic literature review and research agenda. *International Journal of Management Education, 24*(1), 101287. DOI: 10.1016/j.ijme.2025.101287

Xiao, Y., Li, D., & Guo, K. (2025). Generative AI-powered non-player characters in digital storyline-based learning: An innovative approach to EFL writing. *Innovation in Language Learning and Teaching*, •••, 1–15. DOI: 10.1080/17501229.2025.2545397

Xiao, Y., Li, D., & Guo, K. (2025). Using ChatGPT to bring non-player characters to life: Effects on students' storyline-driven game-based writing learning. *Computers & Education, 238*, 105414. Advance online publication. DOI: 10.1016/j.compedu.2025.105414

Xinlin, J., Wenting, L., Shah, K. A. M., Na, M., & Shah Alam, S. (2025). Transforming hospitality decision-making: The impact of generative AI on cognitive alignment and adaptive intelligence. *Journal of Quality Assurance in Hospitality & Tourism*, 1–35. DOI: 10.1080/1528008X.2025.2528044

Xu, M., Luo, Y., Zhang, Y., Xia, R., Qian, H., & Zou, X. (2023). Game-based learning in medical education. *Frontiers in Public Health, 11*, 1113682. Advance online publication. DOI: 10.3389/fpubh.2023.1113682

Xu, Y., Sun, J., & Peng, J. (2025). Present and future trends of virtual simulation in education: A bibliometric analysis. *Education for Information, 41*(4), 277–301. DOI: 10.1177/01678329251329554

Yao, Y., Zhu, X., Xiao, L., & Lu, Q. (2025). Secondary school English teachers' application of artificial intelligence-guided chatbot in the provision of feedback on student writing: An activity theory perspective. *Journal of Second Language Writing, 67*, 101179. Advance online publication. DOI: 10.1016/j.jslw.2025.101179

Yasir, G. M., Shaheen, A., & Hafeez, M. (2021). A Systematic Review on Digital Game-Based Versus Traditional Learning Approaches. *Global Social Sciences Review, VI*(IV), 124–135. DOI: 10.31703/gssr.2021(VI-IV).12

Yeung, A. S., Jin, P., & Sweller, J. (1998). Cognitive load and learner expertise: Split-attention and redundancy effects in reading with explanatory notes. *Contemporary Educational Psychology, 23*(1), 1–21. DOI: 10.1006/ceps.1997.0951 PMID: 9514686

Yıldırım, İ., & Şen, S. (2021). The effects of gamification on students' academic achievement: A meta-analysis study. *Interactive Learning Environments, 29*(8), 1301–1318. Advance online publication. DOI: 10.1080/10494820.2019.1636089

Yildiz Durak, H., & Onan, A. (2025). A systematic review of AI-based feedback in educational settings. *Journal of Computational Social Science, 8*(4), 96. DOI: 10.1007/s42001-025-00428-1

Yim, I. H. Y. (2024). A critical review of teaching and learning artificial intelligence (AI) literacy: Developing an intelligence-based AI literacy framework for primary school education. *Computers and Education: Artificial Intelligence*, *7*, 100319. Advance online publication. DOI: 10.1016/j.caeai.2024.100319

Yim, I. H. Y., & Su, J. (2025a). Artificial intelligence (AI) learning tools in K-12 education: A scoping review. *Journal of Computers in Education*, *12*(1), 93–131. DOI: 10.1007/s40692-023-00304-9

Yim, I. H. Y., & Su, J. (2025b). Artificial intelligence literacy education in primary schools: A review. *International Journal of Technology and Design Education*, *35*(5), 1–30. DOI: 10.1007/s10798-025-09979-w

Yim, I. H. Y., & Wegerif, R. (2024). Teachers' perceptions, attitudes, and acceptance of artificial intelligence (AI) educational learning tools: An exploratory study on AI literacy for young students. *Future in Educational Research*, *2*(4), 318–345. DOI: 10.1002/fer3.65

Yin, R. K. (2018). *Case study research and applications: Design and methods* (6th ed.). SAGE.

Yoon, B. (2023). Research synthesis on culturally and linguistically responsive teaching for multilingual learners. *Education Sciences*, *13*(6), 557. DOI: 10.3390/educsci13060557

Yuan, B., & Hu, J. (2025, December). Generative AI as a tool for enhancing reflective learning in students. In *2025 IEEE International Conference on Teaching, Assessment, and Learning for Engineering (TALE)* (pp. 1-6). IEEE. https://doi.org/DOI: 10.1109/TALE66047.2025.11346600

Zacharia, Z. C., & Olympiou, G. (2011). Physical versus virtual manipulative experimentation in physics learning. *Learning and Instruction*, *21*(3), 317–331. DOI: 10.1016/j.learninstruc.2010.03.001

Zahra, I., & Neo, M. (2024). Transforming education with collaborative games: An interactive learning ecosystem to foster students' critical thinking and problem-solving skills. In *ICERI2024 Proceedings* (pp. 2439–2447). IATED.

Zainuddin, Z., Chu, S. K. W., Shujahat, M., & Perera, C. J. (2020). The impact of gamification on learning and instruction: A systematic review of empirical evidence. *Educational Research Review*, *30*, 100326. DOI: 10.1016/j.edurev.2020.100326

Zajda, J. (2021). Constructivist Learning Theory and Creating Effective Learning Environments BT - Globalisation and Education Reforms: Creating Effective Learning Environments. In Zajda, J. (Ed.), (pp. 35–50). Springer International Publishing., DOI: 10.1007/978-3-030-71575-5_3

Zão, H. (2025). AI and Marketing: Bridging the Gap Through a Game-based Tool Among Higher Education Students. *Comunicar*. Babu, M. S. (2025). AI-Driven Educational Assessments: Navigating the Intersection of Innovation, Equity, and Ethical Concerns for Future Learning. *Journal of Cultural Analysis and Social Change*, 1368–1382. Bharathi, G., Chandra, I., Sanagana, D. P. R., Tummalachervu, C. K., Rao, V. S., & Neelima, S. (2024). AI-driven adaptive learning for enhancing business intelligence simulation games. *Entertainment Computing, 50*, 100699. Bhuvaneswari, G., & Kumar, T. P. (2025). The game of language learning and rewiring biocognitive receptors. *MethodsX*, *14*, 103143.

Zarandi, N., Soares, A. M., & Alves, H. (2024). Student satisfaction and co-creation behavior in game-based learning in the context of higher education. *Journal of Marketing for Higher Education*, 1–22. DOI: 10.1080/08841241.2024.2351118

Zawacki-Richter, O., Marín, V. I., Bond, M., & Gouverneur, F. (2019). Systematic review of research on artificial intelligence applications in higher education: Where are the educators? *International Journal of Educational Technology in Higher Education*, *16*(1), 39. Advance online publication. DOI: 10.1186/s41239-019-0171-0

Zebek, N., & Saygi, E. (2024). Gamification in education: Why where, when, and how? - A systematic review. *Games and Culture*, *19*(2), 237–264. DOI: 10.1177/15554120231158625

Zhai, X., Chu, X., Chai, C. S., Jong, M. S. Y., Istenic, A., Spector, J. M., Liu, J.-B., Yuan, J., & Li, Y. (2021). A review of artificial intelligence (AI) in education from 2010 to 2020. *Complexity*, *8812542*(1), 8812542. Advance online publication. DOI: 10.1155/2021/8812542

Zhang, D., Zhao, J. L., Zhou, L., & Nunamaker, J. F.Jr. (2004). Can e-learning replace classroom learning? *Communications of the ACM*, *47*(5), 75–79. DOI: 10.1145/986213.986216

Zhang, F., & Jiang, T. (2024). Influence of blended learning on students' self-efficacy: An empirical study based on CESIM simulation course. *Higher Education and Practice*, *1*(1), 45–52. DOI: 10.62381/H241108

Zhang, K. (2025). Enhancing critical writing through AI feedback: A randomized controlled trial. *Behavioral Sciences (Basel, Switzerland)*, *15*(5), 600. Advance online publication. DOI: 10.3390/bs15050600 PMID: 40426378

Zhang, M., Ran, C., Liu, F., Yin, M., Cui, S., Li, C., & Li, B. (2025). Hello! AI: An Interactive Rhyme-Based Game for Children AI Literacy Education. *International Journal of Human-Computer Interaction*, •••, 1–26. DOI: 10.1080/10447318.2025.2574514

Zhang, Y., Gao, M., Zhuge, J., & Ye, S. (2024). Strategic-oriented multiteam system cohesion and enterprise investment decision: Evidence from CESIM platform online simulation experiment. *International Review of Economics & Finance*, *95*, 103386. DOI: 10.1016/j.iref.2024.103386

Zhan, Y., Boud, D., Dawson, P., & Yan, Z. (2025). Generative artificial intelligence as an enabler of student feedback engagement: A framework. *Higher Education Research & Development*, *44*(5), 1289–1304. DOI: 10.1080/07294360.2025.2476513

Zhan, Y., & Yan, Z. (2025). Students' engagement with ChatGPT feedback: Implications for student feedback literacy in the context of generative artificial intelligence. *Assessment & Evaluation in Higher Education*, 1–14. DOI: 10.1080/02602938.2025.2471821

Zhan, Z., Tong, Y., Lan, X., & Zhong, B. (2022). A systematic literature review of game-based learning in Artificial Intelligence education. *Interactive Learning Environments*, *32*(3), 1137–1158. DOI: 10.1080/10494820.2022.2115077

Zha, S., Bragdon, M. M., Gong, N., Wang, J., Leavesley, S., Eaton, R., & Bosarge, E. (2025). A case study of integrating AI literacy education in a biology class. *International Journal of Artificial Intelligence in Education, 35*(4), 2453–2477. DOI: 10.1007/s40593-025-00476-8

Zheng, Y., Zhang, J., Li, Y., Wu, X., Ding, R., Luo, X., Liu, P., & Huang, J. (2024). Effects of digital game-based learning on students' digital etiquette literacy, learning motivations, and engagement. *Heliyon, 10*(1), e23490. Advance online publication. DOI: 10.1016/j.heliyon.2023.e23490 PMID: 38187224

Zhu, Z., Hall, C. M., Koupaei, S. N., Lin, F., & Wang, Z. (2026). Influence of AI on usage intention in tourism and hospitality education: The mediating role of perceived trust. *Current Issues in Tourism*, 1–14. DOI: 10.1080/13683500.2026.2622507

Žilak, M., & Car, Ž. (2025). A framework for improving accessibility of serious games in handheld augmented reality based on user interaction data. *Applied Sciences (Basel, Switzerland), 15*(4), 2161. DOI: 10.3390/app15042161

Zimmerman, B. J. (2002). Becoming a self-regulated learner: An overview. *Theory into Practice, 41*(2), 64–70. DOI: 10.1207/s15430421tip4102_2

Zsigmond, I., Metallidou, P., Misailidi, P., Iordanou, K., & Papaleontiou-Louca, E. (2025). Metacognitive monitoring in written communication: Improving reflective practice. *Education Sciences, 15*(3), 299. DOI: 10.3390/educsci15030299

Zulkarnain, I., Sitepu, Y. S., Sutatminingsih, R., & Rajagukguk, M. (2024). Student's digital literacy competence and its implications for the learning process. [IJERE]. *International Journal of Evaluation and Research in Education, 13*(2), 997. DOI: 10.11591/ijere.v13i2.25767

Zvereva, G., Hamari, J., Pirkkalainen, H., & Xi, N. (2026). Gamification for ethics literacy. *Journal of Educational Technology & Society, 29*(1), 291–331.

About the Contributors

Leslie Haas earned her doctorate in Supervision, Curriculum, and Instruction from Texas A&M University–Commerce. She is Professor of Education and Division Chair of Education at Texas A&M University–Texarkana and serves as Co-Editor of the International Journal of Game-Based Learning (IJGBL). Her scholarship centers on literacy, game-based learning, and culturally responsive pedagogy, with a particular emphasis on technology-enhanced and multimodal approaches. She has co-authored and edited multiple books and chapters exploring gamified literacy practices, disciplinary literacy, and strategies for promoting equity in diverse classrooms. Internationally recognized for her work connecting popular culture, fanfiction, and digital storytelling to literacy instruction, Dr. Haas has presented at leading conferences and published widely in both research and practitioner venues. In addition to her scholarly contributions, Dr. Haas has extensive experience in curriculum design, program development, and faculty mentorship across K–12, undergraduate, and graduate education. She has served on editorial boards, reviewed for leading journals, and provided leadership in higher education and professional associations. Honored for excellence in research, teaching, and technology integration, she continues to advance innovative approaches to literacy that prepare learners to thrive in a rapidly evolving world.

Jill Tussey earned her doctorate in Curriculum and Instruction from the Capella University. She is Associate Professor of Education and Division Chair for Literacy, TESL, and Early Childhood at Buena Vista University, as well as Co-Editor of the International Journal of Game-Based Learning (IJGBL). Her research explores literacy education through the lenses of student engagement, digital literacy, social-emotional learning, and the influence of socioeconomic factors on learning. Dr. Tussey has authored and co-edited numerous books, chapters, and peer-reviewed journal articles that highlight innovative and equitable practices in literacy instruction. She is a frequent presenter at national and international conferences, sharing strategies to support diverse learners across educational contexts. Beyond her publications, Dr. Tussey contributes significantly to academic leadership and professional service. At Buena Vista University, she fosters faculty collaboration, curricular innovation, and program development in teacher education. She also serves as an editor, reviewer, and evaluator for literacy-focused journals and academic programs. Her work consistently reflects a commitment to expanding access to meaningful, engaging, and socially responsive literacy experiences that empower learners and educators alike.

***

Vinsens is an emerging researcher affiliated with the Department of Computer Science, Esa Unggul University. His academic interests include Artificial Intelligence, Business Information Systems, Human-Technology Interaction, Social Networking, and Risk Management. Despite being an undergraduate student, he has actively engaged in collaborative research, academic writing, and scientific discussions in technology-related disciplines. He is passionate about bridging the gap between digital innovation and human behavior in organizational and societal contexts. His goal is to contribute to impactful, interdisciplinary knowledge through research and academic publishing.

Dandi Akbar is a researcher and writer in the field of information systems with a strong interest in artificial intelligence, data science, and business intelligence. His work focuses on the intersection of digital technologies, data driven decision making, and organizational systems, with particular attention to how intelligent systems can support effective and responsible information management. Through his research and writing, he explores both the technical and strategic dimensions of information systems, aiming to contribute insights that are relevant to academic discourse as well as practical implementation in contemporary organizations.

Ashraf Alam is currently serving as an Assistant Professor in the Department of Education at NIT Calicut, Kerala, India. He has been recognised among the World's Top 2% Scientists by Stanford University and Elsevier. His academic contributions include more than 75 Scopus-indexed publications and over 100 conference presentations delivered at national and international academic forums. His work has appeared in reputed research publication platforms including Elsevier, Springer, Taylor & Francis, CRC Press, Routledge, Atlantis Press, Springer Nature, Palgrave Macmillan, and IEEE. He earned his Ph.D. from IIT Kharagpur, where his research engaged with foundational concerns in educational policy, curriculum design, educational technology, philosophy of education, innovation in education, educational administration, governance, and pedagogical transformation. His work is grounded in a transdisciplinary orientation that draws from educational sciences, digital pedagogy, curriculum theory, learning analytics, sustainability education, instructional design, artificial intelligence, ethics of technology, and socio-technical studies. Dr. Ashraf's scholarship strives to interrogate and expand the boundaries of educational thought by examining the epistemological, ethical, and social dimensions of digital and post-digital pedagogies. His work critically engages with the changing nature of knowledge production, learner agency, pedagogical mediation, and institutional transformation in technologically saturated educational environments. He is particularly invested in advancing inclusive digital learning, gamified instructional strategies, AI-mediated educational ecosystems, and ethically governed technology integration in education. His research agenda is animated by the pursuit of design-oriented, ethically attuned, and contextually responsive frameworks that can support meaningful educational reform. Through his work, he seeks to contribute to the development of pedagogical models that are not only technologically innovative but also socially just, epistemically inclusive, developmentally sensitive, and aligned with the broader goals of sustainable and human-centred education.

Ashleigh Bridges brings eight years of experience in K–12 education to her role in higher education. She began her career teaching 9–12th grade English, where she gained ESL certification and discovered a passion for co-teaching. This experience inspired her to pursue and earn her certification in special education during her time as a secondary English teacher and working on her first Masters in Curriculum and Instruction. Ashleigh went on to teach secondary English resource classes for 9th and 10th grade students, deepening her expertise in supporting diverse learners. After completing her second Master's degree in Educational Leadership, Ashleigh transitioned into leadership roles beyond the classroom focusing on supporting diverse learners and those who teach them. She served as the Autism Program Coordinator for 19 school districts in the Texarkana area through a Texarkana ISD grant. Following this, she became an Assistant Principal for Special Populations, overseeing special education, Section 504, and Emergent Bilingual programs at the middle school level. During this time, she also achieved National Board Certification in Exceptional Needs Specialist, further strengthening her commitment to inclusive education. Currently in her second year of teaching in higher education, Ashleigh is also pursuing her doctorate in Curriculum and Instruction with a focus in Special Education. Her dissertation research examines how to better support teachers working in inclusive settings and, in turn, how to improve support for students in those classrooms. She has presented at CSOTTE, NCTE, DADD and TASH. She currently has two publications focused on inclusion; both published with TxEP. Her professional journey reflects a strong commitment to inclusion, collaboration, and advocacy for all learners.

Tendai Charles is an Assistant Professor of Education at the British University in Dubai. He holds an MSc in Data Analytics & Social Statistics from the University of Manchester and a PhD in Education from the University of York. He is an accredited researcher with the Office for National Statistics and is a Fellow of the Royal Statistical Society. He is a post-positivist researcher who specialises in evidence-based education and uses computational statistics for secondary data analyses.

Michelle L. Conrad, Ph.D., is a Professor and Graduate Program Coordinator for Career and Technical Education at the University of Central Missouri. She teaches courses for new CTE teachers from industry, as well as advanced coursework in curriculum development theory and research. Dr. Conrad has worked with the Asia Society and Longview Foundation developing global competency resources and trainings. She has also served as a consultant for the Missouri Department of Elementary & Secondary Education's new CTE teacher induction programs and on Missouri CTE curriculum development and revision projects, as well as for the Association for Career & Technical Education for online learning courses. She has published three books titled, "Curriculum Development & Design in Career & Technical Education", "25 Ways to Start Your Days: CTE Bell Ringers", and "Instructional Strategies for Career & Technical Educators".

Nabat Erdogan, Ph.D., is an Associate Professor and Graduate Program Coordinator for Master of Science in Education (MSE) in English Language Learners (ELL) at the University of Central Missouri (UCM). Dr. Erdogan earned her first Ph.D. in Linguistics from Azerbaijan University of Languages in Baku, Azerbaijan, in 2008, and her second Ph.D. in Teaching English to Speakers of Other Languages (TESOL) and English from the University of Missouri - Kansas City, USA, in 2018. With her twenty-seven years of experience in Linguistics and TESOL, Dr. Erdogan brings a wealth of expertise and experience in curriculum development and pedagogical strategies tailored to meet the diverse needs of English Learners (ELs). Her research and publications focus on comparative linguistics, applied linguistics, syntax, phonetics, pragmatics, second language literacy, and the use of generative Artificial Intelligence (AI) in language teaching and learning. Dr. Erdogan's award-winning book titled "Applied Linguistics for Teachers of Culturally and Linguistically Diverse Learners" combines linguistic theory and practice and offers practical approaches and techniques of teaching English to ELs.

César A. García-García is a researcher and faculty member in the Department of Information Sciences and Technological Developments at the University of Guadalajara, Mexico. His work focuses on serious games, artificial intelligence–ready educational systems, and instructional design for multidimensional literacy development across STEM, safety, energy, and health domains. He has led and participated in interdisciplinary projects integrating simulation-based learning, learning analytics, and ethical AI considerations to support inclusive and applied education.

Jossy P George is currently serving as the Dean & Director at CHRIST (Deemed to be University), Pune Lavasa campus. He has a dual master's degree in Computer Science and Human Resources from the USA and has done his FDPM from IIM, Ahmedabad. He was awarded a Doctorate in Computer Science by CHRIST University, Bengaluru, on Image Processing for the paper titled "Development of Efficient Biometric Recognition Algorithms based on Fingerprint and Face", and his research activities continue to focus on algorithms for improved accuracy in biometrics. He has also completed major research work on the topic of "Technology in Higher Education". He has published many papers both in national and international journals and has also successfully filed for patent applications. In addition to this, he is the author of two motivational management books. As an educator, he has been working with CHRIST University (previously Christ College), Bengaluru, and other associated institutions since 2002 in various capacities. In his current capacity as Dean & Director, he continues to strive towards CHRIST's motto of Excellence & Service. He resolutely believes in a holistic approach to education and is motivated by this to encourage the students of his institution to excel at both academic and non-academic pursuits.

K. Balamurugan is a highly regarded academic and researcher with over 29 years of expertise in Information Technology and Computer Science. Currently, he is an Associate Professor in the Department of Information Technology at K.S.R. College of Engineering (Autonomous) in Tiruchengode, Namakkal Dt, Tamil Nadu. He completed his B.E. in Electronics and Communication Engineering from Kumaraguru College of Technology in 1995, M.E. in Multimedia Technology from the College of Engineering, Guindy, Anna University, in 2003, and earned his Ph.D. in Information and Communication Engineering from Anna University in 2018.

Ganesh Kumar K working as a Professor in the department of Information Technology, Velalar College of Engineering and Technology, Thindal, Erode, Tamilnadu, India with 16 years of teaching experience. He has published 15 articles in various national and international level journals. He is an active review member in various reputed journal. He has guided more than 25 undergraduate and 15 post graduate level students projects.

Kaviya M A is a pre final year B.Tech. Information Technology student in Velalar College of Engineering and Technology.

Carrie May is a doctoral student in the Educational Psychology Department of the College of Education and Human Development at George Mason University, Fairfax, Virginia.

Keerthana N V is an Assistant Professor with 8 Years of experience in teaching and 1-year experience in research (IUCAA LIGO Data Centre, Pune). Her area of interest is Network Security, Blockchain, and Machine Learning Algorithms. She is pursuing PhD at Anna University in Blockchain Security. She has work experience in high-performance computing (HTCondor) for the LIGO INDIA Project.

Fakira Mohan Nahak, Professor & Director, PR & Media Communication, Manipal University Jaipur

Norma Yolanda Ochoa-Ramos is a biologist with a Master's degree in Biosystematics and Natural Resources Management. She is currently a PhD candidate in Functional and Applied Ecology at the University of León (Spain). Her academic and professional experience focuses on environmental impact assessment, ecological land-use planning, bioclimatology, vegetation analysis, and spatial analysis using GIS. Her research interests include bioclimatic classification, vegetation ecology, ecosystem management, and climate change.

Hemlata Parmar, a luminary in the field of computer Science and Engineering. Her Journey is defined by a constellation of achievements from prolific publications and patents to enlightening guest lectures. Yet, her brilliance is matched only by her unwavering commitment to human ethics. With a heart as vast as her intellect, she champions women's empowerment, bridging the gap with empathy and insight. In every endeavour, she embodies the perfect fusion of academic process and compassionate advocacy, inspiring generations to come.

Alexandra Patzak is an assistant professor in the Educational Psychology Department of the College of Education and Human Development at George Mason University, Fairfax, Virginia.

Alejandro González Pérez holds a PhD in Functional and Applied Ecology from the University of León, awarded with an International Mention. His extensive academic background includes a BSc in Biology and two Master's degrees: one in Advanced Studies in Flora and Fauna, and another in Teacher Training. He has further honed his expertise through specialisation courses in leadership, digital competencies, and environmental data analysis in R, complemented by research stays at international educational institutions. He is multilingual, proficient in Spanish, English, German, and French. His professional experience encompasses research projects in ecology, bioclimatology, and modelling, supported by a solid and growing record of scientific production and participation in congresses. He has delivered over 400 hours of teaching and co-supervised both Bachelor's and Master's theses. He is recognised for his capacity for teamwork, commitment to continuous learning, and dedication to maintaining up-to-date knowledge in his field.

Carimo Rassal earned his PhD in Tourism from the Faculty of Economics, University of Algarve, Portugal. He holds a Visiting Adjunct Professor position at the University of Algarve, enriching the academic community with his knowledge and experience. With a research affiliation as an integrated researcher at CIDEHUS - Interdisciplinary Center for History, Cultures, and Societies of the University of Évora, he actively pursues academic excellence. Boasting over 30 years of experience in the field, he is regularly sought after as an expert consultant for institutional and business projects nationally and internationally. His key areas of expertise include strategic consulting, training, and human resources development within the tourism and hospitality sectors. This work is funded by the Foundation for Science and Technology (Portugal), under the project UID/00057/2025 -

Carolina L. Recio-Colmenares is a researcher and faculty member in the Department of Basic and Applied Sciences at the University of Guadalajara, Mexico. Her academic work focuses on educational innovation, science education, and the integration of digital technologies to support learning in health and STEM-related contexts. She has participated in interdisciplinary projects addressing instructional design, serious games, and evidence-based educational interventions, with particular interest in inclusive and applied learning environments.

Roxana B. Recio-Colmenares is a faculty member and researcher in the Department of Basic and Applied Sciences at the University of Guadalajara, Mexico. Her work centers on science education, health-related learning, and the design of instructional strategies supported by digital technologies. She has contributed to interdisciplinary initiatives involving serious games, simulation-based learning, and educational innovation aimed at improving disciplinary literacy and inclusive educational practice.

Gusti Muhamad Sardana is a researcher in artificial intelligence and early warning systems at Esa Unggul University, Jakarta, Indonesia. His research interests include machine learning, intelligent monitoring systems, sensor-based technologies, and the development of AI-driven early detection solutions. He has been actively involved in academic research and applied projects focusing on predictive analytics, real-time monitoring, and the integration of intelligent systems to support risk mitigation and rapid response mechanisms. His work reflects strong analytical thinking, technical expertise, and a commitment to innovation in intelligent detection and monitoring technologies. Gusti actively contributes to collaborative research initiatives and scientific publications aimed at advancing the application of artificial intelligence in early warning systems and smart monitoring environments.

Binastya Anggara Sekti has been a lecturer at the Faculty of Computer Science, Esa Unggul University, Jakarta, since 2016. He is actively involved in the Artificial Intelligence and Information Security Study Group. He holds a Bachelor's degree in Informatics Engineering from the Bandung Institute of Technology and a Master's degree in Information Systems Management from Trisakti University, Jakarta. Prior to entering academia, he accumulated over 25 years of professional experience as an IT practitioner in various companies across Jakarta. His work focused on developing data centers for internet service providers and delivering IT solutions for the manufacturing and oil & gas sectors. His research interests include artificial intelligence, cybersecurity, and the development of IT infrastructure.

Yuankun Yao, Ph.D., is a Professor of Education and Graduate Program Coordinator for Master of Arts (MA) in Teaching and Master of Science in Education (MSE) in Curriculum & Instruction at the University of Central Missouri. He earned his Ph.D. in Educational Administration, Curriculum and Instruction from the University of Nebraska-Lincoln, with a focus on Educational Assessment and Evaluation. He currently teaches educational assessment and research methods for graduate students. He is a certified reviewer for What Works Clearinghouse and a long-time reviewer of AERA conference papers. He has published in Action in Teacher Education, Educational Measurement: Issues and Practices, Educational Research and Evaluation, Studying Teacher Education, International Journal of Multicultural Education, Journal of Educational Research and Policy Studies, Journal of Personnel Evaluation in Education, Multicultural Perspectives, and Reading Psychology. He has also been actively involved at the Association of Teacher Education, serving as the chair of the S-STEP (Self-Study of Teacher Education Practice) SIG group, a member of the Inquiry Initiative, and a member of the Billy G. Dixon Distinguished Program in Teacher Education (DPTE) selection committee.

Farrah Zafar holds a PhD in Education with a concentration in TESOL from The British University in Dubai. She also holds an M.Phil in English Literature and an MA in English. Her academic work focuses on English language teaching and learning, particularly willingness to communicate, learner engagement, and classroom interaction. Her research interests include TESOL, language pedagogy, and technology-enhanced language learning.

Index

A

B

C

D

E

F

G

H

I

K

L

N

P

R

S

T

U

V

W

www.ingramcontent.com/pod-product-compliance
Lightning Source LLC
LaVergne TN
LVHW060255011026
849161LV00011B/2717
* 9 7 9 8 3 3 7 3 7 4 7 2 7 *